IRAQ: FROM SUMER TO SADDAM

Also by Geoff Simons and published by St. Martin's Press

LIBYA: The Struggle for Survival

Iraq: From Sumer to Saddam

Geoff Simons

Foreword by Tony Benn, MP

St. Martin's Press   New York

First published in the United States of America in 1994
Reprinted 1994

Printed in Great Britain

ISBN 0–312–10209–7

Library of Congress Cataloging-in-Publication Data
Simons, G. L. (Geoffrey Leslie), 1939–
Iraq : from Sumer to Saddam / Geoff Simons ; foreword by Tony
Benn.
p.   cm.
Includes bibliographical references (p.   ) and index.
ISBN 0–312–10209–7
1. Iraq—History.   I. Title.
DS70.9.S56   1994
956.7—dc20   93–13871
                                                            CIP

Contents

Foreword

The 1991 Gulf War was hailed by many people, including those who prided themselves on their liberal outlook, as the first example of the New World Order made possible by the end of the Cold War.

We were told that the international community, using the United Nations as its founders intended, would defeat and probably overthrow a brutal dictator by means of weapons of clinical accuracy, deploying the minimum force possible, and hence pave the way for democracy and a lasting settlement of the problems of the Middle East.

It is now clear that what happened was very different from this official explanation of events.

The United Nations was actually taken over and used by the United States to secure its strategic oil supplies at a time when the USSR was disintegrating. The bombing was on a horrific and quite unnecessary scale which inflicted untold suffering on the Iraqi civilian population both at the time and subsequently.

A feudal king in Saudi Arabia was protected and the undemocratic Al-Sabah family was re-installed in Kuwait; Saddam's harsh regime, originally built up with enthusiastic Western help, was actually consolidated in Iraq; and the double standards of the West, with respect to the Palestinians, stand out more glaringly than ever.

When a superpower war machine gets going and the media puts itself at the disposal of the political leaders and generals who are cranking it up, all understanding is driven from the airwaves and the newspapers to ensure public support for that war. So it was during that short and bloody conflict.

No-one was allowed to hear about the long history of Iraq or its civilisation, its relations with its neighbours or what happened when Britain governed it. All parallels with other Western military interventions and non-interventions were discouraged, as were comparisons with the conduct of Israel or Turkey.

There was tight censorship of the war reports and then a deadly media silence about the carnage caused by the bombing and the suffering that followed, so that we were never permitted to hear of the many thousands of civilian deaths for which we were collectively responsible.

That whole horrific story and the background which explains it has been waiting to be told. Here Geoff Simons tells the Iraq story with scholarship, clarity and great moral force, making this a book for the general reader as well as for the academic student of the Arab world and its relations with the West.

TONY BENN

Preface

The 1990/91 Gulf crisis stimulated Western interest in Iraq and yielded a number of books (most listed in the Bibliography). These volumes, almost without exception, followed a common pattern: whilst often outlining the circumstances of the crisis (sometimes giving historical background), there was rarely any attempt to chart in detail many of the historical events that would inevitably fuel future tensions in the region.

Nor, in my view, was adequate attention ever given to the United States, a principal player in the crisis. It was increasingly recognised – who could deny it? – that the US had aided Saddam in the Iran/Iraq war and after, that Washington had given Saddam the 'wrong signals' prior to the invasion of Kuwait, and that Washington had then worked hard to suborn the UN Security Council. Even so, the ethical discourse was inadequate.

Hence this book was written to position the 'Iraq Question' in a broad historical and ethical context. The ambitious breadth has inevitably entailed the reluctant sacrifice of much detail. It seems to me none the less that there is enough here to expand the moral universe of conventional discourse – about both Iraq and broader political questions. We need to reaffirm the principle that the protocols of international behaviour are properly sanctioned by ethics, not by the perceived self-interest of this or that state, even if a hegemonic power.

GEOFF SIMONS

Acknowledgements

I am grateful to Tony Benn MP for enthusiastically welcoming this book and for writing the Foreword. His achievements are many and too rarely noted. Above all, his example will always help to sustain the subversive idea that the proper spirit of politics is morality, not the tawdry obsession with an accountant's balance sheet.

I appreciate also the work and commitment of Christine Simons. Her support through the writing and production of this book has been invaluable. She too believes that there is more to politics than money-grubbing exploitation and the propaganda designed to protect it.

GEOFF SIMONS

Introduction

When Iraq invaded Iran in 1980 – to begin a war that would last most of the decade – the West was not too concerned. A nominal consensus to prevent arms reaching both sides in the conflict was systematically violated in various ways. In particular, the United States developed a manifest 'tilt' towards Iraq which resulted in both covert and overt aid, a posture that was to become highly controversial after the 1990/91 Gulf crisis.

Iraq had, in its aggression against a sovereign state, violated the United Nations Charter. The West made no effort to activate the Security Council in a violent response to the Iraqi invasion. There was no prospect of launching missiles and bombers against Baghdad, no prospect of a US-orchestrated coalition turning the Iraqi deserts into killing fields.

Iraq's 1990 invasion of Kuwait – an act that grew directly out of the Iran/Iraq war – was however an entirely different matter. Soon Iraq was branded a 'pariah nation', its leader a 'new Hitler'. The scene was set for a devastating but brief war, with hundreds of thousands of (mainly Iraqi) casualties, vast regional ecological damage, immense harm to many Third-World economies, and prodigious dissipation of treasure.

In Part I (Chapter 1) a description is given of the state of Iraq and Kuwait in the immediate aftermath of the war: the fruits of comprehensive bombing, ground battles, massacre and torture. Then attention is given to some of the (Western) lies and unanswered questions, the clues to hidden agendas, the mounting evidence of double standards. A post-war chronology is presented which ends with how the defeated Saddam consolidated his post-war power while the victorious George Bush passed into history.

Part II (Chapters 2 to 7) gives a history of the region now known as Iraq. It is difficult to comprehend the richness of this multifaceted historic culture; to grasp how tribes, peoples and nations clashed and cross-fertilised in one of the principal crucibles of world civilisation. Irrigation specialists from ancient Sumer, the architects and astronomers of Babylon, siege engineers from China, the Abbasid scholars and law-givers, Alexander and Kublai Khan, Tamerlane and Saladin – all left their indelible marks. From the Code of Hammurabi to the polities of the Caliphate, the Ottomans and the British Empire, systems of ethics and law, the impact of Judaism, Islam and Christianity – all are touched upon, too briefly but enough to give a flavour of the myriad cultures to which Mesopotamia (later Iraq) was exposed.

The rise of Arab culture and its decline are charted (Chapter 3) with attention to the life of Mohammad, the birth of Islam, and the Arab conquests. The dynasties of the Caliphate that came to influence much in the enduring cultures of modern Syria and Iraq – and much in the historic pride in the Arab nation – are described. Then the Mongol horde and fresh sackings of Baghdad, as a prelude to the Ottoman conquest (Chapter 4) and the impact of Western colonialism (Chapter 5) – both of which Arab nationalists would learn to confront with a resurgent self-confidence and growing success.

Today, at a time when the West pretends to be concerned at the plight of the Iraqi Kurds, it is useful to highlight the enduring Western hypocrisy. In the 1920s the British used machine guns and bombs to suppress both the northern Kurds and the southern marsh Arabs. Colonel Bousett, a medical officer with the Royal Artillery, then noted in his diary that the burning Arab villages made a 'wonderful sight at night'. Poison gas was a particularly useful weapon (Winston Churchill: 'I am strongly in favour of using poisoned gas against uncivilised tribes . . . gases can be used which . . . spread a lively terror'). General Sir Aylmer Haldane suggested that gas was particularly useful in the hilly country of the Kurds, whereas 'in the hot plains . . . the gas is more volatile' (see Lawrence James, *Imperial Rearguard*, 1988). (Today the Turkish regime continues to repress its own Kurdish minority, a sustained policy that has involved torture, mass killings and the forcible emptying of 1000 Kurdish villages; and which in June 1993 led Kurdish protesters to occupy government buildings in eighteen cities in Germany, France and Switzerland. The Turkish suppression of its Kurds is never denounced by Western governments. Turkey is a NATO member and of crucial strategic importance.)

Iraq then moves from British-imposed monarchy to an independent republic (Chapter 6), and thence into the era of Saddam, heir not only to Hammurabi and Nebuchadnezzar, but also to political brutalities, Machiavellian plotting, and the naked consolidation of power. Saddam practised torture, exterminated rivals, and gassed his countrymen.* At the same time he stimulated pride in some sections of the Iraqi people, giving a boost to Arab nationalism and anti-Zionism throughout the region. The West too found reasons to support Saddam Hussein, perceiving that the Iranian ayatollahs who had recently and roughly evicted the pro-West shah might

---

*Saddam immortalised Halabja by his gassing of the Kurds in 1988. In one important account the Kurds died of Iranian- not Iraqi-delivered cyanide gas, with other doubts expressed about Iraqi culpability (see Bennis and Moushabeck, eds, *Beyond the Storm*, p. 311). However, here and elsewhere I have echoed the conventional Western account of Halabja as clear evidence of Saddam's perfidy.

be best tamed by the Iraqi despot. But Saddam then trod on sensitive US toes by (briefly) deposing the Kuwaiti al-Sabahs (which was of no concern to Washington) and taking command of Kuwaiti oil (which concerned Washington greatly). The scene was set for war.

Chapter 8 describes how Washington gave a 'green light' to Saddam, seemingly encouraging the invasion of Kuwait, before setting out to subvert the United Nations so that Iraq could be 'legally' and unambiguously crushed. A chronology of the war is given, ending in the 'turkey shoot' massacres perpetrated by Christian forces in their new crusade against a Muslim foe. The Kuwaiti and Iraqi deserts were turned into mass grave-yards, while the West rejoiced at its self-proclaimed virtue and its much-advertised prowess in the fine art of human slaughter.

There had been an orgy of killing, visited largely on hapless Iraqi conscripts trapped in the desert far from home. We should remember this. Saddam immortalised Halabja. Soon afterwards, the US-led forces immor-talised the slaughters of Fallujah, Amiriya and Mitla Ridge. And remember Milan Kundera who said (in *The Book of Laughter and Forgetting*, p. 5): 'The struggle of people against power is the struggle of memory against forgetting'. The present book – in recording various historical themes and details of recent events – is intended in part to jog the memory.

Part I

Iraq in the New World Order

1 After the 1991 Gulf War

Let me also make clear that the United States has no quarrel with the Iraqi people.

President George Bush, 1991

The prosecution of the 1991 Gulf War by the US-led coalition was intended to serve a number of purposes. It was useful to demonstrate to the world that any grave threat to American interests would not be tolerated, particularly where these required the unimpeded supply of fuel to the world's most energy-profligate nation. It was useful also to signal the new global power structure, the 'New World Order' in which a post-Cold War United States could operate without the bothersome constraint of another global super-power. It was essential in these circumstances that Iraq be mercilessly crushed. As the American academic and dissident Noam Chomsky pointed out, the much weaker opponent 'must not merely be defeated but pulverised if the central lesson of World Order is to be learned: we are the masters and you shine our shoes'.[1]

There were other purposes: some obvious and some less so. The Americans did not disguise their delight at being able to experiment with a new generation of high-technology weapons. It was helpful to be able to test such devices on the flesh and fabric of a vulnerable state that was obligingly bellicose and conveniently racially different from the United States. Another factor, rarely discussed, concerned strategic matters of an altogether different kind. Japan remains massively dependent on the huge oil tankers that ply the routes from the Gulf: how prudent for the United States to maintain a stranglehold on the crucial energy supply to a principal economic competitor in the rapidly developing tripolar system of world commerce.[2]

It would be a mistake to believe that the primary purpose of the US-initiated war on Iraq was the expulsion of Saddam Hussein from Kuwait. The expulsion was in fact no more than a means to various ends: it is plain enough that *the United States has no principled (as opposed to tactical) objection to aggressions by sovereign states against others*, and so the reasons for the onslaught on Iraq must be sought elsewhere. The US did not work to activate the United Nations in military opposition to the Israeli invasions of Lebanon and other Arab lands; to the Indonesian invasion of East Timor; or to the various South African invasions of Namibia, Angola

3

and Mozambique. Indeed, there is evidence that it conspired, to varying degrees, in such invasions; and, of course, the US itself has invaded many sovereign states (notably Grenada and Panama in recent years). Moreover, in order to protect the war on Iraq, the US sanctioned fresh contemporary or subsequent aggressions: further Israeli incursions into Lebanon, the Syrian onslaught on East Beirut, and the (post-Gulf War) Turkish invasion and occupation of northern Iraq.

The war on Iraq, realistically viewed, was designed to protect US hegemony over oil (with the broad strategic aims that this implies), to educate the world about post-Soviet political realities, to test new anti-personnel and other weapons, and to justify the absurdly high levels of investment in US military power. A further aim was to bolster the reputation of a US president beset by the 'wimp factor' and the prospect of a presidential election in 1992. No-one doubted that, whatever the Gulf War's other useful effects, the reputation of President George Bush had been much enhanced. Commentators queued up to proclaim the inevitability of Bush's re-election in November 1992. Thus, in an observation that was typical for the times, the respected journalist Mike Graham felt able to declaim: '. . . after winning the war against Iraq and presiding over the death throes of communism, Bush knows that he barely has to lift a finger to be returned to power in next year's elections'.[3] The little-known Arkansas governor, Bill Clinton, could be discounted since there were already 'whispers about secret affairs and illegitimate children . . . he appears vulnerable to the media inquisition that inevitably will occur if he runs'. In any event, 'no matter who gets the [Democratic] nomination, he is unlikely to become president . . .'[4]

Efforts to improve the image of an unimpressive American president must be judged less important than those designed to safeguard traditional US interests. Individuals come and go, but attempts to sustain hegemonic power must be maintained over decades. Iraq had tasted the fruits of US strategic calculations.

THE FACE OF IRAQ

Massacre

One of the most significant factors of the Gulf War was the speed with which the US-led coalition was able to achieve air supremacy. Iraqi air defences were systematically devastated, many of the targets being attacked time and time again. Within a matter of days it became clear that Iraqi aircraft were unlikely to engage allied planes and soon, with the speedy and comprehensive destruction of the multilayered Iraqi anti-aircraft systems, allied aircraft were able to range and bomb at will. What this meant in human terms is hard for distant and comfortable observers to imagine. Tens of thousands of hapless Iraqi conscripts, many of them from groups known to be persecuted by Saddam Hussein, had no choice but to sit in the wastes of Iraq and Kuwait until the bombs fell. Here they were forced to suffer napalm, cluster bombs that shred human flesh, the air-fuel explosives (virtual mini atom bombs) that incinerate some and asphyxiate others, and the carpets of 'earthquake' bombs laid down by B-52s – all the obscene paraphernalia that in earlier days had killed perhaps three million people in Korea, Laos, Cambodia and Vietnam.

The relatively brief war saw no first-hand journalistic accounts of the scale of the slaughter: one of the key lessons that Washington had learned from Vietnam was the tactical need to exclude journalists from the scenes of horror.[5] After the war, accounts appeared in the press, but few of these attempted to depict the numbers of the Iraqi casualties or the enormity of what had been accomplished. At Basra, the journalist Karl Waldron picked his way for 'perhaps 100 yards, trying to count the corpses, but it was a hopeless task. There were not enough whole bodies left to count'.[6] Most of the slaughter was intentional, a matter of military planning; but some of it was accidental, as when the marketplace of Fallujah was bombed. Abdullah, the grandson of Terfeh Mehsan, is – we are told – a 'handsome but frail boy of 12 . . . Where his legs used to be, Abdullah has two little stumps, the skin flayed with septic cuts'.[7] Some of the accounts describe the destruction of the convoys desperately attempting to flee from Kuwait; as, for example, on the doomed road to Umm Qasr: '60 miles of carnage . . . scores of soldiers lie in and around the vehicles, mangled and bloated in the drifting desert sands'.[8] We were left in no doubt about the face of Iraq in March 1991:

At one spot, snarling wild dogs have reduced two corpses to bare ribs. Giant carrion birds claw and pick at another; only a boot-clad foot and eyeless skull are recognisable.

One flat-bed truck has nine bodies. Each man clutches the next. Their hair and clothes are burned off, skin incinerated by heat so intense it melted the windscreen on to the dashboard.

Another body hangs from the driver's seat of a shrapnel-riddled front-end loader. Half a corpse sits in a truck with twisted metal for an engine. Blowing sand laps at other bodies on the roadside.[9]

Such reports soon stimulated discussion as to what might constitute a war crime. Thus the correspondent Denis Knight (*The Guardian*, 5 March 1991) suggested that the deliberate massacre of thousands of fleeing soldiers might qualify. And what of the specific weapons used? Paul Flynn, British Member of Parliament, cites a report that fuel air explosives were 'designed to produce nuclear-like levels of destruction without arousing popular revulsion'; and comments (*The Guardian*, 21 June 1991) that the 'cluster bombs, daisy cutters and fuel air explosives should not be classed as conventional weapons . . . They are massacre weapons'. He adds that the British government has wilfully refused to recognise 'the holocaust results of the Gulf War. The most recent estimate is that 100,000 to 200,000 Iraqis were killed and 300,000 to 700,000 injured. Most of them Shia and Kurdish conscripts'.

In no estimates are there fewer than tens of thousands of Iraqi casualties. The journalist Christopher Bellamy, after some preliminary computations, suggests that this 'still leaves a huge number [of Iraqi soldiers] missing' (possibly approaching 200,000).[10] British estimates, cited soon after the end of the war, suggest at least 90,000 Iraqi soldiers killed; with a French military expert estimating as many as 150,000 Iraqi fatalities.[11] When Beth Osborne Daponte, a demographer at the US Census Bureau, published her own estimates of 158,000 Iraqis, half of them women and children, killed in the war and its aftermath, efforts were made to fire her. Her boss, Barbara Torrey, accused Daponte of using 'false information' and of 'untrustworthiness and unreliability'. Lawyers from the American Civil Liberties Union (ACLU) then threatened legal action, whereupon Daponte was reinstated. She later commented: 'They wanted to suppress the figures because I had broken them down to show how many women and children had died . . . I find it extremely disturbing that the US Census Bureau tried to suppress and delay the release of information that is embarrassing to the current administration. Government employees should not be fired for speaking the truth . . . in this case the figures were clearly politically embarrassing.'[12]

Ken Livingstone, British MP, pointed out (*The Independent*, 11 March 1991) that most of the 'vast slaughter' took place when the Iraqi government had already declared its willingness to withdraw from Kuwait and when in any case the Iraqi army was in a state of disintegration. And Marjorie Thompson, Chair of CND and the Committee to Stop War in the Gulf, commented in letters to *The Independent* (6 March 1991) and *The Guardian* (7 March 1991) that the slaughter of the fleeing Iraqis was an unforgivable act that will come to rate alongside Dresden and Hiroshima 'as one of those acts no one in the world will be found to justify'. In one report,

Robert J. Lifton, Professor of Psychiatry and Psychology at the City University of New York, and director of the Centre on Violence and Human Survival, quoted a taxi-driver who had summed up 'accurately enough' the character of the one-sided conflict: 'This ain't no war. It's just us dropping bombs and killing people.'[13] Here it is suggested that much of the slaughter could have been avoided if the war had been ended earlier, as the Soviet Union and other states had urged, while still achieving the goals laid down by the United Nations; and perhaps the war itself could have been avoided altogether 'by pressing sanctions and a diplomacy of common security'.[14]

Further reports indicated the extent to which the war had been fought against human beings, rather than simply against tanks and other weaponry. Thus some discussion was provoked by the revelation that the American army had used earthmovers and ploughs mounted on tanks to bury thousands of Iraqi soldiers alive.[15] One attack of this sort resulted in thousands of Iraqi dead and wounded, with not a single American fatality. Colonel Lon Maggart, commander of the US 1st Brigade, estimated that his forces had buried about 650 Iraqi soldiers; and Colonel Anthony Moreno, commander of the 2nd Brigade, commented: 'For all I know, we could have killed thousands . . . What you saw was a bunch of buried trenches with people's arms and things sticking out of them'. Such improvised mass graves, to which must be added the bulldozing of thousands of Iraqi corpses at the end of the war, are part of the post-war face of Iraq and Kuwait. And there are many other characteristic features in the erstwhile battlefields: not least the massive detritus of beaten armed forces, the inevitable residue of unexploded ordnance, and the radioactive waste left in the desert by the allied forces.

In November 1991 it was revealed in a secret report by the United Kingdom Atomic Energy Authority that the allied armies had left forty tons of depleted uranium ammunition on the battlefield.[16] Here it was suggested that the long-term health of thousands of Kuwaitis and Western clean-up teams could be threatened, with the chemically toxic and radioactive waste passing into the water supply and the food chain. The report estimated that US tanks fired some 5000 depleted uranium rounds, US aircraft many tens of thousands of rounds, and British tanks 'a small number'. The tank ammunition alone, it was reckoned, contained more than 50,000lb of depleted uranium, enough material to cause '500,000 potential deaths'. A particular hazard would exist in the form of the uranium dust produced when the uranium shells hit and burned out Iraqi armoured vehicles. Ingested in sufficient quantities, the uranium dust would cause kidney failure and a range of cancers. In March 1993 an Associated Press (AP) report, citing research by the Boston-based National Toxics Campaign Fund (NTCF), stated that thousands of Gulf war veterans may be suffering from radiation sickness after being exposed to US uranium-tipped weapons (*The Guardian*, 19 March 1993). The NTCF chairman John O'Connor, referring to the widespread chemical contamination caused by the US in the Vietnam War, commented: 'What we have here is a new problem which we believe could be the Agent Orange of the nineties'.

It can be assumed that many of the Iraqi casualties were caused by inaccurate bombing: the US forces, while at first lauding the reliability of the 'smart' weapons, later came to admit the massive number of inaccurate targetings. Thus in one classified US analysis, the computer-navigated Tomahawk cruise missiles hit their targets just over 50 per cent of the time.[17] The 'smart' laser-guided bombs launched from the US F-117A Stealth attack jets hit their targets in only about 60 per cent of the missions flown, in contrast to the 90 per cent claimed earlier.[18] In any case, of the 88,500 tons of bombs dropped on Iraq and Kuwait, only 6520 tons were precision-guided, and 70 per cent of the total 'missed their targets', according to a defence expert quoted by *The Washington Post*.[19]

At the end of the war, wrecked armaments, unexploded mines and other munitions, radioactive debris and mass graves littered the Iraqi and Kuwaiti deserts. It was also suspected, though not at that time known for certain, that the American forces had drawn up plans for the contingency of launching chemical and nuclear attacks against Iraq. Thus Major Johan Persson, a liaison officer at a Swedish army field hospital, declared in interviews in Stockholm that he had seen official guidelines about the use of nuclear and chemical weapons in certain circumstances.[20] Declared Major Persson: 'There was such an order. I saw it. I had it in my hand. It was the real thing.' When US Secretary of State James Baker met the Iraqi foreign minister Tariq Aziz on 9 January 1991, days before the start of the US-led bombing of Iraq, Baker declared: 'We know that you have a vast stock of chemical weapons . . . Our sincere advice to you is not to even think of using them. If you do, or if we feel that you did, then our reply will be unrestrained. I hope I am understood well.' The authoritative commentator Mohamed Heikal noted Aziz's understanding 'that Baker was hinting at the use of nuclear weapons'.[21]

It was also known that the infrastructure of the Iraqi state had been comprehensively devastated, though detailed reports had yet to emerge. At the end of the war the toll of US casualties was small; to the hundreds of thousands of Iraqi dead, wounded and traumatised, tens of thousands more casualties were to be added.

Desolation

The six weeks of allied air raids had destroyed the bulk of the electrical power stations that supplied hospitals, water pumping facilities, sewage treatment plants and water purification facilities; in addition, these various facilities had often been totally or partially destroyed by the bombing. A consequence was that many parts of Iraq had to face a public health crisis of vast proportions. In the immediate aftermath of the war the residents of Baghdad, having had no electricity or running water since the onset of the bombing in mid-January, had to rely for drinking water on the Tigris river, now being fouled by gushing streams of raw sewage. Iraqi and international health authorities predicted that unless sanctions on Iraq were lifted the capital and other major cities would soon be facing outbreaks of cholera, typhoid, hepatitis and polio. Dr Mohammad Ani, the Iraqi director for immunisation and primary health care for the ministry of health, commented: 'We are being killed indirectly.'[22] The Rustumiya and Sarafiya sewage treatment and water pumping stations had been attacked with allied missiles and bombs, and nearby water treatment plants were working at about one-quarter of capacity. Raymond Naimy, an official of the United Nations Children's Fund (UNICEF), commented that Baghdad's water supply had been cut by 90–95 per cent, and a World Health Organisation (WHO) delegation noted a fourfold increase in the number of children being treated for diarrhoea.[23]

In March 1991 Dr Roger Vivarié, of the Paris-based Médecins Sans Frontières, reported: 'The situation in Baghdad and in Falluja, 80km from the capital, which was visited by our team, was already very difficult a week ago. Hospitals, once among the most advanced and best equipped in the region, now lack the most elementary working tools. There is no infrastructure, no running water, no food and no medicine. All sanitary infrastructures have gone and not a single hospital is in a position to provide the most elementary of services.'[24] The UN special envoy, Martti Ahtisaari, reported that Iraq was in a 'near apocalypse': Iraq was like a patient whose central nervous system had been destroyed. Ahtisaari warned that since the country's energy systems had been so badly damaged by bombing, food aid alone would not be sufficient to avert disaster. The UN sanctions committee was urged to respond to the crisis by declaring that an 'urgent humanitarian need' existed throughout Iraq. In his UN-sponsored report, Ahtisaari himself commented: 'Nothing we had seen or read had quite prepared us for the particular form of devastation which has now befallen the country . . . the recent conflict has wrought near-apocalyptic results upon the economic infrastructure'. Moreover, 'sanctions decided upon by the Security Council

... seriously affected the country's ability to feed its people'; all sources of fuel and power and modern means of communication were now 'essentially defunct', with the telephone system and the mail service destroyed; the supply of food to private citizens had been reduced to 'a trickle'. There was a real risk of widespread deaths through disease and perhaps starvation. Ibrahim al-Nouri, the director of the Iraqi Red Crescent, was reporting on cases of cholera and typhoid detected in several towns, and urging international aid organisations to send water purification chemicals to help combat the diseases. Relief officials in Jordan were commenting that Iraqi hospitals had been forced to halve rations for their patients.

In Basra and other cities women were forced to wash clothes and kitchen utensils in water contaminated with raw sewage, with the incidence of disease sharply increasing because of the shortage of food and the lack of clean water for drinking. All but two of the city's filtration plants were destroyed, and cholera and typhoid, not yet at epidemic proportions, were increasing. Said al-Tamimi, a medical engineer, was quoted: 'A friend of mine brought me a bucket of water from the mains supply in which was swimming a little snake.' The death rate, particularly among children, was rapidly increasing: the main bridges across the Tigris, the Euphrates and the Shatt al-Arab had been destroyed, making it impossible to take children to hospital where, in any case, virtually all normal services were impossible. At the same time it was impossible to monitor with any accuracy the incidence of the burgeoning cholera epidemic, since during the war and the ensuing civil unrest most of the laboratory equipment used to measure the disease had been destroyed.

In a damning article in *The New York Times* Zbigniew Brzezinski, the former national security adviser to President Carter, shattered the US claim that the war was fought with discrimination to minimise civilian casualties. He emphasised that damage-toll 'raises the moral question of the proportionality of the response' to Saddam Hussein's aggression against Kuwait. The respected British journalist Peter Jenkins, commenting on the Brzezinski report and other material, noted that the peace 'has turned into a nightmare, the continuation of the war by other means'.[25] Joost Hiltermann, Middle East organiser for Physicians for Human Rights (PHR), commented: 'The bombing was called surgical, but we're calling it neurosurgical: with extraordinary accuracy the allied bombs took the brain out of the country's ability to survive'; and PHR president Jack Geiger, having toured the region of Basra, described the effect as: 'Bomb now, die later. You don't kill people, you just cause the system to collapse.' The main themes of the PHR report were familiar enough: malnutrition, diarrhoea and dehydration among the children; dangerous drinking water; and a crippled economy.[26]

In the same spirit a Harvard medical team visiting Iraq found that the death rate of children under five was two to three times higher than before the war. They estimated that over the coming year a further 170,000 children would die because of the problems caused by the Gulf War: the massively dislocated social infrastructure and the harshness of the enforced sanctions. Now typhoid and cholera epidemics were flaring up throughout the country, with hospitals – lacking antibiotics, infant formula, medicines, bandages and other supplies – unable to treat malnourished children. One Baghdad hospital reported 30–35 new cases of cholera a week during April 1991; and infectious typhoid patients were being discharged in all regions because of a shortage of chloramphenicol, the drug needed for treatment. Dr Megan Passey, the leader of the Harvard team, said that the report would be presented to UN agencies, the US Congress and international relief agencies.[27]

In May 1991 Iraq declared it was desperate for access to its overseas assets, now frozen by the US-dominated Security Council, in order to pay for the next four months' food supply. Deals had been signed with Australia and Canada for the import of 1.5 billion tons of wheat, half the country's needs, but the orders were dependent on Iraq gaining access to its foreign assets. It soon became clear that the United States, Britain and France were in no mood to lift the sanctions on Iraq, while at the same time Washington began pressing for a 50 per cent levy on all future Iraqi oil revenues. In June the Soviet Union, backed by China and India in the Security Council, urged some relaxation of the punitive sanctions on Iraq, if only to allow the purchase of food and medicines. On 12 June Britain blocked an Iraqi move for the unfreezing of currency printed in Britain for the purchase of food, but the Security Council's sanctions committee agreed that thirty-one countries could release Iraqi assets to facilitate the purchase of food, medicines and other essential supplies. At the same time it was clear that this measure was insufficient to meet Iraq's growing humanitarian needs. Figures provided by the Iraqi health ministry suggested that many patients were dying from infectious diarrhoeal diseases; death from such a cause was rare in 1990 but in the post-war period deaths were running at about thirty-two per thousand admitted to hospital (in April and May 1991, 17,000 people were admitted). At Baghdad's main hospital for infectious diseases the staff acknowledged that they were treating many suspected cholera cases, as well as typhoid and meningitis.[28]

Dr Michael Viola, an American professor of medicine and microbiology who visited Iraq along with two other New York physicians, reported on the severe epidemic of several diseases, a situation now aggravated by malnutrition ('You don't need statistics. It's everywhere'). The journalist

Patrick Tyler, who visited dozens of paediatric and infectious-disease wards across the country, encountered more than one hundred cases of marasmus, a condition of progressive emaciation caused by advanced malnutrition: 'Typical symptoms are a gaunt skeletal look and distended stomach. There were also many obvious cases of kwashiorkor, an advanced form of protein deficiency in toddlers seldom seen outside drought-stricken areas of Africa.' Dr Amera Ali, a physician at Ibn Baladi Hospital in Baghdad, commented that if all the marasmus cases were admitted, 'the hospitals would be full in one day'.[29] In July 1991 the UN sanctions committee rejected an Iraqi request that $1.5 billion-worth of oil be sold to buy food and medicine.

By August, according to official Iraqi sources, more than 11,000 people had died of starvation. The poor were at particular risk from malnutrition and disease: there was no suggestion that the Ba'athist leadership, against whom the sanctions were supposedly directed, was going hungry. Soon Western aid donors were warning that unless international sanctions on Iraq were eased the country could face malnutrition and disease on an unprecedented scale. UN officials confirmed the fresh incidence of marasmus and kwashiorkor, and reported infectious diseases such as typhoid, hepatitis, meningitis and gastroenteritis surging out of control. Washington and London continued to block a relaxation of sanctions on the grounds that the Iraqi authorities were refusing to co-operate with UN officials required to inspect Iraq's surviving military facilities. In July a UN mission led by Prince Sadruddin Aga Khan issued a report on 'humanitarian needs in Iraq', compiled following 'observations and conclusions drawn from on-the-spot evaluation'. The report declared that sanctions were having a substantial effect on the living standards of the civilian population. Damage to water treatment plants and the international block on the supply of spare parts had cut off an estimated 2.5 million Iraqis from the government system they relied upon before the war. The 14.5 million Iraqis continuing to receive water via the pre-war system were now receiving less than a quarter of the pre-war amounts, and this was of doubtful quality. Raw sewage continued to flow in city streets and into rivers used for washing and drinking, resulting in unprecedented levels of infectious diseases, including typhoid and cholera. The international blockade on spare parts meant that medical, surgical, dental and laboratory equipment could not be maintained, and that the electrical supply for most agricultural purposes was running at about one third of the previous year's. The price levels of wheat and rice – the two normal staple foods – remained at 45 and 22 times their pre-war levels, with government rationing providing only about one third of the typical family's food needs. Almost half of the nation's 900,000 telephone lines had been damaged beyond repair, and all the international communications facilities had been destroyed.

The Sadruddin mission urged that Iraq be allowed to import $1 billion-worth of spare parts and other materials to begin the restoration of the oil industry; that immediate steps be taken to alleviate the priority needs identified by the mission in the areas of food supply, medicine, water and sanitation, power generation, telecommunications and the oil sector; that food imports, to meet the minimum consumption requirements, be allowed; that imports of fertilisers, pesticides, animal feed and drugs, machinery and spare parts needed to repair the irrigation and drainage system be allowed; and that imports should also be permitted for the repair of surgical, dental and diagnostic equipment, for ambulances, for water pumping and treatment facilities, for the sewage system, for electrical generation, for the oil industry, and for telecommunications.

On 26 August 1991 Iraq reported that more than 14,000 children had died because of the lack of drugs since the United Nations imposed the trade embargo. A month later, publicity was given to the results of the study carried out by the 87-member Harvard Study Team which investigated some 6000 Iraqi households. The earlier enquiry carried out by the same team found that the child mortality rate had doubled. Now it was found that the death rate of under-fives had trebled and amounted to tens of thousands.[30] Disease was rampant, with widespread epidemics of typhoid and cholera. There was also a major increase in domestic violence, with 'the highest rate of war-related psychological trauma ever found in a post-war study'.[31] At the same time the UN Secretary-General, Javier Perez de Cuellar, was urging the Security Council to allow Iraq to sell increased amounts of oil to provide revenue for humanitarian purchases.

In November 1991 there were reports of food riots in Baghdad and other Iraqi cities, with particularly serious disorder in the Baghdad (Shia) suburbs of Thawra and Khadhimaya.[32] Prices of some essential foods had risen a hundredfold. Fifty kilogram bags of sugar and rice were now costing 500 dinars, equivalent to two months' salary for a professional. The Iraqi government, faced with a partially collapsed currency, ordered the major Rafidain Bank to accept currency known to be counterfeit. On 14 November the Iraqi agriculture minister, Abdul Wahab al-Sabagh, declared that thousands more children and old people would starve unless UN sanctions were lifted soon: '. . . only fifteen per cent of our people can afford to buy food on the free market. The rest must accept hunger. That is the reality of the embargo'. Iraq had been allowed to import 100,000 tonnes of grain over the eight-month period since the end of the war, but the normal national requirement was 200,000 tonnes a month: 'Today we have a great lack of food and medicines. We lack spare parts for agricultural machinery. We lack fertilisers and pesticides as well as spares to get our power stations and oil refineries working again. We are a country that lives in the dark . . . we need pumps to bring the water to the fields and these require electricity which we do not have.' At this time the United Nations was expressing a willingness to allow Iraq to raise revenues to buy food and other essential goods, provided that the UN was allowed to supervise food distribution and secure reparations for the victims of the Iraqi aggression. The British Overseas Development Minister, Lynda Chalker, announced that further action might have to be taken against Saddam Hussein unless he agreed to the UN terms for oil sales.

On 20 November 1991 the director of Oxfam, Frank Judd, having just visited the region, called for a big international humanitarian effort to help the millions of Iraqis suffering malnutrition and now facing a winter without adequate food, medicines or housing.[33] Now children with matchstick limbs and distended bellies, 'like drought victims from Ethiopia', could be seen in Baghdad and other Iraqi cities. A doctor in a Baghdad hospital commented: 'It's a vicious circle. They get weaker and weaker from lack of food. Then they are susceptible to disease because they have no immunity, and that weakens them even more.' Britain had agreed a release of £70 million-worth of Iraqi assets to buy the freedom of the businessman, Ian Richter, but there was no control over how the money would be used: it was unlikely that the plight of the needy would be alleviated, and in any case President George Bush had asserted that the UN economic embargo must remain in effect. Again there was no suggestion that the measures were hurting the Ba'athist leadership. Some 30 per cent of all Iraqi children were now malnourished, with infant mortality trebled since the Gulf War.[34]

The situation in Iraq following the war was plain enough. The US-dominated Security Council was insisting that *de facto* biological warfare be waged against the impotent and traumatised Iraqi people, not against the Ba'athist leadership who alone were culpable. By now the reports were frequent and unambiguous: the UN sanctions – whatever the callous machinations of Saddam Hussein – were bringing disease, malnutrition and starvation to virtually an entire nation. Louise Cainkar, director of the Chicago-based Database Project on Palestinian Human Rights, having spent several weeks conducting fieldwork in Iraq, reported in detail on the effects of the UN-imposed sanctions on Iraq.[35] In Basra she encountered 'the same scene I was to see over and over again . . . Iraqi women holding thin, bloated and malnourished children . . .'. On 20 May 1991 President Bush declared that the trade embargo would continue: 'We don't want to lift these sanctions as long as Saddam Hussein is in power.' And in the same spirit, the deputy national security adviser, Robert Gates, nominated by Bush to head the CIA, stated that the Iraqis would 'pay the price while he [Saddam Hussein] is in power'.[36]

Maintaining Sanctions

While few observers doubted the deteriorating plight of the ordinary Iraqi people, and while Bush repeatedly emphasised that the option of further military action against Iraq was still open, the punitive sanctions – including a (*de facto* if not *de jure*) ban on imports of food and medicine – remained in place. WHO and UNICEF had warned of the 'catastrophe' that would beset Iraq if sanctions were not lifted, but Washington and London remained largely oblivious to this concern. In May 1991 the White House spokesman Marlin Fitzwater repeated the familiar refrain that 'All possible sanctions will be maintained until he [Saddam Hussein] is gone.' There was plenty of evidence that sanctions were devastating the Iraqi people, but no evidence that they were undermining the Ba'athist regime.

The deteriorating health of the Iraqi population became increasingly obvious through the summer of 1991, though the US and Britain – as lead players on the Security Council – seemed reluctant to agree any relaxation in sanctions. These countries even went so far as to block Iraq's unilateral efforts to export $1 billion-worth of oil to buy food and other essential products, such as water purification tablets. A few states connived with Iraq to break the UN-imposed sanctions, but Iraqi imports remained only a fraction of pre-war levels. Jordan, for instance, was found to be trading with Iraq in violation of UN stipulations, as shown by an Iraqi–Jordanian Joint Committee documents, with minutes signed by Abdul Wahid al-Makhzumi, adviser of the Central Bank or Iraq, and Dr Ibrahim Badran, under-secretary of the Ministry of Industry and Trade for Jordan.[37] In July there were signs that the US and Britain were prepared to allow Iraq to sell some oil for humanitarian purposes, provided such activity could be closely monitored and regulated to bring reparations to some of those who had suffered because of the Iraqi aggression. There were signs also that the enduring US hostility to Iraq, evidenced by threat of further military strikes, was now being countered by other Security Council members unwilling to see further conflict in the Gulf. On 29 July Maurice Gourdault Montagne, a spokesman for the French government, urged the Security Council to ease the trade embargo against Iraq. This pressure, combined with the entreaties of WHO and UNICEF, had some effect: on 15 August 1991 the Security Council authorised Baghdad to sell up to $1.6 billion-worth of oil to help pay for desperately needed food. The deal, under strict UN control, was seen as a one-off humanitarian gesture. Other resolutions passed at the same time fixed a ceiling of 30 per cent on the amount of annual Iraqi oil sales used to pay reparations; and condemned Baghdad's failure to co-operate with UN inspectors responsible for destroying Iraq's clandestine nuclear weapons programme.[38] It was soon being pointed out that the UN concession was totally inadequate, with even Secretary-General Perez de Cuellar commenting that the restrictions on the permitted oil sale would provide the Iraqis with 'substantially less than the minimum food import requirements'.[39] The Iraqi government, perhaps predictably, condemned the half-hearted UN gesture as an interference with Iraqi sovereignty.

On 4 February 1992 the Iraqi ambassador to the UN, Abdul Amir al-Anbari, declared that Iraq would not resume talks on possible oil sales: 'We decided that the talks were no longer useful or productive given the conditions imposed by Security Council resolution 706, which renders the production of Iraq oil a non-profitable enterprise and the Iraqi oil non-marketable.' However, by the end of March, agreement had been reached between the UN and the Iraqi authorities on the terms that would govern the resumption of Iraqi oil sales. Such agreement came too late to save many thousands of Iraqi deaths: a senior Iraqi health official, Abdul Jabbar Abdul Abbas, reported that in the first four months of 1992 the UN economic sanctions had caused nearly 41,000 deaths, including 14,000 child fatalities. And UN officials estimated that nearly five million children in the Middle East would spend their formative years in deprived circumstances as a result of the Gulf crisis. Thus Richard Reid, the UN Children's Fund director for North Africa and the Middle East, commented that: 'We can speak with alarming, grave assurance of a lost generation.' On 3 September 1992 Britain ruled out any easing of sanctions on Iraq, instead warning Iraq against any attempt to interfere with the aerial exclusion zone over southern Iraq (see below). A few weeks later, the Harvard research team published their estimate that 46,900 children under the age of five died in Iraq between January and August 1991 as an indirect result of the bombing, the civilian uprisings and the UN economic embargo.

Iraq, claiming purely humanitarian motives, made frequent requests for an easing of sanctions. Thus in November 1992, for example, Tariq Aziz visited New York to ask the UN to relax the current restrictions, but the Security Council issued a statement saying that Iraq had only partially complied with UN demands and so there could be no relaxation of sanctions. It was now clear that the comprehensive embargo was drastically affecting every aspect of Iraqi life. There were serious and worsening shortages of food, medicines and the spare parts needed to repair the national infrastructure (sewage plant, hospitals, water purification systems and the like). Before the war children were given government-supplied meals at school but this was no longer possible; and the embargo, extensive enough to cover imports of paper, meant that newspapers were reducing their number of pages and editions, and that the book trade had virtually collapsed, massively hampering education at all levels. Ian Katz, reporting for *The Guardian* (29 January 1993), describes how the resilient Iraqi people are struggling to cope with appalling difficulties: thousands of engineers and doctors are unemployed, a pharmacist tells how she can only service a quarter of the prescriptions brought to her, a dentist describes how she cannot any longer obtain the necessary anaesthetics. And there is the frequent suggestion that the repression by Saddam's regime is a lesser evil than Iraq's constant humiliation at the hands of the West.

The West, for the most part, continued to pay little attention to the privations brought to the Iraqi people by the seemingly permanent sanctions. Hugh Stephens, the co-ordinator for the unofficial British Commission of Inquiry for the International War Crimes Tribunal, noted (in *The Independent*, 15 February 1993): 'Iraq is inhabited not only by its president, but by 18 million people who, in systematic contravention of Article 54 of the 1977 Geneva Protocols, are being subjected to hunger as a means of war, are being deprived of essential medical supplies and are facing the destruction of services essential to civilian life.' There were few signs that the bulk of the Iraqi people were blaming such privations on Saddam.

THE FACE OF KUWAIT

Iraqi Terror

Kuwaitis suffered through the war and its aftermath, first persecuted throughout the period of the Iraqi occupation and then hounded and tormented by their own countrymen. To these sufferings were added the horrors of the allied bombing – many of the selected targets were in Kuwait itself – and the wanton destruction perpetrated by the fleeing Iraqi forces. Kuwait, like much of Iraq, was a devastated land littered with the detritus of war: unexploded mines and other ordnance, wrecked military and civilian vehicles, fragments of radioactive shells, burning wells, massive pollution, and the grim residue of human body parts and decaying corpses.

There was soon ample evidence of the brutalities inflicted by Iraqi troops on their helpless Kuwaiti captives. These included, in the words of an

Amnesty International (AI) report, 'the detention without trial of thousands of civilians and military personnel . . . widespread torture . . . and the extrajudicial execution of hundreds of unarmed civilians, including children'. In addition there was widespread destruction of property and extensive looting, particularly of food, medicines and medical equipment. By November 1990 Amnesty had received the names of more than 875 Kuwaitis said to be in custody, and official Kuwaiti sources estimated that between 6000 and 7000 Kuwaiti military personnel had been taken to Iraq. A memorandum issued by the Kuwaiti Red Crescent described the daily attacks carried out by Iraqi soldiers:

> Arrest and torture threatened every individual. Young men were shot near their homes and in front of their families, and this method was used to terrorise the people and to eliminate the young men on the pretext that they worked in the resistance.

Former detainees interviewed by Amnesty declared that they were not brought before any judicial authorities, and that they were denied visits from lawyers, doctors or family:

> I was interrogated about the resistance. They applied electricity to my chest, head and arms. I felt paralysed for nearly three days. They also poured an acid-like liquid on my back and used a pincer-like device which they placed around my fingers and tightened. I was released after my friends paid a bribe.

There is more of such testimony in the report issued by Amnesty at the end of 1990. In the abbreviated version of the report no less than thirty-six categories of torture are listed, for some of which Amnesty had obtained photographic evidence. (Those interested in this catalogue of horror should consult the AI report.) There were reports of extrajudicial executions following such 'offences' as:

> Trying to flee Kuwait;
> Giving medical treatment to suspected opposition activists;
> Refusing to allow medical equipment to be looted from hospitals;
> Carrying large amounts of money;
> Carrying the Kuwaiti flag or photographs of the emir of Kuwait;
> Refusing to demonstrate allegiance to Saddam Hussein; and
> Delivering food to people's homes.

People were too frightened to remove bodies from the streets; but, despite this, the morgues were soon full. Hospital refrigerators intended for food were used to hold the accumulating number of corpses, and at the same time many bodies were cast into mass graves. Some of the atrocity stories – for example, the Iraqi theft of hospital incubators – were later identified as black propaganda, but there can be little doubt that the bulk of the reports of Iraqi brutalities were substantially true. In one graphic account the respected Middle East journalist Robert Fisk describes how an entire Kuwaiti family disappeared after Iraqi soldiers came knocking at the door.[40] This was only one of many families treated in such a fashion ('they took 14 Kuwaiti families from Mishrif alone. No one has seen them since'). Many other accounts have recorded the brutalities suffered by the captive population at the hands of a cruel and increasingly demoralised occupying force.

Kuwaiti Terror

The liberation of Kuwait did not herald peace for all Kuwaitis. Many of the people living in Kuwait were foreigners with few civil or political rights in the emirate.[41] The war had exacerbated tensions in the Kuwaiti community, with some groups – especially the Palestinians – regarded with at best suspicion, at worst hatred. The PLO, desperate for some sort of tactical victory in the Middle East, had expressed support for the Iraqi invasion, and many Kuwaitis assumed that the Palestinians in their midst would have welcomed a victory by Saddam Hussein. The result was a further round of human rights violations, with the Kuwaitis – many observers would say understandably – playing the part of persecutors.

Many Palestinians who had fled to Jordan and elsewhere at the start of hostilities were now struggling to return to their former jobs in Kuwait. At the Kuwaiti embassy in Jordan many signed a 'book of congratulations' in the hope that this gesture would guarantee their safe return, but the Kuwaiti ambassador, Suleiman Alfassam, seemed less than enthusiastic about re-storing jobs to all of the 400,000 Palestinians who had worked in pre-crisis Kuwait: 'Why don't the Palestinians go to Iraq or to Libya? Gaddafi has said he'll take them. In the old days we had hundreds of thousands of Egyptians, Indians and Asians. With our new life, I don't think we need the whole bunch back again.' And he added, 'Don't blame us if there are a few reprisals.' In fact there was already the possibility of a civil war in Kuwait between the Kuwaitis and the Palestinians. Kuwaiti and Saudi soldiers were reported to be victimising the Palestinians as supposed supporters of Saddam Hussein, a situation that was set to escalate in the immediate post-war weeks. One young Palestinian showed a journalist the welts and bruises he had received at the hands of the Kuwaiti army,[42] and soon there was a proliferation of such accounts. At the time of the Iraqi invasion there were 800,000 Kuwaiti citizens in a country of two million, with the 400,000 Palestinians the largest minority group. Now they were forced to look to their own survival.

One Palestinian father told how his son had been taken away by Kuwaiti soldiers on the first night after the Iraqis were driven out of the emirate. When the man went to the police station to enquire he was told: 'Go away or I will shoot you.' In similar fashion a Palestinian doctor who had helped the Kuwaitis throughout the period of the Iraqi occupation was taken away by Kuwaiti soldiers and never seen again. The chief of the International Committee of the Red Cross in Kuwait City, Walter Stocker, commented that he could not comment on the numbers of Palestinians charged with collaboration with the Iraqis: 'the situation is still very touchy'. It was now being reported that dozens of Palestinians were disappearing 'into a secret web of interrogation, torture, detention, deportation and in a few cases death'.[43] Palestinians were being picked up at random, tortured for hours, days or weeks, and then shot dead and buried in unmarked graves. Arab medical workers and grave-diggers testified to seeing the bodies. The body of one man, his hands still handcuffed behind his back, was delivered to Kuwait City's Mubarak al-Kabir hospital. He had been shot in the thighs and the shoulder, and his head had been smashed so severely that the entire back of his skull was missing. Hospital workers had no doubt that the man was a Palestinian tortured and killed by Kuwaiti soldiers.[44]

The Kuwaiti minister of state for cabinet affairs, Abdul Rahman al-Awadi, said he did not think that 'purposely organised torture by the government' was taking place, but said he would not be surprised 'if there is some hard handling for personal reasons'. At the same time government officials were talking of the need to 'clean out' the Palestinian suburbs, a process that could be heard 'every night in the sound of gunfire from the Palestinian neighbourhoods'.[45] Palestinians who had lived in Kuwait for years, sometimes for decades, had now lost all security. There were growing numbers of disappearances, and the threat of a new forced mass exodus, another flood of impoverished refugees across the unstable Middle East. Many of the Kuwaiti Palestinians were now hiding at home, out of sight of the roaming vigilantes. If, reasoned the Palestinians, they could survive the period of martial law then things may improve. Human rights groups were expressing growing concern at the random detentions, torture and executions in Kuwaiti police stations, army camps, hospitals and schools. Middle East Watch had estimated some 2000 people detained and forty executed since the expulsion of the Iraqis, with beatings and torture common.[46] Palestinians, some of whom had sheltered Kuwaitis during the Iraqi occupation, were abused in food queues, told to 'ask Saddam' to give them food. Others were beaten in police stations until they could not walk. A father collecting the body of his son from a police station found that he had been burnt and beaten all over; a cousin said, 'his father fainted when he saw him'. Kuwaiti Palestinians acknowledged that there were some collaborators but maintained that most Palestinians were opposed to the Iraqi invasion.

On 25 March 1991 Kuwaiti officials in the justice ministry announced that about 700 Arabs, mostly Palestinians and Iraqis, were to face trial for war crimes and collaboration. Human rights groups estimated that there were about 2000 foreign Arabs in detention, most of them being tortured on a daily basis, and it was thought that a substantial number of these would face trial in special courts. If convicted, the accused would face up to fifteen years in a Kuwaiti jail or execution. The Kuwaitis also opened an exhibition of Iraqi torture tools, found at a police station in the Surra neighbourhood after the Iraqi retreat. Now US officials in Kuwait were becoming increasingly alarmed at the scale of Kuwaiti brutalities, particularly when it emerged that members of the al-Sabah royal family had formed 'goon squads' to carry out attacks on Palestinians, so giving explicit sanction to the brutal behaviour of Kuwaiti soldiers and armed civilians. Said Colonel Ron Smith of the 352nd Civil Affairs Command, working with the Kuwaiti police: 'We're putting severe pressure on them, telling them "you don't want to look like Iraqis".' The US ambassador to Kuwait, Edward Gnehm, reportedly warned Sheikh Saad al-Abdullah al-Sabah, the crown prince, that human rights abuses would lessen international support for Kuwait: 'There is credible information that there have been some abuses. I have furnished the government with the names of places and people. The government has never denied that these things are going on.'[47] Efforts to end the abuses seemed largely ineffectual. Beatings and disappearances were continuing throughout Kuwait, with mutilated bodies being dumped in the streets, and bands of armed Kuwaiti men touring the streets with the express intention of raping foreign women. In one report, a rape crisis was 'sweeping unchecked across the recently liberated emirate, worse than anything experienced during the Iraqi occupation. It has led to calls for a special force to protect women from the uniformed thugs who roam the streets and knock on doors in search of easy prey.'[48] Said a Kuwaiti-born Palestinian, writing under the pseudonym of Khaled Ghaleb: 'I ask my Kuwaiti friends: is what you are doing any better than what Saddam did?'[49]

Large metal cages had now been constructed for use in the Kuwaiti courtrooms to hold the accused Palestinians, Iraqis and others who had confessed under torture. It was expected that some of the accused would face execution, though the method of killing had not yet been determined. Traditionalists were said to favour public hangings in Safat Square, near the Sheraton and Plaza hotels, with bureaucrats preferring the compound of Al Salibiya prison, to which the public could be given access for the occasion. Many of the prisoners, denied access to family or lawyers, were being held in the notorious G-1 detention centre, the headquarters of the Kuwaiti National Guard, often in underground cells, 'hidden from the prying eyes of the International Red Cross'.[50] Amnesty was now reporting that hundreds of people were being held in 'deplorable conditions' at a military prison outside Kuwait City: scores of prisoners had been extra-judicially killed, with many others routinely tortured with beatings, electric shocks and the denial of food and water: 'Victims have been gunned down in public, and taken away, tortured and killed in secret. Hundreds of victims were plucked from their homes, taken from the streets, or arrested at checkpoints, many to be tortured in police stations, schools and other makeshift detention centres.'[51] Again, there were reports that the Kuwaiti royal family was implicated in the torture of Palestinians, many of whom had remained loyal to Kuwait throughout the period of the Iraqi occupation.[52] The International Committee of the Red Cross was warning the Kuwaiti government and its allies that reprisals against Palestinians and other civilians were violations of international law, though such warnings seemed to do little to influence the course of events.

On 19 May 1991 the Kuwaiti authorities began the trials of 628 accused men, mostly Palestinians and Iraqis, for allegedly helping the Iraqi forces during the invasion. Soon the sentences were being handed down: two Iraqi brothers were given twelve years each for possessing four decorative bullets on a key ring; and a Palestinian, Adnan Abed Ali-Hussein, was sentenced to fifteen years in jail for wearing a T-shirt carrying a picture of Saddam Hussein. Monitoring agencies described the trials as scandalous, while Western diplomats noted that they were unsatisfactory. Later, under mounting international pressure, the Kuwaiti government agreed to review some of the verdicts of the martial law courts.[53] In September 1991 the human rights group Middle East Watch accused the United States of ignoring the murder, torture, arbitrary detentions and deportations in Kuwait: 'The reinstated Kuwaiti government has trampled on [human] rights at nearly every turn, often with the use of violence.' The martial law tribunals, declared the group, were a charade, with confessions forced through torture and the right to consult lawyers denied; and with some of the arbitrary deportations involving dumping people in the middle of a mine-infested desert without food, water or medicine.

The Kuwaiti abuses of human rights persisted throughout 1992. There were reports of hundreds of Asian maids and nannies being beaten and raped by their wealthy Kuwaiti employers, and then being further sexually abused by Kuwaiti soldiers.[54] One case involved a 20-year-old Sri Lankan, Singala Bolasi, admitted to hospital with broken ankles and severe internal bleeding after her Kuwaiti employer had first raped her and then thrown her over a balcony. An appeal was made to the Kuwaiti emir, but the authorities took no action.[55] In September 1992 various UN bodies were expressing concern at the fate of the remaining Palestinian community in Kuwait. Tens of thousands of Palestinians, many of them having worked in Kuwait for many years and maintained their loyalty to the regime, had been deported and dumped in the desert. Most of the former Palestinian neighbourhoods in Kuwait have now been emptied of residents. In late 1992 plans were announced to turn the Palestinian suburb of Hawaii into an amusement park.

In January 1993 it was reported that Kuwait was continuing its systematic deportation of undesirable groups. A Captain Khalid Hussein, a local Kuwaiti police commander, was quoted: 'They are Palestinians, Jordanians but most are badouns.'[56] The stateless *badouns* (the term means 'without') often served in the Kuwaiti armed forces, even in the war against Iraq. But even this did not entitle them to remain in Kuwait, and their forced departure has left Kuwait with a massive gap in its armed forces: down from a pre-war total of 25,000 to less than 16,000 today. Kuwait has rejected offers of armed assistance from Egypt, Syria and Oman, seemingly only trusting its Western allies.

One estimate suggests that Kuwait has lost some 800,000 of its pre-invasion inhabitants, nearly half of these evicted as belonging to countries that were deemed to have supported Iraq. There are serious gaps, not only in the armed forces, but also in such service sectors as health and education; and trade has been hit. It is often suggested that the Kuwaiti authorities can no longer afford to maintain comprehensive public services because so much oil revenue has disappeared through corruption. It is now generally acknowledged that Kuwait carried out its own brand of 'ethnic cleansing' – before the term became current with the collapse of Yugoslavia – by expelling 360,000 Palestinians from their homes after the liberation of Kuwait. It is also recognised that as 'gold-plated Kuwait rots from within' the corrupt al-Sabahs, still undemocratically ensconced in power, have little public support. The ruling sheikhs continue to involve themselves in financial scandals (for example, the celebrated case revolving around the London-based Kuwait Investment Office) while foreign women in their country – mostly Filipinos, Indians and Sri Lankans – tell horrific stories of seemingly unrestricted rape and brutalisation. The al-Sabahs, for the moment, serve Western interests and so, for the moment, are secure.

POST-WAR CHRONOLOGY

In most Western propaganda the 1991 Gulf War had a tidy ending (though the carefully cultivated depiction did not last long): the Iraqi forces had been comprehensively routed, Saddam Hussein had been crushingly evicted from the sovereign emirate of Kuwait, and the casualties had been 'mercifully light' (the Iraqi dead and injured were rarely included in the tallies). Now it was the task of the United Nations to 'build the peace', a job which somehow lacked the self-righteous energy and commitment that the US-led war had enjoyed. Soon it would be found that the peace was a far from tidy affair.

Once President Bush had declared a suspension of hostilities the Iraqi ambassador to the United Nations, Abdul Amir al-Anbari, declared that Iraq would co-operate over the return of allied prisoners and in other ways. There were signs that the embargo on food and medicine to Iraq would soon be lifted, though most other restrictions on the country would be maintained while Saddam Hussein remained in power. At that time it was also being suggested that Iraqi oil sales might be permitted as a way of securing reparations for Kuwait and other injured parties. At the same time, in late February 1991, the coalition allies began suggesting that the Iraqi people should rise up and overthrow Saddam Hussein and his tyrannical regime. The peace would be easier on Iraq, declared Western politicians, if Saddam were to go. On 28 February 1991, soon after the cessation of military action, Prime Minister John Major told the House of Commons that Iraq would remain an 'international pariah' while Saddam Hussein remained in power. In the same spirit a spokesman for the Israeli prime minister, Yitzhak Shamir, continued to demand the overthrow of Saddam Hussein, urging Iraqi commanders to demonstrate 'courage, desire and ability' to bring him down.

On 1 March 1991 President Bush announced that allied commanders led by General Norman Schwarzkopf would soon be meeting Iraqi military leaders at a secret Kuwaiti location to agree the terms of a ceasefire.

Already, despite the hype that would soon follow, Bush was sensing that the allied victory was only partial: after the Second World War there had been a 'definite end' but now 'we have Saddam Hussein still there'. Again, he commented that the US had no claims on Iraqi territory and did not intend to target Saddam Hussein, but 'nobody can be absolved of responsibility under international law' – a remark that encouraged people to contemplate the possibility that the Iraqi leader might be tried for war crimes, if ever he could be brought before a suitable court. Speculation was also encouraged about US intentions regarding the presence of American troops in southern Iraq and the circumstances under which Bush would resolve to restart hostilities: the US defence secretary, Dick Cheney, declared that if Iraq were to take any military action 'probably what we would do is open up the air campaign again'. There was growing talk also about the prospects for a lasting peace in the Middle East. Despite all the Western denials, Saddam Hussein had succeeded in establishing 'linkage' between the Gulf crisis (now only partially resolved) and the lasting Arab–Israeli dispute. Douglas Hurd and other Western politicians now seemed prepared to agree that Israel's security should be guaranteed in return for an Israeli withdrawal from occupied Arab lands.

In early March there were growing reports that Saddam was facing revolts, encouraged by the West, in various parts of Iraq. The Iraqi regime was losing control of the northern Kurdish provinces and the southern Shia regions, while bedraggled soldiers returning from the front staged impromptu anti-Saddam demonstrations in Baghdad. A former Ba'athist leader exiled in London commented: 'The situation is deteriorating very quickly. The army is retreating in chaos and without real command. The intelligence apparatus is still sustaining Saddam in Baghdad, but I expect the situation will soon deteriorate there too.'[57] There were in fact many signs that Saddam Hussein was losing control, not only in the far-flung northern and southern reaches but in his Baghdad heartland itself. One report suggested that 'all Ba'athists' were taking off their uniforms and fleeing, and that there was general chaos and disruption. Effigies of the Iraqi leader were being smashed on the streets and civilians felt able to shout that 'Saddam is finished!' A spokesman for the Kurdish Democratic Party (KDP) said: 'Our people are moving in the towns more easily than before'; and noted that there had been fifty organised attacks against Ba'athist leaders, with the Ba'athist headquarters in Kirkuk attacked with grenades. Opposition Iraqi politicians began to believe that a new leadership would emerge from the demoralised Iraqi army and that this new faction would unite with Kurdish and Shia activists opposed to the regime.

In Nasiriyeh hundreds of army deserters routed Iraqi government forces, just as in Basra dissident military factions looked like securing the region, the headquarters of Iraq's 3rd Army Corps. On 4 March, aware of this growing danger to the regime, Saddam pledged to pardon all deserters and urged them to rejoin their units; but the revolts spread, particularly among the Kurdish regions and the southern areas with a Shia majority. Saddam then moved to buy off the dissenting factions: monthly bonuses were offered to conscripts and five times as much (100 Iraqi dinars) to serving members of the Republican Guard. Food rations were increased by a quarter, while at the same time stern measures were taken – where possible – to crush the burgeoning uprisings throughout the country.

The allies had now formalised the ceasefire terms: a ceasefire line was defined, a sixth of Iraq's territory was placed under the control of allied forces (including 100,000 US troops), and each side was required to keep its troops at least one kilometre and its aircraft at least six kilometres from the line. Allied aircraft continued to fly over the whole of Iraq. Eleven members of the UN Security Council voted in favour of the new resolution, with Cuba opposing it and China, India and Yemen abstaining. The text referred to the 'definitive end to the hostilities' but it was assumed that the allies would resume military activities if the Iraqis broke the terms of the ceasefire. The resolution noted that the earlier provisions authorising the use of force 'remain valid'. All member states and specialised UN agencies were called upon to assist the reconstruction of Kuwait, but the US resisted an Indian appeal for the embargo on food, water and fuel to Iraq to be lifted. It was clear that Washington wanted the war on the Iraqi people to be continued by other means. Again the idea was floated that eventual oil revenues might be used to fund reparations to Kuwait and other injured parties. Already Western companies were scrambling to secure lucrative contracts for the rebuilding of Kuwait.

Uprisings against Saddam Hussein continued throughout Iraq, with the rebels, having been exhorted by the allies to overthrow the regime, repeatedly asking for military assistance. On 3 March resistance leaders met US forces at Safwan, the site of the ceasefire talks, and asked the allies for bomber support to fight off the Republican Guards moving from the north to crush the rebellion. Refugees – many of them expatriate workers released from prisons in Basra – told of widespread civil turmoil in southern Iraq. It was said that some 1400 prisoners had been freed from Basra's main prison after police had been shot dead by rebels, and that disturbances were taking place in many other towns and cities of the Tigris–Euphrates valley, including al-Kut, al-Nasiriyah, al-Amarah, Suqash Shuyukh and Ali al-Gharbi. A farmer and rebel leader, Mamad Ibrahim Wali, declared: 'There are many dead – maybe hundreds. The opposition control all the city [Basra]. All offices of the Saddam party, police stations, security areas, are all hit by the opposition.'[58] There were also signs that Iran was intervening in the situation to aid the southern Shia rebels. On 7 March President Rafsanjani, in an address to Saddam Hussein, urged him not to stain further 'your bloodied hands by killing more innocent Iraqis. Yield to the people's will and step down'. This declaration was accompanied by reports that 'tens of thousands' of armed men had moved from Iran into Iraq, raising the prospect of another Iran–Iraq war and an intensified Iraqi civil conflict fomented by outside interests. It was significant that the Basra rebels were loyal to the Shi'ite cleric Ayatollah Baqr al-Hakim, whose father, Mahdi Hakim, had been executed by the Ba'athist regime. Now there was speculation that a provisional government of 'Free Iraq' might be formed in the territory occupied by the US forces. Kurdish rebels were said to have seized control of the northern town of Sulaimaniya, while the Basra rebels were fighting off an attack by Republican Guards and clashes continued in the area of Baghdad. Ayatollah Hakim, referring to the uprisings as a *jihad* (holy war), urged Saddam Hussein to quit power and called on Iraqi army units to join the revolt and to ignore orders issued 'to the detriment of the nation'. A Sairi official in Beirut reported that units of guerillas were now in Baghdad, 'working to assassinate Saddam Hussein'. At the same time it was becoming increasingly clear that Washington was reluctant to become involved in the uprisings throughout Iraq. Thus a US military source commented on the American refusal to give arms to Iraqis struggling to overthrow the regime: 'We're sticking out of this. They're doing real fine all by themselves right now.'[59]

On 11 March 1991, following meetings in Damascus, representatives of nineteen political parties and movements – all opposed to Saddam Hussein – met for a two-day conference in Beirut, in optimistic preparations for assuming power in Baghdad. This was, however, a fragile union, split by religious and political differences and incapable of producing a coherent plan for the exploitation of the nationwide turmoil in Iraq. The Iraqi opposition failed to name any permanent leadership, failed to identify a useful strategy, and failed to channel the energies of the disparate groups. Said one of the Syrians, in manifest frustration, at the Beirut conference: 'You have to do something concrete when there is an uprising. If you don't show any practical reaction, it will be seen as a failure to help them.'[60] Where the delegates did agree was on the evident lack of US commitment to the opposition cause. Said one delegate: 'What are the Americans up to? The American army allowed the Republican Guard to pass down the road to Basra to attack our fighters there. Why did they do that? I thought the

ceasefire agreement said there should be no movement of forces. Do the
Americans want Saddam to stay in power?'[61] On 12 March a senior US
diplomat revealed at least one strand in American thinking: 'Better the
Saddam Hussein we know than an unwieldy coalition, or a new strong man
who is an unknown quantity.'[62] Now the rebels – in Basra and elsewhere –
were being crushed: some, according to witnesses, being hanged from tank
gun barrels, others being burnt alive. The rebels in Basra were doomed but
the Kurds, with their long history of revolt, continued to fight – despite the
US refusal to help for fear of offending Turkish sensitivities (see below).
A report on Tehran Radio claimed that loyal Iraqi troops had killed 16,000
people in the Shia towns of Najaf and Karbala.

By the end of March Iraqi opposition leaders were claiming a number
of significant successes. In a final offensive the Kurds had taken control
of Kirkuk, Iraq's main northern oil city, and the surrounding oilfields,
including the main complex of the Iraqi Oil Company. Iraqi helicopter
gunships had been shot down and the rebels were holding 9000 prisoners-
of-war. Kurdish Radio was instructing rebels to bring Iraqi prisoners to
Arbil, where 'we will judge them'. The Kurds were now claiming to hold
about one tenth of the land area of Iraq, including the region of Kirkuk,
Sulaimaniya, Arbil, Dahuk and parts of Mosul. In Baghdad the regime
was re-establishing control and in the south the Shia rebels were coming
under increasing pressure. The United States gave every sign of political
uncertainty. The Bush administration had refused to talk to the opposition
groups, a policy that was coming under increasing criticism. Thus Laurie
Millroy, from the Washington Institute on Near East Policy, commented
that the US government was 'paying the price for an inexplicable failure
to talk to the Iraqi opposition . . . With tens of thousands of people dying
within Iraq, we should be giving close air support to the rebels'. But it was
not difficult to find evidence for US strategic confusion. A Congressional
official went on the record: 'The question we are asking is "Do we want
either the Kurds or the Shias to succeed? Is it in our interest to turn Iraq
into Lebanon?" Quite honestly, I don't believe we know what to do.'[63] It
did seem clear the American forces were content to allow Iraqi helicopter
gunships to attack Kurdish and Shia positions. One report suggested that
Saddam Hussein's forces had used Scud missiles – supposedly all destroyed
in the Gulf War – and fixed-wing aircraft – supposedly banned under the
ceasefire terms – in the mounting counter-offensive to regain Kirkuk.

The extent of the US betrayal of the Iraqi rebels was now manifest to all.
The word 'betrayal' ran through the headlines of Western newspapers; the
Kurds, it was recorded, had not asked for much but the world 'gave them
nothing'; efforts to help the rebels had been 'thwarted'; the US 'stands by';

'Read my lips: no action'; 'George casts morals away'; and, declared journalist Andrew Stephen, 'the President is turning a blind eye to genocide because he really is a wimp'.[64] The Iraqi people had struggled to rid themselves of Saddam Hussein, as exhorted to by the West, but now Washington was 'looking the other way'.[65] In one area the US did act: it cut off aid to an impoverished Jordan to punish that country for King Hussein's support for Saddam during the Gulf War (before this measure was enacted the Jordanian economy was in crisis with unemployment running at nearly 30 per cent). Eventually the US, under mounting pressure, agreed to establish Kurdish enclaves in northern Iraq, to protect the refugees and to safeguard the UN relief efforts. Some observers suggested that this was only a token gesture – since a much greater area was already under the control of the rebel Kurdish forces. And in any case the Western forces were planning to leave the area, at which time the Kurdish people would again be at the mercy of Saddam.[66]

The turmoil in Iraq continued through June, though it was clear that Saddam had reasserted his authority in Baghdad and most of the country outside the Shia south and the Kurdish north. The US, shamed into some response to the plight of the Iraqi people, had delayed its withdrawal from the Kurdish zone, though UN efforts to supply protection and relief were near to collapse through lack of funds (the US remained a massive debtor state in the United Nations). Competing victory parades were held in Washington and New York, with President Bush declaring 'there's a new and wonderful feeling in America'. A week later Saddam Hussein – using tanks, armoured vehicles and helicopter gunships – was launching a fresh onslaught on the southern Shias.

The allies were faced with a dilemma. A speedy withdrawal of forces from the northern towns – a policy favoured by Washington – would only appear to compound the manifest betrayal of the rebel forces. Yet the US had no stomach for a prolonged stay, and it was increasingly being argued that it was up to the Kurds and the other dissident groups to sort out their own problems. In fact the Kurdish rebel leader, Massoud Barzani, had already been negotiating a peace deal with Saddam Hussein. This, Washington hoped, might help the US to extricate itself from an expensive and unwelcome commitment. The Barzani–Hussein deal stipulated that Kirkuk would be jointly administered by Kurds and the Iraqi government, though the West predictably expressed doubts that the deal would survive a US withdrawal from the northern towns; and Barzani too had problems in selling the agreement to other Kurdish leaders. Burhan Jaf, working with Barzani in the Kurdish Democratic Party (KDP), claimed that the deal would be endorsed since it gave the Kurds much of what they had been seeking; but Jalal Talabani of the Patriotic Union of Kurdistan (PUK), the second largest Kurdish faction, found the proposed agreement 'unacceptable'. The deal, if signed, would have granted the Kurds control over the northern provinces of Dihuk, Arbil and Sulaimaniya; partial control over the local police and army groups; a separate budget funded from Iraqi oil revenues; and elections within three months, the new head of the Kurdistan Executive Council to become a senior member of the Iraqi government. Barzani, supporting the agreement and suspicious of Western intentions, commented: 'Nobody has told me anything. There are just statements that they will not abandon the Kurds.'[67] Soon there were signs that the agreement would not be implemented; Saddam, seemingly moving the goalposts, began insisting that the Kurds cut all links with their allies, inside and outside Iraq, hand over their heavy weapons, and stop broadcasting from their two radio stations. Western suspicions about Saddam's duplicity seemed to be justified.

Now the West had its own agenda. Fresh attention was being given to the rooting out and destruction of Iraq's 'weapons of mass destruction' – with particular focus on Saddam's residual nuclear potential. By the end of June the Iraqi authorities were being warned about the consequences that would follow any refusal to co-operate with UN weapons inspectors, with publicity given to evidence that Saddam was trying to hide the fruits of his nuclear research. On 30 June 1991 President Bush declared that the US and its allies had full authority to use force if necessary 'to solve one way or another' Saddam Hussein's alleged nuclear potential: 'We feel the authority exists' for a military strike. In fact Resolution 687 (the ceasefire resolution agreed by Iraq) provided for the destruction of biological, chemical, ballistic and nuclear weapons, though whether the resolution authorised the use of force was less clear. *The Washington Post* (30 June) was in no doubt: 'Continued evasion of the conditions of the ceasefire and resistance to them, would justify further resort to military force by the allies.' At the same time there were moves to establish a strike force – of possibly 5000 American, French and British troops based in Turkey – to protect the Kurds.

It now seemed obvious that Saddam Hussein was consolidating his power within Iraq, a situation that many observers – but seemingly not all – viewed with impotence and frustration. Allegations of an Iraqi nuclear arms programme were being hyped as a justification for a further military strike against Saddam, though the motives behind this US suggestion were clearly political. In mid-July Washington began a propaganda exercise to prepare the American public and the rest of world opinion for the start of another air offensive against Iraq, a plan that looked set to go 'far beyond the stated reason of destroying Iraq's surviving nuclear research facilities'.[68] Despite all the carnage of the Gulf War, Saddam was intact, a circumstance that Bush regarded with deep distaste: '. . . so there is now a prospect of renewed conflict'.[69] The pull-out of Western troops from northern Iraq was expected to end by 16 July, though it was hoped that the rapid reaction force in Turkey would keep Saddam's troops away from the Kurds (one Kurd commented: 'People are frightened about what will happen when the Americans leave but they are too tired to run away again'). Bush in the meantime continued to seek support – not least from the Group of Seven (G7) nations – for a renewal of air strikes against Iraq if Saddam refused to co-operate with UN nuclear inspectors. The Iraqi leader, in an obvious attempt to forestall a renewed US-led onslaught, invited the Arab League to send an inspection team to Iraq to show that no nuclear facilities were being hidden from the UN officials. UK Foreign Secretary Douglas Hurd, ever the reliable US ally, declared at a G7 meeting in London on 16 July that Britain would be prepared to take part in renewed bombing raids on Iraq. All this despite General Norman Schwarzkopf's claim, six months before, that Iraq's nuclear capability had been thoroughly damaged and would not be effective for years to come.

In fact a UN nuclear inspection team reported in mid-July that most of Iraq's nuclear equipment had been destroyed during the Gulf War, and what remained could not be used to make nuclear weapons. In a televised speech to the Iraqi people Saddam Hussein said 'the aggressors have destroyed what we have built in 23 years'; and he went on to promise prosperity and political democracy. However, the legitimate opposition parties continued to be ruled out since loyalty to Ba'athism was still demanded; and there were few signs of the promised free press. A week later the Iraqi government issued a further decree forgiving army deserters and government opponents, despite (or because of) fresh battles in northern Kurdish towns. By the end of July more than 20,000 Kurds had fled the city of Sulaimaniya and were heading towards the Iranian border. The US declared that there were no plans to despatch troops from the mobile force in Turkey to protect the new wave of refugees. The new deadline of 25 July for full Iraqi disclosure of the country's nuclear plan had passed, and for a time the Iraqis were nervously scanning the skies in expectation of a further wave of bombing strikes (one woman commented: 'We are all very nervous, knowing what happened after the last ultimatum on 15 January').

The allies continued to monitor the Iraqi troop build-up in the north of the country, an evident prelude to a further offensive against the Kurdish-held regions. Still there was no decision to send Western ground troops back into action, though in mid-September the US decided to send air units back to the Gulf to pressure Saddam Hussein into observing the UN resolutions that he had seemingly ignored since the ending of hostilities. President Bush, describing himself as 'plenty fed up' with Saddam, insisted that the new move was not a threat: 'There's just firm determination he complies with the UN mandate.' An announcement was made that US aircraft, believed to include F-117A Stealth bombers and F-15 jets, would be despatched to Saudi Arabia over the next few days, and that the Saudis would receive at their request Patriot missiles as a 'safeguard' against possible Scud attacks. Contingency plans, 'Operation Determined Resolve', for a fresh air strike against Iraq were hinted at, with Defence Secretary Dick Cheney commenting that 'It is very important he [Saddam] understands he has no choice but to comply with the resolutions.' Now hundreds of thousands of Kurds, forced to flee from towns and villages, were facing a bleak time in the mountains. The West seemed largely indifferent to their plight and there were constant threats of further military attacks by Iraqi forces. The UN took steps to tighten the inspection of alleged nuclear facilities in Iraq, and President Bush yet again declared how resolved he was: 'I've never been more determined. We are prepared to use military force to see he does comply. And when a President makes a statement like that, he ought not to do it without being willing to back it up.'[70] On 23 September Iraqi soldiers confiscated several car-loads of nuclear-research documents from UN inspectors, again increasing the tension between Baghdad and Washington. The inspectors, the Iraqis claimed, had not documented what they had taken or issued receipts, so in taking back the documents Iraq had not breached its obligations under the Security Council resolutions. Again President Bush condemned the Iraqi action, but by now his words were appearing increasingly hollow: 'This shows that we cannot compromise for a moment in seeing that Iraq destroys all of its weapons of mass destruction and the means to deliver them, and we will not compromise.' In fact the Iraqi move had clearly left Bush 'flummoxed'.[71] United Nations inspectors were held under virtual siege in a Baghdad car park for several days and Washington seemed powerless to act. Eventually the inspectors were released, agreement was reached on the provision of receipts for confiscated documents, and the Iraqi authorities gave permission for UN helicopters to explore Iraq in search of 'weapons of mass destruction'. The incident had run its course.

There was dispute as to how close Iraq had come to developing a workable atomic weapon. David Kay, the leader of the UN team, commented that Iraq had been within two months of making a nuclear device at the time of the outbreak of the Gulf War, an observation that was rejected out of hand by the International Atomic Energy Agency (IAEA), the UN body responsible for inspecting Iraq's nuclear facilities. The Agency revealed that the Iraqi development programme had hit several problems and that a much longer development period would have been required. It also emerged that of the forty-four UN inspectors detained by Baghdad, only three came from the IAEA, the rest seconded from the member states of the UN Security Council; and that the inspectors, often American, had more of an interest in communicating with Washington than in conveying their findings to the various UN centres. By now there was further fighting between Kurds and Iraqi troops, with reports of at least one massacre by Kurds of sixty Iraqi prisoners and civilians. Of this the US State Department spokeswoman, Margaret Tutwiler, felt obliged to say: 'We are deeply distressed by this account, and will be talking to Kurdish opposition representatives.' She added that Washington was also concerned about reports of indiscriminate Iraqi shelling of Kurdish civilian areas. As many as 50,000 Kurds were now reported to be fleeing from their homes to escape the renewed fighting. At the same time Saddam Hussein moved to intensify the food and fuel blockade of the Kurdish regions as winter closed in. On 12 November the Kurdish leaders agreed to withdraw their guerrillas from the northern towns if Iraq would lift the economic blockade: the main thrust of the Kurdish revolt had been starved into submission.[72] Still the blockade persisted – an Iraqi blockade of Kurdistan within the UN blockade of Iraq – and on 28 November KDP leader Barzani again went to Baghdad in desperation to search for a negotiated settlement.

By now many of the Kurds were in an appalling predicament. Tens of thousands of men, women and children were struggling to survive in mountain camps beset by snow and freezing temperatures. In early December UN officials were reporting some 200,000 Kurdish refugees fleeing Iraqi army attacks in northern Iraq and straining relief efforts beyond their capacity. The dreaded word '*anfal*' on the lips of a refugee was quoted as an emotive synonym for genocidal massacre.[73] Grim reports came from one Kurdish region after another. In Sayed Sadiq, east of Sulaimaniya, 60,000 Kurds were struggling to build a camp in the freezing rain; 8000 refugees were driven to the town in the last week of November. In the province of Arbil 60,000 Kurds, clutching only what belongings they could carry, headed for the mountains after Iraqi troops had ordered them to leave their villages. The United Nations High Commissioner for Refugees (UNHCR) struggled to organise relief for hundreds of thousands of displaced villagers forced to survive in ramshackle tents in fields of mud and on the icy mountains. According to one estimate, some 182,000 Kurds had 'disappeared'; and an aid worker commented, noting the absence of clean water in the improvised camps: 'Only the toughest of these kids can expect to survive the winter.'[74]

Margaret Tutwiler commented: 'The United Nations people there on the ground tell us they believe they can handle this situation. It is something that is a concern to us, and something that we are obviously watching closely.' The Kurds were increasingly forced to recognise the American 'do-nothing policy': they needed to know 'whether the US would like them to sign an agreement with Baghdad, but the US refuses to express any official opinion on the matter'.[75] Few observers of the Kurdish plight doubted that the UNHCR programme was too little, too late; and moreover that the enduring UN sanctions on Iraq were hurting most of all the Iraqi opponents of Saddam Hussein.[76]

The Iraqi leader himself continued in characteristic fashion to use stick and carrot, with stick predominant. In a move to reduce the tension between the Ba'athist regime and the Kurds he sacked the long-serving health minister, Abdel Salem Mohammad Saad, and replaced him with the Kurdish labour and social affairs minister, Umeed Madhat Mubarak. At the same time Saddam released 2300 prisoners, including four hundred Kurds, from the Abu Ghraib Jalik jail, west of Baghdad, so fulfilling one of the Kurdish conditions in the autonomy talks being held with the Iraqi leadership. In December 1991, according to Iraqi opposition sources, eighty Iraqi officers who had tried to stage a coup against Saddam Hussein were executed. The officer, Mufleh al-Rawi, who exposed the coup plans was later decorated by Saddam.

On 19 January 1992 details of a Saudi plan to topple the Iraqi leader were published in *The New York Times*, and the US administration seemed split over the merits of the scheme. The idea, scarcely original, was that trouble should be fomented in northern and southern Iraq, forcing Saddam to use troops stationed around Baghdad, whereupon they could be picked off by air strikes. The US defence secretary Dick Cheney commented that 'If we were engaged in such plans, obviously I couldn't talk about it'; but added that in any case Saddam's days were numbered: 'He's in considerable difficulty. His economy is a shambles. He doesn't control the north and has only weak control of the south. He does not have a power base in Iraq that allows him to survive long-term.' The CIA director, Robert Gates, had recently emphasised the desirability of ridding the world of Saddam Hussein, though President Bush himself continued to seem undecided about a course of action. A week later, Iraqi dissidents produced an Iraqi army video showing brutality against Shia captives. The interior minister, Ali Hassan al-Majid, and another senior Iraqi, Mohammad Hamza al-Zubeidi, were shown kicking and otherwise abusing the prisoners, all of whom were in civilian dress. At one point Majid says: 'Let's execute one so the others will confess'; then he says to one of the terrified captives: 'Where are your friends? If you don't tell me I'll kill you right now.'[77] Another report highlighted the growing number of Kurdish casualties from some of the twenty million Iraqi mines planted in Kurdistan in the 1980s.[78] By now the Kurdish population was in an increasingly desperate plight, with thousands of people facing starvation and the health and other support services near to collapse.

The UK foreign secretary, Douglas Hurd, was now warning Iraq that the blockade of Kurdistan must be halted or air strikes would follow. At the same time the UN Security Council issued a statement declaring that if Iraq refused to co-operate with UN weapons inspectors, 'serious consequences' would arise, though no effort was made to explain what these might be. It was also announced that the American CIA and the British MI6 were spearheading an effort to topple Saddam Hussein. One American source revealed that $25 million, much of the cash from Saudi Arabia, would be spent over the next year to oust the Iraqi leader: 'This is on the front burner for President Bush right now. He wants Saddam out before the [presidential] elections in November.'[79] In February 1992 CIA chief Robert Gates met intelligence leaders in Israel, Egypt and Saudi Arabia to discuss the covert plans. Kurds from northern Iraq had been flown to Saudi Arabia for training in communications, tactics and weapons. It was also reported that the British government was forcing the pace. Said one Pentagon source: 'You Brits were really annoyed when we called a ceasefire so early. Now you have been driving hard to finish the job in the way you wanted in the first place.'[80] President Bush at that time decided that Saddam Hussein was 'brutal and cruel', adding that 'the best thing that could happen would be for him to go out of there so we could start new relations with Iraq'. Bush continued to seek support for fresh bombing raids on Iraq but seemed unable to secure either an international consensus or agreement within the US administration.

Thomas Pickering, US ambassador to the United Nations, then predicted to the Security Council that 'March [1992] will be the month of Iraq'. Saddam, it was declared, was still refusing to co-operate with UN weapons inspectors, and President Bush moreover was in evident electoral trouble at home. In such circumstances he clearly relished the prospect of another military confrontation. Now it seemed that he had the pretext, though there had been many similar excuses in recent months. Rolf Ekeus, the Swedish diplomat in charge of disarming Iraq, had reported to the Security Council that he was up against a brick wall because of Iraqi intransigence: Saddam would only agree to co-operate if the economic embargo were lifted. Thomas Pickering dubbed the Iraqi posture 'totally unacceptable'. On 9 March Tariq Aziz, now first deputy prime minister, flew with

Mohammad Saad al-Sahhaf, another senior Iraqi official, to plead the Iraqi case at the United Nations. Meanwhile the Iraqi newspaper *Babel* was commenting that, in view of the deteriorating conditions in the north and south of Iraq, an explosion was 'inevitable in those areas if they are ignited by the fire of foreign plotters'. On 11 March Security Council members warned the Iraqi delegation of the possibility of fresh bombing raids on Iraq. The next day, six B-52 strategic bombers of the US 42nd bomber wing arrived at RAF Fairford, Gloucestershire, giving rise to speculation that they were preparing for a strike on Iraq; the US aircraft carrier *America* moved into the Gulf to send a 'clear signal' to Iraq; and a Cable News Network (CNN) report suggested that the US Defence Department had drawn up a list of Iraqi targets for attack by air and Cruise missiles. Said a White House official: 'Both Libya and Iraq have ignored carrier movements – and paid for it.' The USS *America* was reported to be carrying 150 Cruise missiles and eighty aircraft, supported by deep-strike F-111F bombers and F-117A Stealth bombers in Turkey. Paul Rogers, a defence analyst at Bradford University in the UK, declared: 'The US is ready for two things: to start air strikes, including having a go at Saddam's deep military bunkers and to contain anything that Iraq would do in retaliation.' David Kay, the former leader of the UN inspection team, commented in characteristic mood that now there was no choice but to take military action against Iraq: 'I have grave fears that we would see a wave of massive proliferation if Iraq is allowed to continue thumbing its nose at the UN.'[81] To forestall the likely bombing attacks, Iraq agreed to destroy its Scud-making equipment; the US remained sceptical that the assurances would be honoured.

On 28 April 1992 crowds of Iraqi demonstrators in Baghdad, Tikrit (Saddam's birthplace) and elsewhere in the country celebrated the Iraqi leader's 55th birthday: 'Bush! Bush! Listen carefully: We all love Saddam!', 'Our blood, our soul, we sacrifice to Saddam!' The road to Tikrit from Baghdad was clogged with buses filled with people attending the demonstrations. In the Tikrit sports stadium scores of people were assembled into columns and marched past Izzat Ibrahim, the vice-chairman of the Revolutionary Command Council. Vividly-clad folk dancers enacted a piece entitled 'The Village Hears of the Birth of Saddam'. Few observers doubted – despite the obvious orchestration of events – that Saddam had retained (or rebuilt) a degree of popularity among certain sections of the population, and that he was very much in charge of the Iraqi state.[82] A fortnight later he moved to frustrate the fresh Kurdish elections, seen in Iraq as an illegal step towards independence. Kurdish officials reported that the Iraqi army had warned them that if they attempted to participate in the planned elections their villages would be shelled by artillery. And it was not only Saddam who had an interest in frustrating the Kurdish moves towards democracy: it was reported that warplanes from Turkey had bombed villages in Iraqi Kurdistan in a concerted effort to disrupt the proceedings (see 'The Turkish Factor' below).[83] In the event it was the apparent delibility of the imported 'indelible' ink – for marking voters' wrists – that forced the Kurds to postpone their elections.

When the Kurds eventually went to the polls on 19 May 1992 – with a heavy turnout among the 1.1 million eligible voters – they cannot have imagined that a virtual dead heat between the leading contenders would have resulted. Most voters indicated that they were supporting either Massoud Barzani's Kurdish Democratic Party (KDP) or Jalad Talabani's Patriotic Union of Kurdistan (PUK), the KDP favouring renewed autonomy talks with Saddam Hussein and the PUK rejecting any accommodations with the current Iraqi regime. When the results were declared, all parties – the KDP, the PUK and the smaller parties (Mahmud Osman's Socialists and Khaled Osman's Islamic faction) – made charges that the others had practised fraud, with multiple voting on a massive scale. An independent observer, Michael Meadowcroft of the Electoral Reform Society, commented: 'We have monitoring reports on more than half of the voting stations, and on not a single one of them is there any suggestion of any intimidations of voters whatsoever. Nor is there any suggestion that any kind of double or multiple voting took place in any significant degree whatever.' At the same time it was reported that, because of the paucity of polling stations, thousands of would-be voters who had queued for hours were unable to vote before the polls were closed. Barzani won the most votes (466,879–44.58 per cent, against Talabani's 44.33 per cent) but failed to secure the conclusive mandate for renewed talks with the Iraqi regime. However, the holding of the election was perceived as giving the Kurds a new self-confidence. Saddam Hussein had been unable to disrupt the elections (as indeed had Turkey and Iran, both equally opposed to the development of Kurdish autonomy). Saddam maintained what pressure he could on Iraqi Kurdistan, and continued to confront the dissident Shias, the 'marsh Arabs', in the south.[84]

In early June the Bush administration proposed that $40 million should be spent on covert aid in 1993 to oust Saddam Hussein. 'What we need,' declared an organiser of the self-styled opposition Iraqi National Congress, meeting in Vienna, 'is a plan to get rid of the pig [Saddam Hussein].'[85] Some days before the conference convened, a CIA report concluded that Saddam was stronger now than he was a year ago; a senior US official commented privately: 'We expect him to stay.' The US administration would continue to fund efforts to topple the Iraqi dictator, but with a feeling of growing impotence. A prime mover of the Vienna meeting, Ahmed Chalabi, revealed that Saddam had managed to outplay the Americans: 'He kept sending officers to Saudi Arabia, who told America they were credible and were planning coups. Then he sent them directly to the Americans. They followed a lot of red herrings.'[86] On Iraqi television Saddam, ridiculing the idea of a coup, said to vice-president Izzat Douri amid much laughter: 'I will make a coup and you will help me!' In July there were reports of an actual coup bid, again defeated by Saddam.[87] And suggestions of US involvement were confirmed by an American official: 'There was a plot . . . we were involved.'[88]

Again tensions were developing between Iraqi officials and UN arms inspectors: on 5 July, with the Iraqis preventing UN access to a government building, the UN team leader Karen Jansen said that the two sides were 'in a stand-off'. The Iraqi agriculture minister, Abdul Wahab al-Sabagh, declared that Iraq would not authorise the search of a 'civilian ministry which has nothing to do with the United Nations and its resolutions'; and he accused the UN of being a tool of the United States, with the Bush administration 'using international terrorism' against Iraq. A few days later, Saddam Hussein was denouncing the United Nations as 'an advertising agency' for the United States, at the same time calling for the overthrow of the rulers of Kuwait and Saudi Arabia: 'What is needed is a *jihad* to purge the Arab nation of these treacherous leaders who have become a shameful burden on our region.' Tension further increased when a UN guard, a Fijian, was shot dead by an unknown gunman in northern Iraq.[89] The Iraqi authorities then agreed that the disputed Agriculture Ministry in Baghdad could be searched by 'impartial' (that is, non-American) experts.

Yet again the prospect of a new Gulf war loomed. White House spokesman, Marlin Fitzwater, commented: 'We're serious about this. I won't comment on military decisions but all options remain open.' The Bush administration had secured the agreement of the British to participate in a fresh air war against Iraq, and the Democratic presidential candidate Bill Clinton had given his backing to the use of force. It was reported that the new war against Iraq would begin with Cruise missile strikes as the first stage of an escalating campaign. A US source declared: 'We are not talking of a surgical strike here. It is to make the Iraqis realise that if they do not comply, more is coming.' Said Bill Clinton: 'Let Saddam Hussein make no mistake. Even during an election campaign, Americans are united on this issue. If the UN decides to use force to ensure Iraqi compliance with the ceasefire agreements, I will support American participation.'[90] Bush, increasingly unpopular in national opinion polls, faced a dilemma – not eased by anti-Bush car bumper stickers seen around the US: 'Saddam Hussein still has a job. Do you?' By now it was being suggested that air strikes on Iraq could start within days, though Bush still seemed reluctant to issue an ultimatum.[91] Talks at the UN had failed to resolve the crisis over arms inspection, and Bush was now holding meetings with senior military advisers. Secretary of State James Baker joined in by declaring to Iraq that the US and its allies were 'very serious'; while the tenacious British MP, Tam Dalyell, pressed for a recall of Parliament before British troops were again committed to military conflict. (It was also revealed at this time that Major Karen Jansen had the previous year consulted a Maryland psychic in an extra-sensory search for Iraq's weapons of mass destruction.[92])

On 26 July 1992, under threat of further bombing attacks, the Iraqi authorities agreed to let UN inspectors enter the Agriculture Ministry, provided the inspectors were not from countries involved in the Gulf War. The deal gave the UN access to the disputed building, but Saddam had seemingly secured control over who should be in the inspection teams. The West celebrated Saddam's 'climb down', while Iraq rejoiced with equal enthusiasm at Saddam's 'victory over the UN'. The delay had obviously allowed the Iraqis to remove any incriminating evidence from the building in question, but Washington was keen to play down what was increasingly being seen as a humiliation for the US. The US national security adviser, Brent Scowcroft, commented: 'That doesn't end it. That deals with the tip of the iceberg.' The Americans also tried to disguise their minor tactical reverse by completing their preparations for seventeen days of war games, involving 2000 marines, in Kuwait. On 28 July tens of thousands of Iraqi demonstrators marched through Baghdad, chanting 'Bush, Bush, listen with care – we all love Saddam Hussein!' The American bluff had been called. Bush ordered another carrier battle group into the Gulf and sent a Patriot missile system to Kuwait, but it seemed that yet again the prospect of further hostilities in the Gulf had been averted.

Whilst the UN–Iraqi dispute was developing, the position of the Kurds continued to deteriorate. It increasingly appeared that the Kurds had been 'left in limbo' by the United Nations, with various relief agencies gradually phasing out their operations. Aid workers had been terrorised by Iraqi attacks, and the new UN–Iraqi deal had seemingly left the Kurds even more exposed.[93] Now the US had agreed to talk to members of the Iraqi opposition – James Baker granted an audience to a carefully selected group of two Kurds, two Shia Arabs and two Sunni Arabs – but few observers thought that anything useful would come out of the meeting (in one account the unprecedented meeting did no more than reveal US 'desperation' to find any group that might topple Saddam). While these talks were in progress it was reported, to no-one's surprise, that nothing of interest had been found in the Baghdad agriculture ministry; and that, more significantly, Washington was yet again gearing up for bombing strikes on Iraq.[94] At the same time the Iraqi forces seemed to be massing for a further onslaught on the Arabs of the southern marshes.[95] The US continued with its war games in Kuwait and, in the face of yet more Iraqi non-compliance in Baghdad, made further threats, with Marlin Fitzwater again running through the familiar liturgy: 'No one should be of any apprehension that there are ways to seek a very forceful compliance' (which presumably meant that Baghdad would be bombed if it did not behave itself). Again the Iraqi authorities were digging in their heels, this time refusing UN access to government ministries. The Iraqi information minister, Hamed Youssef Hammadi, was adamant: 'We reject categorically visits to the headquarters of ministries because the aim . . . is to hurt Iraq's sovereignty and independence . . . As far as other places, the inspection teams can visit any place in the country.' Again the crisis was defused only when agreement was reached on the use of non-American inspectors.

On 9 August 1992 the Iraqi authorities cut the telephone links to the holy city of Najaf, and imposed a curfew, in an attempt to prevent thousands of mourners turning out for the funeral of the Grand Ayatollah Abdel Qassem al-Khoei, a renowned Shi'ite scholar. The authorities called for three days of mourning, but the intended plans for a public funeral after the brief family ceremony were cancelled after police visited the family home. The death of al-Khoei occurred at a time of growing reports of renewed attacks on the southern Shias, and as the main aid channels to the northern Kurds were drying up, a year after the withdrawal of allied troops from the region. The allies were now warning Saddam to stop the air attacks on the Shias, with the implied threat of air strikes against Baghdad if the warning were not heeded. Again, President Bush seemed uncertain how to proceed. A new bombing strike on Iraq, far from being politically advantageous as election day approached, would now reek of opportunism; and the very charge of such politicking was clearly having a deterrent effect on the White House. On 16 August Bush commented: 'From now on some will accuse us of political opportunism for every move that I make. That's unfortunate but it's not going to deter me from doing what is right, regardless of the political fall-out . . . There will be no politics and I will do what is right for the United States and in this case for the rest of the world.' Said Pentagon spokesman Pete Williams: 'You can't let Iraq . . . draw a red line around buildings.' This was the start of the crucial Republican convention in Houston. Many observers speculated that a bombing strike on Baghdad, a useful diversion from Bush's domestic problems and his poor poll ratings, would make the affair go with a swing. Unfortunately for President Bush there was too much speculation along these lines: the timing would be so transparently contrived as to be massively counter-productive. Yet again the military plans, by now doubted by no-one, failed to come to fruition. The Republican convention, with less than three months to go to election day, was a lacklustre affair.

President Bush had been massively embarrassed by leaks of his new bombing plans.[96] The publicity had effectively stopped the scheme dead in its tracks; so a new ruse had to be cobbled together – one that might yet allow the assembled US forces to attack the recalcitrant Iraqi leader. The new idea was that a 'no-fly zone' could be imposed over southern Iraq – nominally to protect the Marsh Arabs, whose desperate plight had been well known for many months, but hopefully to provoke Saddam Hussein into a response that would justify an air war on Iraq (and a consequent improvement in Bush's dismal poll standing). Again it was easy to wonder about the timing of the announcement: why now, when humanitarian aid officials had been trying to alert the West to the predicament of the southern Shias for more than a year? There was also a strange hiatus, yet to be explained, in the procession of US comments on the new policy. After the initial declaration of intent by the United States, the British premier John Major was left to make the announcement of allied agreement on the idea of the no-fly zone over southern Iraq. John Major, obedient as ever, made the announcement – and then, for a brief but embarrassing period, was left high and dry. President Bush made no comment on John Major's announcement, and doubts grew as to whether allied agreement had actually been achieved. Marlin Fitzwater did not help America's pliant British allies when he commented that 'a final collective decision has yet to be made'.[97] The most likely explanation for the unaccustomed US reticence was that the Bush administration was making a clumsy effort to avoid the familiar charges of politicking in the run-up to the election. The message seemed to be: 'Let the Brits do the talking and we'll climb on board some way down the tracks!'

Some observers were beginning to point out that the US-inspired imposition of a no-fly zone was in fact a violation of international law, a decision not covered by the requisite UN resolutions on Iraq – though we can hardly expect such niceties to have deterred Washington. The UN was not consulted on the 'no-fly' idea, nor did 'any UN Security Council resolution authorise the actions in the name of the besieged Marsh Arabs and rebel Shias'.[98] The UK foreign minister, Douglas Hurd, went so far as to admit that 'Not every action that an American government, a British government or a French government takes has to be underwritten by a specific provision in a UN resolution', adding the proviso that we should 'comply with international law' (though no argument was advanced as to how the imposition of a no-fly zone met this requirement).[99] Again it was easy to depict the new Western initiative as arbitrary, 'political' and probably unjustifiable in international law.

One suggestion was that the imposition of the no-fly zone – to cover seven million people in 35 per cent of Iraq's territory – would stimulate the demoralised Iraqi army to overthrow Saddam. Said one jubilant Iraqi opposition leader: 'Saddam is being challenged in a very fundamental way – inside Arab Iraq. This is not just a plan to protect the Shias. It is a plan to get rid of Saddam.' Again the various battle scenarios were rehearsed in the press. US fighter-bombers would shoot down Iraqi aircraft flying in their own country but below the 32nd parallel; British Tornados would be required to fly reconnaissance missions. Paul Rogers, the conflict analysis expert at Bradford University in the UK, commented that if hostilities developed: '. . . the US forces, while still far smaller than during last year's war, could opt for wide-ranging attacks on Iraqi ground troops. They could target munitions dumps, bridges, power supplies and air bases, command and control centres and even a full range of targets in Baghdad.' The US calculation seemed to be that a new conflict with Iraq would help Bush in the run-up to the November election, provided the responsibility for a new war could be levelled at Saddam rather than at a transparently politicking president. Soon there were fresh reports of planned air strikes on Baghdad and speculation about how the imminent war was designed 'to save the President's skin'.[100] Iraqi newspapers carried a flood of declarations of support for Saddam Hussein from marshland tribal leaders and reports of mass pro-Saddam demonstrations in the southern parts of Iraq. At the same time the Iraqi deputy prime minister, Tariq Aziz, spoke of the 'criminal plan' [the no-fly zone] which was aimed at 'carving up Iraq on a sectarian and racial basis'. There was also mounting evidence that other Arab states were suspicious of Western intentions. Saudi Arabia seemed reluctant to let British aircraft use the Dhahran air base, though discussions were continuing; Egypt expressed polite reservations; and Syria, which had fought against Iraq in the Gulf War, joined Jordan, Sudan, Yemen and Algeria in denouncing the latest Western plans. Only Kuwait, among the Arab states of the region, supported the imposition of the no-fly zone.

What had seemed a promising plan for the resurrection of Bush's presidential ambitions was now seen as an empty gesture. The American columnists Rowland Evans and Robert Novak remarked that 'the removal of

Bush's nemesis [Saddam Hussein] is seen by Baker as one-shot success – the only one – that could transform Bush's campaign overnight.' But the announcement of the plan had been badly handled ('All at half-cock as usual,' said a US official); the Western allies were forced to declare that they were not divided in their approach; Western commentators were querying the legal basis of the plan; the Arab states were denouncing the Western intentions; and Saddam Hussein, despite many earlier miscalculations, was too canny to hand Bush a presidential re-election on a plate. Behind many of the Arab and Western doubts was the suspicion that Washington would be seeking to dismember Iraq, a modern version of the colonial boundary-drawing of the 1920s, the arbitrary creation of state frontiers that had stored up so many problems for the future.

The Western aircraft began their patrols over southern Iraq and, to likely American disappointment, all was reported quiet.[101] At one level, the supposed protection of the southern Arabs from Saddam's aircraft, the plan was working; at another, the re-election of George Bush, it was not. Again, we were reminded of new plans to attack targets in Iraq, many of them outside the newly defined security zone.[102] There were no signs of the hoped-for army rebellion against Saddam, and even some of the Iraqi opposition members had become silent, unhappy to countenance what might emerge as a *de facto* partition of Iraq. There were signs however that Saddam was consolidating his power. The Iraqi army was being rebuilt, unrest in most parts of the country had now been crushed, and the Saddam 'carrot' – a well tried ploy – was much in evidence, particularly in some areas of southern Iraq, where the purblind Western strategists could discern nothing but suppression. Sheikhs from many of the southern tribes had 'been wooed with cash and cars. In Laladel, a village on the edge of the marshes, a sheikh last week fingered the keys to his new saloon and pledged his loyalty to Saddam'. He commented that 'Saddam is paying attention to us. My people have a hospital and schools.'[103] And with the carrot, the stick . . . while sheikhs were being given car keys, dissident factions – in any case, according to Baghdad, only a small minority – were being routed. Washington had no doubt whatever that it would view a further Iraqi offensive in the southern marshlands with grave concern. Thus the US national security adviser, Brent Scowcroft, commented on the NBC's 'Meet the Press': 'I wouldn't want to say exactly what we'd do but I think that Saddam ought to take the prospect very seriously.'

In early September 1992, Washington was in fact boasting little evidence of an Iraqi offensive against the southern Shias.[104] In a letter to Congress, President Bush himself tacitly admitted that he had no evidence of Iraqi repression of the southern Arabs, and confirmed that there was currently no bombing of citizens in the marsh areas.[105] However, evidence supplied by the human rights group Middle East Watch and by the British MP, Emma Nicholson, suggested that Saddam had responded to the imposition of the no-fly zone with massive repression of the Arabs in the region. Said Nicholson, newly returned from the Iraqi marshes: 'Saddam has stepped up his onslaught on the marshes since the enforcement of the no-fly zone. I travelled through marshes smoking from ground-launched bombardments from missiles and tank cannon'; and Middle East Watch, reporting 'new massacres', described how 2500 men, women and children had been rounded up in the Nasiriyeh area, and later executed nightly in groups of one hundred at a time.[106] At the same time there was mounting evidence of the desperate plight of the Kurds in the north. Baghdad had refused to renew an agreement on the UN humanitarian aid programme in northern Iraq and some UN staff had been denied visas. Some 750,000 Kurds – virtually cut off from vital medical, food and fuel supplies – were most at risk as they faced yet another harsh winter. A confidential UN report, entitled *Winter Survival Plan*, commented on how the Kurds were now facing a winter of 'unbearable hardship', with most people in northern Iraq lacking the income for even the 'bare necessities' of life.[107]

At the end of September more than 170 delegates from all the main Iraqi opposition groups met in Salahuddin, the first time that such a meeting had been convened inside Iraq. The aim at this northern Kurdish resort was to demonstrate that the opposition Iraqi National Congress (INC) was now a coherent body that could pose a serious threat to Saddam Hussein. If the INC succeeded in this task, Western governments would finally be able to reckon with a realistic alternative to the current Iraqi government. Ayad Rahim, one of the youngest delegates, commented on what he perceived to be the new atmosphere among the opposition factions: 'Before we never dared talk to each other. Now the barrier of fear has been broken. That was what buttressed Saddam. That was what made us brain-dead for twenty years.' Now it was decided that the conference would elect a three-man leadership: a Sunni, a Shi'ite and a Kurd; and that also a 174-member generally assembly and a 25-member executive council would be elected. The delegates recognised above all that without a show of constructive unity it would be impossible for the INC to attract the vital Western support.

There were few signs that the West was prepared to give realistic support to the beleaguered Kurds and the other Iraqi minorities. Nor were other states in the region interested in encouraging the development of Kurdish autonomy. In November 1992 the Turkish prime minister, Suleiman Demirel, visiting Iran, invited the foreign ministers of Iran, Syria and Saudi Arabia to a conference on the Kurdish question. An official source commented that 'both Ankara and Tehran oppose a federated Kurdish state . . . they feel that regional countries should start having a say in the way things are shaping up and that "outside influences" [the West] are a negative element for the security and stability of the region.' At the same time the Turkish high command was announcing that it had 20,000 troops in northern Iraq, a blatant occupation of sovereign territory that the West pretended not to notice.

Saudi Arabia alone was unenthusiastic about the proposed conference, discerning a 'Turkish–Iranian–Syrian agreement to limit the intervention of the Western states in Iraq' (the Saudis could be relied upon to protect US hegemony in the region). Now the threat loomed of fresh tensions between Iran and the West and even between Turkey and other members of the NATO alliance. In 1975, in an earlier betrayal, the US decided to abandon the Kurds. Now such Kurdish leaders as Massoud Barzani had little doubt that the Western powers were running true to form. Winter was again threatening post-war Kurdistan, Saddam was impeding UN aid efforts, and stocks of fuel and food were critically low.[108] On 14 November 1992, Turkey, Syria and Iran held a meeting of foreign ministers in Ankara to discuss how to prevent the creation of an independent Kurdish state in northern Iraq. In particular they declared their intention to oppose the development of a Kurdish parliament and the emergence of a federal Kurdish state. At the same time it was clear that Turkey was reaching an accommodation with the Iraqi Kurds in order to oppose more radical Kurdish factions. Turkish commanders had reached a pragmatic agreement with Kurdish leaders Barzani and Talabani for a security zone to protect Turkey from the Marxist Kurdistan Workers' Party (PKK). Thus, while opposing the emergence of an independent Kurdish state, Ankara was giving tacit recognition to the autonomy of the northern Iraqi Kurds. Various commentators (for example, Yalcin Dogan in the Turkish national daily, *Milliyet*) saw such moves as giving impetus to the emergence of a Kurdish federal state.

By the end of November UN trucks were again struggling to reach some of the 3.5 million people in Iraqi Kurdistan. At the same time foreign aid workers were being intimidated in the north, a grenade had been tossed into the offices used by one aid agency, and a UN representative had been killed – possibly murdered – in a traffic accident. Demirel, in a visit to London, declared to Prime Minister John Major that Iraq must not be divided, that Turkish forces would remain in Cyprus, and that air sorties over northern Iraq from Turkey might not be allowed to continue. This last would mean that it would be even more difficult to convey aid to the Kurds via the northern Turkish route. In one incident six UN trucks had been bombed in Arbil, an event that aid workers found difficult to explain. A measure of co-operation with Baghdad had been secured and a Western diplomat commented: 'It would seem strange if the Baghdad government, having agreed to this aid and after helping it go through, should then blow it up.'[109] By the middle of December it was obvious that the UN aid effort, facing sabotage and with wholly inadequate funds, would not be able to meet the desperate Kurdish needs. The UN Security Council, at the behest of the US, had again insisted that no relaxation of sanctions on Iraq be allowed – with the absurd consequence that UN aid efforts were massively hampered. On 8 December 1992 Oxfam commented that the imposition of Security Council sanctions on Iraq had worsened the plight of people 'throughout Iraq' and for millions of them 'life remains enormously difficult'. It was noted that thousands of young children had died from the combined impact of war and sanctions.

Now it was clear that the Western allies – despite the illegal no-fly zones over the northern and southern areas of Iraq – remained unwilling to oppose Saddam's repression of the Kurds and Shias. Saddam had been emboldened by the limited air strikes in the south (see 'The Bush Finale', below), and a third of the army was now concentrated in the north, waiting for orders to attack the important Kurdish towns that had achieved a measure of independence from the central Iraqi government. At the same time it was reported that about 150 Kurdish separatists, half the population of a rebel camp in the eastern mountains, had been killed by Turkish air raids, an event that received little publicity in the West.[110] Estimates suggested that the particularly vulnerable Kurdish groups numbered some 750,000 people, with 270,000 'vulnerables' in Arbil province alone; and that even the official 'vulnerables' would only receive supplies to meet a third or a quarter of their 'basic survival needs'.[111] Again there was further evidence, if more were needed, that the UN blockade on Iraq, coupled to Saddam's internal blockade, was bringing immense hardship to the Iraqi people. And again the clear paradox – the Swedish diplomat Jan Eliasson, negotiating for the UN, had agreed a 'Memorandum of Understanding' with Saddam (an agreement that expired at the end of March 1993) to allow the shipment of aid into the Kurdish areas, while at the same time the UN expected the international blockade on Iraq to be maintained.[112]

In early February Tariq Aziz, Iraq's deputy prime minister, indicated that the two Britons jailed for entering Iraq illegally – Paul Ride and Michael Wainwright – might be freed if Britain was prepared to unfreeze Iraqi assets for humanitarian purposes. A spokesman for the British Foreign Office announced that all the Iraqi assets held in Britain would remain frozen until the Iraqi government complied with all UN resolutions. This was the familiar formula, increasingly threadbare, that was being used to prolong the international blockade against the entire Iraqi people. It seemed increasingly no more than a vindictive Western policy, arguably illegal in international law, which continued to consign vast numbers of ordinary Iraqis to disease and death, and which did nothing to achieve the declared aim of eroding the security of Saddam Hussein.

The irony of the broad political situation was manifest to all. Saddam Hussein – in US terms comprehensively defeated in the Gulf War – was succeeding in consolidating his power, while George Bush, the nominal victor, seemed about to pass into history. The election success that a year ago had appeared a foregone conclusion would soon elude the US president. There were moreover fresh allegations being made that were helping to erode the moral posture of the Western leaders.

THE SADDAMGATES

The United States

The United States was accustomed to providing arms and other support to military dictators and despotic regimes around the world – principally as a matter of policy in the Cold War but also in the service of other strategic requirements. Weapons were supplied to the Iran of the ayatollahs with the aim of securing the release of American hostages, an event that was significant in the context of the Iran–Iraq war.[113] At the same time, because of the US 'tilt' towards Iraq as a defender of the Gulf states against Islamic fundamentalism, Washington was prepared to countenance both overt and covert aid to Saddam Hussein over many years. Much of this activity was widely known in the period leading up to the 1991 Gulf War (see Chapter 7), but it was only after the war that the extent of the earlier covert aid to Saddam was exposed in the public domain. The controversy – 'Saddamgate' (or 'Iraqgate') – continued through 1992 and may be judged partly responsible for Bush's election defeat.

Even before the start of the 1991 war the extent of US support for Saddam was being publicised. It was now known that Saddam Hussein had 'the fruits of a secret six-year intelligence exchange with the United States to draw on as he fights American forces, thanks to Ronald Reagan, William Casey and aides'.[114] Saddam had long received 'coaching from the CIA and the State Department' in the assumption that Iraq could be drawn into a useful relationship with the United States. Intelligence data was routed to Baghdad via the American embassy in Amman, with King Hussein of

Jordan personally overseeing the sensitive operation: 'By 1985, Mr Casey had opened a CIA shop in Baghdad to manage the traffic'. Over the next few years, in the run-up to the invasion of Kuwait, Washington approved $1.5 billion-worth of exports with potential military uses to Iraq.[115]

It was also emerging that immediately prior to the invasion of Kuwait the Bush administration was still giving substantial support to Saddam – yet another reason why he may have believed that the projected invasion would be tolerated by Washington (see Chapter 8). The very day before the invasion of Kuwait the Bush administration approved the sale of $695,000-worth of advanced data transmission devices to Iraq. In the fifteen days preceding the invasion Washington approved licences for $4.8 million in advanced technology products; on one day, 17 July 1990, the Bush administration agreed the sale of $3.4 million-worth of computers to Iraq.[116] Washington was also obstructing an investigation into Iraq's central role in a $4 billion bank fraud involving the Atlanta branch of Italy's state bank, the Banca Nazionale del Lavoro. The US senator Henry Gonzales, chairman of the House Banking Committee, involved in investigating this scandal, declared that he had been urged by the White House, the CIA and Secretary of State James Baker not to continue his enquiries.

On 27 April 1992 the published minutes of a US agriculture department meeting held in October 1989 showed that officials had evidence that US loan guarantees to Iraq, intended for food purchases, were being used by Saddam to build up his military power. It had already been revealed, in investigations by Henry Gonzales, that Iraq had systematically subverted the $5 billion food aid programme; and that this was well known to the Bush administration. The independent Wisconsin Project on arms control published a list of nuclear and missile-related exports to Iraq up to 1990, all licensed by the US government. It was also emerging, significantly enough, that *a Watergate-style cover-up was being organised by the White House*, under the control of Nick Rostow, general counsel to the National Security Council (NSC) and Boyden Gray, Bush's White House general counsel. Senator Gonzales published evidence to show that:

President Bush and Secretary of State James Baker appeased Saddam and misled Congress, despite knowing that Iraq was working to acquire nuclear weapons and that US laws were being broken.

US intelligence was secretly supplied to Saddam weeks before the invasion of Kuwait, a fact that CIA director Robert Gates concealed from a Senate panel.

Commerce Department records of US military exports to Iraq were altered, deleted or seized.

Investigations into illegal money-laundering and the use of food aid to the Iraqis to buy weapons were deliberately obstructed.

Gonzales himself, a Democrat in Congress for more than thirty years, summarised the indictment: 'Behind closed doors, and out of sight of the people and the Congress, they [Presidents Bush and Reagan] courted Saddam Hussein with a reckless abandon that ended in war and the deaths of dozens of our brave soldiers and over 200,000 Muslims, Iraqis, and others.'[117]

It also emerged, in May 1992, that President Bush had been forced to grant an extraordinary executive 'waiver' exempting eleven senior officials from conflict of interest laws after the invasion of Kuwait. A confidential memorandum to Robert Kimmitt, the then under-secretary for political affairs at the State Department, revealed that the conflict of interest was so severe that the officials would have been barred from 'current US policy-making, discussions, decisions and actions in response to the Iraqi invasion'; and that 'because of the breadth and sensitivity of the waiver, the White House is currently unwilling to distribute copies to the affected individuals'. The suggestion was that the officials in question – one of whom was known to be James Baker – had private business holdings and other interests that necessitated the waiver. Gonzales demanded an independent counsellor to investigate this affair: 'There is a problem of perception when the president surrounds himself with cabinet officials that have serious conflicts of interest regarding one of the most important areas of US foreign policy.' On 18 May Margaret Tutwiler stated that the waiver covered the entire cabinet and senior government officials.

On 9 July 1992 the House Judicial Committee in Congress asked for a special prosecutor to be appointed to investigate whether government officials broke the law in helping Iraq in the run-up to the invasion of Kuwait. White House presidential counsel Boyden Gray was named as a target of the projected enquiry: 'There is a clear need to investigate possible criminal violations by high-ranking officials' (Jack Brooke, committee chairman). It was already clear that the investigation would be wide-ranging; Brooke commented: 'Apparently there was a large amount of that so-called food that turned into military equipment. It left as food and arrived over there as tanks. Now it turns out that Mr Gray's shop in the White House may have been up to their ears in attempts to influence the BNP [Banca Nazionale del Lavoro] prosecution.'[118] On 21 July Henry Gonzales disclosed further documents indicating that US intelligence agencies had obtained abundant evidence of Saddam's vast network set up to buy Western military technology.[119] In September it emerged that the Scud missiles fired at Israel and

Saudi Arabia during the Gulf War were financed in part by US money, with the secret knowledge of US government and Italian bank officials.[120]

In October, as various US government departments struggled to cover their tracks, a bitter feud developed between the CIA and the Justice Department over improper loans to Iraq – with each accusing the other 'of withholding information from federal prosecutors.'[121] By now it seemed that criminal indictments of senior Bush officials were increasingly likely. A respected American columnist Jim Hoagland commented: 'The Iraq cover-up is unravelling with stunning speed as the Bush administration dissolves into warring clans more worried about staying out of jail than promoting the re-election of President Bush.' The Justice Department had announced that it was going to investigate itself, the FBI and the CIA over the cover-up of the improper BNL loans to Iraq; and the FBI had announced it would investigate the Justice Department. The Democrat Senator Bill Bradley expressed a widespread view when he commented that the Bush administration seemed to be 'unravelling', while many observers were sensing that it would be impossible to keep the whole affair under wraps if Bush were to lose the November election. 'The first thing a Clinton administration will do is throw open the executive-branch files on Iraq and Iran and anything else they can think of,' said one administration official.[122]

The United Kingdom

Britain, as befitted America's smaller partner in the Iraq affair, was able to boast its own home-grown Saddamgate. Like its US equivalent, the British Saddamgate ran back over time.* In 1984 Sir Geoffrey Howe, then foreign secretary, issued ministerial guidelines on trade with the warring Iran and Iraq. These involved – as John Major was to declare to Liberal Democrat leader Paddy Ashdown in November 1992 – 'a ban on the export of lethal equipment and on defence equipment that would significantly enhance the capabilities of either side to prolong or exacerbate the conflict between them'. The Howe guidelines, which most observers found unexceptional, were not observed: between 1987 and August 1990 Britain, shadowing the US's pro-Iraq posture, supplied Saddam with much of the equipment he sought, including Matrix Churchill machine tools to make shells, Philips Scientific technology to aid nuclear development and Plessey communications facilities – all secured with financial credits supplied by the generous

---

*In view of the US Saddamgate it seemed ironic that British firms were the largest contingent of a US 'blacklist' of organisations supplying arms to Iraq.

British taxpayer. So it was that in the Gulf War the British forces were obliged to face British-made (and US- and British-funded) armaments. This politically embarrassing state of affairs soon pushed British ministers into a wide-ranging and inept cover-up attempt, just as Bush administration officials had responded with their own lies and evasions.

The pivotal trial – that of three former executives of Matrix Churchill – was initiated in February 1991 by UK customs officials investigating violations of export controls. In April it was announced that the former defence minister, Alan Clark, would be required to give evidence. It was also said that Clark had given 'a nod and a wink' to British firms seeking government approval for the export of armaments-making equipment to Iraq: '*Clark strenuously denies the claim*'.[123] At that time UK customs investigators also moved to arrest four more senior managers, including the chairman of BSA Tools, and the chairman and commercial manager of Wickman Machine Tool. (It was also reported that the Birmingham-based aerospace company, Bimec Industries, which had supplied a 'metal treatment plant' to an Iraqi armaments factory, had provided funds to the British Tory Party.)[124] With the Matrix Churchill trial in prospect, evidence of other cases of UK support for Saddam's armaments development began to emerge. It was revealed that Douglas Hogg, then a trade and enterprise minister, had in 1989 approved a grant of £2 million to the Gateshead factory of Flexible Manufacturing Technology (FMT), a firm building specialised equipment to supply the Iraqi army with a mobile rocket-launch system similar to the MRLS (Multiple Rocket Launcher System) used by the allies during the Gulf War.[125] By now it seemed clear that the British government was providing licences for the export of a wide range of equipment that the Iraqis were using to build up their military potential.

In August 1991 it emerged that Britain had supplied Iraq with substantial amounts of uranium suitable for the manufacture of nuclear weapons. The trade and industry secretary, Peter Lilley, commented that only 'tiny amounts' of uranium had gone to Iraq, but after press revelations that some eight tonnes of depleted uranium had been exported to Iraq on Department of Trade and Industry (DTI) licences between 1988 and 1990, with mustard gas and nerve gas ingredients shipped to Iraq over the same period, Lilley admitted that an error 'had crept into the memorandum supplied by his department giving details of materials licensed for export to Iraq'.[126] It also emerged that UK Customs and Excise officers had destroyed detailed records of British arms and chemicals exports to Iraq through the 1980s.

In October 1992, with the Matrix Churchill trial drawing to a dramatic conclusion, Alan Clark now admitted that British exporters had been advised to stress the peaceful aspects of the machinery they wanted to export to Iraq, even though it was known that such machinery could also be used for military purposes. Paul Henderson, the former managing director of the company, testified that the DTI had condoned the sale to Iraq of machine tools it knew could be used to manufacture armaments.* There was also testimony that Mark Gutteridge, a former employee of Matrix Churchill, had passed intelligence information to MI5, as indeed did Paul Henderson. An MI5 officer, testifying from behind a screen, agreed that there was no doubt from information supplied by Gutteridge that the Matrix Churchill machine tools were to be used by Iraq for the production of armaments. Alan Clark was now prepared to declare in court that the guidelines restricting trade with Iraq were *'elastic . . . tiresome and intrusive'*; and that Western interests were 'well served by Iran and Iraq fighting each other'. Clark also testified that suggestions that nothing should be said about the equipment's military uses was *'a matter of Whitehall cosmetics to keep the record ambiguous'*. And he also admitted, using a phrase that came to symbolise the emerging character of the affair, that his failure to make any reference to the possible military uses of the machine tools was no more than being 'economical . . . with the *actualité'*.

The situation now rapidly escalated. Alan Moses QC, for the prosecution, declared to Mr Justice Smedley that the evidence no longer sustained the charges against the three former Matrix Churchill executives. In particular, the evidence of Alan Clark was 'inconsistent with his statements, both in the written statement and in his interview with the officer of Customs and Excise in 1992'. According to Henderson's solicitor, Irwin Mitchell, the government's policy to breach the (UN and British) arms embargo on Iraq was revealed in the 500 pages of secret papers disclosed to the defence on the orders of Mr Justice Smedley – despite the strong resistance of cabinet ministers, Kenneth Clarke, Michael Heseltine and Malcolm Rifkind, together with Tristan Garel-Jones, minister of state at the Foreign Office. The court heard that exports to Iraq were approved in private meetings between ministers, including the then minister of state at the Foreign Office, William Waldegrave (Irwin Mitchell: 'Much time was spent by civil servants, in compliance with ministerial wishes, to keep these developments secret'.)[127] The former Matrix Churchill executives were acquitted.

The government documents, coupled with the unambiguous House of Commons statements made by ministers, showed official duplicity at the

---

*In February 1993 US government sources revealed that MI5 and MI6, as early as 1987, were passing information to US intelligence that Matrix Churchill was selling arms-related equipment to Iraq (*The Guardian*, London, 16 February 1993).

highest levels. Opposition leaders suggested that Prime Minister John Major must have known of the clandestine shipment of arms-related equipment to Iraq, and there was a growing clamour – in the light of mounting evidence – that individual ministers, including John Major, answer the accumulating charges of misrepresentation and mendacity. On 10 November 1992 Major responded by announcing that an independent judicial enquiry into the whole affair would be conducted by Lord Justice Scott. Sir Nicholas Lyell QC, the attorney-general, announced that the enquiry's precise terms of reference still had to be discussed, but it already seemed clear that (1) witnesses were to be invited, not compelled, to testify, and (2) testimony would not be under oath (so ruling out the possibility of later perjury charges). If – as more than one observer asked – ministers had lied to the Commons, and been prepared to let innocent men go to jail to save their own reputations, might they not be equally tempted to lie to a toothless judicial enquiry?

The government decision to opt for a judicial enquiry had the intended effect that embarrassed ministers were no longer required to respond in the House of Commons to questions on the matter. Now it could all be left to the Scott deliberations, a useful ploy for the government but one that did not stop press speculation (until opposition MPs ran out of steam and journalists lost interest) and a number of hasty books.[128] Already it was possible to piece together a web of government mendacity that enjoyed increasing exposure by the day. Alan Clark had already admitted stretching and bending the defence guidelines, and many other ministers were found to be implicated in the pragmatic sale of arms-linked hardware to Saddam Hussein. (The announcement in February 1993 that Clark was not to be prosecuted for the manifest inconsistencies in his testimony seemed to many observers the sure sign of an official cover-up.) William Waldegrave, while Foreign Office minister of state, had expressed concern that stopping the trade with Iraq 'could force Matrix Churchill to close . . . causing us to lose intelligence access'. Lord Trefgarne, the minister for trade, approved export licences for the shipment of Matrix Churchill machine tools to Iraq, knowing that they were destined for an Iraqi bomb-making factory. Such details, and much else, were revealed before the abortive trial of the Matrix Churchill executives – Peter Allen, Paul Henderson and Trevor Abraham – collapsed, causing immense humiliation to a rattled government.[129]

It also emerged that Nicholas Ridley, then trade and industry secretary, had written to Prime Minister Margaret Thatcher to warn that Britain would lose as much as £1 billion if arms sales to Iraq were stopped, and that 'Whitehall cosmetics' had been applied – with the approval of Foreign

Secretary Douglas Hurd – to keep the records deliberately ambiguous.[130] Further reports suggested that Matrix Churchill had been involved in Iraq's plan to develop nuclear weapons, and that British intelligence agencies used the criminal Bank of Credit and Commerce International to fund arms sales to Iraq.[131] Soon the finger of guilt was also pointing at Prime Minister John Major, who was forced to declare – somewhat pathetically for a head of government – that he had never been told that his ministers and officials had illicitly connived at breaches of defence guidelines.[132] Observers inclined to believe his disclaimer: at least catalogues of the 'guilty' tended not to include John Major.[133] In fact documents released after the collapse of the Matrix Churchill court case suggested strongly ('beyond reasonable doubt', according to Labour's trade and industry spokesman, Robin Cook) that Major had misled MPs over Britain's role in arming the Iraqis.[134]

Over subsequent weeks there was further information released to the media, fresh allegations about official mendacity and predictable government denials. The Chilean businessman Dr Carlos Cardoen, who had procured weapons for Iraq through the 1980s, claimed that he had briefed the US and British governments throughout the entire period; Howard Teicher, a former member of the White House-based National Security Council, stated that Margaret Thatcher's son had been involved in Middle East arms deals ('I read of Mark Thatcher's involvement in arms deals in diplomatic dispatches from embassies in Europe and Saudi Arabia. We were very surprised to see him play a personal role'); and Matrix Churchill, citing the government's Export Credit Guarantee Department (ECGD) approved insurance cover, claimed £4 million from the government (i.e. from the British tax-payer) after Saddam defaulted on payment for equipment supplied to Iraq. In the House of Commons the Labour MP Ken Livingstone suggested that there was 'overwhelming circumstantial evidence' connecting Mark Thatcher with weapons exports to Iraq; and the Labour MP Tam Dalyell declared that even if the prime minister was ignorant about what was going on 'Mr Hurd was a very different kettle of fish because few men have come to the office of Foreign Secretary with a greater knowledge of world affairs'.

There were reports that Matrix Churchill had supplied nuclear components to Iraq, and now the International Atomic Energy Agency was demanding an investigation.[135] Evidence emerged that Britain had supplied equipment to aid Saddam's poison gas programme, with the government insuring the exports knowing full well that they were destined for an Iraqi 'chemical weapons factory'; and that arms exports destined for Iraq were approved *after* the invasion of Kuwait.[136] It seemed increasingly unlikely that the terms of reference of the Scott enquiry would allow a proper investigation into the enormity of the case in hand – involving as it did a former prime minister, the current prime minister, many current cabinet ministers, the security services and many key officials in various government departments. Robin Cook, Labour trade spokesman, voiced widespread fears when he commented: 'What we see at the end of the day will depend on negotiations with Lord Justice Scott and the government . . . The inquiry is staffed by the same treasury solicitors that advised those government ministers not to disclose documents in the Matrix Churchill case.' The holding of the enquiry had largely defused the issue. Lord Justice Scott would take months to deliberate, and few observers believed that his final report would condemn John Major, Baroness Thatcher and a whole raft of senior government figures.

As the time approached for the start of the formal hearings before the Scott Inquiry there were already signs of the difficult times ahead. In a case that bore striking similarities to the Matrix Churchill affair, government lawyers were refusing to release official documents which could overturn the convictions of four former Ordtech executives, accused of selling arms to Iraq (*The Guardian*, 22 April 1993). At the same time it emerged that Ministry of Defence documents requested by the Scott Inquiry had been destroyed or lost.* Defence Minister Jonathan Aitkin admitted that some of the papers could not be found, but said in reply to a Parliamentary Question that it would be 'inappropriate' to give further details. The tone was set. The Scott Inquiry began its formal hearings on 4 May 1993, with the final report anticipated by the end of the year.

OTHER EXPOSÉS AND UNANSWERED QUESTIONS

The Saddamgates are special, bearing as they do on the very integrity of government (on 15 November 1992 Brian Walden, prestigious broadcaster and ex-Labour MP floated the suggestion that the British Saddamgate showed that the UK government was 'fundamentally corrupt'). There are other matters – admissions, exposés and unanswered questions – that, while of less import than the Saddamgates, deserve attention. Some such matters – the lies of war propaganda – are characteristic of all military conflicts throughout history. (Other contentious matters of weight – the possible 'green light' given to Saddam by the West to sanction his invasion of

---

*The Observer, 2 May 1993; *Business Age*, July/August 1993.

Kuwait, the suborning of the UN by the United States, etc. – are considered in Chapters 7 and 8.)

On 20 January 1991 General Norman Schwarzkopf declared triumphantly that 'we've destroyed 29 Iraqi aircraft – with not one air-to-air loss on the part of the coalition' – even though he knew the statement to be false. At the start of the Gulf War an Iraqi MiG-25 destroyed a US navy plane in a dogfight, but the Pentagon denied the loss for the sake of a 'clean' record. Michael Scott Speicher, the pilot of the US FA-18, was killed in the encounter on 17 January 1991, and so became the first American casualty of the Gulf War.[137]

At least some of the Western propaganda about Iraqi atrocities in Kuwait appears to have been false. In particular, the story that babies had been taken out of incubators and left 'on the cold floor to die' seems to have been complete fabrication. The allegation appeared in an Amnesty International report and was much cited by President Bush in his efforts to stoke up righteous anger in the United States. Yet subsequent investigations by human rights groups and other interested parties appear to indicate that this alleged 'baby massacre' did not happen.[138]

The much-vaunted Western technology, for most of the time dauntingly superior to what the Iraqis possessed, suffered various failures which were not revealed until after the war. The decision to conceal the Speicher death derived from the US impulse to portray their technology as invincible, a war requirement that some observers may well still seek to justify and which meant that other equipment shortcomings were not revealed until the war was safely won. A Pentagon report publicised in July 1991 reported shortcomings in mine clearing, supplies of tank ammunition, tactical intelligence and other areas. *The Washington Post* noted that officials squabbled bitterly about the sort of attention they received in the report, but it still remained obvious that 'the US military was in places . . . extremely vulnerable and ill-prepared'. US command and control systems were highly reliant on vulnerable satellite communications exposed to jamming, and the US forces themselves were unable to encrypt satellite signals because of inadequate equipment hastily acquired at the start of the conflict. In addition, there were various unfortunate incidents, including one in which seven US combat engineers were killed while stacking cluster bombs.[139] American Abrams tanks seemed very vulnerable to relatively unsophisticated Iraqi fire, and the gas turbine engines used more fuel than expected. RAF Tornados were not always downed by enemy fire: sometimes they unaccountably flew into the ground or were destroyed by their own munitions. And it was suggested that British Tornados flew unnecessary missions to help the RAF win 'political' battles in Whitehall; that is, to enable the air vice-marshals to resist the *Options for Change* reductions in air force spending planned by the government.[140]

It was also reported that the US navy was investigating allegations of war crimes made against its own forces. An anonymous letter, written by a sailor on the guided-missile frigate USS *Nicholas*, alleged that US forces had opened fire on Iraqis trying to surrender, killing five Iraqis and wounding others. Admiral Eugene Carroll, of the Washington think-tank, the Centre for Defence Information, commented that the US military's record in investigating its own breaches of international law is 'abysmal', and he added: 'I would feel a lot more comfortable if we were talking to all the people involved, rather than just our own side.'[141] Another report revealed that American pilots flying combat missions in the Gulf were routinely being given the sleeping drug Halcion, banned in Britain and known to be associated with amnesia, paranoia attacks and violent behaviour.[142]

Another highly contentious issue was the question of 'friendly fire' deaths. It was reported that US tanks, artillery and other weapons managed to destroy more than thirty American tanks, armoured personnel carriers and other vehicles that in total carried more than 175 soldiers. It is significant also that US forces succeeded in killing more Americans than did the Iraqis; said one US army officer: 'Right now we estimate that more than fifty per cent of the ground war casualties were from friendly fire. It probably will go higher.'[143] Most American families of the victims of friendly-fire incidents have not been informed of the circumstances of the deaths. At the same time it was being reported that the US had performed an almost flawless feat of arms. Thus Dick Cheney was telling Congress that 'there are no confirmed reports of penetrations by Iraqi projectiles of M1-A1 Abrams tanks' – while Lisa Applegate had information about the death of her husband on an Iraqi battlefield: 'His tank burned for 48 hours and they couldn't get him out until after the fire was out.'[144] In fact Sergeant Applegate's tank was hit by a sabot round fired by another US Abrams tank, some army experts reckoning that 'most of Applegate's body was sucked through the three-inch hole by a vacuum' created as the 'Silver Bullet' [a two-foot steel dart tipped with depleted uranium] passed through. Mrs Applegate said. 'The coffin didn't weigh anything.'[145]

One of the most contentious cases of friendly-fire deaths concerned the killing of nine British servicemen by US aircraft. An American report on the incident was not made available to the relatives of the nine dead, and from the start of British efforts to uncover the truth there was persistent stalling on the part of the US authorities. Archie Hamilton, the British minister of state for the armed forces, while obviously disinclined to make a fuss, admitted that 'there were still many questions that remained unanswered'.[146] At the Oxford inquest hearing on 11 May 1992 the legal representatives of the victims' families claimed that there were 104 inconsistencies in evidence submitted by the US authorities. It was also stated at the inquest that the US pilots ignored a range of specified Gulf war procedures. Of one report of the pilots' action, Wing Commander Brian Carmichael, the chief British air liaison officer in the Gulf, commented: 'If the report is true then the procedures were not followed adequately or correctly.'[147] On 12 May John Major revealed that the defence secretary, Malcolm Rifkind, had pressed the US government to send the pilots to the inquest. However, Washington refused, whereupon British officials obediently commented that they understood the Pentagon's wish to preserve the anonymity of the pilots. Geoffrey Robertson QC, for the families of the British casualties, commented on the 'staggering discrepancies' in the written evidence submitted by Washington. US Defence Secretary Dick Cheney said that it was 'important not to subject the pilots to what could well turn into a media circus'.

In the event the inquest jury decided that the nine British soldiers were unlawfully killed – which meant in effect that the two pilots had committed manslaughter. There were immediate calls for the British Director of Public Prosecutions to begin extradition proceedings, though by now it was clear that the supine British government would refuse to encourage any further attention to the matter. Geoffrey Robertson declared that the pilots were 'guilty of manslaughter by gross negligence', but neither he nor the families had any further recourse. The US cover-up was set to move into history.[148] On the 19 May 1992 John Major and Malcolm Rifkind made it clear that – despite the 'unlawful killing' verdict – the British government would not be putting any pressure on the United States to encourage the two pilots to give evidence or to take any other action against them. Anne Leech, whose son was among the men killed, commented on the American attitude: 'They know that the information they gave us and the statements made by the two American pilots were a pack of lies. They have given us absolutely nothing so far. They know that a lot of questions were raised at the inquest and they should answer them.'[149] In his book on the Gulf War, Sir Peter de la Billière gives six inconclusive pages to this incident ('. . . we were left knowing that we would have to investigate the matter in more detail if we were to have any chance of establishing exactly what happened');[150] in his own volume, General Schwarzkopf dismissed this 'upsetting development' in two sentences.[151] (The American propensity for causing friendly-fire deaths was shown yet again when, on 2 October 1992, a US aircraft carrier accidentally fired missiles at a NATO Turkish destroyer, killing the ship's commanding officer and four crewmen.)

Another unanswered case involving legal action is that of civilian BA Flight 149 which – with more than 300 passengers and crew aboard – arrived in Kuwait hours *after* the Iraqi forces. In August 1992 it was reported that legal proceedings against British Airways were under way in Britain, France and the United States. One suit filed in San Diego, California, alleged that BA 'knew or should have known of the hostile invasion of Kuwait by Iraqi armed forces, and the resultant eminent danger to the lives and safety of plaintiffs'. Wilful misconduct and negligence were alleged. Lawyers for the plaintiffs claimed that passengers overheard an argument among crew members over whether the plane should take off from Heathrow at all, in view of the situation in Kuwait. In the event the 337 passengers, along with seventy-seven BA staff, were prevented by the Iraqi military from taking off from Kuwait City to continue their flight. Thirty-six passengers, all but two of them British, were taken to Baghdad for use as human shields. A BA stewardess was raped by the Iraqis.[152]

Why was British Airways not warned that the invasion had taken place? Why was Flight 149 not diverted to a safer airport (in any case it was destined for Kuala Lumpur)? The flight arrived in Kuwait two hours after the start of the Iraqi invasion. Was there not ample time to warn the BA flight crew of what had become a hazardous region? Or, as has been alleged, were British and American intelligence using the BA flight to bring their own people into Kuwait? Was BA Flight 149 a 'Trojan horse'? A BA man has said that a group of twelve young men who arrived at Heathrow to pick up the flight were 'obviously soldiers – you get used to recognising them'. Allegations have also been made that these men 'melted away' as soon as the plane landed, so avoiding capture by the Iraqis. The journalists Mike Jempson and Andrew Marshall established that:

There was ample time for the British embassy in Kuwait to warn BA before the plane landed.

Passengers were told by Ministry of Defence personnel held captive with them that the plane was 'talked down' by British military staff.

BA Flight 149 was the only one to land after the start of the invasion.

The dozen men believed to be soldiers had been booked in from Hereford, the base of the Special Air Service.

A member of the Kuwaiti royal family, thought to have a military role, was on the plane with his bodyguard.[153]

The British Foreign Office refused in August 1992 – two years after the incident – to comment on the circumstances surrounding BA149, apart from referring to earlier inconclusive ministerial statements. These statements 'appear to contradict each other as well as evidence obtained' by various journalistic investigations.[154]

In March 1993 fresh evidence emerged to cast doubt on statements made by Prime Minister John Major and Baroness Thatcher on the fate of Flight 149 (*The Independent on Sunday*, 7 March 1993). Documents newly obtained from US intelligence services under the Freedom of Information Act confirmed that the British government knew about the Iraqi invasion of Kuwait at least three hours before BA149 was due to land. It is hard to avoid the conclusion that intelligence reports should have provided ample time for the aircraft to be diverted. In June 1993 British Airways took steps to ban the release of information about Flight BA149.

Other court cases in the UK have involved some of the eighty-eight Iraqis, Palestinians and Yemenis interned by the Home Office at the start of the Gulf War. The men were wrongly arrested, denied their legal rights, and threatened with deportation. After several weeks of imprisonment the deportation threats were lifted. The Home Office subsequently initiated 'a top-level internal inquiry into what Whitehall is describing as the worst intelligence débacle for years'.[155]

THE TURKISH FACTOR

Turkey,* another coalition ally and NATO member, was pursuing its own agenda of violence and repression – in circumstances that bore an alarming resemblance to Saddam's war on his own minority ethnic groups. The Turks had long been intent on repressing their own Kurdish minority (in some areas the Turkish Kurds had been granted fewer rights than their Iraqi counterparts), and one consequence of the Gulf War has been to give the Turks a freer hand in repressing Kurdish culture, destroying Kurdish villages and waging war – sometimes across the border into Iraq – against the organised Kurdish resistance. In March 1991, following the ending of

---

*Turkey, as a strategic Western asset, affords a good example of how the US is prepared to rewrite history in the interest of *realpolitik* objectives. In a sustained genocide that began on 24 April 1915 the Turkish army began the systematic massacre of hundreds of thousands of Armenian Turks: men, women and children. When Hitler was planning his 'final solution' to the Jewish Question he asked: 'Who remembers the Armenians now?' The United States does not. When in 1990 Senator Robert Dole moved a resolution for US recognition of the 1915 massacre, Senator Robert Byrd urged caution: 'I say we ought to stop, look and listen before we take a fateful step here to offend a friend, to offend an ally.' The resolution was defeated by 51 votes to 48. Washington had decided that the Armenian massacre, cynically consigned to oblivion by Adolf Hitler, had never happened.

the Gulf War (and true to a long Turkish tradition), the Turkish army was firing on Kurdish nationalists in southern Turkey: two people were shot dead and twenty were wounded by the Turkish security forces. Turkey – in the interest of dismembering a bellicose Iraq – had shown some support for Kurdish independence in Iraq, but conservative Turkish factions reckoned that such a move would strengthen the dissident Kurds within Turkey. There was already conservative hostility to the efforts of the Turkish president, Turgut Ozal, to lift a Turkish law banning the Kurdish language. There were already signs that the Turkish Kurds were being emboldened by the partial political successes of their brothers across the border in Iraq.[156] Reports in April told of Turkish soldiers stealing blankets, sheets and food from terrified Kurdish refugees in southern Turkey.

On 5 August 1991 Turkish F-4 and F-104 fighter-bombers flew ninety-two sorties into northern Iraq to bomb Turkish Kurdish rebels. At the same time a Turkish land invasion penetrated as deep as eleven miles into Iraqi territory in an attack on guerrillas belonging to the Kurdistan Workers' Party (PKK). It was also declared that Turkey intended to mount a permanent occupation of parts of northern Iraq – as a deep 'buffer zone' – to prevent further infiltration of its territory. On 7 August the prime minister, Mesut Yilmaz, said: 'We are declaring a 5-kilometer region along the border a buffer zone. Everyone who steps into that area [without permission] will be fired upon.'[157] Over the subsequent months there were further Turkish raids on the Kurds in Iraq, some of the attacks being made on the 'safe havens' set up by the allies at the end of the Gulf War for the protection of the Kurds.[158] In one account no less than three thousand Turkish troops invaded Iraq in an attempt to root out PKK guerrillas. Estimates suggested that more than one hundred Kurdish civilians had been killed by Turkish artillery fire.

The Kurdish resistance was still able to mount offensives against the regular Turkish forces. On 25 October as many as 500 PKK guerrillas mounted an attack on Turkish soldiers across the border, whereupon Turkey immediately retaliated with F-104 planes and helicopter-borne troops making raids on Kurdish positions. The Kurds had planned their raid to coincide with the aftermath of Turkey's parliamentary elections, narrowly won by the conservative Suleiman Demirel. The new government was considering the idea of conciliation with the Kurds, but there were loud public demands for an all-out war against the Kurdish minority. Again the conflict threatened the involvement of other states in the region. Turkey's ambassador in Damascus had already informed the Syrians that Turkey might feel forced to attack Abdullah Ocalan's PKK camp in the Syrian-controlled Bekaa Valley, and that if Turkey did not receive Syria's co-operation, 'it would seek help from Israel'. There were also reports of

Turkish brutality against Kurdish civilians, with mass executions and bodies flung into mass graves.[159] On 5 May 1992 a British delegation, led by Lord Avebury, chairman of the Parliamentary Human Rights Group, called on the government to impose economic sanctions on Turkey for its torture and massacre of Kurdish civilians. A week later, Kurdish civilians were again being bombed by Turkish planes. Clashes continued throughout 1992 with some eighty-two combatants killed on 29 September in the worst single engagement of the war.

Now the Iraqi Kurds, fearing for their own survival, were co-operating with the regular Turkish forces to defeat the radical PKK. President Ozal met an Iraqi opposition coalition that Kurdish leaders hoped to establish as a US-backed provisional government in northern Iraq, though he was quick to support the preservation of Iraq as a unitary state and the maintenance of Turkish-dominated land in northern Iraq. By now it was abundantly clear to independent observers that the West, so exercised about Saddam's persecution of his own Kurdish minority, had no interest in Turkey's repression of its own Kurds.[160] A bloody battle at the end of September left some two hundred dead, mostly PKK insurgents, as it became increasingly clear that military force alone would be unlikely to quell the rebellion.

On 23 October, five thousand Turkish troops drove into northern Iraq in search of PKK guerrillas, Turkish planes having bombed Kurdish camps for the previous two weeks. It was reported that Turkish bombing raids on PKK bases had killed many Iraqi Kurds, a circumstance that hardened Iraqi feelings against the PKK insurgents.[161] By the end of October Turkish troops had advanced ten miles into Iraq on a twenty-mile front, according to official Turkish statements, and there were growing signs that the PKK were trapped between the Iraqi Kurds and the regular Turkish forces. Now the Turks were admitting to controlling some sixty-two square miles of Iraq, on two main fronts. But now it seemed that Turkey had gone too far: the Iraqi Kurds were outraged at the extent of the Turkish invasion and were calling on Western countries to insist on an early Turkish withdrawal. Now, with the West looking the other way, it seemed clear that Turkey intended to consolidate a permanent annexation of substantial tracts of Iraqi territory.[162]

Early in 1993 there were some signs of a willingness to negotiate an end to the military conflict between the PKK and the Turkish government. The PKK leader, Abdullah Ocalan, declared that he wished to negotiate and would mount no attacks during the celebrations for the Turkish New Year of Nowrug on 21 March. Now it seemed that both the war-weary PKK and their Syrian backers had an interest in a truce. Still Ocalan maintained that if the Turkish government continued to say to the Kurds 'you don't exist', there would be a return to 'continuous war' (*The Guardian*, 18 March 1993). Within weeks, the conflict had resumed.

THE SURVIVAL OF SADDAM

At the end of the Gulf War it seemed unlikely that Saddam would survive. The army appeared to be fragmented and demoralised, the infrastructure of the country had been massively damaged, there were still tens of thousands of US troops in southern Iraq, and the country remained under tight economic blockade. The Ba'athist regime – now forced to confront widespread riots and obvious disaffection in Baghdad – was facing unprecedented threats. Much of a devastated Basra was in rebel hands and it appeared unlikely that Saddam would be able to re-establish his control over the northern Kurds. Western leaders, rejoicing at their evident military victory, urged the Iraqi people to rise up and depose their brutal and discredited leader. But it soon became apparent that Saddam, having made many miscalculations over his invasion of Kuwait, had given thought to his post-war survival. In particular, he had husbanded enough of the Republican Guard to ensure his protection in a devastated and demoralised land.

Saddam began his efforts at post-war reconstruction with a cabinet reshuffle. Tariq Aziz, the foreign minister who had shuttled round the world in a vain attempt to prevent the war, was made deputy prime minister – to some observers a meaningless post. Saddoun Hammadi, a Shia, was promoted to the position of prime minister; and Taha Yassin Ramadan, a Kurd, was elevated to the new post of vice-president. Some exiled opposition figures claimed that Latif Jasim, the former information minister, had disappeared without trace. Soon – as part of his 'carrot' theme – Saddam was encouraging Iraqi journalists to write freely: 'Write what you like. If you get it right, take the credit. If you get it wrong, I'll take the blame.' There were in fact signs of a partial liberalisation, with Iraqi newspapers carrying measured criticism of shortages and high prices. Saddam also tried to bolster Iraqi morale by pretending that Iraq had won the war. Thus on the eve of the first anniversary of the invasion of Kuwait he declared: 'We look at victory in its perspective as an historical duel, not as a fight between one army and several others. You are victorious because you have refused humiliation and repression . . . and clung to a state that will strengthen the people and the [Arab] nation for ever. We don't have the feeling that we were not victorious in the historical duel.' Then there were more ministerial changes.

On 3 September 1991 Iraq's Revolution Command Council (RCC)

issued a new law legalising opposition parties, though only the Ba'ath Party was allowed to operate in the armed forces: 'The Ba'ath Party should be in the armed forces to defend the revolution and prevent any military coup.' The new law stipulated that a party could be founded by a minimum of 150 people aged at least 25, but that it could not be established on the basis of race, regionalism, sectarianism or atheism. In a significant shift of policy, religious parties – provided they were not sectarian – were now allowed to operate; and party members receiving funds from abroad would face life imprisonment (not, as formerly, the death penalty). At the same time there was talk of multiparty elections being held by the end of the year. However, Western-style democracy would not be allowed. In a speech lasting several hours, delivered in September at a top-level meeting of the Ba'ath Party, Saddam stated that anyone aspiring to Western values 'would not be allowed . . . to take any post in leadership'. The Iraqi leader was now giving every sign of consolidating his control over the regime, though some of his own diplomats were deserting him: staff at various Iraqi embassies defected and the Madrid embassy was closed down after the last three diplomats disappeared to seek refuge somewhere in the Gulf area.

Saddam now felt strong enough to pressure the British government into releasing some Iraqi assets in exchange for freeing a British businessman. On 23 November 1991 Ian Richter, jailed by the Iraqis for five years on bribery charges, was celebrating his release after Britain had allowed Iraq access to £70 million-worth of assets. There were signs of factional squabbles in the Iraqi leadership – with at least one account of a gun-battle involving Saddam's bodyguards – but it seemed clear that now Saddam was 'in complete control of the country outside Kurdistan'.[163] Syria was now moving closer to Iraq, opposing UN Security Council threats of fresh military action against Baghdad and growing increasingly suspicious of American intentions to turn the Middle East into a US 'security zone'. In March 1992 Damascus resumed its mail and parcel services to Baghdad, and Syrian newspapers and television were instructed to end their verbal attacks on Saddam Hussein. It was significant that Syria also declined to celebrate the February anniversary of the liberation of Kuwait. American efforts to intercept the North Korean ship carrying Scud missiles to Syria had enraged the Ba'athist leadership in Damascus. In an address to the Syrian parliament President Assad denied that the ship had been carrying missiles but commented: 'We have missiles and will bring missiles according to our needs.' Then he attacked US hypocrisy. Israel was being allowed to produce 'all types of weapons, especially missiles' while Washington was trying to prevent Arab states from doing the same: 'That is not international legitimacy. That is the law of the jungle. The law of wild animals.'[164]

In May the senior UN aid official Robert Hauser, director of operations for the World Food Programme, declared that there was now little malnutrition in Iraq: 'The vast majority have adjusted to the government rationing system. People eat less and throw away less, but I have not seen people as wasteful as in Iraq before the wars.' The rationing system was equitable and well organised, with the overall situation in Iraq 'only one per cent as serious as in Somalia or Sudan'. In June a classified intelligence report, a National Intelligence Estimate presented to President Bush and his chief aides, declared that Saddam Hussein was stronger than he had been a year earlier. Some of the country's infrastructure had been rebuilt by importing goods via Jordan, in violation of UN sanctions, and hidden Iraqi reserves had been tapped. The report also stated that the continued imposition of sanctions would cause the conditions for most people in Iraq to worsen, so increasing the pressures on Saddam. A Bush administration official commented: 'The main point is that Saddam is still there and we expect him to stay. It used to be that people were saying that the sanctions were making him weaker. They're not saying that any more. He is clearly stronger than he was a year ago'; and in the same vein James Lilley, assistant secretary of defence for international security affairs, declared: 'As long as he's able to get enough stuff to buy off his cronies, the Republican Guard, his chances of staying in power are pretty good. From what I've seen recently, it doesn't look like he's going to fall any time soon.'[165]

Much of the problem, from the Washington perspective, was that Saddam was succeeding in escaping the intended sanctions stranglehold. In July CIA chief Robert Gates flew to Jordan to urge King Hussein to allow on-the-spot inspections of lorries carrying the bulk of Iraq's trade with the rest of the world. US intelligence sources were blaming Jordan for allowing middlemen to supply Iraq with howitzers, steel cables and rods, tyres, cement and other equipment that could be used for military purposes. The Jordanian response was to insist that the Iraqi borders with Syria, Turkey and Iran were equally permeable. In one substantial account a detailed description was provided of how Barzan Tikriti, Saddam's half-brother, was running a world-wide sanctions-busting operation from Switzerland,[166] and it was increasingly being recognised that Iraq was now selling millions of gallons of oil in violation of UN sanctions and with the apparent compliance of Turkey.[167]

In August dozens of Iraqi businessmen were executed for profiteering and hoarding basic commodities, whereupon Saddam was forced to send an envoy, Ahmed al-Zubeidi, to Amman to reassure terrified Iraqi traders. On 12 August Saddam promised a crackdown on 'irresponsible government officials' as part of a plan to help the economy: 'Measures taken by the leadership to protect the interests of citizens and future measures that will be taken in this respect aim at protecting all the sons of Iraq from the devious people.' Said Saddam: '[the corrupt officials] will be dealt with the same way we dealt with corrupt businessmen'. On 20 August a British expatriate, Paul Ride, was jailed for seven years in Baghdad for allegedly entering the country illegally; and a week later a second Briton, Michael Wainwright, was facing similar charges in a Baghdad court. Wainwright was sentenced to ten years in jail, a 'totally disproportionate' term that provoked 'the strongest possible protest' from the UK Foreign Office. Three Swedes, arrested for entering Iraq on 3 September, were each sentenced to prison terms of three years.

On 18 September 1992 it was announced that Iraqi engineers and builders, working round the clock, had succeeded in rebuilding Saddam's main palace, the massive 'Home of the People' on the southern bank of the Tigris River. The army newspaper *al-Qadissiyah* declared that the speedy reconstruction of the bombed palace was 'a loud reply to rancorous and malevolent enemies'. Saddam was also spending vast sums on the construction of a modern Babylon. Huge artificial mounds carry terraced trees and flowers, in imitation of ancient Babylon's Hanging Gardens, with palaces and recreation centres overshadowing the remains of the monuments to Nebuchadnezzar's greatness. Placards decorating the entrances to the ancient city proclaim: 'From Nebuchadnezzar to Saddam Hussein, Babylon rises again'. Of Saddam's plans to revive an international cultural festival in the ruins of ancient Babylon, Hamed Youssef Hammadi, the Iraqi minister of culture and information, has declared: 'The Babylon festival will underline that the torch of life will not be extinguished no matter how hard the enemies like Zionists and [their] agents try to stop the march. This festival . . . is a defiance . . . of the forces of evil and conspiracy against our country.'

There were now fresh UN moves to help the Kurds, Shias and other Iraqi groups again facing a harsh winter, with Washington urging the use of frozen Iraqi assets to pay for weapons inspections and humanitarian aid. Iraq in turn threatened that it would not co-operate with the 'winter survival programme' if the Security Council decided to go ahead with plans to seize Iraqi assets. It also announced that it was seeking UN agreement to export $4 billion-worth of oil to pay for humanitarian aid and to fund the implementation of UN resolutions against Iraq. Any attempt to seize the frozen assets would be 'bank robbery, Texas-style' and 'an act of illegal confiscation'. On 2 October 1992 the UN Security Council passed the planned resolution (14–0 with China abstaining) for the confiscation of frozen Iraqi oil assets, an unprecedented UN initiative. Iraq had been able to use some foreign funds to purchase humanitarian supplies exempt under the UN sanctions. Now such a facility was blocked, with all the relevant funds having to go through the US-controlled UN agencies. Washington had succeeded in performing its Texas-style 'bank robbery'.

The Iraqis continued – in the teeth of sanctions, with their assets frozen and with oil sales limited – to rebuild their country, to repair the massive damage caused by forty-three consecutive days and nights of bombing. By October 1992 Iraqi engineers had succeeded in repairing all but one of the bridges in Baghdad, the 14-storey telephone exchange – bombed to a concrete shell – had been restored, and the many gutted ministries had been rebuilt. The main Baghdad power plant was working at 90 per cent of its pre-war capacity and oil production was back to around 800,000 barrels a day (though overseas sales were still prohibited). The six-lane highway from Baghdad to the Jordanian border – once littered with bomb craters – was now again a smooth super-highway. Developments were continuing on the 'Third River' project, a 350-mile canal that will tap the Tigris–Euphrates basin to reclaim land. It was obvious that Saddam Hussein was a key motivating factor in the reconstruction of Iraq. Those around him have said: 'Saddam never, ever, gives up . . .' – a mentality which, according to the journalist Marie Colvin, has proved 'crucial to the rebuilding of Iraq. He went from the Mother of all Battles to the Mother of all Reconstructions without missing a beat'.[168]

Ordinary Iraqis continued to face massive problems, not least the repression visited on dissident groups, but it would be wrong to doubt the pride felt by many Iraqis in the speedy rebuilding of their country – in the face of sanctions and continued Western hostility. (In some cases the Western policy on Iraq worked to damage Western firms: for example, by 1993 the freezing of Iraqi assets was driving some thirty British companies close to ruin.) On 18 October 1992 the head of UNICEF reached agreement with senior officials in Baghdad on reviving aid to Iraq. Said the UN official, James Grant: 'It is a programme for all of Iraq, including the three northern governorates [areas controlled by the Kurds].' Two days later, to the outrage of UN officials, the United States moved to block the humanitarian agreement, saying that it made too many concessions to Baghdad. As the desperate Kurds in the mountains faced yet another cold winter, Washington had again demonstrated the character of its political priorities.

At the end of October the strengthened opposition Iraqi National Congress (INC) completed its conference in Salahuddin in northern Iraq. Now

it was conceded that the INC had little organised support within most of
Iraq, though there was still hope of fresh Western support that might make
the difference. Saddam Hussein gave no sign that he was troubled by the
INC efforts in the north. He had survived – despite everything – and it
looked as if he would remain in power for the foreseeable future. The
rebuilding of Baghdad, while much of the rest of Iraq remained desolate,
was increasingly advertised as a propaganda success. For example, on
21 January 1993 there were celebrations in Baghdad to mark the reopening
of the Bilady baby milk factory, destroyed two years ago by US bombs
and missiles. The prime minister Mohammad Hamza al-Zubeidi presided
over the inauguration of the plant, while an anti-aircraft crew swivelled
their gun on a US-supplied Jeep and children from the Saddam Kinder-
garten chanted: 'With our spirits and our blood we will sacrifice ourselves
to you, O Saddam!' [169] At the same time there were frequent reports of the
rising tide of crime in Baghdad and elsewhere, of Basra still awash with
untreated sewage (a UNICEF water and sanitation officer, Kazim Hallal,
declaring that 'the people here are drinking sewage'), and the hospitals
still having to contend – in the teeth of a *de facto* UN embargo on medical
supplies – with epidemics of cholera, hepatitis and malaria. Dr Aladin
al-Fadhli, a hospital director, was quoted: 'It is a catastrophe for me as a
doctor to watch people die unnecessarily. It is not humanity for anyone
to do this. We feel that the war did not end with the bombing and shelling.
It is not finished.'

The US-inspired sanctions – in late-1993 running into a fourth year –
ensured that Saddam, well cushioned in Baghdad, would continue to preside over a demoralised and suffering country racked by crime, destitution
and disease. [170] It was becoming increasingly clear that there was little
reason for continued sanctions. There was broad Iraqi compliance with UN
resolutions and no suggestion that Iraq was about to embark upon further
aggression. UN inspectors had commented, for example that Saddam's
nuclear intentions were no longer a threat, that the destruction of mustard
gas stockpiles was progressing well and that nerve gas stocks had been
destroyed (*The Independent*, 20 March 1993). On 19 March 1993 UN
experts arrived in Baghdad to remove Iraq's stockpiles of irradiated uranium. In such circumstances of broad Iraqi co-operation with UN inspectors
it was hard to see why the Iraqi population should continue to be punished
with sanctions. Any independent observer might have thought that the
Iraqi people had suffered enough, but there was more to come. A frustrated
George Bush, smarting under the fact that Saddam had outlived his term
in office, could not resist the temptation of launching a final punitive attack

on Iraq. A fresh military onslaught – some observers noted – would have the additional consequence of locking president-elect Clinton into a violently anti-Saddam posture.

THE BUSH FINALE

Since the end of the 1991 Gulf War George Bush had smarted in relative impotence on the Iraq question. The dissident uprisings in the Kurdish north of Iraq, in Basra, in the Shi'ite south – all verbally supported by the Western coalition allies – had failed to dislodge Saddam Hussein. Nor had the Iraqi army risen up to depose the tyrant. Bush had dramatically personalised the Gulf conflict, and yet the demonised Iraqi leader was still in place. What could be done?

There were few options. It would not have been possible to organise a second coalition onslaught on Iraq: there were too few grounds for such an attack and the Arab states that had reluctantly supported the original coalition would not support a further US-inspired adventure. In the dying weeks of his administration George Bush had no recourse but to invent fresh Iraqi sins as a prelude to US air strikes on selected Iraqi targets. Of course there would be further Iraqi civilian deaths but at least George Bush would have relieved some of his personal frustrations by giving Saddam a 'bloody nose' or a 'spanking'. The excuse for a fresh US military attack was Iraqi 'violation' of the so-called 'no-fly zone' in southern Iraq. What this meant in fact was that if Iraq chose to fly aircraft over certain parts of its own land then US fighters, illegally violating Iraqi air space, would shoot them down.

The no-fly zones had no legal status. There is no reference to the no-fly zones – in either the north or the south of Iraq – in any UN resolutions. Only one resolution – Resolution 688 (5 April 1991) – condemns (rightly) the repression of the Iraqi people in many parts of Iraq, and 'demands' and 'insists' that Iraq undertake certain actions in this connection. But 688 was passed under the humanitarian chapter (Chapter 1) of the UN Charter, not under the chapter (Chapter 7) that allows for military action in the event of non-compliance. Resolution 688 contains no clauses that specify what action should follow in the event of Iraq's non-compliance with its various requirements. If it were demonstrated – as it well could be – that the Iraqi authorities had violated the terms of 688 then the proper course would be a further Security Council resolution authorising action. The US, fearing that they would not command the support of the Council in a resolution

authorising further military action against Iraq, decided not to approach
the UN on the matter: George Bush liked the idea of unilateral military
action that could be taken promptly and without the bothersome need for
legal justification. And once a military action had been taken, other military
initiatives could follow.

On 27 December 1992 US fighters challenged two Iraqi aircraft flying
over southern Iraq. One of the US F-16 fighters fired air-to-air missiles
which brought down one of the Iraqi planes. Commentators were quick
to point out that the US action had no legal basis: thus the no-fly 'zone
was established unilaterally . . . not by a separate resolution . . . Thus the
US action in shooting down the Iraqi MiG appeared questionable in terms
of international law.'[171] President-elect Bill Clinton issued a statement
saying that he supported 'efforts to bring Iraq into compliance [with UN
resolutions]'. At the same time the Iraqis denounced the act as 'flagrant
aggression', declaring that they would take 'suitable' action to respond
to 'this aggression over our national territory'. Nizar Hamdoon, the Iraqi
ambassador to the United Nations, denied that Iraq was seeking a new
military confrontation with the US and declared that Baghdad would not
be lodging a formal complaint to the UN. Soon Washington was expressing
its concern that there were Iraqi SAM ground-to-air missile batteries along
or below (the reports varied) the 32nd parallel that defined the border of
the illegally-defined no-fly zone in the south. Thus Marlin Fitzwater, White
House spokesman, declared: 'We're monitoring the missiles. We're very
concerned. We're still considering our options.' On 6 January 1993 Iraq
was given forty-eight hours to withdraw the missiles or face air strikes by
the US, Britain and France – an ultimatum that again encouraged comment
about the legality of the US-defined no-fly zones ('The zone has never
been officially approved by the UN').[172] Two days later Iraq announced
that it had withdrawn the missile batteries to less threatening positions,
and US reconnaissance aircraft and spy satellites were working to check
whether Washington still had a pretext to launch military strikes against
Iraq. On 10 January American defence officials were admitting that the
Iraqi leader had complied with US orders.[173] Soon Washington had contrived fresh grounds for a US–Iraq confrontation.

Saddam was now pressing ahead with his plan to drain the southern
marshes, a scheme that had agricultural implications and likely strategic
consequences for the beleaguered marsh Arabs. It was now being widely
reported that this 'Third River' project would drastically affect the livelihood of the marsh dwellers – further evidence of Saddam's perfidy. What
was less often noted was that this development scheme was based on a 1951
report ('Control of the Rivers of Iraq') by Frank Haigh, a senior British

engineer formerly with the British Indian administration (see *New Scientist*, 17 April 1993). A principal purpose then, as now, was to capture the marsh waters for irrigation. At the same time, Saddam was keen to suppress the recalcitrant tribes in the marshes. An important report in *The Observer* on 28 February 1993, by Middle-East correspondent Shyam Bhatia, revealed 'the full barbarism of Saddam's onslaught' on the marsh Arabs.*

There were also reports of further Iraqi incursions into Kuwait, events that seemingly were inflated out of all proportion by Western commentators in the effort to justify a fresh allied military response. It was reported that Iraqi troops or unarmed technicians (the reports varied) had ventured into Kuwait to retrieve Iraqi material (including missiles and other weapons) from warehouses near the border. In fact the newly (and illegally) demarcated border between Kuwait and Iraq was not due to come into force until 15 January and the Security Council had allowed Iraq, until that date, to remove its equipment from the area, providing it received prior clearance from the UN.[174] Thus what some US officials were trying to inflate into a second invasion of Kuwait was no more than an Iraqi failure to say 'please' before retrieving material, as agreed with the Security Council, from what was still Iraqi territory.

On 10 January Iraq imposed its own no-fly zone, denying UN officials permission to fly from Bahrain to Baghdad in protest at the continuing ban on flights by Iraqi Airways. At the same time Washington was making fresh charges that allied flights over southern Iraq were again being threatened by SAM missile batteries (which most independent observers agreed were obsolete systems lacking spare parts). Now the points were clocking up – a fresh 'invasion' of Kuwait, clapped-out SAMs threatening allied aircraft in Iraqi air space, further restrictions on UN inspectors. But did such trivia amount to a justification for further bombing raids on Iraq, with the inevitable civilian deaths that such a course would involve? Washington thought so, and so did UK Foreign Secretary Douglas Hurd: 'I don't think anyone who is concerned with international law . . . could argue that the Iraqis can be allowed to get away with what they did.' On 13 January 1993 some 114 aircraft, including British Tornados, carried out air strikes on southern Iraq. Use was made of French Mirages and at least thirty-five aircraft, carrying 2000lb laser-guided bombs and Harm missiles, operating from the USS *Kitty Hawk* in the northern waters of the Gulf. Early reports said that civilians had been killed in a residential area of Basra.[175] Marlin

---

*In March 1993 there were reports that Washington was considering bombing the massive earth dykes that were draining the waters of the Iraqi marshes (*The Observer*, London, 7 March 1993).

Fitzwater, spokesman for George Bush, declared: 'We stand ready to take additional forceful action with our coalition partners.' A USA Today/CNN/ Gallup poll found that 83 per cent of respondents approved of the bombing of Iraq, with 59 per cent saying that the bombing should continue until Saddam was toppled from power. A large majority (75 per cent) of those favouring further bombing were not deterred by the possibility of 'substantial US casualties'.

Now Washington was advancing a further ground for military attacks on Iraq. Baghdad was instructed to close down six ramshackle police posts in the UN-controlled demilitarised zone by midnight on 15 January – or face military retaliation. George Bush was now scraping the barrel. The six Iraqi positions had been in existence for a year, during which time the US had orchestrated the redrawing of the Kuwait/Iraq border in favour of Kuwait, and the presence of the posts had seemingly caused Washington no problems throughout the entire period. Suddenly the presence of a few Iraqi policemen, in a few dilapidated offices that the US and Kuwaiti authorities had known about for many months, were to be used as a further pretext for American aggression.[176] When it was revealed by the White House that the earlier bombing raids had missed at least half their targets there was new speculation that there would be further air attacks 'to finish the job'. At the same time the first of some 1250 US troops were arriving in Kuwait to protect the emirate from imaginary dangers. A partial climb-down by Saddam on the question of flights by UN inspectors seemed unlikely to prevent fresh US air attacks. Now it was being reported that US generals were urging Bush to bomb Baghdad.[177]

The Pentagon had admitted the poor performance of its planes in the earlier bombing raids, when the bombs missed a third of their targets altogether and only destroyed a few of those they hit. It was also announced in the US that the British Tornados had missed half their targets, contradicting British claims of their good performance. Said a UK Ministry of Defence official: 'It's very, very silly to get into the game of numbers.' With Washington and London smarting under such evident failures it seemed unlikely that fresh air strikes would be long delayed.

On 17 January 1993 President Bush, supported by Britain and France, fired some forty cruise missiles at a factory on the outskirts of Baghdad. It was announced that the Tomahawk weapons had been launched from the Gulf and the Red Sea to destroy the Zaafaraniyah 'nuclear fabricating plant' which had already been the subject of UN weapons inspections. The al-Rashid hotel in central Baghdad was also hit, resulting in the deaths of two women receptionists and the wounding of thirty-one people.[178] Even while the cruise missiles were hitting Baghdad the Iraqi police posts on the border were being dismantled, according to UN officials. The little-publicised fact also emerged that Kuwait itself had failed to comply with UN requests to remove its own police posts in the disputed area.[179] On 18 January there were further air strikes on southern Iraq to destroy the targets missed in the earlier bombing raids.

The Bush finale had failed to impress many world leaders. The Arab states remained significantly quiet and Russia demanded a meeting of the Security Council and a clearer indication of allied objectives. A few more innocent Iraqis had been killed and wounded; Saddam Hussein was yet more securely ensconced in power, and George Bush found yet again that personal spite was no substitute for useful policy. Again, the West had demonstrated its hypocrisy and double standards, reacting disproportionately to minor irritations. Now Baghdad was offering a 'ceasefire' – though it was manifestly too weak to respond in military terms to Western aggression – and hoping to cultivate fresh relationships with the new US administration.

ENTER BILL CLINTON

On 4 November 1992 George Bush – after a dismal year of health worries, a stagnant economy, collapsing social services and negative campaigning – was defeated by the Democrat Bill Clinton, governor of Arkansas. In Baghdad the people cheered in the streets; in Kuwait they were dismayed. President Saddam Hussein rejoiced by firing shots in the air during a visit to the desert city of Ramadi. Said Saddam: 'Bush fell a long time ago, when he decided to bomb Baghdad.' A few days later the Iraqi newspaper *Babel*, owned by President Saddam's eldest son Udai, commented in an editorial that the Iraqis 'will deal with the new administration'. Here, above the signature of Nouri al-Marsoumi, the under-secretary of the Ministry of Culture and Information, it was stated that Iraq should prove to the new administration that US interests 'can be guaranteed in balance with the interests of the region's peoples'.

President-elect Clinton announced that 'America has only one president at a time . . . and even as American administrations change, America's fundamental interests do not'. There would, declared Clinton, be 'essential continuity of American foreign policy'. In an interview with Trude Feldman for *The New York Times*, in answering the question 'What was President Bush's biggest foreign policy mistake?', Clinton replied:

His policy toward Iraq before and after the Gulf War. For example, he made a basic mistake in being so friendly toward Saddam Hussein, extending agricultural credits that will never be paid, providing technology which Saddam used in his weapons programme, and sending signals that must have given Saddam the impression that he had a good chance to be able to invade Kuwait and get away with it – because of the way we coddled him. That was the mistake. Then, as soon as the war was over, out of fear that Iraq would break up, we let Saddam attack the Kurds in the north and the Shi'ites in the south until the international press and our allies forced us to get back in and try to change it. For the first year after the war, we were not nearly as insistent as we are now that the terms of the ceasefire resolutions be observed.[180]

Bill Clinton had won thirty-two states and Washington DC, taking 370 of the 538 electoral-college votes, the best performance by a Democrat since Lyndon Johnson's landslide in 1964. Clinton had secured what seemed a convincing victory. Viewed in other terms, he had won with only 43 per cent of the popular vote on a 55 per cent turn-out, high by recent standards. This meant that Bill Clinton had been elected president of the United States with only 23.6 per cent of American men and women supporting him. It remained to be seen what foreign policies – including those bearing on Saddam Hussein's Iraq – would be adopted by a new American president supported by fewer than one in four American adults.

The signals coming from president-elect Clinton suggested that not much would change. In a major interview Clinton appeared to be suggesting that the Bush approach to Iraq would be maintained:

Q: Would you be willing to enter into a shooting war?
A: I have to say I wouldn't rule anything in or out.
Q: Could you imagine ever having normalised relations with Iraq as long as Saddam is in power?
A: I can't imagine having normalised relations with Iraq with the sort of behaviour that characterises what they did.[181]

While US aircraft continued to range over substantial tracts of Iraq in the run-up to the Clinton inauguration, the president-elect resolved not to waver on the question on Saddam. On 18 January Baghdad reported twenty-one further Iraqi deaths caused by US bombing, while Clinton declared: 'The policy of this country will remain American policy after 20 January.'[182]

Baghdad greeted the inauguration of President Bill Clinton with the hope that it would open a new chapter of relations between Iraq and the

United States (while the Iraqi journal *Al-Jumhouriyah* suggested that for George Bush 'suicide is the best remedy'). The Iraqi information minister, Hamed Hammadi, declared: 'We hope that President Clinton will seek to establish a relationship of equality that ensures the legitimate interests between Iraq and the Arabs on the one hand, and the US on the other.' However, the first day of the Clinton administration was marked by further air strikes against Iraq, though suggestions were made that Clinton had not been consulted.[183] Iraq was now insisting that it was keeping out of the (illegal) no-fly zones, as a gesture of goodwill to the new US president, and Washington found itself in the uncomfortable position of having to admit that some of the recent bombing strikes had been carried out in error.[184]

In mid-February 1993, President Saddam Hussein – in a peace gesture that President Clinton could probably have done without – praised Clinton's opposition to the Vietnam war and urged him to display similar wisdom in dealing with Iraq. At the same time Hikmet Cetin, Turkey's foreign minister, declared that Iraq had pulled all its missiles out of the southern and northern no-fly zones, withdrawn troops from the north and closed all radars (Cetin: 'By this attitude, Iraq wants to give a message to the new Clinton government'). There were no signs that such peace moves – if such they were – stimulated any constructive response from President Bill Clinton.

On 29 March the White House press secretary, Dee Dee Myers, declared that it was 'inconceivable that Saddam Hussein could remain in power if he complied with all UN resolutions'. The aim of using sanctions to force Saddam's overthrow remained US policy.[185] One point, rarely discussed, was that to allow Iraq to trade its oil would 'inevitably depress' world prices as the extra volumes were made available.[186]

Sporadic military attacks against Iraq were maintained. On 9 April American fighters dropped cluster bombs on sites in northern Iraq, after US claims that their aircraft had encountered Iraqi ground fire.[187] An Iraqi foreign ministry spokesman denied the American accusations, declaring that if Iraq had wanted to change its ceasefire policy, 'it would have announced it at the highest level'. Little publicity was given in the West to the fate of an eight-year-old Iraqi boy killed by a US cluster bomb.[188]

In May 1993 there were reports of Iraqi plans to assassinate George Bush on his visit to Kuwait the previous month.[189] It was also reported that the Pentagon had discounted Iraqi involvement and that US Defense Department officials cited by NBC television news had said 'evidence for the plot was questionable and that heavy-handed Kuwaiti interrogation tactics [a euphemism for torture] made testimony by the prisoners useless'.[190] All the suspects had been tortured, defence lawyers had no access to their clients until the day of the trial, and a US State Department source admitted that the confessions were useless in view of the Kuwaiti methods used to obtain them.[191] Amnesty International expressed concern that the suspects would be executed following unfair trials that denied basic human rights.

The Iraqi information minister Hamed Youssef al-Hummadi dismissed the charges: 'The sheikhs of Kuwait, in co-ordination with American intelligence, are plotting another deception to fool American public opinion in order to justify a new aggression on Iraq and tighten the economic siege imposed on it.' No-one familiar with US disinformation campaigns (see, for example, Woodward, *Veil*, 1987) can doubt that the Iraqi statement was possibly true.

On 27 June, in the middle of the night, twenty-three US cruise missiles were launched on Baghdad in retaliation for the alleged plot three months earlier. Few independent observers believed that the declared target, the Iraqi intelligence headquarters, had been seriously damaged. It was agreed that some of the missiles had hit residential areas and that there were civilian fatalities, including children and Leila al-Attar, an Iraqi painter revered throughout the Arab world.

The evidence for the plot submitted by Madeleine Albright at the United Nations – including photographs of an 'Iraqi' device with markings in English! – was widely recognised to be inconclusive. Even *The New York Times* commented that to swallow the US case 'as it stands requires a leap of faith and a complete suspension of political cynicism'.[192] President Bill Clinton, despite the totally specious citing of Article 51 of the UN Charter, had committed a gross violation of international law, killed more innocent civilians, dismayed his erstwhile Arab allies, ensured that the tortured suspects in Kuwait stood no chance of a fair trial, further undermined the authority of the United Nations, and given a significant boost to Saddam Hussein.

On 1 July 1993 it was reported that the United States, Britain and France were finalising new plans, without UN authorisation, for a fresh 'full-blown air attack' on Iraq.[193] Such plans, coupled with – in the words of a UN report – *'politically motivated sanctions . . . imposed to create hardship'* in a manner that could not spare *'the vulnerable'*[194] (my italics) left no doubt what the Iraqi people were expected to endure under the US-defined New World Order.

Part II

The History of Iraq

2 The Ancient Crucible

The region of the world that the ancient Greeks called Mesopotamia (land 'between the rivers') and that we know today as Iraq was a fount of civilisation – a veritable crucible, cockpit, cradle, womb of cultural progress (the metaphors run through the books). Here it was that restless tribes and peoples jostled for land and power, contending with their neighbours, being shaped by defeats, successful conquests, and the collisions of different cultures. Here it was that the first cities were born, writing began, and the first codified legal systems were established. Here it was – through such ancient lands as Sumer, Akkad, Babylonia and Assyria – that the vital cultural brew was stirred, the quite remarkable concoction from which Western civilisation would emerge. We often tend to begin the chronicle of Western culture with the achievements of the classical world but it is worth remembering that the Greco-Roman states owe much to the ancient worlds of Egypt and Mesopotamia, as far removed in time from them as Greece and Rome are from the nation states of the modern era. We may reflect also that a modern Iraqi is entitled to contemplate with awe and pride the fructifying richness of the cultures that first emerged in his land more than five thousand years ago.

BEGINNINGS

The first settled communities of the Near and Middle East were established during the 8th and 7th millennia BC. They typically relied upon cereal cultivation and the range of developing technologies that went with it. Mudbrick villages were built and rebuilt on geographically favoured sites, producing prominent mounds that were well signalled in many regional languages and dialects (for example, by *tell* in Arabic). The earliest settled sites were not far from the original mountain homes of the wild ancestors of wheat and barley, where rainfall was adequate or where floodplain irrigation could be developed. The two most famous sites of this type were Tell es-Sultan (Jericho) in the Jordan valley and Catal Huyuk in the central plain of Turkey. Such sites, embryonic towns, were characteristically defended by walls enclosing agglomerations of houses so tightly packed that some could be entered only by the roof. Trade developed between such settled communities, including those on the Mesopotamian

plains, and the way was prepared for the development of literate, technological and stable cultures.

The geography of the great Tigris–Euphrates Valley, the land of the so-
called 'Twin Rivers' at the heart of Mesopotamia, manifestly favoured the
emergence of civilised communities – as did, for similar environmental
reasons – the Nile Valley and the Indus Valley. The great river system of
the Tigris, the Euphrates and their tributaries made cultivation possible and
facilitated trade – and the associated cultural infusions – with all the most
important regions of the ancient world: Persia, India, Anatolia, the Levant
and, via the Mediterranean, Egypt and all the states of southern Europe.
As the settled communities became largely self-sufficient, through agriculture and the raising of livestock, their populations increased and there was
a pressing need to expand into new lands. One region for fresh settlement
was the upper valley of the Tigris and Euphrates, an area where the rainfall
was adequate for cultivation. In the 6th millennium BC there were many
thriving settlements in this area, though much of the lower valley was still
sparsely populated, the home of scattered nomads and marsh dwellers.
Much of the Mesopotamian plain was too dry for successful cultivation
without irrigation, and by about 5000 BC farmers were building primitive
dykes and canals, just as elsewhere efforts were being made to drain the
wetlands.

Many of the early prehistoric settlements quickly disappeared, buried
below alluvial silt or submerged by fresh villages erected on their ruins.
The common need to maintain an effective irrigation system would have
led to a degree of social organisation and developing technology, features
that would have been stimulated by the ever increasing populations. The
most successful settlements grew into royal or sacred cities – such as Eridu,
Ur, Uruk, Nippur and Girsu on the central Mesopotamian plain. It is Eridu
that is often cited as providing the best evidence of cultural continuity from
the first peopling of the region through to later historic times. The inhabitants of Eridu knew that Enki, god of wisdom and sweet waters, had taught
human beings the arts of writing and geometry. A succession of temples
was built, each raised above its predecessor and enshrining the new principles of a developing architecture. One of the later temples was about
eighty feet long, with its mudbrick walls strengthened by buttresses, the
whole structure set upon a substantial platform, the first stage of the mighty
ziggurat. By about 4000 BC religious commitment was stimulating innovations in architecture, imaginative mythology and social organisation.

The Sumerians, responsible for one of the first great explosions of
culture on the Mesopotamian plain, were wandering shepherds who came
to the region about 3500 BC. They came to dominate the whole of the

lower valley, though rarely venturing further north. Their language was without known relatives, and their sculpture is too stylised to provide many clues about their origins. Once they had invented writing they described themselves as the 'black-headed people'. They shared the plain with settlers from many different regions, resulting in tensions and conflicts as populations grew and technology advanced. The early village settlements had developed into substantial towns and cities, laying the foundation for the city states that would later emerge. The way was prepared for the organisation of armies, equipped by technology and sanctified by religion. The military clash of cultures was to become one of the principal features of early Mesopotamian life, a further incentive for material invention and religious devotion.

SUMER

The descendants of the early Stone Age farmers struggling to subsist on the edges of the marshes became known as the Sumerians, the inhabitants of Sumer. At that time most of the world's population were nomads, moving from one area to another in search of the necessary resources. They followed the wild herds through the seasonal migrations, clothing themselves in animal skins and seeking shelter in caves and crude lean-to structures. The settled communities were at first rare and insecure, though some evolved into larger stable communities. Some relied on a single prized commodity, such as salt (at Tell es-Sultan) and obsidian (at Catal Huyuk), used in the manufacture of mirrors, jewellery and knives. If communities were to be more durable they needed to develop more flexible economies; they needed to become more self-reliant. In fact the people of the Middle East were among the first to domesticate sheep and goats and to cultivate crops of wheat and barley. No longer were such people threatened by the whims of passing traders or the exhaustion of a local commodity.

The Sumerians, building on the achievements of their ancestors, worked to irrigate a difficult terrain and so to bring vast areas of alluvial desert into cultivation. The resulting surplus of grain gave the Sumerians time and resources for ambitions beyond mere subsistence. They became traders and merchants, artisans and engineers, and in due course scribes, the complex order of social classes sustained by the many developments in farming production. Sumerian scribes became the first people known to have written down epic poems, a type of recorded history, and to have speculated on the meaning of life.

The farmers began by simply carrying water to where it was needed, a laborious task that necessarily limited the area that could be irrigated. Next they diverted water from the rivers by means of small mud dams that directed the flow into well-placed ditches. From here the *shaduf* (a counter-weighted bailing bucket) was employed to convey the water into irrigation channels. The Sumerians also invented the plough, at first nothing more than a tree branch pulled by one person and pushed by another, but later, during the 4th millennium BC, they invented a cópper plough that could be pulled by oxen. By 3000 BC ploughs made of bronze, an alloy of copper and tin, helped the Sumerian farmers to work large plots of land. And the successes in agriculture yielded many further developments. Planners and engineers were needed to lay out the patterns of dams and dykes, just as mathematicians were required to calculate rates of water flow, distances and the angles of slopes. Instruments were developed to aid such computations, which in turn led to observations of the sun and moon to develop a reliable calendar, whereupon farmers could be advised when to plant and harvest their crops.

The invention of the wheel is often attributed to the Sumerians, its first form probably being used in pottery making. Then they thought of throwing the potter's wheel on its side and using it for locomotion. This again extended the scope of Sumerian agriculture by enabling farmers to work land far from their villages: an ox or donkey hitched to a wheeled cart could move a much heavier load than could be carried on its back or dragged on a sledge. The invention of the wheel, we may surmise, also assisted in the construction of the stepped ziggurats, the ever larger temples built on the Sumerian plain. The interiors of the ziggurats were adorned by frescos and sculptures, a further indication of the importance of the temples in Sumerian culture. A priestly class farmed extensive tracts of land connected to the ziggurats and used the produce to support themselves and other citizens deemed to be in special need. The temple staffs expanded over the years and the ziggurats themselves came to function as centres of urban life. Administrators, accountants and priests all came to enjoy a well-rewarded existence and there were, in addition, a vast army of singers, musicians, cooks, weavers, cleaners and others, all drafted to serve the expanding religious culture. Agricultural activity was increasingly consigned to slaves, who toiled with evident success. It is recorded that soon after 3000 BC the temple in the city of Lagash was producing a daily bread and beer ration for around 1200 people, a significant achievement for the times.

The successes of the Sumerian economies gave a great stimulus to the greatest innovation of all, the invention of writing. To keep track of the expanding flow of products it was necessary to develop some means of keeping a permanent record. Thus the earliest written works were no more than inventory lists, charting the fluctuating contents of storehouses, but once a flexible system of writing had been invented it went far beyond the needs of straightforward economic administration: for the first time it was possible to use a symbolic system to record legends, poetry and historical detail. The earliest scripts were pictographic symbols used for individual words and concepts but such cumbersome systems eventually gave way to systems of symbols used for sounds. The Sumerians evolved one of the most successful systems, where clay tablets carried wedge-shaped impressions made by a stylus. This 'cuneiform' system (Latin *cuneus* = wedge) was later adopted by the Akkadians, the Babylonians, the Assyrians, the early Canaanites, the Hittites and the Hurrians; and so served Semitic, non-Semitic and Indo-European languages.

It has been suggested that the evolution of Sumerian writing was shaped in part by the limitations of the recording medium. Thus when the Sumerian scribes were required to speed up the recording process they would attempt to 'scrawl' hurriedly, when taking dictation or wishing to complete an onerous writing task in a short time. Since, however, the pen or stylus was a rigid, wedge-ended tool it would not easily make curves in soft clay as the substance would easily 'pile up' and so convey an unclear impression. The solution to this problem of 'speed writing' was to develop stylised versions of the original pictographs, the particular forms being determined by the shape of the stylus.[1] It is interesting that the Sumerian language survived in the later Babylonia as the language of religion, law and international diplomacy, much in the way that Latin had a residual function in medieval Europe. Since Sumerian is not a Semitic language the later Babylonians and Assyrians who, with the Jews and the Arabs, have Semitic languages, had problems when they tried to record their own speech in Sumerian script, a difficulty that can be appreciated if we think of trying to write English in Chinese ideographs.[2] It is of course likely that Sumerian pictographs evolved from much earlier systems of representation. As early as 8000 BC farmers in the region were using small clay tokens of different sizes and shapes to keep a record of their commodities, and much later it was the custom for tokens to serve as a virtual bill of lading to accompany goods being traded. With the more convenient clay tablets the Sumerian merchant could make a numerical sign to indicate the items bought or sold, a simple pictograph being added to represent the token. And further refinements in format and style made for greater convenience. The first pictographic tablets carried vertical columns starting at the right, but to prevent the scribe's hand from smudging previously incised signs the format was changed

to writing in horizontal rows from left to right. The original stylus was a
simple point, apt to raise bumps and ridges, but by 2500 BC it had assumed
its wedge-shaped (cuneiform) character.

Sumerian writing was used for centuries as a tool of commerce, a means
of defining contracts and bills, of recording shipments and receipts. Later it
became an instrument of religion, a way of recording magic formulas,
ceremonial procedures, sacred legends, prayers and hymns. By 2700 BC
there were great libraries in various Sumerian towns; at Tello, for example,
archaeologists discovered 30,000 inscribed tablets set one upon the other
in neat and logical arrays. And by 2000 BC the Sumerians were attempting
to record their history and details of the present for the instruction of
future generations. As happens in all ancient traditions some of the works
disappear beyond recall but are quoted in later accounts surviving in fresh
cultures. Thus in some Babylonian chronicles there are useful extracts from
Sumerian works that long since ceased to exist. An original tablet found at
Nippur carries the Sumerian prototype of the famous *Epic of Gilgamesh*
which was recast in later years for a Babylonian audience. Some of the
original fragments contain dirges that embody the rhetorical trick of chanting repetition with slight variations from one group of lines to the next.
Such creations were prayerful invocations, the heartfelt words of pious
supplicants.

Gilgamesh and other Sumerian works prefigure biblical tales and the
chronicles of classical Greece. We learn from the 3500-line poem that King
Gilgamesh of Uruk wandered the earth, like Homer's Odysseus; and another Sumerian character, like the Old Testament Noah, survived a great
flood. Other texts offer practical advice – to farmers and other practical
people struggling to succeed in a difficult world. Thus one text comprises
more than one hundred lines telling the reader how to do well in agriculture.
He should, for example, protect his young seedlings by uttering the appropriate prayer to Ninkilim, the goddess of field mice and other vermin; and
he is advised to harvest the barley 'in the day of its strength', before it
begins to bend under its own weight. Many farmers, not having attended
the Sumerian *edubba*, the world's first formal school, would not be able
to read or write the cuneiform script. The students had to pay for their
instruction, and so tended to come from the wealthy and high-ranking
families. Only males could expect an education and they were subject to
a harsh discipline: one *edubba* student recorded that he was beaten four
times in one day.

Many of the tablets were destroyed by the conquerors of the great
Sumerian cities, or the chronicles were carried off if they were reckoned

to be of value. One such conquest is recorded in the Sumerian *Lamentation over the Destruction of Ur*, which includes the words:

How, O Sumer, are thy mighty fallen!
The holy king is banished from his temple.
The temple itself is destroyed, the city demolished.
The leaders of the nation have been carried off into captivity.
A whole empire has been overthrown by the will of the gods.

The 'holy king' is Ibi-Sin, the deified monarch of Ur who ruled from 2029 to 2006 BC. The Elamite invaders from the east overran Sumer, sacked the temple of Ishtar, and carried off the idol of the goddess. However, the cult of Ishtar, the Sumerian Aphrodite, survived into Christian times.

The tablets have also helped researchers to define the sequence of dynasties in ancient Sumeria. The royal inscriptions, treaties, administrative accounts and word lists have aided scholars in their efforts to comprehend the Sumerian *King List* that was compiled in the 2nd millennium. (The Early Dynastic period is reckoned to run from around 3000 BC to the accession of Sargon of Akkad in 2340 BC.) The celebrated *List* provides the names of the early Sumerian kings, details of the length of their reigns, and occasional notes on their most significant achievements. The *List* is deemed 'quite useless' for chronological purposes because the early reigns, like some biblical lives, are absurdly long and some contemporary reigns are given as succeeding one another.[3] Here, like many later dynasties outside Sumeria, there is assumed to be a divine right of kings; and, like the Old Testament deluge, there is mention of a great Flood that 'swept over the land'. Silt deposits have been found at the sites of Ur and other Sumerian cities but there is no evidence of a single massive deluge that affected all the land.

Sumerian culture was focused on the great cities, such as Eridu (in modern times, Abu Shahrein), Ur (Makayyar), Uruk (Warka, the biblical Erech), Larsa (Senkereh, the biblical Ellasar), Lagash (Shippurla), Nippur (Niffer) and Nisin. The ancient cities are buried beneath the sand and under the later urban developments that in modern times were given new names. Ur, perhaps the most famous of the cities, came to be called by the Arabs after the mighty ziggurat hill, *Tell al Muqayyar*, the Mound of Pitch. This great urban site ('of the Chaldees') was supposedly the home of Abraham, and so it has significance for both Semitic and non-Semitic religions.[4] The mighty Ur of the 3rd millennium BC was built around the mudbrick ziggurat dedicated to the moon-god Nanna and his wife Ningal.

The famous mound rose to some twenty-five metres in stepped terraces, and the structure was surrounded by a dense crush of houses, shops and bazaars – a town of more than 30,000 people.

Ur, like Tell es-Sultan and Catal Huyuk, was a walled city with apertures in the perimeter for road and water-borne traffic. Two great canals ran outside the walls, connecting Ur with the Euphrates and thence the Persian Gulf. A third waterway ran from one of the canals to a placid harbour well within the city walls, allowing Ur's artisans and farmers to trade effectively with the outside world. Beyond the walls lay the vast system of irrigation ditches, the ambitious agricultural development that sustained the wealth of Ur and the other Sumerian cities. However, other tribes too were to be impressed by such progress.

AKKAD

Great tribes, sometimes as federated unions comprising entire nations, moved with restless energy through the ancient Middle East. Expelled from their homes by invaders or seeking expansionist conquests of their own, they inevitably came into collision with the settled urban communities, of which the Sumerian developments were the most successful examples. They had created a rich agricultural economy and an unprecedented urban civilisation: suddenly they were to encounter the onrush of warlike hordes hunting for loot and land. It was one such confrontation around 2500 BC that came to threaten the existence of the Sumerian urban system. The Sumerians called the invaders the Amurru, who were probably the same Semitic tribes that the Hebrews referred to as the Amorites or Canaanites.[5] In any event, they swarmed across the open Mesopotamian plains, capturing the ancient cities, killing the local kings, and then settling down to enjoy the fruits of their conquest. It was the collision of the Sumerian civilisation with the culture of the conquering tribes that was to generate the civilisation of Babylonia.

The leader of the warlike tribes was Sargon (dubbed I, to distinguish him from the later Assyrian leader, Sargon II, who ruled from 721 to 705 BC). He has been depicted as the child of nomadic pastoralists who moved across the plains, and as a man who became cup-bearer to a king of Kish. Thereafter he rose from courtier to king, of Kish itself and of Akkad (the Sumerian Agade) which he founded. Sargon I reigned for fifty-five years (2302 to 2247 BC), fought thirty-four successful wars (mostly against Sumer), and ultimately succeeded in uniting the great regions of Mesopotamia into one vast kingdom, the later Babylonia that would comprise the southern Sumer and the northern Akkad.

The Sargon dynasty lasted until 2108 BC. The rulers and the key administrators, like the language, were Semitic; but the arts, sciences and religion were Sumerian, adopted *in toto* by the conquerors. The Akkadian military vigour and the sophisticated Sumerian civilisation provided a unique mix of talents well equipped to expand an empire towards Egypt in the west and India in the east. Sargon had conquered Sumer at some cost. It had taken three massive campaigns involving many battles to overthrow one of the Sumerian kings. Thus a Sumerian inscription notes: '. . . he conquered Uruk and broke down its walls . . . Lugalzagesi, King of Uruk, he took prisoner in battle and brought him in fetters to the gates of Enlil' (to Ekur, the national shrine at Nippur). After this victory Sargon launched further campaigns – as far as the Cedar Forest of Lebanon, into the region of the Mediterranean, along the Persian Gulf, perhaps as far as Oman and Bahrain.[6]

The empire was inherited by Sargon's two sons, Rimush and Manishtusu, who were forced to fight continuous campaigns – against desert nomads, against Elam, and against the discontented Sumerians – to maintain control over Sargon's conquered lands. During a spate of tribal warfare Rimush was killed, to be later avenged by Manishtusu who managed to defeat most of the national enemies (and who in consequence became known throughout the empire as 'great king'). Sargon's grandson Naram-Sin came to the throne in 2260 BC, ruled for thirty-seven years, and called himself 'king of the four quarters of the world' and master of 'lands that no king before had ever conquered'. Following his father Rimush, Naram-Sin built temples in Nineveh, suggesting that the Akkadians had conquered much of Assyria. As in early Sumeria, religion served to consolidate and unify the political state; and as a further 'social cement' Akkadian, the language of the conquerors, became the official tongue of the empire. Shar-kali-sharri, Naram-Sin's son, faced a host of military problems in his efforts to maintain the empire.

BABYLONIA

Babylonia emerged historically and ethnically from the union of the Sumerians and the Akkadians, a merging in which the Semitic Akkadian strain proved dominant. The military success of the Akkadians against the Sumerians led to the establishment of Babylon as the capital of lower

Mesopotamia. Babylon was to flourish for almost two thousand years from about 2225 BC to its conquest by Alexander the Great in 331 BC. The biblical scribes of the Old Testament reckoned that the Euphrates, on which Babylon was sited, ran through the Garden of Eden.[7] The Greeks declared that Babylon contained two of the Seven Wonders of the World, and the Romans saw it as 'the greatest city the sun ever beheld'. The outer defences of the city were ten miles in circumference, fifty feet high, and fifty-five feet deep – and by the first century BC the walls were all that survived.[8] According to the Greek historian Herodotus, born around 490 BC at the town of Halicarnassus on the south-west coast of Asia Minor, the vast city of Babylon lies in the form of a square 'with sides nearly fourteen miles long and a circumference of some fifty-six miles, and in addition to its enormous size it surpasses in splendour any city of the known world'.[9] A broad moat surrounded the city: as the moat was dug the removed earth was formed into bricks, and then 'using hot bitumen for mortar the workmen began by building parapets along each side of the moat, and then went on to erect the actual wall'. Four-horse chariots could turn on the tops of the walls, which carried a hundred bronze gates in the full circumference.

At the start of the history of Babylon stands the great figure of Hammurabi (2123–2081 BC), a conqueror and law-giver through a reign of some forty-three years. He was depicted on seals and inscriptions as a youth full of fire and skill, a great warrior who crushes all his enemies, who marches over mountains and never loses a battle. Under Hammurabi the tumultuous states of the lower valley were forced into unity and disciplined by the famous Code. The diorite cylinder carrying the engraved Code of Hammurabi, conveyed from Babylon to Elam around 1100 BC, was unearthed at Susa in 1902 (it is now in the Louvre).

There is full acknowledgement of the role of the gods but the Code is essentially a body of secular legislation. Enlightened laws accompany barbarous punishments, and the primitive *lex talionis* and trial by ordeal are set against complex judicial procedures that have a modern ring. In all there are 285 laws arrayed systematically under the headings of Personal Property, Real Estate, Trade and Business, the Family, Injuries, and Labour. The Code, from which the Mosaic Code borrows or with which it shares a common source, is more enlightened than many judicial systems that were to follow in the centuries ahead.

Hammurabi retained the principle of the *lex talionis* ('an eye for an eye') but he sought to reduce its impact. Misdemeanours that formerly attracted mutilation or even death were now punished by fines, an advance that has been interpreted as a great civilising influence. The Sumerians long before had discovered the advantages of paying a wronged person compensation instead of waiting for the aggrieved party to exact revenge, and Hammurabi developed this idea into a penal sanction. It has been suggested that this development encouraged the emergence of the entire fabric of law, with all the associated apparatus of lawyers, solicitors, juries and the complex fabric of jurisprudence in civilised societies.[10]

The idea that justice should be tempered with mercy was a Babylonian innovation, a vital contribution to the morality of law. But the idea was expected to apply only in domestic situations: there was no thought that one's enemies should be treated with compassion. This attitude accords well with how Middle Eastern rulers were in general expected to slaughter their opponents, even innocent non-combatants. Thus the Old Testament Lord of Hosts urges his followers to 'go and smite Amalek, and utterly destroy all that they have, and spare them not; but slay both man and woman, infant and suckling, ox and sheep, camel and ass'.[11] However, in urging a just approach to family morality Hammurabi laid the basis for a moral general social compassion, a position that is well represented (though often impotent) in the modern world. Here Hammurabi followed a much earlier Sumerian code, the earliest known legal canon, that attributed to Ur-Nammu who founded the Third Dynasty of Ur (2113–2096 BC), and who included the stipulation that 'the orphan is not to be given over to the rich, nor the widow to the powerful, nor the man of one shekel over to him of one mina'. It is clear that there were compassionate law-givers long before Hammurabi.

The Code bears importantly on aspects of marriage and women's rights (innovations here are sometimes contrasted with much repressive legislation in later Christendom). The 136th clause, for example, declares that if a man abandons his wife, leaving her without proper support, she is then free to remarry without being involved in the complexities of the courts. In the same spirit the 124th clause of the Code states: 'if a woman hates her husband and refuses him his conjugal rights, her case shall be examined in the district court. If she can prove she has kept herself chaste and has no fault while her husband has been unfaithful and so has demeaned her, she shall not be punished but may take her dowry and return to her father's house.' (Though this still smacks of sexism it should be set against a grossly anti-feminist Christianity happy for almost two millennia to tolerate marital rape.)

Hammurabi concludes his Code with the words:

> In my bosom I carried the people of the land of Sumer and Akkad . . . in my wisdom I restrained them, that the strong might not oppress

the weak, and that they should give justice to the orphan and the widow . . . Let any oppressed man, who has a cause, come before my image as king of righteousness! . . . In the days that are yet to come, for all future time, may the king who is in the land observe the words of righteousness which I have written upon my monument!

Today there is a sad irony behind such words, despite their noble ring. Babylon did not endure 'for all future time': it was destroyed first by the Assyrian king Sennacherib in 689 BC, rebuilt under the rule of Nebuchadnezzar II, was conquered by the Persians under Cyrus the Great in 538 BC, and was again subdued by Alexander in 331 BC. In the 3rd century BC Babylon was largely overtaken by Seleucia as the commercial centre of the region. The classical author Zosimus, alive during the reign of Julian the Apostate, wrote that in AD 363 the remnants of Babylon had been made into a royal game reserve for the Persian king Shapur I. The grandest city of the ancient world had been allowed to decay.

Hammurabi had aimed to lay the basis of a state that would endure 'for all future time', but the glory of the empire scarcely survived his death. His son, Samsu-iluna (1749–1712 BC), faced fresh revolts in southern Macedonia and new invasions from the north. The state of Babylonia survived until 1595 BC when the capital was sacked by the Hittites, a nomadic horse-breeding tribe of Indo-Europeans. Their warrior-chieftains ('kings') thought in basic military terms wherever the tribe settled: they were quick to organise massive fortifications linked by subterranean tunnels. It was inevitable also that they would absorb much of the culture of the Babylonians, adopting, for example, their systems of writing and the fabric of their law. When King Mursilis I led his Hittite warriors to end the Hammurabi dynasty it may have been expected that a new line of rulers would be established. However, Mursilis was forced to withdraw his army, and soon afterwards he was assassinated. Other tribes rushed to fill the Mesopotamian vacuum, among them the Hurrians and the Kassites.

These tribes swarmed down from the eastern heights, skilled charioteers eager to exploit a Babylonia mortally wounded by the brief Hittite conquest. For four centuries after the collapse of Babylon the region was ruled by a Kassite dynasty. The new conquerors adopted the Akkadian language, with the use of Sumerian reserved for religion, law and learning. The temples and palaces built by the Kassites at the new capital of Dur-Kurizalgu were designed and constructed in traditional Babylonian style. Little is known about the history of this period though the names of some of the self-styled kings have survived: Nazi-nugash (1350–1345 BC), Nazi-marrutash (1323–

1298 BC) and Kashtiliash IV (1242–1235 BC). The Kassites ruled inconclusively for about six hundred years, and some centuries of confusion followed their demise.

ASSYRIA

The Assyrians ('children of Ashur') were a Semitic race, at first colonists from Babylonia and its subjects. Later, around 1300 BC, they rose up and conquered Babylon. The state of Assyria grew around four cities watered by the Tigris and its tributaries: Ashur (later Kala'at-Sherghat), Arbela (Arbil), Kalakh (Nimrud), and Nineveh (Kuyunjik, near to Mosul). Archaeologists have found obsidian knives at Ashur, along with black pottery with geometric patterns that suggest links to central Asia. A town has been unearthed at Tepe Gawra, near the ancient site of Nineveh, for a long time the capital of the Assyrian empire. The town – with its many temples and tombs, its combs and jewellery, and the oldest dice known to history[12] – dates to around 3700 BC. The Assyrian kings were first based in Ashur, but then built Nineveh (named after the god Nina, the equivalent of the Babylonia Ishtar), as a more secure retreat from the invading Babylonians. Here at the height of Ashurbanipal's power 300,000 people lived and Assyria's 'Universal King' was recognised by all the western Orient.

At the time of the Kassite conquest of Babylonia Shalmaneser I united the northern city states and made Kalakh his capital; his successor, Shalmaneser II (860–825 BC), fought successfully against Babylonia and also forced King Jehu of Israel to pay him tribute.[13] The reign of the Assyrian king Tiglath-Pileser I is thought to have been particularly grand. One of his inscriptions, doubtless penned by a loyal scribe, declares: 'In my fierce valour I marched against the people of Qummuh, conquered their cities, carried off their booty, their goods and their property without reckoning, and burned their cities with fire – destroyed and devastated them . . . The people of Adansh left their mountains and embraced my feet. I imposed taxes upon them.' Such accomplishments were commonplace for a man said to have slain 120 lions on foot, and eight hundred from his chariot. He is said to have conquered more than forty nations, including the Hittites and the Armenians, to have intimidated Egypt into sending him placatory gifts (including a live crocodile), and to have captured Babylon. Some of his victories were short-lived: Babylon rose up, defeated his armies and pillaged his temples – only to be conquered yet again, with the swing of the pendulum, by later Assyrian kings. For a while Sammuramat ruled as queen mother, providing a frail basis for the Greek myth of Semiramis, so attractively depicted by Diodorus. Then a new king, Tiglath-Pileser III, organised fresh armies to subdue Syria and Babylonia, after which he died peacefully in bed. His successor, Sargon II (721–705 BC), took power via a palace *coup d'état* and then set about consolidating the conquest of Babylonia.

The son of Sargon, Sennacherib (705–681 BC), put down the usual revolts throughout the empire, but inconclusively attacked Jerusalem and Egypt (the Egyptians attributed their success to field-mice who obligingly devoured the quivers, bow-strings and shield-straps of the Assyrians at Pelusium). Sennacherib is said to have sacked some eighty-nine cities and and 820 villages, captured 7200 horses, 11,000 asses, 80,000 oxen, 800,000 sheep, and 208,000 prisoners. His conquests induced Byron to write:

> The Assyrian came down like a wolf on the fold,
> And his cohorts were gleaming in purple and gold,
> And the sheen of their spears was like stars on the sea
> Where the blue wave rolls nightly on deep Galilee. . . .

Yet again Babylon was singled out for special attention. Sensing Babylon's restlessness under Assyrian control Sennacherib sacked the city, slaughtering all the inhabitants until mountains of corpses were piled high in the streets. The palaces and temples were pillaged, the treasures looted and the supposedly omnipotent gods destroyed or carried in triumph to Nineveh: the great god Marduk became a menial servant to Ashur. Sennacherib then set about rebuilding and expanding Nineveh, using the spoils of his conquests to fund ambitious civic schemes. He diverted rivers to protect the city, reclaimed desert land, and was assassinated by his ambitious sons in 681 BC. Son Esarhaddon (681–669 BC) seized the throne and soon began the task of rebuilding Babylon, so wantonly devastated by his father. Then he annexed Egypt, rendering Assyria the undisputed master of a vast empire; restored the captive gods to Babylon; and, in a remarkable gesture for a semi-barbarous world, offered food and other resources to the famine-stricken people of Elam. He perished on his way to suppress an Egyptian revolt, and the control of Egypt was to last in all a mere fifteen years.

Ashurbanipal (669–626 BC), son of Esarhaddon, was the last of the great Assyrian kings. In 648 BC he crushed a fresh rebellion in Babylon and managed to retain control of the Elamites. But Ashurbanipal (the Sardanapalus of the Greeks) had lost Egypt and there were signs that the empire was beginning to fall apart. Despite this, it was inevitable that an

Assyrian king would glory in the triumphs that had been accomplished. A scribe recorded Ashurbanipal's destruction of Elam where the royal leaders were forced to drag Ashurbanipal's chariot through the streets of Nineveh. Then the head of the Elamite king was struck off and later brought to Ashurbanipal as he banqueted with his queen in the palace gardens, whereupon the head was raised on a pole in front of the guests, later to be fixed over the gate of Nineveh to rot away. Dananu, the famous Elamite general, was flayed alive and then bled like a lamb; his brother, perhaps more fortunate, had his throat cut before his body was chopped into pieces for distribution as souvenirs throughout the land. In the glow of such a triumph the Assyrian empire had never seemed more secure, but it was starting to disintegrate.

Ashurbanipal had performed as befitted an Assyrian king. He has functioned as brave conqueror and wise statesman, and was proud of his knowledge of books and academic accomplishment:

I, Ashurbanipal, understood the wisdom of Nabu the god of wisdom, I acquired an understanding of all the arts of tablet-writing . . . Marduk, the wise one of the gods, presented me with information and understanding as a gift . . . I understood the craft of the wise Adapa, the hidden secrets of all the scribal art; in heavenly and earthly buildings I read and pondered; in the meetings of clerks I was present; I watched the omens, I explained the heavens with the learned priests, recited the complicated multiplications and divisions . . . The beautiful writings in Sumerian that are obscure, in Akkadian that are difficult to bear in mind, it was my joy to repeat . . . I had the learning that all clerks of every kind possess when the time of their maturity comes . . .

Despite all this learning, real or imagined, Ashurbanipal was not able to lay the basis of a durable state. In his old age he laments: 'I cannot do away with the strife in my country and the dissensions in my family; disturbing scandals oppress me always. Illness of mind and flesh bow me down; with cries of woe I bring my days to an end. On the day of the city god, the day of the festival, I am wretched; death is seizing hold upon me, and bears me down . . .' This sad lament, contained on the last of Ashurbanipal's inscribed tablets, represents more than the dismal thoughts of a man forced to face his own mortality. There were broader issues at stake: Egypt had freed itself from Assyrian control, and Babylon was preparing for a further rebellion against the Assyrian dynasty, a revolt that would prove the most decisive of them all. Assyria had been weakened, at least in part, by its very successes. Countless destitute captives had been brought into the empire: with a vast dissolute population at its heart, the Assyrian state lost its national unity. The once impressive army was increasingly reliant on alien elements, and even the prodigious Assyrian resources were progressively dissipated in endless wars.

In 626 BC Ashurbanipal died, though it is not known how.[14] Fourteen years later the Babylonian king Nabopolassar (625–604 BC), in league with the Cyaxares-led Medean army and a force of Scythians from the Caucasus, launched an effective onslaught on the Assyrian cities of the north. Nineveh was subdued as ruthlessly and effectively as the Assyrian monarchs had once sacked Susa and Babylon. Nineveh was sacked in 612 BC, a comprehensive devastation recorded in the Old Testament Book of Nahum.[15] The city was completely destroyed, the people killed or enslaved, and the palace that Ashurbanipal had so recently built was pillaged and then totally demolished. When the archaeologists uncovered Kalakh, another of the main Assyrian cities, its main fort was six feet deep in the ashes of the final conflagration. Ivory inlays from the furniture stored there were found among the ashes, the gold leaf stripped from the ivories, a few strands around the nail heads signalling the violence of the city's last hours. In one great cataclysm Assyria had collapsed, destined to have no further part in history.

Nabopolassar ended the Assyrian control of Babylonia and created the Chaldaean empire. When he died he bequeathed the liberated empire to his son Nebuchadnezzar II, the villain of the Old Testament Book of Daniel. In his inaugural address to the god Marduk he praised the deity for his sublime appearance and then declared: 'At thy command, O merciful Marduk, may the house that I have built endure forever, may I be satiated with its splendour, attain old age therein, with abundant offspring, and receive therein tribute of the kings of all regions, from all mankind.' He did much to realise his great ambitions; as warrior, statesman and builder he has been rated among Babylonian kings as second only to Hammurabi. He crushed an Egyptian force that was conspiring with the Assyrians against him, and brought Palestine (after the siege of Jerusalem in 586 BC) and Syria under his control. Enjoying the protection of Nebuchadnezzar, Babylonian merchants were again in charge of all the trade in the region.

He took tribute and raised taxes to spend on civic projects, as Hammurabi had done. He built new temples and palaces, embellishing all new buildings with frescos and sculptures; like Hammurabi, he remembered to keep the priests well fed. Again Babylon had become the grandest metropolis in the ancient world. The building bricks often carried brilliantly coloured enamel tiles of blue, yellow or white, embellished with glazed relief shapes of animals and human beings. Most of the bricks recovered from the site of Babylon bear the words: 'I am Nebuchadnezzar, King of Babylon'.* In the centre of the city a lofty ziggurat was raised, to a height of 650 feet, and came to serve as the best candidate for the 'Tower of Babel' in Hebrew legend (*Babel* does not mean confusion or babble, as the myth claims, but the Gate of God). The great temple of Marduk was situated south of the ziggurat, and this and other temples were joined by a spacious 'sacred way' flanked by walls bearing brightly coloured lions to protect the sanctity of the site. At the end of the 'sacred way' was erected the resplendent Ishtar Gate, a double structure carrying tiles adorned with animals and flowers. Close by were the Hanging Gardens, built by Nebuchadnezzar for one of his wives, a Medean princess who pined for her native hills. Hydraulic engines were used to carry water to all the tiers of the gardens. Seventy-five feet above the ground, shaded by tall trees and surrounded by fragrant flowers, the women of the royal harem were allowed to walk unveiled, far from the common eye. But the glories of Nebuchadnezzar were not to last: even before he died there were signs of dissolution and decay, even the suggestion that he became insane.

Thus in the Book of Daniel, uncorroborated in this particular by any other sources, we read:

> . . . there fell a voice from heaven saying, O king Nebuchadnezzar, to thee it is spoken: Thy kingdom is departed from thee. And they shall drive thee from men, and thy dwelling shall be with the beasts of the field: they shall make thee eat grass as oxen . . . The same hour was the thing fulfilled upon Nebuchadnezzar: and he was driven from men, and did eat grass as oxen, and his body was wet with the dew of heaven, till his hair was grown like eagles' feathers, and his nails like birds' claws.[16]

We may speculate that Nebuchadnezzar was punished, forced to endure some sort of exile, but later in Daniel he seems to acknowledge that his mind had been disordered: '. . . my reasons returned to me . . . mine honour and brightness returned to me . . . and I was established in my kingdom'.[17] In any event Nebuchadnezzar's recovery, if such it was, did little to secure the empire.

Soon after the death of Nebuchadnezzar the Babylonian army was falling into disorder; the traders were interested only in profiteering; and the parasitical priestly class did no more than accumulate treasure, a beckoning

---

*Saddam Hussein, seeking a similar immortality, has followed Nebuchadnezzar's example and inscribed building blocks with his name.

finger to envious peoples beyond the gates. When Cyrus, at the head of a disciplined Persian army, stood outside Babylon in 538 BC, the gates were opened to him; and for two centuries Babylonia was ruled as part of the Persian empire. Then Alexander the Great came to Mesopotamia, conquered Babylon in 331 BC, and soon afterwards died following a banquet in the palace of Nebuchadnezzar – killed, some commentators have decided, by alcoholism. Babylon survived the death of Alexander, though it had sunk into a period of irreversible decline. In 50 BC the great Sicilian historian Diodorus commented of Babylon: 'only a small part of the city is now inhabited and most of the area within its walls is given over to agriculture'; and in the same vein St Jerome (AD 345–420) wrote: 'The whole area within the walls is a wilderness inhabited by all manner of wild animals.' Perhaps ancient Babylon ended its days as nothing more than an abandoned desolation.

THE JEWS

In about 1850 BC a man called Abram (later Abraham) left his home in Ur – at the imagined prompting of God – and travelled to the land of Canaan, today's Israel. He believed, as have many ambitious individuals throughout history, that God had promised the land to him and his descendants, a certain recipe for conflict in both the ancient and modern worlds. (The situation is further exacerbated by the fact that Christians and Moslems also see themselves as the children of Abraham.) The Israelites, tribal descendants of Abraham, subsequently moved to Egypt in about 1700 BC where they were forced to endure a deteriorating condition that by 1250 BC amounted to little more than slavery. In due course Moses, again seemingly aided by a powerful god, helped the Israelites to escape their bondage and to emerge as an independent people. For a while they lived as nomads on the Sinai peninsula but later decided to travel to what they dubbed the Promised Land, then occupied by the settled Canaanites. Moses died before reaching Canaan and it was Joshua who in about 1200 BC led the twelve tribes of Israel in a merciless war of conquest. When a city was conquered it was entirely demolished: men, women, children and animals were massacred and the city was reduced to rubble. It is enough to cite one of the many Old Testament accounts.[18]

Strife continued in the newly-won lands, partly because some of the Israelites were too easily seduced by the prevailing pagan cults. A measure of unity had been accomplished under David and Solomon but then the religious divisions in the Holy Land were paralleled by political strife.

The northern tribes broke away to form the Kingdom of Israel which was thereafter set against the smaller Kingdom of Judah in the south. This schism inevitably weakened the Israelites and in 722 BC the Kingdom of Israel was conquered by the Assyrian king Tiglath-Pileser III: the ten northern tribes of Israel were carried off, forced to assimilate into the Assyrian empire, and in consequence they disappeared from history. The surviving Kingdom of Judah was appalled at this tragedy and took what steps it could to avoid a similar fate.

For more than four hundred years Jerusalem had been the capital of the Judean nation: David had ruled there and the descendants of Aaron had served in its Temple. But in 589 BC the great king of Babylon, Nebuchadnezzar launched a savage attack against the city, in part to counter an alliance between certain Jewish elements and the Egyptians conspiring against his rule. Most of the inhabitants of Judah were deported to Babylonia, leaving behind only the sorry remnants of a once proud people: thus began the Babylonian captivity. Nebuchadnezzar was content not to annihilate the entire population of Judea. Realising that if he removed the princes and priests the rest of the people would incline to keep the peace, he left a proportion of the population undisturbed. He also appointed Gedaliah, a member of one of the few surviving prominent families, to rule Judea but this puppet leader was soon murdered by a patriotic descendant of the House of David. This forced the men surrounding Gedaliah, fearing Nebuchadnezzar's wrath, to flee to Egypt for sanctuary. Jeremiah accompanied them, continuing through his old age to urge his people to return to the worship of God and the observance of Mosaic traditions. The Jewish calendar still commemorates the anniversary of Gedaliah's murder, the day following Rosh ha-Shanah, the day that marked the final collapse of the first Hebrew Commonwealth. Thus the Jews themselves 'completed what the Babylonians had begun'.[19]

The Jews in Babylon were divided about their future. The Babylonians, true to their times, were merciless conquerors: typically, they slaughtered or thrust into slavery the bulk of the populations in the lands they subdued. But survivors brought to Babylonia were often permitted to build new lives in their exile. As conquered peoples they remained second-class citizens but they were sometimes assigned (heavily taxed) land or allowed to work as traders in the cities. Some of the Jews brought to the mighty land of Babylonia were seduced by the fresh opportunities that they found. It now seemed clear that though 'the Judeans as a group seemed to have no future at all'[20] many individual Judeans were able to adjust to their new conditions.

In 538 BC Cyrus the Great of Persia defeated the Babylonian armies. Babylon collapsed, Bel and Marduk were shown to be impotent, and the

Jewish exiles were free to return to their own land. However, not all the
Babylonian Jews were keen to return to Judea. Many now owned land or
were prosperous in trade, and what would they find when they returned? In
fact forty-two thousand Babylonian Jews decided to return, taking with
them all their possessions and funds donated by the Jews who decided not
to make the journey. After several months of arduous travel they rejoiced
when they reached the land of their fathers (the song in the Book of Psalms,
chapter 126, celebrates the return to Zion: 'Then was our mouth filled
with laughter, And our tongue with singing . . .'). But there were still many
problems to face: Judea, unsurprisingly enough, was now peopled by
other settlers, and the Babylonian Jews argued among themselves. Moreover, Persia did not welcome the idea of an independent Jewish state.
Internal divisions and the hostility of foreign neighbours impeded all efforts
to establish an independent Israel, a situation that persisted up to modern
times. With the Bar Kochba rebellion of AD 135 the Palestinian Jews
struggled to throw off the Roman yoke, with the dire result that the Palestine community was thrust into poverty and obscurity. Emperor Hadrian
decided that if the Jews would not submit to Roman rule then Judaism
would have to be destroyed. Hence he prohibited the practice of the Jewish
religion, banned circumcision and Sabbath observance, made studying the
Torah a capital offence, and banned the use of the calendar for the celebration of Jewish holy days. In these circumstances the Jews who had remained
in Babylonia, seemingly less pious and less committed to the ideal of an
independent Jewish state, assumed a central place in the preservation of
Jewish culture.

The importance of Palestine had always been recognised. Thus a modern
Jewish historian comments:

> . . . Palestinian intellectual and religious activity far outstripped similar
> activity among the Jews who remained in Babylon . . . after making a
> number of steps forward in the development of Judaism, the Babylonian
> community became tired and sat back to let Palestine do the rest . . . The
> Babylonian Jews . . . were always interested in study. Their intellectual
> activity, however, was not as profound or as intensive as in Palestine.
> When a man showed an unusual desire to continue his studies, he would
> go to Palestine, and sometimes he would remain there . . .[21]

None the less, the prevailing circumstances of Palestine made a 'transfer of
leadership'[22] from Palestine to Babylonia inevitable. A Palestinian Talmud
had grown out of the work of Palestinian scholars but by the fourth century

AD the Babylonian schools had become so dominant that the competing Babylonian scholars came to the fore: in the Middle Ages, at the peak of rabbinic Judaism, even the Palestinian Jews accepted the Babylonian Talmud as their code of law.

The strong Jewish community remained in Mesopotamia over the centuries – despite the rise of Islam and the caliphate, despite the Arab dominance and the shaping of Iraq in the modern world.[23] It is a singular paradox, considering the modern Arab–Israeli confrontation, that Jewish hopes were sustained largely in the land that became known as Iraq: 'The credit . . . for giving Israel its all-important start, physically and culturally, belongs to ancient Mesopotamia.'[24]

THE PERSIANS

Persia began its rise to prominence in the 7th century BC, becoming by the 6th century the dominant power of the ancient Near Eastern world. Long before that time there were tribes and peoples in the region competing for power and influence and injecting important ingredients into the cultural crucible. Perhaps the most important of these early regions was Elam, situated in the territory of what today is Iran and dating as far back as the 4th millennium BC. Its capital was Susa and what we know of this town and its people comes largely from extant Babylonian sources. The relevant texts say little about the Persian interior in those early days, since the Babylonians were mainly interested in the tribes that confronted them at their borders: for example, the Elamites, the Kassites, the Lullubi and the Guti.[25] The Elamites and the other tribes threatened the Mesopotamian plains, and one of the Elamite inscriptions is in Sumerian, establishing that they had significant contact with the Babylonians. Other inscriptions written in the Elamite script have appeared alongside Akkadian texts. Elam had developed a national identity and made regular forays into Babylonian territory. Thus the Elamite king Puzur-Inshushinak raised an army and invaded Babylonia, reaching as far as Akkad and encouraging such tribes as the Lullubi and the Guti to attempt similar ventures.

At their height the Elamites conquered much of Babylonia, their capital, Susa, surviving through six thousand turbulent years of history, through all the great empires of Babylonia, Egypt, Assyria, Persia, Greece and Rome (as late as the fourteenth century AD Susa survived under the name of Sushan). Susa was captured and sacked by Ashurbanipal in 646 BC and he carried in his train a vast booty of treasure back to Nineveh. This was yet another pendulum swing in the ancient turmoil of the Middle East. In the 2nd millennium BC the Elamites had become masters of Babylon and Uruk, only to be thrown back and forced to suffer the depredations and humiliations that they had brought to others.

Around 1500 BC the Medes and Persians had migrated to the Iranian plateau, and in the 7th century BC the first Persian dynasty was founded by Achaemenes. The dynastic line was to include Cyrus the Great, who founded the Persian Empire. Cyrus (550–529 BC) overthrew the Medean king Astyages in 550 BC and conquered Lydia in 546 BC. Then he decided to give his attention to Babylon. Herodotus described some aspects of the campaign.[26]

The Babylonians had anticipated the Persian advance and launched the first attack, but they were defeated and forced to retire inside the city defences. Babylon then contained provisions for many years and there seemed no alternative to a lengthy siege, but then Cyrus diverted water from the Euphrates to enable Persian troops to wade through the newly shallow river into the city. The Babylonians were taken by surprise: '. . . owing to the great size of the city the outskirts were captured without the people in the centre knowing anything about it; there was a festival going on, and even while the city was falling they continued to dance and enjoy themselves, until hard facts brought them to their senses'. The last Babylonian king Nabonidus (556–538 BC), who ruled with his son Belshazzar, had been perceived to be weak, now increasingly preoccupied with worship of the god Sin and with his 'archaeological' research into ancient monuments. Babylon fell without much resistance, the royal citadel alone holding out for a few days. Cyrus, with typical clemency, spared the king and even joined the national mourning when Nabonidus died in 538 BC, the following year.

Cyrus represented himself to the Babylonians more as a liberator than a conqueror, but still the legitimate successor to the crown. He took the title of 'king of Babylon, king of the land', and he returned to their rightful temples all the statues of the gods that Nabonidus had conveyed into the capital. At the next New Year Festival, Cyrus, following the custom of the traditional Babylonian kings, took the hand of the god Bel and so legitimised a new Babylonian dynasty. He also issued a decree freeing the Jews from their Babylonian captivity, stipulating that a high Persian official should accompany the Jews that decided to return to the Promised Land, to ensure that his wishes were fulfilled. The Jewish exiles hailed Cyrus as a liberator and sang songs of joy to celebrate the end of their bondage. Their joy, as we have seen, was short-lived.

Cyrus remained well-regarded, and not only by the Jews, who called him 'the anointed of the Lord'; the Persians called him 'father', and the Hellenes whom he conquered regarded him as 'master' and 'law-giver'. He was a great conqueror but generally compassionate towards defeated enemies, to whom he often extended the hand of friendship. After Cyrus the Persian empire was ruled by Cambyses II (529–522 BC), who had killed his brother Smerdis to gain the throne. Thereafter the dynasty continues up to the time of Darius III (336–330 BC); an inscription on a high cliff between Kermanshan and Hamadan – in Old Persian, Babylonian and Elamite – declares that Darius was the ninth Achaemenian king, a number that includes both branches of the dynasty. As with most of the ancient rulers Darius was forced to wage repeated battles to protect his reign: in his first two years as king he is said to have defeated nine rulers in nineteen battles. In such confrontations Darius was victorious, but in a series of battles – in 334, 333 and 331 BC (this last at Gaugamela) – he was defeated by the Macedonian Greeks led by Alexander the Great.

THE GREEKS

When Alexander the Great (Alexander III) inherited the throne from Philip II, his murdered father, he took over an empire that had just succeeded in subduing the states of mainland Greece. He then, aged about twenty, launched a vigorous crusade to punish the Persians for Xerxes' invasion of Greece some 150 years earlier. He encountered Darius first at Granicus in 334 BC and defeated him; battle was again joined against the Persians in 333 BC, this time in Syria (at Issus), and Alexander was again victorious; and Darius was finally comprehensively defeated in 331 BC, forcing him to flee to Bactria where he was assassinated in 330 BC. Now Alexander became master of the entire Persian empire, including the great plains of Mesopotamia. When he died in Babylon in 323 BC he was thirty-five years old.

Alexander's empire did not survive him: his surviving commanders were ambitious to command nations rather than armies. There were serious political divisions in the empire and these led to the Battle of Ipsus in Phrygia, Asia Minor, in 301 BC. Here Antigonus I was killed by Lysimachus and Seleucus, and the vast empire created by the Macedonian Alexander was at an end. Three kingdoms emerged from the political confusion: a Macedonian monarchy in Europe, a Ptolemaic monarchy in Egypt, and a Seleucid monarchy in Asia. Seleucus had taken command of the calvary formations of Persian nobles after the capture of Susa and he had converted them into a disciplined body of several tens of thousands of warriors. As satrap of Babylonia he finally inherited the bulk of the Achaemenian empire, but without Egypt, Palestine, southern Syria and parts of Asia Minor.

The Hellenistic Seleucid dynasty (312–64 BC) ruled over the Iranian world, Babylonia, Phoenicia and the cities of Asia Minor. Now the influence of classical Greece, working through the Macedonians and the Seleucids, was helping to shape the culture of Mesopotamia.

ROMANS AND PARTHIANS

The Seleucids were now in a position to administer the vast areas of Asia Minor conquered by Alexander the Great, but no sooner had they assumed power than they experienced great problems in holding together the empire. In Bactria – the region that today is northern Afghanistan and the southern (erstwhile) USSR – the Seleucid rulers were confronted by the Persians. An accommodation was reached and for a time the Greeks and Persians – representing two entirely different social and political systems – accepted a mutual understanding. Then the Parthians erupted on to the scene and forced a separation between the Bactrian Greeks and the rest of the Seleucid empire: in 256 BC Bactria became an independent state, but after little more than a century was submerged by the first of a procession of conquerors. In 247 BC Arsaces had founded the Parthian empire, which at its peak in the 1st century BC embraced parts of Persia and extended from the Euphrates to the Indus. Its decline was to begin with defeats by the Romans in 39–38 BC. Parthia was taken over in AD 226 by Ardashir I, founder of the Sassanid empire.

It took the Parthians over a century to recover substantial parts of Persia from the Greeks and to consolidate their western frontiers on the Euphrates (these western regions were to remain in the Persian orbit until the Arab invasion). The Hellenic Seleucus II (246–226 BC) struggled to restore the eastern parts of the empire and the Parthians were forced to retreat before his army, but a revolt at Antioch forced Seleucus to return to Syria and the Parthians rushed back to fill the vacuum. After the death of Seleucus there were further territorial losses in Asia Minor. Between 160 and 140 BC the Parthian leader Mithridates I forcibly annexed many lands – including large parts of Babylon and Assyria – in the west and substantial territories in the east. On the left bank of the Tigris the Parthians established a vast military encampment that later developed into the Parthian capital of Ctesiphon. When Mithridates died in 137 BC the Parthian empire stretched from the Euphrates to Herat (in what today is north-west Afghanistan). On the death of the later king, Mithridates II, the Parthian empire began its period of decline.

The Parthians had succeeded in throwing back the Roman incursions and for more than a century the Euphrates frontier remained secure. The western Semites opposed to Rome – such as the Palestinian Jews, the Syrian Nabateans and the desert Arabs – took heart at the Persian successes. Mark Antony failed in 36 BC in a further attack on the Parthians, and Augustus accepted thereafter the Euphrates frontier as a secure division between the empires. However, in AD 114, at a time of Parthian weakness, Trajan resolved to reduce Parthia to vassalage and to impose a puppet king. Having annexed Armenia as a Roman province he advanced down the Euphrates and the Tigris to take Seleucia and reach the Persian Gulf. He had captured Ctesiphon, the Parthian capital, and made prisoner the daughter of King Osroes. On his journey through Mesopotamia Trajan offered sacrifices in the Babylonian palace where Alexander the Great had died, thus honouring the great conqueror whom he sought to emulate. But his imperial successes were not secure: the Parthians began a partisan war and he failed to take the Parthian fortress of Hatra. Trajan died before he could return to Rome. In AD 165 the Roman general Avidius Cassius again sacked Seleucia and Ctesiphon, a feat repeated yet again by Septimius Severus in AD 198. And yet again the conquest did not hold: the Roman forces were compelled to evacuate the territory and Persia re-established its western frontiers on the Euphrates.

THE SASSANIANS

The Sassanian dynasty, the last in Persia before the Arab conquest of AD 651, began in AD 226 under Ardashir I and it was to experience continual conflict with Rome in the west. There was also internal dissent: Ardashir was forced to confront a coalition of factions ranged against him – which he successfully overcame using bribery and force. His son Shapur inherited a secure empire and was able to force Rome to cede substantial parts of Mesopotamia to the Persians. Thereafter, following the death of Shapur, the Sassanian empire grew weaker and gradually lost territory to the Romans and other forces threatening the frontiers. The Arabs were increasingly involved in Sassanian affairs, securing provinces within the empire and offering help to various dynastic factions. Thus Vahram V (AD 421–38) was forced to seek help from the Arab prince of Hira, a small vassal state to the west of the Euphrates; and Kavad, having invaded Mesopotamia and forced a treaty with Byzantium (the eastern part of the Roman empire), was obliged to seek help from the Arab leader Quteiba to secure his rule. However, such tactics did little to secure the Sassanian dynasty.

The Romans were yet again putting pressure on the western frontier and even nature seemed to conspire against Chosroes II, one of the last Sassanian kings: the Tigris flooded and transformed flourishing land into swamps, causing part of the royal palace at Ctesiphon to collapse. Chosroes refused to sign an agreement with the invading Byzantine emperor Heraclius (610–41), even though his own generals were then campaigning against him. He was killed by his own son who failed to impose order on the contending factions within the empire. The country was engulfed by rivalries, with royal princes crowned, only to be assassinated a short time later. Sometimes women – for example, Boran and Azarmedukht, the daughters of Chosroes – were placed on the throne as prisoners of this or that rival faction; and the great military leaders also tried to seize the crown. The Sassanian state crumbled into a chaos of petty states, helpless to resist the Arab conquest. The Persian commander Rustam was killed on the field of battle at Qadisiyah in Mesopotamia and Ctesiphon was soon captured, a vast amount of treasure falling into the hands of the Arabs. The last of the Sassanian kings, the child Yazdgard, raised a fresh army but was crushed by the Arabs on the plain of Nihawand. The empire had fallen, yielding to the fanatical onslaught of the Bedouin. It was the start of the Arab conquest, an irresistible wave of expansion fuelled by the passion of a new religion.

3 The Arabs, Islam and the Caliphate

The turbulence in ancient Mesopotamia lasted for four millennia: it generated massive cultural advances and all the misery and destitution (less frequently noted) that are inevitably associated with the ravages of military conquest. This dramatic historical phase may be regarded as drawing to a close with the reverses suffered by Rome and Persia. Soon a new power would burst forth, fuelled by fresh beliefs able to supplant, but not wholly to extirpate, the prevailing religions of the region – pagan creeds, Zoroastrianism, Judaism and Christianity. Soon a nomadic nation would be exploding from Arabia to challenge Persia in the east and to extend as far as Spanish Cordoba in the west.

ARAB ORIGINS

The first appearance of the name *Arab* is on an inscription of the Assyrian monarch Shalmaneser III who in 853 BC defeated an alliance of states in which King Ahab of Israel was supported by a certain 'Jundibu the Arab'.[1] Various writers have noted that Jundibu (or Gindibu) provided a thousand camels for the allied forces. Thereafter many Assyrian and Babylonian inscriptions refer to the Aribi or Arabu. The Arabs themselves first used the term in an inscription in the Nabataean script which records the deeds of a certain Arabian ruler, the supposed 'King of all the Arabs'. Two races have been identified as inhabiting the broad expanse of Arabia in ancient times. One such group were the inhabitants of the rain-fed uplands in the south, in the region of what today is the Yemen; the other group were nomads, wandering with their livestock over the great deserts that stretch from the Euphrates to the centre of the Arabian peninsula. These latter have been depicted as the true Arabs.[2] They were subservient to their Assyrian overlords and paid tribute in the form of camels and other animals. Thus in the Old Testament we learn that 'some of the Philistines brought Jehoshaphet presents, and tribute silver; and the Arabians brought him flocks, seven thousand and seven hundred rams, and seven thousand and seven hundred he goats'.[3] (The Arabs were later called Ishmaelites, since the Jews came to see the Arabs after the rise of Islam as fellow-descendants of the patriarch Abraham via his son Ishmael.)

The word 'aribi', as it appeared in the inscriptions and writings associated with the region of the Fertile Crescent, generally referred to desert peoples in general but particularly to the nomads and tribes that came from Arabia. One Assyrian inscription dating from around 700 BC suggests that the Aribi were regarded as akin to slaves, and a later inscription records punitive campaigns waged against the Aribi to stop them preying on caravans.[4] During this period there is no specific reference to Arabia *per se*; we may speculate that it was later named as the land of the Aribi. It was largely the inhabitants of the coastal strips that used the word 'aribi' to denote the nomads of the great inland deserts. In fact the word itself and its many variations derived from a Semitic root suggesting nomadism (*abar* = 'to pass'). After about 550 BC, at about the time of the Persian invasion, the term *aribi* disappeared from the literature and inscriptions of the Fertile Crescent. The Persians later came to call the land across the Gulf 'Arabaya'; and *Arabia* first appears as a term in the Greek writings. Thus Herodotus and the later Greek and Latin writers used the terms 'Arab' and 'Arabia' to include all the desert areas of the Middle East inhabited by the speakers of Semitic languages.[5] (The word 'Semitic' – deriving from Shem, the eldest son of Noah, from whom all the Semite peoples are said to be descended – was coined by the German historian Schlözer to describe the tongues of Syria, Arabia and Mesopotamia that later spread into North Africa.) Hence an Arab was essentially a nomadic inhabitant of the Arabian peninsula. Long before the days of the Islamic expansion the Arabian nomads had travelled to other lands, and sometimes settled there.

The settled communities continued to have contact with their Bedouin cousins as they moved restlessly across the lands of the Middle East and north Africa. This led to yet more cultural cross-fertilisation: the nomads of Arabia became increasingly aware of Hellenic ideas and encountered also the complicated beliefs of the Jews (themselves great travellers) and the early Christians. In one view the ancient Hebrews were also Arabs, inhabitants of the Arabian peninsula.[6] The Arab nomads, accustomed to fighting for bare subsistence in a desolate environment, were associated with brigandage as a means to survival; or as an alternative they would move into communities overcome by internal conflict or decimated by disease. It was inevitable, in such difficult circumstances, that there would be tensions between the various Arab groups; at the same time a sense of kinship, ebbing and flowing, has always survived in what today we recognise as the historic Arab nation.

The early nomads who wandered across the deserts of the Arabian peninsula helped to provide the matrix of the Arabian civilisations that would follow. In particular, the emergence of a multilayered clan system, allied to a powerful framework of religious commitment, was to become a defining feature of Arab society. The need to survive was a primary requirement: strong clan bonds established a basis of security for the ambitions of the group, and in due course the clan system evolved into the complex tribal configurations that persist in the modern world. The tribes traditionally focused on the raising of flocks and herds, and on the periodic raiding of their more sedentary neighbours, a practice that came to be irrevocably associated with the name of the Bedouin (from the Arab word 'Badawiyin', originally meaning 'people who appear in open country', such as the desert expanses).

The early Arabs were also keen traders, as attested by the ancient caravan routes that cross Arabia in all directions: commerce between the fierce nomads, who may sometimes have pillaged for booty, and the more placid settlements was a typical and important feature of the Arab world. The Old Testament records how a travelling company of Ishmaelites took part in this trade, coming from Gilead 'with their camels bearing spicery and balm and myrrh, going to carry it down to Egypt'.[7] At Petra in southern Jordan there was a flourishing Arab trade centre until the Nabataean kingdom was subdued by the Romans in AD 105 to become part of the Provincia Arabia. Again the cultural collision led to the absorption of fresh ideas, some associated with monotheism (the Romans, at least in their pagan incarnation, were scarcely monotheists but the idea of a one and only supreme deity at the head of the pantheon was well established, as was monotheism in Judaism and Zoroastrianism). Some of the Arabs who farmed in the peninsula had adopted Judaism (though some of these may have been Jews expelled from Palestine by the Romans); and by the 4th century AD many of the Arabian settlers had abandoned traditional animism and polytheism in favour of belief in a supreme god dubbed *al-Rahman*, 'the Merciful'.[8] The ground was well prepared for the coming of Islam.

The Arabic language was originally common to the entire Arabian peninsula but the tribes eventually developed their own dialects and variations, encapsulating their own unique experiences and adding foreign accretions. The language reflected many interests: it at once celebrated the heroic history of the tribes and reflected with due solemnity on man's awe and predicament in the face of nature. Arab poetry is immensely rich and fecund, a circumstance rarely acknowledged in the West. Poetic expression could be used for both story-telling and ordinary conversation. An enquiry or a chance encounter might stimulate a rendering of the *qasidah*, a lengthy discourse in several phases, all intended to amuse and entertain the listener. In such a fashion the business of everyday intercourse could be embellished with poetic and narrative invention. Small surprise, some observers may note, that the Arab mind is sometimes captivated by the seductive power of rhetoric.

The poetic tradition helped to frame the character of the classical Arabic language, from which the modern vernaculars derived; and helps also to fuel the common awareness of Arab nationhood. The roots were established in Arab prehistory but the developing culture would only come to maturity via the power of a new creed and the dynamic of a new wave of conquest.

MOHAMMAD

Mohammad was born in or near the year AD 570.[9] His parents belonged to the aristocratic Quraysh tribe of Mecca, a group that included traders who had forged useful agreements with the pastoral tribes around Mecca and in Syria and south-western Arabia. Mohammad's parents died early and he was put in the care of a tribal wet nurse who looked after him in the desert until he was six. Thereafter he came under the charge of an uncle and a grandfather, later to be educated for a life in Meccan commerce. When he was about twenty-five Mohammad married Khadija, a Quraysh business woman fifteen years his senior. He helped her look after her trading interests but despite such practical affairs he is said to have led a mystical and solemn life. Held in high esteem, even at an early age, Mohammad was called 'The Honest One'.

Little is known about Mohammad's life between the time of his marriage and the visionary experiences that were to transform him and change the world. Khadija, still involved with the camel trade, bore him two sons (who both died in infancy) and four daughters. The marriage of his daughter Fatima to Ali was of great importance, for Mohammad's descendants of this line are specially revered, and the Shias regard the descendants of Ali and Fatima as the true heirs to the Caliphate, with all the secular and religious privileges that this implies.

When he was about forty years of age he experienced what believers have regarded as contact with the supernatural, with the 'one true God'. In one version of this Night of Power (or Destiny), Mohammad sees an angel (perhaps Gabriel) in the shape of a man, calling him to become the messenger of God. In another version he hears the angel telling him to recite certain verses. At first he resists, and then a physical presence forces him to utter sublime and ominous verses that convey the anger of an omnipotent God resolved to punish mankind for the paganism of Arabia. Then Mohammad felt a great upsurge of emotion and quickly fell into a trance. When he recovered he was a transformed man, convinced that he had been chosen as the Prophet of Allah, the only true God.

Three years after the angelic vision, Mohammad received the divine order to preach, to proclaim in public what he had been newly taught by God (Allah). He then began teaching that God was One, that the idols must be swept away, that the righteous dead would rise again to eternal happiness, and that the idolaters would be consigned to hell-fire. He claimed that sometimes the Archangel Gabriel spoke to him as one person to another, and that sometimes he heard an inner voice. With each fresh revelation Mohammad would recite a new verse which his disciples would learn by heart and which would eventually come to form part of the Koran. He further claimed that his faith was not new, but simply the correct religion of Abraham that had been distorted by the Israelites. He claimed no more than to be a conduit for God's Word, to be merely reciting verbatim what he was told. He called the new creed *Islam*, surrender to God. Those who followed the true path would be known as *Muslims*, surrendered persons.[10]

When Mohammad died in 632 there was no established Muslim code of laws and no provision for the succession. Mohammad had left no sons and there were no protocols for the election of the next leader of Islam and the growing Muslim movement. The Meccan and Medinese authorities conferred, whereupon Mohammad's father-in-law, Abu Bekr, was appointed – or appointed himself – *Caliph*, the successor.

THE FRAMEWORK OF ISLAM

Mohammad had left no son, no obvious successor, and no body of rules to define the polity of an Islamic state: much of this would come later. What he had left was a multifaceted legacy: the surviving impact of his own personality and authority, and the Koran, to believers the manifest Word of God. The testimony of Mohammad, conveyed to and repeated by the early Muslims as largely an oral tradition, was not consolidated until much later. Until that time there were the shifting tales, doubtless acquiring variations from one telling to another and attracting accretions that would have been quite new to the Prophet. The early Muslims had the tales, conveyed in all the richness of the Arabic language, the essence of the remembered sermons, and the enduring recollection, in the minds of followers, of the person of the Prophet. He would have served as an example, as he still does, if not a god then a supreme model of virtue and insight for all mankind. Those who remembered Mohammad would have tried to behave as he did, to approach human problems in the spirit of the Prophet: over time 'there evolved a type of human personality which may well be to some extent a reflection of his'.[11] Such circumstances, we may assume, were significant shaping factors in the personalities of modern Arab rulers wont to claim descent from Mohammad.

There is also the question of the originality (or otherwise) of the Koran. The text states that Mohammad did not himself write down the words contained therein; so others must have done so, and what do we know of their credentials? They cannot have been directly privy to the divine Word vouchsafed to the Prophet and to him alone. The first Koranic verses would be scratched on stones, inscribed on animal bones, written on palm leaves: any medium, some more durable than others, would be used, and on this uncertain foundation the eternal Word of God was preserved for all the generations of people that would follow. Zayd, one of Mohammad's secretaries, is said to have presented a bunch of leaves carrying the holy words to Abu Bekr, who later left them to his daughter Hafsa, one of Mohammad's widows. It is recorded also that under the caliph Uthman there were at least four rival versions of the Koran in use, though these are no longer extant. Uthman himself established a commission to finalise a text that everyone could agree, but he was unsuccessful: the people of Kufa rejected the 'finalised' edition, preferring another version that was still in use as late as AD 1000. Today we are not surprised to learn that various readings of the 'agreed' texts are individually argued by different scholars, even to the point that there is dispute about particular vowels and consonants. In such circumstances there have always been immense etymological and philosophical difficulties in deciding what message God had conveyed to man.[12]

In the modern world two sects – the Shi'ites and the Sunnis – are of particular significance: they represent the principal divisions of modern Islam, heavily underlining the political schisms in Iraq and other Muslim states. When Ali, the fourth caliph, was assassinated in 661, his son Hasan relinquished any claim to the throne in favour of Muawiya. When Muawiya's son later claimed the caliphate, Ali's second son Husain rose to challenge the claim. One consequence was an armed clash resulting in the massacre of Husain and most of his followers in 680 at Karbala in Iraq. Those who continued to support Ali's line of succession became known as the Shi'ites (from *shia* meaning party, the party of Ali). Shi'ite roots can be traced to Persia, where today they remain a significant faction, sometimes offering support to the Shi'ites in the southern marshlands of Iraq. (With Shi'ism the official religion of modern Iran it is easy to see the antipathy that exists between the Iranian leadership and the government of Iraq, dominated by Sunni Muslims.) Against the Shi'ites the Sunnis believe in the legitimacy of the actual succession of the early caliphs, giving great weight also to the *sunna*, the authentic body of Muslim custom. Since most of the early supporters of Ali were Iraqi the movement developed a parochial political flavour in opposition to the Umayyad Arabs in Syria (see below). In the modern world ninety per cent of all Muslims are Sunni, though most are non-Arabs, while the Shi'ites include a greater proportion of Arabs. Most Muslims in Iran and Yemen, and more than half those in Iraq, are Shi'ite – with small pockets elsewhere in the Middle East and southern Asia amounting to a world total of some 100 million Shi'ites.

The early Muslim world was one of unceasing turbulence. The Roman and Persian empires were exhausted and the time was ripe for a new force to expand and fill the spiritual vacuum. The Muslims seemed riven by factionalism, lacking a codified system of polity and law, and dependent for their strength on what appeared to be the fragile alliances of restless tribal groups. They had demonstrated their fanatical commitment to a new creed, one that had acknowledged links to established religions, but this alone hardly seemed sufficient to fuel a wave of conquest that would shake the world.

THE ARAB CONQUEST

As soon as the tribes of the Arabian peninsula heard about the death of Mohammad the rudimentary Muslim alliance began to fall apart: many tribes renounced Islam and refused to pay the tax, a development known in Arab history as the Apostasy (*Ridda*). Abu Bekr, the ageing caliph, decided to use force to subdue the dissident tribes. The fighting dragged on in some regions but within a year of the Prophet's death the Apostasy had been suppressed; by the summer of 633 Arabia was at peace. Mohammad had enjoined Muslims not to fight each other, and the peace was sustained by the growing tribal acknowledgement of Muslim hegemony in the region. It was this unprecedented peace in Arabia that was to serve as the secure springboard for expansion into the lands beyond. The Arabs began their dramatic expansion with a series of probing raids into Mesopotamia. In 633 the desert to the west of the head of the Persian Gulf was occupied by the large Bedouin tribe of Beni Bekr ibn Wail, formerly loyal to the Arab Lakhmid princes, satellites of the Persian state. Already the pattern was clear: local tribes, fearing subjugation by the Arab onslaught, were quick to offer alliances and to profess Islam.

In 639 the Arab general Muawiya became governor of Syria, the first colony of the burgeoning Muslim empire. The native Aramaeans had long been persecuted by the Roman occupying forces, the sedentary Monophysite Christians and Jews being particularly repressed because of their stubborn unwillingness to accept the demands of the Byzantine church. Many perceived the Islamic conquest, showing as it did a surprising degree of religious tolerance, as a liberation. The co-operation of the Syrian populace with the Muslim conquerors has been seen as sealing the fate of Syria, ensuring the total Arabisation and Islamisation of the country that have endured to the present day.

Arab incursions in eastern Mesopotamia led to further confrontations with the Persians, and in 637 a large Persian force was defeated at the battle of Kadisiya. As in all their conquests the Arabs had relied upon the fanatical energy of their javelin-throwing tribesmen on camels or horses. They would rush forward, hurl their missiles and then retreat to an agreed line, soon to repeat the procedure. When the enemy began to falter the Arabs would then engage them in hand-to-hand combat, inspired as they were with thoughts of a paradise reserved for fallen warriors. In such a fashion the Muslim forces, giving all the appearance of a ragged cavalry, overcame all opposition. Soon they had captured the Sassanid capital of Ctesiphon on the Tigris, near to what was to be the site of Baghdad, the seat of the Abbasid caliphs. Still the Persians tried to counter the Arab expansion into Mesopotamia, launching various attacks on the central plain, but to no useful effect. The Arabs repulsed all the Persian efforts, and Yazdgard, the last of the Sassanid emperors, was killed in 651 as he fled before the pursuing Bedouins. Now the Arabs were able to pour eastward from the river Euphrates: soon they were in control of the whole of the Mesopotamian region, and Syria and Mesopotamia were then fused together into a single province under an Arab governor.

The Apostasy had been suppressed, the whole of Arabia had been won for Islam, and the conquest of Syria and Mesopotamia had laid the basis for an expanding Arab empire. During the decade of Umar's rule (634–44) the subjugation of Egypt and Syria was completed and the Sassanid empire was overthrown. Umar had adopted the title *Amir al Mu'minin*, Commander of the Faithful (*amir* signifying military command), foreshadowing the character of the later Umayyad dynasty. The Sassanid general Rustam had been killed on the plain of Qadisiyah, near Hira, and the young King Yazdgard, obliged at the age of twelve to confront the Arab invasion, was forced to flee to the Zagros mountains before being slain by the pursuing Muslims. In Ctesiphon the untutored desert Bedouins found themselves in a treasure-house of riches: gold and silver, precious jewels and silks, priceless artefacts of all kinds. The Persian forces had been crushed but Umar wisely ruled against any Arab incursions into the heart of Persia itself: it was one thing to conquer Iraq, a Semitic province that had never shown much loyalty to the Sassanids, quite another to battle through mountainous terrain to subdue a large population that would have no cause to welcome an Arab invasion. Umar then arranged for the bulk of the Arab forces to be focused in two cantonments in lower Iraq, the camps at Basra and Kufa which would expand in a few years into large towns.

The Arabs had established an effective dominion over Syria, Egypt and Iraq but there was no prospect of assimilating Persia whose people, conscious of their own imperial past, resented the barbarous race of 'lizard-eating Bedouins'.[13] The Persians adopted Islam, at first reluctantly (as *mawali*, clients of the Arabs, with an inferior status), but later with a growing cultural autonomy. One Persian Christian, a certain Abu Lu'lu'a, taken as a slave to Medina, managed in 644 to stab the caliph Umar six times in the back. Umar, aged fifty-two, took some hours to die: he had enough time to rejoice that his assassin was not a Muslim, and to set up an electoral college (*shura*), including Ali and Uthman, to select the next caliph. The college also included Zubair ibn al Awwam, who had fought in Egypt, Abdul Rahman ibn Auf, and Saad ibn abi Waqqas, the conqueror of Iraq.

SCHISM

Soon after the death of Umar cracks began to appear in the young Arab empire. A new situation was developing, not merely because Islam had lost a wise leader but also because the pace of Arab advance inevitably slowed. It proved impossible to maintain the speed of the early conquests and in the second decade problems emerged that would have taxed the capacities of any leader. The newly-expanded Arab nation rushed towards a crisis that would create permanent divisions in Islam and whose effects are manifest in the modern world.

It was soon evident to the electoral college set up by Umar that there were only two serious candidates: Ali (ibn abi Talib) and Uthman (ibn Affan), both of them members of the Quraysh. The two realistic candidates came from different clans – the Beni Hashim (Ali) and the Beni Umayya (Uthman) – within the Quraysh tribe, and these were the groups that had vied for supremacy before Islam: Mohammad himself had belonged to the Beni Hashim and his principal opponent, Abu Sofian, to the Beni Umayya. This meant that a mere twelve years after the death of the Prophet the old family rivalries were again coming to the fore. Twenty-two years earlier Mohammad had journeyed to Medina to escape the hostility of the Meccans, and in that period of new empire had supplanted the old hegemonies of Rome and Persia. But already the insecurities in the new state were apparent: 'Quraysh had built it and Quraysh were to destroy it'.[14]

The electoral college selected Uthman (644–56) as the third caliph. He was handsome and wealthy, and about seventy years of age. Although of high social standing, he was soon showing the weakness that would help to end his rule. New popular risings broke out in Persia and continued for about five years (644–9); here, as in other matters, Uthman had responded with indecision and nepotism. He had made his own half-brother, Waleed ibn Uqba, governor of Kufa and the military commander in northern Persia (it was remembered that when Waleed's father, Uqba, had been taken prisoner at Bedr and cried out, 'Who will take care of my little children?' Mohammad had replied, 'Hell-fire'). Waleed, a drunkard, was soon removed from his post and replaced by Saad ibn al Aasi, another Umayyid, as was the newly-appointed governor of Basra, Abdulla ibn Aamir. The revolts in Persia had been suppressed and Abdulla had captured Balkh, Herat and Kabul, but such successes did little to quell the growing dissent among the Arabs. Now it seemed clear that only an Umayyid could hope to gain high office, even though it had been the Beni Umayya that had originally opposed Mohammad and the establishment of Islam. The Quraysh, given status because of Mohammad, had long been seen as a natural aristocracy in the movement, but it was the sectional Umayya that was operating as a clique over all Arabs. Uthman himself appeared to be taking orders from the Umayya, a circumstance that alienated many of his nominal followers. In 655 there was an armed revolt in the Kufa camp, and Saad was forced to flee to Medina, soon to be followed by a mutinous army supported by factions from Fustat and Basra. In June 656 a mob of soldiers broke into Uthman's house in Medina and hacked him to death. The third patriarchal caliph was dead.

The assassination of Uthman was a momentous event in early Islam. The murder itself was dramatic enough. When the soldiers broke in they found the old man sitting with a copy of the Koran in his lap. His wife struggled to shield him, and had several fingers cut off for her pains. As the soldiers thrust their swords into Uthman's body the blood of the caliph flowed over the Koran, a nice metaphor on the state of Islam. It no longer seemed that God was guiding the affairs of the Arab nation. At one fateful blow the true nature of the Caliphate was exposed: it was no sacred office, no divinely sanctioned head of a people chosen by Allah to conquer and rule the world. Instead the Caliphate, like all other human institutions, was a prize to be won by the sword. It was Muslims, not infidels, who had murdered the caliph in the holiest city of Islam. The Arab nation had passed through its brief dream, the unreflective state in which seemingly the whole world had lain at the feet of the holy warriors. Now the Arabs were again plunged into fratricidal strife, bloodshed and civil turmoil.

Ali, the first cousin of the Prophet and husband of his daughter Fatima, seemed to be Uthman's natural successor. Five days after the assassination he was approved as the fourth patriarchal caliph and the soldiers returned to their garrisons. But Ali was opposed by the powerful Umayyads, including Muawiya, and by Ayisha, Mohammad's widow. Ali had opposed Uthman's election and he had been in Medina at the time of the assassination. Had he lifted a hand to prevent the catastrophe? Did he intend to punish the assassins? Did he secretly welcome the death of the third caliph? Muawiya, having failed to prevent the murder of his kinsman, now refused to recognise Ali until the assassins were punished. But Ali refused to act and Muawiya accused him of complicity in the murder. Ali had at best shown a lack of resolution in the revolt against Uthman, and his inaction had awakened suspicion. Now Ali, a man of about sixty years of age, found himself increasingly beset by enemies, including Muawiya, the powerful governor of Syria. The bloodstained shirt of Uthman and his wife's severed fingers were smuggled out of Medina and conveyed to Damascus, there to be exposed in the mosque to stimulate public outrage.

After fruitless talks and a battle in July 657, it was agreed that arbitration, on the basis of Koranic law, should be allowed to settle the issue between Ali and Muawiya. Two umpires, one from each side, were selected and the arbitration court met at Adhruh, an old Roman site near the ruins of Petra. Amr was chosen to represent Muawiya, and Ali was forced to select Abu Musa, an independent Kufan leader. Today the details of the deliberations are obscure but it is thought that the court scrutinised the record of Uthman, finally vindicating him sufficiently to condemn the regicides. This implied, in view of Ali's failure to punish the assassins, that his caliphate was invalid – a conclusion that would have satisfied Muawiya, since he himself, at least overtly, was making no claims for the throne. Ali, who had looked like being victorious in battle, was now defeated by arbitration. He rejected the proposal of a *shura* to elect a new caliph, and in consequence further alienated many of his supporters. Several thousand of his followers deserted him and became known as Kharijites ('outgoers' or 'secessionists'), claiming connections with the original Kharijites and destined to have an influence through all the subsequent centuries of Islam.

Ali, increasingly insecure, lost the Hejaz to a local rebellion, and was then forced to move against Kharijites who had established a base at Nahrawan, beside one of the Tigris canals. In July 658, in a bloody confrontation, he crushed the dissenters; but in January 661, while entering the mosque at Kufa, he was assassinated by a fanatical Kharijite. He was the third caliph in seventeen years to be murdered. Now the way was open for Muawiya.

THE UMAYYAD DYNASTY

The supporters of Ali, the *Shia* ('partisans of Ali'), made some efforts to continue the struggle against Muawiya, and encouraged Ali's son, Hasan, to make claims on the caliphate. But Muawiya had already had himself declared caliph in Jerusalem and Hasan was soon persuaded to renounce his claims in exchange for a substantial pension. The Shia built the town of Najaf around Ali's supposed tomb at Kufa: the Shia/Sunni divide had been consolidated and would continue to plague Islam up to modern times. The Arab state, weary of internal strife, was now prepared to accept the rule of the Umayyads: the confrontations were temporarily abated in celebration of the *jama'a* (the return to harmony and agreement). With the death of Ali, the first important phase of the Arab nation came to an end: that of the first four caliphs known to most Muslims as the *Rashidun* (the 'Rightly Guided Ones'), a generous appellation in view of the violence and errors with which their names are associated.

Arabia had lost its political primacy for the Arab nation, though Mecca and Medina retained their unique significance for all Muslims. Now the centre of political power had shifted from Medina, via Kufa, to Damascus in Syria. Muawiya was now set to rule for twenty years as Caliph of Islam. He has been reckoned a successful monarch. His style was that of the democratic Arab leader: he circulated freely in the streets without an escort, winning over enemies and consolidating the loyalty of his friends. He is said to have replied to bitter criticisms with calm conciliation, and throughout the two decades of his power there was no rebellion against him, a remarkable accomplishment for an Arab caliph. He was not averse to bribery, as well as persuasion, to gain allies. When he was rebuked for distributing gifts so widely he was apt to comment: 'War costs more!' Syria was a reliable base for his rule but the turbulent province of Iraq often presented problems and under Umayyad rule it was kept in order by a series of ruthless governors.

The towns of Kufa and Basra were often the sites of disaffection: the civil strife had shattered once and for all the brief unity of the Arab nation, and in any case the restless Bedouins were never content to stay placid under civil government. Such troubles were well contained by the various governors; in particular by Ziyad, who created a *shurta*, a carefully picked bodyguard to control the streets. He also cultivated the friendship of the *sheikhs*, the all-important tribal chiefs, and began deporting the most difficult clans to the far-off region of Khurasan where they were encouraged to settle as military colonists, a robust force on the frontiers of the empire. Muawiya had succeeded in impressing his people and in consolidating Arab control of the provinces; in time-honoured fashion he embarked upon various further military adventures to focus Arab energies.

Muawiya died in 680, and still no rules had been drawn up to control the succession to the caliphate. He had worked with the *shura*, a council of elders, often cajoled into implementing his wishes by pressure from the *wufud*, tribal delegations whom he had bought or persuaded. He had resolved, without dispute from the *shura*, that his son Yazid would inherit the throne but leading Muslims, doubtless aware of the rampant nepotism throughout all the years of the caliphate, were not eager to assume a hereditary entitlement to the caliphate. It is often noted that despite the clan and tribal structure of Arab society there is an aversion to the hereditary right of succession: merit, rather than birth, has often been depicted as giving the best reason for accepting one leader against another.

In fact Yazid was in a weak position: there were many caliphs' sons about, and Yazid was far from uniquely talented. He seemingly had a frivolous disposition, preferring hunting to business and lacking all the authority of his venerable father. Moreover, there were many enemies of the house of Umayyad, and they now saw their chance. Ali's second son Husain was the only surviving grandson of the Prophet, Hasan having died before Muawiya (some said of poison); and Husain was regarded by the Shia as the future caliph. His supporters compelled him to forsake his congenial seclusion in Mecca and to enter the hazardous political fray. Husain was seen as serious and pious, a suitable contrast to the frivolous Yazid. When news that Husain, without an army, was journeying towards Kufa there was general alarm in Damascus: there were memories of earlier strife and it was not difficult to imagine what might happen again. While Husain was still travelling across the desert Yazid appointed Ubaidulla, the son of Ziyad, as governor of Kufa. The new governor could be relied upon: within days he had executed all Husain's principal supporters in the town, and when Husain's small convoy approached Kufa it was suddenly surrounded by a cavalry force of four thousand. Husain gathered around him his band of less than a hundred supporters, and resolved to fight to the death. The Arab archers fired on the convoy for several hours, and one by one Husain's men died around him. His ten-year-old nephew Kasim died in his arms; two of his sons and six of his brothers also perished, until Husain himself, now bleeding from several wounds, stood alone. The troops closed in and struck him down with their swords. Most of the women and children, cowering in the tents, were spared, but all the slain males were decapitated; some seventy heads, including that of Husain, were carried in triumph to Ubaidulla.

In November 683 Yazid died, and the scene was set for further political chaos. Now Yazid's sickly son, Muawiya II, though only a child, was proclaimed caliph but died a few months later, not long after Abdulla ibn Zubair, son of the Zubair who had opposed Ali, made competing claims for the caliphate. These were set aside and the defence of the Umayyad dynasty now depended upon Marwan al-Hakam, a cousin of Muawiya and Yazid. In 684 Marwan was proclaimed caliph in Damascus, but died a year later, to be succeeded by his son Abdul Malik ibn Marwan. Such turmoil had further weakened the Umayyad dynasty, and the position faced by Abdul Malik seemed to be little short of hopeless. In Mecca Zubair made fresh claims and established himself as a rival caliph; the Persian provinces were in anarchy; and in turbulent Iraq the Shias and the Kharijites had begun open rebellion.

Abdul Malik, supposedly a shrewd and competent politician, first consolidated what forces remained loyal to him, and then began a fresh invasion of Iraq (which now was showing increasing allegiance to the anti-caliph Abdulla). Abdul Malik took Kufa in December 691, killing the brother of Abdulla ibn Zubair in the process. The loss of Iraq seriously weakened the position of Zubair in Mecca, and in 692 Abdul Malik felt strong enough to send an army to recapture the Holy City. Kufa had been lost to the caliph, run by the rebel Mukhtar – who assured his followers of the imminent coming of the *Mahdi* (the promised redeemer) – for eighteen months; but in 687 Mukhtar and his principal lieutenants had been killed, and now it was time to tackle Mecca. The siege lasted for a full eight months. The famous Umayyad commander Hajjaj ibn Yusuf had placed mangonels (wooden rock launchers) on the surrounding hills, and Mecca was forced to suffer a constant bombardment. Eventually Abdulla ibn Zubair, rapidly losing heart, consulted his mother, whereupon the woman, a daughter of Abu Bekr, declared: 'If you are conscious of your right, you will die like a hero!' So Abdulla ibn Zubair donned his armour on 3 October 692 and rushed out of the Meccan stronghold to face the Syrian army. He was first hit by a missile in the face, and then fell, sword in hand, riddled by arrows. Mecca was taken and, as befitted the times, Abdulla's head was duly presented to Abdul Malik in Damascus. Now that the caliph could rule without a serious rival a second *jama'a*, signalling peace and accord, was declared.

Suleiman ibn Abdul Malik (715–17), the brother of Waleed, succeeded him as caliph. His reign witnessed the second great Arab siege of Constantinople, which lasted for two years and which was no more successful than the first. The Byzantines employed 'Greek fire', apparently based on naphtha, which could be ejected from nozzles and poured from the battlements on unfortunate soldiers struggling to mount the walls. The Arabs were further handicapped by a harsh winter (716–17), when thick snow covered their lines for three months; and by an attack in the rear by the Bulgars, persuaded to enter the fray by the Isaurian Emperor Leo. Suleiman died in Damascus in 717 while the fighting outside Constantinople was still in progress, and his successor, Caliph Umar ibn Abdul Azeez, sent instructions for the Arab armies to return to Syria. The new caliph also did all he could to end the historic feud between the Beni Hashim and the Beni Umayya, making fresh efforts to conciliate the various factions (for example, when the Kharijites again rebelled in Iraq he invited them to send delegates to Damascus to explain their grievances). But his efforts were unsuccessful, a failure that was to contribute to the eclipse of the Umayyad dynasty.

It was now becoming clear that a more effective leadership of the Arab nation might be offered by another branch of the family of Mohammad, the descendants of his uncle Abbas. Elements of this family branch and their supporters created a political organisation with its centre at Kufa. They sent as their emissary to distant Khurasan a man called Abu Muslim, who may have derived from a Persian family. Umar had died after a brief reign, and his successors – Yazid II and Hisham, another son of Abdul Malik – while seeming to secure the empire were marking time before the establishment of a new dynasty. The caliph Hisham died in 743 and the Umayyads began their irreversible decline. Waleed II, the next caliph, was reputedly a drunkard and blasphemer: he survived fifteen months only, and on 17 April 744 his head was paraded through Damascus on the point of a lance. His successor, Yazid III, who had organised the revolt, died in October 744 after ruling for a mere six months. During this period, Abu Muslim had been forming an army to challenge the Umayyad dynasty. From Khurasan the army first marched to the west, engaging Umayyad forces in a number of battles. The demoralised Umayyad forces were repeatedly defeated in a series of confrontations in 749–50; and the last Umayyad caliph,

Marwan II, was chased into Egypt and there killed. In Kufa the new leader of the Arab nation was proclaimed: Abdul Abbas, a descendant not of Ali but of Mohammad's uncle, Abbas.

THE ABBASID DYNASTY

The Abbasids were quick to move their capital from Syria to Iraq, a decision that was to involve the creation of Baghdad in 762. This meant that now Muslim power was focused on the former Sassanid territories (southern Iraq, Persia, Khurasan and the land that stretched into central Asia), rather than on the eastern Mediterranean countries or the Hejaz; the Maghrib, now more distant from the centre of Muslim power, became less important. Persians were key players in the Abbasid *dawla* – to the point that some early observers saw the cultural transformation in Islam as a victory for Persian Aryans over Arab Semites. There was still a substantial Arab presence in the movement but now Islam was more cosmopolitan. The Arab tribes had been at the heart of the early imperial expansion, but now Persians were streaming into the public service: a new class of officials, merchants and landowners was evolving, with the *ulama* corresponding 'socially, though not religiously, to the priesthood of Christendom'.[15] A new office (Wazir or Vizier), with the authority of a vice-caliph, was created and the caliph himself was encouraged to retreat, in the manner of the old Sassanid shahs, into the heart of his palace, secure from the common eye. The trend towards oriental despotism, already discernible under the Ummayads, was accelerated under the Abbasids: the new caliphs 'seemed to have inherited the sacred absolutism of the kings of Nineveh, Babylon and Persia'.[16] The official executioner stood by the throne and symbolised the monarch's total power over his subjects, unprotected as they were by any law or constitution. One of the first decisions of Abdul Abbas (749–54) was to kill Abu Muslim and others who had helped the Abbasids to power: there must be no threat to the crown. Some family members were appointed as governors, as were others from Persian families newly converted to Islam and with a tradition of involvement in state affairs. Some freed slaves were appointed as officials.

The caliph Abdul Abbas, the first Abbasid Prince of the Faithful, died of smallpox on 9 June 754 (he had already earned the nickname of Saffah, the 'shedder of blood'). He was succeeded by his brother Abu Jafar, who was proclaimed caliph in Kufa with the title of al-Mansur (the Victorious). Mansur's most celebrated act was the creation of Baghdad; according to al-Tabari, Mansur had spent 'the sweetest and gentlest night on earth' at the site of a priest's church. Everything he saw pleased him, whereupon he declared: 'This is the site on which I shall build. Things can arrive here by way of the Euphrates, Tigris, and a network of canals. Only a place like this will support the army and the general populace.' He allocated funds for the building of the city, even laying the first brick with his own hand: 'In the name of God, and praise to Him. The earth is God's; He causes to inherit of it whom He wills among His servants, and the result thereof is to them that fear Him . . . Build, and God bless you.'[17]

Baghdad was situated on the site of an ancient Persian village on the west bank of the Tigris, near the old Persian capital of Ctesiphon. The great city of Baghdad (to be known as the Round City or the City of Peace) was to emerge as the most splendid metropolis of the time. Its diameter was some two miles, and there were three concentric walls, each with four gates controlling the highways that radiated from the caliph's palace at the centre of the city to the four corners of the Muslim empire. The proximity of the Tigris and the Euphrates, feeding the complex system of irrigation canals, enabled the surrounding countryside to support the large city; grain could be brought down from Jazira in northern Iraq, camels could ply trade overland with Persia, and ships could sail down the Tigris to Arabia and other lands. Tribute and taxation fed the treasure-houses of Baghdad, and the city developed as the heart of a vast trading network.

Baghdad reached the peak of its glory under the caliphs Haroun al-Rashid (786–809) and his son al-Mamum (813–33), though there were already signs that the empire was starting to disintegrate (North Africa had become autonomous around 800). Baghdad, at that time, was a focus of power, wealth and religious devotion; often depicted by later writers as a city of pleasure (the nineteenth-century English explorer Sir Richard Burton dubbed Baghdad 'the Paris of the ninth century'). There were mosques and palaces, patios and pavilions, walkways and gardens; and philosophy, science and a literary revolution (the great Arab poet Abu Nuwas was a friend of Haroun al-Rashid). *The Thousand and One Nights* – immortalising the exploits of Aladdin, Ali Baba and Sinbad the Sailor – dates to this period, many of the tales deriving from far afield (Persia, India, Turkey and Greece). The caliphs Haroun and his son often appear in the stories, though some of the main protagonists – such as King Shahryar and the prime minister's daughter Shahrazad (Scheherazade) – carry Persian names.

When Haroun died in 809 the empire was thrown into confusion by a power struggle between his sons, Amin and Mamum. This accelerated the Muslim decline which had already been signalled by the earlier rebellions. Even during the reign of the first caliphs the internal tensions in the Islamic world were plain for all to see. The period of the Ummayads did nothing to heal the divisions at the heart of Islam, and even the world-shaking Arab conquest, though impacting dramatically on all future centuries, seemed only to pile up the forces that in due course would tear apart the empire. The Arabs, fuelled by a potent fanaticism, had exploded out of the desert peninsula to confront ancient empires and sweep across many lands. The sudden ascent of the Arab nation had happened with startling speed; its decline, inevitable and irreversible, would take much longer.

DECLINE

In the autumn of 808 Haroun al-Rashid travelled to Khurasan, where he installed his son, Mamum, as governor. Soon the great caliph Haroun, only forty-five and the greatest emperor of his time, was complaining that he felt tired and unwell; then he found he could no longer stand. On 23 March 809, in a Persian garden outside Tus in Khurasan, Haroun died. Amin was proclaimed caliph in Baghdad – and another Muslim civil war began.

In June 811 Mamum's army inflicted a defeat on the caliph's forces at Rei, and then advanced to Hamadan on the route to Baghdad: the Khurasan forces began their siege of Baghdad on 1 September 812, using mangonels and catapults to bombard the splendid mosques, houses and palaces of Haroun's great capital. At the end of the year-long siege half of Baghdad lay in ruins, the caliph Amin was dead and the rebels had taken the city. But Mamum, now caliph, decided to run the empire from Khurasan: his mother had been a Persian concubine and he was sensitive to his Persian roots. It was not until September 819 that Mamum decided to make his final state entry into Baghdad, after which he made the conqueror of the city, Tahir al-Husain, governor of Khurasan (which before long led to a dynasty in east Persia that was virtually independent of the Baghdad caliphate).

Until his death in 833, Mamum did much to expand the culture of the Baghdad capital. One significant innovation was the so-called House of Wisdom, an institution designed for the translation of foreign works; the Christian Hunain ibn Ishaq was in charge of translating Greek works into Arabic (Aristotle and Plato among the philosophers, Galen and Hippocrates among the physicians). It was via Baghdad that Galen's seven-volume *Anatomy*, translated into Arabic, reached western Europe through Sicily and Spain (Hunain himself produced ten treatises on the eye, the earliest known text of ophthalmology). At the same time the Arabs were making prodigious strides in mathematics and other sciences. They introduced the zero, probably learned from earlier cultures, and established the positional method of computation that came to serve as the basis of modern mathematics ('algebra' and 'algorithm' derive from Arabic roots). The Arabs invented plane and spherical geometry, and also logarithms (this last a corruption of the inventor's name, al-Khawarizmi), with al-Battani discovering the range of trigonometrical relations. Mamum witnessed the building of an astronomical observatory: Arabs accurately computed the circumference of the earth, six hundred years before the European Christians were prepared to admit that it was not flat; and the Arab *Compendium of Astronomy* was in use as a text in Europe up to the sixteenth century. Mamum also saw medical schools opened in Baghdad – Haroun had established the first free public hospital – with doctors and chemists subject to systematic government inspection.[18]

It is sometimes alleged that such cultural progress was one of the reasons for the decline of the Muslim empire: the Arab conquest had succeeded because of the supreme martial qualities of the desert Bedouin, not through the adoption of congenial sedentary activities. In any event, the ethnic richness of the empire could never have existed without the conquest; we may speculate that it was this ethnic mix that made the main contribution to Muslim progress at the height of the empire.

Mamum (813–33) was clearly a great patron of the arts and sciences, but his political competence was less impressive. The caliphate had already lost Khurasan in 820, and Mamum's successor, al-Mutasim (833–42) had little choice but to preside over a progressive disintegration of the empire. In fact the population of Baghdad was now so hostile to the caliphate that Mutasim was forced to transfer the capital to the town of Samarra, lying further north on the Tigris. One of the reasons for the discontent was that the caliph had brought a large number of slave-boys from Turkestan and built them up to constitute the main strength of his local army. A bodyguard of ten thousand Turks had behaved with arrogant excesses towards the people of Baghdad, so generating much hostility and forcing Mutasim to migrate to Samarra. The caliphate did not move back to Baghdad for more than fifty years, until 889. The extended exile in Samarra, sixty-five miles north of the grand capital created by the Abbasids, did not prevent a number of military expeditions.

In 837 the Byzantine emperor Theophilus crossed the Taurus and captured the Muslim town of Zebetra, whereupon the Byzantines carried off more than a thousand Muslim women as slaves and mutilated many men (gouging out eyes and cutting off ears and noses). Mutasim, bent on revenge, crossed the Taurus in 838 with a great army (according to the Arab historian Masoudi, two hundred thousand strong), defeated the Byzantine forces, and took many women and children as slaves. Four years later, the Muslim caliph was dead and the whole imperial structure was set to collapse. Mutasim's successor, his son Wathiq, was cultivated and ineffectual, achieving little in his brief reign. He died in 847, to be followed by his son Mutawakkil (847–61), who tried to curb the growing arrogance of the Turkish soldiery. This led to a mutiny in which Mutawakkil was killed, an event that heralded a further period of anarchy and yet more erosion of the power of the caliphate. The ineffectual caliphs, variously erected and expelled by the army, lost control of the bulk of Persia; and a Turkish soldier, Ahmad Tulun, proclaimed himself master of Egypt and Syria. At the same time a terrible slave rebellion began in Basra and advanced through lower Iraq.

The Zanj (or Zindj) slave revolt shook the entire Muslim world and discouraged thereafter the concentration of large numbers of slaves in one place. The Zanj were black slaves, driven by harsh overseers and in a seemingly hopeless plight; but Muslim missionaries moved into the region, gained converts, and prepared the way for the emergence of the rebel leader, Ali Mohammad (an Iraqi Spartacus), who claimed to be a descendant of the caliph Ali. He sought to restore the purity of Islam, calling himself *Mahdi* (the promised redeemer); his followers called him Master of the Zanj (*Sahib az-Zanj*), and his enemies called him the Rascal (*al-Khabith*). He formed the freed slaves into an army and pillaged the countryside for food and weapons. They captured Basra in 871 and took a number of other towns in southern Iraq, but time and resources favoured the armies of the caliphate: in 883 the caliph's brother finally defeated the Zanj armies, killing Ali Mohammad and his officers.[19]

The Zanj revolt, plus the other reverses in the empire, had exposed the weaknesses of the Abbasid caliphate. Independent states were now being consolidated in Egypt, Persia and elsewhere; and other contemporary revolts, taking inspiration from the Zanj uprising, had merged into a more general rebellion, the Qarmat movement, that helped to shake yet more the structure of the Muslim caliphate.[20] Under the caliph Mutamid some recovery took place: his brother Muwaffak had crushed the slave revolt, the Turkish arrogance had been curbed, and a degree of central authority had been re-established at the heart of the empire. Muktafi (902–8), the last Abbasid ruler for many years, managed to recover Egypt, but with his death the decline of the caliphate continued. The Fatimid anti-caliphate, set up in North Africa in 909, challenged the spiritual credentials of the Abbasids; and in 945 the Buyid clan from north-west Persia seized control in Baghdad – and the political power of the caliphs was finally extinguished. And this was not all. The tenth century also saw an upsurge among the Isma'ilians, the revolutionary wing of the Alid movement: a massive schism broke for generations the spiritual unity of the Muslim *umma*.[21]

If ever there had been the hope of a unified Muslim state, with an agreed polity and a shared religious base, the hope was now shattered. There would always be many races, many disparate political systems and many spiritual exegeses within Islam.

The wild Arab Bedouin, fortified by a fresh millennial creed, had burst out of the Arabian deserts, confronted vast empires and conquered half the known world. In a few short decades the Arab armies had exploded through Mesopotamia to occupy Persia, Armenia, Syria, Egypt, Libya, Tunisia, Morocco and Spain. At its height the Arab conquest ran from Samarkand and the Indian Punjab in the East to Lisbon and Toulouse in the West, and Arabs sailed to occupy Cyprus, Crete, Sicily, Sardinia and Corsica. By 750, little more than a century after the death of Mohammad, at the time when the Abbasids were overthrowing the Ummayad dynasty, the Islamic empire was the greatest civilisation west of China.

The empire, like all empires, could not last. With easy hindsight it is possible to chart the emergence of tensions and dislocations through every historical phase. The early family jealousies, the tribal rivalries, the personal ambitions, the competing ethnic claims in an expanding empire, the many incompatible ingredients poured into the cultural melting-pot – all contributed to the eventual disintegration and dissolution. Separate dynasties gradually broke away from the central control of the caliphate: the Safavids in eastern Persia (867–1495), the Samanids of eastern Khurasan (819–1005), the Tulinids in Egypt (868–905), and the Aghlabids of Tunisia (800–909). But the indelible Islamic influence continued to be felt in all the territories of the erstwhile empire: the people and their rulers in the once subject lands continued with their Muslim devotions, even during the decay and final overthrow of the caliphate. A few areas broke away from Muslim control or retained pockets of religious independence: notably Spain, subject to a Christian reconquest, and various self-sufficient enclaves of Judaism, Christianity and Zoroastrianism elsewhere.

The Arab conquest had succeeded in spreading the frontiers of the Arab nation, now spread over many national states and different political systems; and in conveying Islam to many races and peoples beyond Arabia. The Arabs had begun the spread of Islam; they, with the Persians, had dominated the latter phases of the caliphate. It would soon be the turn of the Turks to impact on the Islamic world.

4 Seljuks, Mongols and Ottomans

END OF THE ABBASIDS

The Abbasids had been the most glorious dynasty in the history of the caliphate; but now, as they came increasingly under foreign sway, their power was dissipated as the empire began to fragment. The Isma'ilians (Ismailis or 'Seveners') had spread throughout the empire their message that the son (Mohammad) of Ismail (the seventh descendant of Ali, the Prophet's son-in-law) would return as the *Mahdi*. Secret cells were formed to spread the word to all the oppressed classes of the Abbasid empire. In consequence, the Isma'ilians were accused of supporting a communist philosophy that included the common ownership of women.[1] The movement was increasingly successful: in 901 the rulers of Yemen were won over, and in 908 the Isma'ilians installed their own caliph in Tunisia, so beginning the Fatimid dynasty (after Fatima, the Prophet's daughter and wife of Ali). In 969 the Fatimids came to power in Egypt and founded Cairo, where they established the al-Azhar University – to become one of the great centres of Islamic learning. Baghdad, now in decline, was briefly occupied by a Fatimid general in 1056.[2]

In the ninth century the Abbasids had developed the practice of importing foreign mercenaries to secure their rule. Such free men were supplemented by Turkish and Circassian slaves specially trained to protect the caliph and his ministers. These guards, known as Mamluks (*mamluk*, 'owned' = slaves), were held to be reliable since they lacked the family ties (and resulting jealousies) that would threaten the dynasty. But as the Mamluks became more powerful their arrogance grew: before long they were operating as a praetorian guard able to make and unmake kings. In 945 the leader of the Baghdad Mamluks took the title *Amir al-Umara* ('Commander of Commanders') to signify his unique role. Now the Abbasids were no more than puppet rulers, destined to survive in name until abruptly crushed by the Mongols in 1258, but lacking all scope for independent action under their foreign masters .

Mamluk armies were periodically despatched from Baghdad to establish a *de facto* Turkish control of neighbouring lands in the name of the Abbasid dynasty. The Byzantine emperor Alexius I appealed in 1094 to Pope

Urban II to send urgent military aid to block the Turkish advance. It was the pope's response to this desperate appeal that precipitated the Crusades.

It was now abundantly clear that the Abbasid caliphs, still nominally in control of the Baghdad regime, were no longer active players on the political scene. They continued to exist as mere 'shadow-caliphs', pathetic imitations of the great Haroun and Mamum, until the time of the Mongol onslaught.[3] But for two centuries it was the Turkish *Amir al-Umara* who held the real reins of power in Baghdad – even to the point that one of the interlopers joined his name to that of the caliph (al-Rahdi, 934–40) in Muslim prayers. Al-Rahdi, eventually killed by the Turkish guard, was regarded by Arab historians as 'the last of the real caliphs': the last to be allowed to deliver the Friday prayer at the Baghdad mosque, the last to be permitted to conduct matters of state. The demise of al-Rahdi saw the death of the last vestiges of power and dignity in the office of caliph.[4] Now the Commander of Commanders (or 'Prince of Princes'), usually unable to speak Arabic, was the *de facto* ruler of the Muslim state.

THE SELJUKS

The Abbasid caliph al-Mustakfi (944–6) surrendered all authority in 945 to Ahmad ibn Buwaih, a Persian tribal chief hostile to the dynasty. Ibn Buwaih had occupied Baghdad unopposed and was quickly proclaimed *Amir al-Umara* and *Muiz al-Dawla* ('one who cherishes the state'). The new master of Baghdad was one of three sons of Abu Shujaa Buwaih, the chief of a warlike horde who claimed descent from the Sassanid kings. It is recorded that even the ready servility of the Abbasid caliph did not satisfy the Persian conqueror. On 29 January 946 Buwaih broke into the palace, dragged the caliph from his throne and across the floor, and then drove him through the streets to the jeers of the soldiers. His eyes were then put out with red-hot irons and he was thrown into jail where he died five years later. Buwaih then installed Mutia as a puppet caliph, reportedly allowing him a daily pittance as pocket money.[5]

So ran the Buwaihid period of Iraqi history which lasted from 945 to 1055. Ibn Buwaih himself died in 967, to be succeeded by his son. He and his successors, aided by the servile Abbasids, ruled Baghdad until the Seljuk Tughril Beg entered the Muslim capital in 1055 and put an end to Buwaihid rule. It had not been an auspicious period. Ibn Buwaih had shown little interest in scholarship or reconstruction, and his son proved a failure. His nephew Adhud al-Dowla had taken power in 975, and succeeded in imposing law and order over much of Iraq and west Persia: he encouraged agriculture, repaired roads and bridges, and rebuilt the cities that had been ravaged by war. But when he died in 983 a fresh civil war broke out. The Buwaihids fought one another throughout the land, plundering the countryside, and doing nothing to protect themselves from an onslaught by another wave of conquerors.

The Ghuzz (sometimes referred to as the Oguz) were a tribe of Turks who grazed their livestock on the steppes north of the Aral Sea: their 'principal occupation' was war.[6] In 1029 they burst into northern Khurasan and began to plunder the land, killing all who tried to oppose them; but when regular forces were sent against them they dispersed, continuing to ravage the territory as marauding bands. In this fashion they continued to migrate towards the west, raping and killing as they went, but vanishing into the night when faced by organised armies. The chiefs of the Ghuzz tribe belonged to the Seljuk family; with two brothers, Tughril Beg and Daud, grandsons of Seljuk, at the head of the marauding bands. In time the groups, bolstered by their predatory successes, became consolidated in larger units and so achieved increasingly significant military victories.

In December 1055 the puppet caliph Quaim begged the Seljuks (who were Sunni Muslims) to end the Shi'ite domination of Baghdad. In due course Tughril Beg arrived on the east bank of the Tigris to find the Buwaihid prince Malik al-Raheem confronting him on the west. When, the next morning, a few bands of Ghuzz soldiers entered the city they were attacked and driven out. Tughril Beg felt strong enough to demand that the young Buwaihid prince report to him immediately to explain what had happened. Malik al-Raheem was arrested and condemned to imprisonment in a Persian fortress; Quaim, having invited Tughril Beg in the first place, now protested but was impotent. The Seljuks moved into the Baghdad palaces, formerly occupied by the Abbasids and the Buwaihids, while the soldiery scattered over the region to plunder, rape and kill.

In 1057 the caliph Quaim, draped in the Prophet's cloak, received Tughril Beg in audience. The caliph had long since abandoned all pretension to secular political power but appeared to have regained some religious prestige. Perhaps Tughril Beg, the untutored warrior from the steppes, was impressed by the descendant of the Prophet's uncle. Tughril Beg died in August 1063, without children and never having learned to read or write. He was succeeded by his nephew Alp Arslan who was immediately plunged into civil war by his brother Qutlumish, who claimed the crown: the brief conflict ended in December 1063 with the death of Qutlumish, whereupon his descendants later established an independent Seljuk sultanate in Asia Minor.

The new Seljuk ruler Alp Arslan was courageous and energetic but, like his uncle, illiterate. With shrewd political insight he arranged marriages between his sons and the daughter of Qara Khan of Trans-Oxania and the daughter of the Sultan of Ghazna: in this way the three principal Turkish dynasties of the time were united, so stabilising the political situation in the East. Elsewhere the Seljuks were soon confronting the Byzantines, keen to protect their frontiers against the new ruler of Baghdad. In a pitched battle on 19 August 1071 at Malazkirt, north of Lake Van, the Byzantine emperor Romanus Diogenes faced a vast Seljuk force of calvary. The Byzantines were eventually shot to pieces by the galloping tribesmen, and the Byzantine emperor was forced to kiss the ground before the barbarian commander. Emperor Romanus was later released for a ransom of five hundred thousand gold dinars: but when he returned to Constantinople, shortly after a palace coup in favour of Michael VII Ducas, he was arrested and then executed. Alp Arslan himself was killed in Persia on 25 November 1072: he had succeeded in refining the administration of the state, had opposed corruption and shown compassion to the poor. His son, Malik Shah, well-educated and interested in scholarship, brought the Seljuk empire to the peak of its greatness. In 1087 the caliph Muqtadi, the grandson of Quaim, married Malik Shah's daughter at a grand ceremony held in Baghdad. In late 1092 Malik Shah returned from a hunting expedition outside Baghdad complaining of a high fever. He never recovered: ten days later, aged thirty-seven, he died. None of his four sons, all still children, could impose order on the empire, and a fresh civil war was stimulated by the competing factions.

The Seljuk leaders, as sultans, had assumed most of the powers of the Muslim caliphs. Now it was the sultans, not the erstwhile Abbasids, who were taking the important decisions on matters of administration and military affairs. The caliphs retained certain religious responsibilities, allowed to comment on matters of Muslim observance, Koranic exegesis, and proper personal behaviour. But the Seljuks had extensively revised the Perso-Islamic administrative framework, injecting Persian culture, and largely eliminating the use of the Arabic language in most cultural and governmental activities. Even where Arabs found themselves in areas with a great Arab majority, they were administered by officials who knew no word of Arabic. The Seljuks also had an interest in pressing religious orthodoxy on the Muslim world: the caliphs enjoyed their reduced areas of religious autonomy but the Seljuks were keen to abolish all Shi'ite influence in religion, politics and military affairs. To this end the Shias were expelled from their posts, and Muslim schools were reorganised to reflect the prevailing orthodoxy. The proponents of Sufi mysticism were allowed to

advertise views regarded as consistent with the wishes of the new establishment, and Sufi orders were encouraged all over the empire as a means
of countering the enduring influence of the Shi'ite polemicists.

The Seljuks had effectively brought to an end the great age of the Arab
nation. But the Seljuks too, like all the previous historic conquerors, had
no permanent hold on power. There were inevitable fractures in the
empire, competing factions and civil wars, and unexpected threats that
would soon burst over the frontiers. After the rule of Alp Arslan Malik the
long Seljuk decline began. The last great Seljuk ruler was the sultan Sancar,
son of Malik Shah who was soon to be faced with the Mongol hordes
exploding into the Middle East: with the death of Sancar in 1157 there was
little left to stand in their way. A new caliph, al-Nazir (1180–1225) had
risen in Baghdad and for a brief period re-established some of the authority
of the old caliphate: the last ties with the Seljuks were broken, and al-Nazir
managed to suppress Turkish dominance in some parts of Iraq and to
discourage the Ismaili Assassins from further terrorist attacks (in return
for recognition of their autonomy). He continued the Seljuk support for
the Sufi mystic orders and for Muslim orthodoxy. But with the death of
al-Nazir and the end of the Seljuks, the way was open to the Mongols.

The Seljuk supremacy had effectively come to an end in 1194, when
the caliph al-Nazir, a member of the Turkish dynasty of the Khwarizm
Shahs, defeated the ruling sultan in Baghdad. So ended yet another significant phase in the history of the region, with the name of the Seljuks
remembered for many conquests and some cultural achievements. They are
also remembered not least because Salah el-Din (Saladin), the great liberator of Jerusalem, the mighty conqueror of the Christian Crusaders, was
himself a Seljuk.

IMPACT OF THE CRUSADES

When the Crusades were launched in 1094 they were advertised as a holy
war (a Christian *jihad*) against Islam, but it was soon clear that a secondary
task was the determination to establish European control over the riches of
the Middle East and beyond. The Crusades lasted for two centuries and for
the most part comprised a struggle between the Christian Europeans and
the Muslim Seljuks. By the twelfth century the Turks had spread through
the region, establishing local sultans or ruling through proxies, such as the
Baghdad caliphs. The indigenous Arab populations had been largely squeezed
out of the centres of power, and now it was left to the Turks to defend the

Fertile Crescent and Asia Minor. There had already been a number of Christian successes against the Muslims: Toledo had been taken in 1085 at the start of the Christian reconquest of Spain; the Genoese took the Arab base of Mahdia in Tunisia in 1087; and the Muslims were expelled from Sicily in 1091. The papacy was pleased by these early victories: there was no difficulty in reconciling the words of the Prince of Peace with the martial exploits of the feudal armies. There was already alarm at the Turkish threat to the Byzantines, and now circumstances were conspiring to encourage a holy onslaught against the Muslim and all his works.

When the Byzantine emperor Alexius made urgent calls for military help to block the advance of the Turks through Asia Minor, Pope Urban II quickly saw how this frantic appeal could be exploited. At the Council of Clermont in 1095 he demanded the launching of a military expedition – not so much to aid the Byzantines as to evict the Muslims from Palestine, the cradle of the Christian religion. The appeal was immensely successful. Its first fruit was the People's Crusade, a vast rabble of men, women and children that fought and looted its way to Constantinople. Some twenty thousand Christian devotees were ferried across the Bosphorus, to be massacred on 21 October 1096 by the Turks near Nicomedia. At the same time four great Christian lords were heeding Urban's message and forming their own armies to confront the Muslim: substantial military contingents, built out of tenants and feudatories, were headed by Godfrey de Bouillon, Duke of Lorraine and of Lower Lotharingia (modern Belgium); Robert, Duke of Normandy, the eldest son of William the Conqueror; Raymond de Saint Gilles, Count of Toulouse and Marquis of Provence; and Bohemond, Count of Apulia, of the Norman House of Hauteville.

At the beginning the forces were fired with much enthusiasm, stimulated as much by Christian zeal as by the prospect of plunder and riches in the East. A modern Lebanese writer comments on the character of the Christian advance: '. . . the Franj* crossed the Bosporus and, despite a blazing summer sun, advanced along the coast. Wherever they passed, they were heard to proclaim that they had come to exterminate the Muslims, although they were also seen to plunder many a Greek church on their way.'[7] The promiscuous nature of the Christian onslaught soon became apparent: the Franj 'passed through several villages, all of them Christian, and commandeered the harvests, which had just been gathered, mercilessly massacring those peasants who tried to resist. Young children were even said to have been burned alive.'[8]

---

*The Muslims regarded all West Europeans as Franks (Franj).

The Crusaders established a series of feudal states along the Syrian coast and in Palestine, aided in their efforts by divisions among the Seljuks and by the seeming indifference to events shown by the Cairo Fatimids and the Baghdad Seljuks. But despite their early successes the balance of power in the region did not favour the Crusaders. It had seemed that the Christian forces had swept all before them, leaving a legacy of hatred throughout the Muslim world that would endure over the centuries. There had been much needless slaughter, often in cold blood. The author of the celebrated *Gesta Francorum* tells how in Jerusalem the Crusaders 'killed everyone whether male or female' – even, the day after the main massacre, slaughtering a group of Muslims who had been granted sanctuary.[9] It was at this time that the crusaders began equating Muslims with 'filth'[10] – a racist ploy still evident in the modern world.*

The Egyptian Fatimids were now becoming increasingly concerned at the Frankish threat, and so decided to seek assistance from other Muslim forces. Rival wazirs in Cairo approached Nuraddin and King Amalric of Jerusalem with the request that they send military aid, Nuraddin sent Shirkuh and his (Shirkuh's) nephew Saladin to Egypt; Shirkuh later reported that Egypt was a country 'without men, and with a precarious and contemptible government'.[11] The caliph Adid accepted Shirkuh as a new wazir and when

---

*Racism has often stimulated repressive and imperialist impulses in Western society. Thomas Jefferson, in common with many of his white friends, regarded blacks as hybrids between white men and apes. In the US conquest of the Philippines, begun in 1898, 'goo-goo hunts' were organised to exterminate the indigenous population, just as in America's later Asiatic wars the enemy was variously depicted as 'monkey meat' (Admiral William F. Halsey), 'Chinks', 'slopes', 'dinks' and 'gooks'. Nelson Mandela condemned the selective Western response to the 'brown skinned' Iraqis, and Noam Chomsky noted that the world campaign against Saddam was the 'world minus its darker faces'. In the US and Britain, Arabs were harassed by the authorities for clearly racist reasons (see, for example, Mowahid Shah, 'The FBI and the civil rights of Arab-Americans', *ADC Issues*, 5, American-Arab Anti-Discrimination Committee, Washington, DC; Patricia Wynn Davies, 'We gave refuge and then locked them up', *The Independent*, London, 1 February 1991; Julie Flint, 'Quiet changes in the rules bar Iraqis', *The Observer*, London, 3 March 1991). The day after the 1991 Gulf War began, a man rang the offices of the American-Arab Anti-Discrimination Committee to say: 'I'm going to be down there in fifteen minutes with a high-powered rifle to shoot you A-rabs' (this example and many others supplied by Jamal Kheiry of the Committee). A professor at California State University, Sacramento, declared to his class: 'All you have to know about Arabs is that they lie, cheat and start rumours.' The Anti-Discrimination Committee publishes a 'hate crimes chronology' to record and publicise the numerous instances of harassment of American-Arabs in the United States: telephone threats, rocks thrown through windows, employment harassment, school harassment (children routinely depicted as 'sand niggers', 'camel jockeys', etc.), letter threats, vandalism, police harassment, assault, shootings, death threats, arson, etc. Such circumstances, little advertised in the West, were an important element in the cultural climate of the 1991 Gulf War and the subsequent enduring punishment of the Iraqi people.

he died suddenly in 1169 Saladin was appointed his successor. In 1171 Saladin felt strong enough to abolish the Fatimid caliphate and to declare himself ruler of Egypt; and when, three years later, Nuraddin died, Saladin took over Syria. He was now in a position to build up the necessary power to drive out the Franks.

Saladin's brother Turanshah had conquered the Nubians; and Saladin himself repulsed Franks, Assassins and Sicilian Normans in their massive naval attack on Alexandria. The Byzantines were defeated at Myriocephalon in Asia Minor by the Seljuks of Rum in 1176, and there were further divisions among the European powers. Venice and Genoa were content to trade in Egypt, a circumstance that led Saladin to boast that Franks were selling him arms to use against Franks. Saladin was now in an increasingly strong position: accepted by orthodox Muslims, he was in effective control of the governments of Egypt, Syria and Iraq and now in a position to challenge the Christian control of Jerusalem.

In 1187 Saladin crushed King Guy's army at Hattin and overran Palestine in a few weeks, a decisive victory that horrified the European powers. There were fresh sermons and fresh military preparations, but little was to be accomplished. A new Crusade was launched, encouraged by Richard the Lionheart of England, Philip II of France and the Byzantine emperor Barbarossa, but this time there were few gains. Saladin had proved too much for the Christian forces and the peace of Ramla in 1192 did no more than consolidate the Muslim victories. It is recorded that Richard the Lionheart, doubtless frustrated by his failures, had three thousand Muslim captives massacred when negotiations with Saladin broke down. The Christian warriors then carefully examined the entrails of the corpses for swallowed gold.[12] Richard then sailed for England, and in November 1192 Saladin made a grand state entry in Damascus. Now his empire included substantial parts of North Africa, Syria, Kurdistan, Egypt and much of Iraq, and there were signs that he had further ambitions: a contemporary Arab historian, Ibn al-Athir, wrote that Saladin was considering widening his empire to include the whole of Iraq and Persia. But a few months later, on 3 March 1193, he died in Damascus.

The Crusades impacted on the Muslim world in many different ways. At the most obvious level many Muslim states were drained of men and material resources in a sometimes desperate effort to repel the Christian invaders: such military demands have often distorted and crippled national economies. And there is also a bitter legacy. It is nicely documented that the historical Muslims were generally tolerant of Jews and Christians (the *dhimmis*, the people of the two other monotheistic creeds), but the Crusades helped to erode this traditional tolerance. There can be no doubt that the

Muslims were brutally treated by the Christian occupying forces. The dreadful testimony of Raymund of Aquiles on the conquest of Jerusalem is only one of many pieces of evidence: 'Wonderful sights were to be seen. Some of our men . . . cut off the heads of their enemies; others shot them with arrows . . . others tortured them longer by casting them into the flames. Piles of heads, hands and feet were to be seen in the streets . . . men rode in blood up to their knees and bridle reins . . . it was a just and splendid judgement of God that this place should be filled with the blood of the unbelievers . . .'. It is useful to remember that the merciless crusades were the first encounters that many Muslims, including Arabs, had with the agents and representatives of Christendom. We are reminded: 'For the Arabs, who of all people have perhaps the most lively feelings of their own history, the aggressive invasion of the crusaders is still a vivid popular myth.'[13]

This all became part of the Arab perceptual frame, the complex fabric of cultural memory used to aid fresh comprehensions. At the time of the first Crusade the Muslim world was more tolerant and more intellectual than medieval Christianity. The Muslim warrior and gentleman Usama ibn Munqidh (1095–1188) comments in his memoirs (in *An Appreciation of the Frankish Character*) that Allah sees the Franks 'as animals possessing the virtues of courage and fighting, but nothing else; just as animals have only the virtues of strength and carrying loads'.[14]

Thus the long-term impact of the Crusades was such as to cause all later generations of Arabs to mediate their perceptions in particular characteristic ways, to absorb information via cultural filters – as do all people in all societies. Saladin remains a historic hero for Muslims, with the inevitable corollary that all Western designs and intentions should be prudently viewed with suspicion. This was one long-term consequence of Byzantine panics and papal appeals, the urgent declamations that led to two centuries of Christian aggression in Muslim lands.[15]

The Crusades also had more immediate consequences. The Muslim world, already in decline, was further weakened. One short-term effect of the Christian onslaught was to make it harder for the Muslims to resist the next devastating foreign invasion. The Mongol hordes were already at the borders of the weary Islamic world.

MONGOL ONSLAUGHT

Soon the Muslim states were to experience the most devastating nomadic onslaught of them all, one that almost engulfed Islam completely. We are in no doubt about the enormity of this invasion: for the Muslim world the Mongols represented a 'disaster',[16] a 'catastrophe'[17] and a 'scourge'.[18] The great chronicler Ibn al-Athir thus begins his account of the Tartar aggression into the lands of Islam:

> For some years I continued averse from mentioning this event, deeming it so horrible that I shrank from recording it . . . To whom, indeed, can it be easy to write the death-blow of Islam and the Muslims . . . O would that my mother had not born me, or that I had died and become a forgotten thing ere this befell . . . this thing involves the description of the greatest catastrophe and the most dire calamity . . . which befell all men generally, and the Muslims in particular . . . since God Almighty created Adam . . . the most grievous calamity recorded was that Nebuchadnezzar inflicted on the children of Israel by his slaughter of them; and what was Jerusalem in comparison to the countries which these accursed miscreants destroyed, each city of which was double the size of Jerusalem? . . . those whom they massacred in a single city exceeded all the children of Israel . . . these [Tartars] spared none, slaying women and men and children, ripping open pregnant women and killing unborn babes. . . .[19]

This was the mission of Genghis Khan: to extend the Mongol empire to the outermost limits, and to leave misery and desolation in his wake. He is said to have declared: 'All cities must be razed, so that the world may once again become a great steppe in which Mongol mothers will suckle free and happy children.'[20] This was the task: to abolish the hated cities and their sedentary occupants, so that free Tartar* nomads would be able to range without encumbrance across the whole of creation. In pursuing his quest Genghis Khan rocked Islam to its foundations and succeeded in extinguishing the weakened caliphate once and for all.

Fresh divisions within the Muslim world were developing, dislocations and enmities that would prevent any unified response to the Mongol threat. Takash had become the Khwarizm shah in 1172, whereupon he occupied Khurasan, crushed the Ghuzz, and in 1194 killed the last Seljuk sultan, Tughril II. Khwarizmian power was now extending into western Persia, threatening a confrontation with the Abbasid caliph, Nazir. Takash soon showed his hostility to Nazir's efforts to consolidate Abbasid religious and

---

*These nomads were called *Tatar* by the Arabs and Persians. The European *Tartar* was an attempt to connect them with Tartarus, following their hellish deeds and infernal cruelty.

political power: he demanded that Caliph Nazir recognise him as the Bagh-dad sultan. Nazir refused and Takash died in 1200, leaving the Abbasids and the Khwarizmians in a state of confrontation. Takash's son Mohammad (1200–20) extended the Khwarizmian control throughout Persia, and with the caliph still refusing to donate the sultanate Mohammad resolved to abolish the Abbasids. In 1217, at a time when Genghis Khan was contem-plating fresh conquests, Mohammad declared Nazir deposed and marched on Baghdad. But the winter checked his advance and there was disruption among his own forces: his army was largely composed of disaffected Turkish slaves, and the leading Muslim clerics were disturbed by his hostil-ity to the caliphate. Then an event occurred that would precipitate the earthquake throughout the Muslim world. A reckless governor at the frontier post of Utrar arrested and then executed a caravan of merchants whom he branded as spies: the merchants had come from the dominions of Genghis Khan.

In February 1220 Genghis Khan and his Mongols, supported by troops from subject Turkish states, crossed the Jaxartes and stormed the great cities of Bukhara and Samarkand. The Khwarizmian shah Mohammad (Ala al Deen Mohammad) quickly appreciated the growing danger, perceived the strength of the forces ranged against him, and ordered his own armies to avoid pitched battles. Many of the towns were well fortified and it was assumed that a series of lengthy sieges would eventually weary the Mongol invaders. But Genghis had brought with him a body of Chinese engineers, and the Mongol siege tactics proved highly effective. The two great cities fell and Mohammad fled to an island in the Caspian, to die in misery a few weeks later. His son Jalal al-Din resolved to resist the Mongol invasion and achieved some successes, on one occasion routing a Mongol detachment sent to capture him, but then he was forced to flee, only just managing to save his life by swimming across the Indus.

Whenever a city was taken by the Mongols the pattern was the same: mangonels were used to bombard the walls, after which slaves were forced to lead the assault. Then all the inhabitants were marshalled outside the city walls, the women to be raped and thereafter all the people – men, women and children – to be butchered. The town was then comprehensively looted, before being burned to the ground. For a period of three years this devastating policy was extended over a vast area of east Persia. The inhab-itants of the region had developed a sophisticated civilisation over a period of a thousand years before the Arab conquest in the seventh century, an event that led to a merging of cultures to create a wealth of Perso-Arabic innovations – in literature and science, in art and civil engineering. Now, over a prodigious area, the gardens and irrigation systems, the libraries and palaces, whole cities lay in ruins, depopulated, an almost universal desolation. The great Persian historian Ala ai Deen al-Juwaini wrote (in his *History of the Conqueror of the World*): 'In the Muslim countries devastated by Genghis Khan, not one in a thousand of the inhabitants survived . . . If from now until the day of the Resurrection, nothing hindered the natural increase of the population, it could never reach one-tenth of its density before the Mongol conquest.' Genghis Khan was satisfied with the destruction he had wrought. He returned to Mongolia in 1225 – to die, aged about sixty, in 1227 while fighting in Kansu in western China.

On his deathbed Genghis Khan divided up the Mongol empire between his four sons: Juji (given the country north of the Caspian), Jagatai (the land east of the Jaxartes), Ogotai (the Imil valley), and Tului (the Mongol homeland around Lake Baikal). As a separate endowment, the conquered lands of Persia and China were given to Ogotai. But it was not that easy to secure peace among the various competing Mongol factions, and soon wars of succession flared up that gave the Muslim world an unexpected respite; it was soon to end. The third son Ogotai had been selected by Genghis as supreme khan, a choice that was resented among the other members of the family. This led to a degree of factionalism that hampered further Mongol ambitions for conquest. The Abbasid caliph Mustansir (1226–42) managed to repulse Mongol invaders on several occasions, though such successes were soon to be overtaken by a new unity among the Mongol forces. On 1 July 1251, Mangu, the son of Tului, was elected by the tribal council to serve as the supreme khan, a decision that united Jagatai and Ogotai against the family of Mangu. But such divisions did not prevent a grouping of Mongol forces to invade Iraq, Syria and Egypt: Mangu's brother, Hulagu, was despatched to the West to extend further the Mongol dominion.

In March 1257, he reached Hamadan, whereupon he sent an ultimatum to the caliph Mustasim (Mustansir's son and successor) in Baghdad, demanding that he come to pay homage. It was impossible for Mustasim (1242–58) to accede to any such demand: the caliph, the proper ruler of the world, could never pay homage to an animist heathen. Mustasim delayed, hoping in desperation that the Muslim princes would come to the aid of their spiritual leader, but Hulagu was not prepared to wait. On 18 January 1258 the vast Mongol army reached Baghdad and immediately deployed large gangs of slave prisoners to build a breastwork and ditch around the city. On 30 January the mangonels began a massive bombardment of Baghdad and within three days the defences were in ruins. At the same time the Mongol engineers were breaking the irrigation dykes to flood the city; many of the panic-stricken inhabitants were drowned in the rising floodwaters. Then the Mongol forces began mounting the shattered defensive walls and Mustasim, now in despair, sent the Nestorian Patriarch to Hulagu to offer a surrender. The Mongol khan ordered Mustasim to come in person to his camp, with his family and all his retinue, and to yield up all his treasure.

The caliph's army was instructed to assemble on the plain outside Baghdad, where all were massacred. Then the inhabitants of the city were told to assemble, when they too were shot and hacked to death, their corpses piled in heaps. The Baghdad palaces, mosques and colleges were then given over to the Mongol soldiery, to plunder at will and to slaughter any surviving Muslims still struggling to hide in the rubble. It is estimated that some eight hundred thousand men, women and children were killed over a period of days in the streets and houses and on the plain outside the city. Mustasim and his sons were taken to a village outside Baghdad, there to be killed in cold blood. It is recorded that in view of the Mongol superstition about shedding the blood of sovereign princes, they were first rolled in carpets before being trampled under the hoofs of Moslem horses (in one version of this account the caliph Mustasim was first sewn up in a sack; in another account the caliph was strangled to death). In such a miserable fashion the Abbasid caliphate was finally extinguished in 1258, and all the glories of medieval Baghdad were reduced to ruins.

The entire Muslim world was horrified to learn of the destruction of Baghdad, while the Christians of the East delighted in the sacking of the great Muslim city – in the spirit of the 'Babylon is fallen!' declaration of the New Testament Revelation (in the merciless destruction of Baghdad a few Christians had been spared). Hulagu had marched off, heavily laden with the Muslim treasures than had been accumulated over five centuries; and soon his armies were in Syria. In January 1260 the Mongols overran Aleppo and the ancient city was forced to suffer all the massacres, plunder and devastation that had ravaged Baghdad. The Ayyubid kings of the various Syrian cities were unable to stem the tide and soon Hulagu was at the gates of Damascus. This great Muslim centre gave in without a fight. Three Christian leaders – the Mongol commander Kitbuga, the King of Armenia and the Frankish Count Bohemund of Antioch – rode in the streets, forcing the Muslims to bow to the cross. Christian opinion was divided (the neutral position of the Acre Franks helped the Muslims), but it was easy to represent the Mongol campaign as an anti-Muslim crusade, 'a pendant to the Frankish expeditions'.

The Muslim world was then helped by a fortuitous event. In 1260 Hulagu received news that his brother, the khan Mangu, had died in China. This meant that again the Mongol empire was faced with the prospect of conflict over the succession. Hulagu favoured his other brother Kublai, but his cousin Berke – the Mongol commander of Russia, who had embraced Islam and was horrified at Hulagu's destruction of the Baghdad caliphate – was supporting a separate claimant. Hulagu also felt threatened by his cousin's supposed ambition to create an independent western Mongol empire; and so he quickly moved the bulk of his army to the Caucasus, leaving only a light force in Syria. The Mamluks, aware of these favourable developments, raised a Muslim army and advanced under the sultan Kutuz to confront the Mongols, now led by Kitbuga, at Ain Jalut ('Goliath's Spring') near Nazareth. This was one of the world's historic battles: after furious fighting in September 1260 Kitbuga was killed and the great sway that the ancestors of Genghis Khan had held over the world was broken forever. At last, after such dreadful carnage and destruction, the Mongol shadow had been lifted.

The Mongols had destroyed a weakened caliphate that had still served as a focus for Islam and Muslim identity: with the decay of the empire the religious role of the caliphate took on a growing significance. The glory days of the Umayyads and the early Abbasids had long since passed into history, but the memory of those times has never faded from Muslim culture. For more than seven hundred years, since 1258, there has been no single focus within Islam for religious and political loyalty; though in the modern world there is talk, from time to time, of reviving the caliphate as a symbol of Muslim unity. And where would it be based: Cairo, Tripoli, Baghdad, Damascus, Mecca, Medina, Riyadh, Teheran, Ankara, Jakarta? The futility of the dream should not be allowed to obscure the importance of the great phases of historic Islam.

OTTOMAN CONQUEST

The Ottomans were a fierce Turkish warrior tribe that originated in the central and eastern Asian grasslands, the homelands also of the Scythians, Huns and Mongols. Like the Mongols they were great horsemen, and their skill with the bow gave them considerable military prowess. Many of the tribes were a racial mixture, some resembling the Chinese in skin colour and facial features, others the Caucasians of the southern steppe. In their westward trek in the seventh century the Ottoman Turks began to penetrate the borders of the Middle East, and within three hundred years they had become the dominant force in what was later Soviet Central Asia. In contact with the fringes of the Muslim empire some of the Ottomans adopted Islam and the caliphs increasingly relied on Turkish Mamluks ('slaves') to consolidate their power. The Mamluks established an Egyptian dynasty, defeated the Mongols, and eventually drove the residual crusaders from the Middle East. By 1366 the Ottomans had expelled the Byzantines from Anatolia and made Edirne (Adrianople) their new capital in the southern Balkans. Constantinople, the Byzantine capital, finally fell to the Ottoman forces on 29 May 1453 and Sultan Fatih ('Conqueror') Mehmet II occupied what was now the capital of the Muslim empire of the Ottomans. The scene was set for further Turkish conquests.

The Mongol conqueror Tamerlane (Timur, c. 1336–1405), a self-proclaimed descendant of Genghis Khan, had taken the throne of Samarkand by 1369 and thereafter led his Turks and Mongols in a series of expeditions that vastly expanded his empire. In one great campaign he fought against Persia and in 1387 had reached the Euphrates river. He then conquered the region of the Caucasus and invaded India in 1398, after which he again turned westward to attack the Egyptian Mamluks in Syria and to defeat the Ottoman Turks in Asia Minor. It was at this time, in 1401, that Tamerlane became yet another conqueror to attack Baghdad and to take the city. He died before launching a planned invasion of China, and his vast empire was divided among his heirs, the Timurids. After the death of Tamerlane's son Shah Rokh (1405–47), who managed to unite much of the eastern part of the empire, the whole region began to disintegrate into local dynasties (including what was to become the Mogul empire in India).

This turbulent period also saw a Persian national revival under the Safavids, a dynasty (1501–1736) founded by Ismail I who conquered most of Persia and added much of Iraq to his empire. In 1508 Shah Ismail took Baghdad and then Mosul, and the bulk of Iraq was united with his Persian conquests. Soon, however, the Safavids were forced to confront the expanding Ottoman empire. From its secure Anatolian heartland the Ottoman state was now spreading over three continents: Asia, Europe and Africa. Sultan Selim I, in a highly successful campaign (1516–17), had captured Syria, Palestine and Egypt; and soon his great successor, Suleiman the Magnificent (1520–66) was to invade Iraq as far as the borders of Persia and also penetrate into central Europe, adding Hungary and other regions to the empire.

Central and southern Iraq, including Basra and Baghdad, were still in the hands of the Safavids – who were even attempting to establish the Shia heresy in place of the orthodox Islam in the region that had once been the very heartland of the Abbasid caliphate. Orthodox teachers were persecuted and many Sunni shrines were desecrated, including those of the revered

Muslims, Abu Hanifa and Abdul-Kadir Gilani. Suleiman, as leader of the orthodox Muslim world, could not remain indifferent to these activities; and in any case there were good economic reasons for an attack on the Safavids of Iraq. He believed that the Safavid control of both Iraq and Persia had hampered trade between the Far East and Europe, while the Portuguese had helped to block the trade routes through a Middle East that was now largely under Ottoman control. So in 1534 Sultan Suleiman, at the height of his powers, decided to punish the Safavids in Iraq. So would begin a Turkish Ottoman occupation of Iraq that would continue, with one brief interruption (1624–38), up to modern times.

In April 1534 Suleiman despatched the Grand Wazir, Ibrahim Pasha to commence the conquest of Iraq. Thus within three months of the signing of the peace treaty with Austria, Ibrahim was marching out of Aleppo to confront the Safavids. At Tabriz a second army was brought up to support Ibrahim's force, Suleiman himself now taking control of the Ottoman armies. He then moved into Persia but it was a difficult journey: the winter was harsh and the Ottomans lost many men and horses and were forced to abandon guns, wagons and other equipment. This led Suleiman to focus his attention on Iraq, with its more congenial climate, and the Ottoman forces were led over the Zagros mountains and on to the Mesopotamian plains. At last the exhausted army reached Baghdad and what was left of the once great city was taken with little opposition. In fact the approach of the Suleiman force had encouraged the city's Sunni religious leaders to lead a popular uprising that massacred most of the Shia soldiers and religious heads that had been oppressing them. Most of Iraq fell to Suleiman within months, though parts of southern Iraq, including Basra, remained in the hands of local Bedouins, until in 1538 this region too was conquered. The threat of a Safavid advance through Iraq into Syria had been removed, and the lands of the old caliphate had been brought under the sultan's control. The orthodox Islam of the Sunnis had been rescued from Shi'ite persecution. Now Suleiman's supremacy in the Muslim world had been confirmed.[21]

Suleiman made a state entry into Baghdad and decided to spend the winter in the city, restoring the orthodox institutions that had been emasculated by the Safavids and building the characteristic Ottoman tax and administrative system in the newly-acquired territories. The Safavids managed to retain control in Azerbaijan, a few enclaves in eastern Iraq, and parts of the southern Caucasus; but their power had been drastically curtailed and Ottomans were secure enough to introduce a regular system of administration throughout the conquered land.

When Suleiman died in 1566 the empire soon began to decay under a series of vicious and incompetent sultans. In 1619 Bekr (the Su Bashi), a captain of the élite corps of Janissaries in Baghdad, staged a revolt and made himself master of the city. An Ottoman army was quickly despatched to re-establish order whereupon Bekr invited Shah Abbas I of Persia to take over Baghdad. Alarmed at this development the sultan offered Bekr the governorship of the city if he remained loyal to the empire, with the result that when Abbas arrived at Baghdad Bekr tried to refuse him entry. But then Bekr's son Mohammad betrayed him and opened the gates to the Persian army. Thus Abbas took Baghdad on 12 January 1624 and set about slaughtering all the Sunni inhabitants of the city; Bekr himself was tortured to death. Abbas also killed, by boiling in oil, all the Janissaries who had supported him, on the grounds that if they had betrayed the Ottomans they could just as well betray him.[22] The Persians then advanced through the rest of Iraq, the Safavids pushing westwards into Anatolia, with only the regions of Mosul and Basra remaining in Ottoman hands. Soon however, with the inevitable swing of the pendulum, the sultans would regain control of Baghdad and the rest of Iraq.

There was an immense popular reaction in Istanbul to the fall of Iraq; the sultan Murat IV was able to survive only by juggling the political leadership, but his position was weakened. In 1625 the Ottomans again tried to retake Baghdad, but while they were able to defeat the Safavid army and lay siege to the city they were compelled to retire when Persian reinforcements arrived. On 26 March 1626 the Ottoman siege of Baghdad was lifted, but the sultan managed to retain northern Iraq, a suitable base for further campaigns against the Persian masters of Baghdad. In November 1638 Murat, at the head of a great army, reached the Iraqi capital; the Safavids put up a strong defence, lasting from 15 November to 25 December, but then the Persian governor was forced to surrender and all the Persians in the city were slaughtered. The Ottomans then sent troops over much of Mesopotamia to suppress the Sunni Muslims, wherever they could be found, and on 17 May 1639 a definitive peace was established between the Safavids and the Ottomans, resulting in the drawing up of borders between Iraq and Persia that have survived with little change up to modern times. Now the Ottomans had secured their hold on Iraq and the unimpeded trade routes to the Persian Gulf were restored. Murat returned to Istanbul and died soon afterwards on 8 February 1640 – of gout, sciatica or excessive drinking.[23]

There now began the long period of Ottoman decline, a process that was to last for the greater part of three centuries. The empire had been at its height under Suleiman* but after his death there were few territorial gains and the fragility of the Ottoman state became increasingly apparent. The war with Venice (1645–64) exposed serious weaknesses in the empire; and soon afterwards the Russo-Turkish war (1676–81) resulted in most of the Turkish Ukraine being lost to Russia. The long slow decay had begun, but it would take the First World War in the twentieth century to finally extinguish the Ottoman empire.

OTTOMAN DECLINE

Many factors contributed to the decline of the Ottoman state, not least the encroachments of other powers, problems with the dynastic succession, and the characteristic problems of administering a vast empire. The harem system ensured that there would be sufficient contenders to guarantee the survival of the dynasty, but this arrangement has also been seen as generating an embarrassment of riches: many factions competed for power and the internal unity of the state was weakened. Sons contended with one another for the throne and on occasion the ambitious offspring did not wait for the death of the monarch. Thus Selim I (1512–20) overthrew his own father, Beyazit II (1481–1512), a coup that created further dissensions in the royal family. Once a man had been declared sultan he would contemplate the task of securing his power base: his brothers may be bought off by being offered key government posts, or they may be murdered, an abrupt means of removing opposition elements. In the fifteenth century fratricide among the rulers of the Ottoman state was an acknowledged part of *realpolitik*; and the practice also enjoyed theoretical acclaim. A *kanun* issued by Fatih Mehmet not only allowed such an action but proclaimed the practice desirable as a means of avoiding civil strife.

It was later decided that the oldest son of the sultan would inherit the throne – a device that seems obvious, if one needs a monarchy at all, to modern observers. The sons of the reigning sultan were maintained on the palace premises, each granted separate quarters called *kafes* ('cages') in the harem sector of the royal establishment. Here the sons would employ both black and white eunuchs to guard the women, a convention that seems to have been imported from Mesopotamia.[24] This arrangement, ensuring that

---

*At his height Suleiman ruled all or part of Hungary, Yugoslavia, Albania, Greece, Bulgaria, Rumania, the Ukraine, the Crimea, Turkey, Iran, Iraq, Syria, Lebanon, Jordan, Egypt, Libya, Tunisia and Algeria.

the likely heirs to the throne were cloistered in their own secluded premises, guaranteed that no sultan from the seventeenth century onwards would have any knowledge of government affairs until he took the throne. Thus the habitual contact with the women of the harem did little to prepare sultans for affairs of state, and the harem itself came to play a significant role in government matters, particularly in the appointment of state officials.[25] This in turn led to a degree of corruption that infected government and had adverse effects on the functioning of the military establishment. From the seventeenth century onwards the sultans found themselves in charge of vast undisciplined forces, far removed from the great ordered forces that had originally secured the frontiers of the empire. With the growing corruption at the heart of the empire many of the distant regions became semi-autonomous, paying tribute only when threatened by Turkish armies, and so adding to the pressures on the state. At the same time the European nation-states were growing in power and influence, by the end of the seventeenth century presenting a multifaceted challenge to Ottoman security.

In Iraq the Ottomans relied on the pasha of Baghdad to maintain the subjugation of the desert Arabs, an increasing disruptive faction through the region. In 1694 the Arabs succeeded in capturing Basra, which was only restored to the sultan after a Persian onslaught on the region. The desert Arabs and the semi-nomadic Kurds were also raiding the caravan routes between Aleppo and Baghdad, so further hampering Ottoman trade. The governors of Sidon and Damascus still struggled to maintain the flow of taxes to Istanbul, despite the growing resentment of the local tribes and religious groups; some areas, such as Mount Lebanon, achieved virtual autonomy within the empire. On many fronts, despite occasional advances, the Ottomans were in retreat.

In 1704 Hasan Pasha Mustafa, the son of a calvary officer (Mustafa Beg), was appointed governor of Baghdad; and for a period of nineteen years he waged endless battles against the desert tribes, managing in such a fashion to maintain the nominal power of the sultan. But in 1723 the Afghan chief Mahmud Khan Ghilzai dethroned the last Safavid shah and proclaimed himself Shah of Persia, whereupon the sultan, hoping to benefit from the resulting confusion, declared war on Persia. Hasan Pasha was thereby despatched with his Baghdad army to invade Persia, but died in the middle of the campaign. His son, Ahmad Pasha, continued with the military expedition for a futile four years, after which peace was agreed on the basis of the pre-war frontier. In January 1733 Mahmud's successor, Nadir Quli Khan, invaded Iraq and lay siege to Baghdad, reducing the city to starvation by July of the same year. The Ottomans, perceiving the catastrophe that faced their Iraqi territories, despatched Topal Othman Pasha (known as

Othman the Lame) to relieve Baghdad. By that time Othman was old and crippled with wounds and had to be carried on a litter over the thousand miles from Istanbul to Kirkuk. On the plain, north-east of Baghdad, Nadir Quli Khan awaited the arrival of the old commander.

On the morning of 19 July 1733 Topal Othman mounted his horse for the first time in the whole lengthy campaign, whereupon his French doctor, Jean Nicodème commented: 'I saw him riding along like a young man, sword in hand, with animated countenance and sparkling eyes.' The battle lasted for a full day. Fifty thousand Persian horsemen drove the Turkish cavalry from the field and two thousand Kurdish infantry deserted the Ottomans in the midst of the conflict. Othman called up Janissaries as reinforcements and eventually the Persian infantry was overcome. Nadir Quli Khan, who had had two horses shot from under him, fled back across the frontier to Persia, and Baghdad was relieved. When the Turkish soldiers entered the city they found that some hundred thousand people had died of starvation. Nadir spent three months raising a fresh Persian army, while Othman's desperate appeals to Istanbul yielded no reinforcements. On 26 October 1733 battle was again joined, Othman was shot dead on the field, and virtually the entire Turkish army was exterminated; but this time Baghdad was not taken. Nadir rushed home to quell risings in Persia, and Ahmad Pasha was left free to govern Iraq until he died in 1747. Now the Ottoman empire was weakened and in disarray, leaving Iraq to be governed as a virtually autonomous province. When Ahmad Pasha died the Sublime Porte struggled to re-establish Ottoman control over the region, but four successive Istanbul nominees failed to establish their authority over Baghdad, forcing the sultan to recognise Ahmad's son in law, Suleiman Pasha, as the new governor.

This meant that what was a Mamluk ('slave') regime was set to rule Iraq until 1831, at which time a terrible attack of bubonic plague devastated the Baghdad population and reduced the city to impotence. In April 1831 between two and three thousand people were dying every day, while the healthy fled the city; civil administration broke down, whole regiments were killed off, robbers ranged the streets, communications collapsed, and all food supplies were exhausted.[26] Then the Tigris burst its banks, flooding the city, and reducing hundreds of houses to ruins. Mamluk culture had been devastated: the diseased and depopulated city was now reduced to rubble, the grand mosques and palaces destroyed, all the silks and satins, the jewels and elaborate artefacts destroyed. In June an Ottoman army, led by Ali Ridha Pasha, arrived outside the city and demanded that the Mamluk ruler, Daud – who had managed to survive the chaos and destruction – surrender himself to justice. However, Daud was pardoned by the sultan and employed in high office until his death in 1851. Twelve pashas – Mamluks and Turks – had ruled Iraq during the period 1750–1831, in which the fortunes of the Ottoman state had continued to deteriorate.

At the same time a Muslim reform movement, founded by Mohammad ibn Abd al-Wabia in the eighteenth century, had been gaining strength in Central Arabia (Wahabism became the religion of the Saudi rulers and so survived as an influential sect in modern Saudi Arabia). At the beginning of the nineteenth century a fanatical Wahabist tribal chief, Mohammad ibn Saud, swept northwards, plundering and killing throughout Iraq and Syria. In 1802 the Wahabists had captured Mecca and Medina, and quickly laid claim to the soul of Islam. The Ottoman sultan Mahmud II, perceiving the Wahabist expansion as both a religious and a political threat, sent Mohammad Ali to crush the uprising: the Wahabis were crushed after fighting that began in 1812 and lasted for six years. However, Mohammad Ali, having been content to function as a nominal feudatory of the Istanbul Ottomans, now decided to rebel; his son Ibrahim Pasha took an army through Syria to defeat the Turkish forces at Konia in Asia Minor. The European powers then intervened to stop the fighting, though Mohammad Ali had already succeeded in annexing Syria to Egypt. When fighting resumed in 1840 Syria was lost but Mohammad Ali secured recognition as the hereditary monarch of Egypt, now virtually independent of the Ottoman state. Mohammad Ali, keen to employ specialist Europeans, had started Egypt on the long path of westernisation, but Syria, Iraq and most of Saudi Arabia were to remain under Ottoman control until the end of the First World War.

It has been pointed out that the heart of the Ottoman state was able to withstand for several centuries 'both external assault and internal subversion'; and that moreover the Ottomans 'displayed a comparable durability in the provinces'.[27] In the nineteenth century the Empire was widely perceived as the 'Sick Man of Europe' (long before this soubriquet was transferred elsewhere); but the sickness was one that 'few other Islamic states would have survived to endure'.[28] It is certainly possible to argue that the Ottomans, in their very longevity, offered unique gifts to Islamic history, but it is unlikely that the survival of Islam depended on the Turks: it would have survived anyway – in Iraq and elsewhere. It had survived many imperialisms in the past, including the Christian imperialism of the Crusaders. Soon Islam would be forced to face the Christian imperialism of the twentieth century.

5 The Western Impact

I do not understand this squeamishness about the use of gas. I am strongly in favour of using poison gas against uncivilised tribes.

Winston Churchill

If the Kurds hadn't learned by our example to behave themselves in a civilised way then we had to spank their bottoms. This was done by bombs and guns.

Wing Commander Gale, 30 Squadron (RAF), Iraq

The Crusades were the first large-scale Western intervention into the Muslim world. Their impact however on the centres of Islamic power was limited: most of the great Muslim cities remained intact and the most impressive Christian victories were in due course thrown into reverse. But the Arabs – with a 'most lively feeling of their own history' – have never forgotten the series of Western aggressions that came to an end more than seven hundred years ago. The leaders of the Arab world still rejoice in the successes of Saladin, still constantly refer to the recapture of Jerusalem from the Christian interlopers, with modern Israel itself depicted as a new crusader state. The Suez expedition of 1956 has been regarded as a Frankish Crusade, akin to the aggression of 1191; and an Arab writer has pointed out that the Turk, Mehmet Ali Agca, who on 13 May 1981 almost killed the Pope, declared: 'I have decided to kill John Paul II, supreme commander of the Crusades.'[1] We are reminded that the schism between the Arab East and the West dates from the Crusades; and that this schism is 'deeply felt by the Arabs, even today, as an act of rape'.[2] The Crusades were the first great Western onslaught on Muslims, but it was in the twentieth century that the most comprehensive Western interventions were to take place – with all the exploitation, miseries and humiliations that this implied.

EARLY INTERESTS IN MESOPOTAMIA

Iraq under the Ottomans had remained one of the most backward regions of the Turkish empire: it was poorly governed and underdeveloped, Ottoman interests generally focused elsewhere. The appointed *walis* (governors) had problems trying to discipline the desert tribes and the settled

Kurdish communities in the north of the country. Some of the *walis* tried to introduce reforms but to little effect. Thus the progressive Midhat Pasha, who in 1869 began a three-year rule, introduced conscription among the local population, built schools and hospitals, and took steps to improve local administration. He also tried to dredge the Shatt al-Arab waterway (the confluence of the Tigris and Euphrates), and encouraged steamers to navigate the major rivers. But though the area remained backward the Europeans were becoming increasingly aware of the region's potential strategic and commercial importance.

Britain already controlled the Gulf and now saw Iraq as the gateway to India, one of the acknowledged glories of the imperial network. Britain helped to establish telegraph and postal services linking major Iraqi cities with Istanbul, the Gulf and India; and increasingly came to regard central and southern Mesopotamia as an obvious British sphere of interest. At the same time France was casting an eye on Mosul in the north, Russia was looking towards the Gulf, and imperial Germany had formed a disturbing alliance with the Ottoman sultan. In 1865, following the death of Feisal bin Turki, a violent contest for the Saudi succession erupted, encouraging the Turks in an attempt to consolidate their power in the region. Britain was alarmed at the prospect of a Turkish presence in the Gulf, and so strengthened its links with Bahrain to counter both Turkish and Iranian ambitions.

As early as 1798 Britain had despatched a permanent agent to Baghdad, a modest response to Napoleon's supposed intention to march across Mesopotamia to India.[3] Subsequently technology and political circumstance conspired to increase British interest in the region. In 1836 the British government decided to fund an expedition to explore the possibility of using steamboats to navigate the Euphrates from its source in Syria to its outlet on the Gulf; and by the 1850s the possibility of expanding railway communications was being considered. Russian encroachments in Persia represented a threat to British communications in the Middle East, and so a plan for a Euphrates Valley railway to link the Mediterranean to the Gulf stimulated much official thought.[4] This official interest acquired further impetus when the 1857 Indian mutiny exposed the shortcomings in Anglo-Indian communications and later when de Lesseps opened the Suez canal, so threatening to give France a sea route to India. The importance of protecting British India was never in doubt; it was to this defence that the 'whole British military and naval machine was heavily geared'.[5] Lord Curzon, Viceroy of India (1899–1905), asserted that 'as long as we rule India we are the greatest Power in the world'.[6] It was this focus on India –

the declared need 'to safeguard all the routes leading to India'[7] – that concentrated British attention on Mesopotamia, apart from any additional strategic or commercial benefits that Iraq might offer. Thus in 1871 a Select Parliamentary Committee was established to explore again the possible benefits to Britain of a Euphrates Valley railway. In fact, none of the schemes materialised in the nineteenth century but the discussions did succeed in convincing the British government that if it did not need to develop the overland route by means of a railway then no other European power should be allowed to control such a development. This conclusion helped to determine British attitudes to a possible Russian railway project and to a more concrete German proposal. In 1888 the Deutsche Bank gained Turkish support for a development proposal; and in 1903 the German financiers obtained a final Baghdad Railway Concession from the Ottoman government, whereupon the British took steps to secure a degree of control over the projected railway.

It is easy to see why Britain would want to protect the trade routes to India. In 1904 India was the largest consumer of British goods[8] – and, perhaps for this reason, a principal concern of the recently formed Committee of Imperial Defence. Between 1900 and 1902, ships totalling 478,000 tons called at Basra, and the vast majority of these flew the British flag. India was second only to Persia as an importer of dates, hides and wool from Mesopotamia; and Britain supplied sixty-five per cent of the Mesopotamian market: most of this trade was cloth exported from Manchester. Within Mesopotamia itself British merchants controlled much of the carrying trade; for example, the Euphrates and Tigris Navigation Company, established in 1859, remained a British family concern. The Company was allowed by the Turkish government to run only two steamers in Mesopotamia, and it was forced to compete with the Oman Steamship Company sponsored by the Turks. The East India Company had installed a representative at Basra as early as 1764 and opened an agency in Baghdad in 1783. The British Consul General at Baghdad maintained his own steamer, the Comet, on the Tigris and in 1800 was protected by his own Sepoy detachment, an official force that by 1904 had grown to a contingent of more than forty cavalry and infantry.

British trading interests in Iraq developed throughout the nineteenth century and there was much optimism that these would expand in the years ahead. It was thought that conservation of the spring floods of the Tigris and Euphrates would improve the grain, rice, cotton and date crops, with technological investment expected to vastly increase crop quality and quantity. It was assumed also that European capital investment would quickly expand Mesopotamia's petroleum production.[9] By 1903 there were many English and German schemes for the development of irrigation and mining works in Mesopotamia, but it was perhaps the presence of oil that above all would give the lands of the region scope for independence but also advertise to the Europeans – and later the Americans – their need to retain control of the region.

THE LURE OF OIL

There had long been hints of the presence of oil in the Arabian peninsula and beyond: travellers' tales and Arabic literature made reference to black oily substances, and bitumen had been used over the centuries for various purposes (the 'Greek fire' used by the Turks against Arab ships probably had a petroleum base). Oil was discovered in Egypt in 1869, though it was not until forty years later, in 1908, that the massive Masjid-i-Suleiman (Temple of Solomon) well in Persia began to flow; thirty years after that an even more fertile well was discovered in Kuwait. These and the many other discoveries of oil in the region ensured that Kuwait, Persia, Iraq and other states would long be the focus of imperial ambitions. The oil bounty that should rightly have liberated the Arab peoples (and the Persians and others) was destined to lead to their subjugation and humiliation. The oil-rich nations of the Middle East have not yet escaped from the predatory designs of powerful Western nations in a shrinking and energy-hungry world.

In 1890 the French geologist Jacques de Morgan, a member of an archaeological team in Persia, observed manifest oil seepages; ten years later he decided to obtain financial backing to explore the matter further. This led to a meeting with Sir Henry Drummond Wolff, sometime British Ambassador to Persia – an encounter that, via further contacts, led to an exclusive concession for a British company to search for oil in Persia. The Russian Imperial government protested but the concession assigning rights to the British firm was signed on 28 May 1901, though the actual exploitation company was not set up until 1903. On 26 May 1908, with the funds almost exhausted and the firm now in a syndicate with the Scotland-based Burmah Oil Company, oil in commercial quantity was found at Maidan-i-Naftun; a year later, in April 1909, the Anglo–Persian Oil Company was founded. One of Winston Churchill's first acts, when made First Lord of the Admiralty in 1911, was to resurrect the Admiralty committee on oil to ensure that British warships would not go short of fuel. Lord Fisher was made head of the Royal Commission on Oil for the Navy, and a group of experts was sent to Persia and the Gulf to assess future prospects in the region. Britain had already perceived the strategic importance of Kuwait and had taken steps to guarantee a lasting British influence. Thus on 23 January 1899 Sheikh Mubarak, the ruler of Kuwait, had been induced to sign an agreement with Britain guaranteeing British protection in return for an assurance that neither he nor his heirs would 'cede, sell, lease or mortgage, or give for occupation or for any other purpose a portion of his territory to the government of any other power without the previous consent of Her Majesty's Government'.[10] This meant that an agreement *in perpetuity* had been made between Britain and successive rulers of Kuwait, despite the ambiguous position of Kuwait in its relations to the Ottoman state. Thus in the nineteenth century Britain saw the strategic and commercial advantages of keeping Kuwait out of Iraqi control. This was to bear directly on the oil question, and on many other matters, in the years ahead. It was not long before Sheikh Mubarak confirmed the terms of the 1899 agreement. British diplomats and oil experts were welcomed in Kuwait, and in 1913 he wrote to Sir Percy Fox, the British Political Representative in the Gulf: 'We are agreeable to everything which you regard as advantageous . . . we will associate with the Admiral one of our sons to be in his service, to show the place of bitumen in Burgan and elsewhere and if in his view there seems hope of obtaining oil therefrom we shall never give a concession to anyone except a person appointed by the British government.'[11] The puppet status of Kuwait was clear.

The British government took a 51 per cent shareholding in the Anglo-Persian Oil Company, via a Parliamentary bill that received the Royal Assent six days before the declaration of War; a further investment of £3 million was made in 1919. Kuwait was set to play a key role in the appreciation of British assets, 'and in affairs which would soon enmesh much of the Arabian peninsula, the USA, Britain and Europe, and many of the greatest commercial enterprises in the Western world, in a relationship that to say the least of it was delicately poised'.[12]

The collapse of the Ottoman Empire created an immediate battlefield for oil diplomacy among the victorious powers. Turkish possessions were being carved up between Britain and France (see the Sykes–Picot Agreement, below), and attention was focused on the possibility of vast oil reserves in the regions of Mosul and Baghdad. The Armenian entrepreneur Calouste Gulbenkian had founded the Turkish Petroleum Company (TPC) in 1914, soon half owned by British Petroleum who had managed to secure the Iranian concession. At the end of the war TPC was divided up, the

German quarter-share being given to France, Gulbenkian retaining five per cent, and the United States being excluded (on the dubious grounds that the US had not declared war on Turkey and so was not interested in the terms of the peace). The Americans were outraged when they learned the terms of the settlement. In 1919 the State Department had begun to assert American legal rights in the occupied Ottoman territories, including the right to carry out archaeological and commercial activities. The question of oil was raised on behalf of the Standard Oil Company of New York, which before the war had held exploration concessions in Palestine and Syria. There was growing interest in the possibility of oil reserves in Iraq and in September 1919 Standard Oil ('Socony') sent geologists to prospect in that region, despite the nominal British hegemony. One wrote to his wife, saying: 'I am going to the biggest remaining oil possibilities in the world . . . the pie is so very big' that everything should be done to 'gain us the rights which properly belong to American Citizens'.[13] The British government, learning of the letter, immediately instructed Sir Arnold Wilson, High Commissioner in Iraq, to forbid the geologists to prospect. The State Department protested but Lord Curzon, the Foreign Secretary, declared that oil explorations were not possible under the wartime restrictions. The Standard Oil Company of New Jersey then entered the fray, deciding that it might be useful to research for oil in Iraq and in March 1919 sending a company executive to the Paris Peace Conference to raise the question with the American delegation.

On 27 April, at the San Remo Conference, Britain and France finalised their agreement to monopolise all Middle Eastern oil. This was intended to be a secret deal to exclude the United States but A. C. Bedford, later the chairman of New Jersey Standard, managed to obtain a copy of the agreement from a member of the French delegation and immediately presented it to the American embassy. The US government did not respond until in the summer of 1920 the terms of the San Remo agreement were made public. At that time, following US protests, Lord Curzon commented that whereas Britain controlled only 4.5 per cent of world oil production the United States controlled 80 per cent and that moreover the US excluded non-American interests from areas it controlled.[14] Bainbridge Colby, US Secretary of State, replied that America possessed only one twelfth of the world's known oil reserves and that the unhampered development of existing resources was essential.[15] The confrontation between Britain and the United States had now reached grave proportions – to the point that British officials suspected the Americans of supporting the Arab revolt (see below) against British rule. A rebel leader arrested in Iraq by British security forces was said to have a letter in his possession proving that the American consul in Baghdad was funding Shi'ite rebels in Karbala.[16]

The American government continued to maintain diplomatic pressure on the British and in due course the Americans were offered shares in the successor company to TPC. Iraq's oil industry was now monopolised by the Iraq Petroleum Company (IPC), jointly owned by the Anglo–Persian Oil Company (later BP), Royal Dutch Shell, an American group (eventually New Jersey Standard Oil and Socony-Vacuum, later Mobil), the Compagnie Française des Petroles (CFP), and Calouste Gulbenkian (still retaining his five per cent share). Gulbenkian also managed to preserve a clause whereby each partner agreed not to seek further concessions in the former Ottoman Empire, a provision that ran against the Americans' 'open door' policy but which guaranteed secure pickings to the US companies in IPC. Now the door was slammed behind the IPC partners and 'the most remarkable carve-up in oil history'[17] (following a line drawn by Gulbenkian in red pencil on the map)* had been accomplished (Gulbenkian: 'never was the open door so hermetically sealed'). The Europeans and the Americans had succeeded in parcelling out Arab resources – in particular, oil – among themselves. The powers that had been victorious in the First World War had little interest in the fact that 'the lands wrested from the Turks were, in fact, Arab lands'.[18] It was also conveniently forgotten that the Arabs had fought on the side of the British and the French on the understanding that Arab independence would be guaranteed after the war. A few Western Arabists (Gertrude Bell, T. E. Lawrence and others) tried to highlight such facts but their efforts were submerged by the *realpolitik* of the day.

The carve-up of Arab lands that followed the ending of the First World War could not have happened in the way that it did without the final collapse of the Ottoman Empire. Many of the factors that led to a division of the spoils were already in place before the war. The pliant Sheikh Mubarak in Kuwait had already consolidated his country as a British puppet, and the British already controlled the Gulf and had extensive commercial interests throughout Mesopotamia. Other powers – France, the United States, Germany and Imperial Russia (soon to dissolve in revolution) – were casting covetous eyes on the region. The pace of technological development and the new demands – not least for oil – that it generated, coupled with the growing tensions between the European powers, had made a fresh political cataclysm inevitable. A host of political players were being sucked into a new vortex. Throughout the war years, as it became increas-

---

*The so-called Red Line agreement

ingly clear that the Ottomans were doomed, the burgeoning patterns of the post-war world began to emerge.

THE DEMISE OF THE OTTOMANS

In the decades before the First World War Britain had tried to ensure that no other European nation would become strong enough to dominate the deteriorating Ottoman Empire, lest such a development threaten British interests in India and beyond. A vast system of outposts had been established to protect the sphere of British control between the Mediterranean and India. Russia and France no longer seemed to pose a serious threat to the British Empire, and Germany was emerging as the sole potential danger to British interests. The Young Turks had formed an alliance with the German Kaiser and there was growing German commercial and political penetration of the Ottoman state. Some efforts were undertaken by the British and Germans, now both aware of the impending crisis, to resolve their commercial conflicts in the territories of the Ottoman Empire; though with hindsight it is easy to see the futility of such attempts. The Germans appointed two British directors to the board of a company intending to operate the Berlin–Baghdad railway; and Germany had no difficulty recognising the manifest British supremacy in Kuwait, the Gulf and in the area defined by the Anglo-Iranian oil concession. When hostilities broke out a few weeks later the Middle East was effectively divided between four influential factions: the Ottoman Empire, now in the German sphere of influence; Egypt, nominally an Ottoman region but in reality a British protectorate; the Gulf, including the coasts of Arabia, under British control; and Iran, now split between Russian and British zones of influence. There was growing westernisation in the region, a development that was already impacting on Islam. Soon powerful Western states would be in conflict with the Muslim Turks, a new confrontation between Christian and Is- lamic forces.

It has been argued that much of the misunderstanding between the West and the Middle East throughout the twentieth century can be traced back 'to Lord Kitchener's initiatives in the early years of the First World War'.[19] Like most Westerners he was ignorant of the Muslim world; he was forced, moreover, to rely upon inaccurate information supplied by his agents in Cairo, Khartoum and elsewhere. He was soon proclaiming that when the war was over it would be up to Britain to seize as much of the old Ottoman Empire as possible. Kitchener was suspicious of the Turkish sultan, still regarded by Sunni Muslims as the caliph, and was well prepared to believe that the head of Islam (wrongly perceived by Kitchener to be a monolithic structure) would be eager to hurl his Muslim warriors against British interests. It was noted with some consternation that British India had seventy million Muslims, some of whom constituted a large part of the Indian army. Could such recruits be relied upon? There were, moreover, millions of Muslims in the Sudan and in Egypt, alongside the Suez route to India. Small British garrisons were expected to keep order in this extended Muslim world: it was not a situation that Kitchener faced with equanimity.[20]

He believed in addition that Russia may come to control the caliph and that, since Russia still wished to take India, this would represent a great hazard to the British Empire. One answer was for Britain to install a puppet caliph: an Arabian would do nicely since, with Britain's control of the Gulf, an Arabian caliph could be insulated from Britain's European rivals. In such a fashion Britain was to gain control of the Muslim world.[21] It was noted that a likely candidate for the role of caliph, Abdullah, the son of Hussein, the ruler of Mecca, had already visited Cairo to suggest that a revolt was imminent in Arabia. In meetings with Kitchener and Ronald Storrs, his Oriental Secretary, Abdullah is thought to have requested British assistance in resisting Turkish attempts to depose his father; the British, it is said, did not respond to such entreaties. It did emerge, however, that Kitchener was keen to enlist Arabian help in the event of a British war that would involve the Ottoman state as a German ally. So Abdullah was asked: 'If war broke out, would the Hejaz support Britain?' The reply was vague but encouraging. Kitchener went further and declared to Abdullah: 'If the Arab nation assist England in this war that has been forced upon us by Turkey, England will guarantee that no internal intervention take place in Arabia.' It has also emerged that as the letter was being translated into Arabic its terms were enlarged, under encouragement from intelligence head Gilbert Clayton, to pledge British support for 'the emancipation of the Arabs'[22] – a cynical bid for Arab support that would entail no commitment to Arab nationalism in the post-war world. Kitchener, with the approval of Sir Edward Grey, the Foreign Secretary, then sent a further statement to strengthen the declaration even more. He promised much of the Arab world ('Palestine, Syria and Mesopotamia') that if the Turkish yoke were thrown off, Britain would recognise and guarantee Arab independence.[23] The promise meant nothing, being no more than a cynical device to win support in the coming war; above all it was to serve as evidence, if any were needed, of British duplicity over Arab interests.

Kitchener's manifest strategy was to secure what allies he could for Britain while envisaging the creation of an Arabian caliphate that Britain would be well placed to exploit in the post-war world. He totally failed to grasp the divisions in the Muslim world; to notice, for example, that the Wahabist Saudis were at the throats of the Sunni rulers of Mecca. He failed also to perceive the swelling force of Arab nationalism, the burgeoning tide that would generate an Arab revolt soon after the end of the war and which in due course would drastically weaken Western efforts to maintain an unchallenged grip on Arab resources. In the short term there was time to deploy military power to secure the British hold on Mesopotamia.

In the autumn of 1914 an Indian Expeditionary Force (IEF 'D') was despatched to Mesopotamia, a development that would ultimately confirm Britain's claim to a mandate over Iraq.[24] It is important to realise that the despatch of the Force 'was not a response to any particular act of Turkish aggression'.[25] The sending of a British military contingent into Mesopotamia was discussed as early as August of that year, and full Cabinet sanction for the operation was given on 2 October. The contingent left India on 15 October and proceeded to the Shatt-al-Arab waterway after news was received that the Turks had bombarded Odessa on 29 October. It was not until 5 November that war was declared on the Ottoman Empire.

There has been much speculation about the purposes behind the despatch of IEF 'D'. Was it simply an imperialist gambit, as some have argued? Or was the aim the conciliation of the Arabs, whose support was being sought for a possible war against the Turks? Why, if so, was it assumed that the Arabs would welcome an extension of British power in Mesopotamia? Liddell Hart suggested that IEF 'D' was despatched to protect the Abandan oil stores and the Persian petroleum fields at the head of the Gulf from Turkish attack.[26] In any event the Force did succeed in establishing British control over Iraq, whether or not this was its main purpose.[27]

The activities of IEF 'D' were soon only a small part of a much wider struggle. In November 1914 the Turkish sultan, playing up his role of caliph, declared a *jihad*, exhorting all Muslims to take up arms against Britain, France and Russia. Such an uprising would have been extremely awkward for the French in North Africa and for the British Empire, with its large numbers of Muslims; Kitchener was not the only observer to realise what a unified Muslim revolt against the imperial European powers would mean. In an attempt to prevent any such development the British had begun the dissemination of pro-British propaganda in Arab regions and began also building up contacts with the Sharif Hussein of Mecca – in the hope that an Arab uprising against the Turks could be organised.

The British military contingent (IEF 'D') was landed at Basra, which it took without difficulty. T. E. Lawrence ('Lawrence of Arabia') commented: 'The enemy troops in Irak were nearly all Arabs in the unenviable predicament of having to fight on behalf of their secular oppressors against a people long envisaged as liberators, but who obstinately refused to play the part. As may be imagined, they fought very badly. Our forces won battle after battle till we came to think an Indian army better than a Turkish army.' But this good fortune, from the British point of view, did not last. There soon began 'our rash advance to Ctesiphon, where we met native Turkish troops whose full heart was in the game, and were abruptly checked. We fell back, dazed; and the long misery of Kut began.'[28] Several thousand British troops had occupied Basra, following the bombardment of the Turkish fort at the mouth of the Shatt-al-Arab by the British gunboat, the river sloop *Odin*. The early Turkish counterattacks were repulsed with ease and the British force began the long advance towards Baghdad.

The British commanding officer, Sir John Nixon, encouraged the officer in the field, Major-General Charles Vere Ferrers Townshend, to move along the Tigris towards central Iraq; but the terrain was difficult and the force, despite its early victories, was ill-equipped for such an advance. The troops had to contend with a land of swamps and desert; and, in the absence of mobile hospitals and adequate medical supplies, with debilitating flies and mosquitos. At a time when Townshend's supplies were becoming seriously depleted he encountered a well-equipped Turkish force. At Ctesiphon, some twenty-five miles south-east of Baghdad, half the British force was wiped out; and on 25 November 1915 Townshend, now hundreds of miles from his Basra supply base, began his long retreat. He soon learned that 30,000 Turkish troops were being sent to reinforce the 13,000 that he had confronted at Ctesiphon; his own poorly-equipped force now numbered about 4500. After a hundred-mile retreat, during which Townshend lost a thousand more men, he decided to make a stand at Kut el-Amara, a village set in a loop of the Tigris. There followed a virtual siege of the miserable British force, now compelled to endure a predicament that would last for 146 days until, on 26 April 1916, the War Office in London proposed to Townshend that Captains Aubrey Herbert and T. E. Lawrence negotiate a surrender on his behalf.

The Turks were eventually offered £2 million to let Townshend and his men go free on parole. They rejected the offer, whereupon the British force – by now diseased, starving and totally demoralised – destroyed their guns and surrendered unconditionally. There had been attempts to relieve the besieged troops (supplies parachuted to them had blown off-course and the Turks had spread chains across the Tigris to stop riverboats laden with supplies), but now the pathetic survivors of the once-ambitious force had to rely on the mercy of the Turkish victors. Townshend was allowed to travel to Istanbul where he was to live in luxury; his wretched soldiers were sent on a long death march – 100 miles to Baghdad and a further 500 to Anatolia – to be put to work as slaves on the railroads. The 'long misery of Kut' was at an end. Townshend had lost 10,000 men, and a further 23,000 casualties were inflicted on the British forces that struggled to relieve him. The losses, albeit horrendous, would not long delay the British occupation of Iraq.

Baghdad fell to the British in March 1917, and by the end of the war the British forces were in control of most of Iraq. The British military efforts had been aided to a large degree by the Arab revolt against Ottoman forces in Arabia and the Hejaz, but in Mesopotamia few Arabs had fought on the side of the allies. T. E. Lawrence observed: '. . . till the end of the war the British in Mesopotamia remained substantially an alien force invading enemy territory, with the local people passively neutral or sullenly against them. . . '.[29] The evident promises from Kitchener on Arab independence had encouraged Sharif Hussein to contemplate a general revolt against the Turks, but the eventual Arab response to his appeal did not spread beyond the Arabian peninsula. The 'passively neutral' Arabs of Mesopotamia may have sensed British duplicity more quickly than did the leaders of Mecca.

Sharif Hussein himself worked hard through 1915 to secure the assurances that he required from the British government, though it has been suggested that at that time Britain 'had no clear policy towards the Arabs or for the future of the Ottoman provinces in Asia after Turkey's defeat'.[30] It seems clear with hindsight that the British were motivated by no more than a cynical pragmatism, uncommitted to any theories on Arab independence, and that such a posture would inevitably come to be viewed as unprincipled. Sir Percy Cox, the chief political officer of the Mesopotamian Expeditionary Force, had been keen to enlist Abdul Aziz ibn Saud, a key leader in central Arabia; and so sent Captain W. H. I. Shakespear to speak for Britain at the Saudi court. In January 1915 Shakespear was killed by opponents of the Saudi regime, whereupon the British government – under prompting from the Cairo-based Arab Bureau – decided to focus its attention on enlisting the Hejaz Hashemites under Sharif Hussein to lead the Arab revolt. The Ottoman sultan had already called for a *jihad* against the allies; it would be useful, London thought, if the allies could parade their own Muslim leader, the very Sharif of holy Mecca.

Sir Mark Sykes (later to achieve everlasting fame or notoriety through the Sykes–Picot Agreement, see below) had reported to the British government that the Arabs were of prime importance to the allied war effort; and that in consequence agreement should be reached with Hussein. Lord Curzon, the former Viceroy of India, had commented that no promises should be made to the Arabs because they were 'a people who are at this moment fighting against us as hard as they can'.[31] But Kitchener was keen to develop the Hussein connection and he was prepared, as we have seen, to encourage promises to the Arabs, however vacuous such commitments would later prove to be. Sir Henry McMahon, the High Commissioner in Cairo, then resumed correspondence with Mecca – in a series of letters that have received endless scrutiny and diverse interpretations from every political camp. Hussein had written McMahon a letter in which he accused him of 'lukewarmth and hesitancy' because of the British reluctance to consider territorial boundaries and frontiers; and Hussein hinted that he was being pressured by others ('our people') to seek clarification from the British government. Hussein's aim was to secure British support for Arab independence throughout the Ottoman lands: from Mersin in the north, the Iranian frontier in the east, the Mediterranean in the west and the Indian Ocean to the south; with Aden alone allowed as a temporary exception. The audacity of such a demand may well have alarmed the British but the times were difficult and there was a war to be won. In a historically crucial letter, dated 24 October 1915, McMahon pledged the support of the British government for Arab independence, subject to various crucial qualifications; and commented in connection with the two Vilayets of Baghdad and Basra that 'the Arabs recognise that the fact of Great Britain's established position and interests there will call for the setting up of special administrative arrangements to protect those regions from foreign aggression, to promote the welfare of their inhabitants and to safeguard our mutual interest'.

The British attitude to Arab independence meant that none of Hussein's demands could be accepted *in toto* but at the same time it was important to create the impression that Britain supported the emancipation of the Arabs then living under Ottoman control. In the most pessimistic interpretation, 'Britain did not bind herself to support Hussein's claims anywhere at all'.[32] However, some Arab observers seemed only to notice that 'Great Britain is prepared to recognise and uphold the independence of the Arabs in all the regions . . .', and not mark the careful caveats. Hussein perceived the ambiguities in some of McMahon's words and readily acknowledged the weight of the British occupation of Iraq but he also went to pains to point out that the Iraqi provinces were once an important part of the Arab Empire, the first centre of Arab culture, and it would be 'impossible to persuade or compel the Arab nation to renounce the honourable association'. Here it was: the Sharif of Mecca, in the face of British imperialism, was even forced on the defensive in trying to argue for Arab independence in the ancient and historic land of the caliphs.

It was also clear that Hussein's position was weak because he could not command the support of all Arabs. He ruled only in the Hejaz, a relatively small area, although of immense religious significance. The imam of Yemen remained pro-Turkish; various Arab sheikhs on the fringes of the Arabian peninsula had treaty obligations to the British government; and ibn Saud in the Arabian interior was a bitter rival to Hussein. Furthermore the Sharif of Mecca had little direct contact with the Syrians or the Arabs of North Africa; Jemal Pasha was able to declare in Damascus in January 1915 that 'the Turkish and Arab ideals do not conflict. They are brothers in their strivings, and perhaps their efforts are complementary'. (Jemal later adopted a policy of repression that included public executions in the centre squares of Damascus and Beirut.) However, despite the weakness of Hussein's position and his doubts about the British commitments on independence, he seemingly felt that there was more to be gained by opposing the Ottomans than by seeking yet more clarification from McMahon and the British government.

On 16 June 1916 Sharif Hussein raised the flag of the Arab Revolt and quickly overcame the small Turkish garrison in Mecca. Hussein was now committed to an Arab involvement in the war, in the hope of wider political gains in the post-war world. But for a time there was no wider Arab involvement; the Arab Revolt that Britain had encouraged as essential to its war aims was confined to the Hejaz. On 2 November 1916 Sharif Hussein's followers proclaimed him 'King of the Arab Countries', a title that was rejected by Britain and France; in January 1917 they both agreed to recognise him as King of the Hejaz. It was soon to emerge that Britain and France were developing their own schemes for the shaping of the post-war world, and these had little to say about Arab independence.

The Arab Revolt had contributed to the demise of the Ottoman Empire and it had advertised – partly through the efforts of T. E. Lawrence – the Arab thirst for independence in Arab lands. But many of the early hopes behind the Revolt remained unrealised. At the purely military level Hussein's expectations were not fulfilled by the event. The Arab Bureau had argued that an uprising would immediately win support throughout the Muslim and Arab worlds, and Hussein and Feisal had reported that they would be joined by 100,000 Arab troops – which would have represented about a third of the Ottoman army's fighting strength. It was also reported that Hussein expected to be joined by no less than 250,000 troops, almost all the combat troops in the Turkish army. None of this materialised. No Arab units of the Ottoman forces, and no political or military leaders, defected to the allies. Outside the Hejaz 'there was no visible support for the revolt in any part of the Arabic-speaking world'.[33] Hussein relied solely on a few thousand tribesmen, massively supported by British funds. Half a century later, when a Bedouin sheikh was asked if he remembered Lawrence, he replied: 'He was the man with the gold'.[34] The Bedouin tribesmen, the core of the Hussein military contingent, were ill-equipped to deal with modern warfare; and despite their skilful and courageous guerrilla raids they were sometimes near to collapse as a fighting force. The French and the British were compelled to take action on occasion to ensure the survival of the Revolt.[35]

The military limitations of the Arab Revolt, despite its clear contribution to the allied victory, helped to weaken Hussein's political position. What had been intended as a dramatic demonstration of Arab unity as a weighty factor in post-war diplomacy had done no more than demonstrate the factionalisms and divisions in the Arab world. Kitchener need not have worried about the imagined solidarity of the Islamic peoples; even the Arabs, with their shared ethnic identity, were unable to unite around the Word of the Prophet. This of course well suited the European powers. Kitchener, McMahon and others had speculated on the possibility of Arab independence, and used the idea in cynical *realpolitik* to aid the allies, but there was no commitment, no promise to Hussein or to any other Arab leader. The British and French had their own post-war political agenda: its framework had been drawn up during the war, some years before the final collapse of the Ottoman Empire. The agreement that encapsulated this agenda laid the basis for the colonial interregnum of the inter-war years. It demonstrated yet again – if anyone outside the Arab world was interested – the characteristic duplicity of the European powers.

THE SYKES–PICOT AGREEMENT

Britain, serving also the French interest, had been happy to seduce the Arabs into supporting the allied cause; at the same time taking pains to avoid any firm commitment on Arab independence. There had been the suggestion – to Hussein and others – of Arab emancipation but without the substance. There had been no treaties, no binding agreements, no unambiguous promises that the Arabs could exploit in helping to shape the post-war world. It was not hard to find Europeans who were proud of having won the war without having incurred any embarrassing political debts; and even during the war the shape of diplomatic things to come was being made clear. Thus Gilbert Clayton, commenting on the McMahon efforts, commented that 'Luckily we have been very careful indeed to commit ourselves to nothing whatsoever';[36] and Sir Edward Grey, the Foreign Secretary, observed to Austen Chamberlain on the vexed question of

Arab independence that 'the whole thing was a castle in the air which would never materialise'.[37] At the same time McMahon himself seems to have been concerned lest rising Arab aspirations turned out in fact to cause problems for Britain. In the event both Britain and France were determined not to be cheated of the fruits of the anticipated victory over the Ottoman Empire.

The French government, well aware of the strength of the British presence in Mesopotamia and the Gulf, was already charting out its own favoured spheres of influence. On 10 December 1915 McMahon cabled the Foreign Office to acquaint the British government with the diplomatic efforts of Albert Defrance, the French representative in Cairo: '. . . I am informed that he sent a few days ago for a leading Arab notable of Damascus now in Egypt, and told him as follows: "You can tell all your friends here from me, and I tell you this in my capacity as representative of the French Government, that Syria shall never be part of an Arab Empire. Syria will be under the protection of France and we shall shortly send an army to occupy it. . ."'.[38] If the British were to hang on to Iraq then France was to have Syria. The suspicions of the British government regarding French intentions were confirmed by the appointment of François Georges Picot as their representative (McMahon: '. . . Picot is a notorious fanatic on the Syrian question and quite incapable of assisting any mutual settlement on the reasonable commonsense grounds which the present situation requires').[39] It was time for the British and French governments to agree their carve-up of the post-war Middle East in the perceived interests of their two countries. The Arabs of course would be left out of all the political horse-trading on the future of their own lands.

George Clerk, a British Foreign Office official, proposed that it was time for the two governments to negotiate and that the views of Sir Mark Sykes, a Member of Parliament and Middle East expert, should be heard (Sykes 'Was better informed about the state of Middle East politics than anyone else in London';[40] perhaps more importantly, as Clerk emphasised, he was 'highly qualified to speak from the point of view of our interests'). Picot and Sykes met on 21 December and began the talks that would in due course yield the agreement that would bear their names. For three days at the beginning of January 1916 Sykes went to the French embassy to negotiate, reporting at night to Kitchener and Lieutenant-General FitzGerald; in this way a draft memorandum was hammered out that would form the basis of the Anglo-French understanding on the division of spoils in the post-war world.[41] France was to be given a Greater Lebanon and an exclusive influence over the rest of Syria; a sphere of French influence would also extend to Mosul, while Britain would retain the two Mesopotamian provinces of Basra and Baghdad. A compromise was reached on Palestine: Britain was to be given the ports of Acre and Haifa, and also a territorial region that would facilitate the building of a railway to Mesopotamia; while the rest of the country was to be assigned to some sort of international administration. In the remaining areas, where the Arabs were to be allowed some small degree of control, an effective British or French influence would be maintained. The arrangements 'could not possibly have been accepted by Hussein'[42] – and so the British and French governments decided to keep the Sykes–Picot agreement secret for the time being. France had been given a vast area of influence in Syria and northern Mesopotamia, and now the way was clear for a massive British colonisation of Iraq. The Arabs – and those few Europeans prepared to treat with them fairly – were not to be told about the carve-up. Even McMahon was left out.

The Sykes–Picot memorandum and the accompanying map – approved by the British and French cabinets in early February 1916 – were circulated in Whitehall to those individuals thought likely to be sympathetic or unlikely to rock the boat; but care was taken to shield the proposals from rejection by Hussein or representatives of genuine Arab opinion in Cairo and elsewhere. But even in these carefully controlled circumstances official British opinion was divided on the terms of the proposals: 'The comments which survive in official files are almost all hostile'.[43] Such objections were kept secret, as were the terms of the Agreement. The important consideration, from the Anglo-French perspective, was to maintain a pliant Sharif of Mecca – by lying to him, if necessary – while determining what would happen to Arab lands in the post-war world. McMahon could be better used to placate the Arabs if he too were kept in ignorance about the terms of Sykes–Picot, and those officials who knew about the proposals could be relied upon to dissemble when occasion demanded. Thus Sykes himself was despatched in early 1917 to allay Hussein's reasonable misgivings about Anglo-French intentions. The British and French governments were well prepared to deceive their allies and their own high officials in the cynical pursuit of political advantage.

When, two years after it had been agreed by the British and French cabinets, the Sykes–Picot Agreement was made public it was not the only cause of Arab anguish. On 2 November 1917, shortly before Hussein learned of the secret agreement, a letter from Foreign Secretary Arthur Balfour to a leading British Zionist Jew, Lord Rothschild, was published. This important document, to be known as 'the Balfour Declaration', stated:

His Majesty's Government view with favour the establishment in Palestine of a National Home for the Jewish people, and will use their best endeavours to facilitate the achievement of this object, it being clearly understood that nothing shall be done which may prejudice the civil and religious rights of existing non-Jewish communities in Palestine or the rights and political status enjoyed by Jews in any other country.

It was not explained how a Jewish homeland could be created in a region already occupied by Arabs without prejudicing 'the civil and religious rights of existing non-Jewish communities . . .'. The terms of the Sykes–Picot Agreement were to be abandoned within a few decades with the gradual decay of British and French imperial power; but the baleful consequences of the Balfour Declaration persist nearly eighty years after its first publication.

COLONIAL INTERREGNUM

Assuming the Mandate

At the end of the war the Arabs still had hopes for political independence. There were suspicions about British and French intentions but the situation in the Middle East seemed fluid. The Ottoman Empire had collapsed and a centuries-long occupation of Arab lands was at an end; perhaps, after all, Arab emancipation would emerge from the chaos and confusion of the post-war world. In fact the European powers had carefully charted the way ahead. Arab nationalists had rejoiced at the defeat of the Turkish state but they were soon facing a fresh imperialism. In Syria there was wild Arab rejoicing once it was clear that the country had been liberated. Apart from the horrors of war there had been a plague of locusts that had caused widespread famine; out of a total population of four million between 300,000 and 500,000 people had died. But the terms of Sykes–Picot were already being applied. The French had no intention of allowing an Arab Syria to emerge from the ruins, and when the French objected to the flying of Feisal's flag over Beirut the British soon ordered its removal. The French had soon assumed administrative control of the whole coastal area from Tyre to Cilicia in Asia Minor. Towns in the Syrian interior were controlled by Feisal but he was heavily dependent on British officers for the task of administration, while an Anglo-Indian control had been consolidated throughout most of the allocated regions of Mesopotamia. Now Britain was in a strong position to protect its widespread interests in the Middle East.

The region saw the production of cotton for Lancashire factories, the production of oil in Iran and later in Iraq, the ongoing investment in Egypt and Mesopotamia, and the development of markets for manufactured goods. British strategic interests were protected also; its role as a Mediterranean and a world power was consolidated, with focus on the sea-routes to India and the Far East through the Suez Canal and on the development of air routes across the Middle East. Military bases in the Mediterranean and the Indian Ocean were strengthened, and airfields were established in Egypt, Palestine, Iraq and the Gulf. What had originally been the Ottoman province of Syria had now been divided up into four separate political entities – Palestine, Lebanon, Transjordan and a much-reduced Syria – for the advantage of Britain and France. Transjordan had not previously existed, 'even in the imagination of the Arabs',[44] but had been created solely to serve British colonial designs. It was usefully situated between the Mediterranean ports of Palestine and the oil fields of British-controlled Iraq. Moreover, it bordered the Arabian peninsula: if the Suez Canal should become blocked Britain could pipe its oil across Transjordan to tankers at the ports on the Mediterranean coast. The British sought to consolidate their grip on Transjordan by installing Hussein's son Abdullah as king, just as they installed Feisal as king of Iraq after he had been thrown out of Syria by the French (see below). With Hussein now the monarch of Hejaz, and his sons conveniently planted in Transjordan (later Jordan) and Iraq, it seemed that Britain's control of the area – from the Nile Valley and the Mediterranean to Iraq and the Gulf – was secure.

Britain had now consolidated its colonial grip on Iraq, a poorly developed area of deserts and swamps, with a population divided between the Shi'ite and Sunni sects and riven by private blood feuds and sullen resentment of any occupying powers. In the north lived another faction, seemingly of much interest to European observers in the 1990s: 'Peasant and townsman alike reciprocated the hatred of the 700,000 Kurds, half-Moslem, half-animist, who glowered down on them from the mountain fastnesses of the northeast'.[45] At that time Baghdad depended for commercial and administrative leadership – as it had done on occasions in the past – on its literate Jewish minority. In the last Ottoman official yearbook for the *vilayet* of Baghdad the Jews in the city were given as numbering 80,000 out of a total population of 202,000; with the Sunnis, Shi'ites and Turks amounting to 101,400 *in toto*. When Baghdad fell to the British in March 1917 the Jews were the largest single group. When, in 1926, the Baghdad Chamber of Commerce was established, five of the its fifteen-member administrative council represented Jewish merchants; there were four Muslim representatives, three British, one Persian and so on. There may have been serious practical difficulties in arranging for Arab control of Baghdad, even if the

British colonial authorities had so wished. In fact the British cabinet was prepared to tolerate the idea of a puppet Arab state 'to be administered in the vilayet of Baghdad behind the Arab façade as far as possible as an Arab province by indigenous agency and in accordance with existing laws and institutions'. But even this suggestion, issued by London on 29 March 1918, was too much for Sir Percy Cox, now the civil high commissioner under the Indian Army for occupied Mesopotamia. He warned in a curt note on 7 April that any suggestion of Arab rule would simply prolong the chaos of the Turkish withdrawal, and declared that he would run the country under tight military control, the only 'practical' approach. Cox later wrote: 'By the end of the war the people of Mesopotamia had come to accept the fact of our occupation and were resigned to the prospect of a permanent British administration; some, especially in Basrah and the neighbourhood, even looked forward with satisfaction to a future in which they would be able to pursue their commerce and agriculture with a strong central authority to preserve peace and order.'[46] When Cox went to Teheran in May 1918 to serve as British minister to Iran his responsibilities were delegated to Lieutenant Colonel Arnold Wilson, a career officer now to serve as acting civil commissioner.

Wilson, like Cox, was horrified at the idea of Arab self-government, even condemning the proposal that puppet Hashemite monarchs – Abdullah and his brother Zeid – be installed in 'Upper' and 'Lower' Mesopotamia. However, Wilson did agree to hold a plebiscite to determine Arab opinion – provided that his officers guarantee the result. He instructed them to conduct the poll 'when opinion is favourable', to ensure that the 'right' answers emerged from the most reliable sheikhs. This splendid effort to ascertain the popular will yielded the unsurprising conclusion that the people were keen to reject a Hejazi ruler in favour of the British, a result that delighted Curzon and persuaded him that there was much to be said for firm rule in Mesopotamia. A tight administration, along the proven Indian lines, was introduced and strengthened: Indian civil servants worked under senior British officials, with the very titles used by the bureaucracy in New Delhi – political officer, revenue officer, judicial officer, civil commissioner – now introduced to Iraq. That was not all. The Iraqi people suddenly found themselves subject to laws based on the Indian legal code and obliged to handle the Indian currency based on the rupee.

Civil commissioner Wilson had as his assistant the celebrated Gertrude Bell, a well-known writer about Arab countries. She too had been prepared to rule out Arab self-determination, commenting that 'the people of Mesopotamia, having witnessed the successful termination of the war, had taken it for granted that the country would remain under British control and were as a whole content to accept the decision of arms'. It was alarming to Wilson, Bell and others of their ilk that international figures such as Woodrow Wilson opened up, in their talk of national self-determination, 'other possibilities which were regarded almost universally with anxiety, but gave opportunity for political intrigue to the less stable and more fanatical elements'.[47] Bell commented in a letter to her father that the provincial magnates in Iraq were strongly opposed to an Arab government: 'They say they don't want to be rid of one tyranny in order to fall into the clutches of another.'[48] Iraq had never been a political entity, in part because they 'have no conception of nationhood yet.'[49] Gertrude Bell ruled out the possibility of a native uprising against British rule; Arnold Wilson disagreed with her and was right (see below). As a prelude to the Arab uprising that would take place against British rule in Iraq an Arab independence party was founded in 1919.

While Feisal was in Paris the Arab nationalist society al-Fatah formed a party which soon gained Feisal's support on his return to Syria. Feisal managed to organise elections throughout Syria, but in some areas they were blocked by the French. Then a General Syrian Congress met in Damascus and demanded the recognition of the independence of Syria (including Palestine) and Iraq, the repudiation of the Sykes–Picot Agreement and the Balfour Declaration, and the abandonment of the mandatory system under which France and Britain had unilaterally assumed responsibility for the control of Arab lands. Feisal, by now well aware of the power of the European states, returned to Paris in November to negotiate a compromise with Clemenceau, pending a final settlement that would suit the British and the French. But Feisal's followers in Damascus refused to accept any such compromise and in March 1920 exhorted the Syrian Congress to declare the independence of Syria. At the same time a meeting of Arab Iraqi leaders proclaimed Iraq's independence under Abdullah as king.

This was the greatest challenge to European hegemony in the Middle East since the end of the war; and Britain and France responded quickly. They immediately repudiated the Damascus resolutions and convened the Supreme Council of the League of Nations. The Council, under the virtual control of Britain and France, delivered its predictable conclusion on 5 May 1920 at San Remo. France was to have mandates for Syria and Lebanon (the partitions of Greater Syria), and Iraq was to remain as a single British mandate; the further British mandate for Palestine was to involve the implementation of the terms of the Balfour Declaration. The situation was clear. Britain and France, as the then great powers, had successfully manipulated the League of Nations to provide a legalistic cloak of respectability for their *de facto* partition of the Middle East. Now Feisal's position in Syria had been totally undermined. The French had achieved a spurious justification for their intended occupation of the whole of Syria, and the British had received a sanction in so-called international law for their occupation of Iraq. Few observers saw any difference in practice between the assigned mandates and the the traditional colonial occupation of subject peoples.

Installing a King

Feisal was now in an impossible position. He had long declared his wish to rule in Syria but the French, having contrived their League sanction, were making it clear that they intended to establish direct control over the whole of the country. He had the option of resisting the French by force, and in fact the young Arab officers under Feisal's command were soon launching attacks on the French positions near the Lebanese border. However, the French were in no mood to tolerate military opposition to the policies thrashed out with the British over several years. On 14 July 1920 General Gourand, the French commander in Beirut, issued an ultimatum to Feisal to accept the mandate and the French occupation of Aleppo and other major Syrian towns. Feisal, with no stomach for a military confrontation with a European power, persuaded the General Congress to accept the French demand; but even this acquiescence was not enough to prevent a French attack. On 25 July French forces, including Senegalese and North African troops from other French-controlled states, marched into Damascus. The Syrian forces, backed by popular resistance, could do little against modern guns, tanks and planes; and the French occupation was soon secure. Feisal was then expelled from Syria and arrived in London at the end of the year; the British were soon concocting a plan that could turn his defeat to their advantage.

There had been some British debate about what to do with Iraq. There was a broad consensus, fuelled by characteristic European condescension, that the Iraqis were not fit to govern themselves; nor, it was assumed, would they be able to do so in the foreseeable future. Some Arabists (Lawrence, Bell, etc.) were prepared to support a measure of Arab independence but this would be subject to British advice: any Arab rulers supported by the British would remain puppets. The India Office, well accustomed to running a colonial administration, had no doubt that Iraq and the Arab regions in the Gulf should be tightly controlled by British officials; most conveniently as appendages of the British-controlled Indian state. The policy, implemented with little regard to local conditions, was destined to generate rebellion.

Winston Churchill, now Secretary of State for the Colonies, decided to call a conference to resolve the Iraq question and other related matters. Churchill had already learned, via Lawrence, of Feisal's views; and it was already clear that Feisal would be amenable to British plans for the Middle East. It seemed that he was prepared to abandon any claims to Syria and to renounce also his father's claims to Palestine. Lawrence had commented to Churchill's private secretary in mid-January 1921 that 'all questions of pledges & promises, fulfilled or broken, are set aside': there was to be a clean slate. It was clear that decisive action had to be taken to impose order on the post-war Middle East. For example, Hussein was now in an escalating conflict with the emir of Riyadh, both British client rulers; and there was the question of what to do with Feisal. In May 1920 a group of Members of Parliament wrote to the *Daily Express* proposing a single ministry for the direction of Middle Eastern affairs. Churchill's response to the evident disorder was to call together 'practically all the experts and authorities in the Middle East' – which, in the terms of the day, meant some three dozen Englishmen, Gertrude Bell and two Arabs (both aides to Hussein). This redoubtable collage, dubbed by Churchill the 'Forty Thieves', met in Cairo in March 1921 to settle the Middle East problems in the interests of Britain; care would be taken not to tread on French toes but little heed would be given to the aspirations of the Arabs. Churchill went so far as to say that the French attack on Syria 'conducted very largely by black African troops' had been 'extremely painful to British opinion' but 'we have these strong ties with the French and they have to prevail, and we were not able to do anything to help the Arabs in the matter . . .'.

On 12 March 1921 the Cairo Conference was formally begun at the Semiramis Hotel. Over the following period some forty or fifty sessions were held, between which Colonial Secretary Churchill escaped to do some sketching, ensconced before the Pyramids in close company with an armoured car. The results of the conference were to a large extent entirely predictable: the broad framework of European colonialism was to be preserved while at the same time both strengthened and rendered more economically manageable. The French, as expected, were to keep Syria and Lebanon, with the British retaining the mandate over Palestine with the declared aim of reconciling indigenous Arab and immigrant Jewish demands (an impossible task). For the first time, Mesopotamia was formally renamed Iraq and given to Feisal – as compensation for his loss of Syria – under British tutelage. What had been dubbed the 'vacant lot' between Palestine, Syria and Iraq, now named Transjordan (or Trans-Jordan, later Jordan) was generously donated to Feisal's brother Abdullah. Abdul Aziz ibn Saud was left without interference in Nejd, though Sir Percy Cox proposed that his British-supplied allowance might be raised to the same level as Hussein's to mollify him for the British machinations with the Hashemite rulers. Ibn Saud was contemptuous of the British plans, at the same time being content to accept his pension: 'We have arrived at a state where feet have assumed the position of heads', with the Sharif's sons no more than 'silly little fools aping English wisdom'; at the same time he observed that 'They have surrounded me with enemies . . . the grey-haired one in Mecca . . . his son Abdullah in Transjordania, his other son Feisal in al Iraq'.[50]

There were disagreements at the conference on whether the Kurdish area in north-west Iraq should be absorbed into Hussein's new state, but it was decided that the Kurds should continue as a separate entity under British jurisdiction. Not much, it was thought, could be done to aid other groups in the area, such as the Assyrian (or Nestorian) Christians driven from their homes by the Turks. Churchill tried also to reduce the economic burden on the British 'policing' of Iraq by shifting the military effort to an airforce-based strategy: Arabs and Kurds would be bombed and strafed by the Royal Air Force (RAF) if they did not behave themselves. It was also thought helpful to invite Abdullah, not yet planted in Transjordan, to assist in securing peace in the area. There was concern that Britain would not be able to hold on to Transjordan without more troops being sent into the area, and it would be difficult to cope with such an extra burden. Moreover, there was fresh British alarm at the news that Abdullah, with thirty officers and two hundred Bedouin, was on his way to attack Damascus, not at all the sort of thing envisaged by the Cairo Conference. Few observers believed Abdullah's claim that he had arrived in Amman 'for a change of air in order to regain his health after an attack of jaundice'.[51] Churchill solved the problem by buying off Abdullah: he was offered Transjordan if he agreed to fall in line with British plans. He would run the area, initially for a six-month trial period, under the control of a British political chief officer and with a useful British financial subsidy. He would also agree to entertain British air bases from which sorties could be launched to punish recalcitrant tribes. The overall plan in Transjordan seemed to be working well, enough to induce Churchill to write to Lord Curzon: 'Abdullah turned around completely under our treatment of the Arab problem. I hope he won't get his throat cut by his own followers. He is a most polished & agreeable person.' The principal remaining task was to implement the agreed time-table for the installing of Feisal in Iraq, if possible in circumstances that suggested popular approval of the event.

The plan was for Feisal, amenable as always, to travel to Mecca and then to despatch telegrams to leading (carefully selected) individuals in Iraq, declaring that he had been urged by his friends to come to Iraq and that after discussions he had resolved to place himself at the disposal of the Iraqi people (Lawrence to Feisal: 'Things have gone exactly as hoped. Please start for Mecca at once by quickest possible route . . . Say only you are going to see your father, and on no account put anything in press'). In such a fashion did colonial Britain manipulate its clients. The schemes did not however always run smoothly. It was soon learned that Sayyid Talib, a political notable in Basra, had agreed with Naqib, an elderly political leader in Baghdad, the terms for a Naqib candidacy for control of Iraq. Now there were signs that the carefully contrived candidacy of Feisal was to be strongly opposed. Ibn Saud had been bought off with cash but there were other problems facing the British scheme: not least that Sayyid Talib had adopted the alarming slogan, 'Iraq for the Iraqis!'[52] It was found moreover that Talib was receiving 'a magnificent reception everywhere'.[53]

The British response to the threat posed by Talib's popularity was to invite him to tea at the residence of Sir Percy Cox in Baghdad. As he was leaving the Residency – Cox himself had not deigned to attend the tea party – Talib was arrested on Cox's instructions, and later deported to Ceylon. The day after the arrest Sir Percy Cox issued a communiqué declaring that the action was necessary in order to preserve law and order. It was then discovered that the arrest of Talib had not materially improved the popularity of Feisal, though the British action had succeeded in defusing the nationalist threat. There was persistent support for Iraqi control of Iraq, and also suggestions for Iraq to become a republic, for the re-establishment of rule by the Turks (who were at least Muslim), and for the continued administration of Sir Percy Cox. Feisal sought advice in London and then travelled at British expense to Basra, having learned while aboard ship that Naqib's Council of Ministers in Baghdad had invited him to be a guest of the nation. Britain pretended indifference, at the same time urging Feisal to campaign so that the gloss of public acceptability could be maintained. The Council unanimously adopted a resolution declaring Feisal the monarch of Iraq, and on 18 August 1921 the Ministry of the Interior announced Feisal's overwhelming victory in the contrived plebiscite. His coronation was held a short time later.

The Ottoman *serai*, the fortress of government buildings dating to the time of Midhat Pasha, was chosen for the royal event. The temperature was high and the Tigris waters had fallen, allowing islets to surface briefly. The purpose behind the pageant was to install a pliant Hashemite king, one suitably sensitive to the proper interests of colonial Britain; but 'The kingdom of Iraq, seen against a scale going back to Ur and Sumer, Babylon and Assyria, would be as brief-lived as one of these summer islands. The kingdom's summer was the forty years of British supremacy in the Middle East'.[54] There were some fifteen hundred spectators: including Sir Percy Cox, his oriental secretary Gertrude Bell, Arab officials, Ottoman deserters, bankers and traders, the various (Muslim, Christian and Jewish) clergies, sheikhs, Kurds and others. And on the dais stood Feisal, 'the sensitive if none too clever Feisal whom Colonel Lawrence had selected as the most suitable leader for a British-promoted side show'.[55] Then an Iraqi shouted a declaration from Sir Percy Cox to the effect that some 96 per cent of the Iraqi people had voted in the plebiscite to chose Feisal as their king. A new flag was run up and the military band, lacking an Iraqi anthem, played 'God Save the King'. On 26 August Gertrude Bell wrote home: 'We have had a terrific week but we've got our King crowned.'

Drawing the Frontiers

The frontiers that came to define the Middle East of the twentieth century were drawn up by Britain and France with the (overt or covert) agreement of some other states.* The cynical definition of such territorial boundaries had inevitable consequences for ethnic rivalries, for spheres of sovereignty and for the areas of Western influence that have so far persisted for nearly eighty years. The creation of Israel in 1948 resulted in more boundary-drawing by Western powers, yet another source of tension in a region long troubled by outside interference.

The territorial definition of the Middle Eastern states has been a prime source of conflict in the modern world. In particular, for our immediate purposes, the frontiers of Kuwait and the associated status of Kuwait as an independent country have encouraged dispute – not only between Iraq and Kuwait, but also between Kuwait and Saudi Arabia.

The original settlement of Kuwait was founded around 1710 when a group of Arabian Bedouins were driven by drought to find new pastures. Among these wandering Arabs were the ancestors of the Al Sabah, the current ruling family of Kuwait, and of the Al Khalifah, the ruling family of Bahrain. The Persians occupied Basra from 1775 to 1779 and Kuwait prospered throughout this period. Basra was then recovered by the Turks, and Samuel Manesty of the East India Company moved his staff and factory to Kuwait in April 1793 to escape the attention of the Ottomans (this event has been adduced as evidence that Kuwait was then independent of Turkish

---

*In 1992 the UN Security Council, under direction from the United States and its Western allies, redrew the Iraq/Kuwait frontiers in violation of UN resolutions.

authority). Despite this independence there is still debate as to the extent to which the Ottomans could impose their wishes in Kuwait. Turkish forces from Baghdad marched through Kuwait in 1798 to attack the Wahabists in Arabia, and there were no complaints from the Kuwaiti rulers. Similarly in 1871 the Kuwaiti Sheikh Abdullah II gave assistance to another Turkish expedition marching through Kuwait to attack the Wahabist forces in Hasa.

When Abdullah died in 1892 the new Kuwaiti emir, Sheikh Mohammad, was advised by Yusuf bin Abdullah al Ibrahim, an Iraqi in the pay of the Turks. It seems clear that Yusuf was conspiring to oust the Sabahs and have himself installed as Turkish governor in Kuwait; at this time the province of Kuwait was in a state of lawless confusion. However, Sheikh Mohammad's younger half-brother, Mubarak, spoke out against the slide into anarchy, whereupon Mubarak was expelled into the desert to restore order if he could, and Yusuf became Chief Wazir of the state. Mubarak resolved to seize power, and one night in May 1896, with a small band of followers, he rode into Kuwait town, shot Mohammad at point blank range and then began a search for Yusuf. The Wazir was not to be found, having escaped to Iraq the previous evening. One of Mubarak's first moves on taking power was to declare Kuwait independent of Turkish control; he even went so far as to impose a levy of five per cent on all imports, including those from Turkish ports.[56] It seemed clear that the Sabahs 'were able to remain virtually independent in return for a nominal acceptance of Turkish suzerainty'.[57] To protect this independence Mubarak sought the support of the British who, after some hesitation, showed themselves willing to enter into an agreement. In 1899 Germany had obtained a concession to build a railway from Constantinople to Baghdad, and since it was obvious that Kuwait would be a natural terminal for such a railway this was quite enough to alarm the British. Mubarak was offered British protection in return for the commitment that he would enter into no territorial deals with any other government. The clear British involvement in an *in perpetuity* agreement would have various consequences throughout the twentieth century.

In December 1901 the Turkish sloop *Zuhaf* arrived off Kuwait with an ultimatum for Sheikh Mubarak; confident of British support he rejected it and the *Zuhaf* withdrew without further action. Then three British cruisers arrived and landed troops to forestall an anticipated Turkish attack from Basra; and in a subsequent action the British sloop *Lapwing* managed to intercept a Turkish force at sea and capture one hundred and fifty armed men. Neither the Turks nor disaffected Kuwaitis made any further efforts to overthrow Mubarak. Subsequent agreements were enacted to strengthen further the Kuwaiti–British links: in 1904 Mubarak agreed not to allow any post offices other than ones appointed by India to operate in Kuwait; in July 1911 he agreed that sponge and pearl concessions would be granted only with British consent; and in October 1913 he made the same pledge on the granting of oil concessions. It now appeared that Kuwait was secure from intervention from Iraq but it was not long before the small state had to confront interference from another quarter.

In November 1915 the Ajman rebelled against ibn Saud and in the subsequent conflict the Saudi forces were besieged at Hufuf, whereupon Mubarak sent a Kuwaiti force to offer active assistance. The Kuwaitis, under Mubarak's second son Salim and his grandson Ahmad al Jabir, managed to raise the siege and rout the Ajman forces. Then the surviving Ajman appealed to Sheikh Salim for sanctuary in Kuwait to escape the wrath of ibn Saud. Salim agreed and was immediately accused by ibn Saud of acting against Saudi interests, a new source of tension that might have been well handled by Mubarak – but Mubarak had died and the news reached Salim as he was marching home. Jabir, Mubarak's eldest son, ruled for a year, during which time he ejected the Ajman from Kuwait and tried to restore the earlier satisfactory relationship with ibn Saud. At the same time further problems, scarcely anticipated, were developing with the British.

In 1918 Britain had imposed a naval blockade on Kuwait to block supplies reaching the Turks via the desert route; and in July Sheikh Salim, Jabir's successor, was told that Kuwait would only be protected if it refrained from any actions prejudicial to British interests. Salim was now expecting ibn Saud to urge the British to revise their view of Kuwait's frontiers to the Saudi advantage. Salim then decided to build a fort near Jabal Manifah to signal the southern limits of his territory, whereupon ibn Saud immediately declared that the proposed site was on his land and ordered a settlement to be built at Jariya Ilya, in an area claimed by Salim. The Kuwaiti ruler then made a show of force near Jariya Ilya, an initiative that invited a dawn attack by ibn Saud's fanatical Ikhwan warriors: the Kuwaitis were almost entirely wiped out and many of their camels were stolen. Salim ordered the building of a defensive wall around Kuwait town, and both he and ibn Saud tried to justify their military postures to the British government. Britain confirmed that it recognised the Kuwaiti frontiers laid down in the 1913 Anglo–Turkish agreement, a treaty that favoured Kuwait against the claims of ibn Saud. In late 1920 there was further conflict between Sheikh Salim and the Ikhwan, led by Feisal al-Duwish. On 10 October 1920 Feisal launched an attack on Jahra, which Salim had to protect if Kuwait town was not to be the next to be attacked. The gunfire could be heard in Kuwait, raising much anxiety, whereupon all the remaining able-bodied men rallied to defend the wall. On 11 October several hundred men were sent by sea and by land to relieve Jahra, but already the Ikhwan forces had been decimated: at a cost of two hundred Kuwaiti men, there were already eight hundred enemy dead on the field, with another five hundred Ikhwan later to die through their wounds. Feisal al-Duwish then negotiated peace proposals, but no longer from a position of strength. Shortly afterwards his forces moved out of Jahra, carrying their spoils and burying men as they died on the march home. In Jahra itself many corpses were disposed of in nearby wells.

The British had not intervened in the battle but had indicated that they could not stand by and watch the destruction of Kuwait town. The RAF had dropped copies of a communiqué over the Ikhwan camp and British warships had arrived off the coast. In one view the Ikhwan attack on Kuwait had not been ordered by ibn Saud, who was still massively subsidised by Britain, and it seems that British officials accepted his denials of responsibility. The ubiquitous Sir Percy Cox declared that the Subaihiyah wells, now the site of an Ikhwan camp, should become an effective 'no man's land' between the two sides, and an uneasy truce ensued. On 27 February 1921 Salim died, to be succeeded by Sheikh Ahmad al Jabir. Ibn Saud at once made placatory noises, suggesting that there was no need for a formal boundary between the two states. This declaration did not satisfy Sir Percy Cox and in 1922 at the Uqair Conference he made efforts to resolve the frontier problem. This conference 'was of paramount importance to Kuwait and, indeed, to the whole of the Arabian peninsula'.[58]

Kuwait and Arabia had an obvious interest in the outcome, as did Feisal in Iraq, now keen to establish his own boundaries and so gain formal recognition by the League of Nations (it was becoming increasingly clear that the Cairo conference had not finished the job). The Iraqi delegate Sabih Beg indicated a region that ran close to the Saudi capital Riyadh, thus taking in the northern half of Arabia; and he also proposed a boundary on the Red Sea and the Gulf region as far as Qatif ('As God is my witness, this and only this is the true boundary and cannot be disputed'). Ibn Saud countered with a grandiose claim that took in much of Syria, a large slice of Iraq and the whole of Kuwait. Sir Percy Cox soon lost patience with all this and declared to ibn Saud that he would not tolerate 'these impossible arguments and ridiculous claims'. He, Sir Percy Cox, would determine the frontiers.[59] He drew a line on the map, denying part of ibn Saud's claim and giving Sabih Beg three hundred miles less than he had demanded. Cox had reprimanded ibn Saud, the Sultan of Nejd and the future King of Saudi Arabia, as though he were a naughty child. A witness to these events, the military attaché Colonel Dickson, later remarked: 'I was astonished to see him being

reprimanded like a naughty schoolboy . . . Ibn Saud almost broke down and
pathetically remarked that Sir Percy was his father and mother who made
him and raised him from nothing to the position he held, and that he would
surrender half his kingdom, nay the whole, if Sir Percy ordered.' But
Sir Percy was keen to placate the Saudi ruler, as Dickson observed: 'To
placate Ibn Saud, Sir Percy deprived Kuwait of nearly two-thirds of her
territory and gave it to Nejd.' Years later, Sheikh Ahmad commented to
Dickson that Britain had sacrificed a small nation to a greater power, and
that this had shaken his faith in Britain. H. St. J. B. Philby subsequently
wrote in a letter to the Dicksons, with regard to the territorial relationship
between Kuwait and Arabia:

> Of course the whole trouble about Kuwait is that it is racially and
> geographically a part of this country, though it is artificially separated
> from it by a political barrier which the British in their folly prefer to
> keep up. You might just as well make Hull and its district an inde-
> pendent principality under German protection . . . [60]

Thus the boundaries drawn up at the 1922 Uqair conference to define
the states of Kuwait, Iraq and Arabia depended upon no more than the
whim and writing hand of High Commissioner Sir Percy Cox. By all accounts the discussions were not extensive; the problems were addressed
in a peremptory fashion that invited no dispute. This is not to argue, in the
context of the tensions of the 1990s, that Kuwait should not have status
as an independent country; but it does suggest that the borders between
Kuwait and Iraq – one of the sources of conflict in the 1990/91 Gulf
crisis – were not well considered in 1922. And there is always the suspicion
that, on a different day and in a different mood, Sir Percy Cox would
have defined a different Middle East.

Iraq had long made claims, on both practical and legal grounds, to
control the territory of Kuwait. It had often claimed, for example, that
contraband goods were being smuggled into Iraq and that Kuwait had no
interest in blocking such traffic. It had also claimed, perhaps more significantly, that Kuwait should be incorporated as an autonomous sheikhdom
within Iraq since, even in the days of Sheikh Mubarak, Kuwait was part
of the Ottoman *vilayet* of Basra (and so in the modern world is rightly
regarded as a part of Iraq). It is interesting to note, in view of such claims,
that in 1930 the British acting High Commissioner in Baghdad '*suggested
to the government of the day that Britain should encourage the gradual
absorption of Kuwait into Iraq*' (my italics); and that representatives of

the British government were contending '*that Kuwait was a small and expendable state which could be sacrificed without too much concern if the power struggles of the period demanded it*'[61] (my italics).

The border issue was one matter that came to influence Arab attitudes to British interests in the area. Another was the evolving policy of the British government on the question of maintaining order among the subject peoples of the colonial lands.

The Shape of Repression

Britain had occupied most of Iraq – even Mosul, formerly claimed by the French.[62] But the British dominance in the area was not sufficient to keep the peace; in 1920, after many signs that a disturbance was imminent, the tribes rose in revolt. The indigenous people, many of them nomadic Bedouin, were not keen to replace rule from Istanbul with rule from London. Many of the officers in Feisal's army had been Iraqis who had witnessed the French attack on Damascus and thereby become sensitised to the claims of Arab nationalism. Now they had returned to Iraq, claiming that Britain had betrayed its pledges on Arab independence and spreading dissent in Baghdad and elsewhere. The British efforts to maintain tight administrative control throughout the country further exacerbated the problems: the tribes had managed to retain a large measure of independence over the centuries, even under the Ottomans, and they were not keen to lose it now.

Britain had apparently been willing to tolerate a Feisal administration in Damascus but now the British government, despite their plans to plant Feisal in Iraq as a puppet, seemed intent on maintaining tight British control throughout the country. It did not help that the British forces were thinly spread, and expected to move speedily from one possible trouble spot to another over an area of 170,000 square miles. The British were aware of the possibility that returning Iraqi officers might stir up trouble and managed to exclude some erstwhile Hejaz officers from Iraq, but many slipped through the net and spread the word about Damascus proclamations demanding Mesopotamian independence. Some of the Iraqi cities saw incidents of violence, and the unrest spread through the tribes as far as Kurdistan. Three British officers were murdered in Kurdistan in the summer of 1919 and the official sent out to take their place was killed a short time later. Soon further killings were being reported – six British officers were killed in one ten-day period – and further skirmishes encouraged the idea that stern measures would have to be taken. Colonel Gerald Leachman, celebrated for his travels and military feats in the eastern deserts, managed to rescue a group of officers attacked by tribesmen, but two of his own officials were carried off and later murdered. Leachman declared that the only way to deal with the tribes was 'wholesale slaughter'.[63]

A full Arab revolt began in June 1920; Gertrude Bell, now shaken out of her complacency, remarked that she was living through a nationalist reign of terror. Military posts were overrun by the Arabs, British soldiers were killed, and lines of communication were severed. In the holy city of Karbala a *jihad* was proclaimed against the British. Leachman was shot in the back by his Arab host, an event that stimulated much talk of 'Arab treachery' and encouraged further efforts to resist British rule. By mid-August 1920 the rebels felt strong enough to announce a provisional Arab government. Increasingly, questions were being asked – many in *The Times* – about the wisdom of British government policy: 'How much longer are valuable lives to be sacrificed in the vain endeavour to impose upon the Arab population an elaborate and expensive administration which they never asked for and do not want?'[64] The India government sent fresh troops to restore order; the towns were quickly secured but the problems in the rural areas proved more intractable. Over a period of months Britain had lost 450 dead and some 1500 further casualties. The British garrisons had often been taken by surprise at the ferocity of the Arab attacks. Thus one of the early engagements occurred at Dair al-Zor on the north-western frontier, when Jamal al-Midafi led a band of three hundred Arabs against British frontier posts. In a typical engagement that 'set the pattern of the emergent rebellion'[65] the defenders were entirely wiped out; over a period of weeks the isolated and undermanned Anglo-Indian garrisons were overwhelmed.

The rebellion spread from one region to another. Soon the entire area of the lower Euphrates was in revolt, with fresh uprisings breaking out around Baghdad. On 13 August 1920 Diltawa fell to the Arabs (or was liberated by them), to be followed by the capture of Baquba and Shahraban. Nationalist guerrillas began infiltrating the Kirkuk region and by mid-August the whole country, with the exception of the Tigris Valley in the south and the heavily controlled urban centres, was in revolt. By February 1921 the revolt had been crushed; against the 2000 or so British casualties between 8000 and 9000 rebels had been killed or wounded. The British forces had been swelled by 25,000 Indian and 5000 British troops, supported by the Royal Air Force; and by early 1921 the Arab invaders of Kifri and Khaniqin were pursued as demoralised outlaws. Punitive expeditions were launched by land and by air against the tribes: whole villages were destroyed by British artillery and suspected ringleaders were shot without trial. By late March the provisional Arab government was no more. The entire operation had cost the British government around £40 million, more than three times the total subsidies for the Arab Revolt against the Ottoman occupation.

Winston Churchill, as Colonial Secretary, was sensitive to the costs of policing the Empire; and was in consequence keen to exploit the potential of modern technology. This strategy had particular relevance to operations in Iraq. On 19 February 1920, before the start of the Arab uprising, Churchill (then Secretary of State for War and Air) wrote to Sir Hugh Trenchard, the pioneer of air warfare. Would it be possible for Trenchard to take control of Iraq? This would entail 'the provision of some kind of asphyxiating bombs calculated to cause disablement of some kind but not death . . . for use in preliminary operations against turbulent tribes'.[66] Churchill was in no doubt that gas could be profitably employed against the Kurds and Iraqis (as well as against other peoples of the Empire): 'I do not understand this squeamishness about the use of gas. I am strongly in favour of using poison gas against uncivilised tribes.' Henry Wilson shared Churchill's enthusiasm for gas as an instrument of colonial control but the British cabinet was reluctant to sanction the use of a weapon that had caused such misery and revulsion in the First World War. Churchill himself was keen to argue that gas, fired from ground-based guns or dropped from aircraft, would cause only 'discomfort or illness but not death' to dissident tribespeople; but his optimistic view of the effects of gas were mistaken. It was likely that the suggested gas would permanently damage eyesight and would 'kill children and sickly persons, more especially as the people against whom we intend to use it have no medical knowledge with which to supply antidotes'. Churchill remained unimpressed by such considerations, arguing that the use of gas, a 'scientific expedient', should not be prevented 'by the prejudices of those who do not think clearly'. In the event, gas was used against the Iraqi rebels in 1920 with 'excellent moral effect',[67] though gas shells were not dropped from aircraft because of practical difficulties.

Squadrons of the Royal Air Force had already been active in policing Iraq and Kurdistan before the start of the Arab rebellion in 1920. Thus Lieutenant-General Aylmer Haldane had praised the 'admirable work of . . . the RAF under extremely arduous conditions'[68] after British aircraft had bombed the Kurds in the winter of 1919/20 and in the spring of 1920. RAF squadrons were also used to protect the British line of communication between Baghdad and Mosul, and to bomb and strafe the Sufran tribe in the Diwaniyah area. Today in 1993 there are still Iraqis and Kurds who remember being bombed and machine-gunned by the RAF in the 1920s.[69] A Kurd from the Korak mountains of Kurdistan commented, seventy years after the event: 'They were bombing here in the Kaniya Khoran . . . Sometimes they raided three times a day.' Wing Commander Lewis, then of 30 Squadron (RAF), Iraq, recalls how quite often 'one would get a signal that a certain Kurdish village had to be bombed . . .', the RAF pilots being ordered to machine-gun any Kurds who looked hostile. In the same vein, Squadron-Leader Kendal of 30 Squadron recalls that if the tribespeople 'were doing something they ought not to be doing then you shot them'. Similarly, Wing-Commander Gale, also of 30 Squadron:

> If the Kurds hadn't learned by our example to behave themselves in a civilised way then we had to spank their bottoms. This was done by bombs and guns.

Wing-Commander Arthur Harris (later 'Bomber Harris', head of Wartime Bomber Command) was happy to emphasise that 'The Arab and Kurd now know what real bombing means in casualties and damage. Within forty-five minutes a full-size village can be practically wiped out and a third of its inhabitants killed or injured . . .'. It was an easy matter to bomb and machine-gun the tribespeople because they had no means of defence or retaliation. Iraq and Kurdistan were also useful laboratories for new weapons; devices specifically developed by the Air Ministry for use against tribal villages. The ministry drew up a list of possible weapons, some of them the forerunners of napalm and air-to-ground missiles:

> Phosphorus bombs, war rockets, metal crowsfeet [to maim livestock] man-killing shrapnel, liquid fire, and delay-action bombs. Many of these weapons were first used in Kurdistan.

There was no doubt that in the circumstances British technology, exploited in the full wisdom of British politics, was highly effective for colonial control. Gertrude Bell was one of those who was much impressed by the power of this mechanism for administrative supervision. Thus in 1924 she described an RAF demonstration, even more remarkable than the performance 'we saw last year at the Air Force show because it was much more real':

> They had made an imaginary village about a quarter of a mile from where we sat . . . and the first two bombs dropped from 3000 feet, went straight into the middle of it and set it alight. It was wonderful and horrible. Then they dropped bombs all round it, as if to catch the fugitives and finally fire bombs which even in the brightest sunlight

made flares of bright flame in the desert. They burn through metal and water won't extinguish them. At the end the armoured cars went out to round up the fugitives with machine guns. I was tremendously impressed.[70]

The British government, despite some divisions, deemed it necessary to use any available means to suppress the Kurdish and Iraqi tribes since they manifestly refused to acquiesce in British rule. The decision to instal Feisal as an 'independent' Arab ruler had convinced no one, just as no one believed that the League mandate for the British administration of Iraq was in any way different to traditional colonialism. General Haldane commented in March 1922 that 'the King here is very widely regarded as a British puppet'.[71] On 25 June 1920 Lord Curzon had declared quite openly in the House of Lords that it was a mistake to suppose that 'the gift of the mandate rests with the League of Nations. It does not . . . It rests with the powers who have conquered the territories, which it then falls to them to distribute'.[72] These were the circumstances in which the mandates were 'conferred upon and accepted by' Britain and France. The reality was, in the early 1920s and for some years after, that Feisal was a puppet, that Iraq was a British colony, and that it was necessary – in traditional colonial thought – to suppress the indigenous peoples as a requirement for maintaining a grip on the occupied land.

The need to maintain control of Iraq – by now much disputed in Britain – did not prevent speculation as to why the rebellion had occurred. There were many possible culprits: the Turks (in particular, Enver Pasha and Mustafa Kemal), Feisal himself (who by now was less enamoured of British designs), Arab nationalism (defused, but far from extirpated, by the exile of Talib), the Germans, the Americans (in the shape of Standard Oil), the Jews (still influential in Baghdad), and the Bolsheviks (at whose door any perfidies could be laid). Whatever the source of British colonial difficulties it seemed that pressure of circumstance, especially the cost of maintaining the Iraq occupation, would soon force London to revise its colonial posture, not only in Iraq but elsewhere.

The RAF continued to serve in the colonial territories as an instrument of control, and it was increasingly viewed as a cost-effective force. When John Salmond, the first Air Officer Commanding, took control of all the military forces in Iraq he found himself in charge of eight squadrons of aircraft, nine battalions of British and Indian infantry, local Iraq Levies, a number of armoured cars, pack artillery and supporting units. By the end of 1922 the Turks were again threatening Mosul and in the event of an attack Salmond intended to use RAF bombers to disrupt the Turkish advance. First he launched a bombing campaign against Turkish positions in northern Iraq and achieved considerable success: by the end of October the RAF had driven the Turks from the Rania, Koi Sanjak, Quala Diza and Bira Kapra districts, and the immediate threat of a Turkish advance had been removed.[73] In November 1922 an Allied–Turkish Peace Conference opened in Lausanne and the Turkish demands for the Mosul *vilayet* soon became clear. The conference adjourned in early February 1923 and the British quickly moved two columns of imperial troops into Kurdistan to strengthen the British negotiating hand. Rebel positions were bombed and the Kurdish leader, Sheikh Mahmud, was forced to flee across the Persian border. Turkish irregulars were expelled from Rowanduz on 24 April, just prior to the resumption of the conference. Now, in the interest of local British hegemony the state of Kurdistan was abolished as a political entity.

The Treaty of Sèvres between the Allies and the Ottoman Turks, agreed 10 August 1920, had forced Turkey to renounce all non-Turkish possessions. Apart from consolidating the British and French mandates the treaty recognised the independent Kurdish state of Kurdistan. However, the agreement was rejected by the Turkish nationalists led by Kemal and it was superseded by the Treaty of Lausanne. In April 1923 the state of Kurdistan, recognised at Sèvres, ceased to exist. The Kurds, with no political focus, were now distributed over the states of Iraq, Turkey, Iran and the Soviet Union (western observers may think it ironical that Kurdish rights were best protected in the USSR). The British negotiators at Lausanne had treated the Kurds as some HM government representatives came to think Kuwait might be treated, as 'a small and expendable state which could be sacrificed without too much concern if the power struggles of the period demanded it.' The problems that Sir Percy Cox had already laid up in southern Iraq with his cavalier attitude at Uqair were being well duplicated in northern Iraq by the Lausanne negotiators. The immediate *realpolitik* requirements took no account of ethnic histories, legitimate sovereign needs or the manifest pressures of natural justice. Britain, in sole control at Uqair, and in concert with the other powers (France, Belgium, Germany, Italy and Japan) at Lausanne had managed to contribute in substantial measure to many of the problems that would afflict the area for the rest of the century.

Britain continued to maintain the tight administrative control on Iraq, despite the cost and the growing alarms at home. In one view, the air power of the Royal Air Force was 'the midwife of modern Iraq' (Omissi, p. 37), since without the RAF the whole region might have been engulfed by a revived Turkey. British air power remained active in the area throughout the 1920s and early 1930s. In the late 1920s the RAF defeated the Ikhwan raiders who were challenging the power of ibn Saud in Arabia. Violet Dickson, the widow of Colonel H. R. P. Dickson records how Britain insisted that Kuwait must not help the rebels: '. . . Harold as Political Agent was concerned at the possibility that they would cross into Kuwait to feed their flocks and herds – as indeed they did during 1929, and again in January 1930 . . . Harold was told to warn the rebels that unless they withdrew they would be bombed by the RAF from Iraq.'[74] In July 1931 the RAF flew demonstrations over Euphrates towns to intimidate the supporters of an Iraqi general strike, and in 1931/32 British aircraft bombed Sheikh Ahmad's Kurdish rebels in Barzan. The continued presence of the Royal Air Force in the region, even after Iraq had secured its nominal independence, was assumed to be a powerful deterrent to what Winston Churchill was pleased to call 'uncivilised tribes'.

TOWARDS INDEPENDENCE

Most Westerners who bothered to contemplate the matter viewed the prospect of Iraqi independence with a mixture of alarm and disdain. Was it not obvious 'that the "wogs" would never succeed in managing their own affairs'?[75] Many would have agreed with Wing-Commander Gale (30 Squadron, Iraq) when he talked about 'the gutter rats who were the Arabs – and they *were* gutter rats'.[76] And even Westerners disinclined to use such invective have been ready enough to assume 'that the Arabs do not know what is best for themselves and that only the West can take efficient measures to deal with a critical situation . . . it illustrates the unconscious Western conviction that the peoples of the Middle East are incompetent to handle their own affairs . . .'.[77] The British government, doubtless to a degree sharing such traditional colonial attitudes was, however, under growing economic pressure and mounting domestic criticism. What benefits was Britain deriving from the occupation of Iraq? Could not British influence in the region be preserved in a less costly and less overt way? It was time to take stock of government policy on Iraq and to maintain Western control in other ways.

A constitutional assembly was convened in 1924, and in October a twenty-year treaty of alliance was signed by Britain and Iraq. This Anglo–Iraqi treaty was designed to safeguard British rights in Iraq, including military bases. In March 1925 the first Iraqi parliamentary elections were held, under British supervision, and Iraqi ministers became responsible for a two-chamber parliament. Already, however, there were signs that the tide was starting to move against the traditional colonial presence: it was only under heavy British pressure that the Iraqi parliament was able to stave off radical demands for complete independence. By the late 1920s Britain, now growing weary of the colonial commitment, was ready to abandon the mandate, assuming that British interests in the region could be protected. But Arab nationalists were growing increasingly wary of the possibility of British imperialism being maintained in other ways. In 1930 a further Anglo–Iraqi treaty was concluded, one which this time was expected to last for twenty-five years. The two countries agreed to consult with each other to harmonise their foreign policies; and again Britain would be allowed to retain air bases on Iraqi soil while providing a military mission to help train the newly-constituted Iraqi army. Key British interests were preserved but the 1930 treaty also specified certain restrictions on British power in the region. In part the agreement was designed to lead to Iraqi independence in 1932 and membership of the League of Nations in the same year. At the same time the British mandate, a cover for covert colonialism, was ended and Iraq joined the League in October under British sponsorship, a ploy to maintain continuing influence over the rapidly evolving Iraqi administration. In 1932 there were already signs that Iraq was aspiring to the leadership of the Middle East, a putative ambition that was not unwelcome to the British Foreign Office. If British influence in Iraq could be maintained then a strong Iraq would help to sustain the British presence in the area. The Saadabad Pact – which in 1932 brought together Iran, Turkey and Iraq – helped to reinforce Britain's presence in the Middle East.

Many of the old mandate responsibilities had now been jettisoned, mainly because Britain was increasingly alarmed at the financial burden (which by 1930 had been reduced to less than £500,000 per annum).[78] The 1930 treaty safeguarded British oil interests, partly by the continuing sovereign rights at two military bases (Habbaniyya, fifty miles from Baghdad; and Shaiba, near Basra) and partly by the entitlement to use Iraqi facilities in time of war. A constitution had been drawn up in 1924 to protect the (British-supported) monarch, but various debilitating conventions were written into this political framework. The upper chamber was appointed and dismissed by the king, with elections to a lower chamber strictly controlled by the government. Until constitutional amendments were introduced in 1943 the king could appoint the cabinet but not dismiss it, a provision that encouraged political intrigue and frequent resorts to violence.

Feisal lived to see Iraqi independence and membership of the League, but died the year after, in 1933. His son, Ghazi I, became king and lasted until the onset of the Second World War; Ghazi supposedly had nationalist inclinations but lacked authority and between the years 1936 and 1941 there were seven political coups. Rule was autocratic: no independent political parties developed and the successive governments worked hard to control the results of elections. In April 1939 King Ghazi was killed in an automobile accident, to be succeeded by his infant son, Feisal II, under a regent; the new Feisal was to last until 1958. Politics throughout the period was a class-based affair, with rival politicians keen to stir up tribal feelings in support of one faction or another. Now a group of reformist intellectuals and nationalist army officers had emerged to challenge the old-style politicians favoured by the British. In 1936 these new political elements seized power under the leadership of General Bakr Sidqi, who was assassinated ten months later, so establishing the precedent for one political coup after another. In December 1938, in the last of the pre-World War Two coups, General Nuri al-Said seized power, aided by an army faction known as The Seven. This development was not uncongenial to British interests: Nuri was staunchly conservative and pro-British, with no inconvenient notions about liberal democracy or a free press. He promised to end press restrictions and to advance the cause of parliamentary democracy, but during his period of office, power remained in the hands of the same clique of sheikhs and landowners, a group that supplied the few dozen politicians who in turn filled all the cabinet posts. Nuri built up alliances through nepotism and corruption, instead of making any efforts to reform and reconstruct the system. Such matters were of little interest to Britain, still working to maintain influence in the region. London was particularly gratified that Nuri broke relations with Germany upon the outbreak of World War Two, despite much popular opposition to his stand. (It is of interest that ibn Saud, long a British client, was quick to do deals with the fascists. He had already concluded an arms agreement with Mussolini, and in July 1939 did a deal with Hitler for the supply of 4000 German rifles, ammunition and the building of an armaments factory near Riyadh. At the same time ibn Saud ratified a treaty of friendship and trade with Japan who was making a bid for a Saudi oil concession. Through all this, ibn Saud maintained undying loyalty to the British government, remaining, in the words of one historian, 'clearly adept at being all things to all men'.)[79]

In Iraq Nuri used the outbreak of war as an excuse for further repression. He crushed all political dissent in the cabinet and in the country at large, and encouraged the British, still exerting influence through covert means, to work through his selected appointees in political posts and the administration. At the same time the various nationalist factions were being inspired by Nazi successes to adopt a more vigorous anti-British line. There was still resentment at the evident British presence and some observers saw an alliance with Germany as a means of evicting Britain once and for all. In March 1940 Nuri fell from power and Rashid Ali al-Gilani, a former

National Brotherhood anti-British agitator, became prime minister and soon demonstrated that he saw a German victory as a way of ridding the country of the long-lived British domination. When France collapsed in 1940 Britain demanded more military bases in Iraq, a demand that Rashid immediately rejected; while proclaiming that Iraq had the right to remain neutral Rashid encouraged his nationalist supporters to cultivate friendly relations with Italy and Germany. Then Britain tried to exhort the Iraqi regent, Abdul Illah, to dismiss Rashid from office, but the nationalists managed to force Abdul to flee the country. Rashid Ali, his anti-British posture in no doubt, then created a National Defence government with the prime aim of furthering the Arab nationalist cause.

Rashid Ali, by now thought to be 'in German pay',[80] conspired with three senior army officers to form what became known as the 'Golden Square' – a group that became increasingly ambitious despite Rashid's reservations. He and his foreign minister, Tewfiq Suwaidi, pondered on whether to support the Axis powers wholeheartedly or whether to try to preserve some residual relationship with the British. The Axis pressure became more insistent and Rashid responded by cutting off the oil pipeline to the Mediterranean, whereupon an elated Hitler ordered Vichy arms to be sent from Syria to Baghdad and German military advisers to be despatched to help Rashid retain power. On the night of 1/2 April 1941 the Golden Square began mobilising their forces and ejected the prime minister, Taha al-Hashimi, from office. Britain watched these developments with growing alarm. On 8 April Field-Marshal Auchinleck sent a message to Major-General Wavell conveying proposals that he (Auchinleck) and Lord Linlithgow, the Indian viceroy, had devised to address the mounting problem in Iraq. An infantry brigade and an artillery regiment, then in ships destined for Malaya, were to be sent to Basra; additional troops – enough to bring the Basra force up to division strength – were to be despatched within three weeks; four hundred British infantry were to be flown to Shaiba, equipped with Vickers guns and light machine guns. Wavell then signalled to Auchinleck: 'This proposal involves critical decision. It is just probable that this force might suffice to swing scale in Iraq . . .'

On 18 April an unopposed British brigade landed at Basra; the Golden Square was taken by surprise and Britain had the advantage. A force of 9000 Iraqi troops was hastily mobilised to confront the British force of 2250, but the British successfully resisted the attack. On 28 April, three days after Rashid had signed a secret agreement with the German and Italian representatives in Baghdad, he learned that a second British force was due to arrive at Basra the following day. Sir Kinahan Cornwallis, the British representative in Baghdad, warned Rashid in vain of the grave consequences that would follow if Rashid opposed the landing of the second force from India. In a rapidly deteriorating situation about 250 British women and children were sent from Baghdad to the British base at Habbaniyya, now entirely sealed off, trapping 2200 troops and 9000 civilians. The Habbaniyya forces had no artillery and only eighty-two obsolete or training aircraft; the base commander duly reported that the situation was 'grave' and that it seemed that the 'Iraqi attitude is not bluff and may mean definite promise Axis support'. In fact the Axis powers had already promised Rashid substantial financial aid, other support, and – as a gesture to his Arab nationalist aspirations – a United Kingdom of Syria and Iraq under the Iraqi monarch.

Two days later some nine thousand Iraqi troops had occupied the plateau overlooking the airfield. There were then, according to Churchill, 'fruitless parleys, and at dawn on 2nd May fighting began'.[81] The besieged British forces were successful: the defenders of Habbaniya 'without doubt turned the tide in Iraq and prevented the country, its oil resources, and its access to the Persian Gulf, from falling under Axis control. It was an important little battle'.[82] Thirty-two of the Habbaniyya aircraft and eight Wellingtons from Shaiba began bombing the Iraqis on the plateau, whereupon the Iraqis began shelling the cantonment. The RAF flew nearly two hundred sorties on the first day, losing five aircraft in the process, while inside the base there were thirteen fatalities and twenty-nine wounded, bad enough but a surprisingly low tally for the Iraqi artillery. Air Vice-Marshal Smart then developed an offensive to disable the Iraqi Air Force and the enemy lines of communication; bombing raids were launched against the Rashid airfield, near Baghdad; against the Baghdad Falluja road; and on the Iraqi forces still occupying the plateau. By now Blenheims and Hurricanes had arrived from Egypt and begun low-level machine-gun attacks on a small Luftwaffe detachment on the airfield at Mosul. It was soon clear that the Axis support demanded by the Iraqis was not forthcoming (the Panzer commander, General Heinz Guderian was later to comment: 'A German attempt to secure a foothold in Iraq was carried out with insufficient force and failed'), and the Iraqi resistance to the British forces began to crumble. The ground troops withdrew from the Habbaniyya plateau, abandoning large quantities of useful arms and other equipment; and the RAF, British infantry and the Iraq Levies launched an attack on Iraqi forces on the Falluja road, resulting in the capture of twelve officers and three hundred other ranks. Another Iraqi column moving up from Falluja was also attacked with bombs and machine guns: ammunition stocks were hit, lorries were set on fire, and more prisoners were taken. On 7 May 1941 Churchill cabled Wavell: 'Your vigorous and splendid action has largely restored the situ-

ation. We are all watching the grand fight you are making. All possible aid
will be sent. Keep it up.'

It was clear however that Wavell's position was weaker than the military
victories might have suggested. The British forces were thinly spread over
a wide area and there was concern at the possibility of a repeat of the
disastrous Mesopotamian campaign of the First World War. Churchill's
priorities were clear and he cabled to Wavell that his 'immediate task is to
get a friendly Government set up in Baghdad and to beat down Rashid
Ali's forces with utmost vigour'; Wavell responded that he would do his
best 'to liquidate this tiresome Iraq business quickly'. There were now
alarming signs that German aircraft based in Aleppo were beginning to
operate more freely over Iraq; on 13 May a Luftwaffe force headed by
Major Axel von Blomberg, the son of the German field-marshal, flew to
Baghdad and Rashid and other notables waited on the airfield to greet the
arrivals. As Blomberg's Heinkel landed it was mistakenly fired upon by
Iraqi police Levies and the Major was killed. This accident put an end to
German efforts to establish a military foothold in Baghdad; thereafter
the RAF attacked the pro-German Iraqi forces with mounting success. On
19 May troops from Habbaniyya, supported by relief forces, launched a
successful attack on Falluja, forcing an Iraqi withdrawal and taking some
three hundred prisoners. A week later the British force set out from Falluja
to advance on Baghdad but progress was hampered by extensive flooding
and many blown-up bridges over the canals. But by now the RAF had
destroyed the remnants of the Luftwaffe in Iraq and Rashid Ali could
expect no relief.

On the night of 29/30 May 1941 Rashid, accompanied by the German
and Italian ministers and some thirty of his closest supporters, fled across
the frontier into Iran. The Mayor of Baghdad sued for peace and on the
morning of 31 May an Iraqi deputation met the British representatives
(Major-General Clark, Air Vice-Marshal D'Albiac and Major Glubb) to
arrange the terms of the armistice. Sir Kinahan Cornwallis was collected
from the embassy, until then under siege. A few days later a residual group
of Rashid supporters rampaged through the Jewish quarter of Baghdad,
looting shops, destroying houses and killing anyone they encountered; more
than 150 Jews were killed. A commission set up to investigate these horrific
events concluded that the principal cause was the Nazi propaganda that
had been disseminated during the period of Rashid's rule, but no attention
was given to 'the most bizarre and astonishing aspect of the whole affair,
namely that the riots took place *after* the pro-Nazi regime of Rashid Ali
was toppled and in full view, so to speak, of the British, the Regent and

the loyalist army and police commanders'.[83] It seems that the British were reluctant to put forces into the city because, in the words of one British intelligence officer, this would have been 'lowering to the dignity of our ally, the Regent, if he were seen to be supported on arrival by British bayonets'.[84] Thus, for appearances sake, the Baghdad Jews were forced to suffer a pogrom, the climax of the period of severe persecution under Rashid. The British triumph 'was somewhat marred . . .'.[85]

The pro-Nazi regime in Baghdad was at an end. The reinstated regent appointed Nuri al-Said as prime minister, and Iraq had fallen yet again under British influence. But the British hegemony in the region, preserved despite the burdens and the tribulations of the Second World War, was soon to be shaken: fresh waves of Arab nationalism were about to break.

6 From Monarchy to Republic

THE GROWTH OF NATIONALISM

Nationalist factions were agitating for Arab independence in the time of the Ottomans, particularly in the nineteenth century when the empire was running into irreversible decline. In the twentieth century the British found it useful to encourage Arab nationalists to revolt against Turkish rule, though seeking at all times to contain Arab aspirations for genuine independence. Feisal would be allowed his brief moment of glory in Damascus, before being crushed by French military forces while the British observers, under whose tutelage Feisal had acted, would be happy to wring their hands. The subsequent planting of Feisal in the newly-defined Iraq was never intended by the British as a gesture to Arab independence, rather as a means of securing British influence over the former Ottoman *vilayets* of Mosul, Baghdad and Basra. Now, after the costly suppression of the Iraqi rebellion in the 1920s, British writ would run from the Kuwaiti coast on the Gulf to the Kurdish mountains and the Turkish border in the north.

The assumption of the mandates by France and Britain, under the convenient legalistic cloak of the League of Nations, represented no more than a continuation of colonial control in a garb that might be more acceptable to an international community growing increasingly sensitive to nationalist demands. Even the United States, not keen to advertise its growing economic imperialism, could pose as a friend of colonised peoples – a posture soon seen to be threadbare as the competing imperialisms continued to decay. The Arabs and other subjugated nations were becoming increasingly restive: the authority of the traditional colonialist regimes had evaporated for ever and there was new scope for national emancipation. It has been suggested that Feisal himself 'never abandoned his pan-Arabism', though his early experiences 'made him more cautious and explicitly gradualist'.[1] He never escaped from the orbit of British influence, and he died soon after Iraq had achieved its nominal independence as a sovereign state; but he helped to unify the disparate regions of what had been Mesopotamia, so preparing the ground for the integrated Iraq of the modern world (today, in 1993, the West appears to see advantages in a freshly-fragmented Iraq). Feisal managed to achieve the abrogation of the British mandate, though Britain had every intention of maintaining its control in less costly ways, and he saw recognition of Iraq by the League of Nations; a dubious benefit in circumstances where the League (like today's United Nations) was largely a tool of the great powers. Britain had protected most of its regional interests by negotiating the 1930 Anglo–Iraqi treaty, an agreement supported by some Iraqi nationalists but denounced by pan-Arabists as yet another colonial ploy. Moreover, the French and British mandates over Syria and Palestine were still intact, so stimulating the growth of nationalist movements that were to have a powerful regional impact. In Iraq itself the securing of independence had generated a new complex of political forces: the army, still advised by the British, was increasingly assuming a political role; socialists, communists and other radicals were urging a transition to genuine independence; and pan-Arabist idealism was developing with a fresh vigour. Syrian and Palestinian exiles in Iraq – including Haj Amin al-Husseini, the Mufti of Jerusalem exiled by the British for his nationalist agitations, and the Syrian nationalists Shukri al-Quwatli and Jamil Mardam – encouraged expectations of a radical transformation of the region. The pro-German Rashid Ali, who had confronted the British in 1941, was later deemed responsible for the 'first revolution for Arab liberation', though it was not made clear how he would have subsequently resisted the blandishments of his Nazi paymasters.[2] In Damascus a committee was set up to support Iraqi nationalists and to further the cause of the pan-Arabist movement. This body, set up by Michel Aflaq and Salah al-Din al-Bitar, is now seen as the direct precursor to the Ba'ath Party, the pan-Arabist faction that was later to acquire power in both Syria and Iraq (and number Saddam Hussein among its most powerful members).

Feisal had also stimulated pan-Arabist awareness by appointing leading ideologues, such as the Syrian Satia al-Husri, to the fledgling Iraqi civil service. Husri arrived in Iraq in 1921, acted as a general adviser, became one of the first Iraqi directors general of education, and later served as dean of the Law College which educated many of Iraq's first generation of modern politicians. The British deported Husri in 1941 as part of a general purge following the Rashid confrontation. In this fashion Iraq demonstrated its capacity to stimulate pan-Arabist sentiment, despite what may have been seen as a 'communal mix' that 'did not lend itself to such a project'.[3] Husri himself, influenced by traditional German philosophy, believed that nations were organic entities having an objective significance independent of people's subjective feelings. The nation was the primary existential focus, logically prior to statehood, geography and even religious identity: Islam was not incompatible with Arabism, but there was an Arab identity long before the birth of the Prophet. A principal task for Husri was to combat what he discerned as foreign influences amongst the Arabs, with the objective of confirming and developing a manifest Arab identity.

It seems clear that Husri was a moderate, or at any rate a pragmatist, despite his capacity to enrage the British authorities. But he was keen to work through the existing structures of society, an approach that also earned him the condemnation of leftist radicals. The educational system, for Husri, must seek 'the cultivation of the enlightened and ruling class on the one hand, and the attempt to spread education among all the nation's classes on the other, in the knowledge that the latter could not be achieved before the former'. The removal of illiteracy was secondary and 'without large benefit' unless it could be used to generate publications suitably addressed to the 'commoners'. It is easy to see why Iraqi radicals perceived the Feisal–Husri approach as one designed to serve the social and political interests of the ruling class. The approach aimed at the gradual transformation of society, in ways that did not entail the violation of the social organism; society had to be coaxed and cajoled to change, never forced. But for many of the new radicals this was a depressingly ineffective formula. Iraqi society desperately needed far-reaching reform – to abolish the divisions between rich and poor, to transform the inadequate social institutions, and to create a genuine Arabist consciousness as a necessary step towards effective pan-Arabism.

Feisal himself was well aware of the extent of his own political failure. He had succeeded in introducing a measure of social integration and in stimulating Arabist awareness, but he died in 1933 recognising how much there was yet left to accomplish. Feisal had always depended on the support of army officers, as well as on the approval of the British military presence; he had been assisted in the 1916 Arab revolt by ex-Ottoman officers, and by 1921 his officers were one of the most highly-educated sectors of the Iraqi population. Of the fourteen Iraqi prime ministers between 1922 and 1932 (i.e. for virtually the full period of the Feisal monarchy), nine were ex-Ottoman officers 'who shed their uniforms for politics and personal gain'.[4]

The predominance of the army in Iraqi politics derived directly from the British approach adopted during the period of the mandate. Britain had no interest in encouraging the education of the Iraqi people, whatever Husri may have urged on the basis of philosophic principle. The obvious priority for a traditional colonial power interested solely in strategic and colonial advantage was to organise pliant armed forces able and eager to protect the status quo. Britain helped Feisal to develop the armed forces to complement (and sometimes to supplant) the British forces in the area. And in addition there were the Iraq Levies, an all-Arab Shi'ite force recruited from the area of the lower Euphrates that could be relied upon to provide 'excellent service' and to show 'steadfast loyalty' to their British officers.⁵ Thus for obvious colonial reasons Britain was largely responsible for the militarisation of Iraq during the period of the mandate.* The weighty role of the military in Iraqi politics – both before and after the death of Feisal – was largely an outgrowth of British policy.

There were other influential factors. The mandate years had stimulated nationalist and pan-Arabist feelings, and these were to be increasingly reflected in the post-independence years.

TOWARDS THE COUPS

The years of the Feisal monarchy saw great turbulence in Iraq, but the post-Feisal monarchy witnessed even more violence and terror. The full period of the British-imposed monarchy (1932–58) saw coups, assassinations and public executions; dissident groups were persecuted and there were anti-Jewish pogroms; uprising followed uprising until a group of 'Free Officers' overthrew the monarchy. Some of the key events through this period are shown in Table 6.1.

In the 1920s the British imported into Iraq 'Western-devised political forms . . . into a tribal society ethnically and theologically fragmented with an urban crust of sophisticated largely Turkish educated leaders'.⁶ In 1924 the Organic Law constitution, allowing the king considerable political powers, was introduced as a means of protecting both the newly-planted monarchy and the enduring British presence. Two political parties (the Ahd al-Iraqi and the Hara al-Istiqlal), created in Ottoman times to protect Arab rights from erosion by the Turks, were now augmented by the arrival of three other parties: the Watani (National) Party, the Shaab (People's) Party and the Taqqadum (Progressive) Party. After the conclusion of the 1930 Anglo-Iraqi Treaty the parties regrouped, with Nuri al-Said reforming the Ahd and members of the Shaab and Watani coming together to form the anti-government Ikha al-Watani (National Brotherhood) Party, which expressed hostility to the treaty, declaring it a betrayal of Iraqi independence. Once Iraq had gained its nominal independence in 1932 these parties, their principal objective seemingly accomplished, withered away. The Iraqi Communist Party (ICP), despite many setbacks, persisted but other parties emerged only after the Second World War.

---

*Just as Britain trained officers of the Iraq Republican Guard and supplied military equipment through the 1980s.

Table 6.1   Chronology of key events through the period of the
Iraqi monarchy (1921–1958)

27 August 1921	Feisal installed as King of Iraq; accompanied by supporters from the time of the Arab revolt; the Syrian Satia al-Husri arrives to take charge of the Iraqi education system.
10 October 1922	The first Anglo-Iraq treaty, designed to safeguard British interests, signed.
16 November 1930	New Anglo-Iraqi treaty, giving Britain favourable terms on termination of the mandate, ratified.
3 October 1932	Independent Iraq admitted to the League of Nations.
8 September 1933	Feisal dies, to be succeeded by his son Ghazi.
29 October 1936	Bakr Sidqi overthrows the government and promises social reform.
11 August 1937	Sidqi assassinated by army officers; six more coups follow in rapid succession.
1 April 1941	Government of National Defence formed by the pro-German Rashid Ali; pro-British Iraqi politicians flee from Iraq.
19 May 1941	Rashid forces routed by the British; Rashid flees to Tehran; the regent and pro-British politicians reinstated.
1 June 1941	Scores of Iraqi Jews and their supporters killed in Baghdad pogrom; British forces fail to intervene.
24 July 1943	A small group calling themselves the Arab Ba'ath (Resurrection) Party issue their first statement in Damascus.
April 1947	The first congress of the Ba'ath Party, representing a new membership of several hundred, held; Ba'ath ideas begin to spread abroad.
20 January 1948	A massive urban uprising against a proposed treaty with Britain begins. The Iraq Communist Party (ICP) emerges as the main organising force.
14 February 1949	Faud and other leaders of the ICP publicly hanged in Baghdad; in 1949 Ba'ath ideas begin to spread through Iraq.
1956	Nasser nationalises Suez Canal, and Egypt invaded by a coalition of forces. Soon afterwards Saddam Hussein, aged about twenty, joins the Iraqi branch of the Arab Ba'ath Party (ABSP).
14 July 1958	Two hundred 'Free Officers' overthrow Iraqi monarchy; Brigadier Abd al-Karim Kassim emerges as prime minister and commander-in-chief.

The monarchy had been reluctantly accepted in Iraq despite British efforts to create the impression that it was a popular institution. Feisal himself had been regarded as a skilful and experienced politician, with his son Ghazi I (1933–39) seen as competent but unpopular. When, after his brief reign, Ghazi was killed in a car crash many Iraqis blamed the British for his death.[7] Feisal II (1939–58), four years old, inherited the throne and reigned with Abd al-Ilah, Ghazi's cousin, as regent. Abd al-Ilah was incompetent, unpopular and staunchly pro-British: Britain could feel that Iraq was safe in his hands. Many of the early supporters of the monarchy were Arabs who had chosen a career in Ottoman service and who had later joined the Arab group known as The Covenant; this body included Nuri al-Said, Jamal al-Midafi and the brothers Taha and Yasin al-Hashimi. Some of the older notables in Iraqi society were slow to appreciate that the Turkish system had gone for ever, and they were resentful of the young ex-Ottoman officers who had come to Baghdad with Feisal.

Many of the conservative notables came from Sunni *sayyid* families, and the political élite of Feisal's Iraq came to have a strongly Sunni orientation. Over the period 1921–36 seventy-one per cent of cabinet posts were occupied by Sunnis and only twenty-four per cent by Shias (this Sunni dominance of the political hierarchy was continued under Saddam).[8] In 1928 less than a third of the elected deputies were Shias, a reflection in part of the suspicion with which they were regarded: in 1923, for example, they had organised demonstrations with the aim of toppling the government. The Shia involvement in government increased through the later years of the monarchy and between 1947 and 1958 four Shia politicians managed to become prime minister. Such men were however well prepared to tolerate the prevailing hierarchy: they functioned as individuals rather than as representatives of the Shia population and they never challenged the Sunni ascendancy. Between 1921 and 1958 eighty per cent of the five major posts (premier, finance, interior, defence and foreign affairs) were held by Sunnis; and the Sunni dominance was even greater at the provincial level (in 1933 thirteen out of fourteen provincial governors, and 43 out of 47 heads of districts, were Sunni).[9]

Throughout the period of the monarchy there were constant reshuffles of existing ministers – so that the fifty-nine cabinets averaged only eight months each. A basic caucus of 166 men were involved in these reshuffles, some of the individuals holding many of the available posts over their political careers. Nuri al-Said himself, to the evident satisfaction of the British, held some 47 cabinet posts and other names are common: Umar Nadhari (21 posts), Tawfiq al-Suwaydi (19), Ali Mumtaz al-Daftari (18) and Jamil al-Midafi (19).[10] It has been argued that the frequent changes in government were not a sign of political instability; every election was a mere ritual tightly controlled by the government.[11] Iraqi politics was more about personalities than about policies, though there were political differences about such issues as the relationship of Iraq to Britain, the status of minorities and the role of education. Before Iraq achieved independence in 1932 the principal political division focused on the extent to which co-operation with Britain was acceptable; after 1932 the British connection was still an issue but other matters emerged, not least the relationship between the landowning élites and the mass of the population.

In education Husri had emphasised a language-based Arabism. His successor in the 1930s, Mohammad Fadhil al-Jamali, was interested in the generation of vocational skills but was keen also to use history teaching for the inculcation of Iraqi patriotism. Sami Shawkat, who controlled the Iraqi education system in the late 1930s tried to spread the idea that Iraq would be the architect of the future unity of the Arab world. This was the ambitious ground on which, decades later, Saddam Hussein, however fruitlessly, would try to build. It was also the foundation that, throughout the Hashemite years, various ambitious politicians would seek to exploit to personal advantage. There were many pecuniary fruits to be derived from a successful political career: bribery was commonplace, as were speculation in land and partnerships with commercial organisations (in the 1950s the Geylani family were the Pepsi Cola agents for Iraq). None of these self-interested developments seemed to change the basic structure of the Iraqi state: the constitution imposed in 1924 under the watchful eye of the British government remained unchanged for much of the Hashemite period.

In fact the first draft of the Iraqi constitution was written by the British Colonial Office, using the Austrian constitution as a model. Feisal favoured an alternative version based on the 1876 Ottoman constitution – since the Turks were necessarily more sympathetic to the protection of Muslim institutions. Various constitutional drafts shuttled between Baghdad and London until an amalgam was agreed. The Iraqi constitutional assembly convened in 1923 passed the electoral law, ratified the 1922 treaty with Britain and approved the constitution. Nationalists perceived that the treaty had been designed to favour Britain, and so mounted whatever opposition they could: the treaty was approved only after intervention by the high commissioner who threatened reprisals against anyone who voted to defeat the treaty (when the vote was taken there were many abstentions). The final constitutional document drew on the 1831 Belgian constitution and incorporated significant British and Ottoman adjustments. A constitutional monarchy had been established but one in which the king was granted extensive powers: he was allowed to promulgate all laws; to convene and adjourn the legislature; to appoint parliamentary members; to act as commander-in-chief; and to approve the appointment of the prime minister, other cabinet members and all other government appointments. If for any reason parliament was not sitting then the king was allowed to enact laws through royal decree, though the laws so proclaimed required later parliamentary approval (scarcely an onerous condition since the king's parliamentary placements could always be relied upon).

In the two-house legislature the king appointed all senators but the deputies were elected. An effort was made to guarantee civil rights, with all Iraqis declared equal before the law. Islam became the official state religion, and Arabic the official language. The Christian and Jewish communities were permitted to hold their own religious councils; and the official Muslim legal system was built around both Sunni and Shi'ite courts. The voting system – which in any case was not directly representative – did not extend to female suffrage; and it was possible for Sunni notables, Shi'ite religious leaders and the tribal sheikhs to rig the elections as they saw fit. Behind the details of the written constitution there lay ample scope for the preservation of the status quo, an arrangement manifestly to be desired by Britain. Of the three principal influences on the government 'The authority of the British civil servants representing London was the strongest'.[12] The other influences were the king, who in any case was a British placement, and the nationalists, who endlessly sought means of reducing the British influence. In one view it was only the skill of Feisal that succeeded in moderating the various extremist elements and avoiding an insurrection.

Britain, having wrested control of Mosul from France, still faced opposition from Turks unwilling to accept their loss of hegemony in the region. Kemal Ataturk, now heading a new Turkish government, was unwilling to relinquish his claims to Mosul; and so Britain referred the matter to the League of Nations, usefully dominated by the great powers. A commission of enquiry appointed by the League predictably decided in favour of Britain, whereupon the issue was brought before the Permanent Court of International Justice; this body, set up in part by the British, predictably agreed with the commission findings. In December 1925 the League Council awarded Mosul to British-controlled Iraq, with the condition that Britain would guarantee protection for the Kurds (the indigenous minority in the region) until 1950.* The dispute encouraged Britain to draw up a new treaty with Iraq, not least to consolidate the international recognition that Mosul was no longer within the sphere of Turkish control. The 1930 Anglo–Iraqi treaty, negotiated under a British Labour government, became the basis for Iraq's independence and admission to the League of Nations. The main thrust of the treaty was a further explicit protection for British interests, enshrined in a set of provisions that were bitterly opposed by the Iraqi

---

*A principal Turkish claim was that the Kurds were ethnically-related 'mountain Turks', an ironic claim in view of the modern Turkish persecution of the Kurds.

nationalist community. It was agreed that Britain would retain control (albeit covert) of Iraqi foreign and military affairs. Iraq became committed to 'full and frank consultations' in all matters of foreign policy and agreed 'not to adopt in foreign countries an attitude which is inconsistent with the alliance'. In the event of international emergency (its character undefined), Iraq was pledged to offer Britain 'all facilities and assistance', including ports, railways and airfields. Britain would be allowed to maintain military bases in Iraq, and Britain alone would be responsible for training the Iraqi armed forces; selected Iraqi officers would be trained in Britain, not least as an undeclared means of ensuring the correct political orientation of the most powerful element in Iraqi society. Even after independence Britain 'continued to play a dominant role in Iraq . . .'.[13]

After 1932 there was a shift in emphasis in Iraqi politics. Some of the momentum had gone from the independence movement: British covert control was a much more effective mechanism for protecting British interests than was a glaring military occupation that could be readily identified and attacked. The Ikha al-Watani (National Brotherhood) Party declined after independence but remained the largest political faction until 1936. A principal element in its strategy was to attack minorities as scapegoats, a ploy that led to the massacre in 1933 of the Nestorian Christians (the 'Assyrian peril'). These Assyrians (not to be confused with the ancient Assyrians) had been employed as British-protected Levies, used to suppress Iraqi nationalist uprisings, and had thus incurred the hatred of the nationalist forces. Four hundred Assyrians were mercilessly slaughtered in their villages, an affair that attracted international odium but did little damage to the aspirations of leading nationalist politicians. General Bakr Sidqi, the main architect of the Assyrian massacre, was now in the political ascendant. The army's massacre of the helpless villagers 'enhanced its public image and brought fame and promotion to the commanders of the expedition . . .'.[14] Conscription, formerly opposed, was now introduced 'with acclaim' and the army's strength rose from less than 12,000 at the end of 1933 to 15,000 at the end of 1935; on the eve of Iraq's first modern military coup the Iraqi army numbered around 20,000.[15]

On 29 October 1936 the Kurdish Bakr Sidqi led a *coup d'état* against the Iraqi government and installed a civilian administration of reformist ministers headed by Hikmat Suleiman. The ministers were drawn from the *al-Ahali* group (named after their newspaper), many of whom had been educated in European universities. In 1934 some of the Ahali had flirted with socialism; thus Abd al-Fattah had been impressed by what he had learnt about the Soviet Union while he was a graduate student at

Columbia University, and Mohammad Hadid had become a disciple of the left-wing British socialist Harold Laski at the London School of Economics. The Ahali called their philosophy *shaabiya* ('populism'), to convey something of the contempt it attracted from the ruling factions.

The Ahali and Bakr Sidqi did not make good bedfellows. In March 1937 General Sidqi, an admirer of Benito Mussolini, launched a savage attack on the liberals and socialists, an onslaught that led to protest strikes throughout the country. There were demonstrations and stoppages at the port of Basra, at the National Cigarette Factory in Baghdad, at the Iraq Petroleum Company installations in Kirkuk, and at many other industrial sites.[16] The strikes were vigorously suppressed, the Ahali leaders resigned in disgust, and for a brief period Sidqi was in sole command of the country. A few months later he was assassinated by a group of his own officers; in August 1937 the first modern military regime in Iraq was brought to an end, whereupon 'the army became virtually the sole deciding factor in the rise and fall of almost all Cabinets from 1937–1941.[17] Bakr Sidqi had laid down the pattern for a succession of military governments, and for the next few years half-a-dozen military coups kept the country in a state of political turmoil.

After the 1941 coup led by the pro-German Rashid Ali, his subsequent defeat and the re-establishment of British control most of the subsequent government coalitions until the 1958 revolution were controlled by Nuri al-Said (often as head of the government). In April 1946, as soon as it was announced that democracy under the reign of Feisal II would be restored (with a virtually unchanged constitution), five political parties became active: the Istiqlal (Independence), the Ahrar (Liberal), the al-Watani al-Democrati (National Democratic), the Ittihad al-Watani (National Union) and the Shaab (People's) parties. Three of the new groupings adopted socialist slogans, though none of these parties could boast a large following. The reliably pro-British Nuri worked to rally the conservative old guard against the young radicals, though it became increasingly obvious that his main interest was in protecting the wealthy classes. The Istiqlal rightists were largely discredited because of their suspected involvement with Axis agents during the war, and the Liberals were ineffectual. The National Democrats managed to consolidate their position as the strongest party on the left, though this group also was suspended in 1948–9 during the imposition of martial law. An outlawed Communist Party continued to agitate, though forced to remain underground until the 1958 revolution. Soon all the political groups and parties would be forced to confront the rise of the Ba'ath movement.

THE EMERGENCE OF BA'ATHISM

The two recognised founders of the Ba'ath movement came from the al-Maydan area of Damascus, the quarter known for its militant opposition in the 1920s to the French occupation: Michel Aflaq had a Greek Orthodox background, and Salah al-Din al-Bitar traced his descent to a long line of Sunni notables. Thus it was a Christian and a Muslim, meeting in Paris for the first time in 1929, who were to create the political movement that would come to dominate Syria and Iraq in the modern world.

Aflaq and Bitar together founded the Arab Students Union in Paris, and set about reading Marx, Nietzsche, Lenin, Gide, Tolstoy and others. There is some suggestion that Aflaq may have been interested in the philosophic vitalism proposed by the French thinker Henri Bergson, a doctrine that has been used to celebrate the creative function of mass action. But he never acknowledged being influenced by Western writers, even declaring in one interview that he had not followed Western currents of thought since the time of the onset of the Second World War.[18] When the two men returned to Damascus after their four-year sojourn in Paris they contributed regular items for the weekly communist journal *al-Taliah* but did not join the Syrian Communist Party: Aflaq denied any such connection but never disguised his admiration for communist discipline and militancy. Aflaq and Bitar had resolved to devote their full energies to politics: one of their first political acts was to create the Syrian Committee to Aid Iraq during the Rashid Ali episode, a body that was later seen as the organisational precursor of the Syrian Ba'ath Party.

The Party was officially founded in 1947 by Aflaq, Bitar and Jallal Said, an intellectual with a landowning background. The principal inspiration behind the Ba'ath philosophy was that of pan-Arabism: the individual Arab states were regarded as 'regions' of the Arab nation, itself a permanent entity in history. It was emphasised that it was not Islam, the Word of the Prophet, that created the peoples of Arabia, North Africa and the Fertile Crescent, providing them with the Arabic language and Arabic culture; rather it was the Arab nation that generated Islam and all that flowed from it. This suggests a secular focus: the central significance of Islam is acknowledged but there were Arabs before there were Muslims – the Arab states will be liberated when the moral power of the Arab nation is exerted; Islam will contribute to this world-wide emancipation, but there will also be other contributing elements. The perceived Arab decadence will be overcome 'through a purifying and spiritual action, not religious but moral'.[19] The spiritual power will derive from the Arabist consciousness, the awareness of being Arab; and this will achieve the liberation of the individual through social justice. It was declared, not without cause, that the imperialist powers were responsible for the break-up of the Arab nation; and that the overriding Ba'athist aim was the uniting of the various 'regions' of the Arab nation.

In its early years the Ba'athists supported various Hashemite schemes for the uniting of Syria with Jordan or Iraq, then British puppet regimes. The Ba'ath slogan 'One Flag, One Army, One King, One Arab World!' led many of the movement's detractors, especially the French, to accuse the Ba'ath of following a British agenda for the consolidation of the pro-British Hashemite territories. Pan-Arabism continued as a discernible theme in all subsequent Ba'athist groups and parties, though the aspiration became diluted with time: in particular, a bitter rivalry developed between Syria and Iraq for possession of the Ba'athist soul.

Both Aflaq and Bitar ran unsuccessfully for the Syrian parliament on three occasions (1943, 1947 and 1949), after which Aflaq declared he would never stand again. Bitar, very much the practical party organiser in the 1940s and 1950s, managed to get elected in 1954 as a deputy for Damascus and he subsequently held various ministerial posts. Aflaq served as a minister for one three-month period but he had great standing as a theorist of integrity, ascetic and incorruptible, well able to inspire the party faithful. One writer has commented that the Ba'ath was 'Michel Aflaq writ large',[20] an acknowledgement of his enduring significance in the movement. His first programmatic statement for the Arab Ba'ath movement was issued on 24 July 1943. The five banner headlines clearly show Aflaq's priorities at that time:[21]

1. We represent the Arab Spirit against materialist Communism.
2. We represent living Arab History against dead reaction and artificial progressivism.
3. We represent the whole nationalism expressive of the personality against verbal nationalism, which is in conflict with the totality of conduct.
4. We represent the message of Arabism against the craft of politics.
5. We represent the new Arab generation.

Aflaq uses the phrase *al-ruh al-arabiyya* ('Arab Spirit') to allow for the possibility of hostility to the nation's enemies (an option that the Christian 'love' might be deemed to prohibit, despite the practical sanction for Holy War). The 'Spirit' here denotes an energising historical force which, for Hegel, resides in the state but which, for Aflaq, resides in the nation; it is the *risala khalida* (the 'eternal message') of the nation. He proposes that Arab nationalism is not an idea, a mere creed that would add yet one more Arab sect to the ones that already exist. Arabs must forget such ideas and seek to rediscover their original relationship with their original nature. Only in this way can 'living Arab history' be used to reconstitute the eternal Arab Spirit: the emphasis here is on *culture* rather than on *politics*. There is emphasis also on the uniqueness of nations, the importance of conquering degenerate society, and the use of the concept of 'eternity' in helping to define the essence of the nation.

It is easy to portray Aflaq as an absolutist. In one interpretation the nation 'is the sum of those who have the right kind of faith'; and the objectivity of the nation is defined 'entirely subjectively, albeit in the "feelings" of only one man: the Leader'.[22] The state can have internal and external enemies, and the moral order is absolute. The words of Sami Shawkat, a precursor of Aflaq and a protégé of Husri, are now rounded out into a comprehensive doctrine, the detailed creed that helped to inform the declaration issued at the formal inauguration of the Syrian Ba'ath Party in 1947. Here it is stated that 'all existing differences between the members of the nation are superficial and false, and will be dissipated with the awakening of the Arab soul'; 'Whoever has called for, or joined a racist anti-Arab grouping, and all those who immigrated to the Arab homeland for colonial purposes' are excluded from the Arab nation (Article 11); political rights are restricted to those 'who have been faithful to the Arab homeland and have separated from any sectarian grouping' (Article 20); and the state is responsible for all freedoms and all intellectual work (Article 41). At the same time the Ba'ath remains a socialist party: '. . . It believes that the economic wealth of the fatherland belongs to the nation' (Article 26); while at the same time being prepared to protect property and inheritance, 'within the limits of the national interest' (Article 34), as natural rights.

It is easy to see Aflaq's thought as one of the shaping forces in the brutal intolerance of modern Syria and Iraq. The pan-Arabist fervour was nurtured in the colonial period; there was little in this historical phase to encourage moderation or respect for foreign interlopers.

The Iraqi Ba'ath Party was founded in 1951 and by 1954 had attracted some five hundred members.[23] By 1957 the Iraqi Ba'ath had joined the National Front (which already included the Communists, the Istiqlal and the National Democratic Party). This was a mixed bunch, preventing an easy focus for political commitment. There was no 'indubitable focus of political authority. No one person, force or institution dominated the scene'; and the specific Ba'ath claim – '300 active members, 1200 organised helpers (*ansar*), 2000 organised supporters and 10,000 unorganised supporters'[24] – would have been very difficult to verify. In July 1958 the Iraqi revolution swept away the monarchy and drastically curtailed British influence. But the revolution was made by army officers largely unconnected with formal political groupings. The Ba'athists would have to wait for some years before achieving power.

THE ISRAEL FACTOR

In September 1947 Britain announced its intention to give up the Palestine mandate on 15 April 1948. At that time the United Nations had made no detailed proposals for the partition of Palestine: there was no indication of how the partition would be financed or performed, and Britain had refused to participate in the proceedings of the UN Palestine Commission set up to supervise the transitional period. Britain seemed intent simply on divesting itself of power as quickly as possible, keen to hand over power on a piecemeal basis 'to whichever community was locally in the ascendant . . .'.[25] This was a recipe for internal disorder and a full-scale civil war broke out with the abrupt withdrawal of the British administration. The United States vacillated and then called for a truce and further consideration of the issue by the UN General Assembly.

The Zionists, eager to establish their new state, redoubled their efforts: the terrorist Irgun and Stern gang, now collaborating with the Haganah, began implementing the Plan Dalet for the seizure of most of Palestine. Attacks were launched on strategically situated Arab villages whose inhabitants were forced to flee land that their families had occupied for centuries. An Arab Liberation Army of some 3000 volunteers tried to preserve the status quo but were unable to resist the superior Zionist forces. Arab morale collapsed in the face of this Zionist offensive and psychological warfare that spread reports that Irgunists had massacred 250 inhabitants of the Deir Yasin village on 10 May 1948. Soon the Zionists, in direct contravention of the terms of the UN-sponsored partition, had taken Tiberias, Haifa, Acre, Jaffa and most of Arab Jerusalem. The last British high commissioner, quick to wash his hands of the whole affair, left Palestine on 14 May and the mandate was at an end.

On the very day that modern Israel was born five Arab armies massed on the frontiers, determined to restore the Palestinian land to its traditional Arab owners. The apparent Arab unity in fact disguised deep divisions; there was no overall command structure and the various Arab forces were incapable of acting in concert. Some 60,000 Jewish troops were able to confront forces deployed by Egypt, Transjordan (the Arab Legion), Syria,

Lebanon and Iraq; and to secure a remarkable victory. The confrontation ended in January 1949, by which time only a fifth of the land area of Palestine remained in Arab hands, and the number of Arabs in the territory conquered by Israel had fallen by between 700,000 and 750,000.[26]

The UN mediator, Ralph Bunche, negotiated separate armistices between Israel and the Arab states (except for Iraq which however withdrew its troops from around Jerusalem). Despite UN efforts no peace treaty was concluded, the Arab states refusing to consider such an agreement unless the new Israeli government agreed to accept all the Arab refugees wishing to return to their homeland. Resolutions before the UN General Assembly affirming the Arab right of return or adequate compensation for their confiscated property were constantly passed; and it was on the understanding that Israel would observe such resolutions that the new state was admitted to the United Nations on 11 May 1949. However, Israel – insisting that the rights of refugees could only be considered as part of a general peace settlement – guaranteed that the impasse would be complete. Now half of the Palestinian Arabs had become victims of the cavalier British surrender of the mandate and UN machinations that took too little account of local ethnic history or the need for a settlement that would be likely to secure peace for future generations.

These events exacerbated the persecution of the Jews that was already under way in Iraq and other parts of the Arab world. After the crushing of Rashid Ali and the end of the Baghdad pogrom the Jews experienced a period of relative quiet throughout most of British-occupied Iraq; but with the ending of the war fresh troubles began. On 2 November 1945 the Misr al-Fatat ('Young Egypt') fascist-style nationalists staged anti-Jewish riots in Cairo; Jewish property was destroyed, an old-people's home was wrecked, and a synagogue was set on fire. On 5 November Iraqi Arab nationalists were calling for similar demonstrations on the streets of Baghdad, but on this occasion the Iraqi Minister of the Interior imposed a ban and further anti-Jewish actions were prevented. However, the Iraqi authorities were growing increasingly resentful of the Zionist presence in their midst, and with the recent creation of the League of Arab Nations it seemed clear that the Palestine question was the issue that could best serve the cause of Arab unity.

In Baghdad strict censorship on all contacts by Jews with relatives and friends in Palestine was imposed. Letters were seized and filed, to be used later as supposedly incriminating evidence against the Jewish community. British officials assisted in this persecution, collecting sacks of mail and handing them over to the Iraqi authorities.[27] The British themselves had long been hostile to Jewish immigration in the Middle East, even though the Palestine Jews had allied themselves with Britain in the struggle against Nazism. Such immigration was seen as 'a serious menace' to British interests, and as early as May 1942 when the death trains were rolling across Europe Britain reaffirmed its policy of 'taking all practical steps to discourage illegal immigration to Palestine' and of doing 'nothing what-ever . . . to facilitate the arrival of Jewish refugees in Palestine'.[28] In these circumstances the repressive measures adopted by the Iraqi authorities against the Jewish community were not unwelcome to British officials.

Steps were taken to reduce the number of Jews in many occupations, with individuals either dismissed or forced to resign. An American report prepared in 1945 highlighted efforts to reduce the number of Jewish civil servants in Baghdad, and at the same time efforts were being made to restrict Jewish trade: merchants in the export–import business failed to receive the necessary enabling documentation and many were forced to join with Muslim businessmen in order to stay in business. Restrictions were placed on the number of Jews admitted to schools and institutions of higher learning, and teachers who had arrived from Palestine were dismissed. The proportion of Jewish teachers in Jewish schools was reduced, while Muslims were brought in to fill the vacant posts. In 1944–5 out of sixty students admitted to the Royal Medical College only seven were Jews, with the Law College only admitting nine Jews in the new class of three hundred students.[29]

Fragile Baghdad administrations saw advantages in scapegoating the Jewish community. It was often acknowledged that Jews had lived in Iraq for centuries, though Zionism had now arrived to threaten Iraqi interests. Thus Mohammad Fadhil al-Jamali, then Director-General of the Iraqi Ministry of Foreign Affairs, testified in March 1946 that Jews had been living in Iraq 'for thousands of years' as 'our brethren . . . in perfect peace and harmony . . .', but that political Zionism had come 'to poison the atmosphere'; Iraqi Jews, he declared, felt 'embarrassed at what the Zionists stand for and at the bitter relationship that exists between us and the Zionist Jews'.[30] The Anglo-American Committee of Enquiry received such testimony and also statements from Jews, fearing reprisals for adverse comment, declaring that all was well. But as the Committee was completing its investigations there were fresh rumours of anti-Jewish riots, following the publication of a Shi'ite *fatwa* (religious edict) prohibiting the sale of land to Jews throughout the Arab world. In addition the Iraqi authorities were among the first to comply with a resolution of the Arab League Council urging Arab governments to take further repressive measures against Zionism. Travel restrictions were imposed on all but wealthy Jews, and at the same time Nuri al-Said declared that the Jews in Muslim countries were 'hostages'. Jewish participation in demonstrations against the 'Portsmouth' treaty being negotiated between London and Baghdad angered the pro-British establishment which led to further anti-Jewish feeling.

Once the partition resolution on Palestine was published Iraqi 'volunteers' were despatched to protect the Palestinian Arabs; and the Chief Rabbi Sassoon Kadouri was forced to issue a statement in Baghdad condemning Zionism and declaring support for the Arabs in the Palestine dispute. Pressure mounted for a military attack on Israel; demonstrators paraded the slogan 'Death to the Jews!' through the streets of Baghdad; and on 27 April a synagogue was attacked and looted. On 15 May 1948 a contingent of Iraqi troops moved into Palestine and martial law was declared throughout Iraq. Censorship was tightened, military courts were established, and a concentration camp was established in the southern desert to hold dissidents. At the same time an article of the Iraqi Criminal Code was modified so that 'Zionism' could be added to the list of proscribed doctrines. Jewish civil servants were dismissed from their posts; even Ibrahim el-Kabir, the Controller-General of the Iraqi Ministry of Finance, was discharged on pension soon after arriving in Britain to negotiate a new financial agreement. In July 1948 the Minister of Defence prohibited Jewish-owned banks from dealing with foreign financial institutions,[31] and in October the Minister of Finance declared that all Iraqi Jews living abroad must return to Iraq by a particular date or face the forfeiture of their property. It is obvious that the anti-Jewish measures were designed in part to secure revenue for the Iraqi state. Thus 'by the end of October a total of £20,000,000 had been collected from the Jews in fines and by a rich variety of means and excuses . . .'.[32] In the immediate post-war years Iraqi Jews in their thousands struggled to emigrate to Israel (one massive airlift was dubbed 'Operation Ezra and Nehemiah'), though often forced to sacrifice most of their property. The Iraqi government, not without significant British support, had consolidated an anti-Jewish posture that was to endure through all the subsequent decades.

The invasion of Palestine (Israel) by the Iraqi military forces in 1948 had set the pattern for further interventions that would take place in the years ahead. None of the interventions led to permanent Arab advances in the region; nothing, it seemed, could be done to recapture the territories lost to the Israelis in the various Arab–Israeli wars. In due course Egypt was to negotiate the return of Sinai, lost in a later war, but all the military endeavours of the Arabs seemed fruitless.

On 14 May 1948 an Iraqi expeditionary force moved into the West Bank region and tried to bridge and ford the Jordan in the area of Gesher; but when robust resistance was mounted by the settlers of Gesher and by units of the Golani Brigade the Iraqis were forced to withdraw, later deciding to cross the river in an area already controlled by the Arabs. The Iraqi force of an infantry brigade and an armoured battalion moved south to the Damya and Allenby bridges and crossed the Jordan to Nablus. On 25 May, after awaiting reinforcements, the force advanced from the hills of Samaria past Tulkarem towards the Mediterranean – with the aim of cutting Israel in two. The Jewish village of Geulim was taken, and on 28 May Iraqi spearheads reached Kfar Yona and Ein Vered, also bringing Kfar Javits under attack. Then the Iraqi forces were brought to a halt, only six miles from the Mediterranean, by the Jewish Alexandroni brigade which managed to recapture Geulim.

The Carmeli brigade, led by Colonel Mordechai Makleff, then mounted an attack on the advanced Iraqi position. Iraqi resistance, supported by aircraft, was strong, while the Israeli artillery could not reach the Iraqi forces preparing for a counterattack. However, despite Israeli difficulties the Carmeli force persisted and succeeded in recapturing the town of Jenin on 3 June. The Iraqis soon brought up reinforcements and retook the town, inflicting heavy losses on the retreating Israeli forces. On 4 June the Alexandroni brigade managed to capture Kakun, north of the Natanya–Tulkarem road, and repeated Iraqi counterattacks were successfully repulsed. Many such encounters were inconclusive; areas were lost, retaken and lost again. The eventual outcome, following considerable Israeli gains throughout the whole of Palestine, was the complete withdrawal of Iraqi and other Arab forces from the few areas still held. This pattern of Arab defeat was to be repeated in all the later Arab–Israeli wars.

Iraqi forces, along with other Arab contingents, were involved in the Sinai campaign of 1956, following the seizure of the Suez Canal by President Nasser of Egypt (see below). An Iraqi division moved to enter Jordan as a prelude to an attack on Israel; but in the event this and other Arab moves failed to deter the Israeli attack on Arab positions throughout the region. Similarly, in the 1967 Six-Day War the Israeli Air Force destroyed the bulk of Egypt's air power on the morning of 5 June, and then dealt with the air forces of Jordan, Syria and Iraq, destroying vast numbers of aircraft on the ground. Still the Arab air forces managed to mount offensive operations, though without much useful effect. Syrian aircraft attacked the oil refineries at Haifa Bay and bombed an airfield at Megiddo; Jordanian planes strafed the Kfar Sirkin airfield; and Iraqi aircraft bombed the Mediterranean town of Natanya. Such efforts merely encouraged the more powerful Israeli Air Force to concentrate its attack on the vulnerable Arab air forces. Soon substantial numbers of Iraqi aircraft had been destroyed; the Jordanians lost twenty-two Hunter fighters, six transports and two helicopters, virtually wiping out the entire air force; and the Syrians lost thirty-two MiG-21s, twenty-three MiG-15s and MiG-17s, and two Ilyushin Il-28 bombers, representing two-thirds of the air force's total strength. By the end of the second day of the war the Arabs had lost 416 aircraft, 393 of which had been destroyed on the ground; a mere twenty-six Israeli aircraft had been lost in action. Fifty-eight of the Arab aircraft lost were downed in aerial dog-fights.[33]

The Six-Day War saw Iraqi forces moving into Jordan: in addition to Jordan's 270 tanks and 150 artillery pieces there was an Iraqi force of an armoured brigade and three infantry brigades. In the subsequent ground battles between the Arab and Israeli forces the brigade promised by the Syrians to President Nasser never materialised; and the Iraqis, though now stationed in Jordan, did not enter the conflict. The Israelis completed their conquest of the West Bank: King Hussein, dragged into war on a wave of Arab hysteria, had now lost half his kingdom. Jordanian casualties were reckoned at more than six thousand killed and missing; Israeli losses were some 550 killed and 2500 wounded.[34]

A war of attrition then developed through the 1960s as a prelude to the 1973 Yom Kippur War. In December 1968 the Iraqi expeditionary force in Jordan began shelling Israeli towns, whereupon the Israelis responded with artillery barrages of their own and an air attack on the Iraqi force, killing eight troops, wounding fourteen, and inflicting considerable damage on vehicles and other equipment. Between September 1968 and March 1969 there were some 534 hostile actions against Israel: 189 emanated from Jordan, 123 from the Gaza Strip, 47 from the Suez Canal area, and 29 from the West Bank.[35] The Palestine Liberation Organisation (PLO) also began terrorist operations against Israeli interests abroad, starting with the hijacking of an El Al airliner to Algeria in July 1968. The PLO, in part funded by Libya's Colonel Muammar Gaddafi, also helped train and supply terrorists for operations in overseas countries. It is useful to remember, in this context, the terms of the UN Security Council Resolution 242, passed on 22 November 1967. It declared that fulfilment of the principles of the United Nations Charter required the creation of a just and lasting peace in the Middle East, and that this required the implementation of both of the following:

1. The withdrawal of Israel's armed forces from territories occupied in the recent conflict.
2. Termination of all claims or states of belligerency, and respect for and acknowledgement of the sovereignty and territorial integrity and political independence of every state in the area and their right to

live in peace within secure and recognised boundaries free from
threats or acts of force.

The UN Secretary-General appointed the Swedish diplomat Gunnar Jarring
to work for the implementation of the resolution. His efforts were largely
in vain but in 1979 the first peace treaty of the Middle East was secured;
not however before yet another Arab–Israeli war had been fought.

The 1973 Yom Kippur War derived from the circumstances that surrounded the settlement of the 1967 Six-Day War: President Sadat of Egypt
had resolved to recover the area of Sinai for the Egyptians and the other
Arab lands lost to the Arabs in 1967. Again considerable forces were
ranged against Israel, including an Iraqi armoured brigade with 130 tanks
and a mechanised brigade with fifty tanks which arrived in the first week
of the war (week ending 11 October); a few days later another armoured
brigade with 130 tanks arrived in Syria to supplement the Iraqi forces
already there. On 12 October Iraqi tanks advanced towards the southern
flank of the Israeli forces moving to threaten the military camps to the west
of Damascus. When, later that day, the first Iraqi tanks confronted Colonel
Uri Orr's 79th Brigade some seventeen Iraqi tanks, fired on from 300 yards
distance, were knocked out and the Arab force ground to a halt. In a
subsequent engagement Iraqi tanks from the Third Armoured Division, now
reinforced by its Sixth Armoured Brigade, ran into an Israeli trap: eighty
Iraqi tanks were destroyed and the remaining forces retreated in total
disorder, with an entire brigade destroyed in only a few minutes and not
one Israeli tank hit. This was the first major armoured battle of the Iraqi
army, and it was a disaster.

Subsequent engagements were, from the Iraqi point of view, more successful but still relatively unimpressive. The Iraqis had displayed considerable logistical ability in moving two armoured divisions nearly four
hundred miles from Iraq, and in speedily activating one of these for a
military engagement, but their performance in combat against the Israelis
was less impressive. The 'mediocre ability' of the Iraqi Army in battle
has been contrasted with the 'logistic feat' of organising 'the move of
formations to the Golan Heights in such a comparatively short time'.[36]

The Yom Kippur War failed in its primary task of achieving an immediate restoration of Arab lands. At best the war may be seen as having
contributed to the agreement, brokered by President Carter at Camp David
in 1979, between Begin and Sadat when Egypt regained control of the Sinai
area. The legacy of Yom Kippur, like the bitter legacies of earlier Arab–
Israeli conflicts, was yet more anguish and resentment, the unstable mix
of passions still only partially addressed in the 1990s.

PRELUDE TO SUEZ

The British impact on Iraq was first to consolidate, and later to exacerbate, the social divisions that were bound in due course to lead to political upheaval. Thus, under the British, local notables were able 'to acquire vast semifeudal estates and to reduce "their" tribesmen to the status of debt-bonded serfs'. Rural areas became divorced from the rest of the national economy, a development which 'tended to arrest the emergence of capitalist relations of production in the countryside' and to generate 'severe distortions in the country's economic and political systems . . .'.[37] By 1960 more than two-thirds of all cultivable land was divided into some 3400 estates, with a half of such land owned by about 2500 people (out of a national population of around seven million). The position of the (often absentee) landlords was strengthened under British rule, just as much of the population was kept poverty-stricken; in 1957 the bulk of the rural population of 3.8 million was landless. On occasions the peasants struggled to rebel, but on the whole they were passive, inarticulate, resigned and apathetic; in medical terms the Iraqi peasant was seen as 'a living pathological specimen'.[38] The real powers in the country, sustained by the armed forces, were 'the monarchy and its entourage, the great landowners, the Iraq Petroleum Company, and the British economic and military domination'.[39]

A mere two per cent of the landowners owned more than two-thirds of all the useful land, with the sharecropper peasants massively exploited, forced to provide up to two-thirds of their produce to the landlords. Under the terms of a 1951 law unoccupied state lands were to have been given to peasants who would then be aided with state grants, but in the subsequent years little of the land had been distributed and inadequate irrigation schemes ruined the soil (as at Dujaila). In 1952 unrest grew among the peasants when they heard about the land reforms in Egypt, and soon thousands were fleeing to the cities to escape rural destitution. Through the 1950s massive slums spread around Baghdad, with the hovel inhabitants periodically swamped by muddy overflows from the Tigris. One keen observer described the prevailing conditions: 'There is much trachoma and dysentery, but no bilharzia or malaria, because the water is too polluted for snails and mosquitoes. The infant mortality is 250 per thousand. A woman has a 50:50 chance of raising a child to the age of ten. There are no social services of any kind . . . On the adjacent dumps dogs with rabies dig in the sewage, and the slum-dwellers pack it for resale as garden manure.'[40]

This was the social framework that was congenial to British investors and sustained by British arms; and to those Europeans and Americans with a proper interest in wider political matters. In the 1950s such matters related to the strategic exigencies of the Cold War and to the troublesome ambitions of local nationalist leaders, such as President Nasser in Egypt.

In early January 1953 the US Secretary of State Byroade and the British Foreign Office reached agreement on the joint approach to be made to President Neguib of Egypt on the related issues of the Suez Canal base, Middle Eastern Defence, and Western economic and military support for Egypt. This was all part of the US strategy for countering the Soviet threat (real or imagined), but it did not always enjoy the unqualified support of the British. In fact President Eisenhower and John Foster Dulles went cold on the terms of the joint approach to Egypt, arguing that a settlement between Britain and Egypt on Suez might be achieved without guaranteeing Egypt's commitment to the Middle Eastern Defence Organisation.[41] In May Foster Dulles visited Neguib, Nasser and other Egyptian leaders in Cairo to be told by Nasser that the US proposals for the defence of the Middle East were the 'perpetuation of occupation'; and he added: 'I can't see myself waking up one morning to find that the Soviet Union is our enemy . . . I would become the laughing stock of my people if I told them they now had an entirely new enemy, thousands of miles away, and that they must forget about the British enemy occupying their territory.'[42] The Revolutionary Command Council (RCC) of Egypt was encouraging guerrilla actions against the British in   the Canal Zone, and the British were contemplating military action, including the reoccupation of Cairo and Alexandria. Such developments were hampering US plans to involve Egypt in an alliance for the defence of the Middle East. Indeed Foster Dulles suggested that Turkey, Pakistan, Iran and Iraq be organised in a 'Northern Tier' defence organisation, a comprehensive system that would overlap other defensive arrangements and provide yet another bulwark against the possibility of Soviet expansion. Turkey was already a NATO state; Pakistan had 'martial and religious characteristics' that could be exploited; Iran could be an asset provided the US could 'concentrate on changing the situation there'; and Iraq, with its 'forward-looking' government, was the Arab country 'most plainly concerned with the Soviet threat'.[43]

The Dulles scheme suited the ambitions of Nuri al-Said, interested as he was in establishing Iraq as the leader of the Arab world. He was also interested in replacing the 1930 Anglo–Iraqi treaty with arrangements that were better suited to the rapidly changing conditions of the modern world: even the staunchly pro-British Nuri was not wholly reliable. In January 1955 the Turkish prime minister Adnan Menderes visited Baghdad for talks, and soon the US was urging Turkey to bring Iraq into the Turkish–Pakistani Pact, yet another route for tying Iraq into a pro-NATO alliance. Egypt remained a problem. The Muslim Brotherhood had tried to assassinate Nasser, and he subsequently removed General Neguib from power. There were no signs that President Nasser was eager to enter any manifestly anti-Soviet defence arrangements; instead he emphasised that an Arab–Israeli settlement was a precondition for any Egyptian military involvement with the West.

Nuri al-Said concluded his agreement with Turkey; after all Britain's traditional opposition to Turkish access to Mesopotamia, Turkey was now to be allowed to transport military equipment through Iraq. It seemed that Britain was faced with a rapidly crumbling Middle East deployment: Nasser was refusing to contemplate the presence of foreign troops in peacetime, so undermining the British protection of the Suez Canal; and the 1930 Anglo–Iraqi treaty was due to expire in 1957. Steps would have to be taken to bolster the traditional British influence in the area. On 14 January 1955 the British foreign secretary Sir Anthony Eden, soon to be premier, wrote to Nuri, applauding the Turkish–Iraqi announcement and implying that it was time for a new Anglo–Iraqi agreement. A month later the British Cabinet approved Eden's suggestion of negotiations for a new Anglo–Iraqi treaty and, with little choice in the matter, acceded to the newly-hatched Turkish–Iraqi Pact.

Britain's formal accession to the new Turkish–Iraqi agreement succeeded in converting the Pact into a broader arrangement, the Baghdad Pact, developed from Dulles' 'Northern Tier' concept. Now the West had succeeded in organising the required anti-Soviet alliance. The Baghdad Pact included Iraq, Turkey, Pakistan, Iran and Britain; and the United States soon became involved in its activities. Iraq and Britain encouraged Kuwait to join the Pact but Sheikh Abdullah refused, knowing full well the instability of Nuri's unpopular regime and having doubts about the value of a union involving such disparate states. President Nasser was quick to condemn the Baghdad Pact, a position that was popular with many Iraqis 'as much as with other Arabs'.[44] Nuri, sharing John Foster Dulles' obsessive anti-communist feelings, had taken Iraq into a Pact 'to which most Iraqis were opposed'.[45] *The Times* (London) noted that 'Since Nuri Sa'id returned to office all political parties have been dissolved, including his own . . . a new press ordinance has reduced the number of newspapers . . . The colleges and schools have been purged . . . The dismissed teachers and students, and also the civil servants dismissed . . . have been made liable under an amendment to the army law for nine months' military service'.[46] The Baghdad parliament, surrounded by troops and tanks to prevent any disturbance, ratified the Baghdad Pact after ten minutes' discussion. The Pact's 'Special Agreements' and 'Memoranda' were concealed from the parliament because Nuri had no confidence that even his hand-picked deputies would accept them. Nuri, with British support, had ensured that the democratic cause of anti-communism was well served.

Britain had been obliged to hand over its two air-bases to Iraq, though British military assistance was promised in the event of an attack (presumably by the Soviet Union). The day after the Baghdad Pact was agreed, Eden succeeded Churchill as British premier. The United States continued to maintain pressure for the rapid development of the new defence agreement; and Nasser continued to condemn the Pact. The scene was set for a new confrontation in the Middle East.

The Arab–Israeli dispute was now presenting difficulties to a Washington administration keen to support the Pact. Pro-Israeli lobbyists in the US were nervous of an agreement that seemed to lock declared anti-Zionists into a pro-Western defence arrangement: what, for example, would happen in a dispute between Israel and Iraq? Such considerations made a US accession to the Pact impossible, but Washington continued to support the new agreement in less formal ways. At the same time it emerged that Britain and the United States might be secretly planning an Arab–Israeli settlement based on territorial concessions by Israel.[47] Following the secret ALPHA talks regarding such a settlement, Washington agreed to join the Baghdad Pact once an Arab–Israeli agreement had been concluded (a forlorn hope). The British would support the preliminary statement by Foster Dulles, and the US would finance the provision of British Centurion tanks to Iraq and offer military support to Britain in the event of fresh fighting in the Middle East. However, events were now moving to outflank such nice calculations.

On 22 August Israeli patrols crossed into Egypt and occupied positions in the Gaza Strip, whereupon Nasser launched small-scale *fedayeen* raids into Israel. David Ben-Gurion, only four weeks after agreeing to head a new Israeli administration, managed to obtain cabinet approval for an attack on Egyptian positions at Khan Yunis; thirty-six Egyptians were killed. After it emerged that France was reportedly offering Mystère IV fighters to Israel and that the US had no interest in servicing Nasser's defence needs, Egypt agreed an arms deal with the Soviet bloc for submarines, 100 tanks, MiG-15 fighters, Il-28 bombers and other aircraft; Soviet specialists would set up the equipment in Cairo and train Egyptians in its use. An uneasy stalemate between Egypt and Israel had developed, and for a time the political focus shifted to Jordan. Here nationalist disturbances supported by Egypt and Saudi Arabia were threatening the Hashemite throne of King Hussein, long a British client. Jordan was, moreover, being pressured by Britain to develop the Iraqi–Jordanian axis as a further defensive arrangement that would not involve expanding the Baghdad Pact.

In the deteriorating Jordanian situation General John Bagot Glubb, head of the Arab Legion, quickly asked London for reinforcements. Four days later, on 11 January 1956, the British government approved the despatch of two paratroop battalions to Cyprus, with another battalion on notice in Britain. RAF aircraft were transferred from the Habbaniyya base in Iraq to Amman, and an armoured regiment stationed near Aqaba prepared to move north. London gave authorisation for retaliatory strikes against Saudi troops, now massed in strength on the Jordanian border. The threat to Jordan was short-lived and soon the British Embassy was reporting a stabilised situation. But King Hussein's vulnerability had only served to increase Iraqi involvement in Jordanian affairs, a development that was not unwelcome to the British; the Iraqi government was encouraged to enter into economic agreements with Jordan, and the Iraqi diplomatic mission in Amman was promoted to embassy status. Such moves were seen by London as linking (an Iraqi-controlled) Syria and Jordan with the Baghdad Pact, isolating Egypt and Saudi Arabia, and consolidating Western hegemony in the region. In an effort to influence Syrian opinion, Iraq considered increasing its subsidies for pro-Iraqi Syrian newspapers and politicians, encouraged visits by Syrian students and dignitaries to Iraq, and established a new radio station to beam Iraqi propaganda throughout the region.[48] In a subsequent dispute with Washington over the question of Saudi hegemony over the Arabian peninsula, the Foreign Office official Evelyn Shuckburgh allegedly commented: 'America might wake up and realise that Iraq represents the solution of the West in the Middle East.'[49] In any event, the British remained convinced that an Iraqi–Jordanian axis would block Nasser's ambitions in the region.

On 14 March King Hussein met King Feisal II of Iraq, Crown Prince Abdullah and Nuri al-Said for talks at an Iraqi oil-pumping station. Hussein deemed the talks 'most satisfactory', as one fruit of the meeting was agreement on the establishment of a joint Iraqi–Jordanian defence council. A week later the US Joint Chiefs of Staff urged Washington's adherence to the terms of the Baghdad Pact, and at the same time a US planning group of the Middle East summarised measures that could be taken against Nasser. London then issued an *aide-mémoire* to inform the Americans of Britain's own long-term programme against the Egyptian president, after which CIA Director Allen Dulles called for an urgent meeting on the Middle East. The meeting was held on 24 March 1956 and it was attended by the Dulles brothers, James Angleton, CIA Director of Counterintelligence (and the chief CIA contact with Mossad), CIA Middle East specialist Kermit Roosevelt, Herbert Hoover Jr (Foster Dulles' secretary), Assistant Secretary George Allen, William Rountree (Allen's deputy for

Near Eastern affairs), negotiator Francis Russell, and Herman Phleger, the chief legal officer for the State Department. From this meeting emerged Operation OMEGA, a framework for Anglo–American co-operation against President Nasser. On 28 March Foster Dulles informed Eisenhower of a range of anti-Nasser policies that would 'in the main be coordinated with the United Kingdom'.

The measures to be adopted included: the continued denial of export licences for arms shipments to Egypt, a continued delay in concluding the negotiations on the High Aswan Dam, a continued delay on consideration of Egyptian requests for grains and oil, and a continued delay on decisions regarding economic aid. One specific positive provision was the expansion of radio facilities in Iraq to counter Egyptian broadcasts; and, excepting Iraq and Saudi Arabia, the Arab states adjoining Israel would not be allowed to import US arms. Export licences for the shipment of any major military items to Israel would be denied, but 'We would, however, be sympathetic if other Western countries wished to sell limited quantities of defensive arms to Israel'.[50]

The OMEGA memorandum had also confirmed the pivotal position of Syria in the Middle East, a further reason for encouraging Iraqi influence in the region. The West had long been interested in establishing a reliable right-wing regime in Syria but, despite all the efforts of London and Washington throughout 1955, no suitable leader had been found. When in August Shukri Quwatli, supported by the Saudis and the Egyptians, won the presidential election Britain and the US were encouraged to give fresh consideration to Iraq's wish for an Iraqi–Syrian political union. On 4 October Nuri al-Said informed the British and American ambassadors that Syria was in the grip of 'an evilly-disposed minority' and that Iraq 'could not allow the situation to deteriorate much further'. If the Syrians refused to 'get rid of subversive elements and those unfriendly to Iraq' then Nuri, he declared, 'would want to intervene in Syria, if necessary by force'.[51] The Foreign Office was opposed to overt Iraqi action but the FO official G. G. Arthur proposed a plan, to be run with the US and the Iraqis, for an eventual Iraqi–Syrian union. Bribery was to be organised within Syria, by or on behalf of Iraq, with the Syrian army the main target; the Iraqi forces were to be built up; pro-Iraqi propaganda was to be organised in Syria; the Syrian economy was to be subordinated to Iraq's; Saudi influence in Syria was to be countered by overt and covert measures; and propaganda was to be spread in Iraq to convince the people of the benefits of a stable and friendly Syria. Shuckburgh and Macmillan saw this as a 'Machiavellian scheme' to foster an Iraqi–Syrian union, but in the event the prospect of such union was not welcome to Washington: it was obvious that there would be Saudi opposition to any scheme that might produce 'a Greater Iraq' and Israel would be nervous of Iraqi forces on its borders.

The British were by now growing increasingly concerned at Nasser's evident drift to the political left. Harold Macmillan, then foreign secretary, declared to Ambassador Makins in Washington: 'We are afraid that Nasser, whether innocently or deliberately, is dangerously committed to the Communists. Consequently, we believe it would be advantageous, in any event, to overthrow him if possible.'[52] A three-phase plan of operations was proposed by George Young, the MI6 Deputy Director responsible for Middle Eastern operations, and Nigel Clive, MI6's political officer. The first phase would involve the overthrow of the Syrian government; if necessary, relying on joint action with Iraq, Turkey and 'possibly' Israel. Turkey would set about creating incidents on the Syrian border, while Iraq would do the same using local tribes; at the same time the pro-Iraqi Partie Populaire Syrienne would move into Syria from the Lebanon. In this way 'a firm pro-Iraqi government' could be induced to emerge as an 'extension of Hashemite influence'. Then Britain would exploit splits in the Saudi Royal Family to bring about the fall of King Saud; if the CIA did not want to become involved the British might undertake joint action with the Iraqis. Then, to counter the likely Egyptian response to such events, specific measures would be taken against Nasser, including the possible use of force to overthrow the Egyptian government. Washington was not impressed with this multi-phase scheme, seeing various threats to its own interests in Saudi Arabia.

When, on 26 July 1956, President Gamal Abdul Nasser declared that his government was taking over the operation of the Suez Canal the CIA stepped up its own plan, Operation STRAGGLE, for a coup in Syria. The CIA had carefully bribed Syrian army officers to stage the coup; but these men, assigned major roles in the operation, reported to Syria's intelligence head, Colonel Sarraj, handed over their bribe money and named the CIA officers involved. The American army attaché Lieutenant Colonel Robert Molloy, the CIA officer Francis Jeton (officially Vice-Consul at the US Embassy) and the celebrated Howard Stone (with the title of Second Secretary for Political Affairs) were branded *personae non gratae* and expelled from Syria in August. The US State Department denounced Syrian accusations of a coup attempt as 'complete fabrications' and immediately expelled the Syrian ambassador and a Second Secretary from Washington. President Eisenhower disingenuously commented in his memoirs that 'The entire action was shrouded in mystery'.[53]

President Nasser had taken over the running of the Suez Canal, thus opening up a new phase in the politics of the Middle East. For wider reasons of *realpolitik* the US decided to criticise the joint British–French–Israeli military action that followed and Nasser was able to proclaim a nationalist triumph, a dramatic example of political emancipation for subjugated peoples throughout the world. The Anglo-American plans for Nasser's overthrow had come to nought; the careful (and often confused) framing of political alliances throughout the region had done nothing to prevent Nasser's dramatic action. Efforts to link the Middle Eastern states – most of them monarchies – in military compacts to serve Western Cold War interests had achieved little. Soon the West would have to confront another blow to its traditional hegemony in the region: the overthrow of the pro-Western Hashemite monarchy in Iraq.

REVOLUTION AND AFTERMATH

The Suez affair had already eroded Western confidence in the region and now the consequences were spilling over into various states. In Lebanon the conflict intensified between the Lebanese and Arab nationalists belonging to many disparate groups. This in turn encouraged an increased involvement in the dispute by Syria, now part of the United Arab Republic (UAR), keen to support the Arab nationalists against the pro-Western President Camille Chamoun. This Lebanese leader, sensitive to the requirements of *realpolitik*, had exploited the powers of his Maronite presidency to rig the elections in favour of his pro-Western supporters, a tactical ploy that the Lebanese Muslims were powerless to resist. The West found such arrangements congenial and may have encouraged Nuri al-Said of Iraq to support Chamoun's democratic endeavours. If so, then the West helped to tip Nuri's already corrupt regime over the edge and to extinguish the pro-Western Iraqi monarchy.

In Iraq Brigadier Abdul Karim Kassem had formed an equivalent of Egypt's 'Free Officers' organisation, and when Nuri made clear his intention to help Chamoun the Kassem faction staged a successful rebellion to depose Nuri and King Feisal II. Now decades of careful political manipulation by the West were at an end. In the summer of 1958 Nuri had perceived that if the Lebanese civil war resulted in a victory for the pro-Nasser Arabs then Iraq would be isolated. He had already given Chamoun moral and monetary support in May and June, and resolved in July to deploy an army division to Jordan for possible use against Syria. At the same time he made plans to travel with Feisal to Ankara to discuss the Nasser problem at a routine meeting of the Baghdad Pact; Nuri was in no doubt that Adnan Menderes, the Turkish premier, shared his hatred of communism.

On the morning of 14 July army contingents headed by Kassem and Abdul Salaam Arif, ignoring instructions to by-pass Baghdad on their way to Jordan, entered the Iraqi capital. The army seized the radio station and Arif broadcast a dramatic call to revolution. Then soldiers invaded the young Feisal's temporary palace (pending the construction of a larger one on the Tigris) and quickly overcame the royal bodyguard. Feisal and many of his supporters, men and women, were shot dead and the corpse of the pro-British former regent Abdul Ilah was dragged through the streets. Nuri himself tried to escape but was killed when his man's shoes were seen protruding from a woman's *abba*. At first he was buried in a shallow grave but later the body was dug up and repeatedly run over by municipal buses, 'until, in the words of a horror-struck eyewitness, it resembled *bastourma*, an Iraqi sausage meat'.[54] A Baghdad street, formerly carrying Feisal's name, was now dubbed Gamal Abdul Nasser, after the assumed victor of the Iraqi revolution.

Western leaders were shocked at this turn of events. The United States, fearing the collapse of other pro-Western factions in the Middle East, acceded to President Chamoun's request and rapidly despatched 14,000 marines to Beirut. This force, twice the size of the entire Lebanese army and supported by a vast American armada, appeared off the Lebanese coast on 14 July in response to Chamoun's desperate telegram requesting assistance. It was well known that Chamoun, in response to US pressure, had rigged the election of June 1957 to ensure acceptance of the Eisenhower Doctrine: the notion that the American president was entitled to use the 'armed forces of the United States to secure and protect the territorial integrity and political independence of such nations, requesting such aid, against overt armed aggression from any nation controlled by International Communism'. Some observers felt that the election had been rigged too successfully: almost every opposition figure was excluded from the parliament, a bizarre situation that simply exacerbated existing tensions. Even the Patriarch of the Maronite Christians, who may have been assumed to be fervently pro-Chamoun, spoke of forty years' work 'ruined in a month', of 'a country divided against itself'. An armed rebellion had erupted on 12 May, a major pipeline was cut, and the US Information Library was burned. To US strategies the need for American intervention was obvious. The Iraqi revolution added fresh impetus to plans that were already well under way.

When the US troops, equipped with atomic howitzers, landed in Lebanon – 'to protect American lives' and 'to encourage the Lebanese government in defence of Lebanese sovereignty and integrity' – the US government declared it would not invade Iraq unless the new government failed, as *The New York Times* reported, 'to respect Western oil interests'. On this occasion the US forces were not required to act; the massively unpopular Chamoun was ditched by the United States, which then set about building relations with General Chehab, the new Lebanese leader. At the same time the US government was contemplating an invasion of Iraq: there was 'strong consideration' among United States government leaders of 'military intervention to undo the coup in Iraq'.[55] The US ambassador Gallman received a communication from the State Department advising him 'that Marines, starting to land in Lebanon might be used to aid loyal Iraqi troops to counter-attack'; but it was soon admitted that 'no one could be found in Iraq to collaborate with. Everybody was for the revolution'.[56] The reasons were not hard to discern: ninety per cent of Iraq was illiterate; average life-span was twenty-six years; and there was almost universal hatred of the Baghdad Pact. In 1959 Iraq withdrew from the Pact and it was renamed the Central Treaty Organisation (CENTO).

There seems no doubt that the US and Britain would have invaded Iraq in 1958 if there had been any reasonable hope of restoring the monarchy.[57] But it was now clear that Hashemite rule was at an end in Baghdad. The Hashemite monarchy, with Western military aid, was managing to survive in Jordan; but now Britain was no longer able to play 'an active and major part in Arab politics'.[58]

Whatever the personal ambitions of Kassem and Arif, the Iraqi revolution was at least in part buoyed by a wave of popular unrest. One observer noted that 'The hatred of Nuri and of the land-owning Arab Sheikhs and Kurdish Aghas who made up his party was pathological'.[59] On 18 June, a month before the coup, some 4000 people had demonstrated in Diwaniyah, and a three-hour battle had resulted in forty-three police deaths, with 120 wounded and the arrest of five hundred demonstrators. The Iraqi Communist Party worked to mobilise the masses around the 'national democratic movements', but in the event the revolution was led by the army, an inevitable circumstance in a highly militarised society where ordinary people had few rights and few powers. On the afternoon of 14 July, as soon as it became clear that the coup had been successful, martial law was declared and tanks were stationed at key points in Baghdad. The new Kassem regime then broadcast a radio statement:

The affairs of this country must be entrusted to a government emanating from the people and working under its inspiration. This can only be achieved by the formation of a popular republic to uphold complete Iraqi unity, to bind itself with bonds of fraternity with Arab and Muslim countries, to work in accordance with UN principles, to honour all pledges and treaties in accordance with the interests of the homeland, and to act in compliance with the Bandung Conference resolutions. This national government shall be known from now on by the name of the Iraqi Republic.[60]

The military had made the coup but the 'initiative and participation of left and democratic opposition parties, organised in a National Front' had transformed the event into 'something close to a popular revolution'.[61] In the face of the possibility of a Western invasion, following the American and British troop landings in Lebanon and Jordan, Nasser flew to Moscow to secure Soviet protection for the new Iraqi regime. The UN Secretary-General Dag Hammarskjold, working through an Emergency Session of the General Assembly, managed to defuse the crisis created by the Anglo-American troop movements. He brought the Western and Arab views together and in due course Britain and the United States agreed to withdraw their forces.

The new Iraqi Republic was ruled by a military Revolutionary Council headed by Kassem (now premier), and a cabinet of conservative National Democratic Party (NDP) and middle-class independents. A range of social and political policies were introduced that received wide support, particularly since they reflected the demands of the pre-revolutionary independence movement, sensitive as it was to the residual British presence and the pro-Western orientation of the Baghdad Pact. The new measures included: withdrawal from the Baghdad Pact and the Sterling Area; the final removal of British military bases; the building of diplomatic and trading relations with socialist countries; land reform to improve the lot of the peasants; negotiations with the Iraq Petroleum Company (IPC) for a greater share of oil royalties; a housing programme for the slum-dwellers around Baghdad; a freeing of all political prisoners; a new constitution; recognition of trade unions, peasant unions and other popular bodies; a 15 per cent limit on profits from consumer goods; reduced rents; and large cuts in the price of food and other necessities. However, it was one thing to issue a radical programme of reform, quite another to see its effective implementation. One immediate test of the character of the Revolution was the question of the new regime's attitude to the union of Egypt and Syria: if Iraq were to join the United Arab Republic (UAR) then Nasserite policies would inevitably impact on the Iraqi Republic. In this dilemma lay the first clues that the Revolution was not necessarily a pro-Nasser crusade.

In fact the new Iraqi regime came to represent a challenge to Nasser's leadership of the Arab world, and even to the existence of the UAR. It was clear to the Communists and other radicals in Iraq that subservience to

Nasser would result in their persecution; they had supported the revolution and were not eager to welcome what they saw as a new looming tyranny. Kassem himself was not keen to acquiesce in subservience to Nasser, and so he united with the Communists in opposing *wahda* (union). This meant that now *wahda* was being adopted as a rallying cry against the left since for many 'union with Egypt was the lesser evil' in the face of radical social reform or a government that would contain Communists.[62] The new Iraqi leadership was soon offering Syria, no longer challenged by the Hashemite Iraqi–Jordanian axis, a chance to escape Egyptian influence by joining a larger association of Arab states: the doctrine of pan-Arabism was still a potent force but it inevitably took on a new flavour following fresh political turmoil in the area. A joint Arab resolution at the United Nations was taken as a UAR attempt to isolate the Iraqi regime and to shift UAR attention towards the Saudi monarchy and the surviving Hashemites in pro-British Jordan. But the Saudis and the Jordanian Hashemites were not keen to welcome an anti-Iraqi alliance; Iraqi independence, they felt, would represent insurance for their own.

Cairo, now seeing the Iraqi regime as a threat to its own dominance in Syria, began attacking what it chose to regard as the 'communist menace' in Iraq. The United States welcomed the Egyptian posture as a 'bulwark against communism', and on 22 December 1958 Mohamed Heikal, a Nasser spokesman, wrote in *al-Ahram* that although the communists 'had fought alongside the nationalists in violent struggles against imperialism, imperialist agents and feudalists, this struggle is now finished or about to finish'. On 23 December President Nasser declared that Arab communists were enemies of Arab nationalism and Arab unity; and a week later mass arrests of communists were undertaken throughout Syria and Egypt. Plans to overthrow the Kassem regime were soon under way.

In March 1959 a pro-*wahda* revolt was staged in Mosul, inspired by the Syrian and Iraqi Ba'ath factions with Egyptian support. The Ba'ath aim was to bring Iraq into the UAR so that Syria and Iraq together could challenge Nasser. The Egyptian supporters of the revolt had their own agenda. A pro-Nasser Iraqi, Colonel al-Shawaf, led the revolt and it was only suppressed with much bloodshed, an event that encouraged CIA Director Allen Dulles to comment that the situation in Iraq was 'the most dangerous in the world today' and that the communists were close to a 'complete takeover'. The revolt was crushed by the Iraqi army which enjoyed the critical support of Kurdish peasants and Arab workers in Mosul, forced to confront army officers backed by rebel soldiers. The collapse of the confused Ba'ath Nasserist revolt ended for the time being any Syrian ambitions of becoming part of a wider Arab commonwealth; Syria had no choice but to remain subservient to Egypt within the narrow UAR confines. At the same time both Kassem and King Hussein were seeking to exploit the Palestine question to their own advantage, both claiming to speak for Palestinian liberation against the counter-claims of the pro-Nasser groups proposing that a liberated Palestine would sit well in the UAR. Kassem argued for the creation of an independent Palestinian Republic and proposed the building of a Palestine Legion. And while Hussein was claiming exclusive Jordanian sovereignty over Palestine, Nasser was taking steps to organise Palestinians in Gaza and Syria into a Palestine National Union. By 1960 hostilities between Jordan and the UAR had escalated to the point of sabotage and assassinations.

In Iraq, despite the protestations of Allen Dulles, the ICP had no plans to take power by force; in fact, the communists were happy to rely on elections in which they expected to win many seats. There were further riots in July 1959 when pro- and anti-government forces clashes in Kirkuk, leading to thirty-one people killed and 130 injured. In September Kassem had Said Qazzaz, the Minister of the Interior under Nuri al-Said, executed – partly to reassure leftist public opinion of his support. The Ba'athists took this gesture as a sign that Kassem still wanted to maintain the support of the communists, and in October a Ba'athist assassination attempt against Kassem was carried out. One of the would-be assassins was a young Saddam Hussein.

Kassem was by now more interested in suppressing the communists, whom he perceived as a growing threat to his regime, than in honouring the political promises of the Revolution. In 1960 more than 6000 trade unionists, many of them communists, were dismissed from their posts and the government took charge of unions and professional organisations, after systematic attacks on the homes and offices of democratic leaders. The non-communist newspaper *al-Istiglal* (February 1961) saw this process as violating the freedoms of the voters 'by blackmailing them in their means of livelihood and hurling them into prisons and places of detention'. Leftist newspapers were restricted and the licence of the troublesome Kurdish Democratic Party (KDP), founded in 1945, was revoked. The early hopes of the Revolution had all but evaporated.

The new-found hostility of the Iraqi regime to the ICP presented many problems, not least because only the disciplined communist organisations 'could provide large numbers of staff well enough educated to fill the offices that had been purged of their prerevolutionary personnel'.[63] The ICP had a wide popular base and extensive links with many front groups: such as the Peace Partisans, the People's Resistance Movement, the Federation of Peasants' Organisations, the Defence League for Women's Rights, the

Democratic Youth Movement, the Students' Union and many others. The extent of the communist involvement in post-revolutionary Iraqi society gave the ICP a unique status, one that it was difficult for Kassem and his supporters to erode without extensive repression.

Various coups were attempted against Kassem in the period between 1958 and 1963 (the Mosul revolt was only one such attempt). He had managed to alienate various powerful factions, including the Ba'ath, but he had also built some support among particular groups in society. He had introduced an extended social welfare scheme which included increased spending on health, education and housing, and this was accompanied by price and rent controls. The gains were far short of the expectations in the early heady days of the Revolution but under Kassem social welfare spending as a proportion of the budget doubled.[64] Gains were made in land reform; in some of the provinces (for example, in Kut and Amara, where the largest estates existed) the peasants were taking the law into their own hands and seizing land from its nominal owners. Now land over certain limits (250 hectares for irrigated land, and 500 hectares for rainfed land) could be expropriated with compensation, and then distributed for cultivation in small lots (twelve hectares irrigated, and twenty-three hectares rainfed). Peasants granted land became members of co-operatives. In fact, the legal entitlements were only slowly implemented and the period of the Kassem regime saw few substantial advances in land redistribution.

The consolidation of the revolutionary government stimulated further Iraqi claims for the territory of Kuwait. In 1958 Kassem negotiated a £66 million loan from the Soviet Union to fund the building of a port at Umm Qasr, close to Kuwait's northern border. A year later, in May 1959, what some observers saw as an Iraqi 'plot' to infiltrate Kuwait was uncovered, and two hundred Iraqis found camping in the desert were arrested by Kuwaiti forces. Violet Dickson records how 'These poor folk, in their mat and wood huts, were ordered to move . . . Their new camp was a quagmire . . . Now they were told again to move, lock, stock and barrel, into a wired-in enclosure out at Asherij point . . . in October 1961, I drove out . . . to visit them. The camp where they had been was bare . . . nobody I spoke to knew anything about them'.[65] Later the Iraqis were tracked down near Daugha ('. . . it seemed to me that they were being very badly treated').

In June 1961 the Iraqi government ordered a build-up of troops on the Kuwait border; and on 19 June, six days after Kuwait had signed a defence agreement with Britain, Kassem called a press conference at which he declared that since Kuwait was a part of Iraq he would demand every inch of its territory. He denounced the new Anglo–Kuwaiti agreement as a 'specially dangerous blow' against the integrity and independence of Iraq, and condemned equally the 'illegal 1899 agreement' between Kuwait and Britain. General Kassem also warned the present ruler of Kuwait not to transgress against the people of Kuwait, *who were Iraqis*, or he would be dealt with as a 'mutineer'.[66] The next day, with the Kuwaiti government declaring its determination to defend its territory, a memorandum was issued in Baghdad asserting that *'Kuwait is part of Iraq'* and going on to declare: 'There is no doubt that Kuwait is part of Iraq. This fact is attested by history and no good purpose is served by imperialism denying or distorting it.' On the same day King Saud, he himself having been given vast swathes of Kuwaiti land by Sir Percy Cox in 1922, expressed support for 'fraternal Kuwait'. The Arab League described the Iraqi claim as a 'surprise', and the pro-Western Shah of Iran expressed his willingness to exchange diplomatic missions with Kuwait. President Nasser 'joined other leaders of Arab states in expressing cordial greetings to Kuwait. Iraq did not seem to be overburdened with friends'.[67] The Lord Privy Seal, Edward Heath, emphasised Britain's obligation to support Kuwait, and the UAR issued a statement repudiating the 'logic of annexation' among Arabs.

Soon British warships, despatched from Hong Kong and Singapore, were heading for the Gulf. Saudi troops arrived in Kuwait and closed the border with Iraq, while Iranian launches, carrying supplies to Kuwait, were attacked by Iraqi patrol boats. On 1 July the British government declared: 'HM Government had informed a number of friendly governments in Middle East and elsewhere of its deep concern at the situation and expressed to them the hope that they will use their moderating influence with the Iraq government, so that Kuwait may continue her development as an independent Arab state among nations of the world.'[68] On the same day *The Times* (London) decided that Kassem did not intend to put pressure on Kuwait 'to the point of military attack'. By 4 July Royal Marines from HMS *Bulwark* had landed in Kuwait, and US ships were ready to evacuate American personnel; there were further reports that additional British troops with tanks and armoured vehicles were on their way or had already landed. Prime Minister Harold Macmillan declared: 'The government earnestly hopes that counsels of moderation will prevail in Baghdad. Our forces are there purely for defensive purposes, in accordance with our treaty obligations. They will be withdrawn as soon as the ruler considers Kuwait is no longer threatened.' Two days later the Iraqi forces on the border were increased and British troops began laying mines in northern Kuwait. By 7 July there were 6000 British troops in Kuwait, with Britain putting before the UN Security Council a resolution denouncing the Iraqi posture. The Council, at a time when the USSR was still a permanent member was soon deadlocked, and Kuwait suggested an Arab League force to replace the

British presence. A week later, one third of the British force was leaving, its mission accomplished. Kassem blustered that 'If Iraq had chosen to use force, she could have taken Kuwait long ago' – but he took no action. David Holden, the *Sunday Times* Middle East correspondent, noted that Kassem 'was scared off'.[69] The Iraqi leader had at least demonstrated *'that the game of bluff can cause a mighty stir in the region of the Gulf* (my italics).[70]

In a few dramatic years General Abdul Karim Kassem had behaved ruthlessly, working hard to suppress opposition from some quarters and to buy off opposition from others. He had laid the basis, in some areas, for genuine social reform; but had also succeeded in alienating many of his own supporters – in Iraq and elsewhere in the Arab world. But however he had proceeded he would have antagonised the West: he had abolished the pro-British Hashemite monarchy and remained bitterly opposed to imperialism throughout all his political life. In attacking the ICP he had alienated powerful factions that might have protected him from a coup, but the Ba'athists in alliance with various pan-Arabist groups now saw no impediment to a coup attempt against Kassem.

On 8 February 1963 Kassem was toppled in a coup led by Abdul Salaam Arif, Kassem's former collaborator, whom he had first purged and then imprisoned. In 1958 Kassem had spared Arif's life; now Arif resolved on the execution of Kassem. And again the shadow of Western complicity in the overthrow of the Kassem regime was not hard to discern. A few days before the coup Kassem had announced the formation of a national oil company to exploit the oil areas he had expropriated in 1961 from foreign companies (amounting to 99 per cent of their concessionary areas). On 4 February, four days before the coup, in an interview with *Le Monde*, Kassem revealed that he had received a threatening note from the US State Department. According to the Paris weekly *L'Express*: 'The Iraqi *coup* was inspired by the CIA. The British government and Nasser himself . . . were aware of the *putsch* preparations. The French government was left out.'[71] As thousands of Iraqis were massacred following the coup, *Le Monde* reported from Washington: '. . . the present *coup* is not regarded as a menace to US interests; on the contrary, it is regarded as a pro-Western re-orientation in the Middle East'.[72]

The Kassem regime, the first republican government of Iraq, had been crushed – probably with the assistance of the West – after a few short, tumultuous years. Now the Iraqi Ba'ath Party, the Party of Saddam Hussein, was in power. Saddam would have to wait many years before becoming master of the Party; until that time he and his fellow Ba'athists would learn to cope with threats and setbacks. In the brutal theatre of Iraqi politics Saddam Hussein would learn a ruthless pragmatism.

THE BA'ATHISTS IN POWER

President Kassem, it is said, had deluded himself into thinking that he could not be overthrown. In fact an onslaught was launched against the Ministry of Defence, which he had turned into a mini-fortress, and he died in the attack on his headquarters[73] (or he was executed afterward).[74] The coup that had brought the Ba'ath Party to power had been dubbed 'fascist'[75] – and there can be no doubt that it was supported by many of the opponents of the (supposedly) leftist revolution of 1958. Kassem had been opposed by disgruntled army officers and by erstwhile political collaborators (such as Abdul Salaam Arif), purged soon after the Revolution. The plot against Kassem also received the support of Kurdish groups, despite the fact that the Ba'athist publication *al-Ishtiraki* ('The Socialist') had recently depicted the Kurdish movement as a 'suspect colonialist movement', with the Ba'athists criticising Kassem for not dealing harshly enough with the Kurds.[76] Kassem, while retaining support in some of the poorer sections of Iraqi society, had alienated himself from many of the popular factions that might have offered some protection to his regime. While he may have thought that he had quelled opposition and secured the Revolution he had in fact grown progressively more isolated.

A principal organiser of the coup was Ali Salih al-Sadi, the secretary of the Ba'ath Party, who had built up contacts with other groups; in particular, with the officer class waiting to exact revenge on Kassem for purging and executing members of the military. The Ba'ath itself had several factions: Sadi was regarded as a political radical, heading the wing that was strongest among the civilian section of the movement and in the Ba'athist militia, recruited from the Azamiyya area of Baghdad, a Ba'athist stronghold. A more moderate faction, strong in the army, was opposed to the fervour of the radicals and 'no more than lukewarm sympathisers with the aims of the Party'.[77] Arif, as president of the National Council of the Revolutionary Command (NCRC), headed the new regime; and Ahmad Hasan al-Bakr, once (like Arif) a minister in the Kassem government, was now prime minister. Of the eighteen NCRC members, sixteen were Ba'athists; and the Ba'ath Party also held twelve of the twenty-one seats in the cabinet, including the posts of prime minister, and the ministers of defence (Salih Mahdi al-Amash) and the interior (Sadi). Tensions soon developed between Arif and other Council members: over how far to carry the fresh wave of purges, over the degree of socialism that should be introduced (many of the Ba'athists were committed socialists), and over the extent to which Arab unity (especially with Egypt) was desirable.

In the event, many of the revolutionary forces that had formerly struggled against imperialism, the monarchy and the exploitation of the poor were now subjected to harsh persecution. The Ba'ath Party itself later acknowledged the severity of this repression. Thus in January 1974, at the Eighth Regional Congress of the Ba'ath Party, the Political Report observed that in the revolution of February 1963 'blood was shed freely' and that 'this time power must be taken over without such bloodletting as would spoil the image and divert the course of the Revolution'.[78] The brutality that marked the coup was well reported at the time.[79] Concentration camps and torture centres were set up, and the National Guard roamed the streets making arrests, beating suspects, and carrying out arbitrary executions. Batatu has highlighted the torture chambers in the Baghdad Qasr al-Nihayah (Palace of the End), used for detention and interrogation since the end of the monarchy.[80] Later mass graves were discovered where prisoners had been buried alive. The main targets of the persecution were the leaders of the trade unions and other leftist democratic bodies, such as the Iraqi Women's League, the General Union of Students of the Iraqi Republic (the GUSIR), and the Iraqi Communist Party (ICP). There is some evidence that the American CIA was involved in the mass slaughter of the communists.

The Ba'athist leader Michel Aflaq had commented in an interview that 'Communist Parties will be banned and suppressed with the utmost severity in any country where the Ba'ath Party comes to power'[81] – and this was clearly a posture to which the United States was not entirely unsympathetic. Mohamed Heikal later commented on the authority of King Hussein of Jordan that 'an American espionage service' (almost certainly the CIA) had conveyed to the Iraqi Ba'ath Party the names and addresses of Iraqi communists.[82] The Ba'athist National Guard, thus briefed by US spies, carried out mass arrests and summary executions. The ICP later claimed that some five thousand Party members had been killed, either resisting the fascist coup or in the subsequent terror witch-hunts from house to house. Such claims were confirmed by other sources.[83] Many of the killings were carried out with the utmost brutality; for example, Husain Ahmed al-Rahdi, the first secretary of the ICP, was tortured for fifteen days in the Qasr al-Nihayah dungeons, before being crushed to death. The regime announced on 7 March 1963 that his 'execution' had taken place after a trial (that had never taken place).

The brutalities of the Ba'athist regime aroused international protests. Committees were set up to protect human rights in Iraq, including a British group chaired by Lord Chorley, with the Labour MP William Griffiths as its secretary and the novelist Ethel Mannin as treasurer; and including committees set up in France and Italy. Iraqi workers struggled in impossible circumstances to resist the Ba'athist takeover, as did the Kurdish people, themselves now subjected to a programme of genocide. On 10 June 1963 the Ba'aths declared all-out war on the Kurds, with tanks and aircraft sent to raze Kurdish villages and to kill hundreds of men, women and children. The military governor of Northern Iraq issued an uncompromising statement: 'We warn all inhabitants of villages in the provinces of Kirkuk, Sulaimaniya and Arbil against sheltering any criminal or insurgent and against helping them in any way whatsoever. We shall bomb and destroy any village if firing comes from anywhere near it against the army, the police, the National Guards or the loyal tribes.'[84] Despite such repression the new regime was insecure: divisions within the ruling Council soon tore the leadership apart and the new Ba'athist regime collapsed.

The regime had tried to consolidate its position by expanding the National Guard; several thousand young men, tempted by the prospect of sharing in Ba'athist power, were quickly enrolled, but they were no more than – in the words of an Iraqi communist leader – 'adolescents befuddled by jingoistic propaganda, declassed elements and all sorts of riffraff'. The Iraqi army soon came to regard the National Guard as a serious threat to its own position. There were moreover international tensions that were working to destabilise the young Ba'athist regime. The Syrian Ba'ath Party, encouraged by the success of its Iraqi counterpart, launched a coup in March 1963 against the parliamentary regime in Damascus, again with the support of Nasserite army officers. With the Ba'ath movement (theoretically) committed to Arab unity, talks began in Cairo in April with a view to expanding the scope of pan-Arabism. However, Nasser had been forced to witness the collapse of the UAR when Syria seceded in 1961, and he now had no interest in propping up a Ba'athist expansion that might threaten his own position. The protracted talks served to discredit the Ba'ath negotiators whom Cairo Radio depicted as inexperienced adolescents manipulated by the sinister Michel Aflaq. Soon it was clear that such discussions, far from expanding Ba'athist power, would serve only to weaken the new Iraqi regime.

Throughout the summer of 1963 tensions grew in the Iraqi Ba'ath: the National Guard continued to antagonise the army, and political differences in the ruling Council were exacerbated in regard to both domestic and international policies. The scene was set for the overthrow of yet another Iraqi regime.

On 18 November 1963 the Iraqi army, including some disaffected Ba'ath officers, launched a successful coup. As was the pattern, tanks were stationed at strategic points in Baghdad and suspected supporters of the regime were arrested. The headquarters of the National Guard were hit by rockets, and the new Ba'athist leadership, only recently appointed, was rounded up. All political parties were banned, fresh levels of press censorship were imposed, and a new military regime began consolidating its power. The discredited NCRC was abolished, and a National Revolutionary Council (NRC) put in its place. The new council quickly assigned powers to the flexible Abdul Salaam Arif, formerly president of the NCRC; and, trying to emulate Nasser's rallying of mass support, Arif created a new Iraqi Arab Socialist Union, which would contain all the previous political parties. As part of its new socialist programme the Arif government nationalised all banks, insurance, steel, cement, tobacco, food, tannery and construction companies. Such dramatic moves did little to solve the Kurdish problem, to improve the ailing economy, or to resolve the continued divisions between the Ba'athists and the pro- and anti-Nasserites. Ahmad Hasan al-Bakr, the former Ba'athist premier, was assigned the rank of ambassador at the ministry of Foreign Affairs; and the Nasserites, heartened by the collapse of the former Ba'athist regime, made further efforts to achieve unity with Egypt. Soon links were being proposed between the prestigious Arab Socialist Union in Egypt and Arif's new Iraqi Arab Socialist Union. The jails remained full of political prisoners, many of them now tortured at the hands of the Public Directorate for Security. On 29 April 1964 a Provisional Constitution was announced: it failed to end the State of Emergency and stated that there would be a three-year transition period before the return to normality. The prime minister assumed the powers of the Military Governor General, the military courts became State Security Courts, and the premier was also granted powers to suspend all civil laws. A military regime, albeit one of a different complexion, was again consolidating its position. The Ba'ath's first attempt at government in Iraq had lasted nine months.

In September 1965 the pro-Nasser premier Brigadier Abdul al-Razzaq attempted a coup against President Arif, with the aim of seeking immediate unity with Egypt; the attempt failed and Razzaq fled to Cairo to be granted political asylum. It was now thought useful to have a civilian premier, and on 21 September Abdul al-Rahman al-Bazzaz was appointed prime minister, despite his suspected links with reactionary supporters of the monarchy. Bazzaz then attempted to move the Iraqi economy to the right, encouraged joint ventures with foreign companies for the exploitation of raw materials and making some efforts to dismantle the public sector. The hesitant steps to distribute land to the peasants were abandoned, while massively increased compensation was paid to the large landlords. Arif remained president and commander-in-chief until he was killed in a helicopter crash on 13 April 1966, whereupon, after a brief power struggle, his brother Abdul al-Rahman Arif became president, defeating the Iraqi nationalist Uqaili. The emergence of the new Arif, altogether a less colourful figure than his brother, encouraged Razzaq to attempt yet another coup, again unsuccessfully. Bazzaz was dismissed as premier in August, to be followed by a procession of military governments keen to co-operate with foreign companies intent on securing economic advantage in Iraq. In March 1967 Arif himself became prime minister before handing over to Tahir Yahya, but such moves did little to preserve the Arif regime: in July 1968 two coups in rapid succession toppled Arif and again the Ba'athists were in power, this time to stay.

On 17 July 1968 a coup was staged by General Ahmad Hasan al-Bakr, supported by Michel Aflaq and Saddam Hussein. Arif was allowed to go into exile, and the prime minister was put on trial. Within a month Bakr had sacked his entire cabinet for its 'reactionary tendencies', appointed himself prime minister and commander-in-chief, and selected a new cabinet of Ba'athist radicals. In one view the new regime 'prepared itself for its task of containing and defeating any attempt at popular revolt and true democratic changes'.[85] Now Bakr was ruling without a parliament, at the same time stirring up feeling against Westerners, many of whom were expelled from the country. Iraqis with Western wives were purged from government service, and a number of former Iraqi cabinet ministers were arrested as 'counter-revolutionary leaders'. Bazzaz was arrested and show trials were held; following the most notorious of these, fourteen men – nine of them Jews – were publicly executed and their bodies put on public display. By August 1969 about fifty 'spies' and 'counter-revolutionaries' had been executed, many of them Muslim Arabs, as a warning to opponents of the regime. Ordinary citizens were encouraged to attend the public executions: some 200,000 people attended the hanging of the fourteen 'counter-revolutionaries', with Bakr and other leaders making violent anti-Zionist speeches against the backdrop of the corpses dangling from the gallows.

The Ba'athists remained fiercely hostile to any attempt to introduce political democracy. A new Revolutionary Command Council (RCC) imposed a total monopolisation of all media, and arbitrarily introduced laws that facilitated an extension of state terror; ordinary people, mere suspects who were often innocent victims, could be arrested, tortured and executed, with no recourse to law and no chance to broadcast their plight in public. Now the Iraqi leadership was partly 'Tikrit'; that is, many of the key government posts were occupied by Bakr's relatives who, like him, came from the village of Tikrit. Saddam Hussein al-Tikriti, from a Tikrit peasant family, was second-in-command of the Ba'ath Party, its assistant secretary general and also vice-president of the Revolutionary Command Council. Working closely with Bakr, Saddam now conspired to impose the Ba'ath will on the other political factions of the RCC, and on the country as a whole.

Efforts were made to project Ba'athist rule as the will of the people: the concept of 'popular democracy' was advertised, a doctrine which in practice meant no more than one-party rule supported by a network of terrorist organisations used to suppress all political opposition, including even moderate dissent within the ranks of the Ba'athist Party itself. The 'National Security' apparatus, working with such bodies as the Green Brassards, a specially organised militia, imposed a system of state terror to discourage any potential threats to the regime. Throughout 1969 and 1970 there were frequent public executions:

> For eight hours on the day of the hangings, the police virtually handed over central Baghdad to the youths. Directed by Ba'th party commissars they erected the gibbets in flower beds, patrolling the approach roads, controlled the tens of thousands of watchers and chanted for more executions. Each of the three soldiers among the executed had a bandage on an ankle or wrist; the joints were so clearly misshapen that they had clearly been broken.[86]

State propaganda continued to advertise the existence of a supposed 'patriotic front' to unite the various social factions, but it was always made clear that no political factions, trade unions, peasants' groups or other popular organisations could exist outside Ba'ath control. All groups were required to accept total control by the Ba'ath or to face harassment, persecution and abolition. Some factions – the Kurds, the ICP and the pro-Nasserites – continued to challenge the Ba'ath, but their efforts only brought fresh terror, more executions and in 1969 the launching of new military operations against the Kurdish people.

In 1973 an abortive coup led by the Iraqi security chief led to a constitutional amendment giving the president even more power, and to the formation of the cosmetic National Progressive Front. This nominally included the Ba'ath, the ICP and the Kurdish Democratic Party (KDP) but the Ba'ath dominated the Front High Committee, which ensured continued Ba'ath domination of Iraqi politics. The people's popular councils of the Ba'ath gave the appearance of a democratic base to the Party, while the

National Pact, intended to serve as the model for a constitution, defined the Iraqi political system as 'democratic, popular, socialist and unionist . . . guaranteeing democratic freedoms to the masses and to their national democratic forces'.[87] Power continued to reside in the RCC, with all executive power exercised by the government.

Sometimes there were signs that General Bakr and Saddam Hussein had to compromise with other factions in the Front. On one occasion the ICP objected to the Ba'ath being designated the 'leading party' of the Front, and the communists insisted that the Ba'ath leaders give a date by which they would introduce a national parliament. The Ba'ath Party agreed to an inconsequential compromise declaring that the 'Front is led by the parties which form it' – but that 'the Ba'ath enjoys a privileged position within the Front'. In a similar spirit, the Kurds pressed for greater political autonomy, talks with the Ba'athists broke down, and fighting between the Kurds and the Iraqi army broke out again. No-one doubted that it was the Ba'ath Party that dominated the Iraqi regime; having developed and disciplined its own internal structure and operations it now enjoyed a unique status in Iraqi society, perceived as 'an élite party like the [erstwhile] Communist Party of the Soviet Union'.[88] The position of the Ba'ath Party was consolidated in the interim constitution of 1970, in which it was declared that Iraq was a People's Democratic Republic committed to Arab socialism and Islam; under this draft the Revolutionary Command Council, whose members were required to be members of the Iraqi regional command of the Ba'ath, remained the principal authority in the state. In the early days of the Bakr regime a significant number of non-Party men were given government posts, but after 1973 Ba'athists always occupied about two-thirds of all the ministerial positions, including all the key posts. The Ba'athists also developed their own militia, a military organisation independent of the army, reckoned to number some 50,000 men by 1978 but substantially increased through the 1980s.

The 1970s saw increasing tensions between the Ba'athists on one hand and the various contending factions – the ICP, the KDP, the pro-Nasserites, etc. – on the other. In the early 1970s, scores of communist members and cadres were tortured to death, among them Ali Hussain al-Barazanchi, a member of the ICP Central Committee in Kirkuk; and thousands of Kurdish families were deported, some to Iran. Iraqi National Security men were exposed as being responsible for an assassination attempt against Mustafa al-Barzani, the KDP leader, and it was demonstrated yet again that no peaceful settlement of the Kurdish problem was on the political agenda. It was also emerging that a full-scale war with Iran was likely: throughout the 1970s there were frequent confrontations between Iraqi and Iranian forces, as Iran began to see Iraq as 'the main threat to Iranian security'.[89] In 1972 the Soviet–Iraqi treaty of friendship was seen in Tehran as further evidence of the Soviet strategy for encircling Iran; soon there were more than 5000 Soviet military advisers in Iraq, with the Ba'athist regime seemingly having unlimited access to Soviet weaponry.

Iranian leaders had long regarded the Iraqi state as a threat to Iranian interests, even during the period of maximum British influence in the area. In 1941 the British had used Iraq as a springboard to invade and occupy southern Iran; and in 1951–3 the British had again used Iraq as a military base against Iran through the period of the oil nationalisation affair. Iran was also conscious of its ethnic and religious links with the Shi'ites and the Kurds, a majority of the Iraqi population. In 1971 Iraq had severed diplomatic relations with Iran over territorial disputes; and Nasser's death in 1970 had facilitated a speedy *rapprochement* between Egypt and Iran, so weakening the Iraqi position. When the Iraqis insisted that all ships passing through the Shatt al-Arab would have to fly the Iraqi flag and pay tolls to the Basra Port Authority the Iranian authorities declared that any attempt to stop Iranian ships would be considered an act of war. Thus between 1970 and 1974 'Iran and Iraq fought an undeclared and largely unreported war. During that period more than 1500 "exchanges", including full-scale artillery battles, were recorded by the Iranian authorities'.[90] Such events were a prelude to the Iran–Iraq war that was to last through most of the 1980s. Throughout the 1970s and after, Saddam Hussein was a principal architect of Iraqi policies.

Iraq was by now a totalitarian state, intolerant of internal dissent and impatient of disputes with its neighbours. The regime made a pretence of popular support but there were no political mechanisms for ascertaining popular opinion. The modern Ba'athists had learned from the failures of earlier Iraqi regimes: the route to political security was via the complex of state-security organisations, prepared if necessary to use remorseless terror. Accommodations could be made with political factions – if such deals were a means to greater political stability – but the stick was poised, ubiquitous and undisguised, behind every carrot.

Modern Iraqi politics has been shaped largely by the Ba'athist struggle against contending political forces, not least the Iraqi Communist Party, the Kurds and the many putative democratic bodies. The Ba'athist dominance, established for the first time in the early 1970s and signalled by the regime of Bakr and Saddam Hussein, was to determine the character of Iraqi politics in the 1980s and beyond.

THE IMPACT OF OIL

The leaders of the 1958 Iraqi revolution knew well the importance of oil to the national economy. One of the first statements of the National Council of the Revolutionary Command (NCRC) on Baghdad radio was designed to reassure foreign firms. 'The new movement will work to increase our financial potential and guarantee that oil will continue to be exported.' The foreign oil companies in Iraq would be allowed to continue their operations: there were no thoughts yet of a socialist expropriation of foreign assets. Soon however there were moves to restrict the unfettered freedoms of foreign organisations in Iraq. In December 1961 the famous Law 80 limited the concession rights of the Iraq Petroleum Company to the area it was currently exploiting, reserving all rights in the rest of the country to the Iraqi state. Two months earlier, talks between the Kassem government and the IPC had broken down, and there was no doubt that the Company would oppose the new Law. The IPC decided to restrict oil production in Iraq to put pressure on the government through stagnant oil revenues, but 'Law 80 proved to be an irreversible step. Its popularity with the Iraqi people was such that the Ba'ath did not dare to try to rescind it'.[91] An interim compromise encouraged IPC to increase production, with the result that 1963 revenues were more than ten per cent higher than those for the previous year.

Iraqi oil resources had long been of interest to foreign companies. In Ottoman days the Turkish Grand Vizier had promised the Turkish Petroleum Company – formed in 1914 by British, German and Dutch interests – that it would be allowed to exploit Iraq's oil deposits. At the end of the First World War, French interests acquired the German share, an arrangement ratified in 1925 by the pro-British Iraqi government. Pressure from the US State Department resulted in a 23.75 per cent share being allocated to an American group. In 1929 the TPC became the IPC, and a final concession was signed in 1931, just before the close of the British mandate. Iraqi resentment of foreign control of a vital national asset grew, with 'the first demands for nationalisation heard in the early 1950s'.[92] Iraq remained vulnerable to the policies of the foreign companies, and to external political events. In 1956 the Suez crisis drastically affected Iraqi oil revenue: on 31 October the Canal was closed and the Syrian government, protesting at the tripartite invasion of Egypt, stopped the flow of oil from Kirkuk to the Mediterranean. Such events, coupled with the relatively low investment in the Iraqi economy, meant that successive Iraqi governments had little room for manoeuvre in confrontation with foreign interests. The

Kassem regime was the first to seek a reduction in the power of the oil companies.

The government of Nuri al-Said had been negotiating with the IPC, but little headway had been made; the July revolution gave a new impetus to Iraqi demands for increased revenue from the oil resource. Negotiations continued in circumstances of growing tension, with frequent breaks and resumptions, until in 1960 the confrontation was aggravated by the decision of the Basra Petroleum Company (an IPC subsidiary) to stop production at Rumeila as a protest against an increase in port dues. This was one of a number of events that contributed to the passing of Law 80, a dramatic move to cut back the power of the oil companies to exploit Iraqi resources. However, the new law failed to address other contentious issues: the 50–50 profit-sharing arrangement, the exploitation of natural gas, and the Iraqi demand for a 20 per cent share in IPC capital. Such matters, and foreign efforts to achieve amendments to Law 80, were to remain in dispute for the next eleven years. In February 1964 the Iraqi government created the Iraq National Oil Company (INOC), now legally in charge of 'all phases of the oil industry, including exploration and prospecting, production, transportation, refining, storage and distribution of crude oil, oil products and petrochemicals'.[93] But it was one thing to enact laws authorising INOC activities, quite another to ensure that such intentions were realised. The IPC group continued to ignore the INOC provisions, just as it tried to ignore what it regarded as the concession expropriations of 1961. Following the 1958 revolution the new Iraqi regime had helped to radicalise the Arab oil-producing states and to create OPEC (the Organisation of Petroleum Exporting Countries) in 1960. Now the scene was set for a further confrontation with the foreign companies.

In July 1967, during the regime of (the second) President Arif, the Iraqi government enacted legislation to prohibit INOC from granting 'concessions or the like' as a means of developing oil in any part of the country. Then in 1969, as a way of outflanking the Western corporations, the Iraqis turned to the Soviet Union as a route to the development of the promising North Rumeila field; two agreements were concluded, one between Iraq and the USSR and one between INOC and the Soviet Machine Export Organisation. These deals outraged Western interests, causing IPC to threaten to take legal action to prevent the selling of crude oil from North Rumeila, and to reduce output from Kirkuk (and so to cut Iraqi revenue) in contravention of an earlier agreement. The Iraqi government responded on 1 June 1972 by nationalising the Iraq Petroleum Company, though at that time the two subsidiaries – the Mosul Petroleum Company and the Basra Petroleum

Company – were not affected. In the event the IPC had no choice but to accept this situation. It accepted the expropriation of the Kirkuk producing area and surrendered the Mosul company, at the same time paying Iraq $141 million of outstanding debts on the understanding that the Basra company would retain its oil concession. Seven months later the Iraq government nationalised BPC in protest at the support given by the Dutch and US governments to Israel during the June 1973 Arab–Israeli war. Oil from North Rumeila began to flow in April 1972.

Now Iraq had secured considerable economic advantages. The IPC might have expected the unqualified support of the Dutch, British and US governments but it was acknowledged that there was 'some obvious validity in the Iraqi claims against the IPC'[94] and moreover there were rapidly changing geopolitical conditions in the Middle East. These factors combined to encourage Western governments to urge IPC to reach an accommodation with Iraq. The Iraqi regime had at last won some freedom of manoeuvre: it had untrammelled access to its own resources, it could make deals with anyone it wished, and in particular it was now part of international arrangements whereby the oil-producing nations had 'unilateral rights to take whatever decisions they liked on ownership, production and price without reference to the oil companies'.[95] It is not difficult to see how such circumstances generated an abiding resentment in the Western countries that only a short time before had been complacent hegemonic powers in the region.

In 1973, during the turmoil that followed the nationalisation of IPC, Iraq's oil reserves were assessed at 31.5 billion barrels; with an estimate in the early 1980s suggesting reserves of up to 35 billion barrels, on the basis of new fields discovered in the late 1970s.[96] The INOC estimated Iraq's oil reserves in 1983 at 59 billion barrels, and then at 100 billion barrels, after identifying further fields for development.[97] Such resources, even if somewhat optimistically assessed, plus the nation's mineral wealth, 'the vast tracts of land to be reclaimed, the big rivers to be harnessed, and above all the human resources' should facilitate national development 'to benefit every member of an even bigger population' – all brought about by 'the democratic and peace-loving government that the Iraqi people sooner or later will give themselves'.[98] Until that happy time Iraq was forced to accept the political contribution of President Saddam Hussein al-Tikriti.

7 Into the Era of Saddam

In the fourteenth century the Mongol hordes of Tamerlane swept across Mesopotamia, destroying cities and slaughtering entire populations. In 1394, at the small town of Tikrit on the Tigris river, a hundred miles north of Baghdad, the Mongols erected a memorial pyramid with the skulls of their slaughtered victims.[1] The fortress of Tikrit – Edward Gibbon's 'impregnable fortress of independent Arabs'[2] – had fallen to the invaders, but the reputation of the town lived on. Here it was that Saladin was born in 1138. Here it was, some eight centuries later, that Saddam Hussein was born.

SADDAM HUSSEIN AL-TIKRITI

Early Life

Saddam Hussein was born on 28 April 1937 in the village of Al-Auja, in a mud hut belonging to his uncle, Khairallah Talfah.[3] In one account, Saddam's father, Hussein al-Majid al-Tikriti, was killed by bandits around the time of Saddam's birth; in another, it is suggested that Hussein al-Majid simply deserted the family. Saddam's mother, Sabha, was too poor to bring up a child, she gave birth at her brother's house in the Alharah quarter of Tikrit, and her brother-in-law, Hassan al-Majid, named the baby Saddam (meaning 'clasher' or 'one who confronts'). Sabha managed to persuade a married man, Ibrahim Hassan, to abandon his wife and to marry her, whereupon the young Saddam found himself in the charge of a brutal and illiterate stepfather. The family remained poor; the village had no electricity or running water, and Saddam, denied any education, was forced to work as a farmhand. One Iraqi opposition figure has suggested that Saddam was sexually abused by his stepfather but 'it seems unlikely since, once in power, Saddam would almost certainly have killed his stepfather in order to ensure his silence'.[4] (An Iraqi officer, General Omar al-Hazzah, once told a female friend that he had slept with Saddam's mother. The officer, his son and the woman – their conversations bugged by the Mukhabarat – were executed; as was an official who discussed one of Saddam's mistresses.) When Saddam's cousin, Adnan Khairallah (later to become the Iraqi defence minister), started to attend school, Saddam wanted to do the

same but his stepfather had no wish to be deprived of a menial hand; it was
much better to have Saddam continue to steal farm livestock which could
then be resold. But this situation did not last; aged ten, Saddam arrived at
his uncle's house carrying a gun, though it is not known whether Ibrahim
had thrown him out or whether Saddam had simply run away. In any event,
his uncle Khairallah, a fervent Arab nationalist (and also a Nazi sympa-
thiser), enrolled Saddam in the local primary school.

There is no doubt that Khairallah, himself a schoolteacher at that time,
wielded considerable influence over Saddam. Khairallah had been cashiered
out of the Iraqi army for supporting the Rashid Ali coup in 1941, leaving
him with an abiding hatred of Britain and what he perceived as Western
imperialism. Saddam, inspired by photographs of Khairallah in army uniform, desperately wanted to become a soldier but by the time he was sixteen
it was clear that his poor school grades would keep him out of the prestigious Baghdad Military Academy, an institution set up and run largely by
the British. Already Saddam was learning to be self-reliant in the brutal
environment of the streets, and subsequently his lack of a formal military
education came to seem less important than his natural toughness and –
noted by his official biographer – his love of guns. It is said that the young
Saddam was often mocked for being fatherless and that he took to carrying an iron bar to protect himself against attack.[5] And according to exiled
Iraqi observers (perhaps not the most disinterested sources), Saddam used
to enjoy heating the bar and then using it to stab passing animals. Later,
against such testimony, Saddam was to reveal his love for his horse, commenting on the grim reality that 'a relationship between man and animal
can at times be more affectionate, intimate, and unselfish than relations
between two human beings'.[6] When his horse died, Saddam is said to have
been so distraught that his hand became paralysed for more than a week.[7]

In 1955 Saddam, then aged eighteen, followed his uncle to Baghdad and
enrolled at the Karkh high school. These were turbulent times and Saddam
was soon finding political intrigue more attractive than schoolwork. Nasser,
the great hero of Arab nationalism, was buying huge quantities of Soviet
arms; and events were already leading towards the nationalisation of the
Suez Canal and the consequent tripartite military attack on Egypt. In 1956
Saddam was involved in an abortive coup attempt against the pro-British
Iraqi monarchy; and the next year, aged twenty, he joined the Ba'athists. At
that time the Ba'ath Party had a mere 300 members and there were many
competing nationalist organisations. Iraq had recently joined the Baghdad
Pact, under prompting from Britain, and increasingly the Ba'athists were
encouraged to view Egypt as a rival state, a competitor for the soul of
pan-Arabism. In 1958 the non-Ba'athist nationalist faction led by General

Abdul Karim Kassem managed to overthrow King Feisal II, and the Ba'athists saw their chance for power. A hit team – of which Saddam Hussein was a member – machine-gunned Kassem's car in broad daylight (Saddam had already murdered a pro-Kassem communist in Tikrit). The attack was a failure, though keen hagiographers have made what they can of it.

In the official film, *Aliyam Altawilah* ('The Long Days'), made as a non-fiction dramatisation to depict the heroic deeds of Saddam Hussein, the attack on Kassem is shown as a failure – after all, Kassem had survived the hit – but one which added greatly to the glory of Saddam. Here he was portrayed as a bold and heroic figure, unflinching as a comrade uses a razor blade to dig a bullet out of his leg. Saddam later commented to an Egyptian journalist that he had instructed the director to make the film 'didactic, truthful and historically accurate, as well as accessible to the majority of viewers'. The journalist replied that the film 'certainly meets that criterion, except for one scene – when your comrade cuts into your leg using a razor blade to get the bullet out. The actor who was playing your part only grimaces. I think he should scream in pain. It would be more realistic and show people that you, as a human being, have physically suffered'. Saddam, keen to advertise his heroic qualities, then commented: 'I didn't think it was realistic either. I wanted the director to reshoot the scene because I remember the day when it happened. I did not grimace or move an inch until the bullet was out.'[8]

The biographies differ on the point. One suggests that Saddam fainted for some minutes while the bullet was pulled with a pair of scissors; another that he was unconscious for only a few seconds; and another testimony, from the doctor present at the time, reveals that there was no bullet.[9] Other Ba'athists wounded in the attempted assassination of Kassem, some seriously, have received little mention.

Saddam was then forced to flee. He disguised himself as a Bedouin tribesman, swam the Tigris, stole a donkey, and journeyed across the desert to Syria – where he may have expected a sympathetic welcome from fellow Ba'athists. Soon however he left Damascus for Egypt, where he was arrested twice in violent affrays (and threatened with deportation) and where in 1961 he entered the Faculty of Law at Cairo University. At that time he was given an allowance by the Arab Interest Bureau of the Egyptian Mukhabarat and lived comfortably in the Nile-bank quarter of Dukkie. Saddam failed to qualify in law from the University, but some years later was awarded a degree at Baghdad University when he turned up with a well-armed bodyguard to take the examination.[10] Equipped in this fashion with first one degree then a second, Saddam later felt himself well able to comment on legislative and other legal matters.

In 1962, still in Cairo, he decided to marry his cousin, Sajida Talfah, whom he had known since childhood. With surprising attention to custom he contacted Ibrahim, asking him to approach Khairallah on his behalf to ask for his daughter's hand. In the circumstances Khairallah had little option but to give his consent and the marriage took place in Iraq in early 1963. In the wedding photograph Saddam, without a moustache, looks happy and relaxed; there is little hint in this picture of the sinister and brutal personality that was to emerge at the apex of Iraqi politics in the years ahead. Saddam's first son, Udai, was born a year later.

The eventful year of 1963 had also seen the murder of Kassem: this time the Ba'athists were successful. Saddam himself had been growing increasingly restless in Cairo. His allowance was often delayed and he was watched and sometimes harassed by the security services. Once, when Saddam was detained, it was suggested that he was implicated in the murder of another Iraqi political exile; and that he was maintaining politically unacceptable links with foreign powers (even with the Americans).[11] Such circumstances did little to encourage Saddam to remain in Cairo; and the death of Kassem gave further incentive for a return to Baghdad. For several days there had been battles in the streets of the Iraqi capital between Kassem and his supporters, including the communists, and the Ba'athist militia, the National Guard. One estimate suggests that between 1500 and 5000 people were killed in three days of fighting, after which there followed house-to-house searches for communists.[12] Sports clubs, cinemas, private houses and an entire section of Kifah Street were requisitioned by the Ba'athists to serve as prisons and local headquarters. Batatu, relying on official government sources, has written: 'The Nationalist Guard's Bureau of Special Investigation had alone killed 104 persons . . . In the cellars of al-Nihayah Palace, which the Bureau used as its headquarters, were found all sorts of loathsome instruments of torture, including electric wires with pincers, pointed iron stakes on which prisoners were made to sit, and a machine which still bore traces of chopped off fingers. Small heaps of blooded clothing were scattered about, and there were pools on the floor and stains over the walls.'[13] Saddam had nothing to do with these events, but they were orchestrated by the political party in which he was to make his career: there can be no doubt that he was never averse to the pragmatic use of terror to achieve political objectives.

When Saddam returned to Baghdad the newly-installed Ba'athists regarded him as an outsider. He had been too young, before his flight to Syria, to build up an Iraqi power base, and his years in Cairo had kept him isolated from political developments in Baghdad. The party leadership did not recognise Saddam's membership, and even his earlier involvement in the

1958 assassination attempt against Kassem did nothing to enhance his status. He was forced to wait until the Tikritis among the Ba'ath leadership were prepared to nominate him for full membership, and for the time being he had to be content with a minor position working for the Party's central bureau for peasants. According to one testimony he also served as an interrogator and torturer at the infamous Qasr al-Nihayah (the so-called 'Palace of the End', where Feisal II and his family were murdered in 1958).[14] An Iraqi tortured by Saddam had declared: 'My arms and legs were bound by rope. I was hung on the rope to a hook on the ceiling and I was repeatedly beaten with rubber hoses filled with stones.'[15] Many other victims did not survive.*

Party Member

Saddam, helped by his Tikriti origins, did not have to wait long before being accepted into the Ba'ath Party and beginning his speedy rise through the ranks: already the Tikriti officers group included Herdan al-Tikriti, Mahdi Amash, Adnan Khairallah (Saddam's brother-in-law) and the powerful Ahmad al-Bakr. Bakr, one of the Party's most respected military leaders, soon saw advantage in forming an alliance with Saddam; and it is suggested that a marriage between Bakr's son and Sajida's sisters, and marriages between Bakr's daughters and two of her brothers, further helped to propel Saddam to power. Bakr was by now the Iraqi premier and Mahdi Amash was serving as the defence minister; and when in 1965 Bakr became secretary-general of the Party Saddam continued to cultivate his Tikriti

---

*Saddam Hussein has been rightly condemned for his use of torture. It should not be assumed however that the various anti-Iraq states are innocent in this regard. There are copious reports – from Amnesty International and other bodies – exposing the use of torture in such states as Syria, Turkey, Egypt, Israel and Saudi Arabia; and the US also has not been averse to using torture to further its political objectives. For example, in the notorious US-orchestrated Phoenix programme in Vietnam some 20,000 Vietnamese peasants were systematically tortured and then killed. Thus an American military adviser, quoted by Noam Chomsky (*The Chomsky Reader*, 1987, p. 281) stated that 'naturally we kill and torture many Vietcong'. It is now generally acknowledged that the US has funded and trained torturers throughout Latin America and elsewhere. Thus in her copiously researched *Cry of the People* (Penguin, 1980, p. xxiii) Penny Lernoux comments: 'The other integral part of the story of the human rights struggle in Latin America is the verified role of the US Defense Department, the CIA and corporate industry . . . on many occasions Catholic bishops and priests, including US citizens, have been tortured or murdered by organisations funded or trained by the US government, sometimes with the direct connivance of US agencies.' And she declares (p. 157): 'The sickness that has engulfed Latin America, that endorses torture and assassination as routine . . . was to a significant extent bred in the board-rooms and military institutes of the United States.'

connection. The following year he was made deputy secretary-general of the Party: he had already proved his ruthless dedication to the Ba'athist cause, and he was perceived as an asset in intimidating the enemies of the movement (at Qasr he had experimented with torture methods, sometimes offering victims a list from which they would be forced to select their own torture). Promoted to the Regional Command Council, Saddam had demonstrated his industry and imagination. By the summer of 1963, he was urging the need for a special security body, the Jihaz Haneen, that would be modelled on the Nazi SS. Its main purpose would be to protect the Party against the ambitions of the Army's officer corps, an obvious requirement in circumstances where army-based coups against political leaders were always a possibility. Saddam's fears were soon vindicated by the event: in November 1963 the first Iraqi Ba'athist government was overthrown by the army.

Saddam went underground but continued to build up the strength of the Jihaz Haneen, while at the same time plotting ways of ousting President Arif. The Jihaz Haneen (the 'instrument of yearning') would target 'enemies of the people', harassing and intimidating unfriendly factions. Plans for coup attempts against Arif were scheduled for mid-September 1964 at the latest; in one plan, Saddam would lead a group of armed Ba'athists to assassinate the entire Iraqi leadership during a cabinet meeting; in another, Arif's plane would be shot down. Both schemes were uncovered by the Iraqi secret services, resulting in further suppression of the Ba'ath and its leadership. Bakr and many of the other leading members of the Party, though not Saddam, were now in jail; Saddam resolved to stay in Baghdad – defying the orders of the Ba'athist National Command in Damascus – and to continue working for the overthrow of the Arif regime. In mid-October 1964 Saddam's hideout was discovered, quickly surrounded by security forces, and after an exchange of fire he was arrested. His period in jail did nothing to retard his political development: now he could maintain close contact with Bakr and assert his leadership over his fellow prisoners. And his subsequent escape, following a detailed plan, added more grist to the hagiographic mill.

On 23 February 1966 the Marxist wing of the Syrian Ba'ath had staged a successful coup and come to power. Aflaq, Bitar and other traditional Ba'athist leaders were arrested, and now it seemed that the Iraqi Ba'ath, still relatively impotent, was about to be subsumed by the new Syrian regime. Moreover, the success of the Syrian Ba'ath seemingly advertised the importance of the army in achieving a successful coup, and Saddam had no wish to submerge his own power under the ambitions of the Iraqi army corps; he well knew that an independent military faction would not be content for long to co-exist with a civilian government. Therefore Saddam initiated an Extraordinary Regional Congress to determine the way forward for the Iraqi Ba'athists; its main fruit was to lay the basis for the permanent schism between the Ba'ath Parties of Syria and Iraq. From the time of that crucial Congress in September 1966 the unified Ba'ath, with separate regional commands in Syria and Iraq, ceased to exist; both the national parties claimed to be the lawful successor of the original movement, though the unresolved schism was destined to persist into the 1990s, with all the weakening of the Arab nation that this divide implied. Now Saddam was concentrating on developing the Iraqi Party's security apparatus, developing the new Party militia, expanding the Party's national presence, and expelling the remaining leftists from the Ba'athist ranks. Soon the net would close on President Arif.

THE BA'ATHIST COUP

Early Repression

On 17 July 1968 the Ba'athists, with the inevitable army support, made their successful coup. Four senior officers in the Arif regime had been approached for help: Colonel Abdul al-Razzaz Nayif, the head of military intelligence; Colonel Ibrahim Abdul al-Rahman Daud, the commander of the Republican Guard; Colonel Sadun Ghaydan, the commander of the Republican Guard's armoured brigade; and Colonel Hammad Shihab, the commander of the Baghdad garrison. Ghaydan was already sympathetic to the Ba'ath cause, and Shihab's sympathies were reinforced by family connections (he was one of Bakr's cousins); while the others – Nayif and Daud – were prepared to look to their own advantage (Nayif asked for the premiership, and Daud the Ministry of Defence, as the price for their support). Saddam disliked the idea of pressure from army officers but was quick to see the benefits of a tactical accommodation; he declared: 'I am aware that the two officers have been imposed on us and that they want to stab the Party in the back in the service of some interest or other, but we have no choice now. We should collaborate with them but see that they are liquidated immediately during or after the revolution. And I volunteer to carry out this task.'[16] The Party proceeded with the *coup d'état*, the Arif regime was toppled, and on its ruins was established the second Iraqi Ba'athist government.

General Ahmad Hasan al-Bakr became president and commander-in-chief, and remained secretary-general of the Party and chairman of its

Revolutionary Command Council. Saddam became deputy chairman of the Council, and was given control of all internal security matters; Saddam's secret training schools had yielded hundreds of graduates for the security services, including his half-brothers, Barzan, Sabawi and Wathban (Ali Hassan al-Majid, Saddam's cousin and another training-school graduate, was to become involved in the suppression of the Kurds and the invasion of Kuwait). President Arif had been calmly informed by General Hardan al-Tikriti that 'you are no longer President. The Ba'ath has taken control of the country. If you surrender peacefully, I can guarantee that your safety will be assured'; and a few hours later Arif was flying to exile in England. The troublesome Colonel Nayif was invited to Bakr's office after lunch while Sadoun Shakir, one of Saddam's childhood friends from Tikrit, and ten bodyguards blocked off the corridors from Nayif's men. It is said that Saddam then started beating Nayif about the head with a revolver until he broke down: 'I've got four children. Why are you doing this to me?' Saddam replied: 'You and your children will be fine if you leave Iraq and accept an ambassadorship.' After some talk, an honorary position as ambassador to Morocco was agreed, whereupon Saddam insisted on driving Nayif to the airport, passing through army checkpoints manned by Nayif's men: 'Just act normally. Don't forget: the pistol is inside my coat.'[17] Soon after Nayif had been despatched to virtual exile, Saddam sent agents from military security to keep him under surveillance; in July 1978 Saddam's assassins shot him dead on a London street. Daud was instructed to head a military mission in Jordan; in 1970 he was retired from his position and forbidden from ever returning to Iraq. By the end of July 1968 the new Bakr regime had consolidated its power throughout the country. The administration was purged and Bakr supporters put in key positions: Herdan al-Tikriti was made Minister of Defence, with Abdul al-Karim al-Shaykhli the minister for Foreign Affairs. Saddam Hussein, as RCC deputy chairman, now held the second most important post in the ruling hierarchy.

It is easy to see why Bakr wanted Saddam as his deputy. The Tikriti connection was important, Saddam had demonstrated his ruthless competence, and he was not tainted by excessive loyalty to the army faction (the army was helpful in making a coup but disturbing to a civilian regime hoping to retain power). Saddam had contributed little to the primary coup that had brought Bakr to power but, using his command of the security apparatus, he had enabled the Ba'athists to make their 'second revolution' throughout the country, securing the regime and enabling the Party 'to rule rather than merely reign'.[18] Aged thirty-one, Saddam was now in a position to consolidate his own hold on the Party apparatus, until the time when he would be equipped to take over the Presidential Palace.

The new regime had not been established on a wave of popular feeling. The short-lived Ba'athist regime of 1963 was remembered with fear and resentment, and the Iraqi people had no expectation that the new government would do much to improve the quality of their lives. Of the new leaders only Bakr was a national figure, Saddam himself well prepared for the time being to operate quietly in the background. Even the Ba'athist claim, probably exaggerated, of Party membership in 1968 standing at around 5000 does not suggest that the regime had a strong popular base.[19] And it is also significant that by the late 1960s, despite the considerable Shi'ite majority in Iraq, the Ba'ath had become a virtual Sunni party. It was soon clear that the Bakr regime had only a small popular base and ruled through minority factions, a situation maintained only by Saddam's control of the state security apparatus. Now the Jihaz Haneen was the dominant security organ, with Saddam Hussein the only person who could authorise the issue of firearms to Party members. The character of the new regime was soon plain for all to see.

On 9 October 1968, barely three months after the coup, the regime claimed that it had uncovered a major Zionist spy network. Fifth columnists and other 'enemies of the people' were denounced in vitriolic speeches before stage-managed crowds of tens of thousands. On 5 January 1969 seventeen 'suspects' were put on trial.

In fact Saddam had carefully prepared a plot to label and eliminate men he wanted purged. Two years earlier an Israeli agent killed in the Hotel Shattura in Baghdad had been found in possession of an incriminating notebook containing the names of leading Iraqis, including Sadun Ghaydan, then the commander of the Presidential Guard's tank battalion, and Shafiq al-Dragi, head of the Mukhabarat. When the notebook resurfaced in 1968 it included further names, those of men whom Saddam wanted eliminated from the scene. Sadiq Jafer, a trusted member of the Jihaz Haneen, then delivered deliberately incriminating letters, obvious 'plants', to the homes of the targeted men, and immediately afterwards agents of the Mukhabarat arrived to make the arrests. Another Jihaz Haneen member, Salah Omar Ali al-Tikriti, was charged with the task of ensuring that the investigations reached the required conclusion.

On 27 January 1969 fourteen convicted 'spies', eleven of them Jewish, were hanged in public, their bodies left dangling before hundreds of thousands of spectators in Baghdad's Liberation Square. The public turned the public executions into a national holiday with full radio and television coverage. The Ba'ath Party helpfully organised the transport of some one hundred thousand 'workers and peasants' from outside Baghdad so that the appreciative masses could join in the festivities. President Bakr and his deputy, Saddam Hussein, drove round Liberation Square in an open car, members of Shabybabt Al-Ba'ath (a Ba'ath student group) lining the route, as a happy prelude to the executions. Entire families picnicked in the Square as the hangings began. The event lasted for a full twenty-four hours while Bakr made anti-Zionist and anti-imperialist speeches with the corpses dangling behind him. The Egyptian newspaper *al-Ahram* commented that 'The hanging of fourteen people in the public square is certainly not a heartwarming sight, nor is it the occasion for organising a festival'. To the limited international response Baghdad Radio retorted: 'We hanged spies, but the Jews crucified Christ.' And Saddam Hussein later commented that the men were hanged 'to teach the people a lesson'. Anyone thinking of organising a coup should think again; this time the Ba'athists were here to stay.

Saddam continued to purge dissident elements: Jews, Muslims, anyone who might threaten Ba'athist power or his own position. Non-Ba'athists were expelled from state institutions, 'plots' were suppressed, and Saddam gradually tightened his hold on the state machinery. As his power increased, so his reputation for brutality grew. Thus a Shi'ite survivor of Qasr al-Nihayah has commented on how Saddam himself mercilessly killed one of his victims: 'He came into the room, picked up Dukhail and dropped him into a bath of acid. And then he watched while the body dissolved.'[20] Opponents of Saddam may be well disposed to believe such an account, which may well be true; or it may be black propaganda. Another tale, against impossible to verify, shows Saddam in a different light. The Israeli Naim Tawina was jailed in the 1970s as a 'spy', but surprisingly released one day by Saddam: 'Do not touch this man. He is a good man. I know him. Let him go.' Years later, Tawina realised why he had been treated in this manner: he remembered that Saddam had been the youth from whom he had bought cigarettes on a Baghdad street corner many years before, and whom he had often tipped generously. Saddam had remembered and so saved Tawina from further torment in Qasr.[21] This episode, albeit slender evidence, has been taken to illustrate that Saddam is capable of gratitude; and that he does not engage in purges for their own sake. We may conclude that there is much more weighty evidence to indicate the character of the Saddam-sustained regime.

A 'revolutionary court' was set up to deal with 'spies, agents, and enemies of the people'. Here military officers with no legal training were required to hear charges of 'conspiracy to overthrow the government' and 'espionage on behalf of the United States, Israel or Iran'. Key trials were televised so that the Iraqi people could witness the forced confessions. Thus Rashid Muslih, a former minister of the interior, publicly admitted that he had spied for the CIA, and was duly executed. Some who did not confess – such as Abd al-Rahman al-Bazzaz, former premier, and Abd al-Aziz al-Uqayli, former minister of defence – were given long terms of imprisonment.[22] Samir al-Khalil has provided (in a listing citing various sources) details of '*purges of high-ranking officers, Ba'athist Old Guard and politicians of ministerial or higher rank since July 17, 1968*'.[23] Here we find men dismissed from office, imprisoned, exiled, tortured, assassinated and executed; some three dozen men incarcerated after show trials, murdered in prison, shot or stabbed to death, killed with their whole families. Saddam boasted, with good reason, that 'with our Party methods, there is no chance of anyone who disagrees with us to jump on a couple of tanks and overthrow the government'.[24] The military was now subservient to the Ba'athist Party, the officer corps under constant surveillance by Saddam's security services. Then Saddam set about consolidating his power in the civilian areas of the state hierarchy.

Abdullah Sallum al-Samarrai, the Minister of Culture and Information, was relieved of all his responsibilities in March 1970, and then despatched to serve as Ambassador to India; Shafiq al-Kamali, another RCC member, was expelled from the Council; and, after a confrontation with Saddam, Salah Umar Ali was similarly sacked from the Council and relieved of all his ministerial duties. On 28 September 1971 Ammash and Shaykhli were fired, the latter sent out of harm's way to serve as UN Ambassador. Shaykhli had long been an intimate friend of Saddam; together they had made the early attack on Kassem, been exiled in Egypt, imprisoned by Arif, escaped, and worked for the eventual success of the Party. Now it was obvious, if anyone had doubted it, that no-one was safe from Saddam if he sensed a threat to his position. In 1979 Adnan Hussein al-Hamdani, another intimate associate of Saddam and an influential member of the RCC, was executed.

One of Saddam's most significant moves in the early 1970s was against the 'civilian' Abd al-Khaliq al-Samarrai, born in the same year as Saddam and with considerable Party support; like Shaykhli he was seen as a possible contender for the leadership of the Party.[25] In July 1973 al-Samarrai was sentenced to a term of imprisonment; six years later, following fresh allegations against him, he was shot. The practical Saddam had thus eliminated one of the leading theoreticians of the Party, and in this way secured not only his own position but also the presidency of Bakr whom he still seemed content to serve. But in June 1973 a fresh challenge was emerging to confront the Bakr–Saddam leadership. Nadhim Kazzar, the brutal head of the security services under Saddam, had long resented the Sunni leadership of the Party and the privileged position of the Tikritis. On one occasion he recklessly declared that he would 'wipe Tikrit off the map of Iraq'.[26]

Anticipating an inevitable confrontation with Saddam, Kazzar decided to act first. He planned an assassination of Bakr for 30 June 1973, at a time when the president would be returning to Baghdad Airport from a state visit to Poland. However, when the plane was delayed the hit squad, fearing that the plot had been uncovered, fled in panic without informing Kazzar of their moves. It was then Kazzar's turn to flee, taking with him Shihab – the minister of defence, and Ghaydan – minister of the interior, with him as hostages. Saddam quickly organised the seizure of Kazzar and he was pursued by aircraft; in the ensuing battle Shihab was killed and Ghaydan, though wounded, managed to survive by hiding under Shihab's corpse.[27] On 7 July a special court headed by Izzat Ibrahim al-Duri, an RCC member, tried Kazzar and his fellow conspirators. The result was predictable: Kazzar, seven other security officials and thirteen military officers were executed; the next day, a further thirty-six men were put on trial, of whom fourteen were sentenced to death. Saddam had managed to retrieve a situation that had demonstrated possible laxity on his part, and which had even sired rumours that he himself was behind the coup attempt.

Kazzar had suggested before his trial that Samarrai's house might be used as a site for negotiations, and this gave Saddam the chance to target Samarrai as being involved in the plot. Samarrai was tried, found guilty, and sentenced to death – a penalty later commuted to imprisonment after an appeal by Michel Aflaq. Again Saddam, despite a possible failure of his security services, had managed to turn events to his advantage. Yet another threat to his position had been eliminated and the Bakr–Saddam leadership was secure. It was also clear that Saddam was starting to emerge as the dominant man in the Ba'ath hierarchy: Bakr was less robust than Saddam and it was known that most Party decisions were taken jointly between the president and his deputy. Events were slowly but inexorably moving in Saddam's favour.

He had neutralised the political power of the army, infiltrated his own security men into all the state organs, removed all civilian rivals, and increasingly come to dominate the Iraqi president. When Said Muhsin al-Hakim, the world spiritual leader of the Shi'ites, alarmed Saddam by attracting massive public displays of support in Baghdad, Saddam staged a 'spy' confession on television to discredit Muhsin's eldest son as an agent of Iran. Muhsin returned to his home in the holy city of Najaf a lonely and discredited figure. His son was condemned to death *in absentia* by one of Saddam's 'revolutionary courts'; and in January 1988 shot dead in the lobby of the Hilton Hotel in Khartoum by Jihaz Haneen agents who then calmly drove in a diplomatic car to seek the sanctuary of the Iraqi embassy. Other 'traitors' were shot, following cursory trials, after which the families of the victims would be presented with an official invoice to demand payment for the bullets that had killed their relatives. Such tactics were well designed to spread terror in the population and to further impress observers with Saddam's growing power. By 1973 President Bakr, no longer in sound health, was increasingly isolated, with only ceremonial duties and obliged to sign any orders that Saddam wished to implement.[28]

Throughout the 1970s Saddam worked to secure his power base. Already assured of the support of the Jihaz Haneen, he began transferring his relatives from that organisation to command army units, at the same time spending revenue from oil sales to bolster army morale. The army, formerly seen as a threat to civilian power, was now being developed as a useful bulwark against opposition to Saddam. The communists were invited to form a national unity government in collaboration with the Ba'ath, but Saddam had no intention of sharing power with groups outside the Party: at the time he was signing deals with the communists he was promoting a leaflet inside the Jihaz Haneen telling members 'How to Destroy the Iraqi Communist Party' (later he was to launch a violent onslaught on the communists, even though nominally his national unity partners). Ba'athists who suspected Saddam's growing ambition tried to warn Bakr but it was too late. One suggestion made to the president was that a new pact with Syria might serve to curtail Saddam's power, but now there were electronic bugs in every office and every bedroom of Ba'ath leaders; Saddam knew about all the plans and all the suggestions before any move could be made to threaten him.

On National Day, 17 July 1979, Saddam Hussein declared himself president of Iraq. Bakr, said to have resigned 'owing to poor health', was under house arrest. Five days later Saddam carried out a terror purge of the Party in a closed session attended by nearly one thousand cadres. A videotape of these proceedings were later distributed among Party members as a sign of things to come (tape extracts have been shown on British television). At this session, surveyed by a relaxed Saddam Hussein, prominent Ba'athists were forced to read out confessions of their parts in supposed plots (some Syrian-backed) against the nation and its leadership. Saddam himself, in a dreadful exercise of terror, slowly read out the names of the next men to confess. At times he hesitated, moving over names and then returning to them, pausing for maximum dramatic effect. The proceedings went on for days, as gradually a body of 'convicted' men was finalised and forced to face the firing squad. Saddam himself and the surviving members of the Revolutionary Command Council (half having 'admitted' to high treason) formed the firing squad. He had emerged victorious; now there was no-one left in a position to challenge Saddam's authority. He had complete power over the Party, the army, the security services, the courts – over all the organs of the Iraqi state.

Saddam had contrived Bakr's resignation, even at that late stage forced to overcome temporary dissent. Muhie Abd al-Hussein Mashhadi, the RCC secretary-general, had 'suddenly stood up and demanded that they vote on the question of President Bakr's relinquishing his responsibilities in the Party and the State to Saddam Hussein. He insisted that the decision be carried unanimously'. Then he said to Bakr: 'It is inconceivable that you should retire. If you are ill why don't you take a rest?'[29] Saddam's response to this suggestion was immediate. Mashhadi was relieved of all his responsibilities and forced to confess to 'a painful and atrocious plot' against the Iraqi state and the leadership of the Party. At the special closed session of Party cadres Taha Yasin Ramadan, the commander of the Party's militia, demanded that the disloyal Mashhadi confess to his 'betrayal'. Mashhadi had little choice: he delivered a long confession about his part in a Syrian-backed plot designed to overthrow Bakr and Saddam Hussein. Saddam then took the podium, saying how stunned he was to have been betrayed in such a fashion: 'After the arrest of the criminals, I visited them in an attempt to understand the motive for their behaviour . . . They had nothing to say to defend themselves, they just admitted their guilt.' At times, it is recorded, Saddam wept with emotion, using a handkerchief to hide his tears. Then came the slow and theatrical reading of the list of 'traitors'. Saddam paused occasionally to light his cigar, then more names would be read out and the targeted individuals would rise in terror to be led out for execution. If anyone doubted that the era of Saddam had arrived, they knew it now.

The Framework of Policy

When the Ba'ath came to power in 1968 the main policy strategy was to modernise capitalism as a route to prosperity. Iraqi resources had long been exploited by foreigners and it was assumed that progressive policies would work to national advantage without the need for wholesale socialist measures. However, socialist doctrine remained popular in the country and various accommodations were made with the Iraqi Communist Party (ICP) internally and with the Soviet Union abroad. The intransigence of the foreign-owned Iraqi Petroleum Company (IPC) led to its nationalisation by Law 61 on 1 June 1972, though some members of the Ba'ath leadership may well have wanted to avoid such a radical measure. The ICP continued to criticise the undemocratic measures adopted by the Ba'ath leadership, though at that time the wholesale purges that Saddam would initiate were scarcely imagined. The National Action Charter, supported by the Ba'ath–

Communist alliance and signed in July 1973 nominally guaranteed all political and cultural democratic rights, including freedom of action for political parties, the social and vocational organisations, the peasants' organisations, the workers' trade unions, as well as freedom of opinion and belief, freedom of the press and other basic freedoms. The Charter also stipulated an ending of the so-called 'transition period' (which had become an artificial barrier to social and political progress), the 'preparation of the draft of a permanent constitution', the 'elimination of the emergency conditions and the establishment of constitutional organs and institutions, legislative and executive' and the 'implementation of the formula of local government and elected people's councils in all administrative units of the Republic of Iraq'. There was also a stipulation for 'an Executive Regional Authority in the Kurdish region . . .', a pious hope in view of the rapidly deteriorating relationship between the Ba'athist government and the Kurdish Democratic Party (KDP). There were frequent military confrontations from March 1974 to early 1975, with high casualties on both sides and the Iraqi army resorting to the use of phosphorous shells.[30]

In March 1975 the OPEC heads of state met in Algiers, and there the Shah of Iran and Saddam Hussein (then still Bakr's deputy) reached an agreement on the question of border demarcation. The Iraqi government compromised on the Shatt al-Arab waterway, now agreeing that the median line should be recognised as the frontier. A deal was also agreed to 're-establish security and reciprocal confidence along the length of the common borders' and to put 'a final end to all infiltration of a subversive character from either side'. This meant, according to one observer: '. . . an Iraqi concession over the Shatt al-Arab border problem . . . in return for an Iranian undertaking to close the Iranian border to the Kurdish insurgents from Iraq and suspend military aid to them'.[31] In this way, the Iraqi government had further weakened the Kurdish position, and it now felt confident to claim supremacy over its nominal ICP partners. In violation of the Charter the Ba'ath claimed to be the 'leading party' in the life of the 'whole society', after which there was a rapid escalation of persecution of ICP members. By early 1979, under the growing influence of Saddam Hussein the concept of one-party rule was the main theme in statements from Ba'athist leaders. Thus the Party newspaper *al-Thawra* declared on 10 January 1979 that equality 'of the political parties in the Patriotic Front is out of the question . . . and this means that any other ideologies, opinions or practices, disguised as socialism, are impermissible'. Saddam commented in February 1979 during a visit to Basra: 'All citizens are Ba'athists, irrespective of their ethnic origins . . . I am entirely confident . . . that even those who are not organised in other political parties feel the need to be

Ba'athists not only through sympathy and conviction but through their desire to be organised in the Ba'ath Party.' Two months later the ICP was acknowledging that the Patriotic Front coalition had been transformed into 'an instrument of the Ba'ath Party'; in June the ICP Central Committee urged an end to the Ba'ath dictatorship and the creation of a democratic system of government in Iraq. Later in 1979 communist partisans began activities in support of the Iraqi Kurds.

The Ba'athist government, despite its nationalisation of the IPC and its sensitivity to the popularity of socialism, continued to favour the development of capitalist economic structures (and the emergence of a wealthy capitalist bourgeoisie). In the mid-1970s the private economic sector trebled in size, and there was a rapid growth in the number of private middlemen (brokers, consultants, contractors and the like) and senior bureaucrats in the state sector. By 1980, with massive social problems demanding investment, there were some 700 multimillionaires, mostly linked in some way to the Ba'ath Party and to its own version of 'socialism'. In this way an enormous boost had been given to non-productive sectors of the economy, while the multinational corporations from Japan and the West continued to look for commercial opportunities in Iraq (diplomatic relations had been severed with the US at the time of the 1967 Arab–Israeli Six Day War but this had done nothing to restrict Iraqi–US trade). By the late 1970s more than 90 per cent of industrial investment was committed to national capitalist enterprises and foreign multinationals. The Ba'athist leadership saw nothing in this situation to restrict the development of the Iraqi economy or to limit Iraqi independence. A principal aim was to protect Ba'athist power, even if this meant a clear betrayal of earlier egalitarian commitments.

In 1980 Iraq's oil revenues reached $21.3 billion, an ample amount for Saddam Hussein ('The Knight', 'The Leader with a Strategic Mind and Precise Calculations') to strengthen the army and the other state security organs. With predictable oil wealth for the years ahead there seemed little need to begin a genuinely socialist development of the national economy. There was, Saddam perceived, a need for organisational and other changes to further consolidate his grip on power.

As soon as he became president, Saddam merged several ministries, replacing eight ministers and creating new posts: one first deputy premier and five deputy premiers. He moved various family members into key posts (including one of the deputy premier positions and the post of minister of the interior). As a tactical move various Kurds were appointed to senior posts in the Party. Now Saddam and his Tikriti relatives controlled all the key areas of government, though he contrived to disguise this fact by decreeing that family names would be abolished. Everyone was to be issued with a new ID card, and all new birth certificates were to carry only the child's first name and that of the father.

In December 1979 a draft law on a new National Assembly was circulated; it was finally approved in March 1980. This new law, following an RCC enactment in 1970 that a new assembly should be created, stipulated that a 250-member assembly should be elected by secret ballot every four years by all Iraqi citizens over the age of eighteen. However, steps were taken to make it unlikely that non-Ba'athists would be able to stand as candidates. To qualify as a candidate one had to be a native Iraqi of paternal Iraqi origins, not married to a foreign wife and not belonging to a family whose property or land had been expropriated under the various state laws. Moreover – and this was of particular importance – a candidate had to be 'a believer in the principles of the July Revolution' (a condition that effectively banned all opposition candidates). Special committees were established to ensure strict observance of the required conditions, while Saddam himself made the position quite clear: 'We must ensure that the thirteen and a half million [Iraqis] take the same road. He who chooses the twisted path, will meet the sword.'[32] On 20 June 1980 seventeen 'independents' were elected to the 250-member assembly, and Saddam was happy to observe that the Iraqi people supported Ba'ath members and not the candidates from any other political party.

The measures to ensure the practical control of the political system were accompanied by the launching of a vigorous personality cult. Saddam's picture – in many different versions – appeared on postage stamps, on wristwatches, on T-shirts, on street hoardings, in schools, in offices, and throughout government buildings. A reporter for *The New York Times* noted the six portraits of President Saddam Hussein in a government office at the time of the 1980 election, with the Najaf governor declaring that there would be a large turnout to give thanks to 'the leadership of the Party and the revolution . . . They will show that they like and love Saddam Hussein. Saddam Hussein is the hope of the Arab nation and the Arab homeland'.[33] The airport at Baghdad became the Saddam International Airport, and Saddam's birthday became a National Day, despite the fact that Muslims, unlike Westerners, do not customarily celebrate birthdays. It became an offence to insult Saddam. When Saddam visited a school and asked a boy of six, 'Do you know who I am?', and the hapless boy replied, 'Yes, you are the man who makes my father spit on the television every time you appear', the boy's entire family disappeared and their house was razed to the ground.[34]

At the same time, many measures were introduced to portray Saddam as a generous benefactor of the nation. Pay was increased for many wage-earners, with particular attention being given to members of the armed forces. An amnesty was announced for jailed prisoners, apart from spies, economic saboteurs, drug smugglers, and anyone convicted of plotting against the regime. Saddam's personal telephone number was made publicly available and ordinary people were encouraged to call him with their problems (and to report on dissident elements in the community). Saddam's own heroic life story was featured in the newspaper *al-Jumhuriyya*, and a film and an exhibition were on show in Baghdad. The Iraqi people now learned that Saddam was a devoted family man with two sons (Udai and Qusai) and three daughters (Raghd, Rina and Hala), that he would not shrink from sewing on his daughter's button in public, that he preferred bitter black coffee to tea (since he had become accustomed to drinking coffee in jail), and that he liked working in his garden, fishing and looking after the sheep.[35] Sometimes Saddam would disguise his appearance and tour the streets *incognito*, to sound out public opinion, as did the eighth-century Abbasid caliph, Haroun al-Rashid. This was only one clue to suggest that Saddam was well aware of the circumstances of Iraq's glorious past. In 1980 an official two-page statement by the Iraqi government was published in *The Times*; it included the words:

> Iraq was more than once the springboard for a new civilisation in the Middle East, and the question is now pertinently asked, with a leader like this man, the wealth of oil resources and a forceful people like the Iraqis, will she repeat her former glories and the name of Saddam Hussein link up with that of Hammurabi, Ashurbanipal, al-Mansur and Harun al-Rashid? To be sure, they have not really achieved half of what he has already done at the helm of the Ba'ath Arab Socialist Party, and he is still only 44.[36]

This grandiose declaration illustrated well the character of Iraqi politics through the 1980s and beyond, through the period of the Saddam era. Here there was no vacillating politician, tainted by modern ideas of liberalism or democracy. Instead, Saddam Hussein was temperamentally inclined to seek political models in the Mesopotamian past, in the time when 'great men' imposed absolutist regimes on entire populations. If such leaders were loved, all to the good; but above all the authority of the leader must be impressed upon the people – through his use of force, the pragmatic creation of terror, the willingness to strike fear into the heart of the nation.

In these terms, where the sole measure of political success is the gaining and securing of power in the domestic environment, Saddam Hussein has proved to be a dauntingly impressive leader. In one of the world's hardest political arenas, that of an Iraqi state accustomed to coup and counter-coup, Saddam has survived for well over a decade. But even in these amoral terms Saddam's success has been no more than a domestic matter: when he chose to swim in a bigger pond, the ruthless application of force and the chilling use of terror failed to achieve the intended results.

Terror, Law and Order

In common with other absolutist leaders of the twentieth century, Saddam has always believed that 'the road to national servility had to begin with the education of the young'.[37] The young ('the boy and the youth') have not yet been soiled by 'backward ideas'; thus 'the Party and the State should be their family, their father and mother'.[38] Thus the aim is a total indoctrination, with the state the sole arbiter of morality, truth and political propriety. In Saddam's own words: 'You must encircle the adults through their sons . . . Teach students and pupils to contradict their parents . . . You must place in every corner a son of the revolution, with a trustworthy eye and a firm mind who receives his instruction from the responsible centre of the revolution.'[39] And after school and college, membership of the Party is essential for a public career. Indoctrination, Party affiliation, nepotism (with Iraq a Tikriti fiefdom), terror, rewards for service to the state – these are the elements on which the stability of the Iraqi state rests in the 1990s. In particular, the organs of state security, fashioned largely by Saddam himself, are responsible for protecting the Party and the leadership – especially the president.

Principal among such bodies is the *Mukhabarat* (Party Intelligence), a meta-intelligence organ designed to monitor the other policing organisations and to control the activities of state and corporate institutions such as the army, government departments, and the various mass organisations (youth, women, labour, etc.). The Mukhabarat (sometimes called the General Intelligence Department) grew out of the Jihaz Haneen, founded in the mid-1960s as Saddam's secret police. It is significant that this powerful organisation has always been headed by men close to Saddam: his half-brother, Barzan Ibrahim al-Tikriti, ran the Mukhabarat from 1974 to 1983, to be succeeded by Fadel Barrak, a close associate of Bakr and Saddam; at the end of 1989 Saddam's half brother, Sabawi, took over from Fadel Selfeeg, a maternal cousin of Saddam, who had served as acting head for a few months. A 1974 Political Report comments that the 'comrades' of the Mukhabarat have 'proved highly efficient in unmasking foreign and internal plots, and in repressing and liquidating them. This apparatus also played a crucial role in liquidating the espionage networks'.[40] The Mukhabarat, as the supreme overseeing organ, is a highly *political* body, its members selected not only for only their unquestioning loyalty but also for their political knowledge.

The *Amn al-Amm* (State Internal Security) is mainly concerned with domestic surveillance but it has also carried out some foreign missions. It is reported to be run by Saddam's youngest half-brother, Wathban. The Soviet Union helped Saddam to develop this and other state-security organs (just as Mossad and the CIA helped the Shah of Persia to develop Savak). In 1973 – following the 1972 Iraqi–Soviet Friendship Treaty – Saddam worked out a secret intelligence agreement with Yuri Andropov, then KGB head, to facilitate a comprehensive reorganisation of the Iraqi security services. Andropov agreed to supply Iraq with modern surveillance and interrogation equipment, KGB and GRU (Military Intelligence) training for Iraqi personnel, and intelligence information; in return, Iraq would supply intelligence information and assist Soviet agents, via Iraqi embassies, in countries where the Soviet Union had no diplomatic relations.

The *Estikhbarat* (Military Intelligence) controls army security, surveys foreign armies, and runs the military attachés in Iraqi embassies. Along with the Mukhabarat, this organisation runs terrorist operations against Iraqis living abroad and against other selected targets, giving weight to Saddam's threat that 'the hand of the Revolution can reach out to its enemies wherever they are found'. Thus targeted Iraqis have been assassinated in Lebanon, Sweden, England, Egypt, Sudan and the United States, with at least one such murder attempted in Paris. A British court convicted an Iraqi agent of an assassination attempt against Shlomo Argov, Israel's ambassador to London, an event that served as a pretext for Israel's 1982 invasion of Lebanon. A Strategic Work Plan of the Estikhbarat, prepared by operations director Khalil al-Azzawi, was leaked in 1979.[41] Among the various specified aims, the military attaché's office (in any Iraqi embassy) is required to report on 'nuclear, bacteriological and chemical warfare institutions and installations, giving as detailed information as possible on their capacities and stockpiles'. In addition, the 'personal tendencies' of scientists working in such institutions are to be reported, as are full details of naval bases. Iraqi agents are required to discover and report the 'structure of NATO forces . . . particularly in the Mediterranean area'. It is also known that the Estikhbarat provided training and logistical support for the siege of the Iranian London embassy in May 1980.

The *Amn al-Khass* (Presidential Affairs Department) is directly linked to Saddam's office and closely involved with activities of Hussein Kamal al-Majid, Saddam's cousin and son-in-law. This body looks after foreign bank accounts and controls dummy companies for the procurement of contraband items.

The *Amn al-Hizb* (Party Security) is used for the surveillance of Party members, and so aids the supervision of the Party cells and offices throughout Iraq. In addition there are such security elements as the Border Guards, the Mobile Police Strike Force, the General Department of Police, and the General Department of Nationality.[42] And providing an ultimate back-up for the various security bodies are the Party Militia and the Iraqi army.

The various state security organisations and the back-up facilities have helped to sustain totalitarian conditions where there is little regard for human rights. Such bodies as Amnesty International and Middle East Watch (a division of Human Rights Watch) have frequently provided evidence of torture and other forms of repression in Iraq. Thus an Amnesty Report (April 1989), 'Iraq: Children: Innocent Victims of Political Repression', comments that 'the torture and ill-treatment of detainees in the custody of the security forces is routine and systematic in Iraq,' and that 'Among the victims are political prisoners – including young people below the age of 18 . . .'.[43] This document cites earlier Amnesty work highlighting the extent of human abuse in Iraq and calling on the Iraqi government to investigate such abuse.[44] A more recent Amnesty Report (July 1991) comments: 'The violations of human rights perpetrated in the name of the Government of Iraq in the past decade have been regularly documented by various non-governmental human rights and humanitarian organisations. Amnesty International believes that such documentation, including its own reports, reflects only a small part of the actual record of human rights violations in Iraq.'[45] It notes that the number of offences punishable by death has been increased and that now non-violent political activity is a capital offence. Moreover, 'It has carried out thousands of executions, including of children, without trial or following trials which fell far short of international standards for fair trial.'

Middle East Watch noted in its 1990 report 'Human Rights in Iraq', that 'Iraq . . . has become a nation of informers. Party members are said to be required to inform on family, friends, and acquaintances, including other Party members . . . Teachers reportedly ask pupils about their parents' views . . .'. And severe reprisals follow any refusal to inform. Thus the London-based *Index on Censorship* instances the case of a Party member arrested in August 1987 for not reporting jokes about Saddam Hussein made at a gathering. The man, his three sons and a son-in-law were arrested, tortured and executed; and the family's house was razed to the ground. Article 200 of the Iraqi Penal Code 111 specifies the death penalty for the following offences:

Concealment by Ba'ath Party members of their former political affiliations.

Joining the Ba'ath Party while maintaining contact with another political party or organisation.

Leaving the Ba'ath Party and joining another political party.

Persuading a Ba'ath Party member member to leave the Ba'ath party.

The Iraqi Penal Code specifies in all twenty-four activities that carry the death penalty.

The strategy of the Iraqi Ba'ath is plain enough: social control is effectively maintained through surveillance, purges, torture and execution; and through the ubiquitous terror that such things engender in the population.[46] Nor can the Ba'ath's intended victims escape retribution by fleeing Iraq: Saddam's 'long arm' is no respecter of national boundaries. There is already a lengthy catalogue of Saddam's victims murdered abroad. For example, in January 1988 Said Mahdi al-Hakim, the popular Shi'ite leader, was shot dead in a hotel lobby in Khartoum while attending a Muslim conference. In the same month, Abdullah Ali, an Iraqi businessman, was murdered by poison in London; and the wife of an Iraqi dissident was stabbed to death in Oslo. A week later, an Iraqi activist, Kassem Emin, was found with his throat slit in Turkey.

It is interesting that despite Iraqi terror tactics in Britain the Foreign Office and Whitehall seemed reluctant to take action. Thus the British government 'appeared to be prepared to turn a blind eye to Iraq's terrorist activities on British soil in order to maintain the status quo as far as relations with Baghdad were concerned'.[47] Saddam's invasion of Kuwait was to change all this, but even when the *Observer* journalist Farzad Bazoft was hanged in Baghdad, as late as March 1990, the British authorities seemed strangely ambivalent (with stories about Bazoft's background in petty crime appearing in various British newspapers). In February 1990 Iraqi opposition groups in London wanted to hold a press conference and issue a document signed by prominent Iraqi dissidents, warning the British public against the possibility of Iraqi terrorist acts. The Foreign Office urged the opposition groups not to go ahead since they might damage Anglo-Iraqi relations. Two months later, during the countdown to the invasion of Kuwait and with mounting evidence of Iraqi terrorist acts in Britain and elsewhere, Foreign Secretary Douglas Hurd declared in the House of Commons that it would not be appropriate to sever relations with Baghdad. At that time the West still regarded Iraq as an important regional power with massive oil reserves, a useful export market, and a bulwark against the Iranian threat. It had long been known that Iraq was a terrorist state, at one time a host to and supporter of Abu Nidal,[48] and still prepared to send assassins around the world in pursuit of Saddam's enemies. But until its hand was forced in August 1990 the West, as always, was sensitive most of all to *realpolitik* requirements.

The Place of Women

Under the Islamic law of the Ottomans women were not regarded as whole human beings; as in modern Pakistan, a woman's word was reckoned to be worth half that of a man. In the nineteenth century the Turks introduced some reforms but their impact was patchy throughout the empire and any benefits only accrued to upper-class urban women. As late as the 1920s the Turks, now divested of Iraq, introduced a secular legal system that brought benefits to women but other regions of the erstwhile empire were no longer in a position to benefit from such change. The British now ran Iraq under the terms of the mandate and were keen to minimise the extent of social reform. Here the ancient Ottoman legal system was not abolished but merely changed to a small degree, the aim being to avoid any cultural reforms that might appear unpopular or disruptive. Thus in the case of women murdered for having 'dishonoured' their families, one colonial administrator saw the need for a compromise 'between the demands of civilised and of savage tribal justice'.[49] Elsewhere the colonial administrators were keen to point out that 'The Mohammedan of Iraq is naturally suspicious of any innovation connected with his womenfolk'.[50] In 1931 the British authorities in Iraq declared that education for girls would make them 'unfitted for tribal life . . .',[51] though in due course girls were admitted to government schools, following local demands.

Women were active in the 1920 revolt against the British occupation. They variously collected donations, carried supplies to the rebels, created a support group in Baghdad, and took a petition to the British authorities demanding the release of Iraqi detainees and denouncing their ill-treatment by the British forces. In the 1920s Iraqi women agitated for increased educational opportunities, the dropping of the veil, and for recognition as full citizens. The Women's Rising group, founded by Aswa Zahawi, began publishing the journal *Leila* and demanding the right to education and employment. Such activities led to the inevitable backlash, and with the collapse of the 1920 rebellion the ambitious women's movement suffered many reverses (it is useful to remember that at this time women were not yet enfranchised in Britain). The 1930s saw an upsurge in female agitation, new women's magazines (such as *The Modern Woman* and *The Arab Woman*) appeared, and the authorities responded with further blocking manoeuvres:

until as late as 1943 licences were withheld from women's societies, unless they were non-political charities. The Women's League Against Fascism was founded after the abortive coup staged by Rashid Ali, and in the immediate post-war world the possibility of female emancipation through socialism gained a new impetus. Again, the backlash: women agitators were arrested and imprisoned, journals were closed down, meetings were banned, and the burgeoning literacy schools were abolished. In 1948 women took part in demonstrations, supported strikes, and were shot dead in the streets – a degree of turmoil that at times seemed to threaten the monarchy itself. Women were arrested, imprisoned and tortured, but continued to maintain a political presence in such organisations as the Iraqi Communist Party and the National Democratic Party.

In 1952 Iraqi women founded the League for the Defence of Women's Rights, designed to campaign for democracy, national liberation, children's welfare and women's rights. The pro-British authorities refused to recognise the League, and its members were harassed and arrested. After the collapse of the monarchy the League was recognised on 29 December 1958 and held its first congress on International Women's Day, 8 March 1959. When Naziha Dulaimi, the League's president, became Minister for Municipalities in 1959 she was the first woman cabinet minister in the Arab world. Membership of the League grew to around 42,000 but with the growing authoritarianism of the Iraqi regime the League faced increasing difficulties; by the mid-1960s, with growing harassment and physical assaults, the organisation found it hard to continue its activities and before long most of the League's branches had closed down. Under the Ba'ath many League members were arrested and tortured; three members were condemned to be executed but were reprieved following international protest. Today the Ba'ath permits only the well-controlled General Federation of Iraqi Women (GFIW); membership of any other women's organisation is a capital offence.

The main task of the GFIW – according to Law 139 promulgated by the Revolutionary Command Council on 19 December 1972 – is to mobilise Iraqi women 'in the battle of the Arab nation against imperialism, Zionism, reactionism and backwardness', an aim that came before 'raising the level of the Iraqi woman by all possible means'. Emphasis is given to the importance of marriage, procreation and the family (what Aflaq saw as 'the nation's basic cell'). GFIW booklets carry Saddam's picture on the first page, but care is taken to avoid reference to any individual woman by name. It is clear that the Federation, far from seeking the liberation of women, is yet another device for the implementation and expansion of Ba'ath ideology. At the GFIW's third conference, Saddam Hussein spelt out the priority: 'an enlightened mother who is educated and liberated can give the country a generation of conscious and committed fighters' (presumably all male); woman should not seek 'bourgeois' emancipation but should find liberation through 'commitment to the Revolution'; and elsewhere he urged Iraqi women not to try to show that they can do anything that men can.[52] Again the Ba'ath strategy is obvious: women are esteemed to the extent that they serve an ideological purpose, but there are various constraints on genuine female emancipation. Advances in employment and education have been made, but the central Ba'ath intention is to protect the security of the regime. In one view, the 'cooperation of the GFIW with the security forces makes a mockery of their propaganda about women's liberation'.[53]

By 1980, despite the Ba'athist emphasis on the family role of women, there were significant identifiable advances in various industrial and professional sectors: women accounted for 46 per cent of all teachers, 29 per cent of physicians, 46 per cent of dentists, 70 per cent of pharmacists, 15 per cent of accountants, 14 per cent of factory workers, and 16 per cent of civil servants. It is claimed that in the prestigious Ministry of Oil 37 per cent of the design staff and 30 per cent of the construction supervisors were women. The participation of women in the non-agricultural labour force is estimated to have risen from 7 per cent in 1968 to 19 per cent in 1980.[54] The relevant legislation specified equal pay and opportunity measures, positive discrimination for hiring in government departments, paid maternity leave, childcare facilities at the workplace, and a reduced retirement age for female workers. The GFIW, under close Ba'athist supervision, helps to ensure that the intentions behind the legislation are realised. Today the Federation has a branch in each of the provinces of Iraq, with some 265 subsections based in major towns, 755 centres that focus on the larger villages and city quarters with more than 6000 people, and 1612 liaison committees that extend to all the remaining villages and city quarters.[55] In 1978 amendments to the Code of Personal Status were introduced to allow certain departures from the traditional aspects of the Islamic law (*sharia*). These amendments allowed a judge to overrule a father's wishes in the case of the early marriage of a daughter; and to severely curtail the traditional framework of rights held by male kinship groups (uncles, cousins, brothers and so on) over their women. Thus, with the advancement of women in employment and erosion of patriarchal rights, a measure of female emancipation was introduced in ways deemed consistent with the protection of Ba'athist ideology.

Forced marriages have been abolished and the minimum age for marriage has been raised – though it is still relatively easy for a man to gain a divorce but virtually impossible for a woman. Polygamy is allowed with the consent of the first wife, who in any case can be coerced into compliance in various ways; though it has to be said that there is a discernible move away from traditional Islamic practice (a fruit of the secular thread in Ba'athist ideology). In 1977, in a further departure from traditional practice, a law was enacted to regulate the entry of women into the armed forces, with women subject to all military regulations, apart from 'what does not conform with her nature'. It became possible to appoint a woman an officer if she had a university degree in a health-related field, a (Law 131) provision that signalled women's dominant position in the health services. The same pattern was discernible in the popular militia forces, which by 1982 had enrolled some 40,000 women. Here, as in other areas where women have made gains, a seemingly progressive development has to be set against the broader constraints of a totalitarian society. It still has to be acknowledged that the various Ba'athist reforms were 'considerably less radical than the 1956 Tunisian Code, for example, or the Shah's family reforms, to say nothing of Ataturk's radical break with Islamic family law in 1926'.[56] Saddam himself adopted a purely expedient attitude to the advancement of women in society: there was little of principle here, beyond the need to secure the regime and to develop its influence as a regional power. Thus he commented that: 'The unity of the family must be based on congruence with the central principles of the policies and traditions of the Revolution in its construction of the new society. Whenever there is a contradiction between the unity of the family and these new principles, it must be resolved in favour of the latter.' In short, women's advancement must not be allowed to threaten the security of the state. Thus the Iraqi woman must not be advanced in a way that might place her 'in a hostile attitude to the Revolution'.[57]

It further emerged that there was nothing secure in female gains in Iraq. When the regime was under pressure in the immediate aftermath of the Iran–Iraq war (see below), Saddam responded by retreating into age-old patriarchal practices. In a move on 18 February 1990 the RCC decreed that 'any Iraqi who, on grounds of adultery, purposely kills his mother, daughter, sister, maternal or paternal aunt, maternal or paternal niece, maternal or paternal female cousin, shall not be prosecuted'.[58] The effect of such a decree is absolute: any male is authorised to kill any female relative, since no subsequent female testimony would be allowed to count in the balance. The Ba'athist regime had improved the law in certain particulars to free women from the traditional rigours of the *sharia*, but even such advances had always to be set against the horrors of a totalitarian regime.[59] But now there was a further crippling constraint: as a ruthless social palliative Saddam decided to plunge Iraqi family law back into the darkness of medieval Islam.

THE KURDISH QUESTION

The Kurds, of ancient origins, today occupy parts of Iraq, Iran, Syria, Turkey, Lebanon and the (erstwhile) Soviet Union. They are a pastoral nomadic people who – despite frequent historical and modern references to 'Kurdistan' – have never been an internationally-recognised nation or even united under a single government. Of Indo-European stock, the Kurdish people are probably the largest ethnic group never to have achieved national statehood. David McDowall, author of the Minority Rights Group report[60] suggests a total of some sixteen million Kurds, though larger estimates have been given. There are, for example, around 350,000 Kurds working in Western Europe. The Kurdish people live in an area of about 250,000 square miles (640,000 sq. km). About 80 per cent of them are Sunni Muslims, with the rest Shi'ite; and they have claimed kinship with the ancient Medes, one of the founding races of the Persian empire. Their language, which has many dialects, is related to Persian; though the Turks, in the past interested in political advantage over a British-occupied Iraq, have claimed that the Kurds, as 'mountain Turks', have ethnic roots in Turkey (a claim that is rarely voiced today in the context of the Turkish–Kurdish war – see Chapter 1). It has been emphasised that there is no structural relationship between Kurdish and Arabic or between Kurdish and Turkish (moreover, Semitic Arabic and Altaic Turkish belong to very different linguistic families). All this tends to confirm that the Kurds are a well-defined group, with distinct ethnic and linguistic origins.

At the end of the First World War, Kurdish nationalists throughout the Kurdistan region, encouraged by Woodrow Wilson's famous Fourteen Points (8 January 1918),* seized the opportunity to press their claims. However, Britain's main interest lay in the creation of a pliant Iraqi state, a goal that was assisted in no small measure by manifest divisions among the Kurds themselves. In the summer of 1920 the Treaty of Sèvres, to which Britain and Turkey were both signatories, recognised the 'independent states' of Armenia and Kurdistan, but this formal recognition was not destined to be translated into reality. The Sèvres terms, according to which the Kurds

---

*The Twelfth Point declares that: 'the nationalities now under Turkish rule should . . . be assured . . . an absolutely unmolested opportunity of autonomous development'.

would have achieved nationhood, were nullified by the Treaty of Lausanne (24 July 1923), which again cast the Kurds into limbo. Throughout this period the Kurds made frequent attempts to assert their national independence, though repeatedly repressed by the Turks and the British. The Turks denied the Kurds any ethnic or linguistic identity, putting down various risings with great ferocity. The British indicated to the Kurds that they should expect no support from His Majesty's government, and soon were using the RAF to bomb the various Kurdish tribes into submission. In 1922 the mandatory authorities conceded that the Kurds should be granted limited autonomy in northern Iraq, but Sheikh Mahmud Barzinji, whom the British had wanted to instal as a suitable client ruler, seemed reluctant to accept any degree of Iraqi suzerainty. Mahmud's stand seemed to be gaining in popularity, whereupon the British decided to put him down by force. In July 1924 Sulaimaniya was occupied by British troops, and in December the RAF was required to bomb parts of the town. With a measure of stability re-established the pro-British Iraqi regime decided on various prudent gestures to the Kurds; in 1926 it was decided that civil servants in the Kurdish area should be Kurds, that Kurdish children should be educated in Kurdish, and that Kurdish and Arabic should be the official languages of the region. These were significant concessions, although designed largely to take the steam out of calls for a Kurdish homeland. Under the Iraqi monarchy it became the practice to have one or two token Kurdish ministers in the government, and to allow the Kurds a measure of ethnic recognition. Such moves, contrary to Iraqi intentions, served mainly to stimulate Kurdish national aspirations. In 1929, on the brink of Iraqi independence, Kurdish deputies in the Iraq parliament sent a memorandum to the Prime Minister, demanding that the promises made in 1926 be implemented more effectively. Nothing was done, and it soon emerged that the Anglo–Iraqi treaty of 1930 contained no safeguards for minorities, which meant that an independent Iraq would be established with no protection for the Kurds.

Rioting again broke out in Sulaimaniya in September 1930; and Sheikh Mahmud, technically exiled from Iraq, resolved to go on the offensive. Fighting broke out in the spring of 1931, and although Mahmud was comprehensively defeated his efforts stimulated the development of another Kurdish opposition group in the Barzani tribal lands. Mustafa Barzani, the younger brother of the Barzani religious and tribal leader, Sheikh Ahmad, emerged as one of the main Kurdish political leaders. He died in exile in 1979. In 1936 the Barzani brothers were captured and forced to live under a loose form of house arrest in Sulaimaniya, where they came into contact with sympathetic political writers, some of whom came together to form the covert Hewa (Hope) Party in the late 1930s. However, there were various factional divisions in Hewa – essentially between right and left (did the way ahead lie in socialism and revolution or in seeking a useful accommodation with the British?) – and these divisions were to persist in the Kurdish movement through subsequent decades. The Iraqi Communist Party (ICP), founded in 1934, agitated in favour of Kurdish rights, with communist groups set up in Arbil and other Kurdish towns in the early 1940s. Communists edited the first Kurdish political journal, *Azadi*, and an editorial in the first issue (1944) declared: 'We urge the politically conscious among the sons of our people and every sincere Kurd who loves his people and his homeland, not to leave his people unorganised and unprepared . . . we urge him to struggle for democratic parties and associations to organise the Kurdish people, to prepare them and enable them to achieve self-determination so that their unity with the Arabs in Iraq would be a voluntary union based on equality of rights.'[61] It is suggested that the ICP was the first political party 'to develop a coherent policy on the Kurdish question, which generally amounted to a plan for autonomy based on Kurdish self-determination'.[62]

In July 1943 Mustafa Barzani escaped from Sulaimaniya and began organising a further revolt against the British occupation forces. During November and December he made various appeals to the British to support Kurdish claims for autonomy; and then, following correspondence with Sir Kinahan Cornwallis, the British ambassador, made the remarkable promise to obey him, 'whatever your orders may be'. However, any agreement between Cornwallis and Nuri al-Said on the one hand and Barzani on the other did little to pacify the Iraqi government, now worried that any move towards autonomy for the Kurds might simply herald political separatism. In 1945 the government sent 14,000 troops against Barzani's ill-equipped forces, forcing him to flee to Iran in October. With this setback, despite the enforced retirement of Nuri, the Kurdish nationalists were forced to lie low, awaiting the collapse of the monarchy. Already the Iraqi Kurds had won some concessions not granted to their brothers in Iran, Syria and Turkey; and the hope was that a Kurdish victory in Iraq would bring wider successes throughout the whole of Kurdistan.

On 22 January 1946 Iranian Kurds headed by Qadhi Mohammad formed the autonomous Republic of Mahabad in northern Iran. It proved to be short-lived: in mid-March 1947 the Iranian army launched a major offensive against the Kurds which lasted for five weeks. On 31 March Qadhi Mohammad was hanged in public, along with two close relatives and political allies, in the main square of Mahabad. Some months later, four Kurdish ex-officers of the Iraqi army, who had accompanied Barzani to

Mahabad were also hanged, even though they had given themselves up
to the Iraqi authorities. Barzani and some of his closest followers now
decided that it was no longer safe for them to remain in Iraq; in June he
and six hundred men fled across Turkey and Iran, covering more than
two hundred miles over the mountains, to seek refuge in the Soviet Union.
There they remained until 1958.

An Iraqi branch of the Iranian KDP had been established in Mahabad
in 1946 by Barzani and Hamza Abdullah, an associate who later struggled
to establish a branch of the Party in Iraq, but who in consequence succeeded in creating an Iraqi KDP; so was formalised a permanent division
between the Iranian and Iraqi segments of the Kurdish political movement.
At this time there was still a branch of the Iranian KDP based at Sulaimaniya
and led by Ibrahim Ahmad. When Mahabad fell he joined the Iraqi KDP
(known in Iraq as the Hizb al-Party), to be made general secretary in 1951.
Following the 1958 revolution Ahmad sent congratulations to the Free
Officers, and weeks later the new constitution declared that 'Arabs and
Kurds are partners in the Iraqi homeland and their national rights are
recognised within the Iraqi state'. In October, Ahmad went to Prague with
Iraqi passports for Barzani and three of his closest supporters. On 6 October
they returned to Iraq to a rapturous welcome from the Kurds and a cordial
greeting from Prime Minister Abdul Karim Kassem. But the new situation
did not deliver the anticipated fruits.

A struggle for power, centred around the question of whether to join the
UAR, soon developed in the young republic. On this topic the Kurds had
clear views: 'a union of Iraq with Egypt and Syria would scarcely have
helped Kurdish plans since the Kurds in post-revolutionary Syria did not
enjoy even the inadequate recognition of Kurdish linguistic, ethnic and
educational rights which had been afforded to the Kurds in pre-revolutionary Iraq'.[63] Barzani still managed to give unqualified approval to the Kassem
regime, aided by the clear signs that Kassem was not intending to proceed
with any plans for union. Barzani then ousted Ahmad from the KDP
leadership; and in May 1959, in collaboration with the communists, the
KDP published a left-wing manifesto. However, Barzani – along with
Kassem – soon saw disadvantage in close links with the communists, and
in January 1960 the ICP, unlike the Kurdish Democratic Party, was refused
permission to register as a legal organisation. At the same time it was
emerging that Kassem's commitment to the Kurds was limited, a matter
of pragmatic convenience. The situation deteriorated, from the Kurdish
point of view, and the Kassem regime began harassing the Kurdish leadership: Kurdish leaders were arrested in March 1961; the Kurdish newspapers
were banned; and the KDP was prohibited from holding its annual congress

in July. And at a time when conflict was beginning between the Kurds and the Kassem regime there were also tribal confrontations between different Kurdish groups: what had seemed a route to Kurdish unity and independence was rapidly degenerating into factional conflict and state harassment. The Kurds and the central government were in a virtual state of war in 1961, a state of affairs that continued on and off until 1975.

At times, according in part to other demands on the Iraqi armed forces, Iraqi aircraft bombed Kurdish villages indiscriminately (much as the British had done some decades before). Barzani's army, the Pesh Merga ('those who walk before death'), numbered around 50,000 men; and at the peak of their success the Kurds controlled all the mountains in northern Iraq, with Kurdish guerrillas striking as far afield as Mosul, Arbil and Kirkuk, the main cities of Iraqi Kurdistan. Throughout this period various foreign powers (Iran, Israel, the Soviet Union and the United States), seeing advantage in the situation, offered assistance to the Kurds. Casualties between 1960 and 1970 were estimated at 9000 military dead and 100,000 civilian dead (though lower estimates have been given). The Kurds had struggled for more than a decade, at great cost, and it was not clear that anything had been accomplished. Then in March 1970 the Iraqi government offered autonomy to the Kurds, and a new phase in Iraqi-Kurdish relations had begun. Again, however, the promise did not yield reality.

On 11 March 1970, following three months of negotiations between Barzani and the Iraqi government, a joint Manifesto was published that recognised 'the legitimacy of the Kurdish nationality', promising Kurdish language rights, Kurdish representation in government, Kurdish administration of the Kurdish region, and a new Kurdish province based on Dohuk (the reforms went as far as those in the scheme announced on 29 June 1966 by Iraqi premier Abdul al-Rahman al-Bazzaz, who was ejected from office a few months later). Matters seemed to be moving in favour of Kurdish independence, but yet again the paper promises would not materialise.

Soon the disadvantages of the Manifesto, from the Ba'ath perspective, became obvious. A *de facto* recognition of Barzani and the KDP, as the sole administrative authority in the Kurdish area, had been given; and it was clear that this would entail a significant erosion of Iraqi authority in the region. In these circumstances, the Ba'ath had no intention of implementing the terms of the Manifesto, seeing it more as a delaying mechanism: the heat could be taken out of the Kurdish question until the time came to recast the Manifesto in terms more favourable to the Iraqi state. In fact, government attitudes soon became manifest. Kurdish families were evicted from their homes in some areas, particularly around Kirkuk, where the Iraqi government wanted to alter the ethnic balance. Thus in September 1971, for example, some 40,000 Kurds were expelled from the border region near Khaniqin, and forced to settle in Iran, on the grounds that they were not really Iraqis. In the same month the Iraqi government tried to assassinate Barzani, following an attempt on the life of his son. More assassination attempts were to be made in subsequent years.

The Iraqi decision to evict Kurds from particular areas was stimulated by one of the Manifesto provisions: '. . . necessary steps shall be taken . . . to unify the governorates and administrative units populated by a Kurdish majority as shown by the official census to be carried out . . .'. This meant that the Iraqi state had an interest in reducing the Kurdish population in areas over which the government wanted to retain control. Barzani later claimed to have recognised the Manifesto as an Iraqi delaying manoeuvre ('I said this was a ruse. I knew it even before I signed the agreement'), but there had been little scope for negotiation or for controlling the pace of implementation of the provisions. But Barzani, despite his seeming political impotence, was still an irritation to Saddam. While Barzani was talking with eight religious dignitaries, sent by Saddam to discuss the terms of the Manifesto, two explosions rocked the room; two clerics were killed but Barzani survived. His bodyguard opened fire, killing five sheikhs. It later transpired that the clerics had been innocent couriers of bombs hidden in their tape recorders; when the men tried to operate the machines the bombs exploded. Barzani commented: 'Iraq is a police state run by Saddam Hussein who is a power-obsessed megalomaniac. He eliminated Hardan and Amash; he tried to eliminate me; he will eliminate Bakr.'[64] If Saddam needed further reason for suspicion, Barzani soon provided it.

Seeing the futility of his present political course, Barzani moved to develop relations with Israel and with the Shah of Iran. More significantly, he resolved also to establish connections with the United States, a move that Washington was happy to welcome. In May 1972 President Richard Nixon approved a CIA scheme to give Barzani $16 million over a three-year period; this at a time when Saddam was seeking agreements with the Soviet Union. And as if Barzani's acceptance of CIA funding were not sufficient, he then gave an interview to *The Washington Post* in the summer of 1973 in which his intentions were made quite clear. Once the Kirkuk oil fields had been returned to their 'lawful owners', Barzani was prepared to hand over the oil resource to the Americans: '. . . *we are ready to do what goes with American policy in this area if America will protect us from the wolves. If support were strong enough, we could control the Kirkuk field and give it to an American company to operate.*'[65] If Saddam wanted evidence that the Kurds intended to donate Iraqi assets to the imperialist United States, here it was. Barzani, it appeared, was prepared to dismember Iraq as a prelude to rewarding his American paymasters. Saddam responded – in terms that were remarkably similar in tone and intent to statements made in 1992 – by saying: 'We must understand that this country will remain as it is within its present geographic boundaries forever.'[66]

Fighting continued between the Kurds and the Iraqi government through 1973 and after, at times exposing the extraordinary fragility of the Iraqi state. Military clashes, interrupted by the Yom Kippur War in 1973 and by UN peace moves in 1974, were interspersed by several fruitless negotiations. In March 1974 Saddam insisted that government autonomy plans be accepted; Barzani rejected the demand, whereupon the Iraqi government unilaterally implemented its own autonomy scheme. Again fighting erupted throughout the region, and soon the Iraqi army was experiencing serious problems. Iran and Syria – in addition to the CIA – were now supplying Barzani, who by this time was equipped with heavy artillery and surface-to-air missiles. In January 1975 Iran invaded Iraq with two regiments, and the Kurdish threat to Baghdad was the gravest problem that the Ba'ath regime had faced since it took power in 1968. The Iraqi army was facing appalling logistical problems, not least 'a great shortage of ammunition' a situation that was desperate by March 1975, when 'there were only three bombs left for the air force to fight the Kurds'.[67] There was also the growing problem that the Shi'ites, bearing the brunt of the fighting against the Kurds, would become estranged from the Baghdad regime.

For some months it seemed that the Kurds had the upper hand. The Iraqi army was on the verge of collapse and the national economy was in a dire condition. If the Shah of Iran had pressed home the anti-Ba'ath advantage it seems likely that the Baghdad regime would have fallen, but the Iranians had no such ambitions. The Shah wanted to end the Iraqi–Iranian border disputes; and, no doubt to the great relief of the Iraqi government, the Shah signed a pact in March, letting the Ba'ath regime off the hook. The Shah, with his own Kurdish problem, had no wish to advance the Iraqi Kurdish cause (just as today the Turkish government is ambivalent about the rights of the Iraqi Kurds). The Algiers agreement between the Shah and Iraq (with Henry Kissinger, US Secretary of State, a player on the scene) was a devastating blow to Barzani. Iran and the US had decided that it was time to reach an accommodation with Baghdad; and so – in the nature of things – the Kurds were ditched. The Iranians were given free rights of navigation in the Shatt al-Arab, and there were some minor territorial adjustments. More importantly, the Iran–Iraq frontier in the north was closed, so blocking any residual aid from Iran to the Kurds. Now the Kurds were no longer allowed to regroup and rearm in Iran; and they could no longer rely on the vital Iranian military support or on the less important CIA arms and provisions. The Iranian artillery withdrew within twenty-four hours, the heartened Iraqi army picked itself up off the ground, and before long the entire Kurdish resistance had collapsed. Barzani, dispirited and politically impotent, fled first to Iran and then to the United States where he died in 1979. The Iraqis celebrated their victory in the usual way, by executing as many of the rebels as they could catch. The war had cost the lives of some 7000 Iraqi troops and, according to Barzani, around 2000 Kurdish troops; one estimate suggests a higher total of some 20,000 fatalities, with 600,000 refugees.[68]

Barzani, believing in the 'moral obligation and political responsibility' of the United States towards the Kurdish people, had no doubt that he had been betrayed by Washington. His sons, Idris and Massoud, took control of the remnants of the Kurdish Democratic Party; and before long other Kurdish leaders were coming to the fore. Some of the refugees returned to Iraq under a series of amnesties, now forced to accept the measures being implemented by the Iraqi authorities to resolve the perennial Kurdish problem. Any prospect of Kurdish autonomy was now unrealistic. Kurdish groups were systematically resettled in areas that made surveillance easier, and by 1979 some 200,000 Kurds had been evicted from the frontier area, with around seven hundred villages burnt to the ground.

After the 1975 disaster, from the Kurdish point of view, the movement again split into various elements. Idris and Massoud, claiming to be more radical than their father, ran the KDP–Provisional Command, while Jalal Talabani, an old opponent of Barzani, headed the Patriotic Union of Kurdistan (PUK). The fall of the Shah, at first seen as a propitious event in view of the Algiers betrayal, did nothing to advance Kurdish interests; the new theocrats in Tehran had little interest in minority rights. It is significant that the Iraqi Ba'athists have tended to support the Iranian KDP as a useful dissident faction threatening a traditional enemy, whereas for similar reasons Tehran had inclined to support the KDP–Provisional Command; such alignments were particularly evident during the Iran–Iraq war (see below). It is equally significant that Talabani, having taken refuge in 1975 in Syria, was given a Syrian passport by President Assad, with Talabani invited to use his small army of refugees to police the Syrian border against Iraqi Ba'athists: in 1975, tension between Iraq and Syria, competing claimants to the Ba'athist soul, almost erupted in war.

Such developments served to consolidate the fratricidal divisions in the Kurdish movement: even to the point that in 1978 the PUK fought several pitched battles with the KDP (supported by the remnants of the Pesh Merga). In these circumstances it was an easy matter for local states to play off one Kurdish faction against another. Just as the United States used the

Kurds to further its own perceived interests in the region (as it continues to do today), so Iraq and Syria – not to mention Tehran – are apt to see the various Kurdish elements as tools that can aid national policy. Thus the Syrians let Talabani loose in the Iran–Iraq war, inviting him to create disruption in Iraqi Kurdistan and so weaken the Baghdad Ba'athists; just as in 1984 the Iraqis offered Talabani a measure of autonomy in exchange for continued opposition to the Barzanis and the KDP.

The Kurds, in their endless struggle for nationhood and independence, have been systematically repressed and cynically manipulated by states with little interest in minority rights. The persistent efforts of the Kurdish people have yielded a shortlived republic (Mahabad) and many autonomy agreements. In Iraq and the (erstwhile) Soviet Union they won concrete advances, though today such progress is seen with easy hindsight to have been insecure and unstable. States outside the region, especially the US, have seen advantage in pressing Kurdish claims: Washington quickly warmed to a Kurdish leader (Barzani) prepared to donate Iraqi oil resources to American companies. Today it is not hard to imagine that US support for the Kurds, to the extent that such support exists, derives at least in part from American interest in Kirkuk oil.

IRAN–IRAQ WAR

Origins

In history there have been many conflicts between Persia and Mesopotamia; that is, between Iran and Iraq. Competing empires, hungry for land, repeatedly clashed; there were endless disputes about borders, land, navigational rights (in the Shatt al-Arab), sovereignty, and the recognition of minority groups. Some minorities straddled recognised borders, creating fresh tensions, and sometimes external powers – with their own agendas for exploitation and conquest – burst into the region. What some writers, from the comfortable familiarity of the twentieth century, have dubbed the 'first' Gulf war was in fact only one of the many conflicts between the two important states that shared a common border.

Migratory tribes always made it difficult to define fixed boundaries: settled towns were nicely fixed on agreed maps, but wandering nomads always ran the risk of violating this or that frontier agreed by sedentary rulers. And further: nomads sometimes served the cynical interests of national leaders. Look, *there* we have an ethnic presence, so *there* our writ runs. And there was always the question of resources. A land traditionally thought to be bleak and barren would suddenly attract many claims of sovereignty when once oil or other riches were discovered. And this can impact on maritime issues as well as those that only affect dry land. Thus in the spring of 1963 there emerged the difficult issue of Iran and Iran tapping a common oilfield in the central sector of Khaneh and Naft-e Shah, added to the fraught question of exploration for oil in the offshore continental shelf. In February 1969 an Iranian delegation visited Baghdad to discuss offshore exploration, Khaneh oilfield exploration and the demarcation of uncertain frontiers.

On 4 July 1937 Iran and Iraq had agreed a frontier treaty, opening the Shatt al-Arab to all the countries of the world, amending the fluvial frontiers, and confirming the land boundaries defined in earlier (1913–14) accords. Iraq later claimed that the 1937 treaty was signed under duress, and that in consequence its terms no longer applied. Now, in 1969 the Iranians were claiming that Iraq was not observing obligations that still stood, and they repeated their demand for a redrawing of the fluvial frontier. At the same time, one of the periodic Kurdish rebellions blew up in Iraq, encouraging the Shah to press his claims. Tehran then unilaterally abrogated the 1937 treaty, which Iraq in any case was disposed to ignore, and began using the Shatt al-Arab as if it were an Iranian waterway. Iraq lodged complaints with the United Nations, but no action was taken. In time-honoured manner, Iraq then began expelling large numbers of ethnic Iranians and exhorted dissident Iranian groups to rebel against the Shah. Iraq raised also the question of Khuzistan/Arabistan; Iraqi territory, according to Baghdad, that had been yielded to Iran under Ottoman pressure. The Iraqis also set up radio stations to beam anti-Shah propaganda into Iran; and announced the creation of the Popular Front for the Liberation of Arabistan. And on 21 January 1970 Baghdad declared that the Shah had tried to secure a coup led by Major-General Abdul Ghani al Rawi; forty-four conspirators, mostly military men, were executed.

It had already emerged that the Shah was acting as a conduit for arms from Israel and the United States to the Kurdish rebels in Iraq. Britain, the main imperialist power in the Gulf area, was following its plan to make withdrawals from the region by December 1971, with the West already having chosen Iran, usefully led by the pro-Western Shah, to be the new guarantor of the security of the Gulf. The Shah, happy to act as a Western client, decided to acquire some further portions of territory to make the task easier. Thus on 30 November 1971 Iran occupied the Lesser Tunb Island and, following some fighting, took over Greater Tunb. This meant that Arab territory had been usurped by the Shah under instigation from the West; it was not an act designed to please the Iraqis.

These were some of the events that helped to consolidate Iraqi resentment of 'Western imperialism', and which pushed Baghdad into the arms of the Russians. Baghdad responded to the Iranian encroachment by severing all diplomatic relations with Tehran and London, and by negotiating a fifteen-year Treaty of Friendship and Co-operation with the Soviet Union. Iraq and the USSR agreed to make contact in case of 'danger to the peace of either party . . .', and to refrain from joining any alliance directed against the other; moreover, they also agreed to 'continue to develop co-operation in the strengthening of their defence capacity'. The move brought Iran and the US even closer together, with President Nixon announcing in May 1972 that the Shah would be permitted to purchase any non-nuclear weapons, and that the US would help the Shah to instigate Kurdish rebellion in Iraq. The stage was well set for a conflict between the pro-West Iran, guardian of conservative values, and the pro-Soviet Iraq, keen to lead republican Arab nationalism in the area.

In the short term, the Shah backed off from full-blooded support for the Iraqi Kurds, as noted, since he feared a strengthening of his own Kurdish dissidents. The agreement reached on 6 March 1975 between the Shah and Saddam Hussein, both attending an OPEC meeting in Algiers, pledged the signatories to define their river boundaries 'according to the thalweg line' and 'to end all infiltrations of a subversive nature'.[69] A new treaty on the Frontier and Neighbourly Relations was signed by Iran and Iraq on 13 June and ratified three months later. Iraq's concessions on the Shatt al-Arab were matched by Iran relinquishing territory around the villages of Zain al Qaws and Saif Saad. Iraq's weakness, following the draining effects of the Kurdish insurgency (backed by Iran and the US) had forced it to concede Iranian demands on the common waterway, but there was no recipe in this for a stable peace. Indeed, it was already clear that the Iraqi leadership was divided on the issue, and it was only a matter of time before Baghdad would make counter-claims against Tehran.

The 1975 agreement meant that Iraq had again managed to subdue the Kurds but that it 'had apparently lost an unfought war against Iran'.[70] The evident Iranian victory rankled with Saddam Hussein who had been responsible for the 1975 negotiations. He had been forced to accept the 'bitter reality' of the agreement, but this was only a temporary matter; there was 'no question of the Iraqi regime accepting in perpetuity an outcome determined by Iranian *force majeure*'.[71] In December 1980 Saddam commented that Iraq had signed the agreement but 'under conditions we could not control . . . the Iranians used military force against us'.[72] It was obvious that the 1975 agreement, far from being a permanent settlement, was no more than a truce in a long-running contest between Iraq and Iran for supremacy in the Gulf region. The uneasy peace collapsed following the collapse of the Shah's regime and the assumption by Saddam of supreme powers in the Iraqi state. Where the Shah and the ailing Bakr may have wished to preserve a peace, however fragile, the Ayatollah Khomeini and Saddam Hussein had no interest in a compromise status quo.

Since 1965 Khomeini had been living in exile in Najaf where he was closely associated with an Iraqi ayatollah, Baqir al-Sadr, who was keen to establish an Islamic republic in Iraq. In September 1978 the Shah belatedly demanded that Iraq expel Khomeini, whereupon he was exiled to Paris. From the Shah's point of view, this was not a good move. Whereas Khomeini's activities had been subject to surveillance and constraints in Iraq, he now enjoyed much more freedom of movement: Paris was a much better base than Najaf from which to launch a revolution against the Shah. Nor did Khomeini's Paris exile serve Iraqi interests. Baghdad had placated a Shah who was finding himself in an increasingly desperate situation, but at the cost of antagonising a theocratic bigot who was soon to head a powerful state on Iraq's borders. The uneasy peace that followed the 1975 agreement was soon to be shattered by the Iranian Revolution, a turbulent event caused at least in part by the expulsion of Khomeini from Iraq; the Shah had signed his own eviction order.

Khomeini came to power in Iran in February 1979 at the head of a revolutionary Islamic movement. Soon appeals were flooding from Tehran urging that Arab or state nationalism be abolished in Muslim lands in the interest of the higher unity of Islam. In an interview published in a Tehran newspaper, Khomeini declared: 'The Ummayad rule [661–750] was based on Arabism, the principle of promoting Arabs over all other peoples, which was an aim fundamentally opposed to Islam and its desire to abolish nationality and unite all mankind in a single community, under the aegis of a state indifferent to the matter of race and colour . . .'. The Ummayads, Khomeini claimed, were aiming 'to distort Islam completely by reviving the Arabism of the pre-Islamic age of ignorance, and the same aim is still pursued by the leaders of certain Arab countries who declare openly their desire to revive the Arabism of the Ummayads'.[73] There is no doubt that by 'leaders of certain Arab countries', Khomeini had Saddam Hussein in mind: in a Paris interview in late 1978 Khomeini gave as his enemies: 'First, the Shah; then the American Satan; then Saddam Hussein and his infidel Ba'ath Party.'[74]

This theological offensive was not without effect on Saddam Hussein. He declared that the Islamic Revolution, or any other revolution that purported to be Islamic, 'must be a friend of the Arab revolution'; he began praying with greater frequency, at both Sunni and Shi'ite shrines; he made Imam Ali's birthday a national holiday; he resorted to the use of Islamic symbols; and resolved to 'fight injustice with the swords of the Imams', calling at the same time for 'a revival of heavenly values'.[75] But there was no way of preventing a deepening of tension between the Iranian ayatollahs and the Iraqi Ba'athists, following the Khomeini revolution. Differences between the Sunnis and the Shi'ites were exacerbated, and immediately Khomeini took power the new regime in Tehran began inciting the Iraqi Shi'ites to rise up against the Ba'ath government. Soon the Dawa, a Shi'ite party under Iranian influence, was plotting against the Iraqi regime, spreading pro-Iranian propaganda and organising a terrorist campaign. Saddam responded by putting the Ayatollah al-Sadr under house arrest in Najaf; Shi'ite riots followed in Baghdad, which were put down with great brutality. Then Saddam persuaded Bakr to resign and took over the presidency. After consolidating his position he completed the fearful purge of the Party and, in April 1980, had al-Sadr and his sister summarily hanged. Between 15,000 and 20,000 Shi'ites were expelled from Iraq, and hundreds more were arrested, tortured and executed. Saddam was already demonstrating that any threat to Iraq or to his own leadership would be met with the utmost severity. In a matter of months, using all the power of the security services that he had nurtured over the previous decade, he had secured his position.

In March 1980 the Iraqi authorities executed ninety-seven civilians and military men, half of them members of Dawa, now a banned organisation. Dawa activists then began attacking police stations, Ba'ath Party offices, and Popular Army recruiting centres. The repression of the Shi'ites continued and then news leaked out concerning the secret hanging of Ayatollah al-Sadr and his sister Bint al Huda on 8 April. An incensed Khomeini, hearing of the death of one of his principal Iraqi supporters, declared: 'The war that the Iraqi Ba'ath wants to ignite is a war against Islam . . . The people and army of Iraq must turn their backs on the Ba'ath regime and overthrow it . . . because this regime is attacking Iran, attacking Islam and the Koran . . . Iran today is the land of God's messenger; and its revolution, government and laws are Islamic.'[76] Now border skirmishes between Iran and Iraq were happening at the rate of ten a month, and leading Iranian dissidents were being given radio stations in Iraq to beam anti-Khomeini propaganda into Iran.[77] Washington staged an armed rescue attempt to retrieve the American hostages in Tehran, which failed dismally; and a pro-Shah coup attempt on 24–25 May was routed by Khomeini loyalists. A further coup attempt, staged by Shahpour Bakhtiar, the last premier under the Shah, was easily repulsed; and a fortnight later, on

27 July 1980, the last Shah of Iran died of cancer in Cairo. It was obvious to Saddam that he could not rely on Iranian monarchist generals or the imperialist United States to topple the Khomeini regime.

It seemed a propitious time for Saddam to intervene. There were constant reports of friction between the Iranian religious leaders and the then president Hassan Bani-Sadr; the Iranian army, following massive purges, was in disarray; arms had stopped flowing to Iran; and the country was diplomatically isolated. The 'great Satan' was incensed at the overthrow of its long-nurtured client and at the seizing of American hostages; and Tehran's Moscow links had collapsed following the Soviet invasion of Muslim Afghanistan. A friendless and chaotic Iran, starved of supplies and military expertise, seemed an easy target. The question was not whether Iraq should invade, but when.

By August 1980 Saddam Hussein had visited the rulers of Kuwait and Saudi Arabia, who said nothing to deflate his ambitions. Egypt had been suspended from the Arab League following the conclusion of the Egyptian accord with Israel, and there seemed to be a vacancy at the head of the Arab table. Saddam, now promised financial backing from Kuwait and Saudi Arabia, conscious of the deep hostilities between Iran and the United States, believed that he would be able to wage a brief and highly successful campaign. He would be greeted as a liberator by Arabs in Iranian territories and also by the Iranian Kurds struggling for recognition.

On 2 September 1980 Iraqi and Iranian troops clashed near Qasr-e Shirin, and soon afterwards Iranian artillery began shelling the Iraqi towns of Khanaqin and Mandali. On 6 September Iraq threatened to seize vast swathes of Iranian land in the Zain al Qaws region, supposedly granted to Iraq in the 1975 accord, if it was not ceded within a week. Iran responded with increased artillery fire, and Iraqi troops moved to capture a number of border posts. Saddam then claimed – in a televised speech to the National Assembly on 17 September – full control of the Shatt al-Arab, and heavy fighting broke out along the waterway. On 20 September Tehran called up reserves, and two days later Saddam's armies mounted a general offensive. What observers were later to call the 'first' Gulf war had begun. It would last for nearly a decade.

The Shape of Conflict

On 22 September 1980 Iraq's armies invaded Iran along an 800-mile front, from Khorramshahr in the south to Qasr-e Shirin in the north. In October there was heavy fighting around Dizful, Bustan and Susangerd, to the north of Khorramshahr. On 24 October Khorramshahr, Iran's largest port, fell and

Abadan was besieged. Ahwaz, the provincial capital of Khuzistan, was also under threat. By the end of October the Iraqi forces had penetrated 10–20 miles into Iranian territory along the whole front and occupied five Iranian towns. Contrary to Saddam's expectations, the Arabs in Khuzistan/Arabistan did not rise up to greet their Arab liberators but fled in panic from the area. The early Iraqi victories suggested that Saddam would have an easy triumph, but in fact he had made a number of miscalculations.

Saddam had blundered into Iran (as later he was to blunder into Kuwait). Count Alexandre de Marenches, the then head of French intelligence, had Saddam Hussein as one of his 'clients' (the Iraqis bought his villa near Grasse for the Iraq ambassador to France). Marenche commented that the war with Iran 'was born of a terrible misunderstanding'; Saddam, surrounded by nervous sycophants, had been led to believe that 'there would be a popular uprising to applaud the first Iraqi soldier who came over the horizon'.[78]

The Iraqi armies had inadequate leadership and seemingly lacked offensive spirit (just as in the earlier conflicts with the Israelis they had proved logistically impressive but inadequate in combat). At the end of 1980 the major Iraqi offensive, launched after immense preparations, had stalled. The Iranians managed to retain a small area of Khorramshahr and to hold Abadan despite heavy Iraqi shelling. Early in 1981 the Iranians launched a counterattack and drove back the Iraqi forces in several areas. Any Iraqi dreams of a short war, of a speedy victory that would bring easy glory and rich pickings, were at an end. Iraq had launched ten well-prepared divisions against Iran, to be countered by the elements of only two Iranian divisions and a mere 120 tanks at the frontier. Yet already the Iraqi effort had run out of steam. Far from toppling the Khomeini regime, Saddam had helped to consolidate it, to stimulate what the Iranian leadership was able to depict as a blasphemous onslaught on Islam. Khomeini himself denounced Saddam for 'fighting to destroy Islam'; Hashemi Rafsanjani declared that the fact 'we are not making peace stems from the Koran and the honour of Islam and . . . preserving the blood of the martyrs'; and Prime Minister Musavi commented that 'the power of faith can outmanoeuvre a complicated war machine used by people bereft of sublime religion'.[79]

Saddam was forced to seek explanations for the early and unexpected reverses. He decided, according to one observer,[80] that the Iraqi forces had been too widely dispersed, that the Iraqi reservists had been inexperienced, that the Iranians – equipped with better intelligence and better knowledge of the region – had fought more effectively than had been anticipated, and that night attacks by the Iranians had made it difficult for the Iraqi tanks to manoeuvre. It was clear that the Iraqi forces were overstretched and increasingly demoralised; there were desertions in increasing numbers and widespread attempts to evade conscription. There was also the problem of the heavy politicisation of the army under Saddam: no-one had the nerve to query his orders, even if they were manifestly leading to disaster (Marenches: 'This is the tragedy of authoritarian regimes. If the big leader is mistaken, the consequences are incalculable'). From March 1981, against all Saddam's calculations, the Iraqi army was on the defensive. He was even driven to call for a ceasefire for Ramadan, but the call was ignored and in March 1982 the Iranians launched a major offensive.

Iran had already been using its aircraft to good effect, despite Iraqi efforts to destroy the Iranian Air Forces on the ground. Since all the Iraqi air bases were within reach of Iran's warplanes, Saddam decided to despatch most of his 332 combat aircraft to Jordan, Kuwait, Saudi Arabia, North Yemen and Oman (just as in 1991 he would send vulnerable aircraft to Iran).[81] The Iranian Air Force, less keen to shrink from conflict and equipped with some 450 combat aircraft (including US-made F-4s and F-5s), sometimes carried out 150 sorties a day. The Phantom F-4s flew low to avoid Iraqi air defences; and when on 25 September 1980 the Iraqis shelled the Abadan refinery, Tehran despatched 140 aircraft to attack Iraqi oil facilities in Basra and Zubair in the south and Mosul and Kirkuk in the north.[82] Soon afterwards both Iran and Iraq suspended their oil shipments.

In April 1982, as Iraqi military difficulties deepened, Syria moved to close Iraq's oil pipeline to the Mediterranean; economic problems were added to Saddam's military reverses. But other Arab states, fearful of Iranian fundamentalism, rushed to Iraq's aid: King Hussein of Jordan allowed arms shipments to travel through Aqaba (though by now the Soviets had stopped their arms shipments to Iraq); pipelines were hastily built across the desert to the Red Sea, and to the Mediterranean via Turkey; and Kuwait, eager to support Saddam, continued to handle Iraqi exports. The conservative Arab states maintained their subsidy of the Iraqi war effort, amounting over the eight years of the war to some $60 billion. Sudanese troops were despatched by President Numeiri to assist 'sister Iraq', and Egypt's President Sadat agreed in the summer of 1981 that Saddam could conscript Egyptians living in Iraq. One estimate suggests that by 1982 some 20,000 Egyptians, most of them former immigrant workers in Iraq, were fighting alongside the Iraqis.[83]

On 25 May 1982 the Iraqis were forced to retreat from Khorramshahr, and to admit their defeat; in a face-saving communiqué it was claimed that 'Iraq's main task in the war was to inflict the heaviest possible losses on the Iranians. This has been achieved'.[84] Now Basra was under artillery fire and most of the fighting was shifting to the Iraqi side of the frontier. As the Iranians moved into Iraqi territory the Soviet Union decided to resume arms shipment to Saddam; Iraq was still a preferred option to a victorious Iran led by the ayatollahs. Now both the US and the USSR were providing support to Iraq, though Washington was not averse to aiding Iran to preserve balanced levels of slaughter on both sides. And there were other complications. Despite the US membership of the North Atlantic Treaty Organisation (NATO), Turkey (also a NATO member) launched a military attack on northern Iraq. The Turkish military dictatorship, seemingly harbouring ambitions to retake lost Ottoman land, launched 15,000 men (including paratroops and special task forces), backed by 30,000 troops massed along the border, into Iraqi land across the frontier.

It is interesting that this Turkish attack coincided with large-scale NATO manoeuvres close to the Iraqi border, overseen by General G. C. Jones, US Chief-of-Staff. In fact, it is suggested that the attack took place with the agreement of the Iraqi government: Saddam would be free to prosecute the war against Iran while NATO forces attacked the troublesome Iraqi Kurds. It was clear that the temporary advantage to Saddam would result in the loss of northern Iraq to a US–Turkish alliance, Iraqi oil again coming under the control of Western interests. Thus one observer noted close US–Turkish military planning and that 'the Turks want a free hand from Washington to move back into Iraq (taking control of the oil fields around Kirkuk) in the event that the Baghdad government of Saddam Hussein is toppled'.[85] And there was also reference to the top secret CANNONBONE plan, drafted in 1958 by the US Chief-of-Staff, for a US invasion of Iraq.[86]

What was called the 'tanker war' began in 1984. Iraq started attacking Iranian tankers in the Gulf, and also began bombing the main Iranian oil terminal at Kharg island, within easy reach of Iraqi aircraft. Iran responded with attacks on Kuwaiti and other Gulf tankers deemed to be aiding the Iraqi war effort. But both countries found ways round these attacks on their oil facilities; Iraq continued to use the pipelines to the Red Sea and the Mediterranean, and Iran moved its main oil facility to Larak Island in the Straits of Hormuz. Iran used small, less vulnerable, tankers to convey oil from Kharg and other oilfields to Larak where it would then be fed into supertankers. By February 1985 Iranian oil production and export levels had recovered, though Iraq continued to attack facilities on Kharg. One commentator observed: '. . . Iraq's success in penetrating Kharg's defences loomed as a potential turning point in the war, in technical if not yet political terms . . . as the war entered its sixth year, the Gulf sector remained its major flashpoint and the arena most capable of changing the overall course of the conflict'.[87] Iraq continued to attack Kharg, and also Larak and Sirri Island, less vulnerable to Iraqi strikes. By 1987, according to the US

Marine Corps Commander-in-Chief George B. Crist, there had been 132 Iraqi attacks on ships in the Gulf, with forty destroyed or badly damaged; Iran had made some seventy attacks, destroying eleven ships. In January a Soviet missile frigate was escorting four Soviet ships carrying arms to Iraq; and the US, while maintaining its six-ship force in the Gulf, brought the aircraft carrier *Kitty Hawk* and eleven escort ships to the Indian ocean, deployed a carrier task force off the coast of Oman, and began F-111 exercises in Turkey. Britain and France also expanded their forces in the region.

In 1987 the United States agreed to offer protection to Kuwaiti oil tankers in the Gulf, with eleven Kuwaiti ships transferred to American registration. On 17 May an Iraqi Super-Etendard aircraft fired two Exocet missiles at the US frigate *Stark*, apparently mistaking it for an Iranian ship. The ship was badly damaged and thirty-seven American sailors were killed; US–Iraqi relations were such that Washington quickly accepted Iraqi expressions of regret. The Reagan administration voiced no strong criticism of the Iraqi action, and vowed yet again to protect the 'freedom of navigation' in the Gulf against Iranian attacks. US ships were put on maximum alert, and close liaison was established between the American ships, the Iraqi forces, and Saudi and US AWACs (radar aircraft) to avoid a repetition of the incident. At the same time the US massively increased its forces in the Gulf: to forty-two warships and nearly 25,000 troops. Warships were also sent by Britain, France, the Netherlands, Italy and Belgium to supplement the American fleet. It was not obvious what this vast force was expected to do.

When the USS *Vincennes* shot down the Iranian airliner on 3 July 1988 there were more protests from Tehran that the US was aiding Iraq, and the Iranians reacted by sowing mines in the Gulf. The US frigate *Samuel B. Roberts* was badly damaged by a mine, and in September and October there were various military confrontations between Iranian and US forces. The US Navy sank six Iranian warships and patrol boats and attacked two Iranian oil platforms. An Iranian Silkworm missile struck a US-flagged Kuwaiti supertanker, causing considerable damage, and the Reagan administration threatened more reprisal actions. Already the US forces had killed around two hundred Iranian men, and the US Marine Commander General Crist was driven to observe: 'I would suggest they are over there thinking about a way to get back at us.'[88] Saddam's main purpose in beginning the 'tanker war' was to internationalise the conflict, and so to bring other countries, primarily the US, into conflict with Iran. To some extent he succeeded in this objective.

By September 1984 the twenty-two divisions of the Iraqi army comprised some 500,000 men, twice as many as at the beginning of the war and three times its June 1982 strength. The members of the Popular Army, at 560,000 men in early 1984 two-and-a-half times as large as in September 1980, were given two months' training and then deployed to protect strategic targets in Iraq and to service the rear areas of the front lines. University students were conscripted, and the police pressed young men into joining the Popular Army. Tariq Aziz declared in August 1984 that 'Iraq's ability to mobilise manpower is three times that of Iran. We are definitely not suffering from lack of numbers . . .'.[89] Morale had improved from the time of the early reverses; arms were now being supplied from various sources and Baghdad enjoyed what it perceived as virtually unanimous international support. Iran too was more cohesive than formerly, and was acquiring much-needed arms from various countries: Switzerland was providing trainer aircraft, Britain was supplying Chieftain tank parts (at the same time supplying Iraq), and Soviet-made tanks were being obtained from Syria and Libya, two key Arab states that remained hostile to Iraq. Iran appeared to hold the initiative on land, but in the Gulf and in the skies was on the defensive, with Iraqi aircraft now committed to the conflict.

The full-scale 'war of the cities', like the 'tanker war', began in 1984. Iraq launched a number of missile attacks on Iranian cities, including Abadan and Khorramshahr, whereupon Iran used artillery against Basra, Khanaqin and Mandali. In June the United Nations (with mediations from the Saudis, the Kuwaitis and the Islamic Council) managed to secure a ceasefire against civilian targets, but this lasted only until 5 March 1985 when Iraq bombed the Ahvaz steel factory and an unfinished nuclear power plant in Bushahr. Again Basra was shelled and on 11 March Baghdad suffered an air raid, whereupon Iraq launched strikes against sixteen Iranian cities and towns and declared Iranian airspace a war zone, implying that Iranian civilian aircraft would not be safe. On 14 March Iran hit Kirkuk with what was probably a Soviet-made Scud-B missile supplied by Libya, and the next day it was Tehran's turn to suffer an air raid. Then Iran fired four Scuds at Baghdad. Such tit-for-tat actions did little to bring military advantage. What they did do was to kill and maim a large number of civilians: on 31 March Tehran claimed that Iraqi raids had killed 1450 civilians and injured more than four thousand.[90] Some reports suggested that four million people had fled Tehran in the face of the Iraqi missile attacks.[91]

The land war continued to be indecisive, despite fatalities running into hundreds of thousands, with Iran suffering the greater proportion of deaths; and despite the acknowledged Iraqi failure to secure anything like Saddam's original objectives. Now Saddam was fighting merely to prevent the defeat of Iraq, the dream of a glorious victory long since passed. At times, Iraqi defences were overrun by 'human wave' onslaughts involving massive casualties on both sides, and sometimes even Baghdad looked vulnerable. Eventually the Iraqis secured some significant ground victories – in 1988, the first groundwar successes since 1982 – and some observers began to look to the end of the war. There had been a merciless carnage, and nothing had been achieved.

In 1984 UN investigators reported that the Iraqis had used mustard gas and the nerve gas Tabun in Iran. A subsequent UN report (March 1986) concluded that Iraqi forces had deployed chemical weapons in violation of the 1925 Geneva Protocol, and that 'the use of chemical weapons in 1986 appears to be more extensive than in 1984'. Following subsequent visits (in April and May 1987) to both Iran and Iraq the UN inspectors concluded that 'chemical weapons have been used once again by the Iraqi forces against Iranian forces and resulted in many casualties'. Perez de Cuellar, UN Secretary-General, expressed concern that Iraq had continued to use chemical weapons, despite appeals from both himself and the Security Council. In April 1987 Iraqi forces used poison gas against the village of Sheik Wasan in Iraqi Kurdistan; in June 1987 Iraqi war resisters were gas-bombed in southern Iraq; and on 16 March 1988 the village of Halabja in Iraqi Kurdistan, having surrendered to Iranian forces, was gas-bombed in a merciless attack that left 5000 dead and 10,000 wounded (here the casualties were mainly civilians and included many children). Chemical weapons were used in a number of other attacks on Iranian forces; for example, in the battles for the recapture of the Fao Peninsula, Salamcheh and the Majnoon Island, and in the attack on the Iranian town of Mehran.[92]

When in 1988 Iraq began to recapture some of the territory lost to Iran, UN negotiators saw an opportunity achieve a ceasefire: 'even the most extremist factions in Tehran have become less vocal in calling for Saddam Hussein's head on a platter. UN diplomats have seen this as an opportunity worth exploring to recast the UN resolution in a way that both sides could accept . . . '.[93] On 20 July 1987 the UN Security Council unanimously passed Resolution 598 on the Gulf War.

Iran accepted the resolution, with Khomeini still prepared to declare: 'God knows that were it not that all our honour and prestige should be sacrificed for Islam, I would never have consented . . . I repeat that accepting this [resolution] was more deadly to me than taking poison': Khomeini submitted himself 'to God's will and drank this drink for His satisfaction . . . Accepting the UN resolution does not mean that the question of war has been solved. We should be prepared for *jihad* . . . '.[94] One observer commented that the presence of Western warships was not helping the peace process: the 'biggest danger to peace' was not the Iranians or the Iraqis, but 'the gathering of dozens of warships from seven outside nations, all of them steaming up and down the Gulf with limited co-ordination and even less sense of purpose'.[95] Iraq continued to wage war, while declaring itself in favour of Resolution 598; at the same time the Iranians denounced Baghdad and also the United States for keeping warships in the Persian Gulf. Thus Iran's Deputy Foreign Minister noted that 'the USA needs the intensification of tension . . . as an excuse for keeping its fleet in the region'.[96] Even after Khomeini had reluctantly accepted the resolution, Saddam Hussein continued to launch military offensives and to occupy more Iranian territory. In 1984 Iraq seemed to be fighting a desperate war for survival; now Saddam seemed intent on emerging as a victor.

A UN peacekeeping force was quickly assembled and despatched to the Gulf. There was still some fighting as the Iraqis drove Iranian troops out of Kurdistan and continued to penetrate Iran at several points on the central front. The question of sovereignty over the Shatt al-Arab had not been settled, and the Kurds who had been given Iranian assistance in northern Iraq (and who had suffered a NATO-supported invasion) continued to present problems to Saddam Hussein. The war was over, but there had been great costs in both lives and treasure. Some Western estimates put the number of war dead at 367,000 (262,000 Iranian and 105,000 Iraqi); with some 700,000 injured, many badly; the total casualties have been reckoned at over one million. Iran officially stated that they had suffered 123,220 dead combatants, with another 60,711 missing in action. Baghdad declared the much higher figure of some 800,000 Iranians killed in the war.[97] Figures based on estimates made in NATO capitals put the number of Iranian fatalities at between 420,000 and 580,000, with 300,000 Iraqi dead.[98] And to these figures, compiled in 1985, should be added the casualties for three further years of war.[99] At a cost of something in excess of $1,000,000,000,000, nothing had been accomplished except to prepare the way for another Gulf war that would soon convulse the region.

WESTERN SUPPORT FOR SADDAM

Saddam Hussein, as a brutal master of domestic *realpolitik*, has now enjoyed more than two decades of effective power in Iraq: for a decade the powerful and scheming force behind the scenes, and for more than a decade as president. Throughout most of this period – until 1990 – he has been crucially supported by major states in the international community. The players have changed, sometimes moving off-stage, and then reappearing at a later time, according to the demands of business, the perceived self-interest of companies and countries, and the Cold War. But without the massive support – albeit spasmodic and fluctuating – provided over the years by Britain, France, West Germany, the United States, the Soviet Union and other countries, Saddam Hussein would never have been so well equipped for internal repression and for waging war against his neighbours.

When Iraq left the Baghdad Pact in 1958 the Soviet Union became Iraq's chief arms supplier, providing at that time such equipment as MiG-21 interceptors, TU-22 bombers and MiG-23 ground attack aircraft. The Iraqi–Soviet connection was briefly interrupted when the first Ba'ath government came to power in 1963, but then Soviet arms shipments were resumed for the rest of the 1960s. In 1972 Iraq was obtaining 95 per cent of its arms equipment from the Soviet Union, a proportion that had diminished to 63 per cent by 1979, with France a major supplier after 1975. By that time Iraq had decided to diversify its arms supply sources, as some gesture towards its status as a non-aligned state and as a way of avoiding undue dependence upon any one nation. At the same time France has established a posture of independence *vis-à-vis* NATO and was looking for new markets for arms sales. Iraq fitted the bill: it had oil money to spend. When Jacques Chirac was the French premier under the presidency of Valéry Giscard d'Estaing, France agreed to build an experimental nuclear plant outside Baghdad and to supply massive amounts of military equipment. In 1978 French contractors supplied eighteen Mirage F1 interceptors and thirty helicopters, negotiated a deal for the production of the Mirage 200, and concluded a $2 billion deal for the supply of aircraft, tanks and other equipment.[100] This support continued into the early 1980s; on 26 November 1982 President Mitterrand commented: 'We do not wish Iraq to be defeated in this war.'[101] At this time Iraq was buying 40 per cent of France's total armaments exports.

The French had welcomed these arms deals with open arms. When Prime Minister Jacques Chirac gave a press conference in Baghdad on 2 December 1974, after three days of talks with Saddam, the young French premier 'was exuberant', keen to talk of a 'veritable bonanza'.[102] On 3 March 1975 Saddam met Chirac and Giscard d'Estaing in Paris and presented a long list of the weapons he wanted to purchase. Then Saddam flew to attend the OPEC conference in Algiers to agree the accord with the Shah, the controversial agreement that Saddam would later unilaterally abrogate. In early April he visited Moscow to agree a new arms deal and a nuclear co-operation pact with the Russians. Here Saddam secured a Soviet commitment for the training of Iraqi nuclear physicists and for the supply of a research reactor able to produce weapons-grade fuel; at the same time the Soviets demanded safeguards to prevent the production of nuclear weapons. In the 1960s the Arif government had purchased a modest nuclear reactor from the Soviet Union, and this formed the heart of the Thuwaitha nuclear research centre. When Brezhnev and Kosygin met Saddam in April 1975 they seemed reluctant to provide nuclear technology much in advance of the Thuwaitha beginnings, so again Saddam turned to France.

The French subsequently offered Saddam an Osiris research reactor and an Isis scale model, both of which were able to generate quantities of bomb-grade material. Both the systems were designed to operate on weapons-grade uranium, and a one-year supply amounted to 72 kilograms, enough for several Hiroshima-size atomic bombs. The reactor was at first called Osirak, but the two systems were later dubbed Tammuz I and Tammuz II, after the Sumerian corn deity, lover of Ishtar (the Arabs' Athtar), who is brought back from the underworld to symbolise the eternity of the harvest. Saddam's intentions were clear. A few days after visiting the French Cadarache reactor he declared in an interview with the Lebanese weekly, *Al Usbu al-Arabi*: 'The agreement with France is the first concrete step towards the production of the Arab atomic weapon.'[103] While the French were working on the Osirak reactors, Saddam was negotiating a ten-year nuclear co-operation pact with Brazil, who agreed to provide Iraq with large quantities of uranium, reactor technologies, equipment and training. Under the terms of this agreement, nuclear physicists from Iraq and Brazil were to 'exchange visits to research and development facilities'. The United States has claimed that Iraq also signed nuclear deals with India and China, though details have not been published. In 1978 the Italian nuclear body, Snia Techint, a subsidiary of Fiat, agreed to sell nuclear laboratories and other vital nuclear equipment to Iraq. According to Richard Wilson, director of the physics department at Harvard University, the 'Italian Project' was designed to facilitate the manufacture of a nuclear bomb.

When in April 1979 the French contractors had completed the manufacture of the Osirak reactor cores, the French Atomic Energy Commission (the CEA) made arrangements for them to be transported to the Mediterranean port of La Seyn-sur-Mer, to await an Iraqi container ship. An American company, ORTEC (based at Oak Ridge, the home of the first US atomic bomb plant), had supplied a critical germanium detector, and the US company Hewlett-Packard had supplied computers. However, on the morning of 7 April there was an enormous explosion in the CNIM (Compagnie des Constructions navales et industrielles de la Méditerranée) warehouse where the nuclear equipment was stored. The reactor cores were completely destroyed but there was little other damage. A revelation in the German

press a year later indicated that the attack (Operation Big Lift) had been
staged by a seven-man Israeli commando group working for Mossad. An
enraged Saddam Hussein demanded that the French replace the reactors,
and that they supply bomb-grade fuel. Eventually the French complied, the
reactor was built, transported to Iraq, and set to go critical on 1 July 1981.

The nuclear fuel had been installed, the cooling channel was prepared,
and suitable provisions had been made for plutonium production once the
reactor began operation. The Iraqis were negotiating with NUKEM in West
Germany for the supply of depleted uranium fuel pins, and Snia Techint
was completing the last of the on-site reprocessing and fuel manufacturing
laboratories. Iraqi agents had also concluded agreements with Niger, Brazil
and Portugal for the supply of natural uranium ('yellowcake') for use in
the Osirak system for the production of plutonium. In spring 1981 the
International Atomic Energy Agency (IAEA) carried out its regular six-
month inspection of the Thuwaitha plant, and publicly declared that all
was well. However, Robert Richter, one of the IAEA inspectors, suggested
that there were secret Thuwaitha facilities to which IAEA staff had not
been given access. Other officials stated that his fears were groundless and
he was subsequently fired from the Agency. Richter was not the only one
to have anxieties. The Israeli prime minister Menachem Begin decided on
drastic action; with the Israeli chief of staff, General Rafael Eitan, he began
planning a scheme (Operation Babylon) for the bombing of the Osirak
plant.

Begin authorised the building of a full-scale model of the Iraqi plant
so that Israeli pilots could practise bombing it (it was remarked how
closely the Osirak installation resembled Israel's own Dimona nuclear
plant, also supplied by the French). On 7 June 1981 the Osirak facility was
bombed by Israeli pilots flying F-16s and relying on American assistance.[104]
The CIA supplied the Israelis with satellite reconnaissance photographs
that were vital to the success of the mission. The raid was skilfully planned.
When the Israeli pilots were in Jordanian airspace they conversed in
Saudi-accented Arabic and informed Jordanian air controllers that they
were a Saudi patrol gone astray; over Saudi Arabia they pretended to be
Jordanians.[105] The first wave of F-16s punched a hole in the reactor dome,
after which a second wave of aircraft dropped 'dumb' (that is, not laser-
guided) bombs with enough accuracy to destroy the reactor core, its containing walls, and the gantry crane.[106]

The Israeli raid was almost universally condemned, with the new French
premier, François Mitterrand, one of the first to protest. There were hundreds of French workers, and other foreign nationals, at the Tammuz plant
when it was bombed; one Frenchman was killed. Mitterrand made a vague

promise to rebuild the reactor, though few observers took his comments seriously. Washington's support for the raid was undisguised, with President Jimmy Carter later happy to admit US support for this and other controversial Israeli initiatives.[107] In July 1981 Saudi Arabia announced that she would finance the rebuilding of the Iraqi reactor.[108] But nothing came of this promise.

Both before and after the Osirak episode, Western support for Saddam Hussein continued unabated in one form or another. In 1981 French arms sales to Iraq were $2148 million; in 1982 $1925 million; and in 1983 $2000 million. Helicopters and Mirage F-1 fighter-bombers were being supplied, and France also agreed to lend Iraq five Super-Etendard aircraft equipped to carry Exocet air-to-surface missiles (these last arrived in Iraq in October 1983 and were returned to France two years later in accordance with the terms of the loan). A *Le Monde* estimate suggests that France sold Iraq arms to the value of $5.6 billion during the period of the 1980s Gulf War, and negotiated a further $4.7 billion-worth of civilian and commercial contracts.

In 1980 the US company General Electric received American approval to supply engines for Italian warships destined for the Iraqi navy, and in Baghdad a Lockheed sales team was negotiating the sale of helicopters to Saddam Hussein.[109] In 1982 the Reagan administration decided to take Iraq off the list of countries branded as supporters of terrorism, even though it was well known that Saddam was providing refuge for Palestinian terrorists and committing other terrorist outrages. (In 1992, documents declassified under congressional pressure revealed that Iraqi's terrorist activities were well known at a time when the Reagan administration was asserting that there was no evidence to justify branding Iraq a terrorist state.)[110] Full diplomatic relations were restored between Iraq and the United States in 1984, so preparing the way for an escalation of arms sales. In October 1983 William Eagleton, the top US official in Baghdad, suggested that the US should start supplying a wide range of equipment being denied to Iran: 'We can selectively lift restrictions on third-party transfers of US licensed military equipment to Iraq.' This could be done, he suggested, 'through Egypt'.[111] The US also developed an arms interdiction plan (Operation Staunch) to prevent arms reaching Iran. This was a 'final piece of the tilt to Iraq' that the Senate Foreign Relations Committee noted in their 1984 report on US policy regarding the Iran–Iraq war.

In 1982 Washington had decided to clear the sale of 'civilian' transport aircraft to Iraq, and in June 1983 the Reagan administration authorised the supply to Iraq of sixty helicopters for 'agricultural use', machines that were obviously capable of conversion for military use. At the same time Washington provided credit of $460 million for the Iraqi purchase of 147,000 tonnes of American rice. This was an important gesture to Baghdad, boosting Iraqi morale at a time of economic hardship and signalling general US support for Saddam. It was acknowledged in Washington that an Iraqi defeat would be seen 'as a major blow to US interests'. In the autumn of 1983 a study by the US National Security Council reached this conclusion,[112] and Washington decided to formulate plans 'to shore up Iraq morally and materially'.[113] In March 1984 George Shultz commented that 'We wouldn't want to see' an Iranian victory, and so 'we have been deliberately working to improve our relationship with Iraq . . . We have been co-operating with the Iraqis to a certain extent'.[114] In January 1984 Washington branded Iran a terrorist nation, thus denying it access to US products, including arms; and made it plain to various countries – Britain, Israel, Italy, West Germany, Turkey, South Korea and others – that it did not want the supply of arms to Iran to continue.

The US also passed on surveillance information about the Gulf, collected by American-manned AWACs, to Riyadh – in full knowledge that the Saudis were transferring such data to Baghdad. This meant that the US was directly aiding the Iraqi management of the war, a fact later confirmed by Saddam.[115] The Iran-Contra scandal revealed that the US had been providing some illegal assistance to Iran but the pro-Iraqi 'tilt' remained, and survived the end of the war. In the summer of 1990, a few days before the invasion of Kuwait, the US State Department was trying to convince Congress to grant financial credits and other assistance to Iraq. And once the 1991 Gulf War was over, the extent of Western support for Saddam through the 1980s began to emerge. Many countries were involved, but the lead players are those most vociferous in their current condemnation of the Iraqi regime.[116] In the two years before the invasion of Kuwait, the United Kingdom was supplying Iraq with the Cymbeline mortar-locating radar, spares for hovercraft and tanks, encryption equipment, and laser rangefinders; France was supplying missiles, artillery pieces and attack helicopters; and the United States was supplying surveillance computers and avionics spares for naval equipment. The much-vaunted Coalition forces (see Chapter 8), in seeking to expel Saddam from Kuwait, were forced to contend with a wide range of high-technology military equipment recently supplied by the leading Coalition states to Saddam.

In May 1991 it emerged that Douglas Hogg, the UK trade and enterprise minister at the time, had approved a regional grant of £2 million in 1989 that was used to equip Saddam Hussein's army with missiles.[117] The grant was made available to the Gateshead plant of Flexible Manufacturing Technology (FMT), a former subsidiary of Vickers, the defence contractor.

The firm was producing specialised equipment to supply the Iraqi army with a mobile rocket-launch system similar to that used by the allies during the 1991 Gulf War. In July 1991 evidence published by the Commons Trade and Industry Committee revealed that Whitehall had licensed exports of British nuclear and defence equipment to Iraq, in the months before the invasion of Kuwait.[118] The products approved included plutonium, uranium and thorium (used in nuclear reactors), zirconium (used for nuclear fuel casing), armoured vehicles, jet engines, artillery fire-control systems, and mortar-locating radar. The products were licensed for export between January 1987 and 5 August 1990, the date when the United Nations imposed the complete trade embargo on Iraq. The Department of Trade and Industry stated that guidelines on exports to Iraq, published in 1985, were intended to 'prevent the export of lethal weapons or equipment that would significantly enhance' Iraq's military capacity. The report also suggested that Whitehall had ignored an early warning from a Tory MP that British companies might be involved in the manufacture of the Iraqi 'supergun'.

Vital items for chemical warfare weaponry were cleared by the UK government for export to Iraq up to December 1990, despite the widespread knowledge that Saddam Hussein had used gases to kill the Kurdish population of Halabja in 1988. The approved chemicals included more than £200,000-worth of thiodiglycol and thionyl chloride, essential elements in mustard and nerve gases; and their destination was the Iraqi State Enterprise for the Production of Pesticides (SEPP), well known as a manufacturer of chemical weapons. A Commons select committee report revealed that the decision to ban 'a further fifteen chemical weapon precursors' was taken as late as December 1990, and that a further thirteen chemical-weapons ingredients were only banned as late as June 1991. The provision of some nuclear materials was banned only *after* the Iraqi invasion of Kuwait on August 1990.[119] The chairman of the committee declared himself 'astounded' by the findings.

It was revealed also that a British firm, MCP UK Ltd, had been bolstering Saddam's chemical warfare capability by supplying Iraq with nerve gas antidotes. Thus in April 1989 the company sold nearly three tonnes of Cantil and Piptal tablets, valued at £167,000, to Iraq's state drug company.[120] The drugs can be used for medical purposes, but also to protect the body from nerve gas. In September 1991 UK customs inspectors found evidence to indicate that British companies were at the centre of Saddam's nuclear weapons programme. Customs officers raided the Midlands offices of Matrix Churchill and found parts and plans for nuclear centrifuges, vital to the manufacture of nuclear weapons.[121] In fact British companies were among dozens of Western firms named in documents seized in Baghdad by

UN inspectors. In March 1992 the Quaker believer, Robin Robison, who resigned from the top-secret Joint Intelligence Committee (JIC), declared that he had 'seen evidence that the Government was fully aware throughout 1989 that British companies were arming Saddam Hussein, in breach of an international embargo, and well after he had ordered the gassing of his own Kurdish citizens in 1988'.[122] Robison was well placed to have such information: it was his job to analyse computer print-outs of transcripts of electronic communications intercepted by GCHQ. He claimed that it was 'highly likely but not inevitable' that such information would have been discussed by the JIC, and likely that it would have been included in the 'Red Book', a weekly GCHQ intelligence summary seen by the Prime Minister and certain other cabinet ministers. A spokesman for the Cabinet Office stated: 'I think it's highly unlikely we will comment. The so-called JIC is something which doesn't officially exist.'[123]

British support, covert and overt, for Saddam Hussein is nicely paralleled in the United States, though suitably magnified in the most powerful nation the world has known. It is increasingly recognised that Saddam was built up with US billions. Thus Senator Henry Gonzalez, head of a congressional investigation into US policy towards Iraq before the outbreak of the 1991 Gulf War, has commented: '. . . government controls were trampled on . . .', repeating a frequent charge that President George Bush 'appeased' Saddam with loans, technology exports, and intelligence data right up to the time of the invasion of Kuwait. In some accounts, the Iraqi forces actually used surveillance data supplied by the Americans to aid their aggression. Democrat Charles Schumer, at a special house banking committee hearing, declared that 'Saddam Hussein is President Bush's Frankenstein [sic] – a run-of-the-mill dictator the president fed with billions of US tax-payer dollars and turned into a monster'. Democrat Schumer claimed that Deputy Secretary of State Lawrence Eagleburger and other top officials had helped Mr Bush in what was 'at best, improper conduct and at worst, criminal activity. The president's biggest foreign policy success, the Gulf war, was made necessary by the mother of all foreign policy blunders'.[124] The scandal of Saddamgate (or Iraqgate) remained a principle issue through the 1992 presidential election campaign (see Chapter 1).

There are other issues, other iceberg tips. In August 1991 it was revealed that the Bank of England did not act sooner against the criminal Bank of Credit and Commerce International (BCCI) for fear of upsetting Britain's Middle East allies during the Gulf War; [125] just as in 1989 and 1990 the Bush administration turned a blind eye to Iraq's central role in a $4 billion bank fraud.[126] In this latter case, government officials blocked legal action over a scandal involving Italy's state bank, the Banca Nazionale del Lavoro. According to a memorandum leaked to American newspapers, the US State Department prevented charges being made against the Central Bank of Iraq, since it was akin to a government agency and its indictment would set a bad precedent. However, the main purpose behind the blocking manoeuvres was to protect Iraq as the then principal regional opponent of Iranian fundamentalism. Criminal action is of no consequence if there are weightier political matters to consider.

The facts are plain enough. The brutal record of Saddam Hussein throughout the 1980s was well known: all the Western leaders (and the leaders of the Soviet Union) knew about torture in Iraq, about the repression of dissident Iraqi groups, about the persecution of the Kurds and Shi'ites, about the harbouring of Abu Nidal, about the sending of terrorists abroad to bomb and murder, about mutilations and executions, about Halabja, about Iraqi culpability in the invasion of Iran. All this was known: no-one disputed the character of one of he world's bloodiest dictatorships. So how was Saddam rewarded? With loans and credits, with training for his soldiers and scientists, with tanks and armoured vehicles, with designs and equipment for nuclear and chemical plants, with helicopters and modern fixed-wing aircraft, with radar and other communications equipment, with multi-billion-dollar business. There have always been strategic reasons for cultivating dictators; throughout the Cold War the United States tended them with care, training and equipping their security services and armies, intervening where necessary to ensure their survival. But strategy is often a second-order justification, the required framework for the protection of values. The evidence suggests that such values are mostly defined by business. It is still true (however unfashionable to declare it) that free-enterprise business will sup with any devil – even a Saddam Hussein – if there is money to be made.

US BUSINESS AND SADDAM

The supply of arms to Iraq in recent years has been organised largely by Western contractors with governments acting as enabling catalysts: since 1987, for reasons that had little to do with ethics, the Soviet Union was more or less out of the picture. The enabling activities of politicians and government officials, quite apart from matters of national policy, are often less than disinterested. There are massive and complex links between business, military production and procurement, and government policy in all the major arms-supplier states. Corporate directors in the arms companies have often spent time in the armed forces, and have diligently cultivated their connections with the political establishment. And the same circumstances surround Western companies that may not produce arms equipment but which market goods and have obvious strategic significance. We are not surprised to learn that James Baker and George Bush have extensive oil interests; or that George Shultz before he became secretary of state in 1982, worked for the California-based Bechtel group that in the early-1980s won a $1 billion contract with Iraq to build an oil pipeline to Aqaba. In 1984 Bechtel was negotiating with the governments of Iraq, Jordan, Israel and the United States – 'to "create the necessary conditions," as the diplomats liked to say, to ensure the success of the pipeline project'.[127]

It was obvious that Iraq was ripe for development. Thus David Newton, first the US chargé d'affaires in Baghdad and in 1985 promoted to ambassador, commented that 'We are working hard on getting business for US companies'; and he recommended that American firms focus on high technology.[128] The US Commerce Department set about organising trade fairs, despatching businessmen to Iraq, and relaxing the licensing constraints. In 1985 the US supplied $700,000-worth of high-technology equipment to Iraq's French-built defence electronics facility, Saad 13; one $161,550 order was for high-speed capacitors, similar to the krytron triggers used in nuclear weapons.[129] When, on 15 August 1985, Iraqi aircraft successfully attacked Kharg Island they were relying on French and American technology. The laser designator used in the ATLIS (Auto Tracking Laser Illumination System) pod was produced by Martin Marietta in the United States.

The US made many efforts to exploit the commercial potential of the Iraqi market, with no attention paid to Saddam's abysmal human-rights record. One of the most significant efforts to lubricate US–Iraqi relations was the initiative taken by Marshall Wiley, from 1975 to 1977 a US official in Baghdad and in 1979 elevated to US ambassador in Oman. In 1981 Wiley retired from the Foreign Service and joined Sidley and Austin, a substantial lobbying law firm based in Washington. In May 1985 he created the US–Iraq Business Forum, having secured the support of Westinghouse and Mobil Oil as corporate sponsors. He commented that the Iraqis 'were not at ease working with the US private sector because their experience until then had been primarily with the central planning structures of Eastern Europe. So I thought we needed an organisation to help to get to know each other better. That's how I got the idea for the Forum'.[130]

The Forum came to represent a powerful pro-Iraq lobby (including such companies as Exxon, Mobil, Occidental, Texaco, Bechtel, General Motors and the defence contractors BMY, Bell Textron, Lockheed and United Technologies Corporation). Charles Percy, formerly a chairman of the

Senate Foreign Relations Committee, brought in his consulting firm, Charles Percy & Associates; and many companies funded by the Atlanta branch of the Banca Nazionale del Lavoro, later to be involved with the Central Bank of Iraq in the $4 billion bank fraud, joined the Forum. Wiley commented: 'The Middle East has lots of brutal people running countries, but that is not cause to stop all trade.' His connections in government meant that Forum members stood a good chance of securing licences for high-technology deals with Iraq, and thus it was that Saddam Hussein obtained 214-ST helicopters from Bell Textron, the Bechtel-built Aqaba oil pipeline, and military trucks from General Motors. On the occasions when the Pentagon tried to obstruct US–Iraqi deals it was criticised by officials of the National Security Council. Thus in July 1986 Admiral Poindexter, under pressure from the State Department, issued a National Security Decision Directive instructing all government agencies 'to be more forthcoming' in issuing licences for Iraqi deals.[131]

On 17 and 18 March 1988 Saddam Hussein launched his gas attacks to slaughter the Kurdish population of Halabja. Two months later, the US–Iraq Business Forum held a symposium to discuss ways of increasing trade with Iraq, suitably supported by A. Peter Burleigh, the assistant secretary of state responsible for northern Gulf affairs. At the same time the US Commerce Department was approving a wide range of high-technology exports to Iraqi weapons plants. In the months following the Halabja massacre the US government issued licences for the delivery of biological products to the Iraqi Atomic Energy Agency, for the delivery of electronics equipment and machine tools to an Iraqi missile design centre, a bomb plant, a missile factory, defence electronics factories, and a weapons manufacturing complex. In July Bechtel secured a $1 billion deal to provide Iraq with a petrochemicals complex that the Iraqis intended to use in the production of mustard gas weapons, fuel-air explosives and rocket propellants. Towards the end of 1988 the US Commerce Department sponsored a display of US high-technology equipment at the Baghdad Trade Fair, declaring that Iraq was now wide open to US business. Any hint of sanctions against Iraq, as more details of the Halabja atrocities emerged, were quickly squashed by the Reagan administration: legislation would be 'premature', and Marshall Wiley of the Forum commented that sanctions would have no effect on Iraqi behaviour and would shift 'business away from the US . . .'.[132] The US government opposed the introduction of sanctions and encouraged an expansion of trade – including trade in arms – with Iraq. On 4 June 1989, following a personal invitation from Saddam Hussein, Wiley brought a delegation of senior representatives of leading US corporations to Baghdad, with a view to expanding US–Iraqi business. He later observed in the

US–Iraq Business Forum Bulletin: 'In order to keep the delegation at the size requested by the Government of Iraq, only senior executives from Forum member companies with annual sales in excess of $500 million were invited to participate.' The trip include a two-hour meeting with Saddam Hussein and his chief economic adviser, Saddoun Hammadi. One of the members of the delegation was Alan Stoga, a senior associate of Henry Kissinger's New York consulting firm.*

By the late 1980s US–Iraq trade was worth billions, with dozens of the Fortune 500 companies involved. There can be no doubt that Saddam's rapidly enlarged industrial and military strength was created largely through US business ambitions. Other Western powers played their part. France had supplied a wide range of military equipment, loaned some of the most advanced aircraft in the world, and given a boost to Saddam's nuclear ambitions. Iraq was a regular visitor to the British government's huge international arms fair, the British Army Equipment Exhibition (BAEE), organised by the Ministry of Defence; and there were frequent credit guarantees to aid British exports to Iraq. Thus in November 1986 Alan Clark, the minister who headed the UK Department of Trade and Industry, arrived at Saddam International Airport in Baghdad to offer the Iraqi leader a new credit guarantee that brought total British credits to Saddam since 1983 to more than $1.2 billion. Clark, in emphasising that few strings were attached to the British money, knew that it would be used to build Saddam's war machine. After the gassing of the Kurds, UK Trade Minister Tony Newton flew with twenty British officials to Baghdad and offered Saddam Hussein £340 million-worth of British trade credit. The flow of British money to support the Iraqi dictator was not interrupted by Saddam's known genocidal onslaught on minority groups, or by the hanging of *Observer* journalist Farzad Bazoft. Over this period, up to 1990, according to official information supplied to the OECD, Britain supplied Iraq with more than $1.5 billion-worth of high-technology equipment.[133]

As tensions mounted in the Middle East in early 1990 there was growing alarm in the American business community. Suddenly it seemed that all the painstaking efforts of the Forum would be wasted. In the interest of continued business activity something had to be done. On 12 April 1990, less than four months before the Iraqi invasion of Kuwait, Senator Robert Dole of Kansas and Senator Alan Simpson of Wyoming, both very keen to

---

*Two former members of Kissinger Associates joined the Bush administration: Brent Scowcroft, the national security adviser, and Lawrence Eagleburger, number two at the State Department.

expand trade with Iraq, led a group of US senators to visit Saddam Hussein in Mosul. The aim was to safeguard American business interests, President Bush having giving the trip his blessing (even going so far as to talk on the telephone to Mosul to emphasise his support).

Would it, the Senators wondered, be business as usual? They went to some trouble to reassure Saddam about American intentions, whatever irresponsible American journalists might be saying. Senator Simpson declared (in one version of the transcript): 'My advice is that you allow those bastards to come here and see things for themselves.' But, whatever Saddam's thoughts about such advice, events now had their own momentum and were rapidly moving towards a climax. Soon it would not at all be business as usual.

Part III

Towards the
New World Order

8 War with the West

We have about 60% of the world's wealth but only 6.3% of its population. Our world task in this position is to devise a pattern of relationships which will permit us to maintain this position of disparity. We should cease to talk about such vague and unreal objectives as human rights, the raising of living standards and democratisation.

US Policy Planning Staff, Washington
24 February 1948

If Kuwait grew carrots, we wouldn't give a damn.

Lawrence Korb
former US Assistant Defence Secretary
1990

I venture to say that if Kuwait produced bananas, instead of oil, we would not have 400,000 American troops there today.

Congressman Stokes, Ohio
12 January 1991

COUNTDOWN

Preparing the Ground

In the aftermath of the Iran–Iraq war, faced with a disrupted society and a debt-ridden economy, Saddam Hussein strove to achieve a balance between constructive reform and characteristic authoritarian control. As a way of flushing out political opposition within the country, he offered an amnesty to domestic dissidents; at the same time he invited political offenders outside Iraq to return home. In late 1988 Saddam launched 'what seemed an Iraqi perestroika'.[1] A new constitution was promised and also a range of economic reforms that would relax the Ba'athist grip on the nation. There was even the prospect of a new electoral law that would allow the emergence of a multi-party system, and Information Minister Latif Jasim commented that a free press was now a matter of 'paramount interest'. Saddam also tried to build on what he declared as the Iraqi victory over Iran, a supposed triumph that had – according to Saddam – established the Iraqi leadership of the Arab world.

299

He also flew to Cairo to discuss with President Mubarak the creation of a council of the non-Gulf Arab states (Egypt, Jordan and North Yemen) which had supported Iraq during the long conflict with Iran. This followed an earlier proposal by King Hussein of Jordan for the formation of a council of those Arab states outside the Gulf Co-operation Council (the GCC, comprising Bahrain, Kuwait, Oman, Qatar, Saudi Arabia and the United Arab Emirates) which had supported Saddam in the war. On 16 February 1989 the Arab Co-operation Council (ACC) was formed in Baghdad. Mubarak, following talks with King Fahd of Saudi Arabia, refused to agree an integrated military and intelligence structure and the ACC emerged as an organisation committed only to economic and other non-military co-operation. King Hussein envisaged the ACC as an economic union akin to the European Community, a mechanism whereby the rich Arab states could assist the poorer Arab countries throughout the region. North Yemen, a poor state with an unreliable dependence on Saudi and US support, welcomed the formation of the ACC as a means of directing some of its excess manpower to Iraq. Washington too welcomed the development, reckoning that Iraq's strengthened ties with pro-Western Arab states would help to consolidate US hegemony in the region. The US 'tilt' towards Iraq in the Iran–Iraq war, a strategic posture that did not speak to the demands of international law, had already advertised American designs in the Gulf. Now, it seemed, there was further opportunity to secure Iraq in the US orbit.

On 27 March 1989 King Fahd visited Baghdad to sign a non-aggression pact with Saddam, an agreement that received little publicity during the period when Saudi Arabia hosted the forces that were to launch the most devastating onslaught on Iraq in modern times. The pact emphasised the principles of 'non-interference in the internal affairs of the two sisterly countries' and stipulated the 'non-use of force and armies between the two states'.[2] It is interesting to note, in the light of subsequent events, that in February 1989 Saddam offered a similar agreement to the Kuwaiti crown prince and prime minister, Sheikh Saad al-Sabah, during his visit to Baghdad. Saddam also proposed that Iraq lease the offshore island of Bubiyan as a means of strengthening Iraq's access to Umm Qasr. But Sheikh Saad did not respond to these overtures. There were anxieties about Iraq's traditional claims to Kuwaiti territory and there was no wish to antagonise an Iranian leadership that would have resented any strengthening of the Iraqi position at the head of the Gulf. However, an agreement was concluded for Iraq to supply Kuwait with 350 million gallons of drinking water and 500 million gallons of irrigation water daily.[3] This arrangement – first proposed thirty-five years earlier by Iraqi premier Nuri al-Said but rejected by the Kuwaiti Sheikh Abdullah al-Salim – appeared to demonstrate that useful accommodations could be made between Saddam and the ruling al-Sabahs in Kuwait. There were also signs – in addition to the non-aggression pact – that Iraq and Saudi Arabia were continuing with the harmonious relationship that had been established during the Iran–Iraq war.

King Fahd had agreed to supply free building materials for the reconstruction of Basra, devastated during the war. The project, expected to cost around $4.9 billion, was combined with efforts to develop the Umm Qasr and Zubair to enhance Iraqi access to the Gulf. But such development plans, despite Saudi support, continued to be hampered by Iraq's massive debt liability and the continued high expenditure on defence requirements. The austerity programme introduced during the early years of the war was extended, and some 200,000 soldiers were demobilised in a year to reduce the burden of public expenditure. On 17 June 1989 the ACC supported Saddam's claim to the whole of the disputed Shatt al-Arab and his demand to the UN that the war debris be cleared from the waterway. Saddam also pursued his aim of becoming self-sufficient in armaments productions, even going so far as to become an arms exporter.

Thus he began holding international military exhibitions, to attract overseas buyers and foreign revenue. The April 1989 exhibition in Baghdad attracted 168 British companies, including the leading arms producer British Aerospace, already a customer of the Technology and Development Group (TDG, formed by the Baghdad firm Al-Arabi Trading and which had already purchased a number of British engineering companies).[4] At the 1989 fair Iraq exhibited the Assad Babil (Babylonian Lion) tank, a modified version of the T-72, with its electronics and guns manufactured in Iraq; and also a Soviet MiG-23 modified for in-flight fuelling. In July there were reports that the Iraqis had successfully tested an Adnan-1 Airborne Warning and Control System, a modified Soviet Ilyushin Il-76 aircraft.[5] And on 5 December 1989 Iraq launched the Tammuz-1 space rocket from the Al Anbar space centre thirty miles north of Baghdad. Sources at NORAD (North American Aerospace Defence Command) stated that 'three objects had been tracked which had orbited the earth four or five times';[6] but other reports suggested that the rocket had flown for only half a minute before exploding in mid-air,[7] or that it had taken 130 seconds to reach a height of about twenty kilometres before dropping back to the ground.[8] At the same time there were reports that Iraq was co-operating with China to develop nuclear weapons and had developed a network of companies in Europe for the supply of the necessary equipment and expertise. Throughout this period it was clear that Iraq was chafing under its debt burden, with mounting resentment that its oil revenue was limited by OPEC provisions.

In late 1989 Iraq's deputy prime minister Saddoun Hammadi commented that 'Iraq is economically and politically committed to paying back its [non-Gulf] debts, but our country's resources are limited mainly because our oil production share in OPEC is limited'. For this reason the austerity programme would continue, as would the sales of public assets to private citizens; already $2.2 billion-worth of public-sector companies had been sold off.[9] There were also growing tensions between the tens of thousands of demobilised Iraqi troops, many of them unemployed, and the large number of Arab expatriates in the country, most of whom had been well occupied in the civilian economy during the war. The worst clashes broke out between demobbed soldiers and Egyptian workers, resulting in several hundred Egyptian casualties. When, in a further effort to reduce public expenditure, the Iraqi authorities placed limits on the remuneration of foreign expatriate workers – a development that ran against the spirit of the ACC, thousands of Egyptians decided to return home, further exacerbating internal economic dislocations in Iraq and adding to tensions between Baghdad and Cairo. At this time the West was largely preoccupied with the turbulent events in Eastern Europe.

On 16 February 1990, at the second anniversary meeting of the Arab Cooperation Council in Baghdad, Saddam Hussein declared that the developing international situation would result in a weakening of both superpowers in their efforts to dominate the world; and that this presented fresh opportunities for the Arabs: 'Arabs possess an extraordinary ability to accelerate the creation of an international balance . . . because of the region's geography and because of the possession of a source of energy unparalleled in the world. All the major influential powers are affected by this source: be it the US, Japan, Europe or even the Soviet Union'.[10] On 21 February the US State Department, in its annual report on human rights, condemned the Iraqi record: 'For years, execution has been an established Iraqi method of dealing with perceived military and political opponents . . . Both physical and psychological torture are used . . . Given the rigid chain of command within the government, torture could not be practised without the authorisation of senior officials.' The Foreign Affairs Committee of the House of Representatives then proposed a resolution condemning Iraq for its human rights record. Saddam responded at the fourth ACC summit, held on 23/24 February in Amman, by noting that because of America's 'superior position in international politics', the United States 'will continue to be able to depart from the restrictions that govern the rest of the world during the next five years until new balances forces are formed'. The US behaviour was depicted as 'undisciplined and irresponsible', but it seemed that Saddam did not envisage an American attack on Iraq, except via its

Israeli proxy: '. . . Israel might embark on new stupidities . . . as a result of direct or tacit US encouragement'. Washington was 'not interested in peace as it claims'.[11]

On 15 March 1990 the *Observer* journalist Farzad Bazoft, an Iranian Kurd who had lived in Britain for fifteen years, was executed in the notorious Abu Gharib prison in Baghdad as, according to the Iraqi authorities, a 'British spy who works for Israel'. The West protested at Saddam's brutality while the Western press at the same time leaked details of Bazoft's past to smear his reputation. Prime Minister Thatcher professed herself 'horrified and taken aback' by the sentence of death on Bazoft and the sentence of fifteen years in jail on his co-defendant Daphne Parish (since released). William Waldegrave, Foreign Office minister of state, issued a warning to Baghdad, and Foreign Secretary Douglas Hurd requested a meeting with Saddam, which was turned down. Baghdad commented that Iraqi law 'provides for the death sentence on any spy . . . The fabricated clamour against us constitutes blatant interference in our internal affairs'; and Saddam Hussein, on a visit to Riyadh, obtained King Fahd's support for Iraq's right to invoke its laws against those who threatened its security. Other Arab states, including Kuwait and Bahrain, also offered support to Baghdad; and on 26 March the Arab League denounced 'interference in Iraq's internal affairs by Britain and other members of the European Community'. Three months later Saddam commented again on this affair: 'The US and Britain began to talk about ruthless Saddam with no heart when a spy was executed to avoid a return to the time when foreigners ran rampant in this country. We will not allow any foreigner to steal intelligence.'[12]

Various events – the Bazoft affair, the assassination of Gerald Bull (helping in Iraq's 'Project Babylon' for the development of superguns) in a way that was reminiscent of the murder of the Egyptian physicist Yahya Mashad (in charge of Iraq's nuclear programme) in June 1980, and the much publicised arrests at London's Heathrow airport of men trying to smuggle the krytron triggers (for nuclear weapons) to Iraq – were conspiring to suggest a deterioration in Iraqi–Western relations. In addition, the Western media and some elements of the American political establishment were criticising Iraq for its human rights record and political posture, even though no word was being raised against Western allies with equally dismal records. On 2 April Saddam Hussein gave a television broadcast in which he compared the attention given by the Western media to the Bazoft affair to its relative silence over the murder of Gerald Bull. The attempt to block Iraq's acquisition of the high-speed krytrons was part of a 'western–Zionist plot' to deprive Iraq of the means to defend itself and to facilitate an Israeli attack on Iraq. When Saddam declared that Iraq would use 'binary chemical weapons' to attack 'the Zionist entity' if Israel, possessing atomic bombs, dared to launch another military strike on Iraq, Washington branded the speech 'inflammatory, outrageous and irresponsible'. Washington dragged its feet for several weeks and then announced that further credits for American grain would not be forthcoming to Baghdad (at the same time various clandestine deals were being protected). On 21 May Washington announced that it was suspending consideration of Iraq's request for a $500 million loan guarantee from the US Commodity Credit Corporation, a decision that Baghdad took as further evidence of America's growing hostility to Iraq.

Developments in Israel and the Occupied Territories further stimulated Iraqi suspicions that Washington had no interest in Arab rights. On 20 May seven innocent Palestinian workers were shot dead in Rishon LeZion by a young Israeli; seven more Palestinians were killed in the resulting protests. Further riots – in the Golan Heights and in the Israeli towns of Nazareth, Lod, Haifa and Beersheba – resulted in eight more Palestinian deaths with more than seven hundred injured. On 26 May fourteen of the fifteen members of the UN Security Council supported a resolution to send a UN team to the Occupied Territories, but Washington vetoed the move. In this atmosphere Saddam declared on 28 May at a meeting of the Arab League in Baghdad: 'It behoves us to declare clearly that if the Zionist entity attacks . . . we will strike back powerfully. If it uses weapons of mass destruction against our nation, we will use against it the weapons of mass destruction in our possession.' And he also emphasised that Israel's 'aggression and expansion at the Arabs' expense' would not have been possible without America, 'the main source of the Zionist entity's aggressive military force, and the main source of its financial resources'. Nobody, declared Saddam, well aware of the US dependence on Arab energy reserves, 'has the right to enjoy our resources and wealth at the same time he is fighting us and opposing our scientific and technological progress.'[13] However, the threat posed by the 'Zionist entity' would soon, despite Saddam's intentions, recede into the background. The 'economic war' supposedly being waged by Kuwait, supported by Saudi Arabia and the West, against Iraq – plus a host of other Iraqi complaints and grievances – would soon come to the fore.

IRAQ'S GRIEVANCES

It seemed to some observers in the US State Department that in the space of a few short days Saddam Hussein 'had forgotten Israel and become furious with Kuwait . . .'.[14] In fact while Saddam was concerned at the likelihood of another Israeli attack on his developing military capacity, with his nuclear installations at particular risk, he had also long been preoccupied with what he judged to be inadequate oil revenues. It was well known that the main barriers to higher oil prices were overproduction and other manifestations of producer indiscipline within the OPEC cartel. It took no more than one member's willingness to disregard OPEC protocols to start an adverse price trend: international perceptions of oil overproduction would combine with perception of OPEC disunity to depress oil prices yet further – and OPEC members were seldom united in their oil-producing strategies. It was known that the United Arab Emirates (UAE) typically produced more oil than its OPEC allocation, and this – and other departures from OPEC protocols served as a precedent for Kuwaiti non-compliance. The facts are plain. Kuwait was flooding the oil market in violation of the agreed OPEC production quotas. At this time Iraq and Iran had achieved a measure of agreement on oil production; and Saudi Arabia, concerned at its falling oil revenue, was prepared to urge self-discipline within the OPEC framework. Pressure was brought to bear on the small sheikhdoms, urging them to observe prior agreements and to work for the collective benefit of the oil-producing community; but the rich states of Kuwait and the UAE refused to be brought to heel. The consequence was a massive drop in oil prices which 'in turn, hurt Iraq, which was already short on funds'.[15] Iraq's oil revenue then slumped by $7 billion, equivalent to its 1989 balance-of-payments deficit. It could now be argued that Baghdad 'was facing economic suffocation'.[16]

Kuwait, having invested heavily in refining and marketing facilities, derived its income more from the volume of petrol and other products sold than from sales of crude oil, whereas the price of crude oil was the factor of most interest to Iraq. The overproduction of oil by Kuwait and the UAE in the spring of 1990 depressed the oil price well below the OPEC reference of $18 a barrel, agreed in November 1989. On 30 May the Iraqi president commented to participants at an extraordinary Arab summit in Baghdad on 'the failure by some of our Arab brothers to abide by the OPEC decisions when they flooded the world market with more oil than it needed, thereby enabling clients to buy below the fixed [OPEC] price'. He added:

' . . . for every US dollar drop in the price of a barrel of oil, the Iraqi loss amounted to $1 billion annually . . . War is fought with soldiers and harm is done by explosions, killing and coup attempts, but it is also done by economic means sometimes. I say to those who do not mean to wage war on Iraq, that this is in fact a kind of war against Iraq. Were it possible we would have endured . . . But I say that we have reached a point where we can no longer withstand pressure.'[17]

Saddam Hussein, faced with the desperate need to rebuild an Iraqi economy shattered by the war with Iran, well knew the power of the economic tool. During the war, both Kuwait and Saudi Arabia had worked to flood the oil market and damage the Iranian economy by forcing a price collapse from more than $30 a barrel in late November 1985 to less than $10 in early April 1986. In these circumstances, with massive damage inflicted on the Iranian economy, the parallel damage to Iraq's oil revenues was at least in part offset by aid to Iraq from Kuwait, Saudi Arabia, the US and other Western countries.[18] In any reckoning it seemed clear that Kuwait, with the possible involvement of other states, was waging 'a kind of war against Iraq'; and in a memorandum dated 15 July 1990 and addressed to the UN Secretary General, the Iraqi foreign minister Tariq Aziz explicitly named Kuwait and the United Arab Emirates as the 'culprits' in overproduction.

Kuwait, like Iraq, had an interest in trying to make up the revenue lost during the Iran–Iraq war, though its chosen method would obviously damage Iraq. Kuwait had suffered damage to oil installations from Iranian attacks, though losses were small compared to those in Iraq. Kuwait, conscious of its own vulnerability, was concerned also to invest in armaments; and it was also struggling to overcome the effects of a wide-ranging economic scandal (which has received little publicity in the West). In the late 1970s and early 1980s an official stock market, the so-called Souk el-Manakh ('the market where camels kneel'), had developed in Kuwait as a shaky way of speculating in promissory notes. In 1982 the balloon burst, with losses estimated by the Kuwaiti Central Bank at between $80 and $90 billion affecting around six thousand traders and their creditors. Since most of the losses were sustained by wealthy factions sympathetic to the government, the Kuwaiti regime organised a rescue package that used sums amounting to 8 per cent of Kuwait's total reserves. The economy suffered aftershocks for years.[19]

In these circumstances Kuwait was less interested in observing OPEC protocols than in pursuing its own perceived economic interests. Trouble had been brewing for some time. At an OPEC meeting in June 1989 the Kuwaiti attitude had caused general outrage; when the other members objected to the demands made by Ali Khalifa al-Sabah, Kuwait's oil minister, for a 30 per cent increase in Kuwait's allocation, he wrote on the final document: 'Kuwait neither accepts nor is bound by its assigned quota.'

With a Kuwaiti quota of 1,037,000 barrels a day, its actual production was estimated in oil industry reports as 1,700,000 barrels; with a new OPEC-specified allocation of 1,093,000, Kuwait resolved to produce 1,350,000 barrels a day.[20] The other OPEC members, including Iraq, were incensed at the Kuwaiti attitude, and over the following months used argument and threat in a vain attempt to bring Kuwait back in line. The overproduction continued and in early 1990 the price dropped to below $18 for the first time since the previous summer. Following further efforts by Saddam Hussein to stabilise oil prices, the Kuwaiti oil minister declared that OPEC quotas should be scrapped as soon as possible. Both Saddam and King Hussein of Jordan continued to lobby other OPEC members, but to no avail. Kuwait and the UAE continued to produce as they wished, to the point that the price per barrel sank to $11 in June 1990. At this level, Iraqi revenues were such that they could scarcely service current expenses, much less repay foreign loans or fund the required national reconstruction. In June Saddam sent a personal note to the Kuwaiti emir, noting that Kuwait's excess output (then amounting to 600,000 barrels over the OPEC allocation of 1.5 million barrels per day) was having a 'negative impact on Iraq and OPEC's vital interests'; and he addressed a similar letter to the ruler of the UAE.[21]

Kuwait had refused to compromise at the Baghdad summit in May, yet even then the political drift was clear. To give the meeting maximum weight Saddam had insisted that only heads of state attend the crucial talks; of the leaders' colleagues Saddam remarked, 'They don't need to hear the things we have to say.' At first he spoke of Israel but then developed his criticism of the Gulf states, noting at the start that military equipment had been delivered from Dubai to Iran during the Gulf war, and that 'one day the reckoning will come'. Later he addressed the Kuwaiti emir, Jaber al-Sabah, in a face-to-face confrontation: 'The quotas allocated by OPEC stipulated that Kuwait should not exceed a daily production of 1.5 million barrels; in actual fact, it has constantly extracted 2.1 million barrels a day. We are the ones to suffer. We Iraqis want to return to the economic situation that obtained in 1980, before the war against Iran. For the moment we urgently need $10 billion, as well as the cancellation of the $30 billion worth of debts to Kuwait, the Arab Emirates and Saudi Arabia that we incurred during the war. Indeed, brother Arabs, it has to be clearly understood that we are today living through another conflict . . .'.[22] In a belligerent tone Saddam declared that 'War doesn't mean just tanks, artillery or ships. It can take subtler and more insidious forms, such as the overproduction of oil, economic damage and pressures to enslave a nation.' King Hussein then commented that nothing must be done 'to harm the economy of Iraq'.

Those present noted the indifference of Emir Jaber to the Iraqi demands, his reply evincing 'something close to contempt for the Iraqi position . . .'.[23] The subsequent communications through June did nothing to bring the Kuwaitis and Iraqis closer together; the Iraqis were well used to reciprocating the al-Sabahs' contempt by continuing to regard Kuwait as no more than 'a state made out of an oil well'.

In a fresh move to resolve the deteriorating situation, Saddam proposed a new OPEC meeting for the Arab Gulf members (Iraq, Kuwait, Qatar, the UAE and Saudi Arabia). King Fahd agreed to the proposal but then tried to rally the Gulf leaders against the Iraqi suggestion for an increased price of $25 a barrel. Here, as in other matters, Fahd was keen to perform as a Western client; in particular, to safeguard American interests – much of the multibillion-dollar investment of the Saudi royals (and that of the Kuwaiti al-Sabahs) was in American real estate and financial institutions. On 9 July 1990 Iraqi intelligence intercepted a telephone conversation between King Fahd and the Qatari emir, Sheikh Khalifa ibn Hamad al Thani; to Saddam Hussein this seemed conclusive evidence that the two rulers were plotting against Iraq. In the recorded conversation King Fahd commented that the Iraqis 'have lost their temper . . . And you know when someone loses his temper his speech is unreasonable . . . Before you meet with Iraq, all of us must agree . . . as Gulf ministers. Keep quiet even if the Iraqi minister says something bad. These people, the Iraqis, have got themselves into a problem with Israel . . . They have given themselves the same problems as Nasser, and he could not solve them . . .'. With regard to Saddam's proposed summit meeting King Fahd declared: ' . . . But don't think of holding a summit if there's a chance of failure . . .'.[24] The conversation at least demonstrated that Fahd was unsympathetic to Saddam's belligerent posture, that he was anxious about the power of Israel, and that he was prepared to discuss with other Gulf states a way of countering Iraqi designs.

Another document, unknown to Saddam at that time, showed collaboration between the Kuwaiti Security Department (SSD) and the US Central Intelligence Agency (CIA). This memorandum (routinely declared by the CIA to be a forgery) was issued by the SSD director-general, Brigadier Fahd Ahmad al-Fahd, on 20 November 1989 to the interior minister Sheikh Salem al-Salem al-Sabah to summarise agreements reached at a meeting with CIA director William Webster at the CIA headquarters in Langley, Virginia, on 14 November 1989.[25] Paragraph 2 of the memorandum stated: 'We agreed with the United States side that visits would be exchanged at all levels between the State Security Department and the Central Intelligence Agency, and that information would be exchanged about the armaments and social and political structures of Iran and Iraq', with paragraph 5 declaring: 'We agreed with the American side that it was important to take advantage of the deteriorating economic situation in Iraq in order to put pressure on that country's government to delineate our common border.' The last paragraph of the memorandum refers to 'a special telephone' in William Webster's office to allow the Kuwaitis speedy access to CIA headquarters.

This document, if genuine, is an important piece of evidence suggesting a US–Kuwaiti conspiracy against Iraq. The CIA statement, issued by spokesman Peter Earnest on 30 October 1990, claiming that the document was a forgery, does in fact concede that the SSD deputy director paid a visit to CIA director William Webster in November 1989, as the document indicates.

On 11 July 1990 the oil ministers of Iraq, Kuwait, Qatar, the UAE and Saudi Arabia moved some way towards the Iraqi demand of $25 a barrel; there was unanimous agreement on an OPEC production ceiling that would help raise the barrel price to the $18 target set in November 1989. Two days later the Kuwaiti oil minister unilaterally repudiated the agreement. At the same time Kuwait was moving to improve its relations with Iran (still hostile to Iraq) and Egypt was preparing for a visit from President Hafiz Assad of Syria (Saddam's sworn Ba'athist rival). Saddam did not have to be paranoid to believe that various countries were conspiring to damage Iraqi interests. On 15 July Tariq Aziz, the Iraqi foreign minister, sent a letter to Chadli Klibi, the Arab League secretary-general, in which he made assorted complaints against the UAE and Kuwait. He claimed that the two Gulf states were co-operating in 'an unjust policy aimed at harming . . . Iraq'. Their policies had caused a $1 billion annual drop in Iraqi oil revenues; since 1980 Kuwait had been extracting oil from the 'Iraqi Rumeila oilfield' (which extends into Kuwait), resulting in a loss to Iraq of $2.4 billion; through the Iran–Iraq war Iraq had lost $106 billion in oil revenue, a decrease in exports that had benefited Kuwait and the UAE; and the interest-free loans from Kuwait and the UAE to aid the Iraqi war effort could not be regarded as debts ('How can these amounts be regarded as Iraqi debts to its Arab brothers when Iraq made sacrifices that are many times more than these debts in terms of Iraqi resources during the grinding war and offered rivers of blood of its youth in defence of the [Arab] nation's soil, dignity, honour and wealth').[26] On 17 July, in a televised speech, Saddam Hussein issued a warning to Arab states that were conspiring with the US to damage Iraq: 'At the behest of the US, certain Arab states had deliberately overproduced oil in defiance of the will of the OPEC majority. As a result . . . Iraq had been losing $14 bn a year.'[27] The United States, as the sole superpower, wanted a flow of cheap oil; in consequence, 'the policies of certain Arab rulers are American-inspired and detrimental to the interests of the Arab nation.'[28] Kuwait denounced Tariq Aziz's letter to the Arab League, claiming that the Iraqi charges were 'a falsification of reality'. Tension was now growing in the Gulf as it became increasingly clear that Iraq's differences with its neighbours would not be solved by peaceful means.

Iraq continued to nurse various grievances against Kuwait, in addition to the perceived strangulation of the Iraqi economy through the US-inspired overproduction of Gulf oil. The historic Iraqi claims to the territory of Kuwait were an underlying theme to the mounting tension on the Gulf. When Sir Percy Cox, with a cavalier stroke of his pen, in 1922, had delineated the modern borders of Kuwait, Iraq and Saudi Arabia (see Chapter 5) he had given Kuwait a coastline of 310 miles, allowing the much larger Iraq a mere thirty-six miles. Over the following decades, territorial disputes between Iraq and Kuwait broke out on many occasions. On 4 October 1963, following Kassem's overthrow, Iraq recognised Kuwait's independence in exchange for a large cash payment. This deal, however, failed to settle the matter. In 1973 a small Iraqi force briefly occupied a Kuwaiti border post; and on 16 July 1990 Tariq Aziz complained in a letter to the Arab League that the Kuwaiti government had '. . . implemented a plot to escalate the pace of the gradual, systematic advance toward Iraqi territory. The Kuwaiti government set up military establishments, police posts, oil installations, and farms on Iraqi territory'.[29]

There is some weight to the historic Iraqi claim to the territory of Kuwait. Much of the dispute hinges on the extent to which Kuwait was part of the province of Basra within the Ottoman Empire. Britain, as an imperial power concerned with strategic and commercial advantage, had a clear interest in separating Kuwait from the Ottomans (so Britain's modern pronouncements on this matter, manifestly conditioned by an imperial past, should be viewed with circumspection), but it seems that Kuwaiti rulers – despite Britain's best endeavours – were not keen to advertise an explicit break.[30] Kuwaiti ships flew the Turkish flag and the Kuwaiti leaders, even under pressure from Sir Percy Cox, refused to abandon this practice. Sir Percy, as revealed in a memorandum (dated 16 July 1905) to the Indian government's secretary-general, had even gone so far as to propose three designs for an independent Kuwaiti flag. The Kuwaiti sheikh refused to adopt any such symbol of Kuwaiti nationhood, and settled for merely adding the word 'Kuwait' in Arabic to the Turkish flag. After the collapse of the Ottoman Empire all the subsequent Iraqi governments, despite their domination by Western interests, 'from 1921 to the end of the British mandate in 1932, during the rule of King Feisal I, King Ghazi and King Feisal II refused to accept the separation of Kuwait from Iraq'.[31]

There can be little doubt that the territorial dispute has been exacerbated over the years by the original decision of Sir Percy Cox to make Iraq a virtually landlocked country. Basra, serving as Iraq's main port, is situated just below the confluence of the Tigris and the Euphrates and is linked to the Gulf by the much-disputed Shatt al-Arab. Iraq has repeatedly requested that Kuwait allow it to lease the two islands of Warbah and Bubiyan that overlook the approaches to Umm Qasr, one of Iraq's two ports on the Gulf. Kuwait rejected requests made in 1975, 1980 and 1989, decisions that Iraq inevitably viewed as unfriendly. If Iraq had managed to secure access to Warbah and Bubiyan its dependence on the Shatt al-Arab would have been reduced, and this in turn would have defused some of the Iran–Iraq tensions.

In summary it is possible to identify a number of grievances deeply felt by Iraq against Kuwait during the increasingly tense period prior to the onset of the Gulf War. In Iraq's view: economic war was being waged by Kuwait and other Gulf states, with the encouragement of Washington, against Iraq; Kuwait, originally part of the Ottoman *vilayet* of Basra, was now properly regarded as part of Iraq; Kuwait had systematically encroached on Iraqi territory over a period, and deliberately stolen Iraqi oil from the Rumeila oil field; Kuwait, despite Iraq's horrendous losses in the Iran–Iraq war, was refusing to write off Iraqi debts incurred in the defence of the Arab nation; Kuwait, in refusing to negotiate over Warbah and Bubiyan, was insensitive to Iraq's deep-water needs; and in general Kuwait, in its arrogant and uncompromising attitude to negotiations, seemed more interested in following the hidden agenda of its Western backers than in seeking harmonious relations with its neighbours.

A listing of Iraqi grievances is not intended to argue for the legitimacy of the subsequent Iraqi actions. Iraq had clear obligations under the UN Charter (which other nations disregard when they feel like it), under its membership of the Arab League, and following the 1963 Iraqi recognition of Kuwaiti independence. It is however useful to remember the Iraqi grievances, submerged as they usually are under the predictable tide of Western propaganda. And it should also be remembered that Saddam Hussein had little reason to believe that the United States, despite some unsympathetic words and acts, would take action following an Iraqi move against Kuwait: this American 'green light' deserves to be considered.

THE AMERICAN 'GREEN LIGHT'

There were many ways in which the US government and other US institutions aided and abetted Saddam Hussein in the run-up to the invasion of Kuwait. The major (but little advertised) trade association, the US–Iraq

Business Forum (see Chapter 7), numbered many leading American companies among its members, and enjoyed considerable influence in the Washington political establishment. US businessmen, interested only in commercial advantage, had no concern with Saddam's human rights record or with the threat he might pose to neighbouring states. It has been pointed out that Henry Kissinger, for example, was one American businessman among many who sought to benefit from the Iraq connection, for years after Saddam's abuse of human rights was known. After the Iraqi invasion of Kuwait, Kissinger proclaimed that Saddam should be deposed because he 'used poison gas against his own dissident population', but this had not prevented Kissinger's consulting firm 'from continuing to do business in Baghdad for years after Iraq's chemical warfare capability had been unleased against Iraqi minorities (and Iranian soldiers) . . . Hussein was coddled by government officialdom at the urging of his US business partners'.[32] Acknowledged Kissinger clients include a number of companies that have won large contracts in Iraq: Volvo, whose chairman, Pehr Gyllenhammer, sits on the board of Kissinger Associates; Hunt Oil, which sent an executive on the 'blue ribbon' trade delegation to Baghdad in 1989; Fiat, with a subsidiary that has sold weapons to Iraq; Coca-Cola; and the Yugoslav construction company Energoprojekt. Another Kissinger client, Britain's Midland Bank, has also been involved in Iraqi business deals. Henry Kissinger is not the only Western businessman who, content to profit from the Iraqi regime for many years, was forced to perform an ungainly *volte face* following Saddam's inconvenient misjudgements.

The support of US business interests over many years for Saddam Hussein is well documented, part of the general Western support for the Iraqi regime. What is clear also is the extent to which US commentators encouraged Saddam to adopt an aggressive oil pricing policy. In fact, not long before the invasion of Kuwait, Saddam was being urged to take steps to increase his oil revenues. He even commissioned a study from the Washington Centre for Strategic and International Studies, a prestigious foundation with links to Iraq. In a significant article, the Centre's energy security programme director Henry Schuler gave an insight into the secret commissioned study by arguing that the oil exporters were 'leaving money on the table'.[33] The solution, according to Schuler, was for the Arab oil exporters to adopt a more aggressive oil price policy – a recommendation that Saddam Hussein was working hard to implement. At the same time there were a number of diplomatic and political initiatives that further seemed to emphasise America's indifference to (or even sympathy with) Saddam's burgeoning designs.

On 12 April 1990 Saddam met with five US senators: Robert Dole, Alan

Simpson, Howard Metzenbaum, James McClure and Frank Murkowski (see also Chapter 7); the US ambassador, soon to be famous for her own 'green light' to Saddam, was also present. No-one reading the various transcripts of this meeting can doubt the general placatory tone. The US senators even criticised the American press in their attempts to propitiate Saddam, emphasising that there was a difference between the attitudes of the US government and those of journalists. Senator Dole pointed out that a commentator on 'Voice of America' who had not been given authority to talk about the Iraqi government had been removed from his job; and furthermore, 'Please allow me to say that only twelve hours earlier President Bush had assured me that he wants better relations, and that the US government wants better relations with Iraq . . . I assume that President Bush will oppose sanctions, and he might veto them, unless something provocative were to happen . . .'. It was clear, if further evidence were needed, that Iraq's war on Iran, its human rights record, and its increasingly bellicose efforts to impose its will on the Gulf region were not judged to be sufficiently 'provocative'. Ambassador Glaspie then chipped in to affirm that she was certain 'that this is the policy of the US' (that is, that President Bush saw nothing about Iraq that would impede the development of good relations).

Senator Simpson then remarked that the visit had been encouraged by the American president (Bush: 'Go there. I want you there . . . If you are criticised because of your visit to Iraq, I will defend you and speak on your behalf'). And Simpson suggested that Saddam's difficulties (that is, his resentment at being criticised in the West) lay with the Western media (' . . it is a haughty and pampered press; they all consider themselves political geniuses . . . they are very cynical . . .') and not with the American government. Senator Howard Metzenbaum ('I am a Jew and a staunch supporter of Israel') then decided to pay Saddam a compliment: '. . . I have been sitting here and listening to you for about an hour, and I am now aware that you are a strong and intelligent man and that you want peace . . . if . . . you were to focus on the value of the peace that we greatly need to achieve in the Middle East then there would not be a leader to compare with you in the Middle East . . .'.

A fortnight later, on 26 April, the US assistant secretary of state John Kelly testified before a House Foreign Affairs subcommittee on US–Iraq relations. He noted Saddam's growing military power in the region and expressed regret at the hanging of the *Observer* journalist Farzad Bazoft. But such details were no reason for a change in US policies on Iraq. He reiterated the US government's opposition to economic sanctions and even appeared to praise Saddam Hussein for 'talking about a new constitution and an expansion of participatory democracy'.[34] Kelly acknowledged that the US had 'an active program of providing insurance for agricultural credits for Iraq and a modest program of export–import bank guarantees . . . we are not prepared to see economic and trade sanctions legislatively imposed at this point . . . Another result of sanctions would be to worsen the existing imbalance in our trade with Iraq . . . the Administration continues to oppose imposition of legislated sanctions. They would hurt US exporters and worsen our trade deficit . . .'. On 1 May the US secretary of state James Baker appeared before a Senate appropriations subcommittee and, in a careful testimony, backed away from any firm stand against Iraq. After Senator Robert Kasten had highlighted Iraq's willingness to use chemical and biological weapons and its threats to use missiles against Israel he asked: 'What kinds of sanctions is the administration prepared to impose against Iraq for these actions?' Baker then mentioned some measures that had been taken, after which the following exchange took place:

> *Senator Kasten*: You mentioned the fact that in last year's appropriations bill Iraq had been removed from the list of terrorist states. Therefore, Iraq is now eligible for Ex-im Bank loans and a couple of other trade-related programs. Do you believe that we should add Iraq back onto that list of terrorist countries?
>
> *Secretary Baker*: Well, Senator Kasten, I think we have to take a look at that . . . It is a little bit premature of me on May 1 to sit here and make that determination just as we sit here . . .
>
> *Senator Kasten*: . . . There is some legislation . . . that goes significantly beyond that, involving agricultural credits and of other programs.
>
> *Secretary Baker*: That is the CCC [Commodity Credit Corporation, used to finance the purchase of agricultural products] program I am talking about . . . we ought to at least be conscious of the fact that if we take that action with respect to CCC or other economic measures . . . that in all probability our allies will be very quick to move in there and pick up our market share.[35]

The Bush administration continued to argue against the imposition of sanctions on Iraq, and it emerged that the US attorney general Richard Thornburgh had blocked the Atlanta investigation into Saddam's laundering of $3 billion through the Atlanta branch of Italy's Lavoro Bank for the acquisition of American weapons, including components for nuclear devices. William Safire, an ardent critic of Saddam, commented in *The New York Times*: '. . . because the Bush administration does not want to upset the

Iraqi dictator . . . no questions are being asked of the National Security Agency about why it failed to spot the huge transfer of dollars'.[36]

On 24 July 1990 two Iraqi armoured divisions moved from their bases to take up positions on the Kuwaiti border. Later the same day the US State Department spokeswoman, Margaret Tutwiler, asked whether the US had any military plans to defend Kuwait, replied: 'We do not have any defence treaties with Kuwait, and there are no special defence or security commitments to Kuwait.'[37] The next day Saddam Hussein summoned US Ambassador April Glaspie to his office in what was to be the last official contact between Baghdad and the United States before the invasion of Kuwait. Even at this late stage, with an obviously deteriorating situation in the Gulf, Glaspie still made efforts to placate Saddam Hussein.[38] She emphasised that President Bush had rejected the idea of trade sanctions against Iraq, to which Saddam replied: 'There is nothing left for us to buy from America except wheat. Every time we want to buy something, they say it is forbidden. I am afraid that one day you will say, "You are going to make gunpowder out of wheat".' Glaspie was quick to reassure the Iraqi leader: 'I have a direct instruction from the President to seek better relations with Iraq.' And she emphasised that a formal apology had been offered to Iraq for a critical article that had been published by the American Information Agency: 'I saw the Diane Sawyer programme on ABC . . . what happened in that programme was cheap and unjust . . . this is a real picture of what happens in the American media – even to American politicians themselves. These are the methods that the Western media employ. I am pleased that you add your voice to the diplomats that stand up to the media. . . .' Later Glaspie added that 'President Bush is an intelligent man. He is not going to declare an economic war against Iraq . . .'; and then the ambassador produced the much-quoted comment that was perhaps the biggest 'green light' of all:

I admire your extraordinary efforts to rebuild your country. I know you need funds. We understand that, and our opinion is that you should have the opportunity to rebuild your country. *But we have no opinion on Arab–Arab conflicts like your border disagreement with Kuwait.* (My italics)

The point was emphasised: 'I was in the American Embassy in Kuwait during the late 1960s. The instruction we had during that period was that we should express no opinion on this issue and that the issue was not associated with America. James Baker has directed our official spokesman to emphasise this instruction . . . when we see the Iraqi point of view that the measures taken by the UAE and Kuwait are, in the final analysis, tantamount to military aggression against Iraq, then it is reasonable for me to be concerned . . .'. In short, *the US ambassador to Baghdad was here telling Saddam Hussein that he had a legitimate case against Kuwait and that the matter was no business of the United States.*

On 27 July the CIA provided the American government with satellite photographs showing increasing concentrations of Iraqi men and equipment on the Kuwaiti border. Washington issued a warning to Kuwait, Egypt and Saudi Arabia, all of whom – in agreement with the US State Department and the National Security Council – dismissed the idea of an imminent Iraqi invasion, preferring to talk instead of 'Iraqi blackmail'. The intelligence information continued to accumulate, much of it collected by the spy satellites of the National Security Agency (NSA). On 28 July Saddam invited Yasser Arafat to visit Kuwait to tell the emir that 'if he gives me the $10 billion I'm asking in return for the use of the Rumeila oil wells on the border, I'll reduce my troops'. The next day Arafat reached Kuwait City to be told by the emir: 'I don't want to discuss that. In forty-eight hours I'm going to Jeddah for a summit with Iraq. Let's talk instead about the problem of all those Soviet Jews emigrating to Israel.' The PLO leader again tried to raise Saddam's demand but the emir cut him short. By this time the CIA was able to assess the scale of the Iraqi forces massed on the border: 100,000 soldiers including troops of the élite Republican Guard, 300 tanks and 300 pieces of heavy artillery.[39]

The next day, 31 July, the US assistant secretary of state John Kelly entered the Rayburn Building on Capitol Hill to testify before the Middle East subcommittee of the House of Representatives. The aim was to clarify the attitude of the Bush administration to the escalating crisis in the Gulf. Again it is useful to consider the tone and apparent implication of the ensuing dialogue:

> *Representative Hamilton*: Defence Secretary Richard Cheney has been quoted in the press as saying that the United States was committed to going to the defence of Kuwait if she were attacked. Is that exactly what was said? Could Mr Kelly clarify this?
>
> *Assistant Secretary Kelly*: . . . We have no defence treaty relationship with any Gulf country . . .
>
> *Hamilton*: Do we have a commitment to our friends in the Gulf in the event that they are engaged in oil or territorial disputes with their neighbours?
>
> *Kelly*: As I said, Mr Chairman, we have no defence treaty relationships

with any of the countries. We have historically avoided taking a position on border disputes or on internal OPEC deliberations . . .

Hamilton: If Iraq, for example, charged across the border into Kuwait, for whatever reason, what would be our position with regard to the use of US forces?

Kelly: That, Mr Chairman, is a hypothetical or a contingency, the kind of which I can't get into. Suffice it to say that we would be extremely concerned, but I cannot get into the realm of "what if" answers.

Hamilton: In that circumstance, is it correct to say, however, that we do not have a treaty commitment which would obligate us to engage US forces?

Kelly: That is correct.

Hamilton: That is correct, is it not?

Kelly: That is correct, sir.[40]

The statements of Assistant Secretary of State John Kelly, broadcast on the World Service of the BBC, were heard in Baghdad. At a crucial moment, a senior official of the Bush administration had sent Saddam Hussein a signal that the US would not intervene. The American 'green light' for the Iraqi invasion of Kuwait was bright and unblinking.

THE INVASION OF KUWAIT

At the time Assistant Secretary Kelly was declaring that the US had no commitment to help Kuwait in the event of an Iraqi invasion, Kuwaiti and Iraqi officials were preparing for high-level talks in Jeddah.[41] Hours before the meeting, the emir of Kuwait declared he would not be attending, a decision that Saddam took as a slap in the face. The Iraqi leader, smarting under this 'deadly insult', announced that he too would not be taking part in the talks; instead he would send Izzat Ibrahim, his number 2 in the Ba'ath leadership. In this atmosphere the talks were bound to fail.

The Kuwaiti team included the Crown Prince Saad, sent as the emir's deputy; the Iraqi delegation included Deputy Prime Minister Saddoun Hammadi, Izzat Ibrahim and Saddam's cousin, Ali Hassan al-Majid, soon to be appointed governor of Kuwait. The negotiations lasted for about an hour and a half on the evening of 31 July. Izzat Ibrahim recited a prepared speech listing Iraqi complaints against Kuwait, whereupon the Crown Prince Saad refuted the grievances one by one. After some desultory talk King Fahd declared that he would pay a disputed $1 billion to Iraq, 'with no strings attached'. The Iraqis thanked him, after which Fahd retired, leaving the Kuwaitis and Iraqis together. Soon they were in angry confrontation, with Ibrahim making unambiguous threats: 'We know perfectly well how to get the money we need from you and the Saudis.' Saad countered angrily, denouncing the Iraqi threats and reminding Ibrahim that 'Kuwait has very powerful friends. We too have allies. You'll be forced to pay back all the money you owe us'. Soon afterwards, the two delegations parted in total discord.

On 1 August, unable to agree a joint communiqué, the Kuwaiti and Iraqi negotiators left Jeddah for home. Chadli Klibi, the Arab League Secretary-General, learning of the collapse of the talks, then contacted Sheikh Sabah, the Kuwaiti foreign minister, and Emir Abdullah in Saudi Arabia. Both suggested that the next round of talks, scheduled for 4 August in Baghdad, would be more successful (Abdullah: 'Our Iraqi friends were tough, the Kuwaitis too. But it's just the beginning. Let's wait until Baghdad'). US Secretary of State James Baker was in Irkursk, in the heart of Siberia, for talks with the Soviet foreign minister Eduard Shevardnadze.

At 2 a.m. (local time) on 2 August 1990 the Iraqi military began its invasion of Kuwait. Two divisions of the Republican Guard, including armoured brigades, quickly advanced from the frontier to Kuwait City; by 11 a.m. most of the capital's key buildings were in Iraqi hands. The Kuwaiti emir, Sheikh Jaber Ahmad al-Sabah, tipped off an hour before the invasion, fled to Saudi Arabia where he set up a provisional government in exile. President Bush moved to ban all but humanitarian trade with Iraq and to freeze $30 billion-worth of Iraqi and Kuwaiti assets in the United States; Britain and France followed suit. The UN Security Council passed Resolution 660 (in a 14–0 vote, with Yemen abstaining), the first of more than a dozen against Iraq. This initial resolution, passed on the day of the Iraqi invasion:

1. *Condemns* the Iraqi invasion of Kuwait;
2. *Demands* that Iraq withdraw immediately and unconditionally all its forces to the positions in which they were located on 1 August 1990;
3. *Calls upon* Iraq and Kuwait to begin immediately intensive negotiations for the resolution of their differences and supports all efforts in this regard, and especially those of the League of Arab States;
4. *Decides* to meet again as necessary to consider further steps to ensure compliance with the present resolution.

On 3 August, at a meeting of the Arab League, fourteen out of twenty-one members called for an Iraqi withdrawal. Japan, West Germany, Belgium, Italy and the Netherlands took steps to freeze all Iraqi and Kuwaiti assets, and the Soviet Union and the United States issued a joint declaration calling on the world to end arms shipments to Iraq. President Bush, in a revealing observation, commented that 'the integrity of Saudi Arabia' was one of America's 'vital interests', and warned that 'further [Iraqi] expansion would be even more unacceptable'. Two days later, Bush declared that the United States would not accept the accomplishment of a puppet government in Kuwait; and when reporters asked him how he might prevent it he replied, 'Just wait, watch, and learn.' Already there were signs that the US was contemplating military intervention. The countdown to the Gulf War had begun.

THE FABRICATION OF CONSENSUS

The Iraqi invasion of Kuwait set in train a host of events that were to have consequences for the entire world. In particular, the United States – possibly in early August 1990 already working to a hidden agenda – began to orchestrate the 'world consensus' (which in fact was no consensus at all) that was to result in the military devastation of the Iraqi nation. In the hours following the invasion it seemed that the US had not yet decided how to react. It did appear that the Bush administration, despite the 'green light', had been taken by surprise. Only later did the reason emerge: the US had perhaps anticipated Iraqi military action, but only to secure disputed territory and to give Saddam a more convenient access to the Gulf. It was April Glaspie herself who let the cat out of the bag. Interviewed by *The New York Times* in September 1990, she commented: 'Obviously, I didn't think – and nobody else did – that the Iraqis were going to take all of Kuwait.'[42] Did the US administration envisage that Saddam would take only a *part* of Kuwait? Would that have been acceptable if such an Iraqi move had left US oil interests intact? It seemed that the US, as well as Saddam, had grossly miscalculated – but now, with Saddam gaining little support from the world community, President Bush had the chance to turn the affair to political advantage. His reputation had long been bedevilled by the 'wimp factor', despite various military initiatives, including the slaughter of several thousand civilians in Panama. Now Bush had a fresh chance to establish his macho credentials: 'A Third World leader had thrown down a challenge to a president who needed to prove himself.'[43]

Soon Bush was working to stimulate anti-Iraq feeling: amongst Arab states that would have preferred a more cautious approach, and in the wider world community. In a call to President Mubarak, Bush declared that the clear act of aggression 'cannot be accepted', and that he was going to accept Saddam's challenge. He emphasised that the invasion was a direct threat to US interests and that he was being urged to act by Congress, government departments and public opinion. Bush complained that the Arab world had not yet voiced any clear condemnation, a lapse that he clearly intended to remedy at the first opportunity. Even King Fahd – now gravely threatened, according to the emerging American line – had not yet requested US assistance. Bush had himself taken the trouble to contact Fahd, and been horrified at the king's reluctance to demand an American response. The conservative Saudi Arabia, with at that time no real quarrel with Iraq, was being frantically pressured into joining the burgeoning anti-Saddam crusade. If, declared Bush, the Arabs were not keen to look after their interests or to call upon friendly assistance they would have no-one to blame but themselves. Moreover, if the United States did *not* receive requests for assistance it would have no option but to act alone. King Hussein of Jordan urged the US president to delay any military initiative since an Arab solution to the crisis would be preferable, whereupon an irritated Bush replied: 'All right, have your forty-eight hours, but if you Arabs don't make up your mind I don't know who will make it up for you.'[44] At the same time Bush was having to work hard to secure a Saudi 'request' for military protection. Fahd's natural instinct was to handle the situation with maximum caution; he had no wish to jeopardise the Washington connection but was deeply anxious that a massively overt show of support might destabilise the deeply traditional Saudi regime. It was also clear that some members of the Saudi royal family perceived that *Fahd thought that it was Kuwaiti inflexibility that had provoked the Iraqi invasion.*[45] Such a thought would cut no ice with an increasingly persistent President Bush, and gradually Fahd's resistance was worn down. Bush telephoned him repeatedly, insisting that Saddam had ambitions beyond Kuwait (a one-liner hypothesis for which there was no evidence), and all but demanding a Saudi 'request' for American protection. At last, following this persistent pressure, Fahd relented and agreed that US Defence Secretary Dick Cheney could visit Riyadh for talks. Fahd, against his instincts, had stepped onto the slippery slope; the US aim of building an anti-Iraq 'consensus' had achieved its first victory. Soon a weary King Fahd would be 'requesting' American military protection.

The US then hit upon the idea of disguising the Saudi request in a more general call for assistance. The chief of staff John Sununu had perceived Fahd's problem: 'By God, the man needs a cover, an Arab or Islamic cover.' This suggested that it would be easier for Fahd to make his request if it were couched in general terms as a call to all the foreign friends of

Saudi Arabia. So Bush called King Hassan of Morocco and President Mubarak of Egypt to ask whether they would accede to a Saudi request for military protection. They agreed, and Fahd accepted that a US presence on Saudi soil could be disguised – in a propaganda sense – in a broader multinational presence that included some Arab contingents. Cheney, now the scene was set, managed to obtain a speedy agreement in Riyadh; soon American troops and equipment would be flooding into Saudi Arabia. On 7 August, on his way back to Washington, Cheney had brief talks with Mubarak in Alexandria to obtain permission for the aircraft-carrier USS *Eisenhower* to sail through the Suez Canal, so overcoming the long-standing Egyptian policy of banning nuclear-powered ships or ones carrying nuclear weapons. Now the pressures being exerted by Washington on the Arab states and on the wider world community were plain for all to see.

The unremitting pressure on King Fahd had secured the first stage, the access of massive US military forces to the Gulf; and the approach to Egypt had successfully enhanced the American military posture in the region. If Fahd had been worn down by endless badgering and a constant recitation of impending doom, what tactic had been employed to secure Egyptian acquiescence? Simple bribery. In 1990 Egypt had massive debts, the largest in the whole of Africa and the Middle East. Almost $50 billion was owed to the World Bank, and Secretary of States James Baker – President Bush's roving master of creative diplomacy – proposed a bribe (or 'forgiveness') of some $14 billion. At the same time Washington pressured other governments, including Canada and Saudi Arabia, to 'forgive' or delay much of the rest of the Egyptian debt.[46] And where the tactic of bribery worked well with President Mubarak, it could be exploited to equal advantage with other national leaders.*

Turkey, as a compliant NATO member and a strategically well-placed country on the borders of Iraq, was very useful in the anti-Saddam crusade. President Turgut Ozal commented that 'we have benefited from this crisis and made very significant progress towards our goal of modernising and strengthening our armed forces'.[47] Ozal declared that the United States had donated at least $8 billion-worth of military equipment to Turkey, including tanks, ships, helicopters and fixed-wing aircraft (some of which were to be used to suppress the Kurds in Turkey and across the Iraqi border). Washington also agreed to speed up the planned delivery of Phantom bombers, and

---

*Such events also serve to expose one of the key purposes behind the US-dominated supply of economic aid: recipient states are rendered immensely vulnerable to bribery – in terms of debt cancellation – when Washington decides to pursue wider strategic objectives.

to underwrite the building of a Sikorsky helicopter plant in Turkey (this latter worth about $1 billion to Turkey).[48] The US also informed Ozal that Turkey's allocation of US textile exports would increase; and that the World Bank and the International Monetary Fund (both dominated by Washington) would facilitate $1.5 billion-worth of low-cost loans to Turkey. President Bush also agreed to sponsor Turkey's application for membership of the European Community, despite Turkey's appalling human rights record including the persecution of its own Kurdish minority.[49]

Syria's acquiescence in the US strategy was rewarded with a massive supply of arms and aid, and other political concessions, even though the Assad regime was still on the official American list of terrorist states. Noted David Hirst in *The Guardian*: 'The Syrian leader is acknowledged even by his enemies as the Arab world's master strategist: shrewd, stubborn and calculating, inexhaustibly patient and serpentine in biding his time for the main chance and then pouncing on it.'[50] The Gulf crisis had offered President Hafiz Assad a great opportunity. His compliance soon earned him $1 billion-worth of arms and aid through a variety of back doors, primarily Gulf states.[51] The European Community offered Syria – with a human rights record similar to Saddam's – a substantial economic aid package to compensate the Assad regime for the loss of transit trade and the loss of payments sent by Syrian workers in Kuwait.[52] To hedge his bets Assad refrained from the sort of anti-Saddam invective that was flying around the Gulf.

The relatively small-scale Syrian contribution to the US military posture also earned Assad the right to pursue his own regional strategy: namely, the subjugation of much of Lebanon (to Washington the Syrian invasion, in direct violation of the UN Charter, was politically acceptable). James Baker flew to Damascus to discuss with Assad how Syria might aid the anti-Iraq campaign (at the same time enraging the families of the Lockerbie air crash victims who suspected Syrian involvement in the bombing[53]). A consequence of the Baker visit was that Assad was now free to expand his military incursions in Lebanon. When Syrian troops massed around General Aoun's Christian section of Beirut, Assad 'got the green light from the White House to go in and oust the General from power'.[54] Uri Lubrani, the Israeli co-ordinator of operations in Lebanon, observed that the US–Syrian alliance over the Gulf crisis made it easier for Assad to act militarily: 'I have no doubt that the Syrians felt much freer to use force inside Lebanon when they were in an alliance with the United States.'[55] Washington issued no criticism of the Syrian invasion of East Beirut, instead applauding the act as a generous effort to bring order to the region:

'. . . it would be difficult to interpret Syrian occupation of Lebanon for many years any differently from Iraqi occupation of Kuwait . . .'.[56]

When Iran agreed to aid the blockade of Iraq, loans from the US-dominated World Bank were suddenly forthcoming. A Reuter report on 9 January 1990 observed that Iran was 'to be rewarded for its support of the US . . . with its first loan from the World Bank since the 1979 Islamic revolution'. The day before the ground attack on Iraq was launched the World Bank announced its approval for a $250 million loan to Iran. The former US national security adviser Zbigniew Brzezinski warned that one of the 'undesirable and unanticipated side-effects' of the US-led effort in the Gulf would be a new Iranian dominance in the region; also Israel would be tempted to use its force more freely than before.[57]

The permanent members of the UN Security Council – with their power of veto over US-sponsored resolutions – were of particular importance in the US strategy; in fact, they were easy meat. Britain, with its supine foreign policy of simply shadowing Washington, was reduced in foreign affairs to little more than a subdivision of the US State Department; and so could be 'relied upon'. France, more independent, lacked the diplomatic weight or inclination to rock the boat – except in some secondary areas – and never once used its veto to block the procession of anti-Iraq resolutions. The Soviet Union, with its collapsing economy, was particularly vulnerable to bribery, even though President Gorbachev was manifestly more pacific than the US administration. Washington persuaded the Saudi foreign minister, Saud al-Faysalwe, to fly to Moscow to offer a $1 billion bribe,[58] and once Resolution 678 (supposedly authorising the use of force against Iraq) had been agreed by the Soviet Union another $3 billion-worth of aid was provided by the Gulf states. At the same time Washington agreed to review its policy on food aid to the Soviet Union. Javier Perez de Cuellar, the UN Secretary General, 'was surprised by the high degree of co-operation between the US and the Soviet Union . . .'.[59]

China was a special case, the most independent of the permanent members of the Security Council after the US and the most likely to veto the US-inspired resolutions. In fact, China was already in Washington's debt and this circumstance, coupled with additional inducements, ensured that China only abstained – rather than use its veto – on the crucial Resolution 678.[60] China had a particular interest in recovering its international respectability after the Tiananmen Square massacre of June 1989, and it was already grateful that Washington had moved quickly to offer Beijing a diplomatic lifeline (Britain duly made a similar diplomatic move soon afterwards). To ensure Chinese acquiescence – at least a decision not to use its Security

Council veto – a substantial World Bank loan was authorised. Once it was clear that China would not veto Resolution 678 the Chinese foreign minister Qian Qichen flew to Washington to discuss a suitable reward; a few days later, the World Bank deposited a further $114 million in Peking. The Chinese scholar Liu Binyan commented: 'Since August . . . Beijing has skilfully manipulated the Iraqi crisis to its advantage and rescued itself from being the pariah of the world.'⁶¹

The votes of the non-permanent members of the Security Council were also crucial to the United States if the necessary majority was to be achieved. Again the US approach was characteristic: a calculated mix of bribery and threat, directed against some of the poorest members of the world community. Ethiopia was offered an investment deal, with Zaire promised military aid and debt forgiveness. By now, Washington's obsession was so all-consuming that it even tried to bring the long-castigated Cuba on board, despite all the grim history of US-sponsored terrorist attacks on the Cuban economy and the thirty-year-long economic and diplomatic blockade of the island. On 28 November 1990 a meeting took place between US Secretary of State James Baker and the Cuban foreign minister Isidoro Malmierca at an East Side hotel in Manhattan, the first encounter at this level between the US and Cuba for more than thirty years. Cuba, long resolved to survive without American-style generosity, would not be bought. It voted against Resolution 678, as did Yemen. Minutes after Yemen had registered its negative vote, a senior American diplomat told the Yemeni ambassador: 'That was the most expensive "no" vote you ever cast.' Within days the US had stopped its $70 million aid programme to Yemen, one of the poorest countries of the world. The World Bank and the IMF moved to hamper further Yemeni loans, and some 800,000 Yemeni workers were abruptly expelled from Saudi Arabia. It is estimated that the Yemeni 'no' vote – an entirely legitimate sovereign decision under the UN Charter – cost the impoverished Yemen about $1 billion, bringing massive additional suffering to its people.⁶² Zimbabwe, initially hostile to Resolution 678, eventually voted in favour after suggestions to the foreign minister that a projected IMF loan would be blocked; just as the US ambassador in Quito warned Ecuador of the 'devastating economic consequences' that would follow a 'no' vote. The famine-stricken Sudan, rash enough to voice support for Iraq, was denied a shipment of food.⁶³

By dint of threats, bribery and reliance on supine acquiescence the United States had managed to fabricate a bogus consensus. At one level this meant that a pliant Security Council – no longer subject to the possibility of a confident Soviet veto – could be relied upon to serve US strategic interests. Washington, hostile to the UN for most of its history, had not developed a new respect for the international organisation: the Bush administration simply perceived the advantage in pursuing US goals under a legalistic 'flag of convenience'. At another level the fabricated consensus – to be bolstered by the Congress vote – meant that the United States, the one surviving nuclear superpower, was free to wage war against a Third-World country. The legalistic UN camouflage for the American action was not essential – the US would have acted anyway – but it was helpful. Now it was possible to talk of 'UN authorisation', 'UN forces' and 'UN demands'. At the same time there was much talk of the 'allies', of the 'Coalition'. The scene was set. The world did not have to wait long for the performance to begin.

GEORGE BUSH

No-one doubts that President George Bush was a principal player in the Gulf War. But was he the virtuous leader, courageously standing against evil, as he would want us to believe? Or is there another interpretation, more in accord with recent American history and more true to George Bush's record and performance? In fact it is difficult to avoid the conclusion that President Bush, while keen to make moral pronouncements at every turn, embodied above all the gross hypocrisy that has characterised the posture of the United States in the global politics of the modern world.

Noam Chomsky, MIT linguistics professor and dissident writer, has reminded us that at the time of the Gulf War George Bush was the one head of state who stood condemned by the World Court for 'the unlawful use of force'. Bush contemptuously dismissed the Court's demand for the payment of reparations to Nicaragua, while eager to demand reparations from Iraq.[64] In 1975 Bush had become head of the CIA, just in time to support the Indonesian extermination of a third of the population of East Timor. He supported Israel's invasion of the Lebanon, and then opposed UN Resolution 425 demanding an immediate Israeli withdrawal from the territory it had occupied. Under Bush's leadership the CIA launched a massive destabilisation campaign against the democratically-elected leader of Jamaica, Michael Manley; and there is evidence that he knew about, but failed to prevent, the assassination of Orlando Letelier, a former minister in Allende's socialist Chile, in Washington. Bush agreed a flood of military aid into Guatemala, despite proof provided by Amnesty International of 'a government co-ordinated campaign of terror' against its own people. When four American nuns were raped and murdered in El Salvador in 1980, Bush backed UN ambassador Jeane Kirkpatrick who declared that the nuns 'were not just nuns. The nuns were political activists . . .'. After typically rigged elections in the Philippines, Bush flew to congratulate the dictator President Ferdinand Marcos, commenting: 'We love your adherence to democratic principles and to the democratic process.'[65] In December 1989 Bush launched the invasion of Panama, violating the UN Charter and other international agreements,[66] and killing – according to some estimates – up to seven thousand people. Bush then installed Guillermo Endara as president, a man now known to be involved in drug trafficking and money laundering.

In a series of speeches between August 1990 and February 1991, President Bush repeatedly accused Iraq of human rights abuses and violations of international law, and castigated Saddam as 'Hitler revisited'.* Bush frequently cited damning material that he had known about for years but about which he had been silent while the US was supplying Saddam with cash credits, armaments and other equipment. He also had a 'near obsession'[67] with a single Amnesty International report describing Iraqi atrocities in Kuwait. Now – having long ignored the stack of human-rights reports about such friendly countries as Turkey, Syria, Egypt, Israel and Saudi Arabia – Bush was cynically exploiting Amnesty for propaganda purposes. In January 1991 Bush despatched a message to more than 450 college and university newspapers, which included the words: 'Listen to what Amnesty International has documented . . . There is no horror that could make this a more obvious conflict of good v. evil . . .'.[68] He did not refer to what Amnesty had often reported about other states, many of them US allies.

Amnesty's Executive Director John Healey reacted with anger to George Bush's manipulation of Amnesty material for purposes of political propaganda:

> I hope the administration will soon learn that Amnesty members and other student activists can not be misled by opportunistic manipulation of the international human rights movement . . . We can teach our political leaders that people's human rights are not convenient issues for rhetorical arsenals.[69]

---

*The propaganda depiction of Saddam as a new Hitler is ironic in view of the substantial US support offered to historical Nazism. Thus such US companies as ITT, Standard Oil and Ford helped to equip Hitler during the Second World War (Charles Higham, *Trading with the Enemy*, 1983); '. . . the CIA was willing to finance and protect not simply former Nazi and Gestapo men but even senior officers of Adolf Eichmann's SS section Amt IV B 4, the central administrative apparatus of the Holocaust' (Christopher Simpson, *Blowback, America's Recruitment of Nazis and Its Effects on the Cold War*, 1988, p. 245); and Hitler's praise for Henry Ford (*Mein Kampf*, Hutchinson, p. 583) was symbolic of the aid and support that the Nazi despot could rely on from certain powerful American sources.

In a subsequent Congress debate, the republican senator from Oregon, Mark Hatfield, commented: '. . . even the most brutal human rights violations of one nation do not justify an offensive strike against another nation. Indeed, it makes a mockery of the exceptional work done by organizations like Amnesty International to use their documentation of human rights abuses as a convenient justification for launching an attack that will very certainly cause even more suffering . . .'.[70] And the manifest double standard was raised also by Congressman Stokes of Ohio during the debate (12 January 1990) on the so-called 'force' resolution:

> There is no question that the outrageous violations of human rights reported by Amnesty International defy all standards of human rights decency. But I have to wonder where was the outcry from the Administration when three United States servicemen were recently murdered in El Salvador . . . In Guatemala, China, Kenya and South Africa pervasive human rights violations have occurred, and continue to occur . . . I venture to say that if Kuwait produced bananas, instead of oil, we would not have 400,000 American troops there today.[71]

The situation was plain to see. George Bush, with an abysmal human rights record of his own, was eager to point the finger at the 'new Hitler', Saddam Hussein; eager to exploit any propaganda tool to castigate the Iraqi leader for behaviour which Bush himself had tacitly supported a short time before, and which in any case continued to characterise a host of undemocratic authoritarian states that were current friends of the United States. With this gross hypocrisy, in the tattered garb of an adulterated morality, George Bush began preparations for a further devastating war.*

THE CHRONOLOGY OF CONFLICT

2 August to 8 October 1990

The Iraqi invasion of Kuwait, a gross violation of international law, was generally considered to be a 'well planned and efficiently implemented'

---

*There are domestic matters also that should be considered in assessing George Bush's character and performance: for example, the Savings and Loans (S and L) scandal that has cost the American taxpayer more than $500 billion. In this connection the investigative journalist Peter Brewton (in *The Mafia, CIA & George Bush*, 1992) has referred to Bush's 'complicity, non-reaction and denial', describing Bush as a wealthy businessman 'with symbiotic relationships to the Mafia and the CIA'.

operation.[72] By 11 a.m., Baghdad Radio announced that Emir Jaber had been toppled. There had been little resistance, though in any event the Kuwaiti forces would not have been able to fight the overwhelming Iraqi contingents for long. After scarcely any military action Kuwaiti planes fled to Saudi Arabia and Bahrain, just as six months later Iraqi planes would flee to Iran (and be confiscated). Emir Jaber al Ahmad al-Sabah and other members of the royal family rushed by motorcade to the US embassy, where an American army helicopter was waiting for take-off. The Emir, the Crown Prince and a few others piled in and the rest, too numerous for the single machine, began the thirty-mile road journey to the Saudi border.[73] Events had been set in train that in a few short months would result in several hundred thousand Iraqi dead and millions more casualties, with a devastated land and massive ecological damage, turmoil throughout the Arab world, and financial and political reverberations that would shake the global community. The chronology of the conflict (See Table 8.1) shows an escalating tragedy viewed with callous indifference by those few men in a position to shape the course of events.[74]

Table 8.1   From Iraqi Invasion (2 August 1990) to Iraqi Defeat (28 February 1991)

2 August	Iraqi forces invade Kuwait: Emir flees to Saudi Arabia in US helicopter
3 August	Baghdad declares its troops will start withdrawing from Kuwait unless the security of Iraq or Kuwait is threatened
5 August	Bush says Iraqi aggression 'will not stand'
6 August	Saddam reassures Joseph Wilson, US chargé d'affaires in Baghdad, who in turn praises the 'professional standards' of Iraq's ministry of Foreign Affairs
8 August	The puppet 'Provisional Free Government of Kuwait' calls for a merger between Iraq and Kuwait
12 August	Saddam offers peace plan; rejected by Bush
15 August	Iraqi foreign minister, Tariq Aziz, offers talks; rejected by Bush
25 August	UN passes Resolution 665 mandating force to ensure blockade of Iraq
28 August	Saddam starts releasing hostages. King Hussein of Jordan proposes peace plan; accepted by Iraq; rejected by Bush
1 September	Libya proposes seven-point peace plan, including Iraqi withdrawal from Kuwait; rejected by Bush
5 September	Saddam calls for holy war
9 September	Bush and Gorbachev call for unconditional Iraqi withdrawal
12 September	Ayatollah Khamenei condemns US presence in Gulf
19 September	King Hassan of Morocco proposes peace plan; rejected by Bush

24 September	Mitterrand of France proposes peace plan; Iraq responds positively; Bush does not
1 October	Bush says US seeks 'a peaceful outcome'
2 October	Amnesty International reports Iraqi atrocities in Kuwait
5 October	Primakov, Soviet presidential council member, after visiting Saddam, declares himself 'not pessimistic' about a political solution
8 October	Israeli police shoot dead 20 Palestinians and wound 150 at Temple Mount
13 October	Syrian troops invade East Beirut
16 October	US Secretary of State James Baker says sanctions against Iraq 'tightening with increasing severity' have a chance of working
21 October	Edward Heath meets Saddam; secures release of 38 British hostages
26 October	General Zvi Zamir's report absolves Israeli police of responsibility for Palestinian massacre (8 October)
28 October	Gorbachev, after Primakov visit to Baghdad, says Saddam is not intransigent
31 October	Bush decides to secretly double US troops in Gulf to 430 000, to start war in January, and to seek a UN mandate for this action
4 November	Baker discusses war plan with allies
9 November	Willy Brandt meets Saddam; secures release of 206 Western hostages
13 November	Peace initiative by King Hassan fails
16 November	Baker lobbies Security Council for 'force' resolution
21 November	Bush meets Emir Jaber and King Fahd in Saudi Arabia
22 November	Expert witnesses testifying before the US Senate Armed Services Committee show large majority rejecting military option
28 November	Tony Benn, British MP, meets Saddam; secures the release of 15 hostages
29 November	Britain, following fall of Thatcher, restores diplomatic relations with Syria. Resolution 678 (authorising 'all necessary means' to evict Iraq from Kuwait) is passed in the UN Security Council
30 November	Bush proposes talks with Iraq
1 December	Baghdad accepts offer of talks
4 December	Baker criticised by US Senate Foreign Relations Committee for ignoring expert testimony on sanctions
6 December	Saddam decides to release all remaining foreign hostages
9 December	US rejects Iraq's proposed date for talks between Saddam and Baker
15 December	US cancels scheduled Aziz–Baker talks
18 December	Amnesty International reports Iraqi brutalities in Kuwait
23 December	US forces in Saudi Arabia put on high state of alert for a week
30 December	Yugoslav foreign minister, Budimor Loncar, takes Iraqi proposals to Washington; State Department spokesman calls them a 'serious pre-negotiating position'; Bush rejects them
3 January	Bush agrees Aziz–Baker talks in Geneva
4 January	Iraq agrees to proposed talks
9 January	Geneva talks fail

12 January	US Congress authorises Bush to use force in Gulf (Senate vote: 53 to 47, House of Representatives: 250 to 183)
13 January	Anti-war protests throughout Europe. Saddam–de Cuellar talks fail
16 January	US-led bombing of Iraq (Operation 'Desert Storm') begins
18 January	Iraq fires twelve Scud missiles at Tel Aviv and Haifa
19 January	Air sorties against Iraq reach 4000; widespread destruction of Iraq's water, fuel and electrical supplies. Large anti-war protests in US
21 January	Iran protests at scale of US bombing
22 January	Iraq fires three Scud missiles at Tel Aviv
23 January	Air sorties against Iraq reach 12,000; war damage creates 35-mile long, 10-mile wide oil slick in Gulf
28 January	Pro-Iraq general strike in Morocco supported by government
29 January	Iraqi forces capture Saudi border town of Khafji; French defence minister Chévènement resigns in protest at scale of bombing of Iraq
1 February	Allies recapture Khafji
3 February	Allied sorties against Iraq reach 41,000. Pope Paul condemns the war
7 February	Iran proposes peace plan; no response from West. Allies claim to have destroyed 80% of Iraq's bridges
15 February	Baghdad says it is willing to withdraw from Kuwait; Soviet foreign minister welcomes the offer; Bush calls it 'a cruel hoax'
18 February	Gorbachev proposes eight-point peace plan
20 February	Allied air sorties against Iraq reach 85,000
22 February	Bush rejects Gorbachev peace plan
24 February	US-led forces launch ground offensive (Operation 'Desert Sabre')
25 February	Soviet Union proposes peace plan; Saddam orders withdrawal from Kuwait
26 February	Bush rejects new Soviet peace plan. Saddam confirms Iraqi withdrawal
27 February	Kuwaiti and Saudi troops control Kuwait City. Air sorties reach 106,000
28 February	Bush orders ceasefire. Iraq accepts ceasefire terms

Japan, because of the time difference, was the first major state to hear the full details of the invasion; the US was going to bed. A few days later, after much agitation in the world community, President Bush appeared on national television to declare: 'In the life of a nation we're called upon to declare who we are and what we believe. Sometimes these choices are not easy. But today, as President, I ask for your support in a decision I've made to stand up for what's right and condemn what's wrong, all in the cause of peace . . . The mission of our troops is wholly defensive . . . They will not initiate hostilities . . .'. At a press conference on the same day, Bush repeated that the aim of the US military presence was *not to drive the Iraqis out of Kuwait.*[75] The task of badgering King Fahd into 'requesting' US protection had been accomplished, despite Fahd's initial refusal to countenance American troops in Saudi Arabia.[76] And, as the Iraqi forces began looting Kuwait, the US administration developed its plan for the orchestration of its UN 'flag of convenience'.

In a meeting with Joseph Wilson, the American chargé d'affaires in Baghdad on 6 August, Saddam Hussein declared that since 1975 Iraq and Saudi Arabia had enjoyed good relations and that there was no reason why the Iraqi–Saudi links should be harmful to US interests: '. . . there is no danger to Saudi Arabia. If you want to push Saudi Arabia to do something against our interests, that is another thing . . . Kuwait was always part of Iraq . . . But Saudi Arabia is a completely sovereign state. . . ' Saddam also pointed out that his threats against Israel were only intended to deter an Israeli nuclear attack on Iraq. ABC Television had in fact deliberately edited the broadcast interview with Saddam to create the wrong impression, an early indication of the news manipulation that the West would practise to justify the resort to war.[77]

After Saddam Hussein had repeated his assurance that in the appropriate circumstances he would withdraw from Kuwait, Joseph Wilson commented that the Iraqi leader had given him 'a generally assuring picture'; and at the end of the meeting Wilson, the accredited US representative in Ambassador April Glaspie's absence, declared: 'I must congratulate you on the high professional standard with which your Ministry of Foreign Affairs is acting.'[78] At that time, four days after the Iraqi invasion, Saddam Hussein had agreed to a mini-summit to settle the Kuwaiti question, had agreed to accelerate the pace of Iraqi withdrawals (some military contingents had already returned to Iraq), had sent a secret proposal to Washington outlining a package solution, and conveyed various assurances to President Bush. Nothing of this was given attention in the Western media. In one interpretation Washington could have secured the early withdrawal of Iraqi forces but had no interest in so doing: '*Washington and London had decided that Iraq should be dealt with firmly, as an example to others. It was now preferable, from their point of view, that Iraqi troops should stay in Kuwait and take the consequences, even if this made life difficult for the Kuwaitis. Saddam Hussein had stepped into a trap and would have to stay there until the West was ready to finish with him.*'[79] (my italics)

In September 1990 there were further signs (for those who cared to notice them) that Saddam Hussein wanted to leave Kuwait, despite his bluster and repeated claims that many people had always regarded Kuwait as part of Iraq, but that he feared even a withdrawal would not now resolve the crisis he had provoked. He also no doubt felt that a withdrawal with no concession from the Kuwaitis would weaken him in the eyes of the Arab world and possibly even threaten his regime at home. His dilemma was fast becoming acute as it emerged that the Arabs themselves, stymied at every turn by Western impatience, would be unable to find a solution. A group of US senators had flown to the Gulf for talks with various Arab leaders. They had been disappointed that King Fahd had nothing new to say, and incensed that Emir Jaber of Kuwait – with obvious time on his hands – refused to meet them. They had then journeyed to meet President Mubarak in Cairo and President Zayed bin Sultan al Nahayan in Abu Dhabi, the capital of the United Arab Emirates (at this latter stopover, Daniel Patrick Moynihan, the New York Democrat, in response to Sheikh Zayed's praise for the brave Kuwaitis, felt obliged to remark: 'Your Grace, the Kuwaitis left their wives. They left their servants. They took their money and stuffed it in Swiss bank accounts. That is not my definition of courage'.)[80] One of the other members of the US delegation, Senator William Cohen of Maine, later reported to President Bush: 'We visited the Kuwaitis, we saw the Kuwaitis and we realised that Kuwaitis are willing to fight – until every US soldier has dropped.'[81]

By now the US intentions were plain, despite the much-hyped 'defensive' posture of operation Desert Shield: already, in early September, targets throughout Iraq were being selected for a massive bombing campaign, and the battle-worthiness of US troop deployments was being assessed. The Air Force chief of staff, General Michael J. Dugan, reported that the Iraqis had not distinguished themselves in the Iran–Iraq war and that their army was incompetent. Again, such an assessment ran directly against the later propaganda that the valiant American forces would have to contend with a vast and impressive military deployment. By the end of September US intelligence was reporting some 430,000 Iraqi troops in Kuwait and southern Iraq (an estimate that was later disputed), and it was admitted that because the Iraqi forces were digging in (that is, working to secure a defensive posture) an Iraqi invasion of Saudi Arabia was unlikely. Now Saddam, allowed no negotiating loophole, was bogged down; politically unable – because of his miscalculations – to extricate himself, he was forced to witness with growing impotence the deteriorating course of events. The Ba'ath leaders were discouraged from discussing the question of withdrawal, as that would only weaken morale. The Bush administration continued to plan for an offensive initiative, though General Dugan had been fired for letting the cat out of the bag (said a defence department spokesman, the point was not whether Dugan had spoken the truth but that 'he spoke out about items that were not his to discuss on the public record in a very tense situation').

The American people and Congress had at that stage shown their reluctance to agree the war option. A *New York Times*–CBS poll in August 1990 suggested that only 54 per cent of the American people believe that US troops should engage in combat, with a *USA Today* survey finding 78 per cent opposing a first strike against Iraq.[82] President Gorbachev and the UN Secretary-General, both increasingly ineffectual, continued to urge a negotiated settlement, but it was becoming increasingly obvious that the Bush administration was resolutely opposed to any useful negotiations – a situation that was destined to persist throughout the entire period of the crisis, despite occasional bouts of public-relations window-dressing.

On 8 October Saddam saw a glimmer of hope. Following a confrontation in Jerusalem between Temple Mount Faithful activists, a Jewish group led by Gershon Salomon, and devout Palestinians, led by Sheikh Fadhallah Silwadi, the Israelis used tear gas, plastic bullets and live ammunition against the demonstrating Palestinians. By 11.30 a.m. about twenty Palestinians had been killed with another 150 wounded. This 'slaughter on the mount'[83] was the 'bloodiest day of the Palestinian intifada',[84] an event that shocked the world. Would this massacre, Saddam wondered, be enough to shatter the fragile Washington-sponsored coalition in the Gulf? Would it be enough to force the mercenary Arab states to break away from their US paymasters? Saddam's hopes were dashed. A UN resolution condemning the Israeli action was, to the amazement of many observers (and to the horror of the Israeli government), supported by the United States. The Coalition was saved and the preparations for war continued apace.

9 October to 30 November 1990

There were now suggestions, reported in *The New York Times*, that US-led offensive operations would begin on 15 October.[85] This possibility had angered General H. Norman Schwarzkopf, not because he was opposed in principle to the offensive option but because he felt that the massive US forces in Saudi Arabia were not yet ready. On 10 October Marine Major General Robert B. Johnston, Schwarzkopf's chief of staff, met with General Colin Powell, Secretary of Defence Dick Cheney and others at the Pentagon to discuss the details of the planned offensive. Even at this early stage it was obvious that the hype surrounding the 'defensive' Desert Shield was deliberate cover for an altogether different agenda: Iraq – and, where necessary, Kuwait – would be massively bombed as a lengthy prelude to the final ground assault. At this time, while the details of the offensive option were being picked over, Secretary of State James Baker was suggesting that the mandatory sanctions on Iraq were 'tightening with increasing severity' and that they might work, so avoiding recourse to the military option. On 15 October Bush accused Saddam Hussein of war crimes; and, in line with

Margaret Thatcher's suggestion for a UN resolution that would call for the eventual trial of Iraqi leaders, he commented: 'Hitler revisited. But remember, when Hitler's war ended, there were the Nuremberg trials.'[86] It was also emerging at this time that the US administration had actively encouraged Saddam 'to pursue an aggressive policy of higher oil prices' before the invasion of Kuwait.[87]

On 24 October Yevgeni Primakov, Gorbachev's envoy, had his second meeting with Saddam (his first, on 5 October, had left Primakov 'not pessimistic' about a political solution). By now, deserters were swelling the growing anti-war chorus throughout the United States,[88] and Democrats in the US Congress were declaring themselves 'emphatically opposed to any military action'.[89] *On 31 October, before any UN authorisation had been given, Bush secretly decided that the air campaign against Iraq would begin in mid-January 1991, to be followed by a large-scale land offensive.*[90] He also decided that a UN mandate would be helpful window-dressing. In early November Bush made public his offensive intentions, and James Baker began the arm-twisting in the UN to secure the mandatory 'force' resolution. Primakov reported in mid-November that he had seen 'an evolution' of Saddam's position between their two meetings: Saddam, he observed, no longer had any interest in defending his take-over of Kuwait, being more concerned that the West had decided to destroy his regime, whatever action he took.[91] On 20 November a *New York Times*–CBS poll revealed that 51 per cent felt that Bush had not given adequate reasons for his deployment of more than 400,000 US troops in the Gulf; with 62 per cent reckoning that 'protecting oil supplies' was an inadequate reason for going to war. The approval rating for Bush had now fallen to 50 per cent. On 22 November, during his much-hyped Thanksgiving visit to Saudi Arabia, Bush asked the emir of Kuwait: 'When do you want us to go to war?' Emir Jabel al-Sabah replied: 'This minute, before this hour.' Bush responded by saying 'we are going to fight quite soon . . .'; Saddam had made the confrontation 'a question of him or me . . . The future of my presidency and my place in history depends (*sic*) on the outcome'.[92]

Secretary of State James Baker had by now successfully completed one of his primary tasks; that of ensuring, by dint of various bribes and threats (see *The Fabrication of Consensus*, above), that the useful 'force' resolution would be agreed in the UN Security Council. On 29 November 1990 the vote was taken on this crucial Resolution 678, the broadest UN authorisation for war since 1950 (in the case of Korea).[93] The resolution was passed 12 to 2 (Cuba and Yemen), with China abstaining: a predictable outcome following James Baker's creative diplomacy. Resolution 678 made reference to the earlier resolutions; in particular, to Resolution 660, the original demand for the withdrawal of Iraqi forces from Kuwait. It also authorised Member States, 'unless Iraq on or before 15 January 1991' fully implemented Resolution 660 (and all subsequent resolutions), *'to use all necessary means'* to uphold all the relevant resolutions (my italics).

The authorisation of 'all necessary means' has generally been taken as synonymous with authorisation for *force*, a sanction for the military option.[94] In fact this interpretation can be questioned. It relies on the impression that 'all' logically entails every option, without giving due attention to the qualifying weight of the adjective 'necessary'. Who was to decide what was *necessary*? The resolution, despite the requirement that the Security Council 'remain seized of the matter', made no stipulation as to how 'necessary means' would be determined on 16 January 1991, at the expiry of the deadline. Was every Security Council member to make a unilateral estimation? The United Nations itself was in no position to make such an estimation since no relevant protocols had been articulated; and moreover the Military Staff Committee specified in Article 47 had not been established, a manifest violation of the Charter. Nor was there any reference to judgements that might be made by the UN sanctions committee, charged with the task of monitoring the impact of earlier mandatory resolutions intended to compel an Iraqi withdrawal.

These are not minor considerations, but ones directly relevant to the legality of the US-sponsored war against Iraq. It is significant that various Arab experts – including Adnan Pachacchi, Iraqi ambassador to the UN in the 1960s – have argued that the legal basis of Resolution 678 was unsound.[95] But perhaps most significant are the clear signs that even James Baker himself, having negotiated the wording of 678, was not happy that 'all necessary means' was synonymous with 'force'. Thus, in his negotiations with Soviet foreign minister Shevardnadze, Baker *'backed off his own phrase. It was too indefinite . . .'*, though he later *'gave in'*.[96] (my italics)

The situation at the end of November 1990 was that Bush had accomplished all the UN window-dressing he was likely to get. The unsound Resolution 678, in any event secured through threat and bribery, could now be hyped as UN authorisation for a superpower to wage unlimited war on a Third-World nation. There was little attention given in the Western media to the words that appear in the preamble to the UN Charter: *'We, the peoples of the United Nations, determined to save succeeding generations from the scourge of war . . .'.*

1 December 1990 to 16 January 1991

The diplomatic massaging of Resolution 678 through the UN Security

Council did not dispel the doubts in Congress about Bush's Gulf intentions. Thus Robert Dole, then the Republican leader in the Senate, and Richard Lugar, a senior member of the Foreign Relations Committee, demanded a 'put-up-or-shut-up' vote on Bush's policies. By now increasing reference was being made to the 1973 War Powers Act which stipulated that the president should consult with Congress before committing American troops to a combat area, and that if he did send troops he should withdraw them within ninety days unless Congress approved the deployment. Kuwait City, ravaged and pillaged by undisciplined Iraqi forces, had become a 'ghost town',[97] and reports were beginning to accumulate about Iraqi atrocities. Iraqi opposition groups gave signs of greater unity in their aim of toppling Saddam Hussein, and a London-based spokesman for the Kurdish Democratic Party reminded the world that there was 'an Iraqi opposition that speaks for the world'. Speculation was mounting about the likelihood of war but at the same time there was mounting evidence that sanctions were beginning to bite: recent visitors to Baghdad were reporting that the city had run out of bread (though meat was plentiful) and food rationing was 'draconian', with the provision of 'even these minimal rations . . . haphazard' outside Baghdad.[98] A *New York Times*–CBS poll of 1044 people, conducted during 9–11 December, revealed that 48 per cent of respondents believed that the US should 'wait and see' if the 15 January deadline was met, with a larger *Los Angeles Times* poll showing only 37 per cent backing war if Iraq did not withdraw.

On 9 January 1991 James Baker held a six-and-a-half-hour meeting with Tariq Aziz at the Intercontinental Hotel in Geneva.[99] The credibility of Baker, resolved not to negotiate but simply to deliver a message ('Get out of Kuwait by 15th or be forced out!'), was in some doubt as a few months before he had 'viewed Iraq's border claims as a local Arab dispute in which the US should not be involved.'[100] Before long he had emerged from the meeting to declare: 'I heard nothing that suggested to me any Iraqi flexibility whatsoever.' There was also mounting evidence of a split between the UN Secretary-General, Perez de Cuellar, and the US on Washington's handling of the crisis. It was reported that Perez de Cuellar had a *deep distaste for the war deadline* forced by Bush through the Security Council, and that in a diplomatic approach he 'could hardly have done worse than the Americans'.[101] Further evidence emerged in his meeting with Saddam Hussein in Baghdad on 13 January. Here it transpired that Washington had illicitly prevented Tariq Aziz from visiting the United Nations in New York to present the Iraqi case (Perez de Cuellar: '*I tried. I said [to the US] that was not in keeping with the UN's Headquarters Agreement with the United*

States . . .'). A later exchange provided further evidence of Perez de Cuellar's disquiet about US behaviour (*The Independent*, 12 December 1991):

> *Saddam Hussein:* . . . On 12 August we made an initiative. We did not expect it would be accepted in full. However, we never thought it would be turned down without being looked into. The President of the US turned down the initiative while he was on the plane two hours after it was announced and without looking into it . . .
> *Perez de Cuellar:* These were not my decisions, but the resolutions of the Security Council.
> *Saddam Hussein:* These are American resolutions. This is an American age. What the US wants at present is the thing that is passed, and not what the Security Council wants.
> *Perez de Cuellar:* I agree with you. . . .

On 12 January 1991, after furious lobbying by the White House, the US Congress voted to authorise war in the Gulf. The vote was far from overwhelming (Senate: 52 to 47; House of Representatives: 250 to 183), but now Bush had the sanction that he needed. This was the first time since the Second World War that Congress had voted to authorise war, despite Washington's many military engagements, and only the sixth time in its history. Some Congressmen declared that their vote was intended to increase the chance of a peaceful settlement, since now Saddam would know the consequences of a failure to withdraw from Kuwait by the specified 16 January deadline; but, with a different emphasis, White House officials were quick to declare that President Bush now had 'a blank cheque' for any military action.[102] Some observers rated the Senate vote, closer than forecasts, only a 'partial victory' for Bush, less than a 'clear and unequivocal' message to Saddam Hussein,[103] but the die was cast.

The United States, desperate to maintain the Coalition, ignored the Soviet crackdown in Lithuania,[104] just as it had ignored the expansion of Syrian military ambitions in Lebanon. On 14 January France made a further effort to avert war by asking the UN Security Council to endorse a statement that implicitly linked the withdrawal of Iraqi forces to a commitment to hold a Middle East peace conference 'at an appropriate moment'. The plan held no attractions for Washington; a senior US diplomat at the UN declared: 'We intend to block it'; and in this the US attitude was supported by Yuliy Vorontsov, the Soviet ambassador to the United Nations. At the same time the Iraqi National Assembly was voting Saddam Hussein full power to wage war or make peace.

Washington had successfully blocked the French peace plan, with Britain even going so far as to criticise France for bad faith in making the attempt. Perez de Cuellar commented that it was 'perhaps a little late for embarking on any other efforts' to avoid war. President George Bush was reported to be 'at peace with himself'.[105]

16 January to 23 February 1991

The air onslaught on Iraq (Operation 'Desert Storm') began on 16 January 2330 GMT with F-117 Stealth bombers dropping laser-guided Pathway bombs on Baghdad. Then a massive wave of air strikes was extended throughout Iraq and Kuwait, with the USS *Wisconsin* and USS *Missouri*, stationed in the Gulf, firing Tomahawk cruise missiles at such targets as military command centres, airports, missile sites and oil refineries. An initial task was to destroy Iraq's air defence systems so that subsequent bombing raids could be carried out with minimal interference. One of the first targets was the Iraqi airforce headquarters at Habbaniyah, about 60 kilometres from Baghdad, which received a hit from a 2000-pound laser-guided bomb dropped from a radar-invisible Stealth bomber. In the first twenty-four hours of the war, allied aircraft flew 2000 sorties, and more than one hundred Tomahawk missiles, each weighing more than half a tonne, were fired. By the end of February more than 106,000 sorties had been flown and more than 88,000 tonnes of bombs had been dropped.

Within the first minutes of the opening of hostilities the 'idea that a Third World country could absorb and withstand an intensive aerial bombardment by a superpower and its allies began to fall apart . . .'.[106] It was being made clear that this was only the beginning, the first phase of a sustained air assault; US Defence Secretary Dick Cheney told reporters: 'It doesn't end.' Wave after wave of bombers were screaming over Baghdad to attack a broad range of targets. Said Colonel Ray Davies, chief maintenance officer of the US F-15 airbase, 'This is history in the making. It is awesome, absolutely awesome. The ground shook and you felt it. We have been waiting here for five months now and we finally got to do what we were sent to do.' Heavy B-52 bombers, notorious for their carpet-bombing of Vietnam, were being moved forward from their base in the Indian Ocean. On 17 January 300,000 people marched in Berlin, Bonn and other German cities in protest against the war. Anti-US demonstrations took place in Algeria, Morocco, Tunisia and Mauritania; in Libya, a country of 4.5 million, a million people took to the streets to protest. At the UN the Yemeni representative called on the permanent members of the Security Council to 'put an end to the bloodshed and destruction'; and in Amman an official spokesman declared: 'The Jordanian leadership, government and people denounce the brutal aggression against an Arab, Muslim country and people who have always defended their Arab brethren without hesitation.'[107]

On 18 January 'an apparently prostrate Iraq' fired a batch of Scud missiles at Haifa and Tel Aviv (reports varied about how many); in one account, three missiles had landed in Tel Aviv, one in Haifa, three in largely unpopulated areas and one in an unknown area.[108] The Israeli cabinet went into emergency session to decide what action, if any, to take. Washington had urged Israeli restraint as essential to the preservation of the Coalition, though later reports suggested that Israeli warplanes did in fact fly combat sorties over Iraq.[109] President Bush called the Scud attack 'an act of terror, designed to weaken the anti-Iraq coalition', though he refused to say whether the Israelis had provided assurances that Israel would not retaliate. Moshe Arens, the Israeli defence minister, declared: 'We have said publicly and to the Americans that if we were attacked we would react. We were attacked. We will react, certainly.'[110] At the United Nations, peace initiatives by India and Algeria were rejected by the United States.

Saturation bombing raids on Iraqi troops were now being carried out by US A-10 and B 52 aircraft (it was reported that a stick of bombs from a B-52 was able to create a square-mile crater).[111] The first skirmishes between US and Iraqi troops were reported also. On 20 January Iraq fired three Scud missiles at Dhahran in Saudi Arabia, with each reportedly brought down by defensive Patriot missiles (after the war this was seen as a mixed blessing: damage was rendered wider though perhaps lighter, by causing a Scud to disintegrate in flight). Shortly after midnight two more Scuds were detected speeding towards Dhahran, and four heading towards Riyadh. One report suggested that a defensive Patriot missile might have exploded in the outskirts of Riyadh, though official confirmation was not given.[112] On 22 January there were widespread protests at Saddam's decision to parade allied prisoners – three Americans, two Britons, an Italian and a Kuwaiti – on television, an act in violation of the legally enforceable Geneva Conventions. President Bush's approval rating in the United States had now reached 84 per cent. The Iraqi ambassador in London, Azmi Shafiq al-Salihi, summoned to the Foreign Office to be told that Britain regarded the forced presentation of allied prisoners on Iraqi television as a breach of the Conventions, pointed to a newspaper photograph (taken from television film) of a US marine with Iraqi PoWs. The deputy legal director of the International Committee in Geneva, François Bugnon, suggested that the American showing of Iraqi prisoners might be illegal.[113] It was emerging also that the US and Britain had the ending of Saddam's rule one of their war aims, even though this objective was not part of any of the twelve UN resolutions (in particular, this aim did not appear in the crucial Resolution 678).[114] The US confirmed that it intended to put Saddam on trial, and a senior British official declared that Britain 'no longer sees a role for the bedraggled and humiliated leader' that Saddam would have become by the end of the war. On 22 January a Scud missile hit flats in Tel Aviv, killing three and injuring seventy.

The saturation bombing of the Iraqi troops – most of them hapless conscripts – continued round the clock: on 23 January General Colin Powell, talking of the Iraqi army, commented: 'First we are going to cut it off. Then we are going to kill it.' Days later, an Iraqi Exocet attack in the Gulf was foiled, and the allies captured a small island, the first reclaimed Kuwaiti territory in the war. By the end of January a vast oil slick was moving down the Gulf, blamed by the allies on Saddam's 'environmental terrorism' (but after the war found to be caused as much by allied bombing of Kuwaiti oil installations). Declared President Bush: 'It's kind of sick. Saddam Hussein continues to amaze the world. First he uses Scud missiles with no military value whatsoever. Then he uses the lives of prisoners of war. Now he resorts to enormous environmental damage.' On 25 January fresh Scud missile attacks were launched on Israel and Saudi Arabia (with some injuries caused by falling debris after the Scuds had been destroyed in the air). Over the next few days, some one hundred Iraqi aircraft, not risked by Saddam in the air war, flew to Iran for sanctuary.

On 30 January Iraqi troops captured the small Saudi border town of Khafji, using five Soviet T-55 tanks and armoured personnel carriers. After a number of other skirmishes a US captain who had called in punitive air strikes remarked: 'It felt really good. We kicked their asses.' A few days later, after inflicting heavy losses on the Iraqi forces, the allies retook Khafji; and at the same time there were reports that the much-vaunted Tomahawk cruise missiles, 'considerably less accurate than claimed by the allies', were sometimes landing in civilian areas around Baghdad.[115] By now it was clear that massive damage was being inflicted on the whole of Iraq. In one report Iraq would 'take 10 years to rebuild'; in another the country had been 'bombed back to the lowest rungs of the Third World'.[116] Now Iraqi cities were without light or water and with little food. Nguyen Hai Xuan, a Vietnamese civil engineer from Haiphong, who had lived through the B-52 bombing of his home city, commented: 'I thought I was back in Vietnam.' In Baghdad at that time there was no water or electricity, acute shortages of food and medicines, and remorseless bombing around the clock. By now there was increasing speculation about the launching of the ground war that would at last bring matters to a close. United States war planners were well aware that the hot weather was approaching, and that it would be useful to end the war before the start of the holy month of Ramadan on March 17. General Schwarzkopf, according to Pentagon sources, was planning for a mid-February offensive dubbed internally 'the Valentine's Day massacre'.[117] On 5 February Israel launched fresh bombing raids in Lebanon.

In Iraq the devastation continued, with the whole country 'bombed back to last century'.[118] Wave after wave of bombing strikes had destroyed virtually every power station in the country; every public telecommunications building had been destroyed; scores of refineries had gone up in flames; the sewage system had been massively damaged, and even the few pumps that were still functional had no electricity. Direct civilian deaths because of the bombing continuing to mount, with the first evidence emerging of deaths through malnutrition, razed hospitals and disease epidemics. Some bombing strikes on civilians received publicity; most did not. A bombing attack on a bridge in Nasiriyeh on 4 February killed forty-seven civilians and wounded a further 102, with many people tossed into the Euphrates when the bridge exploded and carried downstream.[119] On 13 January four hundred civilians – men, women and children – were burnt to death when US planes bombed the Amiriya shelter in Baghdad.[120]

On 15 February a statement issued by the Iraqi Revolutionary Command Council (RCC) indicated that Iraq was willing to withdraw from Kuwait. President Bush used the 'unacceptable old conditions' in the statement as a reason for dismissing the offer as a 'cruel hoax' (British Prime Minister John Major echoed the US response by dubbing the Iraqi statement a 'bogus sham').[121] The RCC had declared: '*In order to achieve a dignified and acceptable political settlement, Iraq has decided to accept the UN security council resolution No 660 of 1990, including the clause related to an Iraqi withdrawal*'; in rejecting the offer Bush commented: '. . . there's another way for the bloodshed to stop, and that is for the Iraqi military and the Iraqi people to take matters into their own hands, to force Saddam to step aside'.[122] The goalposts had been moved and now there seemed nothing to prevent the US-led land offensive.

On 18 February Tariq Aziz arrived in Moscow to discuss with President Gorbachev the Iraqi proposal for withdrawal. At the same time there were a number of skirmishes on the Iraq border; in one of these a US Apache helicopter accidentally fired missiles at two American armoured vehicles, killing two US soldiers and wounding six (this brought to ten the number of US soldiers killed by 'friendly fire', out of the total of fourteen killed in combat at that stage). In his brief talks with Tariq Aziz, Gorbachev saw what Bush had dismissed as 'a cruel hoax' as 'an important beginning towards peace'; and the Soviet president went further, being prepared to express 'cautious optimism' about Iraqi flexibility.[123] Now Bush was rejecting Soviet support for the Iraqi peace initiative, declaring that there would be 'no concessions and no negotiations'; Perez de Cuellar, UN Secretary-General, threw his weight behind the Soviet efforts, but to no avail. It was clear that Washington was well prepared to override other permanent members of the Security Council and the Secretary-General himself in order to prosecute the planned land offensive. The White House spokesman, Marlin Fitzwater, commented that 'We are assuming that the war will have to be prosecuted to the end,' adding that the US was 'in no way bound' by any deal between Iraq and the Soviet Union.

On 22 February the Soviet Union announced that Saddam Hussein had accepted the fresh Soviet terms for an ending of the Gulf War. This came as 'a stunning blow' for the United States, and in a subsequent telephone conversation Bush raised his 'serious concerns' with Gorbachev.[124] He then publicly overrode the Soviet and Iraqi peace proposals and issued a blunt warning for Saddam Hussein to start withdrawing from Kuwait by noon (1700 GMT) on 23 February or face a massive land invasion. No-one can have expected Saddam to heed the unvarnished US threat, and the RCC issued a predictable statement: 'We confirm that Iraq wants peace and is working to seriously support the Soviet initiative and facilitate its success, but not out of fear of Bush's threat.' Iraqi troops now began firing Kuwaiti oil wells, in addition to those already set alight by allied bombing. There was nothing now to stop the largest land invasion since the Second World War.

23 February to 28 February 1991

Minutes before the US-specified deadline for the withdrawal of Iraqi forces from Kuwait, a Scud missile, the thirty-sixth of the war, was launched against Israel. Then, on 23 February 1991, President Bush gave the order for an all-out war to expel the Iraqis. Washington had decided that the American public and the wider world community would not be told the character of the war that would be waged by a technological superpower against the hapless Iraqi conscripts in the desert. What the journalist and publisher John R. MacArthur called 'Operation Desert Muzzle' meant that 'The American public got only the military view of this war for the most part . . .'.[125] The American public would not be told the true nature of the weapons used, the scale of the American-led slaughter, or the extent to which the United States had violated the Geneva Protocols and other provisions of international law. Powerful military forces, clear victors in the field, often display a purblind indifference to the civilising constraints of ethics and law; the US intended to be victorious.

Within hours, hundreds of allied tanks, supported by virtually unchallenged air power, had swept north into Iraq to arc round towards the surviving Iraqi forces in Kuwait. By the night of the 24 February, reports suggested that allied contingents were already in the suburbs of Kuwait City. A US pilot commented, after a bombing mission over Kuwait, 'It looks like what hell would look like down there. The country is on fire.'[126] On 25 February an announcement on Baghdad Radio stated that Iraqi troops had been ordered to leave Kuwait, a statement that was treated with contempt by the allied command. While battles were raging in the desert a Scud missile hit a US Army reserve barracks in Khobar City, near Dhahran, killing at least twelve soldiers – with a further forty still unaccounted for – and injuring twenty-five more. By now hundreds of thousands of allied troops were sweeping north, destroying hundreds of Iraqi tanks and taking tens of thousands of prisoners. On the morning of 27 February allied tanks began moving into Kuwait City. As the demoralised Iraqi forces struggled to escape from Kuwait there were reports of random killings of Kuwaitis and the burning of some two hundred buildings, including the main hotels, the parliament building and government offices. The Kuwaiti resistance reported that fleeing Iraqis were leaving most of their equipment behind, and that as many as 3000 had surrendered to them. The CBS TV journalist, Bob McKeown, one of the first into the liberated Kuwait City, confirmed stories of executions, rape and torture during the last few days of the Iraqi occupation: 'Everyone has a story to tell about a friend or relative who had been killed.' A Kuwaiti woman said to him: 'If you come to Kuwait, you will say this is not Kuwait at all. Kuwait, it's not Kuwait any more.'

On 27 February a Pentagon official was reported as saying that the war 'could be over within hours'. General Schwarzkopf reported that allied forces had 'rendered completely ineffective over 29 Iraqi divisions' and that there were 'very, very large numbers' of Iraqi dead – though then, as later, he refused to say (even approximately) how many. Tariq Aziz then conveyed a letter to the United Nations, in which Iraq agreed to meet most of the allied demands; White House spokesman Marlin Fitzwater commented that this 'is still a conditional offer and falls far short of what's necessary'. The Security Council issued a statement insisting that Iraq agree to observe all the twelve resolutions imposed since the invasion of Kuwait. Soon afterwards, on the morning of 28 February, President Bush announced that the US and its allies would end combat operations if Iraq laid down its arms.

On television, Bush declared: 'I am pleased to announce that at midnight tonight, Eastern Standard Time (0500 GMT, 28 February), exactly 100 hours since ground operations commenced and six weeks since the start of Operation Desert Storm, all United States and coalition forces will suspend offensive combat operations . . . This war is now behind us. Ahead of us is the task of achieving a potentially historic peace' in the Middle East. The 1991 Gulf War was over.

The character of the war, like the character of the Iraqi atrocities in Kuwait, was plain for all who chose to look: despite all the censorship, all the news manipulation, all the propaganda, what the United States and its allies had perpetrated soon became clear.

The bombing missions over Iraq were a 'turkey shoot . . . It's almost like you flipped on the light in the kitchen at night and the cockroaches start scurrying, and we're killing them.'[127] Long before the end of the war the Iraqi Red Crescent, quoted by former US attorney general Ramsey Clark, estimated Iraqi civilian deaths at between 6000 and 7000 (Clark himself described the bombed-out Basra as 'a human and civilian tragedy . . . staggering in its expanse'). The weapons used were sufficiently modern to achieve their purpose. The laser-guided bombs, much less than 10 per cent of the total tonnage dropped, were accompanied by the B-52 deliveries, massive waves of saturation bombing able to lay out 'carpets' of total destruction in village, town and desert; by the Rockeye cluster bombs, each containing 247 'anti-personnel' grenades that individually explode into 2000 high-velocity razor-sharp fragments (a device that 'shreds people'); by fuel-air explosives (FAEs), dropped to create massive fireballs over Iraqi positions.[128]

A high-tech video, taken at night and shown in a briefing given by the US XVIII Airborne Corps, showed Iraqi soldiers shot to pieces in the dark, some blown apart by cannon shells.[129] The Iraqi soldiers, reported John Balzar of *The Los Angeles Times*, were 'like ghostly sheep, flushed from a pen . . . bewildered and terrified, jarred from sleep and fleeing their bunkers under a hellstorm of fire. One by one they were cut down by attackers they couldn't see or understand. Some were literally blown to bits by bursts of 30mm exploding cannon. One man dropped, writhed on the ground and struggled to his feet. Another burst tore him apart . . .'. One of the US pilots, Ron Balak, commented: '. . . When I got back I sat there on the wing and I was laughing . . . I was probably laughing at myself . . . sneaking up there and blowing this up and blowing that up. A guy came up to me and we were slapping each other on the back . . . and then he said, "By God, I thought we had shot into a damn farm. It looked like somebody had opened the sheep pen." ' Chief Warrant Officer Brian Walker was looking forward to more action: '. . . there is nothing that can take them out like an Apache. It will be a duck hunt'.[130]

Most of the US-led slaughter of Iraqi conscripts by the tens of thousands received no publicity: film shot by the US Army has not been released, and journalists were routinely excluded from most of the killing fields. Two of the massive Iraqi retreats from Kuwait, difficult to disguise because of their scale, received some graphic attention in the Western media. Allied aircraft had arrived as columns of desperate men, carrying their loot from a ransacked Kuwait, queued in military and civilian vehicles to escape back home. The (mostly) American aircraft waited their turn to attack the fleeing Iraqi convoy with cluster bombs, rockets and anti-tank missiles. By the morning of 28 February a section of the Jahra–Basra road at Mitla ridge 'had been turned into a gigantic scrap-yard, with some 2000 military and civilian vehicles destroyed, some charred, some exploded, some reduced to heaps of tangled metal, with dead bodies and their severed limbs scattered all over, some corpses petrified in their vehicles, and others incinerated, with their faces reduced to grinning teeth'.[131] The Mitla massacre of retreating Iraqis was not the only such event in the closing hours of the Gulf War. A similar rout and slaughter occurred on the Jahra–Umm Qasr highway, a coastal road running though the desert. Here too were the masses of destroyed vehicles, the scattered loot, and the charred and bloated corpses. Dogs 'snarled around the corpse of one soldier. They had eaten most of his flesh . . . the dogs had eaten the legs from the inside out, and the epidermis lay in collapsed and hairy folds, like leg-shaped blankets, with feet attached . . .'.[132] The American journalist Bob Dogrin wrote of 'scores of soldiers' lying 'in and around the vehicles, mangled and bloated in the drifting desert sands . . .'. He accompanied Major Bob Nugent, a US army intelligence officer, who commented: 'Even in Vietnam, I didn't see anything like this.'[133]

The retreating Iraqi forces, in total disarray and desperation, were remorselessly attacked over a period of more than forty hours, a 'concentration of killing . . . unequalled since Hiroshima . . .'.[134] The attacking US aircraft participating in the massive slaughter were so numerous that planes had to be diverted to avoid mid-air collisions. Tony Clifton of *Newsweek* reported: '. . . the great red flames and then these weird little contorted figures . . . Next morning we went up to see what we'd done . . . there were bodies all over the place . . . I remember at one point looking down at the car track and I was up to my ankles in blood. The tracks were filled with blood and there were very white-faced men going round saying, "Jesus. Did we really do this?" '[135]

In General Schwarzkopf's own account, an Iraqi representative, Ahmad, at the cease-fire talks asked him why Iraq had been invaded 'after we had withdrawn from Kuwait and announced it on the television and radio'. Schwarzkopf refused to comment, saying only, 'I think we will leave it to history.' And Ahmad replied: 'I have just mentioned it for history.'[136]

The American casualties in the 1991 Gulf War were 137 killed in action (many from 'friendly fire') and seven missing in action. Estimates of the Iraqi casualties range from 50,000 to 300,000 dead, with countless more wounded and traumatised. General Schwarzkopf ordered thousands of Iraqi corpses to be bulldozed into mass graves in the desert – in scenes that must have resembled the disposal of bodies in the Nazi death camps – with no attempt to conduct the body counts and to make the other provisions for the dead specified in the Geneva Protocols. The number of the Iraqi dead and dying – conscripts, professional soldiers, civilians; men, women and children – continued to mount long after the ceasefire, as a bewildered and powerless people struggled to survive in a country that had been comprehensively devastated and which was now being denied the necessities of life. The ordinary people of Iraq, long helpless in the grip of a tyrant, had now been well inducted into the US-defined New World Order.

On 1 March 1991 President Bush declared (on the Middle East): 'There is a better climate now . . . we are going to try to lead.' Then he added, referring to the Arab countries, 'the US wants to be their friend'.[137] In June 1993 the Iraqi justice minister, Shabib al-Maliki, told the UN Human Rights Conference that the continuing sanctions against Iraq, demanded by the US, were a violation of human rights: 'The people of Iraq suffer today from shortages of food, medicine and medical requirements . . . the blockade is causing thousands of lives to be lost.'[138] In September 1993 the Iraqi health minister, Umeed Mubarak, said that more than 300,000 people had died because of sanctions, with 4000 children under five dying every month.[139] The Iraqi claims were supported by the findings of the UN-linked Food and Agriculture Organisation (FAO) and the World Food Programme (WFP). A joint FAO/WFP report stated that sanctions had caused 'persistent deprivation, chronic hunger, endemic undernutrition, massive unemployment and widespread human suffering'; noted many pre-famine indicators; and declared that 'a grave humanitarian tragedy is unfolding'.[140]

Notes

Chapter 1: After the 1991 Gulf War

1. Noam Chomsky, 'The weak shall inherit nothing', *The Guardian*, London, 25 March 1991.
2. In the early 1990s there were many signs of escalating commercial tensions between the United States and Japan. In 1992 there were growing threats of a trade war between the US and Europe. With the Cold War over, the leading commercial players of the world were increasingly able to revert to their traditional practices of economic confrontation.
3. Mike Graham, 'Bush finds comic relief in a ragbag of rivals', *The Sunday Times*, London, 8 September 1991.
4. *Ibid.* Virtually alone among the journalistic pundits, Andrew Stephen (*The Observer*, London, 8 September 1991), while opining that Bill Clinton 'has probably had too many girlfriends for comfort', reckoned that the 1992 election would be 'much closer, much more exciting, than everyone else seems to think'.
5. A detailed account of how journalists were restricted in their efforts to cover the Gulf War is given by John R. MacArthur, *Second Front, Censorship and Propaganda in the Gulf War*, Hill & Wang, New York, 1992.
6. Karl Waldron, 'Splintered remnants of a rout', *The Independent*, London, 4 March 1991.
7. Ed Vulliamy, 'Limbs and lives blasted away by allied bombs', *The Guardian*, London, 5 March 1991.
8. Bob Dogrin, 'Desert claims death convoy', *The Guardian*, London, 11 March 1991.
9. *Ibid.* See also the account by Michael Kelly, 'Carnage on a forgotten road', *The Guardian*, London, 11 April 1991.
10. Christopher Bellamy, 'Arithmetic of death in wake of Gulf conflict', *The Independent*, London, 20 March 1991.
11. Richard Norton-Taylor, 'Allies tot up Iraqi losses', *The Guardian*, London, 1 March 1991.
12. Simon Jones, 'US demographer sacked for exposing Iraqi civilian deaths', *The Independent*, London, 23 April 1992.
13. Robert Lifton, 'Last refuge of a hi-tech nation', *The Guardian*, London, 12 March 1991.
14. *Ibid.*
15. Patrick Sloyan, 'Iraqi troops buried alive say American officers', *The Guardian*, London, 13 September 1991.
16. Nick Cohen, 'Radioactive waste left in Gulf by allies', *The Independent on Sunday*, London, 10 November 1991; Nick Cohen and Tom Wilkie, 'Gulf teams not told of risk from uranium', *The Independent on Sunday*, London, 10 November 1991.
17. Patrick Cockburn, 'Pentagon revises its Gulf war scorecard', *The Independent*, London, 14 April 1992.

347

18. Barton Gellman, 'Study questions famed accuracy of US weapons', *The Guardian*, London, 11 April 1992.
19. *The Washington Post*, 18 March 1991.
20. Richard Norton-Taylor, 'Gulf war allies had nuclear option, claims officer', *The Guardian*, London, 28 September 1991.
21. Mohamed Heikal, *Illusions of Triumph, An Arab View of the Gulf War*, HarperCollins, London, 1992, p. 289.
22. Lee Hockstader, 'Health crisis looms in Baghdad', *The Guardian*, London, 5 March 1991.
23. *Ibid.*
24. Safa Haeri, 'Food and medicines "crucial" to save Iraq', *The Independent*, London, 26 March 1991.
25. Peter Jenkins, 'War continues by other means', *The Independent*, London, 24 April 1991.
26. Ed Vulliamy, 'Doctors find Iraq is slowly dying', *The Guardian*, London, 16 April 1991.
27. Susan Okie, 'Child death rate doubles in aftermath of Gulf conflict', *The Guardian*, London, 23 May 1991.
28. Patrick Tyler, 'Trade ban starves Iraqis', *The Guardian*, London, 25 June 1991.
29. *Ibid.*
30. Sara Helm, 'Child deaths "have trebled" since Gulf war', *The Independent*, London, 20 September 1991.
31. *Ibid.*
32. Helga Graham, 'Starving Iraqis riot as food crisis deepens', *The Observer*, London, 3 November 1991.
33. Sara Helm, 'Oxfam urges action to end Iraqi hardship', *The Independent*, London, 21 November 1991.
34. Marie Colvin, 'Saddam thrives as babies starve', *The Sunday Times*, 1 December 1991.
35. Louise Cainkar, 'Desert sin: a post-war journey through Iraq', in Phyllis Bennis and Michel Moushabeck (eds), *Beyond the Storm, A Gulf Crisis Reader*, Canongate, London, 1992, pp. 335–55.
36. Patrick E. Tyler, 'Bush links ending of trading ban to Hussein exit', *The New York Times*, 21 May 1991.
37. Helga Graham, 'King Hussein bursts sanctions to rebuild Saddam's power', *The Observer*, London, 23 June 1991.
38. Trevor Rowe, 'UN allows Iraqi sale of oil to buy food', *The Independent*, London, 16 August 1991; Mark Tran, 'UN permits sale of $1.6bn of Iraqi oil', *The Guardian*, 16 August 1991.
39. Tony Smythe, 'Oil revenues won't feed Iraq' (letter), *The Independent*, London, 19 August 1980; Leonard Doyle, 'Iraq oil exports "insufficient to prevent famine" ', *The Independent*, London, 7 September 1991.
40. Robert Fisk, 'Families vanish in tragedy without end', *The Independent*, London, 8 March 1991.
41. The character of the Kuwaiti regime had long been apparent. In 1986 the Emir abolished the embryonic democratic system and continued to rule by personal decree. Germaine Greer exposed the 'slave-owners of Kuwait', noting that the Emir is a kinsman of the Kuwaiti princesses, Sheika Faria al-Sabah and

Sheika Samiya, who in Britain subjected their imported slave Laxmi Swami to daily whippings and other torture (*The Independent Magazine*, London, 13 October 1990). The systematic abuse of human rights in Kuwait was well known: 'Now and then the *Kuwait Times* reported spectacular cases of servants thrown from roof-tops, burnt or blinded or battered to death; the systematic abuse they endured was unworthy of remark' (*ibid.*). Laxmi Swami was deliberately starved; if she tried to reach food from a dustbin through a barred window she was beaten 'sometimes with a broomstick or horse-whip, sometimes with a knotted electric flex' (*The Independent*, London, 8 February 1991). The UK Home Office issues visitors' visas to such slaves and denies them the right to work for any other employer. This has meant that over the last fifteen years some 40,000 slaves – owned by Kuwaiti royalty and other rich Arabs – have passed through Britain with no hope of escape or release.

42. Matthew Engel, 'Tensions between Kuwaitis and Palestinians sour peace', *The Guardian*, London, 6 March 1991.
43. Paul Taylor, 'Gun law of avenging Kuwaitis', *The Independent*, London, 20 March 1991.
44. Robert Block, 'Torture of Palestinians "supported by military" ', *The Independent*, London, 21 March 1991.
45. Kathy Evans, 'An emirate unfit for Palestinians', *The Guardian*, London, 13 March 1991.
46. Ian Glover-James, 'Iraqis live in fear as Kuwaitis take revenge', *The Sunday Times*, London, 24 March 1991.
47. John Kifner, 'US warns Kuwait to end Arab reprisals', *The Guardian*, London, 4 April 1991; Kathy Evans, 'Watchdogs on trial of Kuwaiti abuses', *The Guardian*, London, 9 April 1991.
48. Shyam Bhatia, 'Rapists run amok in Kuwait', *The Observer*, London, 14 April 1991.
49. Khaled Ghaleb, 'We toiled for them; now they curse us', *The Independent*, London, 17 April 1991.
50. Shyam Bhatia, 'Kuwaitis pave the way for public hangings', *The Observer*, London, 21 April 1991; Andrew Alderson, 'Rough justice at Kuwait's war-crime trials', *The Sunday Times*, London, 21 April 1991.
51. Michael Simmons, 'Amnesty asks emir to help end torture', *The Guardian*, London, 19 April 1991.
52. Robert Fisk, 'Kuwait's royal torturers', *The Independent*, London, 27 April 1991.
53. John Cassidy, 'Death verdicts fuel anger at Kuwait's chaos', *The Sunday Times*, London, 16 June 1991; Michael Simmons, 'Rights groups outraged by Kuwait trials', *The Guardian*, London, 18 June 1991; Kathy Evans, 'Kuwait moves trials to civilian courts', *The Guardian*, London, 26 June 1991.
54. 'Asian maids flee Kuwaiti terror', *The Sunday Times*, London, 3 May 1992.
55. Liz Thurgood, 'Kuwait "condones" assaults on maids', *The Guardian*, London, 15 April 1992.
56. Kathy Evans, 'Deportations raise fresh questions on Kuwait army,' *The Guardian*, London, 20 January 1993.
57. Julie Flint, 'Iraq in open revolt', *The Observer*, London, 3 March 1991.

58. David Beresford, Alfonso Rojo and Kathy Evans, 'Iraq rebels appeal for allied help', *The Guardian*, London, 4 March 1991.
59. Christopher Bellamy, Annika Savill and Safa Haeri, 'Kurdish guerrillas attack army HQ', *The Independent*, London, 6 March 1991.
60. Martin Woollacott, 'Fragile union to oust a tyrant', *The Guardian*, London, 11 March 1991.
61. Robert Fisk, 'Iraq opposition groups question US intentions', *The Independent*, London, 11 March 1991; Raymond Whitaker, 'US military defends its stand-off role as Baghdad tames rebels', *The Independent*, London, 13 March 1991.
62. Hella Pick, 'Britain and US part over Iraqi rebels', *The Guardian*, London, 13 March 1991.
63. Hugh Pope, John Lichfield, Safa Haeri and John Bullock, 'Washington dithers as Iraqi rebels claim more victims', *The Independent on Sunday*, London, 24 March 1991; Rupert Cornwell, 'Washington trapped by awkward options', *The Independent*, London, 26 March 1991; Martin Walker, 'US fights shy of joining in Iraq civil war', *The Guardian*, London, 28 March 1991; Rupert Cornwell, 'US resolved not to be pulled into Iraq', *The Independent*, London, 1 April 1991.
64. Andrew Stephen, 'George casts morals away', *The Observer*, London, 7 April 1991.
65. *Ibid.*
66. Robert Fisk, *The Independent*, London, 30 May 1991; 31 May 1991; 3 June 1991.
67. Hugh Pope, 'Kurds agonise over pact with Saddam', *The Independent*, London, 26 June 1991.
68. Paul Rogers and Tony Mason, 'Target behind the target', *The Guardian*, London, 13 July 1991.
69. *Ibid.*
70. Rupert Cornwell, 'Conflicting US signals on threats to Saddam', *The Independent*, London, 21 September 1991.
71. Martin Walker, 'Iraqi move leaves Bush flummoxed', *The Guardian*, London, 25 September 1991.
72. Kurt Schork, 'Kurds to pull their troops out of cities', *The Independent*, London, 13 November 1991.
73. David Hirst, 'Kurds trapped between Iraqi army terror and the winter's approaching fury', *The Guardian*, London, 7 December 1991; Kurt Schork, 'Kurds seek safety from snow and Saddam's troops', *The Independent*, London, 7 December 1991.
74. Hirst, 7 December 1991, *op. cit.*
75. David Hirst, 'Fearful time-bomb waiting to explode inside Iraq', *The Guardian*, London, 10 December 1991.
76. David Hirst, 'Kurds stuck in the UN mud', *The Guardian*, London, 11 December 1991.
77. Patrick Cockburn, 'Images of terror from the marshlands of Iraq', *The Independent*, London, 31 January 1992.
78. Patrick Cockburn, 'Kurds reap an endless harvest of Iraqi mines', *The Independent on Sunday*, London, 2 February 1992.

79. James Adams, 'MI6 joins CIA in secret war to topple Saddam', *The Sunday Times*, London, 9 February 1992.
80. *Ibid.*
81. Julie Flint, 'Iraq: US mobilises bombers', *The Observer*, London, 15 March 1992.
82. Patrick Cockburn, 'Saddam whips up a happy birthday for the President', *The Independent*, London, 29 April 1992.
83. Hugh Pope and Patrick Cockburn, 'Ink problem forces Iraqi Kurds to postpone their big day', *The Independent on Sunday*, London, 17 May 1992.
84. Andrew Hogg, 'Marsh Arabs endure revenge of Saddam', *The Sunday Times*, London, 31 May 1992.
85. Julie Flint, ' "Kill the pig Saddam" is enemies' master plan', *The Observer*, London, 21 June 1992.
86. *Ibid.*
87. Julie Flint, 'Unrest spreads in Iraq as Saddam defeats "coup bid" ', *The Observer*, London, 5 July 1992.
88. Patrick Tyler, 'Saddam "purging officer corps" after coup plot', *The Guardian*, London, 7 July 1992.
89. Leonard Doyle, 'UN guard killed as Saddam calls for a holy war', *The Independent*, London, 18 July 1992.
90. Martin Walker, 'Allies ready for new air war in Gulf', *The Guardian*, London, 24 July 1992.
91. Martin Walker, Simon Tisdall and Mark Tran, 'Iraq war could start in days', *The Guardian*, 25 July 1992; Leonard Doyle and David Usborne, 'Baghdad ready to climb down', *The Independent*, London, 25 July 1992.
92. Patrick Cockburn, 'Brinkmanship in Baghdad', *The Independent on Sunday*, London, 26 July 1992.
93. Hugh Pope, 'Aid workers terrorised by Iraqi attacks', *The Independent*, London, 17 July 1992; Chris Stephen, 'UN–Iraq deal leaves Kurds exposed', *The Guardian*, London, 28 July 1992.
94. Christopher Bellamy, 'US and Iraq gear up for new conflict', *The Independent*, London, 31 July 1992.
95. *Ibid.*; Leonard Doyle, 'Iraq "trying to wipe out Marsh Arabs" ', *The Independent*, London, 1 August 1992.
96. Simon Tisdall and Martin Walker, 'President poised to bomb Iraq', *The Guardian*, London, 17 August 1992; Patrick E. Tyler, 'US officials assert that allies will seek showdown with Iraq', *International Herald Tribune*, 17 August 1992; Colin Brown and Patrick Cockburn, 'Allies prepare for air war against Iraq', *The Independent*, London, 18 August 1992.
97. Ian Brodie, 'Bush keeps silent on no-fly zone', *The Daily Telegraph*, London, 20 August 1992.
98. Leonard Doyle, 'UN was bypassed over "no-fly" zone', *The Independent*, London, 19 August 1992.
99. Robin Oakley and Michael Binyon, 'Hurd rejects legal doubts on Iraq force', *The Times*, London, 20 August 1992; Marc Weller, 'Intervention plans lack specific UN sanctions', *The Times*, London, 20 August 1992.
100. Patrick Cockburn and Donald Macintyre, 'Bush plans air strikes on Baghdad', *The Independent on Sunday*, London, 23 August 1992; Patrick Cockburn,

'A secret war to save the President's skin', *The Independent on Sunday*, London, 23 August 1992.

101. Christopher Bellamy, 'All quiet as allied jets patrol skies over Iraq', *The Independent*, London, 29 August 1992.
102. *The Washington Post*, 29 August 1992.
103. Marie Colvin, 'Saddam digs in for a phoney war', *The Sunday Times*, London, 30 August 1992.
104. 'Pilots see no signs of Iraqi attack on south', *The Guardian*, London, 5 September 1992; 'British pilots unable to confirm Iraqi attacks on marsh Shi'ites', *The Guardian*, London, 12 September 1992.
105. *International Herald Tribune*, 18 September 1992.
106. Julie Flint, 'Saddam killing Shias "daily" ', *The Observer*, 4 October 1992.
107. Phil Davison, 'Saddam tightens noose on hungry Kurds', *The Independent on Sunday*, London, 20 September 1992; Hella Pick, 'UN report warns that Kurds could starve this winter', *The Guardian*, London, 28 September 1992.
108. David Hirst, 'A land out on a limb,' *The Guardian*, London, 13 November 1992.
109. Pam O'Toole and Clare Pointon, 'UN lorries bombed in northern Iraq,' *The Guardian*, London, 1 December 1992.
110. Annika Savill, 'Kurds fear for Saddam poised to strike,' *The Independent*, London, 16 January 1993; John Sweeney, 'Saddam's secret war on Kurds,' *The Observer*, London, 24 January 1993.
111. David Hirst, 'Saddam edges closer to the lonely bridge that brings life to the Kurds', *The Guardian*, London, 28 January 1993; 'Kurds build their state in the shadow of Saddam', 12 February 1993; 'A twilight of blood and fear in Iraq', 13 February 1993.
112. John Sweeney, 'Violent birth of unwanted nation', *The Observer*, London, 31 January 1993.
113. 'Irangate' cannot be explored here. For an outline of this controversy in the run-up to the 1992 presidential election, see 'New Iran–Contra revelations pose threat to Bush', *The Independent*, London, 25 September 1992; Peter Hounam, 'Iran weapons scandal closes in on Bush', *The Sunday Times*, London, 4 October 1992; Martin Walker, 'Evidence ties Bush to Iran deal', *The Guardian*, London, 31 October 1992.
114. Jim Hoagland, 'US gave Baghdad military secrets in war against Iran', *The Guardian*, London, 8 February 1992.
115. *Ibid.*
116. Stuart Auerbach, 'US sold high-tech devices to Saddam day before invasion', *The Guardian*, London, 3 December 1991.
117. Simon Tisdall, 'Saddamgate and Mr Bush', *The Guardian*, London, 2–3 May 1992.
118. 'Saddamgate edges closer to Bush as enquiry claims agricultural loans were used for military purchases', *The Guardian*, London, 10 July 1992; Elaine Sciolino, 'House panel urges special counsel for Iraq enquiry', *The New York Times*, 10 July 1992.
119. Elaine Sciolino, 'US was aware the Iraqis were buying technology', *The New York Times*, 22 July 1992.
120. Simon Tisdall, 'Dollars helped to pay for Iraq's Gulf war Scuds', *The Guardian*, London, 17 September 1992.

121. Mark Tran, 'Saddamgate crisis knocks Bush team', *The Guardian*, London, 12 October 1992; Rupert Cornwell, 'Iraqgate feud breaks into open', *The Independent*, London, 12 October 1992.

122. John Lichfield, 'Dog eats dog as Iraqgate dispute grows', *The Independent*, London, 19 October 1992.

123. 'MI5 "knew of British arms trade with Iraq" ', *The Sunday Times*, London, 14 April 1991.

124. John Merritt, 'Scud firm's cash gifts to bolster Tory Cause', *The Observer*, London, 14 April 1991.

125. 'Minister gave £2m grant to Iraqi war rocket firm', *The Sunday Times*, London, 26 May 1991.

126. Tom Wilkie, 'Lilley admits error over Iraq exports', *The Independent*, London, 9 August 1991.

127. Anthony Bevins and Charles Oulton, 'Cabinet broke Iraq arms ban', *The Independent*, London, 10 November 1992.

128. For example, Chris Cowley, *Guns, Lies and Spies*, Hamish Hamilton, London, 1992; David Leigh, *Betrayed, The Real Story of Matrix Churchill*, Bloomsbury, London, 1993; John Sweeney, *Trading with the Enemy, Britain's Arming of Iraq*, Pan Books, London, 1993.

129. Richard Norton-Taylor, 'Trial that blew away a web of deceit,' *The Guardian*, London, 10 November 1992.

130. Richard Norton-Taylor, 'Ridley tried to shield £1 billion Iraq deals', *The Guardian*, London, 11 November 1992; Philip Johnston, ' "Smoking gun" aimed at Major over Iraq arms', *The Daily Telegraph*, London, 11 November 1992.

131. Steve Boggan, 'Company may be linked to nuclear triggers plot', *The Independent*, London, 11 November 1992; Steve Boggan, 'Iraqis used UK parts in nuclear programme', *The Independent*, London, 12 November 1992; Chris Blackhirst, 'Intelligence agencies "used BCCI to fund arms sales" ', *The Independent*, London, 12 November 1992.

132. John Sweeney, Peter Beaumont and Paul Routledge, 'Major: nobody told me', *The Observer*, London, 15 November 1992.

133. In one such listing (*The Sunday Times*, London, 15 November 1992) it was recorded that Clark, Trefgarne, Waldegrave and Ridley 'knew of arms exports [to Iraq]'; that Thatcher, Lilley, Mellor and Sainsbury 'denied arming Iraq'; and that Heseltine, Clarke, Rifkind and Garel-Jones 'signed gagging orders' to prevent the details coming to light.

134. Nicholas Timmins, 'Court documents "prove that Major misled Commons" ', *The Independent*, London, 17 November 1992; Peter Beaumont, John McGhie, Jane Renton and Sarah Whitebloom, 'Major "knew of Iraqi arms deal fears" ', *The Observer*, London, 22 November 1992.

135. Peter Beaumont and Alan George, 'Iraq "got nuclear parts from UK" ', *The Observer*, London, 27 December 1992.

136. John Sweeney, 'Proof of UK aid for Saddam's poison', *The Observer*, London, 7 February 1992; *The Guardian*, London, 23 June 1993.

137. Simon Tisdall, 'Pentagon "covered up" loss of US plane in Gulf', *The Guardian*, London, 16 September 1992.

138. Leonard Doyle, 'Iraqi baby atrocity is revealed as myth', *The Independent*

on Sunday, London, 12 January 1992; Dana Priest, ' "Baby massacre" never happened', *The Guardian*, London, 8 February 1992.

139. Edward Lucas, 'US reveals gremlins in Gulf war machine', *The Independent*, London, 18 July 1991.

140. Alex Renton, 'RAF was fighting war on two fronts in Gulf campaign', *The Independent*, London, 24 May 1991.

141. Edward Lucas, 'US navy looks into war crime allegation', *The Independent*, London, 13 June 1991.

142. Liz Hunt, 'Gulf war pilots used drug banned in UK', *The Independent on Sunday*, London, 17 May 1992.

143. Patrick Sloyan, 'US covers up deaths by "friendly fire" ', *The Guardian*, London, 12 August 1992.

144. *Ibid.*

145. Patrick Sloyan, 'The Silver Bullet in Desert Storm', *The Guardian*, London, 16 May 1992.

146. Jason Bennetto, 'Code word may hold key to British deaths', *The Independent*, London, 23 November 1992.

147. Paul Myers and Martin Walker, 'American pilots who fired on British column "flouted war procedures" ', *The Guardian*, London, 12 May 1992.

148. Michael Fleet and Ben Fenton, ' "Friendly fire" was unlawful killing, says inquest jury', *The Daily Telegraph*, London, 19 May 1992; Clare Dyer, ' "Friendly fire" verdict fails to ease grief', *The Guardian*, London, 19 May 1992.

149. Kathy Marks, 'Bush fails to satisfy Gulf war families', *The Independent*, London, 8 June 1992.

150. General Sir Peter de la Billière, *Storm Command*, HarperCollins, London, 1992.

151. General H. Norman Schwarzkopf, *It Doesn't Take a Hero*, Bantam, London, 1992.

152. Andrew Marshall, 'The strange flight of BA 149', *The Independent on Sunday*, London, 2 August 1992.

153. Mike Jempson and Andrew Marshall, 'Was BA 149 a Trojan horse?', *The Independent on Sunday*, London, 9 August 1992.

154. Mick Jempson and Andrew Marshall, 'Fighters over Kuwait as BA 149 flew in', *The Independent*, London, 30 August 1992.

155. Donald Macintyre and Nick Cohen, 'MI5 on carpet over Gulf detainees blunder', *The Independent on Sunday*, London, 8 September 1991.

156. Hugh Pope, 'Turkey's Kurds scent freedom', *The Independent*, London, 26 March 1991.

157. 'Turkish jets hit Kurds in Iraq', *The Independent*, London, 8 August 1991; Jonathan Rugman, 'Ataturk vision blinded by hatred of Kurds', *The Observer*, London, 11 August 1991.

158. Jonathan Rugman, 'Kurds bombed by Turkey in "safe haven" ', *The Guardian*, London, 12 October 1991.

159. David Sharrock, 'A weekend of brutality in Turkey's Kurdish war', *The Guardian*, London, 21 April 1992.

160. Hugh Pope, 'Ankara hardens line as Kurdish rebellion grows bloodier', *The Independent*, London, 10 September 1992.

161. David Hirst, 'Kurds reluctantly turn on northern kin', *The Guardian*, London, 24 October 1992.
162. Hugh Pope, 'Turks plan to set up "security zone" in Iraq', *The Independent*, London, 6 November 1992.
163. Patrick Cockburn, 'Splits in the ruling clan spell trouble for Saddam', *The Independent*, London, 30 November 1991.
164. Robert Fisk, 'Syria softens stance on Iraq to end honeymoon with US', *The Independent*, London, 13 March 1992.
165. Elaine Sciolino, 'US report shows Saddam rebuilding power in Iraq', *The Guardian*, London, 17 June 1992.
166. Julie Flint, 'The billion-dollar monster who is shoring up Saddam', *The Observer*, London, 26 July 1992.
167. Chris Stephen, 'UN loophole lets through Iraqi oil', *The Guardian*, London, 3 August 1992.
168. Marie Colvin, 'Critics are silenced as Saddam rebuilds Iraq', *The Sunday Times*, London, 4 October 1992.
169. Charles Richards, 'Iraqis receive milk of Saddam's kindness', *The Independent*, London, 22 January 1993.
170. Marie Colvin, 'Iraq's lost legions become the thieves of Baghdad', *The Sunday Times*, London, 31 January 1993; Charles Richards, 'Iraq plagued by wave of violent crime', *The Independent*, London, 1 January 1993; Ian Katz, 'A life of darkness in Iraq's shattered and war-weary gateway to the Gulf', *The Guardian*, London, 6 February 1993.
171. Simon Tisdall, 'Iraq MiG shot down by US jet', *The Guardian*, London, 28 December 1992.
172. David Usborne, 'Allies gave Iraq 24-hour ultimatum', *The Independent*, London, 7 January 1993.
173. James Adams, 'US tells Iraq: no more "cheat and retreat" ', *The Sunday Times*, London, 10 January 1993.
174. Simon Tisdall, 'Iraqi's grab Kuwait missiles', *The Guardian*, London, 11 January 1993; David Usborne and Charles Richards, 'Border raids by Iraq fuel anger in US', *The Independent*, London, 12 January 1993; Hella Pick, 'Iraq pushes UN to limits', *The Guardian*, London, 12 January 1993.
175. David Usborne, Robert Fisk and Christopher Bellamy, 'Allies give Iraq a "spanking" ', *The Independent*, London, 14 January 1993.
176. Robert Fisk, 'Showdown threat to Saddam', *The Independent*, London, 15 January 1993.
177. Patrick Brogan, 'Generals urge Bush to bomb Baghdad', *The Observer*, London, 17 January 1993.
178. Simon Tisdall, 'Missiles hit "nuclear factory" ', *The Guardian*, London, 18 January 1993.
179. Robert Fisk, 'Iraqis remove police posts', *The Independent*, London, 18 January 1993.
180. President-elect Bill Clinton, interviewed by Trude Feldman for *The New York Times*, reprinted in *The Guardian*, London, 4 November 1992.
181. Interview with Thomas Friedman, 'The Clinton inexperience', *The Guardian*, London, 15 January 1993.
182. Simon Tisdall, 'Clinton "will not waver on Iraq" ', *The Guardian*, London, 19 January 1993.

183. Charles Richards and David Usborne, 'Iraq woos Clinton as US aircraft attack', *The Independent*, London, 22 January 1993; Martin Walker and Ian Katz, 'Clinton's US strikes Iraq', *The Guardian*, London, 22 January 1993.
184. Mark Tran and Ian Katz, 'US admits bombing Iraq by mistake', *The Guardian*, London, 25 January 1993.
185. Martin Walker, 'US to stand firm on Iraqi sanctions', *The Independent*, London, 30 March 1993.
186. David Brown, 'Iraq has the oil price over a barrel', *The Independent*, London, 5 April 1993.
187. Simon Tisdall, 'US threatens Iraq after attack on jets', *The Guardian*, London, 10 April 1993.
188. 'Bomb kills child', *The Observer*, London, 18 April 1993.
189. James Adams, 'US planning action over Iraqi plot to kill Bush', *The Sunday Times*, London, 9 May 1993; Colin Smith, 'US: Saddam bid to murder Bush is "act of war" ', *The Observer*, London, 9 May 1993.
190. 'Mystery over Bush plot', *The Guardian*, London, 17 May 1993.
191. Shyam Bhatia, 'Lost in Kuwait with the Crazy Gang', *The Observer*, London, 4 July 1993.
192. *The New York Times*, editorial, 28 June 1993.
193. David Usborne, 'Allies in new Saddam alert', *The Independent*, London, 1 July 1993.
194. Annika Savill, 'UN back-pedals on Baghdad sanctions report', *The Independent*, London, 24 June 1993.

Chapter 2:   The Ancient Crucible

1. James Wellard, *By the Waters of Babylon*, Hutchinson, London, 1972, pp. 83–4.
2. *Ibid.*, pp. 84–5.
3. Jacquetta Hawkes, *The First Great Civilisations*, Hutchinson, London, 1973, p. 63. A translation of the full Sumerian *King List* is included as an appendix in Leonard Woolley, *Excavations at Ur*, Ernest Benn, London, pp. 249–53.
4. Perhaps the most significant archaeological work at Ur was that supervised by Sir Leonard Woolley, beginning in 1922 as the Anglo-American expedition and conducted seasonally for the next twelve years. See, for example, Woolley, *op. cit.*
5. Wellard, *op. cit.*, p. 111.
6. Hawkes, *op. cit.*, pp. 69–70.
7. *Genesis* 2:14.
8. Wellard, *op. cit.*, p. 17.
9. Herodotus, *The Histories*, translated by Aubrey de Sélincourt, Penguin, Harmondsworth, 1954, p. 85. Later historians have found it difficult to accept the dimensions of Babylon claimed by Herodotus. Modern archaeologists have ascertained the size of the city wall but if Herodotus intended to include the surrounding farms and villages then 'Babylon at its height might have been the size of inner London' (Wellard, *op. cit.*, p. 18).
10. Wellard, *op. cit.*, p. 122.
11. I Samuel 15:3. Some observers (e.g. Wellard, *op. cit.*, p. 124) suggest that

Christ urged a generalised mercy to opponents but seemingly neglect such New Testament texts as Matthew 23:33 and Luke 19:27.

12. *The New York Times*, 26 December 1932.
13. A tablet found in the ruins of Sargon II's library at Khorsabad carries an unbroken list of Assyrian kings from the 23rd century BC to the time of Ashurnirari (753–746 BC).
14. Diodorus cities the marvel-loving Ctesias who believed that Ashurbanipal set fire to his own palace and died in the flames. This may be merely a legend.
15. Nahum 3:1–3.
16. Daniel 4:31–3.
17. Daniel 4:36.
18. See, for example, Joshua 8:24, 25, 28.
19. Solomon Grayzel, *A History of the Jews*, New American Library, New York, 1947, p. 29.
20. *Ibid.*, p. 30.
21. Judah Goldin, 'The Period of the Talmud', in Louis Finkelstein, *The Jews: Their History, Culture and Religion*, New York, 1955, p. 115.
22. Grayzel, *op. cit.*, p. 207.
23. Nissim Rejwan, *The Jews of Iraq*, Weidenfeld & Nicolson, London, 1985.
24. E. A. Speiser, 'Mesopotamia: Evolution of an Integrated Civilization', in E. A. Speiser (ed.), *The World History of the Jewish People*, Series I, Vol. II: 'At the Dawn of Civilization', Jerusalem, 1964, p. 265.
25. R. Ghirshman, *Iran*, Penguin, Harmondsworth, England, 1950, p. 50.
26. Herodotus, *op. cit.*, pp. 89–91.

Chapter 3:   The Arabs, Islam and the Caliphate

1. Alfred Guillaume, *Islam*, Penguin, Harmondsworth, England, 1954, p. 1. Elsewhere (e.g. Peter Mansfield, *The Arabs*, Penguin, Harmondsworth, England, 1980, p. 13) there is reference to 'Gindibu the Aribi'.
2. Guillaume, *op. cit.*, p. 1. In another view it is the southern Arabs who are the 'true Arabs', descended from the patriarch Qahtan, as opposed to the *Mustarib* or arabised peoples descended from the patriarch Adnan (see Peter Mansfield, *A History of the Middle East*, Penguin, Harmondsworth, 1991, p. 6).
3. II Chronicles 17:11.
4. Thomas Kiernan, *The Arabs*, Sphere, London, 1978, p. 47.
5. *Ibid.*, p. 48.
6. Guillaume, *op. cit.*, p. 2.
7. Genesis 37:25.
8. Mansfield (1980), *op. cit.*, p. 16.
9. Some sources say 571. There is uncertainty about the early life of Mohammad, the first of his biographers not writing until a century after the Prophet's death. What follows is generally accepted, though there may be elements of legend.
10. John Bagot Glubb, *A Short History of the Arab Peoples*, Quartet, London, 1980, p. 32.
11. Albert Hourani, *A History of the Arab Peoples*, Faber & Faber, London, 1991, p. 19.

12. This means that the supposed Word of God is inevitably defined by human beings. People, rather than divinities, are the *de facto* authorities behind all 'sacred' texts. From this logico-empirical circumstance there can be no escape.
13. J. J. Saunders, *A History of Medieval Islam*, Routledge & Kegan Paul, London, 1965, p. 56.
14. Glubb, *op. cit.*, p. 64.
15. Joel Carmichael, *The Shaping of the Arabs*, London, 1967, p. 118.
16. Saunders, *op. cit.*, p. 103.
17. Muhammad ibn Jarir al-Tabari, *Tarikh*, ed. M. Ibrahim, vol 7, Cairo, 1966, pp. 614–22. English translation, J. A. Williams, *Al-Tabari, the early Abbasi Empire I: The Reign of al-Ja'far al-Mansur*, Cambridge, 1988, p. 145; quoted by Hourani, *op. cit.*, p. 33.
18. There is debate (see, for example, Glubb, *op. cit.*, p. 110) about the extent to which such cultural advances were truly Arab (the discussion often smacks of European racism). Perhaps the inventive scientists and scholars of Baghdad were Persian or Greek or Armenian. The debate is sterile: no race is pure. What is beyond dispute is that staggering cultural progress was made at the heart of the Muslim empire.
19. William D. Phillips, *Slavery from Roman Times to the Transatlantic Trade*, Manchester University Press, Manchester, England, 1985, pp. 76–7. Some authorities (e.g. M. A. Shaban, *Islamic History: A New Interpretation*, Cambridge, 1971) question whether the Zanj were slaves.
20. E. Ashtor, *A Social and Economic History of the Near East in the Middle Ages*, Berkeley and Los Angeles, Calif. 1976.
21. Saunders, *op. cit.*, pp. 125–40.

Chapter 4: Seljuks, Mongols and Ottomans

1. Peter Mansfield, *The Arabs*, Penguin, Harmondsworth, England, 1983, p. 59.
2. The Cairo Fatimids were overthrown by Saladin in 1171, but a Persian/Syrian branch survived, itself yielding separate competing groups (one of which provided the Aga Khans of the present day).
3. A line of such 'shadow-caliphs' survived in Cairo under the protection of the Mamluk sultans from 1261 until the Ottoman conquest of Egypt in 1517.
4. Philip K. Hitti, *History of the Arabs*, London, 1956, pp. 466–70.
5. John Bagot Glubb, *A Short History of the Arab Peoples*, Quartet, London, 1980.
6. *Ibid.*, p. 129.
7. Amin Maalouf, *The Crusades through Arab Eyes*, translated by Jon Rothschild, Al Saqi Books, London, 1984, p. 5.
8. *Ibid.*, p. 6.
9. *Gesta Francorum*, or *The Deeds of the Franks and the Other Pilgrims to Jerusalem*, translated by Rosalind Hill, London, 1962, pp. 91, 262.
10. Armstrong, *op. cit.*, p. 120.
11. J. J. Saunders, *A History of Medieval Islam*, Routledge & Kegan Paul, London, 1980, p. 164.

12. Joachim Kahl, *The Misery of Christianity*, translated by N. D. Smith, Penguin, Harmondsworth, England, 1971, p. 47.
13. Peter Mansfield, *op. cit.*, p. 67n.
14. *Memoirs of an Arab-Syrian Gentleman or an Arab Knight in the Crusades; Memoirs of Usamah Ibn-Munqidh*, translated by Philip K. Hitti, Columbia University Press, 1929; reproduced in William H. McNeil and Marilyn Robinson Waldman (eds), *The Islamic World*, University of Chicago Press, Chicago and London, 1983, p. 185.
15. We have recorded that the Arabs too were once great historic aggressors. They, like the Christians, err in assuming their creed to be a repository of unique virtue.
16. Saunders, *op. cit.*, ch. XI.
17. Glubb. *op. cit.*, ch. XIV.
18. Maalouf, *op. cit.*, ch. 13.
19. Ibn al-Athir, *From Great History, Account of the Outbreak of the Tartars into the Lands of Islam, Under the Year A H 617 (AD 1220–1221)*, from *A Literary History of Persia*, Edward G. Browne, Cambridge University Press, Cambridge, Vol. 2, 1902.
20. Quoted by Maalouf, *op. cit.*, pp. 235–6.
21. Stanford J. Shaw, *History of the Ottoman Empire and Modern Turkey, Volume 1, Empire of the Gazis: The Rise and Decline of the Ottoman Empire 1280–1808*, Cambridge University Press, Cambridge, England, 1976, p. 95.
22. *Ibid.*, p. 194.
23. *Ibid.*, p. 200.
24. N. M. Penzer, *The Harem*, Harrap, London, 1936, pp. 135–6 ('. . . eunuchs were employed in Assyria . . . the "religious" eunuch was gradually moved westward – from Mesopotamia to Syria, from Syria to Asia Minor, and from Asia Minor to Europe').
25. Don Peretz, *The Middle East Today*, Praeger, New York, 1988, p. 60.
26. Glubb, *op. cit.*, p. 237.
27. M. A. Cook, in V. J. Parry, H. Inalcik, A. N. Kurot and J. S. Bromley, *A History of the Ottoman Empire to 1730*, Cambridge University Press, Cambridge, England, 1976, p. 9.
28. *Ibid.*

Chapter 5: The Western Impact

1. Amin Maalouf, *The Crusades through Arab Eyes*, Al Saqi Books, London, 1984.
2. *Ibid.*, p. 266.
3. H. L. Hoskins, *British Routes to India*, London, 1966, p. 64.
4. *Ibid.*, ch. 17.
5. M. and T. Zinkin, *Britain and India, Requiem for Empire*, London, 1966, p. 64.
6. G. N. Curzon, 31 March 1903, quoted in D. Judd, *Balfour and the British Empire. A Study in Imperial Evolution 1874–1932*, London, 1968, p. 231.
7. D. E. Lee, *Great Britain and the Cyprus Convention Policy of 1878*, Harvard, 1934, chs 1–3.

8. D. Dilkes, *Curzon in India*, Vol. 1, 'Achievement', London, 1969, p. 113.
9. S. H. Longrigg, *Oil in the Middle East: Its Discovery and Development*, London, 1954, ch. 1; D. G. Hogarth, *The Nearer East*, London, 1905, ch. 12.
10. H. V. F. Winstone and Zahra Freeth, *Kuwait: Prospect and Reality*, George Allen & Unwin, London, 1972, p. 125.
11. *Ibid.*
12. *Ibid.*
13. William Stivers, *Supremacy and Oil: Iraq, Turkey and the Anglo-American World Order 1918–1930*, Ithaca, NY and London, Cornell University Press, 1982, p. 111.
14. Laurence Evans, *United States Policy and the Partition of Turkey 1914–1924*, Johns Hopkins University Press, Baltimore, Md, 1965, p. 300.
15. *Ibid.*, p. 303.
16. H. V. F. Winstone, *The Illicit Adventure*, Jonathan Cape, London, 1982, p. 348.
17. Anthony Sampson, *The Seven Sisters, The Great Oil Companies and the World They Made*, Hodder and Stoughton, London, 1975, p. 67.
18. Thomas Kiernan, *The Arabs*, Sphere, London, 1978, p. 302.
19. David Fromkin, *A Peace to End all Peace, Creating the Modern Middle East 1914–1922*, Penguin, Harmondsworth, 1991, p. 96.
20. Such anxieties are portrayed in the 1916 novel *Greenmantle* by John Buchan, sometime Director of Information. In this tale a *Mahdi* plots to destroy the British Empire ('There is a dry wind blowing through the East, and the parched grasses wait the spark. And the wind is blowing towards the Indian border').
21. Fromkin, *op. cit.*, p. 98.
22. George Antonius, *The Arab Awakening: The Story of the Arab National Movement*, Capricorn Books, New York, 1965, p. 133.
23. Elie Kedourie, *In the Anglo-Arab Labyrinth: The McMahon–Husayn Correspondence and Its Interpreters 1914–1939*, Cambridge University Press, Cambridge, England, 1976, p. 22.
24. Stuart A. Cohen, *British Policy in Mesopotamia 1903–1914*, published for The Middle East Centre, St Antony's College, Oxford by Ithaca Press, London, 1976, p. 298; the early history of IEF 'D' is described in vol. 1 of F. J. Moberley, *History of the Great War based on Official Documents: The Campaign in Mesopotamia*, London, 1923.
25. Cohen, *op. cit.*, p. 298.
26. B. H. Liddell Hart, *The Real War*, London, 1930, p. 208.
27. Cohen, *op. cit.*, pp. 300–1, argues that IEF 'D' was *not* intended to occupy Iraq.
28. T. E. Lawrence, *Seven Pillars of Wisdom*, Jonathan Cape, London, 1955, p. 59.
29. *Ibid.*, p. 60.
30. Peter Mansfield, *A History of the Middle East*, Penguin, Harmondsworth, 1991, p. 152.
31. Elie Kedourie, *The Chatham House Version and Other Middle-Eastern Studies*, University Press of New England, Hanover and London, 1984, p. 15.
32. Fromkin, *op. cit.*, p. 183.
33. Fromkin, *op. cit.*, p. 219.

34. David Holden and Richard Johns, *The House of Saud: The Rise and Fall of the Most Powerful Dynasty in the Arab World*, Holt, Rinehart and Winston, New York, 1981.
35. Fromkin, *op. cit.*, pp. 225–8.
36. Ronald Sanders, *The High Walls of Jerusalem: A History of the Balfour Declaration and the Birth of the British Mandate for Palestine*, Holt, Rinehart and Winston, New York, 1983, p. 253.
37. Kedourie (1976), *op. cit.*, p. 108.
38. A. H. McMahon to Foreign Office, London, telegram 961, 10 December 1915, FO 371/2486 fo 480.
39. *Ibid.*
40. Jeremy Wilson, *Lawrence of Arabia*, Mandarin, London, 1989, p. 235.
41. The circumstances surrounding the negotiations of the Sykes–Picot Agreement are well described in Fromkin, *op. cit.*, ch. 24; and in Wilson, *op. cit.*, ch. 12.
42. Wilson, *op. cit.*, p. 237.
43. *Ibid.*, p. 238.
44. Howard M. Sachar, *The Emergence of the Middle East 1914–1924*, Allen Lane, London, 1970, p. 366.
45. Quoted by Sachar, *ibid.*
46. *Ibid.*
47. H. V. F. Winstone, *Gertrude Bell*, Jonathan Cape, London, 1978. p. 209.
48. *Ibid.*, p. 219.
49. *Ibid.*, p. 220.
50. Robert Lacey, *The Kingdom*, Fontana, London, 1982, pp. 161–2.
51. Fromkin, *op. cit.*, p. 504.
52. Aaron S. Klieman, *Foundations of British Policy in the Arab World: The Cairo Conference of 1921*, Johns Hopkins University Press, Baltimore, Md, 1970, p. 145.
53. *Ibid.*, p. 146.
54. Desmond Stewart, *The Middle East: Temple of Janus*, Hamish Hamilton, London, 1972, p. 272.
55. *Ibid.*, p. 273.
56. Winstone and Freeth, *op. cit.*, p. 71.
57. Mansfield, *op. cit.*, p. 121.
58. Winstone and Freeth, *op. cit.*, p. 87.
59. *Ibid.*
60. Quoted by Winstone and Freeth, *op. cit.*, p. 90.
61. *Ibid.*, p. 111.
62. When Clemenceau met with Lloyd George on 1 December 1918, Clemenceau asked what changes Britain wanted to the French claims. 'Mosul,' Lloyd George replied. 'You shall have it,' said Clemenceau (quoted in Elizabeth Monroe, *Britain's Moment in the Middle East: 1914–1917*, Johns Hopkins University, Baltimore, Md, 1981, pp. 50–1).
63. H. V. F. Winstone, *Leachman: 'OC Desert'*, Quartet, London, 1982, p. 215.
64. *The Times*, London, 7 August 1920.
65. Sachar, *op. cit.*, p. 372.
66. From the Trenchard Papers, quoted in Philip Knightley and Colin Simpson, *The Secret Lives of Lawrence of Arabia*, London, 1969, p. 139.

67. C. Townshend, 'Civilization and Frightfulness', 148, Wg/Cdr to CAS, 19 February 1920, Trenchard Papers MFC 76/1/36; Martin Gilbert, *Winston S. Churchill*, IV, Heinemann, London, 1975, pp. 494, 810; Companion IV ii, pp. 1066–7, 1083, 1170; quoted in David E. Omissi, *Air Power and Colonial Control, The Royal Air Force 1919–1939*, Manchester University Press, Manchester, England, 1990, p. 160.
68. Quoted by Omissi, *ibid.*, p. 23.
69. Televised interviews were broadcast on Channel 4 (London) in the 'Secret History' programme, 'The RAF and the British Empire', on 6 July 1992. The following quotations in this section are from that programme.
70. *The Letters of Gertrude*, ed. Lady Bell, London, 1947; quoted by Stewart, *op. cit.*, p. 279.
71. Quoted by Omissi, *op. cit.*, p. 30.
72. *Parliamentary Debates (Hansard)*, House of Lords, 5th series, XL (1920), column 877.
73. Omissi, *op. cit.*, p. 32.
74. Violet Dickson, *Forty Years in Kuwait*, George Allen & Unwin, London, 1971, p. 79.
75. Sachar, *op. cit.*, p. 375.
76. Televised interview for Channel 4 (London), *Secret History*, 'The RAF and the British Empire', 6 July 1992.
77. John Bagot Glubb, *War in the Desert, An RAF Frontier Campaign*, Hodder and Stoughton, London, 1960, p. 291.
78. M. E. Yapp, *The Near East Since the First World War*, Longman, London, 1991, p. 70.
79. Lacey, *op. cit.*, p. 257.
80. John Connell, *Wavell, Scholar and Soldier*, Collins, London, 1964, p. 430.
81. Quoted by Connell, *ibid.*, p. 434.
82. *Ibid.*, p. 440.
83. Nissim Rejwan, *The Jews of Iraq*, Weidenfeld and Nicolson, London, 1985, p. 223.
84. Quoted by Rejwan, *ibid.*
85. Martin Gilbert, *Second World War*, Weidenfeld and Nicolson, London, 1989, p. 187.

Chapter 6:   From Monarchy to Republic

1. Samir al-Khalil, *Republic of Fear*, Hutchinson Radius, London, 1990, p. 150; cites also A. Shikara, 'Faisal's ambitions of leadership in the Fertile Crescent: aspirations and constraints', in *The Integration of Modern Iraq*, ed. A. Kelidar, Croom Helm, London, 1979.
2. *Nidhal al Ba'th*, 4th edn, Beirut: Dar al-Tali'ah, 1976, 4:5; quoted by Khalil, *op. cit.*, p. 151.
3. Satia al-Husri, *Mudhakarati fi al-Iraq: 1921–1941*, Beirut: Dar al Tali'ah, 1967, 2, pp. 340–1.
4. Khalil, *op. cit.*, p. 165.
5. R. S. Stafford, *The Tragedy of the Assyrians*, London: George Allen & Unwin, 1935, pp. 63–5.

6. Edith and E. F. Penrose, *Iraq: International Relations and National Development*, London, 1978.
7. Arthur Goldschmidt, *A Concise History of the Middle East*, Westview Press, Boulder, Col. 1979, p. 271.
8. M. E. Yapp, *The Near East Since the First World War*, Longman, London, 1991, p. 73.
9. *Ibid.*, p. 74.
10. *Ibid.*
11. *Ibid.*
12. Don Peretz, *The Middle East Today*, Praeger, New York, 1983, p. 436.
13. *Ibid.* p. 438.
14. Fran Hazelton, 'Iraq to 1963,' in *Saddam's Iraq, Revolution or Reaction?*, Zed Books and CARDRI (Committee Against Repression and for Democratic Rights in Iraq), London, 1989, p. 10.
15. Quoted by Muhammad A. Tarbush in *The Role of the Military in Politics: A Case Study of Iraq to 1941*, London, 1982, p. 94.
16. Hanna Batatu, *The Old Social Classes and the Revolutionary Movements of Iraq*, Princeton University Press, Princeton, NJ, 1978, pp. 442–3.
17. Majid Khadduri, *Independent Iraq: 1932–1958*, London, 1960.
18. Eric Rouleau, 'The Syrian Enigma: What is the Ba'th?', *New Left Review*, 45, September/October 1987, p. 56.
19. Tabitha Petran, *Syria, A Modern History*, Ernest Benn, London, 1972, p. 90.
20. Batatu, *op. cit.*, p. 730.
21. These headlines are quoted and discussed by Samir al-Khalil, *op. cit.*, pp. 191–7.
22. *Ibid.*, p. 196.
23. J. F. Devlin, *The Ba'th Party: A History from its Origins to 1966*, Hoover Institute, Stanford, Conn., 1976, Chapter VII; Batatu, *op. cit.*, pp. 742–3.
24. Batatu, *op. cit.*, p. 808.
25. Peter Mansfield, *A History of the Middle East*, Penguin, London, 1991, p. 235.
26. *Ibid.*, p. 237.
27. Nissim Rejwan, *The Jews of Iraq*, Weidenfeld and Nicolson, London, 1985, p. 234.
28. Bernard Postal and Henry W. Levy, *And the Hills Shouted for Joy*, David McKay Company, New York, 1973, p. 81.
29. Rejwan, *op. cit.*, p. 234.
30. Quoted by Rejwan, *op. cit.*, p. 235.
31. S. Landshut, *Jewish Communities in the Muslim Countries of the Middle East*, London, 1950, pp. 47–8.
32. Rejwan, *op. cit.*, p. 242.
33. Chaim Herzog, *The Arab–Israeli Wars, War and Peace in the Middle East*, Arms and Armour Press, London, 1982, p. 153.
34. *Ibid.*, p. 183.
35. *Ibid.*, p. 207.
36. *Ibid.*, p. 308.
37. Marion Farouk-Sluglett and Peter Sluglett, 'The Transformation of Land Tenure and Rural Social Structure in Central and Southern Iraq c. 1870–1958,' *International Journal of Middle East Studies*, 15, 1983, p. 491.

38. R. Gabbay, *Communism and Agrarian Reforms in Iraq*, London, 1978, p. 29.
39. Marion Farouk-Sluglett, 'Contemporary Iraq: Some Recent Writing Reconsidered,' *Review of Middle East Studies*, 3, 1978, p. 92.
40. Doreen Warriner, *Land Reform and Development in the Middle East, A Study of Egypt, Syria and Iraq*, London, 1987, pp. 181–2.
41. W. Scott Lucas, *Divided We Stand: Britain, the US and the Suez Crisis*, Hodder and Stoughton, London, 1991, p. 25.
42. *Foreign Relations of the United States*, 1952–1954, IX, pp. 27ff.; quoted by Lucas, *op. cit.*, p. 25.
43. *Ibid.*, 379ff.; quoted by Lucas, *op. cit.*, p. 26.
44. Desmond Stewart, *The Middle East: Temple of Janus*, Hamish Hamilton, London, 1972.
45. Hazelton, *op. cit.*, p. 22.
46. *The Times* (London), 23 February 1955.
47. *Israeli State Archives*, 2382/9, Elath to Foreign Ministry, February and April 1955; quoted by Lucas, *op. cit.*, p. 50.
48. Lucas, *op. cit.*, p. 84.
49. Wilbur Eveland, *Ropes of Sand*, London, 1980, p. 160.
50. Quoted by Lucas, *op. cit.*, p. 112.
51. Quoted by Lucas, *op. cit.*, p. 114.
52. Eveland, *op. cit.*, pp. 192ff.
53. Dwight D. Eisenhower, *The White House Years: Waging Peace 1956–1961*, New York, 1965, p. 196.
54. Stewart, *op. cit.*, p. 364.
55. David Horowitz, *From Yalta to Vietnam, American Foreign Policy in the Cold War*, Penguin, Harmondsworth, England, 1967, p. 187.
56. D. F. Fleming, *The Cold War and Its Origins 1917–1960*, 2 vols, Doubleday, New York; George Allen & Unwin, London, 1961, p. 922.
57. Goldschmidt, *op. cit.*, p. 290.
58. Albert Hourani, *A History of the Arab Peoples*, Faber & Faber, London, 1991, p. 368.
59. H. G. Martin, *Middle Eastern Affairs*, March 1959.
60. Edith and E. F. Penrose, *op. cit.*, p. 204.
61. Petran, *op. cit.*, p. 131.
62. Farouk-Sluglett, *op. cit.*, p. 97.
63. Peretz, *op. cit.*, p. 451.
64. Yapp, *op. cit.*, p. 235.
65. Violet Dickson, *Forty Years in Kuwait*, George Allen & Unwin, London, 1971, pp. 210–11.
66. *The Times* (London), 26 June 1961.
67. H. V. F. Winstone and Zahra Freeth, *Kuwait, Prospect and Reality*, George Allen & Unwin, London, 1972, p. 215.
68. Quoted by Winstone and Freeth, *ibid.*
69. David Holden, *Farewell to Arabia*, Faber & Faber, London, 1966.
70. Winstone and Freeth, *op. cit.*, p. 216.
71. *L'Express*, Paris, 21 February 1963.
72. *Le Monde*, Paris, 12 February 1963.
73. James Lunt, *Hussein of Jordan*, Macmillan, London, 1989, p. 73.
74. Yapp, *op. cit.*, p. 237.

75. U. Zather, 'Political Developments in Iraq, 1963–1980', in *Saddam's Iraq, Revolution or Reaction?*, *op. cit.*, p. 30.
76. *Ibid.*
77. Yapp, *op. cit.*, p. 238.
78. *The 1968 Revolution in Iraq, Experience and Prospects: The Political Report of the Eighth Congress of the Arab Ba'th Socialist Party of Iraq*, January 1974, Ithaca Press, London, 1979, p. 30.
79. *Sunday Times* (London), 10 February 1963, talked of an 'open incitement to a massacre'; *Daily Express* (London), 12 February 1963, spoke of hundreds of people 'for whom the future holds only firing squads'; and *Le Monde* (Paris), 14 February 1963, reported '1000 dead in Baghdad alone'; quoted by Zather, *op. cit.*, p. 31.
80. Batatu, *op. cit.*
81. *al-Akhbar*, Baghdad, 24 February 1963.
82. M. S. Agwani, *Communism in the Arab East*, Asia Publishing House, New Delhi and London, 1969. p. 143. This information is confirmed in Edith and E. F. Penrose, *op. cit.*, p. 288.
83. *Economic and Political Weekly*, London, 10 June 1978, p. 932.
84. Quoted by Zather, *op. cit.*, p. 35.
85. Zather, *op. cit.*, p. 41.
86. *The Sunday Times* (London), 28 February 1969.
87. Quoted by Peretz, *op. cit.*, p. 454.
88. Yapp, *op. cit.*, p. 241
89. Amir Taheri, *The Unknown Life of the Shah*, Hutchinson, London, 1991, p. 204.
90. *Ibid.*, p. 206.
91. Zather, *op. cit.*, p. 34.
92. Celine Whittleton, 'Oil and the Iraqi Economy,' in *Saddam's Iraq, Revolution or Reaction?*, *op. cit.*, p. 55.
93. *Ibid.*, p. 63.
94. Peter R. Odell, *Oil and World Power*, Penguin, Harmondsworth, England, 1970, p. 85.
95. *Ibid.*
96. *Iraq*, Country Report, No. 4, 1983, The Economist Intelligent Unit, London.
97. *Petroleum Times*, London, August 1983; *Middle East Economic Digest*, London, 23 December 1983.
98. Whittleton, *op. cit.*, p. 71

Chapter 7: Into the Era of Saddam

1. P. Hitti, *The Arabs: A Short History*, Chicago, Gateway, 1970, p. 248.
2. S. Lloyd, *Twin Rivers: A Brief History of Iraq from the Earliest Times to the Present Day*, Oxford University Press, Oxford, England, 1943, p. 126.
3. There are several biographies of Saddam. The official work is Amir Iskander's *Saddam Hussein: The Fighter, the Thinker and the Man*, Hachette, Paris, 1980; Fouad Matar's *Saddam Hussein – A Biography*, Highlight Productions, London, 1990 is often quoted; and other recent works include: Efraim Karsh and Inari Rautski, *Saddam Hussein, A Political Biography*, Futura, London,

1991 and (with some biographical material) Adel Darwish and Gregory Alexander, *Unholy Babylon*, Victor Gollancz, London, 1991; and Judith Miller and Laurie Mylroie, *Saddam Hussein and the Crisis in the Gulf*, Times Books, Random House, New York. 1990.
4. Darwish and Alexander, *op. cit.*, p. 198.
5. J. Bulloch and H. Morris, *Saddam's War*, Faber & Faber, London, 1991, pp. 31–2.
6. Quoted by Karsh and Rautski, *op. cit.*, p. 9.
7. Iskander, *op. cit.*, p. 19.
8. Quoted by Darwish and Alexander, *op. cit.*, p. 197.
9. Darwish and Alexander, *op. cit.*, p. 200. The doctor who treated Saddam was eventually rewarded by being made Dean of the Medical College of Baghdad in 1968 when the Ba'ath Party took power, a post he held until his break with Saddam in 1979.
10. In one account (Darwish and Alexander, *op. cit.*, p. 201) Saddam turned up at Baghdad University in full military uniform to take the law examination, then placed his pistol on the desk to make him feel 'more comfortable'. He was granted the degree. Four years later he arranged for the university to give him an MA in Law.
11. Bulloch and Morris, *op. cit.*, p. 37.
12. Samir al-Khalil, *Republic of Fear*, Hutchinson-Radius, London, 1990, pp. 29–30.
13. Hanna Batatu, *The Old Social Classes and the Revolutionary Movements of Iraq*, Princeton University Press, Princeton, NJ, 1978, pp. 985–90.
14. Miller and Mylroie, *op. cit.*, p. 31.
15. Quoted by Miller and Mylroie, *op. cit.*, p. 31.
16. Iskander, *op. cit.*, p. 110.
17. Matar, *op. cit.*, pp. 35–6.
18. Iskander, *op. cit.*, p. 111.
19. *The Economist*, London, 24–30 June 1978, p. 78, suggested that the Party membership was around half of that claimed by the Ba'athists.
20. Bulloch and Morris, *op. cit.*, p. 31.
21. *Yediot Acharonot Weekly Magazine*, Tel Aviv, 17 August 1990, p. 13; quoted by Karsh and Rautski, *op. cit.*, pp. 39–40.
22. INA, 14 December 1968, *Baghdad Observer*, 13 December 1968; cited by Karsh and Rautski, *op. cit.*, p. 41.
23. al-Khalil, *op. cit.*, pp. 292–6.
24. *The Guardian*, London, 4 July 1973.
25. A. Baram, 'The ruling political élite in Ba'thi Iraq, 1968–1980: the changing features of a collective profile', *International Journal of Middle East Studies*, vol. 21, 1989, p. 452.
26. Abbas Kelidar, *Iraq: the Search for Stability*, Conflict Studies, No. 59, The Institute for the Study of Conflict, London, 1975, p. 9.
27. These events are described in, for example, *The Times*, London, 9 July 1973; *The New York Times*, 13 July 1973.
28. Darwish and Alexander, *op. cit.*, p. 208.
29. Matar, *op. cit.*, p. 54.
30. *The Times*, London, 13 December 1974.
31. *Middle East Economic Survey*, 7 March 1975.

32. *Al-Thawra*, Baghdad, 3 May 1980; quoted by Karsh and Rautski, *op. cit.*, p. 120.

33. *The New York Times*, 21 June 1980.

34. Darwish and Alexander, *op. cit.*, p. 211.

35. Matar, *op. cit.*, p. 219; *al-Qadisiya*, Baghdad, 14 August 1990.

36. *The Times*, London, 17 July 1980.

37. Karsh and Rautski, *op. cit.*, p. 176.

38. Saddam Hussein, *al-Thawra wa al-Nadhra al-Jadidah*, Dar al-Hurriyah, Baghdad, 1981, p. 149; quoted by Karsh and Rautski, *op. cit.*, pp. 176–7.

39. Saddam Hussein, *al-Dimuqratiyya Masdar Quwwa Li al-Fard wa al-Mujtama*, al-Thawra, Baghdad, 1977, p. 19; quoted by Karsh and Rautski, *op. cit.*, p. 177. 'Teach students and pupils to contradict their parents' – compare with Matthew 10:34.

40. Cited and translated from the Arabic original by Samir al-Khalil, *op. cit.*, p. 15.

41. Cited and quoted by al-Khalil, *op. cit.*, p. 13.

42. Miller and Mylroie, *op. cit.*, pp. 48–50.

43. 'Iraq: Children: Innocent Victims of Political Repression', Amnesty International, MDE 14/04/89.

44. Torture is prohibited under the Iraqi constitution. Article 22(a) of the Constitution prohibits 'any form of physical and mental torture'. Article 127 of the Penal Code prohibits the use of illegal methods to extract confessions, and Articles 332 and 333 lay down penalties for anyone using torture.

45. 'Iraq: The Need for Further United Nations Action to Protect Human Rights', Amnesty International, July 1991, MDE 14/06/91.

46. For details of the shape of such terror see, for example, al-Khalil, *op. cit.*, ch. 2; and Miller and Mylroie, *op. cit.*, ch. 3.

47. Darwish and Alexander, *op. cit.*, p. 227.

48. Patrick Seale, *Abu Nidal*, Hutchinson, London, 1992, pp. 82, 110–13.

49. Colonial Office Sessional Papers, CO 696/3, *Administrative Reports for Iraq 1920*, Mesopotamian Ministry of Justice Reports for 1920, Amarah Division, p. 7; quoted by Deborah Cobbett, 'Women in Iraq', in *Saddam's Iraq: Revolution or Reaction?*, Zed Books and CARDRI (Committee Against Repression and for Democratic Rights in Iraq), London, 1989, p. 123.

50. Colonial Office, *Administrative Reports for Occupied Territories of Iraq*, 1917, Department of Education, Annual Report; quoted by Cobbett, *op. cit.*, p. 124.

51. Colonial Office, *Special Report by His Majesty's Government on the Progress of Iraq 1920–1931* (HMSO for the League of Nations, 1931); quoted by Cobbett, *op. cit.*, p. 124.

52. Saddam Hussein, 'The Revolution and the Historical Role of Women', speech no. 5, in *On Social and Foreign Affairs in Iraq*, Croom Helm, London, 1979.

53. Cobbett, *op. cit.*, p. 129.

54. Amal al-Sharqi, 'The Emancipation of Iraqi Women', in Tim Niblock (ed.), *Iraq: the Contemporary State*, Croom Helm, London, 1982, pp. 83–5.

55. Christine Moss Helms, *Iraq: Eastern Flank of the Arab World*, The Brookings Institution, Washington, DC, 1984, p. 99.

56. al-Khalil, *op. cit.*, p. 91.

57. Saddam Hussein, *On Social and Foreign Affairs in Iraq*, *op. cit.*, p. 31.

58. *The Guardian*, London, 19 April 1990.
59. Cobbett, *op. cit.*, pp. 128–9 gives examples of the torture of women by the Iraqi authorities.
60. Cited by Patrick Brogan, *World Conflicts*, Bloomsbury, London, 1989, p. 296.
61. Majid Abd al-Ridha, *al-Masal al-Kurdiya fi'l-Iraq* (The Kurdish Question in Iraq), al-Tariq al-Jadid, Baghdad, 1975, p. 83; quoted by Peter Sluglett, 'The Kurds' in *Saddam's Iraq, Revolution or Reaction?*, *op. cit.*, p. 182.
62. Sluglett, *op. cit.*, p. 182.
63. Sluglett, *op. cit.*, p. 189; cites Mustafa Nazdar, 'The Kurds in Syria', in Gerald Chailand (ed.), *People Without a Country: The Kurds and Kurdistan*, Zed Press, London, 1980, pp. 211–19.
64. O. Bengio, *Mered ha-Kurdim be-Iraq*, Hakibutz Hameuchad, Tel Aviv, 1989, pp. 67–9; quoted by Karsh and Rautski, *op. cit.*, p. 75.
65. *The Washington Post*, 22 June 1973.
66. Saddam Hussein, *Khandaq Walind am Khandaqan*, Dar al-Thawra, Baghdad, 1977, p. 31; quoted by Karsh and Rautski, *op. cit.*, p. 80.
67. J. M. Abdulghani, *Iraq and Iran: The Years of Crisis*, Johns Hopkins University Press, Baltimore, Md, and Croom Helm, London, 1984, pp. 156–7.
68. Brogan, *op. cit.*, p. 298.
69. Tareq Y. Ismail, *Iraq and Iran: Roots of Conflict*, Syracuse University Press, Syracuse, New York, 1982, p. 66.
70. D. Dowell, *The Kurds*, Minority Rights Group Report 23, London, 1985, pp. 22–3.
71. Shahram Chubin and Charles Tripp, *Iran and Iraq at War*, I. B. Tauris, London, 1989, p. 23.
72. BBC/SWB/ME, 30 December 1980 (A/5); quoted by Chubin and Tripp, *op. cit.*, p. 23.
73. *Jumhouri-ye Islami*, 2 January 1980; quoted by Dilip Hiro, *The Longest War*, Paladin, London, 1990, p. 34.
74. *The Middle East*, 26 July 1982, p. 25; cited by Hiro, *op. cit.*, pp. 34, 274.
75. *Al Hawadith*, 4 January 1980; quoted by Hiro, *op. cit.*, p. 35.
76. *Foreign Broadcast Information Service*, 18 April 1980; *Washington Post*, 18 April 1980.
77. Hiro, *op. cit.*, p. 36.
78. Alexandre de Marenches and Christine Ockrent, *Dans le Secret des Princes*, Stock, Paris, 1986, p. 234.
79. Musavi to the Revolutionary Guards, Tehran: Home Service, 7 January 1985, in FBIS VIII, II-7, 7 February 1985; quoted by Chubin and Tripp, *op. cit.*, p. 42.
80. Helms, *op. cit.*
81. *The New York Times*, 3 October 1980.
82. Dilip Hiro, *Iran Under the Ayatollahs*, Routledge & Kegan Paul, London, 1985, p. 168.
83. *Foreign Report*, The Economist Newspapers Ltd, London, 6 May 1982.
84. *The Times*, London, 26 May 1982; *International Herald Tribune*, New York, 26 May 1982.
85. *New Statesman*, London, July 1983.
86. *Ibid.*

87. Frederick W. Axelgard, 'War and Oil. Implications for Iraq's Postwar Role in Gulf Security', in Frederick W. Axelgard (ed.), *Iraq in Transition*, Mansell, London, 1986, p. 4.
88. *The Daily Telegraph*, London, 3 June 1988.
89. Al Hawadith, 10 August 1984; quoted by Hiro (1990), *op. cit.*, p. 132.
90. *Newsweek*, 1 April 1985, p. 16. Since the start of the war some 7000 Iranian civilians were killed and more than 30,000 injured in air raids, *The Guardian*, London, 9 April 1985; cited by Hiro (1990), *op. cit.*, pp. 135, 279.
91. Brogan, *op. cit.*, p. 264.
92. Jabr Muhsin, George Harding and Fran Hazelton, 'Iraq in the Gulf War', in *Saddam's Iraq, Revolution or Reaction?*, *op. cit.*, p. 237.
93. Hella Pick, *The Guardian*, London, 6 July 1988.
94. BBC World Service, 20 July 1988; *The Independent*, London, 21 July 1988; quoted by Hiro (1990), *op. cit.*, p. 243.
95. Hella Pick, *The Guardian*, London, 6 July 1988.
96. Tehran Home Service, 21 May 1988; quoted by Muhsin *et al.*, *op. cit.*, p. 239.
97. *The Times*, London, 19 July 1987; Tehran Radio, 9 September 1988; cited by Hiro (1990), *op. cit.*, p. 250.
98. D. Middleton, *The New York Times*, 23 September 1985.
99. Another 1985 estimate (L. Bushkoff, *Boston Sunday Globe*, 22 September 1985) puts the total casualties at 1.5 million.
100. R. O. Freedman, 'Soviet Policy Towards Ba'athist Iraq 1968–1979', paper delivered at the Strategic Studies Institute of the US Army War College, Carlisle Barracks, Pennsylvania, 10 June 1980; cited by A. Abbas, 'The Iraqi Armed Forces, Past and Present', in *Saddam's Iraq, Revolution or Reaction?*, *op. cit.*, p. 220.
101. Quoted by Abbas, *op. cit.*, p. 220.
102. Quoted by Kenneth R. Timmerman, *The Death Lobby, How the West Armed Iraq*, Fourth Estate, London, 1992, p. 21.
103. Quoted by Timmerman, *op. cit.*, p. 30.
104. Andrew and Leslie Cockburn, *Dangerous Liaison*, Bodley Head, London, 1992, pp. 323–4.
105. Timmerman, *op. cit.*, p. 100.
106. Richard Wilson, 'A Visit to the bombed nuclear reactor at Tuwaitha, Iraq', *Nature*, 302, March 1983.
107. Jimmy Carter, *The Blood of Abraham, Inside the Middle East*, Sidgwick & Jackson, London, 1985, pp. 45–6.
108. Robert Lacey, *The Kingdom*, Fontana, London, 1982, p. 456.
109. *The Guardian*, London, 2 July 1970.
110. Mark Tran, 'Bush "knew Saddam aided terrorists" ', *The Guardian*, London, 8 June 1992. It was known that Abu Nidal, for instance, was operating from Baghdad until 1983.
111. Quoted by Timmerman, *op. cit.*, p. 119.
112. Richard M. Preece, *United States–Iraqi Relations*, Congressional Research Service, Library of Congress, Government Printing Office, Washington, DC, July 1986, p. 12; *The New York Times*, 11 January 1984.
113. Hiro (1990), *op. cit.*, p. 119.
114. *US News and World Report*, 12 March 1984.
115. *The Guardian*, London, 22 July 1983; *The New York Times*, 29 March 1984.

116. Timmerman, *op. cit.*, pp. 420–3, reproduces a *Mednews* (Middle East Defence News) listing of arms sales to Iraq, 1970–90.
117. 'Minister gave £2m grant to Iraqi war rocket firm', *The Sunday Times*, London, 26 May 1991.
118. Richard Norton-Taylor, 'Iraq arms deals "given all clear" ', *The Guardian*, London, 27 July 1991.
119. John Merritt, 'Fury over poison for Iraq', *The Observer*, London, 28 July 1991; Stephen Castle and Stephen Ward, 'Fury over sales to Saddam', *The Independent on Sunday*, London, 28 July 1991; Tom Wilkie and Alex Renton, 'UK's nuclear exports to Iraq', *The Independent*, London, 27 July 1991; 'Britain shipped 8.6 tonnes of uranium to Iraq', *The Sunday Times*, London, 4 August 1991.
120. John McGhie, 'UK firm sold Iraq drugs to shield nerve gas troops', *The Observer*, London, 11 August 1991.
121. David Leppard and Nicholas Rufford, 'British bomb parts found', *The Sunday Times*, London, 29 September 1991.
122. David Hellier and Rosie Waterhouse, 'British role in supergun "known in 1989" ', *The Independent*, London, 14 March 1992.
123. Quoted by Hellier and Waterhouse, *op. cit.*
124. Simon Tisdall, 'Saddam "was built up" with US billions', *The Guardian*, London, 22 May 1992.
125. Richard Norton-Taylor, 'Action against BCCI "delayed to avoid upsetting Gulf allies" ', *The Guardian*, London, 1 August 1991.
126. Jonathan Cofino, 'US delayed inquiry into Iraq frauds', *The Daily Telegraph*, London, 21 March 1992.
127. Timmerman, *op. cit.*, p. 177.
128. Interview with Baghdad, February 1985; see also Kenneth Timmerman, 'US resumption of ties with Iraq prompting a boom in exchanges', *Atlanta Journal-Constitution*, 17 February 1985; cited by Timmerman, *op. cit.*, pp. 211, 410.
129. Timmerman (1992), *op. cit.*, p. 211.
130. Quoted by Timmerman (1992), *op. cit.*, p. 219. He also lists (p. 424) the seventy-six Forum members, all leading US companies, as of July 1990.
131. Timmerman (1992), *op. cit.*, p. 241.
132. Timmerman (1992), *op. cit.*, p. 307.
133. 'British exports to Iraq', *Mednews*, 2 September 1991.

Chapter 8:   War with the West

1. Dilip Hiro, *Desert Shield to Desert Storm*, Paladin, London, 1992, p. 55.
2. *Foreign Broadcast Information Service*, 28 March 1989.
3. Adel Darwish and Gregory Alexander, *Unholy Babylon*, Victor Gollancz, London, 1991, pp. 238–9.
4. *Ibid.*, p. 164.
5. *The Guardian*, London, 14 March 1990.
6. Quoted by Hiro, *op. cit.*, p. 61.
7. Darwish and Alexander, *op. cit.*, p. 242.

8. *The Times*, London, 7 December 1989; *The Guardian*, London, 18 December 1989.
9. *The Middle East*, December 1989, p. 30.
10. Quoted by Hiro, *op. cit.*, p. 64.
11. *Jordanian Television*, Amman, 24 February 1990; cited by Hiro, *op. cit.*, p. 65.
12. *Wall Street Journal*, 28 June 1990.
13. *Baghdad Radio*, 28 May 1990; cited by Hiro, *op. cit.*, pp. 77–8.
14. Mohamed Heikal, *Illusions of Triumph*, HarperCollins, London, 1992, p. 135.
15. Bishara A. Bahbah, 'The crisis in the Gulf – why Iraq invaded Kuwait', in Phyllis Bennis and Michel Moushabeck (eds), *Beyond the Storm*, Canongate, London, 1992, p. 52.
16. Heikal, *op. cit.*, p. 137.
17. *Baghdad Radio*, 18 June 1990; cited by Hiro, *op. cit.*, pp. 83–4.
18. J. Bulloch and H. Morris, *Saddam's War*, Faber & Faber, London, 1991, p. 175; Danial Yergin, *Prize: The Epic Quest for Oil, Money and Power*, Simon and Schuster, London, 1991, pp. 749–50.
19. Heikal, *op. cit.*, pp. 138–9.
20. *Ibid.*
21. *Foreign Broadcast Information Service*, 28 June 1990; *The New York Times*, 28 June 1990.
22. Pierre Salinger and Eric Laurent, *Secret Dossier, The Hidden Agenda Behind the Gulf War*, Penguin, Harmondsworth, 1991, pp. 32–3.
23. *Ibid.*, p. 33.
24. The transcript is cited in Bulloch and Morris, *op. cit.*, pp. 143–6.
25. The Iraqis, claiming to have discovered the document at SSD headquarters, placed it before the UN Secretary-General on 24 October 1990.
26. Baghdad Radio, 18 July 1990; cited by Hiro, *op. cit.*, pp. 88–9.
27. Hiro, *op. cit.*, p. 89.
28. *The Guardian*, London, 19 July 1990.
29. Quoted by Bahbah, *op. cit.*, p. 51.
30. Heikal, *op. cit.*, pp. 141–2.
31. *Ibid.*
32. Joe Conason, 'The Iraq lobby: Kissinger, the Business Forum & Co', in Micah L. Sifry and Christopher Cerf (eds), *The Gulf War Reader*, Times Books, Random House, New York, 1991, pp. 79–84.
33. Henry Schuler, 'The oil exporters are leaving money on the table', *Arab Oil and Gas Journal*, 1 March 1990.
34. James Ridgeway (ed. and Introduction), *The March to War*, Four Walls Eight Windows, New York, 1991, p. 28.
35. *Transcript of House Subcommittee Hearing on US–Iraqi Relations*, in James Ridgeway, *op. cit.*, pp. 47–9.
36. William Safire, *The New York Times*, 25 May 1990.
37. Ridgeway, *op. cit.*, p. 30.
38. Transcripts of this important encounter are reproduced in various publications: e.g. Sifry and Cerf, *op. cit.*, pp. 122–33; Ridgeway, *op. cit.*, pp. 50–3; Hiro, *op. cit.*, pp. 92–4; Salinger and Laurent, *op. cit.*, pp. 48–63. The

controversial contribution of Ambassador April Glaspie was much discussed after the ending of the Gulf War. In the last of the pre-election debates, televised on 19 October 1992, Ross Perot claimed that the US administration, via Glaspie, had intimated to Saddam Hussein that *he would be allowed to take northern Kuwait*. Perot made great play over the fact that relevant written instructions to Glaspie have not been released by the State Department.

39. Salinger and Laurent, *op. cit.*, p. 68.
40. *Ibid.*, pp. 68–9; Ridgeway, *op. cit.*, pp. 57–8.
41. Salinger and Laurent, *op. cit.*, pp. 70–4.
42. See also *International Herald Tribune*, 20 September 1990.
43. Heikal, *op. cit.*, p. 201.
44. *Ibid.*, p. 205.
45. *Ibid.*, p. 215.
46. *US News and World Report*, 19 December 1990; *The Nation*, 7 December 1990.
47. *BBC Short Wave Broadcasts Summary*, 10 December 1990; cited by John Pilger, *Distant Voices*, Vintage, London, 1992, pp. 138–9.
48. *Middle East International*, 12 October 1990.
49. *BBC Short Wave Broadcasts Summary* and *Middle East International*; Turkish press review, 22 July 1991; cited by Pilger, *op. cit.*, p. 139.
50. David Hirst, *The Guardian*, London, 14 September 1990.
51. *The Nation*, 24 December 1991.
52. Hiro, *op. cit.*, p. 187.
53. See Geoff Simons, *Libya, The Struggle for Survival*, Macmillan, London, 1993, ch. 1.
54. Salinger and Laurent, *op. cit.*, p. 196.
55. *Ibid.*
56. *Ibid.*, p. 197.
57. *The Washington Post*, 15 December 1990; *International Herald Tribune*, 7 December 1990.
58. *The New York Times*, 2 December 1990.
59. Heikal, *op. cit.*, p. 237.
60. It is sometimes argued that an abstention by a permanent member of the UN Security Council counts as a *de jure* veto since it fails to deliver the 'concurring votes of the permanent members' stipulated in Article 27(3) of the UN Charter. This interpretation is supported by the French version of the relevant text: '*Les décisions du Conseil de Sécurité sur toutes autres questions sont prises par un vote affirmatif de neuf de ses membres dans lequel sont comprises les voix de tous les membres permanents*'. However, the practice of not regarding abstentions as vetoes has been recognised as lawful by the International Court of Justice (in the Namibia case, *ICJ Reports*, 1971, pp. 16, 22). This matter invites discussion. What is the value of UN Charter stipulations if political circumstances can override their explicit provisions?
61. Carl Zaisser, *US Bribery and Arm-Twisting of Security Council Members during the November 29 Vote on the Resolution Allowing the use of Force in Ousting Iraq from Kuwait*, 1991; cited by Pilger, *op. cit.*, p. 141.
62. *The New York Times*, 2 December 1990.
63. Pilger, *op. cit.*, p. 142.

64. Noam Chomsky, 'The weak shall inherit nothing', *The Guardian*, London, 25 March 1991.

65. Raymond Bonner, *Waltzing With a Dictator*, Macmillan, London, 1987, pp. 245–6.

66. John Weeks and Phil Gunson, *Panama, Made in the USA*, Latin American Bureau, London, 1991, Appendix 1, 'Violation of International Law', pp. 113–18.

67. Naseer Aruri, 'Human rights and the Gulf crisis: the verbal strategy of George Bush', in Phyllis Bennis and Michel Moushabeck (eds), *Beyond the Storm, A Gulf Crisis Reader*, Canongate, Edinburgh, 1992, p. 314.

68. George Bush, *Iraqi Leader Threatens Values Worth Fighting For*, January 1991; cited by Aruri, *op. cit.*, p. 314.

69. John G. Healey, *Amnesty International USA Response to President Bush's Letter to Campus Newspapers*, 15 January 1991.

70. *Congressional Record*, 12 January 1991, S375.

71. *Ibid.*, H287–288.

72. Hiro, *op. cit.*, p. 103.

73. Salinger and Laurent, *op. cit.*, p. 84.

74. For detailed descriptions of the chronology, from different perspectives, see Hiro, *op. cit.*; Heikal, *op. cit.*; Salinger and Laurent, *op. cit.*; Bob Woodward, *The Commanders*, Simon and Schuster, London, 1991.

75. Woodward, *op. cit.*, p. 277.

76. *The New York Times*, 4 March 1991; see also Hiro, *op. cit.*, pp. 119–20.

77. Heikal, *op. cit.*, pp. 246–7; see also John R. MacArthur, *Second Front, Censorship and Propaganda in the Gulf War*, Hill and Wang, New York, 1992.

78. Heikal, *op. cit.*, pp. 248–9.

79. *Ibid.*, p. 250.

80. Woodward, *op. cit.*, pp. 287–8.

81. *Ibid.*, p. 289.

82. Simon Tisdall, 'Americans urge Bush to be cautious', *The Guardian*, London, 23 August 1990.

83. Marie Colvin, Richard Ellis, Roy Isacowitz and John Cassidy, 'Slaughter on the Mount', *The Sunday Times*, London, 14 October 1990, pp. 16–17.

84. Hiro, *op. cit.*, p. 211.

85. Woodward, *op. cit.*, p. 303.

86. Leonard Doyle, 'Bush accuses Saddam of atrocities', *The Independent*, London, 16 October 1990.

87. Helga Graham, 'US oil plot fuelled Saddam', *The Observer*, London, 21 October 1990.

88. Sam Kiley, 'Deserters swell anti-war chorus across the US', *The Sunday Times*, London, 28 October 1990.

89. Sarah Helm, 'Warning to Bush as anti-war sentiment in Congress grows', *The Independent*, London, 29 October 1990.

90. *The Washington Post*, 2 December 1990; *The New York Times*, 4 March 1991.

91. Interview with Yevgeni Primakov, *The New York Times*, 16 November 1990.

92. Heikal, *op. cit.*, p. 275.

93. Even the legitimacy of that vote was suspect because of the absence of the

Soviet Union from the Security Council when the vote was taken; see also note 60, above.

94. See, for example, Woodward, *op. cit.*, p. 333; Hiro, *op. cit.*, p. 264; Heikal, *op. cit.*, p. 276.
95. Heikal, *op. cit.*, pp. 276–7.
96. Woodward, *op. cit.*, p. 334.
97. Jasper Becker, 'Survivor's stories from a looted city', *The Guardian*, London, 15 December 1990.
98. Helga Graham, 'Blockade chokes Iraq as US loses patience', *The Observer*, London, 30 December 1990.
99. Patrick Cockburn, 'Baghdad divided on hope of averting Gulf war', *The Independent*, London, 9 January 1991.
100. Peter Pringle, 'Anxiety behind Baker's calm', *The Independent*, London, 9 January 1991.
101. Leonard Doyle, 'The man with an eleventh-hour mission', *The Independent*, London, 12 January 1991.
102. John Cassidy, Marie Colvin and Ian Glover-James, 'Congress votes for war in Gulf', *The Sunday Times*, London, 13 January 1991.
103. Andrew Stephen, 'Congress votes for war', *The Observer*, London, 13 January 1991.
104. Annika Savill, 'Iraq crisis stifles US action on Baltic', *The Independent*, London, 14 January 1991.
105. Patrick Cockburn, Annika Savill, Peter Pringle and Leonard Doyle, 'Allies poised for onslaught', *The Independent*, London, 16 January 1991.
106. Heikal, *op. cit.*, p. 295.
107. *The Guardian*, London, 18 January 1991.
108. Martin Walker and David Fairhall, 'Iraqi missiles strike Israel', *The Guardian*, London, 18 January 1991.
109. Hiro, *op. cit.*, pp. 324–5.
110. Michael Sheridan, Peter Pringle and Leonard Doyle, 'US urges Israeli constraint', *The Independent*, London, 19 January 1991.
111. David Rose and Colin Smith, 'Land troops in first border skirmishes', *The Observer*, London, 20 January 1991.
112. David Fairhall, David Beresford and Martin Walker, 'Patriots perform as dictator warns of reserve firepower', *The Guardian*, London, 21 January 1991.
113. Peter Pringle, Colin Hughes, Will Bennett, John Pienaar and Colin Brown, 'Fury at Saddam threat of PoW "human shield" ', *The Independent*, London, 22 January 1991.
114. Martin Walker and Hella Pick, 'British and American aims including finishing Saddam', *The Guardian*, London, 23 January 1991.
115. Patrick Cockburn, 'Tomahawks on Baghdad claim civilian victims', *The Independent*, London, 2 February 1991.
116. Heikal, *op. cit.*, p. 296.
117. Martin Walker, 'US seeks early ground war', *The Guardian*, London, 6 February 1991.
118. Bernd Debusmann, 'Crippled Iraq bombed back to last century', *The Observer*, London, 10 February 1991.

119. Patrick Cockburn, 'Allied raid on bridge kills 47 civilians', *The Independent*, London, 8 February 1991.

120. Martin Walker, Simon Tisdall and David Fairhall, ' "Hundreds killed" in bunker', *The Guardian*, London, 14 February 1991; Christopher Bellamy, Edward Lucas and Leonard Doyle, 'Shelter "a military target" ', *The Independent*, London, 14 February 1991.

121. John Lichfield, Sarah Helm, Harvey Morris and Anthony Bevins, 'US dismisses Iraqi offer to quit as sham', *The Independent*, London, 16 February 1991.

122. Martin Walker, Simon Tisdall, Jane Rosen, David Fairhall and Hella Pick, 'Bush rejects peace "hoax" ', *The Guardian*, London, 16 February 1991.

123. Peter Pringle, Christopher Bellamy, Leonard Doyle and Sarah Helm, 'Last chance to avert land war', *The Independent*, London, 18 February 1991.

124. John Lichfield, Edward Lucas and Peter Pringle, 'Saddam accepts Soviet plan for withdrawal from Kuwait', *The Independent*, London, 22 February 1991.

125. Molly Moore, Pentagon correspondent, quoted by John R. MacArthur, *op. cit.*, p. 159.

126. John Lichfield, Edward Lucas, Christopher Bellamy, Patrick Cockburn, Will Bennett and John Pienaar, 'Allies drive deep into Iraq to cut off Saddam's army', *The Independent*, London, 25 February 1991.

127. Colonel Richard White, US pilot, quoted in *The Independent*, London, 6 February 1991.

128. *The Washington Post*, 16 and 17 February 1991.

129. Reuter pool report, 'Apache pilots in ground attack shooting gallery', *The Independent*, London, 25 February 1991.

130. *Ibid*.

131. Hiro, *op. cit.*, p. 389.

132. Michael Kelly, 'Carnage on a forgotten road', *The Guardian*, London, 11 April 1991.

133. *Los Angeles Times*, 10 March 1991.

134. *New Statesman and Society*, London, 21 June 1991, p. 23.

135. BBC2 television 'Late Show', 8 June 1991.

136. General H. Norman Schwarzkopf with Peter Petre, *It Doesn't Take a Hero*, Bantam Press, London, 1992, p. 488.

137. Martin Walker, Simon Tisdall and Paul Webster, 'Hurd says Saddam must go', *The Guardian*, London, 2 March 1991.

138. 'Iraq complains about sanctions', *The Independent*, London, 23 June 1993.

139. 'Iraq faces health crisis', *The Guardian*, London, 13 September 1993.

140. Special Alert, *FAO/WFP Crop and Food Supply Assessment Mission to Iraq*, Number 237, July 1993.

Bibliography

Abdulghani, Jasim M., *Iraq and Iran: The Years of Crisis* (Baltimore, Md: Johns Hopkins University Press; London: Croom Helm, 1984).

Aldington, Richard, *Lawrence of Arabia* (London, 1955).

Anderson, Ewan W. and Rashidian, Khalil H., *Iraq and the Continuing Middle East Crisis* (London: Pinter, 1991).

Anderson, J. R. L., *East of Suez* (London: Hodder and Stoughton, 1969).

Antonius, George, *The Arab Awakening: The Story of the Arab National Movement*, (New York: Capricorn Books, 1965).

Armstrong, Karen, *Holy War, The Crusades and Their Impact on Today's World* (London: Macmillan, 1988).

Axelgard, Frederick W., *A New Iraq? The Gulf War and Its Implications for US Policy* (Washington, DC: Praeger, 1988).

Bacque, James, *Other Losses, An Investigation Into the Mass Deaths of German Prisoners of War After World War II* (London: Macdonald, 1989).

Barnet, Richard, *Intervention and Revolution* (London: MacGibbon and Kee, 1970).

Baron, Salo W., *A Social and Religious History of the Jews*,
   Vol. I *To the Beginning of the Christian Era* (New York, 1952).
   Vol. II *Christian Era: The First Five Centuries* (New York, 1952).
   Vol. III *Heirs of Rome and Persia* (New York, 1957).
   Vol. IV *Religious Controls and Dissensions* (New York, 1957).

Batatu, Hanna, *The Old Social Classes and the Revolutionary Movements of Iraq: A Study of Iraq's Old Landed and Commercial Classes and of Its Communists, Ba'athists, and Free Officers*, (Princeton, NJ: Princeton University Press, 1978).

Bennis, Phyllis and Moushabeck, Michel (eds), *Beyond the Storm, A Gulf Crisis Reader* (London: Canongate, 1992).

de la Billière, Sir Peter, *Storm Command* (London: HarperCollins, 1992).

Bosworth, C. E., *The Islamic Dynasties* (Edinburgh: 1967).

Bouquet, A. C., *Sacred Books of the World* (Harmondsworth: Penguin, 1959).

Bresheeth, Haim and Yuval-Davis, Nira, *The Gulf War and the New World Order* (London: Zed Books, 1991).

Brittain, Victoria (ed.), *The Gulf Between Us* (London: Virago Press, 1991).

Brockelmann, C., *History of the Islamic Peoples* (New York, 1947).

Buckingham, J. S., *Travels in Mesopotamia* (London, 1827).

Bulloch, John and Morris, Harvey, *The Gulf War* (London: Methuen, 1989).

Bulloch, John and Morris, Harvey, *Saddam's War* (London: Faber & Faber, 1991).

Busch, Briton Cooper, *Britain, India and the Arabs, 1914–1921*, (Berkeley, Calif.: 1971).

Champdor, Albert, *Babylon* (London: Elek Books, 1958).

Chomsky, Noam, *Turning the Tide, US Intervention in Central America and the Struggle for Peace* (London: Pluto, 1985).

Chomsky, Noam, *The Chomsky Reader*, ed. James Peck (London: Serpent's Tail, 1988).

Chomsky, Noam, *Deterring Democracy* (London: Verso, 1991).

Cockburn, Andrew and Leslie, *Dangerous Liaison* (London: Bodley Head, 1992).

Cohen, Hayyim J., *The Jews of the Middle East, 1860–1972* (Jerusalem: 1973).

Cohen, Stuart A., *British Policy in Mesopotamia 1903–1914* (London: Ithaca Press, 1976).

Connell, John, *Wavell, Scholar and Soldier* (London: Collins, 1964).

Contenau, Georges, *Everyday Life in Babylon and Assyria* (London: Edward Arnold, 1954).

Cook, M. A. (ed.), *A History of the Ottoman Empire to 1730* (Cambridge: Cambridge University Press, 1976).

Cottrell, Leonard, *The Anvil of Civilisation* (London: Faber & Faber, 1958).

Darwish, Adel and Alexander, Gregory, *Unholy Babylon, The Secret History of Saddam's War* (London: Victor Gollancz, 1991).

Diakonoff, N. M., *Society and State in Ancient Mesopotamia* (Moscow: 1959).

Devlin, J. F., *The Ba'ath Party: A History from Its Origins to 1966* (Stanford: 1976).

Dickson, H. R. P., *Kuwait and Her Neighbours* (London: George Allen & Unwin 1956).

Dickson, H. R. P., *The Arab of the Desert* (London: George Allen & Unwin, 1970).

Dickson, V., *Forty Years in Kuwait* (London: George Allen & Unwin, 1970).

Dietl, Wilhelm, *Holy War* (New York: Macmillan, 1984).

Dower, John, *War Without Mercy, Race and Power in Pacific War* (London: Faber & Faber, 1986).

Eveland, Wilbur, *Ropes of Sand* (London: 1980).

Farouk Sluglett, M., *Iraq Since 1958: from Revolution to Dictatorship* (London: 1987).

Farrington, Benjamin, *Greek Science* (Harmondsworth: Penguin, 1953).

Fisher, Sydney N., *The Middle East; A History* (London: 1971).

Fleming, D. F., *The Cold War and Its Origins 1917–1960* (New York: Doubleday, 1961).

Fraser, T. G., *The Middle East, 1914–1979* (London: Edward Arnold, 1980).

Freedman, Lawrence and Karsh, Efraim, *The Gulf Conflict: 1991, Diplomacy and War in the New World Order* (London: Faber & Faber, 1993).

Fromkin, David, *A Peace to End All Peace, Creating the Modern Middle East 1914–1922* (Harmondsworth: Penguin, 1991).

Gabbay, R., *Communism and Agrarian Reforms in Iraq* (London: 1978).

Ghirshman, R., *Iran* (Harmondsworth: Penguin, 1954).

Gilbert, Martin, *Second World War* (London: Weidenfeld and Nicolson, 1989).

Glover, T. R., *The Ancient World* (Harmondsworth: Penguin, 1953).

Glubb, J. B., *The Great Arab Conquests* (London: 1963).

Glubb, J. B., *War in the Desert, An RAF Frontier Campaign* (London: Hodder and Stoughton, 1960).

Glubb, J. B., *A Short History of the Arab Peoples* (London: Quartet, 1980).

Goldschmidt, Arthur, *A Concise History of the Middle East* (Boulder, Col.: Westview Press, 1979).

Grayzel, Solomon, *A History of the Jews* (New York: New American Library, 1968).

Guillaume, Alfred, *Islam* (Harmondsworth: Penguin, 1954).

Hamilton, Charles W., *Americans and Oil in the Middle East* (Texas: Gulf Publishing Company, 1962).

Hawkes, Jacquetta, *The First Great Civilisations* (London: Hutchinson, 1973).

Heikal, Mohamed, *Illusions of Triumph, An Arab View of the Gulf War* (London: HarperCollins, 1992).

Helms, Christine Moss, *Iraq, Eastern Flank of the Arab World* (Washington, DC: Brookings, 1985).

Herodotus, *The Histories*, translated by Aubrey de Sélincourt (Harmondsworth: Penguin, 1963).

Herzog, Chaim, *The Arab–Israeli Wars, War and Peace in the Middle East* (London: Arms and Armour Press, 1982).

Higham, Charles, *Trading With the Enemy* (London: Robert Hale, 1983).

Hilprecht, H. V., *The Excavations in Assyria and Babylonia* (Philadelphia: 1904).

Hiro, Dilip, *Iran Under the Ayatollahs* (London: Routledge & Kegan Paul, 1985).

Hiro, Dilip, *The Longest War, The Iran–Iraq Military Conflict* (London: Paladin, 1990).

Hiro, Dilip, *Desert Shield to Desert Storm* (London: Paladin, 1992).

Hitti, P. K., *History of the Arabs* (London: 1956).

Holden, David, *Farewell to Arabia* (London: Faber & Faber, 1966).

Holden, David and Johns, Richard, *The House of Saud: The Rise and Fall of the Most Powerful Dynasty in the Arab World* (New York: Holt, Rinehart and Winston, 1981).

Horowitz, David, *From Yalta to Vietnam, American Foreign Policy in the Cold War* (Harmondsworth: Penguin, 1967).

Hourani, Albert, *Europe and the Middle East* (Berkeley, Calif.: University of California Press, 1980).

Hourani, Albert, *The Emergence of the Modern Middle East* (Berkeley, Calif.: University of California Press, 1981).

Hourani, Albert, *A History of the Arab Peoples* (London: Faber & Faber, 1991).

Hourani, A. H. and Stern, S. M. (eds), *The Islamic City* (Oxford: 1970).

Hussein, Abd Allah ibn, *Memoirs of King Abdullah of Transjordan* ed. Philip P. Graves (London: Jonathan Cape, 1950).

Ionides, M., *Divide and Lose: the Arab Revolt 1955–1958* (London: 1960).

Iskander, Amir, *Saddam Hussein: The Fighter, the Thinker and the Man* (Paris: Hachette, 1980).

Jacobsen, T., *The Sumerian King List* (Chicago: 1939).

Karsh, Efraim and Rautski, Inari, *Saddam Hussein, A Political Biography* (London: Futura, 1991).

Kedourie, Elie, *The Chatham House Version and Other Middle Eastern Studies* (London: Weidenfeld and Nicolson, 1970).

Kedourie, Elie, *In the Anglo-Arab Labyrinth: The McMahon–Husayn Correspondence and its Interpreters 1914–1939* (Cambridge: Cambridge University Press, 1976).

Kelidar, S. (ed.), *The Integration of Modern Iraq* (London: Croom Helm, 1979).

Kelly, J. B., *Arabia, the Gulf and the West* (New York: Basic Books, 1980).

Kennedy, H., *The Early Abbasid Caliphate* (London: 1981).

Kent, Marian, *Oil and Empire, British Policy and Mesopotamian Oil 1900–1920* (London: Macmillan, 1976).

Khaddouri, Majd, *The Gulf War: The Origins and Implications of the Iraq–Iran Conflict* (Oxford: Oxford University Press, 1988).

Khadduri, Majid, *Independent Iraq: A Study in Iraqi Politics from 1932–1958* (London: 1960).

al-Khalil, Samir, *Republic of Fear* (London: Hutchinson Radius, 1990).

Kiernan, Thomas, *The Arabs* (London: Sphere, 1978).

Kinnane, Dirk, *The Kurds and Kurdistan* (Oxford: Oxford University Press, 1964).

Knightley, Philip and Simpson, Colin, *The Secret Lives of Lawrence of Arabia* (London: Thomas Nelson, 1969).

Koldewey, R., *The Excavation at Babylon* (London: 1914).

Kramer, S. N., *History Begins at Sumer* (New York: 1959).

Kramer, S. N., *The Sumerians* (Chicago: 1963).

Kundera, Milan, *The Book of Laughter and Forgetting* (Harmondsworth: Penguin, 1983).

Lacey, Robert, *The Kingdom* (London: Hutchinson, 1981).

Landshut, S., *Jewish Communities in the Muslim Countries of the Middle East* (London: 1950).

Lapidus, I. M., *A History of Islamic Societies* (Cambridge, England: Cambridge University Press, 1988).

Lawrence, T. E., *Seven Pillars of Wisdom* (London: Jonathan Cape, 1935).

Lernoux, Penny, *Cry of the People* (Harmondsworth: Penguin, 1982).

Longrigg, Stephen H., *Four Centuries of Modern Iraq* (London: 1925).

Longrigg, Stephen H., *Iraq 1900–1950: A Political, Social and Economic History* (London: 1953).

Longrigg, Stephen H., *Iraq 1900–1950* (London: 1953).

Longrigg, Stephen H., *Oil in the Middle East* (Oxford: Oxford University Press, 1968).

Lucas, W. Scott, *Divided We Stand: Britain, the US and the Suez Crisis* (London: Hodder and Stoughton, 1991).

Lunt, James, *Hussein of Jordan* (London: Macmillan, 1989).

Maalouf, Amin, *The Crusades Through Arab Eyes* (London: Al Saqi Books, 1984).

Mansfield, Peter, *The Arabs* (Harmondsworth: Penguin, 1983).

Mansfield, Peter, *A History of the Middle East* (Harmondsworth: Penguin, 1991).

Marr, P., *The Modern History of Iraq* (London: 1985).

Matar, Fouad, *Saddam Hussein – A Biography* (London: Highlight Productions, 1990).

McNeil, William H. and Waldman, Marilyn Robinson (eds), *The Islamic World* (Chicago and London: University of Chicago Press, 1983).

Miller, Judith and Mylroie, Laurie, *Saddam Hussein and the Crisis in the Gulf* (New York: Times Books, Random House, 1990).

Monroe, E., *Britain's Moment in the Middle East 1914–1956* (London: Chatto and Windus, 1964).

North, Oliver, *Under Fire* (London: Fontana, 1992).

Odell, Peter R., *Oil and World Power* (Harmondsworth: Penguin, 1970).

Omissi, David E., *Air Power and Colonial Control, The Royal Air Force, 1919–1939* (Manchester: Manchester University Press, 1990).

Oppenheim, A. L., *Ancient Mesopotamia* (Chicago: 1964).

Parrot, A., *Sumer* (New York: 1961).

Parry, V. J., Inalcik, H., Kurat, A. N. and Bromley, J. S., *A History of the Ottoman Empire* (Cambridge: Cambridge University Press, 1976).

Pelletiere, Stephen C., *The Kurds: An Unstable Element in the Gulf* (Boulder, Col.: Westview Press, 1984).

Penrose, Edith and E. F., *Iraq: International Relations and International Development* (London: 1978).

Peretz, Don, *The Middle East Today* (New York: Praeger, 1988).

Petran, Tabitha, *Syria, A Modern History* (London: Ernest Benn, 1972).

Pisani, Sallie, *The CIA and the Marshall Plan* (Edinburgh: Edinburgh University Press, 1991).

Phillips, William D., *Slavery from Roman Times to the Early Transatlantic Trade* (Manchester: Manchester University Press, 1985).

Postal, Bernard and Levy, Henry W., *And the Hills Shouted for Joy* (New York: David McKay, 1973).

Rejwan, Nissim, *The Jews of Iraq* (London: Weidenfeld and Nicolson, 1985).

Rich, C. J., *Narrative of a Journey to the Site of Babylon*, 2 vols (London: 1939).

Ridgeway, James, (ed.). *The March to War* (New York: Four Walls Eight Windows, 1991).

Ringer, Benjamin B., *'We the People' and Others, Duality and America's Treatment of its Racial Minorities* (London: Tavistock, 1983).

Sachar, Howard M., *The Emergence of the Middle East 1914–1924* (London: Allen Lane, 1969).

Saddam's Iraq, Revolution or Reaction? (London: Zed Books and CARDRI [Committee Against Repression and for Democratic Rights in Iraq], 1989).

Salinger, Pierre with Laurent, Eric, *Secret Dossier, The Hidden Agenda Behind the Gulf War* (Harmondsworth: Penguin, 1991).

Sampson, Anthony, *The Seven Sisters, The Great Oil Companies and the World They Made* (London: Hodder and Stoughton, 1975).

Sassoon, David S., *A History of the Jews in Baghdad* (Letchworth: 1949).

Saunders, J. J., *A History of Medieval Islam* (London: Routledge & Kegan Paul, 1980).

Schacht, J. and Bosworth, C. E., *The Legacy of Islam* (Oxford University Press, 1974).

Schwarzkopf, H. Norman with Petre, Peter, *It Doesn't Take a Hero* (London: Bantam Press, 1992).

Shaban, M. A., *The Abbasid Revolution* (Cambridge: 1970).

Shahram, Chubin, and Tripp, Charles, *Iran and Iraq at War* (London: I. B. Tauris, 1989).

Shaw, Stanford J., *History of the Ottoman Empire and Modern Turkey* Vol. 1, *Empire of the Gazis: The Rise and Decline of the Ottoman Empire 1280–1808* (Cambridge: Cambridge University Press, 1976).

Sifry, Micah L. and Cerf, Christopher, *The Gulf War Reader* (New York: Times Books, Random House, 1991).

Sluglett, P., *Britain in Iraq 1914–1932* (London: 1976).

Speiser, E. A. (ed.), *The World History of the Jewish People* (Jerusalem: 1964).

Sprague de Camp, L., *Ancient Engineers* (London: Souvenir Press, 1963).

Stafford, R. S., *The Tragedy of the Assyrians* (London: George Allen & Unwin, 1935).

Stewart, Desmond (with Haylock, John), *New Babylon, A Portrait of Iraq* (London: 1956).

Stewart, Desmond, *The Middle East: Temple of Janus* (London: Hamish Hamilton, 1972).

Stiles, Andrina, *The Ottoman Empire 1450–1700* (London: Hodder and Stoughton, 1989).

Taheri, Amir, *The Cauldron, The Middle East Behind the Headlines* (London: Hutchinson, 1988).

Taheri, Amir, *The Unknown Life of the Shah* (London: Hutchinson, 1991).

Tarbush, Muhammad A., *The Role of the Military in Politics: A Case Study of Iraq to 1941* (London: 1982).

Thomas, D. Winton, (ed.), *Documents from Old Testament Times* (London: Thomas Nelson, 1958).

Thompson, R. C., *On the Chemistry of the Ancient Assyrians* (London: 1925).

Timmerman, Kenneth R., *The Death Lobby, How the West Armed Iraq* (London: Fourth Estate, 1992).

Townshend, Charles Vere Ferres, *My Campaign* (New York: James A. McCann, 1920).

Warriner, Doreen, *Land Reform and Development in the Middle East, A Study of Egypt, Syria and Iraq* (London: 1987).

Wellard, James, *By the Waters of Babylon* (London: Hutchinson, 1972).

Wilson, Jeremy, *Lawrence of Arabia* (London: Heinemann, 1989).

Winstone, H. V. F. and Freeth, Zahra, *Kuwait, Prospect and Reality* (London: George Allen & Unwin, 1972).

Winter, H. J. J., *Eastern Science* (London: John Murray, 1952).

Wittek, R., *The Rise of the Ottoman Empire* (London: 1971).

Woodward, Bob, *Veil: The Secret Wars of the CIA 1981–1987* (London: Simon and Schuster, 1987).

Woolley, Leonard, *Excavations at Ur* (London: Ernest Benn, 1963).

Yapp, M. E., *The Making of the Modern Middle East 1798–1923* (London: 1987).

Yapp, M. E., *The Near East Since the First World War* (London: Longman, 1991).

Index

Index